PEOPLES ON PARADE

PUBLISHED WITH THE SUPPORT OF THE GETTY FOUNDATION

PEOPLES ON PARADE

Exhibitions, Empire, and Anthropology in Nineteenth-Century Britain * SADIAH QURESHI

* * * * * * * The University of Chicago Press Chicago and London * * * * * * *

SADIAH QURESHI is an affiliated scholar in the
Department of History and Philosophy of Science
at the University of Cambridge and the senior research
fellow in the Cambridge Victorian Studies Group.

The University of Chicago Press, Chicago 60637
The University of Chicago Press, Ltd., London
© 2011 by The University of Chicago
All rights reserved. Published 2011.

Printed in China

20 19 18 17 16 15 14 13 12 11   1 2 3 4 5

ISBN-13: 978-0-226-70096-0 (cloth)
ISBN-10: 0-226-70096-8 (cloth)

Library of Congress Cataloging-in-Publication Data

Qureshi, Sadiah.
    Peoples on parade : exhibitions, empire, and
  anthropology in nineteenth-century Britain /
  Sadiah Qureshi.
       p. cm.
    Includes bibliographical references and index.
    ISBN-13: 978-0-226-70096-0 (hardcover : alk. paper)
    ISBN-10: 0-226-70096-8 (hardcover : alk. paper)
    1. Indigenous peoples—Exhibitions—History—
  19th century. 2. Exhibitions—England—London—
  History—19th century. 3. Anthropology in popular
  culture—England—London—History—19th century.
  4. Ethnic performing arts—England—London—
  History—19th century. 5. Human beings—Exhibitions
  —History—19th century. 6. Great Britain—Social life
  and customs—19th century. 7. Great Britain—Race
  relations—History—19th century. I. Title.
    GN36.G72L678 2011
    305.80074'421--dc22
                                    2010040823

This book is printed on acid-free paper.

In memory of MY LOVING GRANDPARENTS

CONTENTS

Ladies and Gentlemen, I Bring You ...

ON THE evening of Monday, May 17, 1847, hundreds of curious people gathered at London's Exeter Hall to see a "spectacle of considerable interest." For days, the press had been touting the opportunity to witness an "extraordinary exhibition," and at last the moment of gratification had arrived. After presenting tickets to gain entry, eager patrons filed in and took their seats. Those prepared to pay the requisite fee of 2 shillings and sixpence were able to avoid the possible rush for seats and take up reserved places; others paid a shilling and were left to find an accommodating spot.[1]

The audience faced a platform on which two men, two women, and a young infant were quietly squatting. Shortly after eight o'clock, a middle-aged man appeared; he introduced himself as the infamous anatomist Dr. Robert Knox and his guests as the fabled "Bushmen" of Africa. Knox then presented a lecture covering their natural historical classification and the foreign policies governing Britain's presence in their homeland. Unfortunately, the "want of physical force" on his part left many straining to hear, and so the spectators continued staring at the diminutive group, which still sat behind him, "wonder-stricken." At about nine o'clock, the lecture ended and Knox announced that the group of "pigmies" would "go amongst the company if not in an obstinate temper." Fearful of being disappointed, spectators enticed the Africans off the stage with money and oranges. The money was placed carefully in a leather pouch by the youngest man; the oranges were eaten "voraciously, peel and all," by the men but in a milder manner by the women. Softened, the two male performers, dressed in "native costume" with a bow slung over the shoulder and arrows stuck in a leather cap, went among the audience and spoke to them with "harangues full of spirit and meaning." Afterward, the men engaged in a debate while the women of the troupe looked on. "The discussion was full of fire, and frequently excited cheers and plaudits," despite taking place in "an assembly that did not understand one word." At the close of the exhibition, the performers were given small gifts, received with kisses on the bestowers' hands and delighted exclamations from appreciative patrons.[2]

Paying to see living foreign peoples perform was enormously popular in the nineteenth century. Throughout the 1800s, for a shilling or more, the public flocked to see, among others, groups of Sámi, Krenak, Inuit, Anishinabe, Bakhoje, Zulus, San, Arabs, Pacific Islanders, Australian Aborigines, Indians, Japanese, Ndebele, Chinese, and "Aztecs."[3] These performers were often colonized peoples who had been specially imported to perform songs, dances, and other ceremonies as demonstrations of their "singular" nature. *Peoples on Parade* explores how such human exhibitions achieved commercial success, the ways in which they developed over the course of the nineteenth century, and their lasting historical significance.

Not only were such shows common but they were profitable, publicly accessible, and among some of the most popular forms of metropolitan entertainment. Many foreign peoples were first exhibited in London. A show's reputation was often built there before making smaller provincial tours; others simply remained in the capital and were regularly reported on by the provincial press. Sometimes, displayed peoples arriving in other busy port cities, such as Liverpool, would be exhibited locally before moving on to London. The San (Bushmen) exhibition at Exeter Hall, for example, was the opening night of Knox's commercial lectures and the group's stage debut in the London season. For subsequent performances, the Africans were exhibited without Knox at the Egyptian Hall in Piccadilly (fig. 1). During these shows the debating scene was followed by a choreographed fight among bushes specially installed within the room and against a painted backdrop of the African veldt.

The sheer size of London's population ensured that the shows were available to a considerable portion of the national population while developing transport links, especially the railways, opened up the possibility of tourists. Showmen vying for patrons' time and money, especially fashionable folk in town for the summer, created the largest competitive entertainment industry in the country.[4] In the early nineteenth century, international warfare, especially the Napoleonic Wars, discouraged people from traveling abroad, thereby stimulating the growth of the internal tourist market. Once the political instability subsided, the industry remained buoyant.[5] Thus, London was both the central node of a national entertainment network and a port conduit for the larger traffic of trade, communication, and industry that was consolidated with the expansion of the British Empire.

Exhibitions of living foreign peoples have been documented since the fifteenth century; however, the nineteenth century witnessed significant changes in the scale and nature of human displays.[6] Up until the mid-1800s, such exhibitions were typically temporary, often lasting only a summer, and usually privately financed. Featuring either an individual or small groups haphazardly brought to the metropolis, they were most commonly staged by entrepreneurial speculators, missionary groups, and itinerant showmen.[7] For example, in 1810 Sara Baartman, better known

FIGURE I
*The Bosjesman, at the
Egyptian Hall, Picca-
dilly.* The San family
that accompanied Dr.
Robert Knox in full
costume and with
their manager at the
Egyptian Hall. (*Illus-
trated London News*,
June 12, 1847, p. 381.
Author's collection.)

by her stage epithet the "Hottentot Venus" and the first celebrity exhibit
of the nineteenth century, arrived in Britain in a joint venture between
herself, her Cape Town employer, and a greatly indebted naval surgeon.[8]
Similarly, in 1822 missionaries arranged for the public exhibition of a
Krenak (Botocudo) family in the hope of securing funds for their return to
South America as future Christian ambassadors among the local peoples.[9]
Knox's exhibition of San exemplified the format of most shows from the
early to mid-nineteenth century in which the proprietor, or a close affili-
ate, provided an introductory lecture followed by a performance or several
tableaux interspersed with explanatory talks. In addition, printed forms of
lectures or pamphlets describing the "manners and customs" of the exhibited peoples were often sold in exhibition venues.

Human displays reached their peak in terms of scale, commercial success, and public access under the aegis of the international trade of Europe, India, America, Africa, and Australia that followed in the wake of the
Great Exhibition at the Crystal Palace in London's Hyde Park in 1851.[10] This
event marked a major undertaking that came to be seen as a model of commercial success melded with philanthropically inspired public education.
Later on, many exhibition organizers harked back to its perceived achievements while at once trying to surpass them. As objects of national policy,
fairs originated as primarily trade and industrial events in France in the
late eighteenth century.[11] They were short-lived events, most often running for six months, and by the late 1800s became commercially success-

Ladies and Gentlemen, I Bring You…

ful, competitive ventures that were inextricably tied to a range of political, scientific, and technological ideals. As early as 1851, contemporary commentators noted the diverse ethnic backgrounds of attendees and the curiosity it stirred from those interested in watching the crowds.[12] From the outset, this was complemented by the inclusion of living foreign peoples among the list of official exhibits.

Originally presented on a small scale as servants and shopkeepers, by the 1880s performers were displaced by the hundreds from their homelands and lived on site in ostensibly authentic "native villages." Within this context, living foreign peoples were transformed into professional "savages" and became tied to new forms of cheap mass entertainment. Simultaneously, importing people also became an organized commercial enterprise that was increasingly regulated and standardized by governmental involvement. For example, Carl Hagenbeck, a German businessman and enormously successful animal exhibitor, took to procuring people for his *Völkerschauen* (people shows) by dispatching specialist agents to collect suitable specimens to display alongside other exotic faunae.[13]

On first acquaintance, the existence, scale, and popularity of human displays is likely to baffle and shock the modern reader. I was appalled that exhibitions of living foreign peoples were ever considered appropriate as either family entertainment or humane treatment—a reaction that I expect most, and most likely all, readers of this work share. For some time, there has been a strong consensus that such exhibitions helped to perpetuate Western, usually imperial, notions of superiority through shaping, reinforcing, and promoting fundamentally hierarchical, racist, and evolutionary arrangements of the world's peoples.[14] Accordingly, the shows have frequently been discussed as examples of populist, spectacular entertainment that were of little, if any, scientific significance, even when scientists are acknowledged as their curators and consumers.[15] While this book does not deny that the shows may be associated with racism or imperialism, it is based on the premise that the associations between displayed peoples, imperialism, and ethnic difference are neither inherent nor self-evident; rather, they must be both created and maintained. Where such associations exist, they are not to be relied on or assumed as explanatory factors but are to be regarded as historically specific developments that require further explanation. As such, in this work the burden of explanation has been transferred to different questions: To whom were the shows available? What kinds of interpretative work were the shows' patrons expected to undertake? What kinds of knowledge did the shows produce and how did this change? Was such knowledge considered at all relevant to issues related to imperialism, science, or race? If so, how was it *made* relevant? In addressing these questions, this book attends closely to the processes involved in producing, promoting, performing, interpreting, and managing the shows across the nineteenth century.

If we consider the San exhibition with which we began, one of its most striking features is the presence of the lecturer and anatomist Knox. He developed a notion of human variety that proposed innate and permanent physiological differences between ethnic groups, thereby warranting, he argued, the division of humans into multiple species. This research and his confident assertion that "race is everything: literature, science, art, in a word, civilization depend upon it" have often underpinned his vilification as one of the most notorious racists of the nineteenth century and, as such, an exemplar of the vehement racism often argued to characterize the late-Victorian age. It is clear that Knox used his lecture as a means to promote his views on human development while simultaneously inviting his listeners to engage with contemporary debates on human variety.[16] Yet, how and why was a lecture on the San, with living performers, considered an appropriate place for such discussion, and were these invitations taken up by anyone? Exploring these issues requires an understanding of how the institutional and methodological criteria for defining scientific investigation were being reforged across Europe in the mid-nineteenth century.

The public face of the sciences became increasingly exclusive as the category of the scientist was both created and widely adopted in Britain from the mid-nineteenth century onward. A paid career in science had existed in France and Germany for several decades, but the gentlemanly practitioner remained the ideal throughout the early 1800s in Britain. In the mid-nineteenth century, men such as the anatomist Thomas Henry Huxley began to campaign for professional positions to be established and opened to men of more modest means. This activity witnessed changes in the spaces that were publicly endorsed as legitimate for the production of reliable natural knowledge. The campaigning led to new forms of exclusion, as paid men of science sought to distance themselves from amateurs, showmen, women, foreigners, and those working outside the institutional domain of the laboratory.[17] Such shifts ensured that what publicly counted as scientific knowledge and who could be a legitimate contributor to its production were both undetermined and hotly disputed. Critically, practices many would now view as pseudoscience, such as phrenology and mesmerism, were considered plausible means of producing natural knowledge in the early nineteenth century because of the radically different disciplinary landscape.[18] Bearing this is mind has allowed the history of science to be opened up far beyond the activities of men in white coats busying themselves in the laboratory; men and women with diverse ranges of skills and expertise are recognized as having contributed to the production of natural knowledge.[19] Furthermore, the spaces used have been identified as ranging from princely courts, domestic abodes, laboratories, pubs, museums, lecture theaters, universities, coffeehouses, and botanic gardens to the field.[20] Building on these developments, the shows may be considered arenas for the production of both intercultural and natural knowledge.

Knox's choice of the San performers as human specimens is indicative of the mid-nineteenth-century interest in redefining the scientific study of human variety while simultaneously forging productive links with the shows. Throughout the eighteenth and most of the nineteenth centuries, scholars redefined the social, political, and physical criteria used to classify humans. In doing so, they changed the repercussions of racialist taxonomies. For example, Christian orthodoxy dictated that humans were considered a single species and often believed to be the product of a single act of Divine creation. In the eighteenth and early nineteenth centuries, differences between peoples were explained using a wide variety of factors, including complexion, physiognomy, physical makeup, language, religion, clothing, and political, social, and economic organization, and usually argued to be the result of environmental influences, not inherent physical differences.[21] Darker peoples' complexion, for example, differed because they lived in hotter climates and were scorched by the sun, while lighter skins and more refined physiognomies were the products of more temperate zones. Similarly, moral and mental development were usually tied to social organization, with hunter-gatherer societies argued to be considerably less advanced than agricultural and commercial nations. By challenging environmental explanations, detractors forced moral and natural philosophers to reassess how human variation was conceptualized. Some even proposed that human variation was significant enough to merit splitting peoples into different species that were unequal in their moral, intellectual, and physical capacities. By the late 1850s and 1860s, this reassessment led to numerous redefinitions of the term *race* and the formulation of new methods for its scholarly study.

Exhibitions of living foreign peoples were far from peripheral to these debates; rather, ethnologists and anthropologists both recognized and exploited the research opportunities that the shows made possible throughout the later half of the nineteenth century. Despite considerable scientific interest in displayed peoples, however, characterizing the shows as inherently "ethnological," "anthropological," or "ethnographic" is potentially problematic.[22] Critically, it risks conflating any discussion of ethnicity with the practices used for its investigation. By the 1840s, "ethnology" had emerged as a historical discipline that used physical, social, and linguistic features to investigate the relationship between different human groups. By the 1860s, "anthropology" was advocated as an alternative approach that encompassed the study of humans in a broader sense and whose early practitioners placed a greater emphasis on synchronic, physiological, and anatomic considerations. Even so, not everyone attending a show was interested in using performers as ethnological specimens, making comparative assessments between ethnic groups or in pursuing further research. Moreover, while foreign peoples were potentially amenable to being used as natural history specimens throughout the period, considerable effort had to be exerted to both create and maintain the association between the shows and scientific research. Assuming the shows were "ethnological" or "anthropological" risks underestimating, or even overlooking, the extent to which the potential utility of performers for scientific research was debated and how their relevance changed as practitioners' theoretical and methodological commitments shifted. In contrast, paying greater attention to if, when, and how performers were used as specimens helps reflect both interpretative diversity in the shows' receptions and contemporary concern regarding the practices of observation, description, and classification that were being mobilized in the production of anthropological knowledge.

Knox's lecture also explicitly associated the San's performance with contemporary debates on foreign policy and British philanthropy. While urging the British to abandon the colonization of Africa in favor of trading partnerships, he noted: "It was not a little singular that, on the same day he should be giving his lecture upon the most striking representative of the dark races of men, that the two greatest societies, the Anti-Slavery and the Aborigines [Protection Society], should be holding their meetings for the benefit of those races."[23] Founded in the 1830s, both societies owed their origins to broader movements focused on improving the lot of enslaved and colonized peoples worldwide.[24] The exhibition's location at Exeter Hall contributed significantly to this kind of politicization. The previous year, the novelist and journalist Charles Dickens had sarcastically located Exeter Hall at the epicenter of an ever-widening circle of influence for the British missionary and philanthropic impulse:

The stone that is dropped into the ocean of ignorance at Exeter Hall, must make its widening circles, one beyond another, until they reach the negro's country in their natural expansion. There is a broad, dark sea between the Strand in London, and the Niger, where those rings are not yet shining; and through all that space they must appear, before the last one breaks upon the shore of Africa.[25]

Meanwhile, just six months after Knox's lecture, the essayist and historian Thomas Carlyle used the anonymously penned and notorious "Occasional Discourse on the Negro Question," later renamed and reissued as relating to the "Nigger Question," to contrast his pro-slavery sentiments with the "Broad brimmed form of Christian Sentimentalism, and long talking and bleating" of "Exeter Hall Philanthropy."[26] Knox's explicit references to foreign policy and his venue's reputation as a bastion of the well-meaning are particularly striking examples of how the shows became fodder for journalists, lecturers, and patrons mulling over issues of wider import. Such political relevance proved vital in both attracting the crowds and shaping the shows' receptions, especially since pleasure and instruction were neither mutually exclusive nor necessarily confined to distinctly separate spaces. Rather, explorations of nineteenth-century mass culture suggest that diverse spaces of nineteenth-century entertainment, from menageries to department stores, were all sites in which social and political orders, often amenable to imperialism, were created or endorsed.[27] Seen in this light, the shows can be characterized as more than entertaining spectacles: they may be recast as intercultural encounters and topical events which both generated and stimulated public discussions on numerous issues, including foreign policy, missionary zeal, and slavery.

Commercial exhibitions of living foreign peoples were embedded within a thriving entertainment market, often making it difficult to know how to distinguish them from other human displays. Throughout the nineteenth century, such shows were most commonly advertised as either exhibitions, levees giving the impression of domestic receptions, or "living curiosities," a broader category that could describe remarkable people and animals ranging from dwarfs to dancing monkeys.[28] Foreign peoples were also exhibited in a whole host of venues such as theaters, museums, zoological gardens, private apartments, international fairs, galleries, music halls, and sporting venues.

Yet despite being exhibited in diverse circumstances and spaces, such displays of foreign peoples have been most commonly compared to, or discussed as, "freak shows."[29] While this has been fruitful in understanding how conventions of representing deviance may have shaped the shows' histories, it has also encouraged, supported, and consolidated the implication that foreign peoples were routinely interpreted as evidently strange, deformed, bizarre, anomalous, or even pathological. The association between "freaks" and foreigners has also been institutionalized in the archives; for example, much of the relevant material in the wonderful John Johnson Collection of Printed Ephemera at the Bodleian Library, Oxford, has been preserved under the organizational subheading of "Human Freaks." Foreign peoples did appear in the same venues and on the same playbills as other human curiosities; in conjunction, ethnic and cultural differences might be, and sometimes were, "cast as a bodily anomaly analogous to physical deformation."[30] Nonetheless, simply placing a Zulu on the same stage as conjoined twins, for example, did not entail that both were marketed or interpreted in the same terms, let alone as "freaks." As such, conceptualizing displayed peoples in terms of the "savage freak show" risks simply equating ethnic difference with "freakishness" while simultaneously homogenizing a dizzying range of differences within the category of the "freakish."[31] Instead, comparisons with other forms of human display are most productive where close attention is paid to tracing how differences between patrons and performers, as well as between competing acts, were created, marketed, and interpreted. Doing so allows for commonalities and differences to be appreciated while also accounting for how patrons made such associations, if and when they did, and showcases the full diversity of the shows' receptions.

Ultimately, exploring the range of ways in which shows were promoted, performed, and interpreted helps focus attention on past perspectives and the shows' experiential dimensions; however, this emphasis raises several difficult issues, most obviously relating to sources. Unfortunately, showmen, spectators, and performers most commonly left few or no records from which we might glean any indication of their encounters with one another or London's entertainment business. Eyewitness accounts are rare and often only to be found in newspaper reviews. Marshaling posters, pamphlets, newspapers, and periodicals helps provide suggestive glimpses, but they must be used with particular caution. As promotional materials they are subject to exaggerating or even falsifying attendance figures and inventing biographical information; but they remain the most readily, and sometimes the only, available documents.

Rarer still, often frustratingly so, are the sources that might be used to reconstruct performers' motivations and perceptions. Increasingly, biographies are beginning to offer a highly productive way to recover performers' agency and often offer surprising insights into their lives as entertainers.[32] Nonetheless, in the absence of diaries and letters, frequently the only materials available are third-party reports of court cases, contracts, anecdotal accounts, or newspaper reviews. Subject to obvious and considerable mediation, all are highly problematic; but if we understand how these archives were formed, they may be used as a resource from which to reconstruct patterns of social organization.[33] In this light, even the rarity or absence of sources can be telling. The sheer lack of materials from which we might recover subaltern perspectives speaks volumes about how they were rarely considered of special interest. Likewise, considering how displayed peoples were made to speak on behalf others can illuminate the patterns of social and political interaction involved in the shows' histories.

Reconstructing past perspectives also raises issues regarding the use of language and material that now bears strongly pejorative connotations. A significant proportion of the sources used in writing this book employ terms such as *savage*, *civilized*, and *heathen*, and ethnic denominators such as *Bushman*, that encapsulate a cultural and religious chauvinism that must now be recognized as deeply offensive and utterly unacceptable. Therefore, throughout the text, such terminology is restricted to quotations or passages in which historical views are reported or summarized. Instead, modern terms are used throughout and only glossed on first use. Consistently limiting the use of historical terms to instances where it is clear that they are being used as actors' categories is intended to help create distance between past attitudes and modern analysis; however, while such considerations are also relevant to the reproduction of images, it is simply not possible to create new visual vocabularies in order to exert the same kind of control as we might over text. This is not to imply that there is a greater immediacy of interpretation associated with images, or that we cannot analyze them in sensitive ways; but it does recognize that even with accompanying analysis, the act of interpretation is always undetermined. Thus, while invaluable in exploring both the advertising and the reception of the shows, the reproduction of images many still be objected to by some on the basis that it allows a form of voyeurism that reenacts the violence done to historically marginalized communities.

I considered omitting any images of displayed peoples, but ultimately decided against it. Participation in the shows, particularly from the mid-nineteenth century onward, became increasingly visual. As production technologies changed to allow cheaper and mass publication, images were used with increasing frequency. This work as a whole, chapter 2 especially, is concerned with the diverse representations of the shows and exhibited peoples that contributed to the creation of potential audiences. In this vein, examining the range of textual and visual material suggests how displayed peoples became both knowable and consumable commodities. Moreover, an analysis of even seemingly innocent images can show just how politically charged they are, albeit subtly so; we may simply not recognize them as such because we lack the strategies for interpreting them (fig. 7 or 10, for example).[34] The limited accessibility of the original material also makes it both useful and instructive for the material to be reproduced here.[35] Just as limiting the use of historical terms is not intended to erase or sanitize past violence, the reproduction of images is not intended to resurrect the shows as an opportunity for modern voyeurism; rather, it is intended to help create a space for respectful interrogation of the primary sources in order to analyze the processes that created and perpetuated the commercial success of human curiosities.[36]

In addition to objectionable overtones, many terms have significantly changed the scope of their meaning. *Race*, in particular, is difficult to define.[37] It originally referred to animals and plants in the context of eighteenth-century agriculture and husbandry. As mentioned, from the mid-nineteenth century onward, scholars were engaged in fierce debates over its exact nature and potential significance. In the modern period, it has come to denote a biogeographically localized set of characteristics that may or may not determine factors such as intelligence and physical ability. Alternatively, it has been argued that "races" are illusionary, since they are not identifiable natural entities but simply locally observable gradations.[38] In addition, there are the modern connotations that are inextricably tied up with *racism* (itself a coinage from the 1930s). As such, *human variety* is used preferentially throughout, and *race* and *racial* are only used as actors' categories or when directly addressing the work of other historians using the term. Within this context, *race* may be an analytical category, an explanatory tool, or a causal factor. In addition, distinctions are drawn between *racialism* and *racialists* on the one hand and *racism* and *racists* on the other. Racialists are taken to subscribe to the view that humans do vary according to "race," with or without inherent physical, intellectual, and moral differences, but that this should not form the basis of social organization. Racists are taken to subscribe to the view that not only can humans be differentiated on the basis of "race," but that this ought to form the basis of social and cultural organization.[39] In this usage, a person who argues that humans are grouped into "races" but argues that this is irrelevant to social organization, since all humans have equal rights, is taken to be distinct from someone who maintains that such variation must form the basis of social and political policy. This distinction is intended to reflect differences of interpretation and commitment that must be accounted for, rather than erased by, historical analysis.

✳

Peoples on Parade takes a tour through London's streets, into its exhibition venues, and through its learned societies and ends with the international fairs of the later nineteenth century. As part 1 suggests, the streets were critical for ensuring showmen's success both in terms of creating a potential clientele and as advertising arenas. Writers produced a literature in which the city's cobbled arteries were transformed into an ephemeral spectacle that dramatized the gamut of global human activity. Here, it was claimed, urban spectators could marvel at peoples, from Anglo-Saxon to Zulu, engaged in the universal business of living. Meanwhile, industrious flyposters ensured the city's walls were teeming with posters promoting the services of workmen and countless medical concoctions alongside playbills of the latest entertainments. Showmen effectively used advertising to secure paying customers from urban spectators who, despite their access to ethnic diversity, wanted to interact with foreign peoples, an act not possible on the street.

Patrons willing to pay a shilling, or more, to meet foreign peoples were just one node in the shows' complex network of showmen, performers, and consumers. Part two recovers their roles and experiences in the shows' histories. Showmen were not only responsible for recruiting performers but essential in mediating the kinds of knowledge the shows produced through providing promotional materials, managing the visual and material cues used in exhibition venues, and giving lectures. Adults and children alike were recruited from all over the globe to be exhibited. Some chose this life abroad, while others were clearly coerced or had little say. Performers found ways to adapt to their environments through learning to speak English, becoming professional entertainers, and even settling down once abroad. Patrons delighted in meeting and mingling with foreign peoples, within both exhibition venues and private appointments. Invariably, they were interested in ethnicity, but they also interpreted the shows as relevant to ongoing political activity, domestic problems, and human development.

For a significant number of patrons, the shows were exciting opportunities to further their scholarly interests in the natural history of humans. Learned societies devoted to the emerging human sciences were especially keen to take advantage of the shows as sources of potential specimens. Part three traces these attempts to establish the shows as observational and experimental resources against the backdrop of the institutionalization of anthropology and the transformation of human displays under the aegis of the international fairs of the latter half of the nineteenth century. In this context, the very nature of human displays metamorphosed, as did their relationship to an increasingly professionalized discipline. Ultimately, reconstructing the shows' original metropolitan context allows for an exploration of their lasting significance, and needs to begin with a short walk through London's twisted streets and alleyways.

PART ONE

STREET SPECTACLES

FIGURE 2

Regent Street and the delights Mr. Pips
failed to notice. (Richard Doyle, "Regente
Street at Four of ye Clocke," *Punch* 17 [1849]:
82. By kind permission of Jim Secord.)

Glimpsing
Urban Savages

IN 1849, *Punch* published a series of extracts from the diary of Mr. Pips titled "Manners and Customs of ye Englyshe." One image accompanying the series illustrates a scene Mr. Pips had witnessed in Regent Street on the way to the theater (fig. 2).[1] Three distinct streams of people are visible in the hustle and bustle. At the top of the illustration, well-dressed, fashionable ladies and gentlemen hurry past one another on the pavement. One woman lingers to window-shop, and bends to gaze longingly through the glass; others engage in conversation as they pass by the novel convenience of the department store. One man casts an appreciative second glance over his shoulder at a passing lady while a nearby dog is locked in combat with the paper bag on his head. Moving from the middle left to the top right, a chaotic maelstrom of people, animals, and vehicles overtake one another on the road. Several horse-drawn coaches appear to clash. One man is almost run down by a stunned horse that has only just managed to cease cantering. The Paddington to Hungerford coach drives on, carrying a shocked and portly man hanging from the back, two women seated inside, and numerous young boys perched precariously on the roof. The coachman snaps the reins to avoid the oncoming, horse-drawn tailor's advertisement. In the top right of the illustration, a police van drives past as a couple attempts to dash past unharmed and unsullied. In the foreground, the other pavement is crowded with a ragged bunch of people. An Irishman smoking a pipe drives by on a donkey. In front of him, men advertise the opportunity to see the smallest dwarf in the world and sea serpents. In the center, a turbaned Turkish street sweeper bows in front of two German men ignoring a begging chimney sweep. Behind them a dashing gentleman sits in his coach. In another coach, further to the right, two women look down disdainfully at the maid talking to them and the poor couple behind. In the bottom right, two boys mischievously tease a fur company's lion, stuffed and manipulated into presenting a friendly face.

By providing a moment frozen in print, *Punch* allowed readers to scrutinize it carefully. Any reader paying attention would have found an image teeming with vignettes of urban life in which people are distinguished by their age, sex, class, trade, and ethnic origin. However, Mr. Pips only mentioned the scene in passing; instead he dwelled on a series of endlessly tedious observations made at the evening opera. The magazine implied that had he attended to the street as much as to the warbling, he might have found the crowd to be the more absorbing show.

Mr. Pips may have paid no attention to the delights Regent Street had to offer, but from the early nineteenth century onward, an urban literature devoted to observing street life appeared in a number of printed forms, including novels, periodicals, and travel journals; in Britain, it frequently boasted that London was *the* world's stage. The most famous consumer this genre produced was the *flâneur*—a rather haughty gentleman who wandered the streets in his intellectual endeavor to survey modernity's multitudes, and whom the literary critic Walter Benjamin classically located in the urban expansion of nineteenth-century Paris.[2] More recently, many elements of *flânerie* have been clearly identified outside this spatial and temporal location.[3] Despite broader definitions, *flânerie* is often still portrayed as the preserve of the independent, often European or American, man and is still most often associated with a natural intellectual aptitude. Yet we can profitably employ the alternative model of an urban spectator: an individual who assigns worth to observing the street, but who is left deliberately undefined by gender, class, ethnic origin, or intellectual ability.[4] Using this model, this chapter examines the writings of nineteenth-century urban spectators to explore how they created a culture of visual inspection that was potentially relevant to the creation of a consumer market for displayed peoples. After all, audiences are not preexisting entities of which showmen, writers, artists, or the like can simply take advantage; instead, they must be created and wooed in order to achieve any measure of public consumption.

In "Passing Faces," a well-known essay in *Household Words* (1855), the self-educated writer Eliza Lynn began with the confident assertion: "We have no need to go abroad to study ethnology. A walk through the streets of London will show us specimens of every human variety known."[5] Everyone could easily spot an Anglo-Saxon, Negro, or Jew, she argued, but closer inspections of Londoners' physiognomies could reveal traces of the Red Indian, Malay, Nubian, Fin, Eastern Tartar, Chinaman, and Lascar. They may have been blended together and "diluted" to varying degrees in succeeding generations of mixed ethnicity, but with a little training, the ethnic archetypes were nonetheless discernible. So why did Londoners pay to see living foreign peoples perform when they lived in a city whose streets were routinely touted as the greatest show of all? By revisiting the nature of Lynn's claims, this chapter explores the relevance of the streets in creating a market for human displays. In doing so, it examines how Londoners became the makers and users of urban spectatorship across social and ethnic divides, beginning with the journalist Henry Mayhew. An indefatigable observer of the working classes, he contended that London was teeming with urban savages, if one only cared to venture into any of the poorer boroughs. Often presented as the first social observer to provide an exploratory account of the London underworld, Mayhew was in fact heir to a long-standing tradition that presented that city's streets as a spectacle and its inhabitants as alien and visually interesting sights. In turn, as Lynn's article suggests, metropolitan demography exhibited striking, but all too often forgotten, ethnic heterogeneity. As we shall see, understanding how these racialized tropes, observational practices, and population differences developed and were self-consciously used is a helpful departure point for understanding how showmen courted their future clientele.

"City Arabs" and "Home Heathens"

In 1853, the *Illustrated London News* launched a searing attack on a "peculiar race" of people that inhabited the metropolis and possessed a "code of morals of their own."[6] Their moral order was the "very reverse" of that "prevalent amongst Christians." These "City Arabs" possessed their own organization, ideas, habits, temptations, tribulations, joys, and sorrows. The "scandal" of Victorian civilization, they committed "ceaseless depredations" and caused greatest anxiety in urban areas, especially Manchester, Glasgow, Birmingham, Liverpool, and London. Although they behaved as "young savages," they could not be hung, imprisoned, or deported. The levels of disquiet they drew even prompted a parliamentary committee to be set up to assess the size of their population and how best to rid the cities of their increasingly visible and problematic presence. One would be forgiven for thinking that these "City Arabs" were recent immigrants facing a torrent of abuse, but they were in fact the urban poor, whose alter ego, the "Home Heathens," betrayed the ambiguous feelings they inspired.

Racialized and alienating images of the urban poor found their most famous proponent in the writings of Mayhew. He found it curious that the poor, one of the largest subsections of London's population, were so visible, and yet "the public had less knowledge [of them] than of the most distant tribes of the earth." To remove such ignorance, he painstakingly gathered tales of street folk into a drama that he hoped would provide a "cyclopaedia of the industry, the want, and the vice of the great metropolis." Notably, he wished to produce "a history of the people, from the lips of the people themselves." However, the lives he documented were so "extraordinary" that he feared that like a "traveller in the undiscovered country of the poor," he must, until "corroborated" by later "investigators, be content to lie under the imputation of telling such tales as travellers are generally supposed to delight in."[7]

Mayhew's work appeared anonymously as a series of weekly articles first published in the *Morning Chronicle* newspaper between 1849 and 1850. He was commissioned in the wake of at least a decade's worth of revelations concerning the conditions of the working classes, including the communist Frederick Engels's *Condition of the Working Class in England* (1844);

government reports on the state of the nation's factories, mines, and potteries (1832, 1842, and 1843, respectively); and the social reformer Edwin Chadwick's official report on the city's stinking effluvia for the Poor Law Commissioners (1842).[8] Nonetheless, the articles caught the attention of the paper's readership and later brought Mayhew into the limelight when they were collated to form the volumes of *London Labour and the London Poor* (1851–52).

Mayhew's choice to discuss the urban poor as resident aliens was facilitated by London's internal geography.[9] The docks in the eastern part of the metropolis, built in the early nineteenth century, were among its poorest and ethnically most varied areas. Further inland and to the west, the economic divide was institutionalized with the architect John Nash's program of improvements, which included the building of Trafalgar Square, Regent Street, and other urban redevelopments in the 1820s. Fashionable society preferred the west and clustered into areas such as Mayfair and Knightsbridge. As the city's property tycoons developed the urban landscape and its factories billowed smoke and ash into the atmosphere, London became ever more polluted. Transport links developed to cope with the demands of commuters, and as the suburbs grew more popular, the urban poor were left to inherit some of the most ramshackle and fetid pockets of the inner city. This internal differentiation lent itself to those, such as Mayhew, who wanted to characterize London as a conglomeration of nations through which one might meander.

Mayhew proposed a fundamental boundary between the civilized and uncivilized that mapped onto the divide between settlers and wanderers.[10] Based on the writings of Scottish naturalist and military surgeon Andrew Smith and Bristolian physician James Cowles Prichard, Mayhew concluded:

(1) There are two distinct races of men, viz.:—the wandering and the civilised tribes; (2) to each of these tribes a different form of head is peculiar, the wandering races being remarkable for the development of the bones of face, as the jaws, cheek-bones, &c., and the head of the civilized for the development of those of the head; (3) to each civilized tribe there is a wandering horde attached; (4) such wandering hordes have frequently a different language from the more civilized portion of the community, and that adopted with the intent of the concealing their designs and exploits from them.[11]

Leaving Britain in 1820, Smith became an expert on the natural history of the Cape of Good Hope while stationed there for sixteen years, and in 1825 became the first superintendent of the South African Museum of Natural History. Reporting on the indigenous African populations, he observed that wandering tribes were usually found at the periphery of settled establishments.[12] Prichard, argued to be the "greatest writer" that "treated of the Science of Ethnology, and investigated and classified the nations

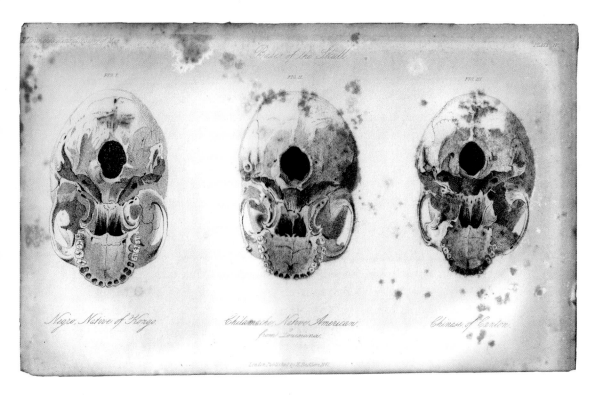

Negro, Native of Kongo.   Chilamache, Native American, from Louisiana.   Chinese of Canton.

FIGURE 3
Three types of humanity as demonstrated by the shape of the jaw from the base of the skull. From right to left, the "Negro, Native of Kongo"; "Chilamache, Native American, from Louisiana"; and "Chinese, of Canton." (James Cowles Prichard, *Natural History of Man*, 2nd ed. enlarged [1845], facing p. 395. By kind permission of Jim Secord.)

and kindreds and tongues of voice-varying men," established his reputation with several important works that helped synthesize the emergent field of British ethnology between 1813 and his death in 1848.[13] His *Natural History of Man* (1843) broadly divided humans into three groups based on a people's means of subsistence as reflected in the shape of the head (fig. 3). Savage or hunting tribes featured prognathous (forward-jutting) jaws and receding foreheads; nomadic or pastoral peoples had broad and lozenge-shaped faces or pyramidal skulls; finally, civilized and agricultural peoples' skulls were elliptical.[14] For Mayhew, these facts were of the "utmost social importance" in making sense of the urban poor, and he found it "curious" that no one had yet applied them to the "explanation of certain anomalies in the present state of society amongst ourselves"—especially since "the points of coincidence [are] so striking that, when placed before the mind, [they] make us marvel that the analogy should have remained thus long unnoticed."[15]

Associating civilization with settled existence and savagery with nomadic lifestyles provided Mayhew with a human social taxonomy that applied across ethnic groups. This allowed him to discuss the urban poor in terms more familiarly seen in discussions of foreign peoples and those alienating the London underworld.[16] London's streets were translated into unknown lands awaiting exploration and the urban poor into a mix of nomads and tribes:

That we, like the Kafirs, Fellahs, and Finns, are surrounded by wandering hordes—the "Sonquas" and the "Fingoes" of this country—paupers, beggars and outcasts, possessing nothing but what they acquire by depredation from the industrious, provident and civilized portion of the community;—that the heads of these nomades [*sic*] are remarkable for the greater development of the jaws and cheekbones rather than those of the head;—and that they have a secret language of their own—an English *"cuze-cut"* or "slang" as it is called— for the concealment of their designs.[17]

Mayhew equated the British upper and middle classes with peoples such as the Xhosa, while London's street folk shared the social role of the Mfengu. By using the similarity of social and cultural practices, such as the adoption of secret languages, and physical features, such as the shape of the skull, he aligned groups across ethnic boundaries. His bivalent taxonomy of settler and wanderer supported social equivalence between the urban elite and settled foreign peoples on one level (or in the center), and the urban poor and wandering foreign peoples beneath them (or on the periphery). Thus, for Mayhew the British class system directly mapped onto the social organization of foreign peoples, and the comparability, once discovered, was of "great service in enabling us to use the moral characteristics of the nomade [*sic*] races of other countries, as a means of comprehending the more readily those of the vagabonds and outcasts of our own."[18]

Equivalence presented Mayhew with a powerful historical element to his argument. In one sense, observing the poor could still support moral lessons in the value of avoiding immoral and therefore degenerative behaviors. However, just as the uncivilized could be raised to worthiness through their salvation, so could the urban poor in order to become the heirs of urban power. The image of London as an organic body with a natural life span was not new. In 1813, for example, Richard Phillips had foretold that as London's size grew,

the houses will become too numerous for the inhabitants, and certain districts will be occupied by beggary and vice, or become depopulated. This disease will spread like an atrophy in the human body, and ruin will follow ruin, till the entire city is disgusting to the remnant of the inhabitants; at length the whole becomes a heap of ruins: Such have been the causes of decay of all overgrown cities. Ninevah, Babylon, Antioch, and Thebes are become heaps of ruins. Rome, Delphi and Alexandria are partaking the same inevitable fate; and London must some time, from similar causes, succumb under the destiny of everything human.[19]

London's future decay became a lasting literary and visual leitmotiv. For example, French artist, engraver, and illustrator Paul Gustave Doré's *The New Zealander* provided one of the most well-known depictions of London's destiny when it originally appeared in *London: A Pilgrimage* (1871).[20] It was based on English historian and essayist Thomas Babington Macaulay's review of Leopold von Ranke's *Ecclesiastical and Political History of the Popes During the Sixteenth and Seventeenth Centuries* (1840) for the *Edinburgh Review*, in which he predicted that the New Zealander would one day visit the future ruins of London, and take his seat on the remains of London Bridge to sketch the ruins of St. Paul's.[21] By clearly allowing the urban poor a culture of their own, even where this apparently undermined, and in doing so reinforced, the traditional values associated with the Victorian middle classes, Mayhew proved ambiguous as to the diachronic state of the poor. Were they an emerging empire or degenerating dynasties? No one knew.

Mayhew's descriptions of costers, street vendors of food items, exemplified his attempt to describe London's streets as a land teeming with forms of life specific to an uncivilized state.[22] For example, the system of concubinage and cohabitation favored by costers over marriage manifested deviance. "The costermongers, taken as a body, entertain the most imperfect idea of the sanctity of marriage," he noted. "To their undeveloped minds it merely consists of one man and woman living together, and sharing the gains they may each earn by selling in the street." Moreover, there was "no honour to the marriage state, and no shame to concubinage." Mayhew admitted that the women were faithful to their "partners," but he also argued that without marriage jealousy was more prevalent. Those costers who were married "strongly resemble[d] the North American Indians in their conduct to their wives." While able to "understand that it is the duty of woman to contribute to the happiness of the man, [they] but cannot feel that there is a reciprocal duty from the man to the woman. The wife is considered as an inexpensive servant, and the disobedience of a wife is punished with blows." For all this violence the women "seem[ed] to like their men better for their being beaten." Feeding this life was the physical indulgence shared by the uncivilized, since "mind, heart, soul are all absorbed in the belly. The rudest form of animal life, physiologists tell us, is simply a locomotive stomach." Since the costers' morality agreed "strangely" with those of "many savage tribes," Mayhew concluded that they were England's nomads.[23] Thus, sensuality provided a powerful means of demonstrating a lack of moral restraint, because the costers' sensorial pleasures, sexual appetites, and lack of formally recognized marital obligations were argued to have usurped the role of reason and more rational forms of social organization. Their alignment with immorality was facilitated by Mayhew's argument that they had "no religion at all, and very little notion, or none at all, of what religion or a future state is."[24] The image of a lowly state in which morality and reason played no part was a common rationale for denigrating many foreign peoples. Not only did it directly contradict traditional criteria of what constituted morality and personal development, it also effectively denied many colonized peoples a culture and so potentially denied their humanity.[25] Religious beliefs, or reputed lack of them, also played a fundamental role in gauging a people's humanity. That Mayhew chose to employ such tropes to discuss London street life is significant because, regardless of ethnic origin, the same modes of establishing states of civilization and social development eventually extended to the urban wanderer.

An Englishman's home may have been his castle, but for Victorians it also indicated his state of civilization.[26] Nineteenth-century writings on foreign peoples regularly employed the distinction between wanderers and settlers to create and maintain human hierarchies. Foreign peoples earned praise for a knowledge of agriculture and for following settled occupations while being criticized for pursuing nomadic lifestyles. Missionaries, for example, encouraged their subjects to adopt the values associated with owning a home and tilling the land in an effort to cultivate civilization.[27] Similarly, those lapsing from a settled lifestyle exhibited signs of a social and moral degeneration from which it was difficult to be rescued. The association between nomads, the poor, and savagery was exemplified by the coinage of the term *Street Arab*. Just five years earlier, the Reverend Thomas Guthrie's pamphlet, *A Plea for Ragged Schools* (1847), passionately argued for establishment of schools for poor children in an effort to save them from lives of crime: "These Arabs of the city are wild as those of the desert, and must be broken into three habits,—those of discipline, learning, and industry, not to speak of cleanliness."[28] The term quickly gained currency and began to be employed in broader debates on the urban poor.

For Mayhew, the urban wanderer was exemplified by the "street-patterer," who took to the streets from a love of "roving" and so demonstrated the propensity to lapse from a civilized into a nomadic state—to pass from a settler into a "wanderer." In London, the love of roving was a trait peculiar to the patterers. Internationally, however, it was hardly extraordinary, since there were countless instances of "white men adopting all the usages of an Indian hunter; but there is not one example of the Indian hunter or trapper, adopting the steady and regular habits of civilized society." Moreover, the nomadic, or vagrant, tribes were, "ethnology teaches us," a "universal type, whether they be the Bushmen of Africa or the 'tramps' of our own country." The innate tendency to rove manifested itself in an indomitable "self-will"; an "innate aversion to every species of government," be it political, moral, or domestic; an "incapability of continuous labour" or residence; and an "unusual predilection for amusements." Mayhew's classification of patterers as lapsed settlers echoed the concern with the moral and social development of foreign peoples, which often coincided with the aim of improvement through missionary benevolence. The patterers reinforced their status as "tribes *indigenous* to the paving-stones" of London with their use of slang.[29] Mayhew argued that the adoption of a secret language was common to nomadic peoples and used as a means of socially excluding the settled/civilized. Therefore, roving was an anomalous, almost pathological, desire that linked humans internationally.

Despite Mayhew's initial explicitness, in the earliest editions of *London Labour and the London Poor* it is difficult to distinguish between his use of ethnological theory and the racialist maxims of many nineteenth-century discussions of foreign peoples.[30] One such example is the iconography of indolence that permeated African travel literature throughout the eighteenth century.[31] It was common to portray many African peoples, most notably the Khoekhoe, as lazy. Peter Kolb's *Present State of the Cape of Good Hope* (1719) became the source of the willfully slothful image in the eighteenth century, and by the nineteenth century the character had stabilized as a stereotype. A German traveler and writer, Kolb argued that the Khoekhoe were "without doubt, both in Body and Mind, the laziest People under the Sun. A monstrous Indisposition to Thought and Action runs through all the Nations of 'em: And their whole Earthly Happiness seems to lie in Indolence and Supinity."[32] The image resonates with a passage in which Mayhew described an Irish neighborhood:

The one thing that struck me during my visit to this neighbourhood, was the apparent listlessness and lazy appearance of these people. The boys at play were the only beings who seemed to have any life in their actions. The women [. . . appeared] as though utterly deficient in energy. The men smoked, with their hands in their pockets, listening to the old crones talking, and only now and then grunting out a reply when a question was directly put to them.[33]

Significantly, Mayhew is describing the Irish, traditionally the focus of much antipathy, but nonetheless, the passage employs traits usually associated with African peoples. In addition to indolence, Mayhew also draws on two of the most common stereotypes associated with the Khoekhoe: a bestial nature exemplified by their use of a system of clicks (frequently not recognized as a "language" by eighteenth- and nineteenth-century commentators) to communicate, and smoking. While the men smoke away the day they are barely able to form words and show a complete lack of interest in engaging with the interviewer. Any ambiguity is removed when Mayhew cannot help thinking that they appear as "inactive as negroes."[34]

Given such resonances, we might argue that Mayhew's choice to flag the work of Smith and Prichard at the start of *London Labour and the London Poor* was a strategic means of providing a validating gloss to his collected writings. For instance, he may have identified traits such as roving and exclusionary use of slang as peculiarly interesting and found that the work of Prichard and Smith offered a respectable ethnological explanation of their existence. Alternatively, as discussed, Mayhew did make sustained use of the division between settled and wandering peoples and street slang, as exemplified in his discussion of costers and street patterers.[35] Moreover, his work is strewn with physiognomic detail. The recurrent use of these specific tropes, especially roving and slang, throughout the larger work may mean that he did read Smith and Prichard and grew interested in their use, and subsequently looked for suitable evidence. In this sense, his consulting Smith and Prichard is likely to have been formative rather than simply limited to a preface that was only added to the collated articles and which had had no real bearing on their content in the original context of weekly newspaper sketches. However, in later editions, the importance of such writings became much more visible.

Between 1861 and 1862, *London Labour and the London Poor* appeared in a weighty four-volume edition that was peppered with explicit references to contemporary travel and ethnological literature. The fourth volume contained an initial section written solely by Mayhew, and the remainder was the work of collaborators. Of this new material, Mayhew worked with the writer and future adventure novelist Bracebridge Hemyng. They addressed the theme of the "prostitute class more generally" by examining the historical and global dimensions of the sex trade.[36] The subsection "Barbarous Nations" made use of the same divide between settlers and wanderers to distinguish between the civilized and the savage and provide cross-cultural comparative assessments of the status of women, arguing that the "points of contrast between barbarian and civilized races display themselves strongly in relation to the condition of the female sex."[37] The broader generalization that women's lives were often degraded in lower developmental stages was substantiated by reference, often with footnotes, to a considerable range of textual and visual material from travel literature, such as Edward Napier's *Excursions in Southern Africa* (1849), Harriet Ward's *Five Years in Kaffirland* (1848), Charles Sturt's *Narrative of an Expedition into Central Australia* (1849), and M. Lucett's *Rovings in the Pacific* (1851).[38] Although not solely the work of Mayhew, the incorporation and prominent references to such work marked its relevance to Mayhew's discussions of urban savages in earlier volumes. Moreover, it provided a sustained indication of how such literature could be used to make cross-cultural comparisons and extend Mayhew's insights to an ethnography of the streets.

Mayhew's wanderings were those of an ethnographer.[39] He did not merely observe but actively participated in the drama that unfolded in the pages of the *Morning Chronicle* every week. When mere glances were not enough to provide the narrative he required, he would approach his subjects and question them on the streets. Alternatively, he would inquire as to their lodgings and follow them there in the hope of obtaining an interview. If he was approached by a beggar, Mayhew would surprise the poor wretch by twisting the encounter into a cross-examination regarding the history of his decline into current circumstances. Mayhew essentially presented these encounters as monologues that happily gushed forth in response to a simple question: how did this happen? Yet this presentation disguises how much of the encounter he actively shaped. Mayhew was obsessed with procuring representative samples of the different occupations he described, and so would carefully select potential interviewees on the advice of gentlemen who were familiar with the trade in question. He cross-examined these individuals either in their homes or at the offices of the *Morning Chronicle*. In this endeavor, he was aided by assistants who checked his statistics and helped him conduct the interviews.[40] Although he did not mention paying any of them, he may have used the possibility of assistance to gain information. One also suspects that in some cases he may have given his subjects some form of remuneration, since he frequently insisted that there were genuine instances of need to be found among the charlatans, in which case one ought to help gladly. Mayhew is often portrayed as a *flâneur* or urban spectator, yet this belies the fact that he frequently transgressed the boundaries within which the spectator functioned, and so may be more productively cast as an urban ethnographer.

By the late nineteenth century, the urban savage had become a malleable cliché that was molded and deployed in the service of numerous causes. In 1890, the social reformer and founder of the Salvation Army, William Booth, published *In Darkest England and the Way Out*.[41] Although founded in 1865 as a Christian missionary society, Booth's organization was restructured on the military model and so gained its more familiar name in 1878. His manifesto was intended to be a rallying cry for the Army's aim of eradicating the twin evils of poverty and vice. For Booth, London's denizens were a "population sodden with drink" and so "steeped in vice" that they had become "eaten up by every social and physical malady." Moreover, "the stony streets of London, if they could speak, would tell of tragedies as awful, of brewing as complete, of ravishment as horrible, as if we were in Central Africa." The "ghastly devastation" had been "covered, corpse like, with the artificialities and hypocrisies of modern civilization"; however, there was hope for delivering the urban poor from the "gloom of their miserable existence" to a state of repentance, recovery, and "higher and happier life."[42] Booth's utopian vision involved progressively moving those adrift in the sea of ruin from the city into farms, and finally overseas (fig. 4). He dreamed of providing salvation by finding the poor gainful employment, training them in agriculture, and offering them the opportunity to rebuild their lives in Britain's colonies.

Booth's project was part of a broader temperance movement and attempts to eradicate the commercial trafficking of sexual acts. Although his reformist zeal firmly targeted domestic problems, in making the arresting comparison with Africans abroad he took advantage of a contemporary best seller by the journalist and explorer Henry Morton Stanley. Stanley had achieved fame in 1871 when he successfully tracked down the missionary and explorer David Livingstone on the shores of Lake Tanganyika. Livingstone had worked in Africa for most of his life but had lost contact with the outside world for six years, prompting Stanley's dispatch and the immortalization of his eventual greeting of the lost man: "Dr. Livingstone, I presume?"[43] Between 1886 and 1889, Stanley trekked across Africa while heading an expedition ostensibly to rescue the governor of Equatoria in Southern Sudan (Emin Pasha) from indigenous opposition.[44] Once back on home ground, he published *In Darkest Africa; Or, The Quest, Rescue, and Retreat of Emin, Governor of Equatoria* (1890).[45] The book was a publishing sensation and sold 150,000 copies in its first year in print alone.[46] Booth's

choice to use the image of urban savagery and his deliberate appropriation of Stanley's popularity resonates heavily with Mayhew's earlier documentary project; *In Darkest London* provides a pregnant indication of how encounters with the urban poor continued to be simultaneously alienated and associated with contemporary literature on the lives of foreign peoples. Meanwhile, it also indicates how the notion of urban savages became tied to wider projects of socialist reform and Christian salvation.

The urban savage also became a staple of visual depictions of London's downtrodden. In the same year that *In Darkest Africa* and *In Darkest England* were published, Stanley married the artist Dorothy Tennant. As might have been expected of the wealthy socialite, the former prime minister William Gladstone and his wife, man of science Thomas Henry Huxley, and the Pre-Raphaelite painters Frances Leighton and John Everett Millais all helped celebrate the nuptials; at the bride's personal invitation, they were joined by a group of ragged children from a local school.[47] Tennant's interest may easily have been more commercial than philanthropic, since she achieved public recognition for her images of London's gamins. In *London Street Arabs* (1890), she confessed to a "strange affinity" with the "dear little children in tatters." Previous images of poor children, she griped, had been "false and made up," because they were all so "deplorably piteous—[featuring] pale, whining children with the sunken eyes, holding bunches of violets to heedless passers-by; dying match girls, sorrowful watercress girls, emaciated mothers clasping weeping babies." As a corrective, Tennant wanted to depict the "merry, reckless, happy-go-lucky urchin." To this end, she kept a "good supply of rags . . . (all fumigated, camphored, and peppered)" in her studio, where she dressed "too respectable ragamuffin[s]" until they looked as "disreputable as you can wish" before committing their likenesses to pen and paper.[48] Despite not being produced in situ, her images frequently portrayed groups of young, happy children playing in the streets, on rooftops, or in other predominantly urban spaces (fig. 5). Compared with Richard Beard's images of the poor (see below, figs. 8 and 9), they are highly sentimentalized. However, Tennant's choice to name her volume *Street Arabs* is suggestive of how conventional the trope of street savages had become in descriptions of the urban poor: while Mayhew and Booth used the image to shock and alienate, in Tennant's hands it became one of harmless and adorable urchins.

Viewing the Londoner as a distinct specimen was not an entirely novel, or a peculiarly nineteenth-century, phenomenon. Throughout the

FIGURE 4
(*Facing*) William Booth's plan for the salvation of those living in "Darkest England." (Booth, *In Darkest England* [1890], foldout plate. Author's collection.)

FIGURE 5
(*Below*) Sentimentalized images of the urban poor. (Dorothy Tennant, *London Street Arabs* [1890], plate 13. Author's collection.)

eighteenth century, a whole genre of works dedicated to presenting the English as alien enjoyed public success. One of the most common tactics employed was to assume a foreign pseudonym and pen a tourist's account of a visit to Europe, or perhaps England. These works capitalized on the inkling that when abroad, tourists were most interested in watching one another. Some of the most famous works adopting this tactic included Montesquieu's *Persian Letters* (translated into English 1722), Oliver Goldsmith's *The Citizen of the World* (1799), and Robert Southey's *Letters from England* (1807).[49] Despite this tradition, Mayhew's references to ethnological theorists were novel. Nonetheless, for all Mayhew's efforts, his work cannot be taken as a new ethnography of urban life. His weekly articles only provided readers with glimpses into London's underworld and, even when collected together, they lack theoretical coherency. Nevertheless, urban spectators, especially Mayhew and his heirs, drew on the figurative "language of colonial expansion and exploration [that] became *the* terminology through which urban social divisions were conceived."[50] Meanwhile, Mayhew and the terms in which he discussed the urban poor were heirs to a long-standing tradition that portrayed London's streets as a spectacle open to visual inspection and consumption.

"We are wanderers; not, I repeat, historians"

In the nineteenth century, London proved to be the biggest city the world had ever seen.[51] In England, the population had expanded dramatically, from 12 million in 1811 to over 21 million in 1851. The greatest growth took place in the cities, especially London. The censuses of 1801 and 1851, for example, recorded the capital's population at 960,000 and 2.4 million, respectively.[52] Migration accounted for a substantial portion of the increase. As rural areas suffered relatively high unemployment, London offered both better wages and prospects. Its status provided writers with the confidence to claim that "London may be considered, not merely as the capital of England or the British Empire, but as the metropolis of the world."[53] Population growth coupled with urban expansion gave rise to the mass urban crowd. A genuinely novel and striking phenomenon, it both intrigued and inspired writers. In response, they produced an urban literature in which the streets were portrayed as a continual, yet ephemeral, spectacle in which spectators voraciously observed the multitudes.[54]

The crowded urban space both alienated and comforted. Strangers to London were at first sight likely to be "impressed with the bustle and confusion that every where prevails," but find themselves "utterly at a loss to account for" all the "apparent hubbub and buz[z] of voices, the runnings up and down, and crossings and jostlings, and rolling of vehicles."[55] The streets teemed with individuals engaged in the universal business of living, but for some this offered no consolation. In *The Prelude* (1799–1805), the Romantic poet and future Poet Laureate (1843–1850) William Wordsworth presented the city as a place of estrangement and emotional desolation.

How often, in the overflowing streets,
Have I gone forwards with the crowd, and said
Unto myself, "The face of every one
That passes by me is a mystery!"
Thus have I looked, nor ceased to look, oppressed
By thoughts of what and whither, when and how.[56]

Metropolitan residents or visitors were forced into consuming the city's peoples and visual space mutely. Passing streams of people of whose histories one knew nothing accentuated the personal feelings of distress or longing for intimacy. The destructive disruption of human relationships such isolation engendered marked the city as dehumanizing. For Wordsworth and many of his fellow Romantics, the only salvation lay in greener pastures and rural idylls.[57] Yet the crowd delighted others. The essayist Charles Lamb loved "the very smoke of London" and had "no hesitation in declaring, that a mob of happy faces crowding . . . give me ten thousand finer pleasures, than I ever received from all the flocks of silly sheep, that have whitened the plains of Arcadia or Epsom Downs."[58] For Lamb, the crowd provided familiarity, and the "happy faces," although they belonged to strangers, confirmed that he was in a bustling, living city.

For those who found London appealing, the city was an unparalleled stage. "Other cities may have been more populous, or more securely fortified," noted John Bee (*nom de plume* of the writer and periodical editor John Badock), but none of these bore favorable comparison with London. "*Delhi* and *Babylon*, what were they? *Paris* and *St. Petersburg*, of what do they boast, that in London we cannot find an overmatch in kind? Happiness, comfort, health, ease, and progressive improvement, are perceptible every where in the faces, the houses, the manufactories, the domestic arrangements of the major part of twelve hundred thousand persons."[59] Similarly, while in other cities one might find "a single feature or lineament of the great picture of man," Scotsman Robert Mudie observed that in London everything of note and worth was present, "all together and at once upon the canvas . . . singularly blended" and "perfect." Furthermore, the city's magnitude rendered it impossible for the author to give anything more than "light and hasty" pencil sketches of its most notable attributes.[60]

As the streets were transformed into a visual cornucopia, sketches of London were increasingly dedicated to the wanderings of spectators. In 1801, for example, Lamb argued that London was "itself a pantomime and masquerade" full of things that worked into "my mind and feed me, without a power of satiating me. The wonder of these sights impels me into night-walks about her crowded street, and I often shed tears in the motley Strand from fullness of joy at so much Life."[61] For him, merely watching others living was a worthwhile activity and one that brought enormous pleasure and comfort. The city stimulated his visual appetite and, as if he were addicted, stirred cravings that could only be fed by taking a walk in the hustle and bustle. Yet, while looking helped quell his stirrings, even London could not satiate Lamb. He was not alone.

The novelty that waited in every corner impelled the urban spectator toward constantly attending to the spectacle of the streets. In 1824, a journalist wrote, "A sameness in London! Preposterous! Every street, every square, every public walk and every theatre, presents novelty and variety. The very shops with their shopmen and shopwomen, their proprietors and customers, offer a world of information and a wide field for remarks." London's variety offered a means to "draw experience and knowledge from every character and from every scene in the drama of existence."[62] By the 1820s, writers employed the mechanics of contemporary forms of display to encode the nature of this spectacle. Mudie presented London as a vast and incomparable panorama where "if one were to take one's station in the ball or the upper gallery of that great edifice [St. Paul's], the wide horizon, crowded as it is with men and their dwellings, would form a panorama of industry and of life, more astonishing than could be gazed upon from any other point."[63] Watchfully wandering the streets ascribed new value to the quotidian: since the Middle Ages, urban literature had used the streets as opportunities for moral instruction, but in the early nineteenth century the emphasis shifted to visual pleasure and transformed the urban landscape into a visual paradise.[64]

The dynamic nature of the crowd allowed onlookers no more than momentary glances at their subjects; thus, urban spectatorship required skills devoted to observing the ephemeral. Wordsworth had lamented the continually fluxing stream of strangers. Similarly, John Fisher Murray, a poet and well-known contributor to *Blackwood's Magazine*, regarded the "crowds of human faces who 'Come like shadows, so depart—' who flit by me in the streets like the faces of a dream, never to be again seen."[65] Like Shakespearean apparitions, they swiftly dissolved, traceless, into the murky fog and darkness; still, for Murray, the lack of interaction proved to be a virtue, since it enabled intimacy "without the trouble of making their acquaintance."[66] Detachment, therefore, functioned as a means of making the spectator feel at ease with little exertion and gain considerable intelligence of the environment without the need for interfering intercourse. The irrelevance of personal interaction for determining peoples' histories also enabled writers to cater to vicarious consumption. In this literary niche, the urban author functioned as a "student of human character" who mediated between street stage, page, and hearth, where the reader, despite never leaving the "easy chair," was able to enlarge the scope of personal experience.[67]

Walking the streets was an art, one that "as a means of avoiding molestation, and to be performed pleasantly," was "an acquisition of no small importance" (fig. 6a and b).[68] The crowd had grown so large that walking had been "reduced to a system in London; every one taking the right hand of another, whereby confusion is avoided." Behavior departing from the

A

B

FIGURE 6A–B

George Moutard Woodward, *The Art of Walking the Streets of London*, 1818. Engraved by George Cruikshank, these prints satirize many of the pitfalls awaiting the careless or uninitiated when taking a walk in the city. (By kind permission of the London Metropolitan Archives, Guildhall Library, City of London, P5386352 and P5386369, respectively.)

usual customs signaled a stranger. Tourists frequently found themselves unacquainted with the conventions of the crowd. Louis Simond, a Frenchman who visited London from 1810 to 1811, felt "alone in the crowd."[69] The German prince Hermann Pückler-Muskau, who partly inspired the character Count Smorltalk in Charles Dickens's *Pickwick Papers* (1837–37), visited London in 1815 and in the 1820s. He found the city a "tumultuous" place where people might be "lost like a flitting atom" if they did not "pass on to the right or left according the rule," leaving most in "continual danger of being spitted on the shaft of a cabriolet driving too near the 'trottoir,' or crushed under the weight of an overloaded and tottering stage coach edifice."[70] Heinrich Heine, a German Jew who emigrated to Paris in the 1830s and visited London in the 1820s, simply lamented, "Oh that confounded pushing!"[71]

Detachment was cultivated not only by the self-fashioning of the observer but by the rules of etiquette. For example, interaction could be initiated by lingering glances, but if unreturned, these could easily be interpreted as staring and thus great rudeness. One might stare only to ward off trouble. Even if the glances were returned, attempting conversation left one open to suspicion as a pickpocket or thievish rogue with similar intentions to cause mischief by creating a diversion, during which liberties could be taken. Visitors to the metropolis were continually warned of the dangers. John Bee foretold, "Mark, reader! whenever you are jostled against, or your heel is trodden upon, you may *suspect* that person, and consider him who is nearest to you on the other side as having robbed you."[72] Gentlemen, especially, were warned of the dangers of helping apparently unfortunate women and the trouble this could cause. Many writers capitalized on these fears, and a whole genre of books regarding unscrupulous street dwellers was published, instructing readers how to avoid strife.[73] Readers were advised to affect "an ease or knowingness" accompanied with an "air of authority." It was also serviceable to "*appear* like a thoroughbred cockney in your gait and manner; perhaps by placing the hat a little awry, and with an unconcerned stare, penetrating the wily countenance of the rogues" so that one might be afforded a valuable opportunity of escaping the countless snares facing newcomers.[74] Thus, the ephemerality of urban spectatorship was born partly of the difficulty involved in establishing social interaction on the street and the assumed contrast between the wily morals of the Cockney and the mannered airs of gentler folk.

Tourists shared British writers' enthusiasm for observing the streets, with their travel accounts presenting London as a city that both repulsed and impressed. Many were taken aback by the dirt. Simond noted that he was "soon lost in a maze of busy, smoky, dirty streets, more and more so as we advanced. A sort of uniform dinginess seemed to pervade everything." However, "through every door and window the interior of the house, the shops at least, which are most seen, presented, as we drove along, appearances and colours most opposite to this dinginess; everything was clean, fresh brilliant."[75] The West, he observed, was "inhabited by people of fashion, or those who wish to appear such; and the line of demarcation, north and south, runs through Soho Square. Every minute of longitude east is equal to as many degrees of gentility *minus*, or towards west, *plus*."[76] Simond was alluding to the physical institutionalization of the divide between rich and poor that had resulted from Nash's urban redevelopment.[77] Thus, Pückler-Muskau observed that London was a "dirty City, swarming like an ant-hill," but "extremely improved in the direction of Regent Street, Portland Place, and Regent's Park. Now, for the first time, it has the air of a seat of government (Residenz), and not of an immeasurable metropolis of 'shopkeepers.'"[78] Likewise, the social activist Flora Tristan, who traveled from France to England in the 1820s and 1830s, observed that the West End was "splendid; the houses are well built, the streets straight but extremely monotonous; it is there that one sees glittering carriages, magnificently dressed ladies, dandies capering on horses of great beauty, and crowds of valets dressed in rich livery and armed with long gold or silver-headed canes."[79] Anishinabe convert, interpreter, and manager of a troupe of Anishinabe performers, George Henry (also known as Maungwudaus), wrote of the city in 1843: "Like musketoes in America in the summer season, so are the people in this city, in their numbers and biting one another to get a living."[80] The numbers similarly impressed themselves on the memory of the Persian prince Najaf Koolee Meerza, who found that the sheer "noise of the carriages and coaches of the great city of London and the voice of its most enormous population" caused the din to be "heard like thunder," even at a distance of "seven parasangs," roughly leagues, from the city.[81] Meanwhile, those who approached London by sea stood in awe of the docks, as from this vantage point it was impossible to detect the city's perimeters, making it appear unbounded.[82]

Despite the bleak weather, miasmic black fog, and pervasive grime, London's sheer size appears to have universally impressed foreign tourists, who also viewed the city as a visual cornucopia. They often felt lost or alone in the crowd and took time to accustom themselves to negotiating the winding, crowded streets. As tourists they were wont to observe the habits and customs of Londoners with an interest and detachment akin to the spectator in British urban literature. Thus, tourists' accounts echoed the ambiguity of British writers' experiences of London. Moreover, they simultaneously confirmed the status of London's streets as a spectacle and, by the early Victorian period, explicitly employed the trope of an international theater to discuss London's streets. The German novelist and poet Theodor Fontane, for example, first visited London in 1844 and noted, "London has made an indelible impression on me. I was amazed not so much by her beauty as by her grandeur. It is a miniature or quintessence of the whole world."[83]

The act of observing the streets involved many elements traditionally associated with the *flâneur* and gained particular currency in the nineteenth century. Urban spectatorship depended on detached observation combined with a vision of the urban environment as a perpetual and ephemeral spectacle. Far from finding this distance alienating, the urban spectator felt at ease with the mass of strangers. However, assuming an isolated presence was not enough to make the streets legible to everyone. One needed judicious care to interpret all that passed correctly; otherwise, spectators might find themselves among apparently uninteresting people and crowded streets of greater inconvenience than pleasure. Nevertheless, for those fortunate enough to possess the required "ray of genius" to light up the stage's significance, life itself seemed to be "compressed" into the "abridgment of a morning walk."[84] Furthermore, for metropolitan spectators, London's streets offered the added advantage of encompassing global human diversity.

A Parliament of Nations

Founded as a port to channel goods for the Romans, London was a cosmopolitan city from the outset. It is difficult to determine the ethnic heterogeneity of the metropolis from figures of resident foreigners alone, since the census defined their status by their place of birth. Therefore, an individual born in India would be classed as foreign regardless of ethnicity, and children born to foreign parents in England would be recognized as belonging to the resident home population. Despite the likely inaccuracies of any estimates, it is clear that by the nineteenth century London was both strikingly diverse and self-consciously recognized as being so by contemporary commentators.

Although most of the inhabitants migrated from the surrounding areas, immigrants formed a significant portion of the population, and were often present in clearly, but informally, demarcated areas of the city. For example, the docks were one of the most ethnically heterogeneous areas of the city, as ships, along with trade goods, brought motley crews.[85] The earliest settlers from overseas were drawn from Scandinavia, the Low Countries, Germany, and France. The physical proximity of these countries allowed southern England and its overseas neighbors to function as a coherent economic region. Others migrated as a result of Britain's historical relationship with their homelands. For example, from the seventeenth through the nineteenth century, many black and South Asian peoples were shipped to England by West Indian sugar plantation owners or colonial officers in India. Some were slaves, while others served in various forms of either paid or indentured labor. Many immigrants also fled in diasporas that were rooted in attempts to avoid persecution following historic upheavals. In the mid-sixteenth century, for instance, Protestants from Germany, France, and the Low Countries fled their respective homelands to escape religious discrimination. Many loyal royalists also left France after the revolution of 1789 and to escape the rapidly escalating violence that so haunted several generations of British writers. Similarly, scores of Americans fled after supporting Britain in the War of Independence, and before the American Civil War (1861–65), many enslaved individuals sought freedom in England.[86]

Jewish and Asian immigrants were among London's largest settled communities. Following the arrival of William the Conqueror, a small Jewish community had formed there, but in 1290 Edward I outlawed Judaism and banished the Jews. In 1656, Oliver Cromwell lifted the ban, primarily to encourage mercantile connections that would revive a flagging economy. Following its readmission, the Jewish community flourished, and by the late seventeenth century synagogues and cemeteries had been established in Spitalfields. Many migrated to avoid religious persecution in mainland Europe, since British rule did not pose any restrictions on the practice of Judaism and so offered relative freedom (but not equality). By the early nineteenth century, Jewish migrants were moving to London primarily for the economic benefits it offered, and by 1815 are argued to have numbered in the region of 25,000.[87] From the seventeenth century onward, many Asians arrived in England as lascars (sailors), ayahs (nannies), and domestic servants for British and Anglo-Indian families returning from India. In the eighteenth century, South Asian servants served as fashionable status symbols for the wealthy British. Once servants had outgrown their usefulness or completed an agreed period of service, most were sent back to South Asia. Others ran away or were sold to serve other families. Some were merely cut adrift and left unemployed, poverty-stricken, and homeless, eking out a living by begging. Early Chinese settlers found themselves in a similar situation. Often sailors arriving aboard trading vessels, they were left in the docks until they could find work elsewhere.[88] The situation was dire enough for the Strangers' Home for Asiatics, Africans and South Sea Islanders to be founded in 1856 to house the growing number of impoverished foreign domestic servants in the East End district of Limehouse. With its foundation stone laid by Prince Albert, the home was intended to fill a need that had "been very generally felt."[89] Once built, "the longing eyes of the starving hundreds of Asiatics in London were hopefully turned to this new building, and daily crowded round its door for help."[90] Others arrived as the wives or children of former nawabs (nabobs) returning from the subcontinent.[91] Smaller communities of Polish, American, and European immigrants were also resident.

The black population proved to be a particularly visible presence. In the eighteenth century, an ornately dressed young black page boy proved to be an indispensable accessory for a lady of fashion. Until the abolition of British slavery, most resident black peoples were in bondage and so of originally African American, Caribbean, or West Indian extraction.[92] The popularity of slaves as servants ensured that even in isolated country residences, black peoples began to penetrate private domestic spaces. In the nineteenth century, many continued in domestic service after having achieved their freedom. Many managed to settle in London, working and intermarrying with the local population; within the lower classes, considerable assimilation occurred. In 1772, with characteristically racist fervor, the antiabolitionist and Jamaican plantation owner Edward Long felt it necessary to attack runaway slaves who upon "arriving in *London* . . . soon grow acquainted with a knot of blacks, who having eloped from their respective owners at different times, repose themselves here in ease and indolence" before finding themselves a paid position, where many "persons of rank and fortune entertain these fugitives on the footing of other servants." Worse still, they "soon intermarry . . . The lower classes of women in *England*," being "remarkably fond of the blacks, for reasons too brutal to mention; they would connect themselves to horses and asses, if the laws permitted them."[93] Long was venting his fury in the wake of the Mansfield judgment, which had been handed down in the infamous case of James Somerset, a runaway slave seeking legal protection from being returned to his former owner. The presiding judge, Lord Mansfield, set a legal precedent by ruling that no slave could be forcibly removed from England.[94] Tellingly, Long's vehemence was directed not just at runaway slaves who failed to respect their owners' property rights but at the resident communities with whom they forged alliances to pursue their freedom.

Almost thirty years later, during an 1805 visit to London, Benjamin Silliman, Yale Professor of Chemistry, Mineralogy and Natural History, also picked up on the visibility of the black presence:

A black footman is considered as a great acquisition, and consequently, negro servants are sought for and caressed. An ill dressed or starving negro is never seen in England, and in some instances even alliances are formed between them and white girls of the lower orders of society. A few days since, I met in Oxford Street a well dressed white girl, who was of a ruddy complexion, and even handsome, walking arm in arm, and conversing very sociably, with a negro man, who was as well dressed as she, and so black that his skin had a kind of ebony lustre. As there are no slaves in England, perhaps the English have not learned to regard negroes as a degraded class of men, as we do in the United States, where we have never seen them in any other condition.[95]

Silliman's surprise is both palpable and, significantly, something he felt would interest his American readers (he was writing for an American publisher). Meanwhile, his observation reflects the broader ethnic diversity of London and the possibilities for cultural assimilation that were available to resident black populations. Accordingly, black faces regularly appear in depictions of London's underworld, where they are found intermingling freely.[96] Some, such as Robert Wedderburn and Olaudah Equiano, having achieved their own freedom, began to campaign for the emancipation of others and achieved prominence as political activists.[97] Those less fortunate might turn to begging. The one-eyed Charles M'Gee and Joseph Johnson, whose hat was unmistakably modeled after a ship, achieved fame for this alone. Londoners' experience of black peoples was inextricably tied up with the practice of performance over a broad range of social situations; black performers ranged from the casual busker in the street to professional musicians and the theatrically inclined. A substantial proportion earned their living as musicians and actors, with some achieving celebrity status: for instance, Billy Waters, a one-legged talented fiddler, and Ira Aldridge, an acclaimed actor. The association between black peoples and performance was strengthened by the significant number of white actors who painted themselves black for theatrical roles. Minstrels, for example, could regularly be found in the streets, where they serenaded passersby. The one exception to this visibility is that of black women. They were a much rarer sight than black men but were still not unknown.

Ethnic diversity extended to the indigenous peoples of Britain. Ethnologists commonly subdivided the population of the British Isles into different human varieties.[98] Thus, the Anglo-Saxons and the Celts were distinct peoples that could easily be distinguished by variations in both facial and bodily formation. Furthermore, the consensus was that they differed in personality, intelligence, and behavior.[99] Within London, despite intermixing, the Anglo-Saxon contingent remained the largest subsection. However, Irish citizens had enjoyed unrestricted access to Britain since the Middle Ages, and so formed a significant portion of British migrants to the capital.[100] From the late eighteenth century onward, cheaper travel and increasing unemployment at home due to changes in the manufacturing and agricultural sectors encouraged Irish emigration. Significant settlement in London began in this period, and Irish immigrants worked principally as unskilled, casual laborers and domestic servants. In the late 1840s, the Great Famine acted as a catalyst, with around 8 million people emigrating, many to London. The Irish community grew particularly strong in Southwark, Whitechapel, and slums such as the St. Giles "rookery" (later abolished to form New Oxford Street). Thus, immigrant communities were particularly visible indicators of larger patterns of migration and urban expansion in the mid-nineteenth century.[101]

The metropolitan population consequently provided an ethnically diverse spectacle, with writers differentiating the variety into fine-grained distinctions that went far beyond divisions based on complexion alone. Such heterogeneity allowed urban writers to claim London as a global microcosm. However, the sheer variety of countless individuals teeming along bustling streets presented would-be social observers with specific needs in order to create order from their experiences. Urban writers following in the footsteps of the *flâneur* laid claim to extraordinary powers of perception that could function instinctually and upon mere glances. However, the majority of the population, lacking such perspicacity, needed more accessible solutions. As the crowd proliferated, technologies developed to allow urban spectators to determine peoples' histories quickly and effectively without inappropriate social interaction.

Reading the Crowds

Urban spectators relied on established conventions in which the body was conceptualized as akin to a hieroglyphic text that could be read by the trained eye. By the nineteenth century, it had become common to argue that a person's outward physical formation reflected the development of inner moral qualities. The head, the seat of the brain and therefore the intellect, achieved particular prominence as an indicator of individual capacity in a range of disciplines. Phrenologists, for example, proposed that the brain could be divided into faculties that corresponded to mental traits. These faculties developed independently of one another, and their physical formation was reflected in the shape of the brain and, in turn, the shape of the skull. Therefore, an examination of the skull (or the bumps on the head) would allow a precise description of an individual's mental capability. In the eighteenth century, Pieter Camper argued that the angle produced by drawing a line along the slope of the brow and down the bridge of the nose could be used to arrange humans along a continuum reflecting degrees of intellectual development. By the 1800s, the facial angle had been adapted to provide a hierarchical arrangement of humanity that reflected the contemporary racialism of human natural history. Similarly, physiognomy capitalized on the premise that intellectual and moral developments were made manifest in an individual's visage. Ancient philosophers had proposed the link, but as a modern enterprise, physiognomy was based on Johann Casper Lavater's *Essay on Physiognomy* (1789–98). The work formally codified existing artistic conventions that were used to signal a person's character through his or her looks. These theories of human development proved significant for the urban spectator, because they were argued to render people's character apparent in their facial features, like words written on a page.[102]

Benjamin Robert Haydon's *Punch; or, May Day* (1829) and Richard Beard's images of London's poor exemplify the conventions used by artists and urban spectators to classify the urban crowd. Haydon, an artist by profession, intended *Punch* to provide a visual synopsis of London's citizens and used established cues to classify the urban landscape (fig. 7). For example, the street sweeper's broom, the street vendor's apples, and the Italian statue seller's figurines all identify their owner's trade. The young pickpocket, almost entirely hidden behind the unsuspecting man watching a puppet show, reveals himself by looking away from his target while a hand grasps at poorly concealed valuables. The lady in the carriage is barely visible, but her dress, compared with the other women, is obviously made of a more delicate, shimmering fabric. Similarly, the Bow Street runner, a predecessor of the policeman, is signaled by his uniform. Others stand out

FIGURE 7
Benjamin Robert
Haydon, *Punch; or,
May Day*, 1829. Hay-
don's painting is
an excellent example
of the visual cues
that nineteenth-
century typological
classifications de-
pended on. (© Tate,
London 2009. Used
by permission.)

because of their ethnic origin. The man dancing in the foreground and the
servant riding aboard the back of the coach are distinguished by their color
alone. The man crouching just in front of the coach, smiling as he watches
his young student stealing, is revealed as Jewish by the stereotyped beard,
cunning expression, and large, irregular nose (see "avarice" and "malignity" in fig. 10).[103] By depicting a crowd differentiated on the basis of class,
gender, trade, and ethnic origin within a single scene, Haydon presented
the visualized equivalent of London's streets in urban literature.

Beard's images of the urban poor were based on daguerreotypes taken
in a photographic studio, and were used to illustrate *London Labour and the
London Poor*. Occasionally, individuals were named in the title of his artwork, or the text allowed them to be identified. Most, such as the long-sheet
seller (ballad seller), spice seller, mud lark (sewer cleaner), old-clothes man,
and rat catcher, were identified only by their trade. As nameless images,
they were intended to function as typological exemplars rather than individualized portraits. *Doctor Bokanky, the Street Herbalist* and *Woman of
the Bosjes Race* present typical examples (figs. 8 and 9). Bokanky's display
box both protects and advertises his concoctions, while his rough, worn

Glimpsing Urban Savages

[39]

DOCTOR BOKANKY, THE STREET HERBALIST.

[*From a Daguerreotype by* BEARD.]

WOMAN OF THE BOSJES RACE.

[*From a Daguerreotype by* BEARD.]

FIGURES 8 AND 9
Richard Beard, *Doctor Bokanky, the Street Herbalist* and *Woman of the Bosjes Race*.
Henry Mayhew's four-volume *London Labour and the London Poor* used such typological images to illustrate the urban poor. They were based on daguerreotypes produced by Beard in his studio. (Mayhew, *London Labour and the London Poor* [1861–62], 1: facing 197 and 4: facing 58. Reproduced by kind permission of the Syndics of the Cambridge University Library.)

clothing betrays his ethnic origin and social status. The San woman was one of a number of foreign peoples in later editions of *London Labour and the London Poor*, including bare-breasted Nubian women making pots, a lady from Borneo, and a Chinese prostitute that appeared in a section devoted to the world's oldest profession.[104] Some of the images were copies from travel literature and were referenced as such. Others, such as the San woman, were directly sourced from daguerreotypes taken by Beard. The San woman, for instance, is shown in the midst of dense vegetation, wearing and squatting on furs and surrounded by firewood. Yet, given Beard's working practices, the original daguerreotype was almost certainly taken in a studio and the model made to conform to expectations of what peoples of her given ethnic group might look like, wear, and own. Significantly, if the model was a San woman, it is highly likely that she was also commercially exhibited, since San individuals were a rare presence in the metropolis.

Both Haydon and Beard drew on art-historical traditions of depicting the urban poor. Haydon owed a great deal to the artist and engraver William Hogarth's images of eighteenth-century London street life.[105] For Beard in particular, the most pertinent images were those of street vendors and hawkers, known as the Cries of London, which were sold in the metropolis from the sixteenth century onward.[106] Hogarth's and Beard's images drew directly from these Cries in both their style and their pictorial content.[107] Originally sold as single sheets featuring an array of hawkers, by the seventeenth century the Cries evolved into ensembles of prints, often by a single artist. By the nineteenth century they were incorporated into dedicated collections of prints or books that documented the lives of the outcast. Hawkers in earlier Cries were shown individually against plain backgrounds. They were distinguished only by the items they sold or occasionally by an item of clothing, such as a milkmaid's apron. By the mid-eighteenth century, their habits were more detailed and they were often depicted in urban areas.

In employing art-historical traditions of depicting the urban poor, Haydon's and Beard's use of face, dress, and occupational effects to classify their subjects meant that both artists were applying the same techniques that were available to the urban spectator. For example, Wordsworth observed that during a walk in the London streets he could

See, among less distinguishable shapes,
The Italian, with his frame of images
Upon his head; with basket at his waist
The Jew; the stately and slow-moving Turk,
With freight of slippers piled beneath his arm!

Briefly, we find if tired of random sights
And haply to that search our thoughts should turn,
Among the crowd, conspicuous less or more,
As we proceed, all specimens of man
Through all the colours which the sun bestows,
And every character of form and face:
The Swede, the Russian; from the genial south,
The Frenchman and the Spaniard; from remote
America, the Hunter-Indian; Moors,
Malays, Lascars, the Tartar and Chinese,
And Negro Ladies in white muslin gowns.[108]

Many ethnic minorities were associated with specific goods or activities. Italians, for example, were identified as selling statues in the summer, while Jews were more commonly merchants.[109] Thus, the Turk, the Italian, and the Jew are respectively defined by the marks of their trade in Wordsworth's poetic autobiography. Meanwhile, other nationalities are distinguished by their physiognomy as bestowed by the sun. As Wordsworth lists the specimens of mankind, from the Swede through to the Negro, he grades them into a spectrum of color from light to dark that in turn reflects the increasing heat of the climates from which they originate.

Similarly, Mudie observed that in London he met with

the bland broad faces, blue eyes, and determined but unspeculative air of genuine England—in one place the winking grey optics, solemn faces, and cautious mien of the pawky Caledonians [Scots]—in another the ferret eyes, and pointed puckered face of Hibernia [Irish], screwed up as if every muscle of it were brandishing a shillelagh … —though you meet with all this, and meet with in every degree, and in every blending; yet it is still true, that for the grand constituent parts of this confusion of characters, and of races you must look to England, to Scotland and Ireland;—to England in a especial manner, because, as is the case with every country, England stamps more or less of her own character, not only upon all who are born within her boundaries, but upon all who reside there for any considerable time.[110]

As a Scotsman, Mudie may have been especially sensitive to the ethnic diversity of the British Isles; nonetheless, he reiterated the common argument that the population of the island group comprised distinct ethnic groups. He used color (the Scots' grey eyes), physiognomy (puckered Irish faces), personality (the cautious Scot), and personal effects (the Irish club) to define subtle differences between metropolitan residents. Interbreeding sometimes blended these features, and the environment added its own imprint; but, he argued, they were still trustworthy indicators of ethnic origin. As urban spectators, Wordsworth and Mudie relied on habit, action, and physiognomy to categorize a range of passersby. The differences they used may have been telling, but were also often subtle enough to require some training to detect and correctly interpret. To cater to these needs, in the late eighteenth and early nineteenth centuries a literature aiming to teach legibility emerged.

One such manual, Thomas Woolnoth's *Facts and Faces* (1854), exemplifies the range of moral and personality traits that physiognomists aspired to encapsulate (fig. 10a–o). The book documented a variety of characteristics using a pictorial example and detailed textual notes outlining the outwardly visible defining features of the inward quality. Cunning, for example, was marked by a great peculiarity in the form of underdeveloped childlike eyes.[111] Avarice manifested itself as "a culprit-like consciousness, giving a piteous and apprehensive look," accompanied by "eyes humid and rheumy, with a timid and tremulous appearance at all times."[112] Significantly, the faces accompanying descriptions of malignity and avarice possessed unmistakably stereotyped Jewish features. Woolnoth, in common with the majority of the literature during the period, supported the training of the eye according to the rational principles of physiognomy in order to read peoples' histories. The popularity of such training is indicated by the number of publications, periodical articles, and pamphlets in circulation that provided their readers with physiognomic expertise and which may be helpfully characterized as "pocket physiognomy."[113]

Training the eye depended on urban spectators comparing instances of variation in the streets with the exemplary types presented in their chosen manuals. Authors such as Woolnoth acted as authority figures who guided the spectators' acts of classification through vicarious ostension.[114] Through repeated acts of seeing and comparing, budding physiognomists

A Avarice   B Cunning in the Imbecile   C Cunning

D Deceit   E Envy   F Gay Conceit

G Grave Conceit   H Ill-nature   I Malignity

J Obstinacy   K Pride   L Resolution

M Sagacity   N Satire   O Tyranny

FIGURE 10A–O

Originally accompanied by detailed textual notes, these images were visual exemplars used to train budding physiognomists. Both "Avarice" (10a) and "Malignity" (10i) feature stereotyped Jewish features. (Thomas Woolnoth, *Facts and Faces*, 2nd ed. [1854]. Reproduced by kind permission of the Syndics of the Cambridge University Library.)

learned to recognize characteristics that were made constitutive of social types, such as "beggar," "Irish," and "Negro," and easily accessible without social interaction. Rather than illuminating inherent, albeit hidden, meanings, the users of these concepts were assigning significance to variations in habit, posture, and physiognomy. New technologies, such as physiognomic literature, created social categories, such as the poorly dressed beggar, because writers like Woolnoth used them as their teaching exemplars and so assigned them a new status within emerging taxonomies of the urban dweller. Once trained, therefore, the urban spectator could classify passing faces into a range of social types quickly and effectively without the need for distracting intercourse. Moreover, while physiognomy was originally developed to detect individual character, over the course of the nineteenth century it became more concerned with defining larger social groups.[115] As such, typological classifications were ideal technologies for the urban spectator and permeated urban literature throughout the early nineteenth century.

✳

Mayhew's urban savage grew out of a long-standing tradition of street ethnography and attempts to classify the ethnically diverse and expanding metropolitan population in both visual and literary materials. From the Middle Ages onward, London had frequently inspired either condemnation or approval; some praised it for its diversity, liveliness, and achievements, while others condemned it as a dehumanizing and festering pustule that bred moral and social degeneration.[116] Ambiguous representations of the city continued into the Regency and Victorian periods. However, a new and novel shared image of the city as an ephemeral spectacle also emerged. Within this new visual economy, wandering the streets gained new intellectual purchase. Metropolitan spectators were especially fortunate, as London, it was argued, was the largest theater of human experience in the world.

In order to render the streets instructive and entertaining, urban literature portrayed the familiar as alien and capitalized on people's interest in observing difference. In the eighteenth century, the genre was almost dominated by British and Continental writers adopting a foreign personality and purporting to be visitors to England. As the cost of travel became less prohibitive, writings of genuine tourists became much more common in the nineteenth century and gave voice to a new type of urban spectator. Tourist accounts frequently confirmed the streets as arenas of prime human interest. Thus, in a range of works, the streets emerged as a visual paradise that provided a continual yet ephemeral quotidian drama.

London's great attraction lay in its sheer size and diversity. The city witnessed by far the largest population and urban expansion of the nineteenth century. Its multitudes alone provided a novel phenomenon that intrigued writers and fed the growing literature regarding the street spectacle, but the city's size also proved to be the basis for another of its greatest assets—diversity. London's streets provided urban spectators with a wealth of people differentiated by their gender, class, occupation, and ethnic origin. A number of identifiable foreign communities were resident in the capital, including significant Jewish, Asian, and black populations. Contemporaries identified distinct ethnicities among the white population too, including the Anglo-Saxon, Celtic, and Irish. As such, walking the streets, it was claimed, was a means of encountering enormous human variety.

In her history of black peoples in Britain, Gretchen Gerzina relates her amazement when she "entered a well-known London bookshop one day, searching for the paperback edition of Peter Fryer's exhaustive *Staying Power: The History of Black People in Britain* and instead of assistance received a stern look from the saleswoman," who promptly replied: "'Madam, there were no black people in England before 1945.'"[117] While the saleswoman's comment may be peculiarly misinformed, it is indicative of a wider neglect of the substantial foreign population that has been resident in London throughout its history and which is particularly pertinent to histories of human display. Foreign people in Britain have often been the subject of histories in which their presence is exclusively documented in an effort to recover the presence of a particular ethnic group. Far less research has attempted to integrate these studies into broader discussions of London's cosmopolitan crowd.[118]

Recognizing urban heterogeneity is critical for histories of human display and would allow the city to be reconceptualized as an intercultural contact zone.[119] Much of the current literature on cultural encounters is located abroad, often at the boundaries of imperial expansion and exploration.[120] This work presents a valuable and sophisticated understanding of encounter, but its international focus has tended to support the neglect of cross-cultural contact in a domestic setting. Such studies might provide rich insights into how foreign peoples lived and settled in nineteenth-century Europe, and how the relationships between migrating populations affected perceptions of corresponding subjects abroad.[121] Unfortunately, neglecting cross-cultural contact in the metropolis has supported the common assumption that displayed peoples were categorized as evidently "savage," alien, or foreign by way of their color alone. For example, it is often assumed that when black peoples were displayed in London it was relatively uncommon to see a black person on the street or that their color ensured their status as alien.[122] Acknowledging the ethnic diversity of London's resident population provides the possibility of more nuanced understandings of why displayed peoples were ever commercially successful.

The visually attentive metropolitan population provided showmen with an ideal potential market for commercially exhibiting human variety.

Urban spectators relied on typological classifications employing physiognomy, dress, and occupational effects as distinguishing markers. These were assigned significance in works that presented readers with detailed instructions on how to utilize the new technologies. The utility and popularity of such taxonomies depended on the ephemerality of the street encounter. Urban spectatorship was the art form of decoding the histories of passersby with whom one was unacquainted and in the briefest of glances. London's populace was, therefore, one that was aware of fine-grained ethnic distinctions and accustomed to quick and effective classification of diverse subjects.

Meanwhile, the heterogeneity of the London populace exposed many to different cultures and possibly whetted the appetite for viewing ethnic diversity. By the mid-nineteenth century, urban spectators were familiar with the notion that knowledge of foreign peoples could elucidate the condition of resident nomads, rendering the shows important for viewing not only difference but similarity. The notion of the urban savage depended on recognizing cultural practices that were common within the different social strata across ethnic boundaries, and human exhibitions provided an arena in which to observe such practices. As such, the shows were sites where a personal identity could be defined in relationship to both foreign and indigenous peoples. Finally, urban spectatorship depended on viewing people as objects available for visual inspection and consumption. Showmen displaying foreign peoples capitalized on this observational practice but charged for the prospect of lingering inspection, an act not possible on the street. However, urban spectatorship alone did not guarantee paying customers for these events; rather, showmen used developing techniques in advertising to translate urban spectators' proclivities into tangible profits.

Artful Promotion

IN 1847, *Punch* published an announcement of one of the season's earliest and most entertaining exhibitions: the billstickers' "pictorial embellishment" of Fleet Street Prison's walls. The weekly magazine argued that the prison walls offered a "powerful counter-action" to the other entertainments on offer and even suggested that an enterprising publisher might profit from producing a catalog of the images (fig. 11).[1] The article's humor depended on the recognition that observing the streets of London was an established practice, both in the imagination and in physical presence. Of particular relevance here is that far fewer people attended an exhibition than knew of its existence, and that the streets were likely to be the first place where consumers were alerted to a new offering. Entrance charges of anything between 1 and 5 shillings often proved prohibitive; however, for the unfortunate many there were numerous other opportunities for consumption without attendance. Knowledge of an exhibition potentially extended beyond those attending to any passersby, since the reproduction and circulation of posters, playbills, and handbills enabled their use as highly visible markers pasted up in the streets surrounding the venue and possibly on the entrance door. Thus, the sheer visibility of the "language of the walls" ensured that the printed materials used to create and disseminate knowledge of the shows were at least as important as the live performances.[2]

Showmen were acutely aware of the need to attract potential consumers, and so were quick to take advantage of advertising's development into a skilled trade from the mid-nineteenth century onward.[3] Previously, most advertising took place within the streets, and few street vendors considered it their full-time trade. Much of it was oral, as sellers "cried" for buyers, but there was some use of printed materials, especially in the late eighteenth and early nineteenth centuries. Billposting was quickly adopted in the early nineteenth century, while sandwich boards first came into use midcentury. In the late nineteenth century, specialized advertising agencies were established, and there were considerable changes to the visual makeup of printed promotional materials, with more frequent use of color,

THE BILLSTICKERS' EXHIBITION.

images, and specialist typefaces. In 1833, a journalist for the *Athenaeum*
confidently described advertising as a trade still in its "infancy," but was
uncertain as to whether it was a science or an art.[4] Considering showmen's
promotional strategies is both revealing and necessary for understanding
the ways in which consumers were persuaded to part with their money;
however, it is critical to bear in mind that this does not equate to an exca-
vation of consumer responses. Rather, a close analysis of promotional materials provides insights into the varied, and often shared, representational
conventions that showmen used to generate public interest and mediate
the ways in which the shows were ultimately interpreted.

The shows' promotional materials have often been ignored by scholars, with many using them as primary biographical or visual sources or
as isolated pieces of evidence (often of the shows' receptions) with little, if
any, analysis of their production, circulation, and use.[5] The exception to
this general neglect is the literature on photography and anthropology.[6]
However, this leaves a wealth of visual material untouched, particularly
from the earlier nineteenth century.[7] In contrast, this chapter explores
how the shows' meanings were shaped for both potential and paying visitors through printed promotional material. In doing so, it draws on the
lessons of museological studies in which it has been shown that curatorial
decisions regarding the context in which an artifact is placed, as well as
its positioning and labeling, can all structure visitor responses.[8] The discussion also adds to recent work that has explored the use of guidebooks
by working-class visitors to the British Museum and the interpretation of
panoramas.[9] Examining promotional material in this vein suggests that it
created a publicly accessible network of artifacts and claims that must be
considered in discussions of how displayed peoples came to be consumable commodities. For instance, the importance of promotional materi-

als depended on the geography of their use; the streets, exhibition venues, and the periodical press were all spaces in which showmen laid claim to readers' attention in an effort to secure custom. Meanwhile, promotional materials effectively extended invitations designed to encourage patrons to interpret the shows within diverse frameworks ranging from travel literature to foreign affairs. By employing these strategies, showmen made these materials of fundamental importance in shaping the shows' receptions while simultaneously implicating them in the creation of broader nineteenth-century attitudes toward human difference.

Advertising Humans

Impresarios used a variety of printed promotional materials to encourage people to part with their money: posters, playbills, handbills, newspaper reviews, and newspaper advertisements.[10] Hurrying pedestrians were offered a visual feast of posters and playbills clinging to the walls of buildings in haphazard arrangements while individuals thrust handbills into their grasp; those at home could peruse a newspaper and select suitable entertainment. Unlike newspaper advertisements, printed advertisements, such as handbills, were not subject to taxation and so provided a less costly alternative. Showmen were so eager to take advantage of the streets in lowering their expenses that billposting, which reached its height in the 1830s and 1840s, prompted Parliament to pass an act requiring permission to be sought before pasting any poster.[11]

John Parry's *A London Street Scene* (1835; fig. 12) evocatively captures this remarkable new advertising culture. The sheer wealth of information that street advertising made available to any literate individual is clear. The posters Parry depicts advertise a range of goods: one suggests reading the *Mirror* magazine (off-center, left in the shadow), another offers new hats for those who find themselves with something looking a little "shabby" (top right-hand corner), a number promote current theater productions at the Adelphi and St. James's, another promises fine singing at the English Opera House (top middle), another a minstrel show with a stylized image of a blacked-up man (bottom right), and another the equestrian show at Astley's while another boldly asks the burning question of the day, "Have you seen the industrious fleas?" (top middle).[12] Although the use of available walls as an advertising arena is evident, Parry also highlights two problems facing showmen using the streets to promote their events. Reading is made difficult by the partial visibility of most of the posters. As soon as promotional materials were made public, they could be buried under another layer of glue and letterpress (although honorable billposters waited until the glue had dried). The billposter creates this dynamic palimpsest by pasting yet another announcement onto the wall, while the scraps of paper littering the pavement and the tattered posters at street level point toward its inevitable destruction. The posters' transience is juxtaposed to the seeming permanence of St. Paul's Cathedral. The direct consequence

of this continual turnover means that viewers of the painting, and by implication the street scene it depicts, must read carefully in order to discern the boundaries and messages of individual posters; just as posters jostle for space, they also vie for attention.

Since promotional materials were not guaranteed effectiveness by sheer numbers or presence alone, their efficacy depended on other innovations; figures 13–16 reproduce typical examples. Their visual impact depended on developments in advertising fueled by the needs of promoters in the nineteenth century.[13] Billposting was a relatively new trade, and

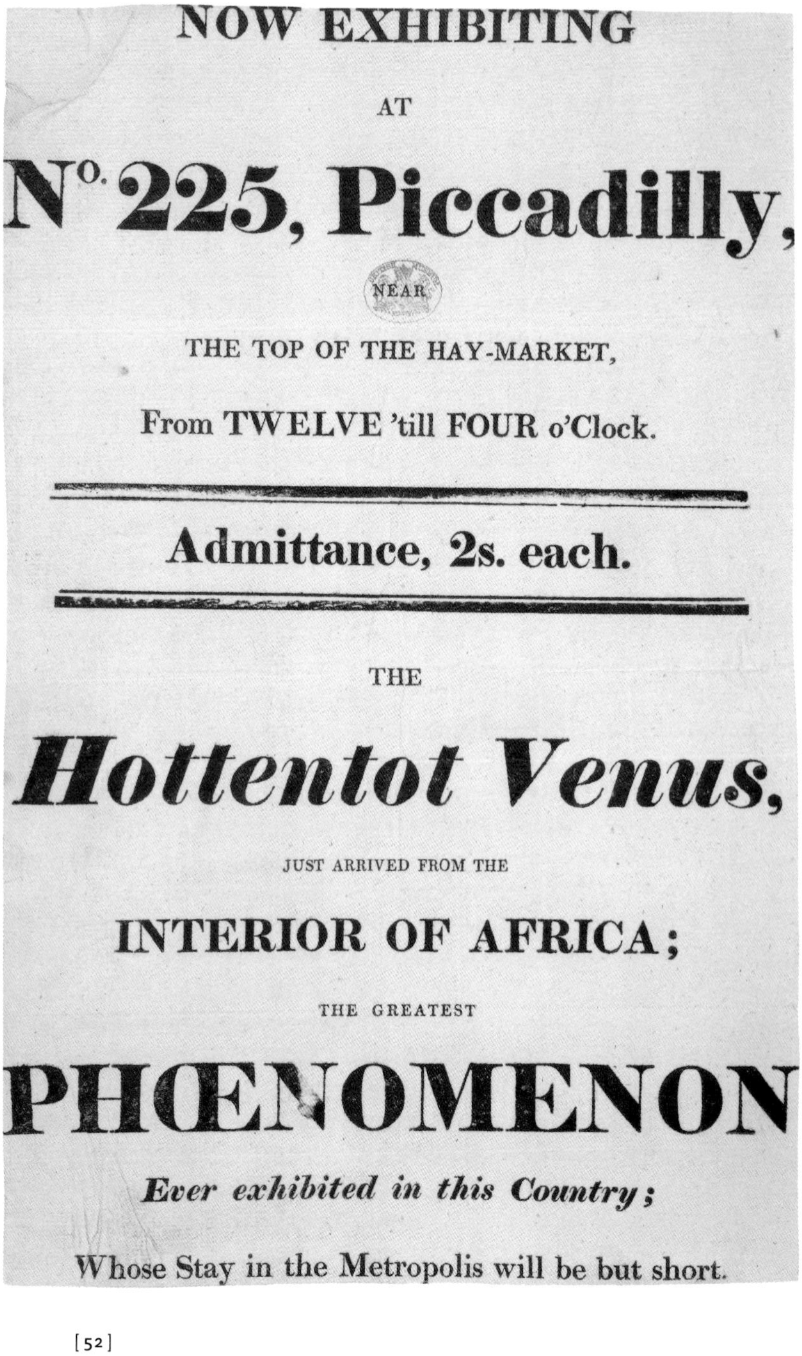

NOW EXHIBITING
AT
N°. 225, Piccadilly,
NEAR
THE TOP OF THE HAY-MARKET,
From TWELVE 'till FOUR o'Clock.
Admittance, 2s. each.
THE
Hottentot Venus,
JUST ARRIVED FROM THE
INTERIOR OF AFRICA;
THE GREATEST
PHŒNOMENON
Ever exhibited in this Country;
Whose Stay in the Metropolis will be but short.

FIGURE 12
(*Preceding spread*) John Orlando Parry, *A London Street Scene*, 1835. Parry's evocative painting captures the importance of the streets as advertising arenas. (By kind permission of Alfred Dunhill Ltd.)

FIGURE 13
(*Right*) A poster advertising Sara Baartman's exhibition, 1810. (Daniel Lysons, *Collectanea*, 2 vols., unpublished scrapbook. © The British Library Board. C.103.k.11[101].)

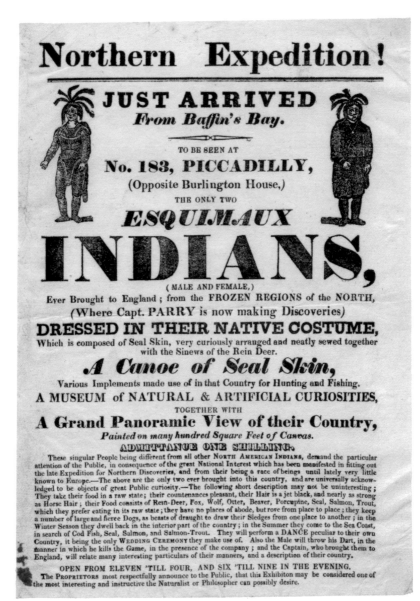

FIGURE 14
Handbill for an exhibition featuring Inuit performers, 1822. The detailed text is typical of early handbills. (By kind permission of the Bodleian Library, University of Oxford, JJ, Human Freaks 4[70].)

over the century posters increased in size from the early theater bills (commonly 8 × 3") to the six-sheet posters (probably 90 × 40") that appeared much later. The innovation of special typefaces suited to advertising facilitated their impact. There were three basic varieties. The first were traditional Roman fonts, in use by about 1806, that greatly exaggerated the contrast between a letter's thick and thin strokes ("Hottentot Venus" in fig. 13). The second were the slab-serif, or Egyptian, typefaces that quickly became popular after their initial appearance between 1815 and 1817. Larger, bolder, and more eye-catching than previous typeface groups, they were characterized by minimal variations in the thick and thin strokes, heavy serifs with squared-off ends, large x-heights, and vertical stress in the rounded strokes ("DRESSED IN THEIR NATIVE COSTUME" in fig. 14 and

Artful Promotion

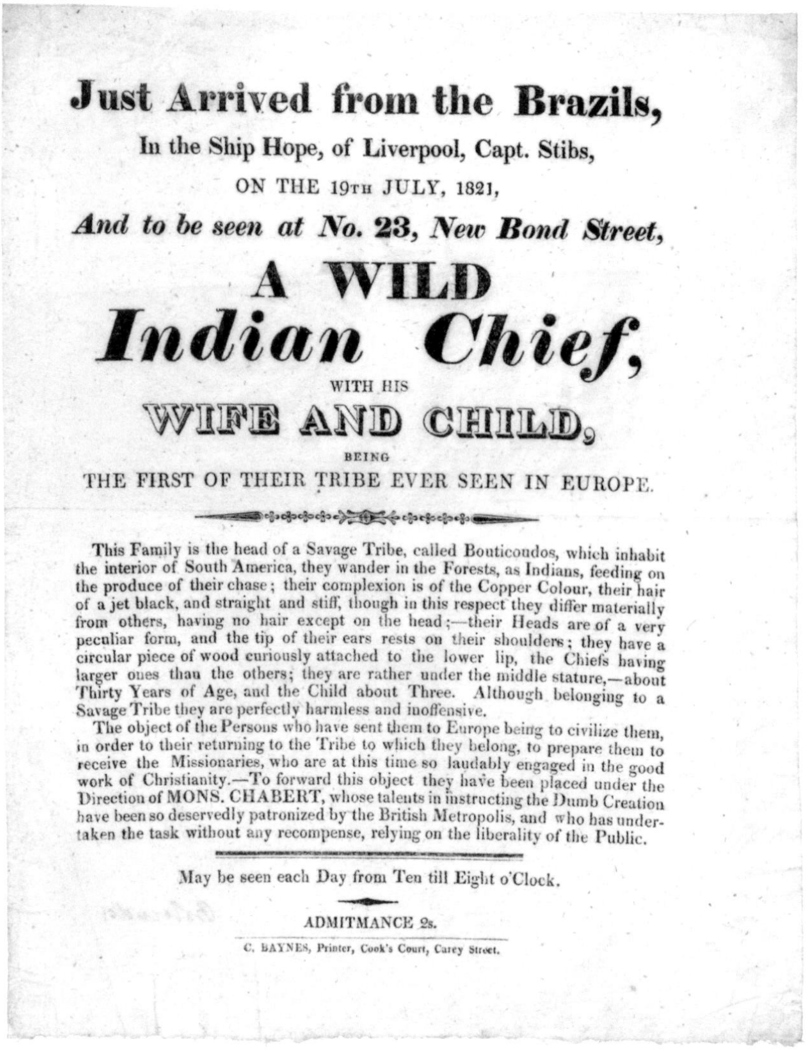

Just Arrived from the Brazils,

In the Ship Hope, of Liverpool, Capt. Stibs,

ON THE 19th JULY, 1821,

And to be seen at No. 23, New Bond Street,

A WILD

Indian Chief,

WITH HIS

WIFE AND CHILD,

BEING

THE FIRST OF THEIR TRIBE EVER SEEN IN EUROPE.

This Family is the head of a Savage Tribe, called Bouticoudos, which inhabit the interior of South America, they wander in the Forests, as Indians, feeding on the produce of their chase; their complexion is of the Copper Colour, their hair of a jet black, and straight and stiff, though in this respect they differ materially from others, having no hair except on the head;—their Heads are of a very peculiar form, and the tip of their ears rests on their shoulders; they have a circular piece of wood curiously attached to the lower lip, the Chiefs having larger ones than the others; they are rather under the middle stature,—about Thirty Years of Age, and the Child about Three. Although belonging to a Savage Tribe they are perfectly harmless and inoffensive.

The object of the Persons who have sent them to Europe being to civilize them, in order to their returning to the Tribe to which they belong, to prepare them to receive the Missionaries, who are at this time so laudably engaged in the good work of Christianity.—To forward this object they have been placed under the Direction of MONS. CHABERT, whose talents in instructing the Dumb Creation have been so deservedly patronized by the British Metropolis, and who has undertaken the task without any recompense, relying on the liberality of the Public.

May be seen each Day from Ten till Eight o'Clock.

ADMITTANCE 2s.

C. BAYNES, Printer, Cook's Court, Carey Street.

FIGURE 15
A handbill for an exhibition of a Krenak family, 1822. Handbills' texts were often excerpted from a show's pamphlet or newspaper review. (By kind permission of the Bodleian Library, University of Oxford, JJ, Human Freaks 4[59].)

"WIFE AND CHILD" in fig. 15). The third basic forms were the sans-serifs, or grotesque, and although they appeared around 1816, they were most popular from the 1830s onward ("ST. GEORGE'S GALLERY" and "ZULU KAFIRS" in fig. 16). Any typeface might also have had additional decoration in the form of engraved lines or motifs around the letters.[14]

All three of these typeface families can be seen in Parry's painting. The artist has used a Roman typeface to sign his name in the center of the composition, while the majority of the typefaces he uses in the posters are Egyptian. The grotesque family is much rarer, but the partially obscured "POMPEII" on the right-hand side provides a good example. The new variations in stroke made these typefaces functionally far more suitable for headlines and display type. Comparing nineteenth-century posters and handbills with an eighteenth-century example makes the differ-

ST. GEORGE'S GALLERY,

HYDE PARK CORNER, PICCADILLY.

Formerly the CHINESE MUSEUM, *(including both Galleries.)*

LAST THREE WEEKS
OF THE
ZULU KAFIRS,
IN LONDON,

Owing to several Continental and Provincial Engagements, this Extraordinary
Entertainment must finally close early in August.

** *In consequence of the increasing interest
excited by this Extraordinary and pleasing Exhibition, arrangements have been made to meet the
Public wishes, by which Visitors will be allowed to see
and converse with this interesting Tribe* DAILY,
FROM ELEVEN TILL ONE O'CLOCK, *during
the short remaining period of their Performance in
London.*

Admission. One Shilling.   The Afternoon Performance in the Theatre will take
place as usual at Half-past Three, and in the Evening at Half-past Eight.

ORDER OF INCIDENTS.
First Part.
Kraal near d'Urban. Port Natal.

Huts erected on the Stage—Zulus heard Singing within—
Zulus come forth. and group themselves outside the Huts—
Hunters arrive—Greetings and Speeches, as they exhibit the
Game—Enter Zulu Woman with her Child. carrying Indian and
Guinea Corn from the Plantation, who feeds her Child from a
Calabash.   II.
Zulu Quarrel. and mode of settling Disputes with Bundles
of Switches—Reconciliation. and Supper.

Umlongo Wam, or Meal Song & Dance.
III.
The Ow Tulaswizwa, or Charm Song

For Protection in the Night—at the conclusion of which some
arrange themselves in prostrate Groups on the Ground, others
crawl into the Huts.
NIGHT—*CLOSE OF THE TABLEAU.*

Second Part.
Morning scene,---Swartz Kop location
NEAR PIETER, MARITZBURG.
II.

Zulus re-assemble and Converse—One of their Kraal Sick—
Witchcraft suspected—The "Imyanger" (Witch Doctor) sent for, in
order to Nooker the Untargartie, or "Smell out the Witch"—Arrival
of the "Imyanger," or "Smeller out"—Sorcerer Denounced—His
Condemnation and Death.
III.
MOVING PANORAMA OF
KAFIR SCENERY!

Kraal—Inanda Location—Zulu Marriage—Puchasing a Wife for
Six Cows—The Ceremony and taking home, with Bridal Song.
IV.
Inhabited Tree in the Basuta Country,

Huts constructed in its branches, exhibiting a contrast to Zulu Kraals—
Zulus assemble for a Hunting Expedition.
V.
Nelson's Kop--Draagenberg Mountains,
Hunting Tramp and Song—Capture of the Reitbok.
SCENE CLOSES.
VI.
THE BUSH.
Preparation for War.—UMSEBEUZA, OR WAR SONG.
Chief's Speech to his Warriors—Warriors' Reply.
LAST SCENE.
KARCLOOF FALL.
ATTACK AND COMBAT.

A DESCRIPTIVE BOOK, containing the History of the Zulu Kafirs, their
customs and their country—is now published, Price 6d. and may be had at the Gallery.

DURATION OF THE EXHIBITION:

Evening, from ½-past **8** *till* **10**;   *Afternoon,* ½-past **3** *till* **5.**
Doors open at 3 and 8.

** Omnibusses from all parts of London pass the Gallery every five minutes.

BACK SEATS, ONE SHILLING.
Front Reserved and Numbered Seats, 4s.   *Unreserved Seats,* 2s. 6d.

Reserved Seats to be obtained at Mr. MITCHELL's Royal Library, 33, Old Bond-st.

Printed by Cramer & Nathn, Silver Street, Golden Square.

FIGURE 16
A playbill for Charles Caldecott's exhibition of Zulus in 1853. Playbills provided an overview of the
show's scenes and may
also have been used as
programs or simply pasted
up outside the exhibition
venues. (By kind permis-
sion of the Bodleian Li-
brary, University of Oxford,
JJ, Human Freaks 4[84].)

ence in readability and stronger visual impact instantly apparent. In the late eighteenth-century example given in figure 17, a considerably larger point size marks the "Beautiful LION, from Algiers" as the star attraction. However, despite capitalization, other headlined exhibits such as the Hunting Tyger, Porcupine, Wandero, and "FEMALE SATYR, or Æthiopian Savage," who "eats, drinks, and sleeps in the human Way," are barely distinguishable from their descriptions. Similarly, the mechanical regularity of newer type styles also made them easier to produce; nonetheless, the production of typefaces remained a relatively laborious process until the late nineteenth century. New typefaces, combined with writing copy so that individual words could be stressed, enabled promoters to consistently emphasize the aspects of exhibitions they considered most enticing or important (usually ethnic origin or, to a lesser extent, venue); it has also been suggested that this practice may have reflected the emergence of a semiliterate public who could quickly gain an understanding of the essential meaning of a poster, even if they were unable to fully grasp the whole text.[15]

The use of images in promotional materials became far more common in the later nineteenth century; until then, they tended to be entirely absent (figs. 13, 15, and 16), very rare (fig. 14), or available as privately produced paintings or prints (figs. 37 and 38). The scarcity of images stemmed partly from the expense of both their production and reproduction until emerging technologies in the later nineteenth century made their reproduction more cost effective. In 1842, the *Illustrated London News* was founded as the first weekly paper to feature images, but the first daily to use them was the *Daily Graphic*, launched in 1889. In the early nineteenth century, both in the press and in promotional materials, images tended to be much rarer and made using cheap woodcuts. Although invented in the eighteenth century, lithography was not commercially viable until the 1820s. The earliest forms of photography, such as daguerreotypes and calotypes, made photography available by 1839 and 1841, respectively. These were routinely used as source material for engraved illustrations from the 1870s and 1880s onward, and by the 1890s were being reproduced as halftone illustrations in periodicals.[16] As the use of images became increasingly common, the amount of textual description on posters started diminishing considerably and, in many cases, barely featured more than an exhibition's name (usually indicating the performers' ethnicity), venue, and possibly the times of admittance.

The promotional materials produced by the flamboyant self-styled showman "The Great Farini" provide an excellent example of the shifting trends associated with the use of images. He exhibited a number of African performers and a troupe of Sámi at the Royal Westminster Aquarium between the 1870s and the 1880s. The handbill for Farini's Friendly Zulus, for instance, dates from 1879 and features a monotone woodcut of a group

1783

To all Admirers of the Wonderful Productions of Nature.
To be feen Alive, from Morning to Night, in the Star-
Yard, Market-Place, Norwich,

A Beautiful LION, from Algiers,

Being the only one alive that travels, and may with Propriety be ftiled, for Pre eminence, or Diftinction's Sake, the
ROYAL LION; and what is very remarkable, he is as tame
as a Lamb to his Keeper.

A Beautiful HUNTING TYGER,

From the Cape of Good Hope. Our learned Authors have
defcribed him through all their Works, as the moft beautiful
cf Animals.

A Curious PORCUPINE, from the Coaft of Africa.

He is covered all over with a Wood of Quills, which he dif-
charges at his Purfuers, one by one, till he leaves himfelf
quite naked.

An amazing large Black WOLF, from Siberia.

The firft of the Kind ever feen alive in Europe. This Creature was taken after feven Days hunting, and is allowed to be
the moft Savage Beaft ever feen alive.

An Aftonifhing Animal, called, The MOON ACT.

A ftrong Refemblance of the Human Species; fuppofed to be
what the Gentoos and Marratas worfhip on the Coaft of Mala-
bar, in the Eaft Indies.

A Beautiful Creature, called, The WANDERO.

Being the only one of that Species ever feen in Europe.

The FEMALE SATYR, or Æthiopian Savage,

From the Ifland of Madagafcar, in the Eaft Indies. This curious Creature is, in many refpects, a ftriking Refemblance of
the Human Species She eats, drinks, and fleeps in the human
Way.

Alfo, two Curious APES, from the Brazils. Remarkable for
their Docility, and Sagacity. With fundry other curious Animals, which the Proprietor has purchafed fince laft Year he was
in this City, which gives univerfal Satisfaction to all Ladies and
Gentlemen who have feen them.

☞ The above Collection is well fecured, and kept clean.

FIGURE 17
Handbill for the
"Beautiful Lion, from
Algiers," 1783. Even
a brief comparison
of this eighteenth-
century handbill
with the nineteenth-
century promo-
tional materials
makes clear the vi-
sual impact of the
new typefaces. (By
kind permission of
the Bodleian Library,
University of Ox-
ford, JJ, Animals on
Show 1[7].)

of Zulu men brandishing weapons while enacting one of their many "WAR
DANCES" (fig. 18). Additionally, Farini produced a set of promotional
photographs of the performers that were sold to the public. Each features
an individual Zulu in full regalia depicted against a painted landscape of
vegetation in the foreground and river valleys in the background (figs.
19a–c). Each photograph was mounted onto a card, the reverse of which
bears Farini's personal stamp, the photographer's details, and instructions
for obtaining additional copies or enlargements from the original negative (fig. 19d). In this guise, Farini's Friendly Zulus became mobile, collect-
able commodities that, by circulating in multiple networks of production
and exchange, acquired a complicated array of meanings.[17]

ROYAL AQUARIUM.
FARINI'S FRIENDLY
ZULUS

Who were originally brought over by Mr. N. BEHRENS,
FROM SOUTH AFRICA for MR. G. A. FARINI.
OF THE ROYAL AQUARIUM, WESTMINSTER.

THE TIMES (speaking of Farini's Zulus) says—"The songs and dances are difficult to distinguish the expression of love from the gesture of martial defiance. Nevertheless as a picture of manners nothing can be more complete; and not the least remarkable part of the exhibition is the perfect training of the wild artists. They seem utterly to lose all sense of their present position; if English actors could be found so completely to lose themselves in the characters they assumed, histrionic art would be in a state, truly magnificent."

ZULUS.

THEIR WAR DANCES
THEIR MARRIAGE FESTIVITIES
THEIR KNOB KERRY FIGHT!
THEIR GRIEF!
THEIR JOY!
AS THEY ARE AT HOME!
AS THEY ARE IN WARFARE!

PRINCESS AMAZULA land her Two Female Attendants.

Special Performances .. ... 2.30. 5.30. 9.30.
ADMISSION, ONE SHILLING.

FIGURE 18
(*Above*) A handbill for Farini's Friendly Zulus. (© The British Library Board. Evan.856.)

FIGURE 19A–C
(*Facing*) Promotional photographs of Farini's Friendly Zulus, mounted to form *cartes de visites*. (Author's collection.)

FIGURE 19D
(*Facing, bottom right*) Reverse side of card onto which the Farini's Friendly Zulus images were mounted. (Author's collection.)

FARINI'S FRIENDLY ZULUS

SAMUEL A. WALKER.   230. REGENT STREET. W.

19A

FARINI'S FRIENDLY ZULUS

SAMUEL A. WALKER.   230. REGENT STREET. W.

19B

FARINI'S FRIENDLY ZULUS

SAMUEL A. WALKER.   230. REGENT STREET. W.

19C

Samuel A. Walker,
Fine Art Photographer
To The Queen, Bishops & Clergy.
230, Regent Street, W.
opposite Hanover Street,
London.

N.B. PORTRAITS OF LADIES CHILDREN & LAYMEN AS WELL AS THE
CLERGY ARE TAKEN DAILY AT THIS STUDIO, ALSO PHOTOGRAPHS
OF EVERY DESCRIPTION.

An enlargement can be made at any time from this Negative Nº 3.

All negatives carefully kept.

19D

Farini's large-format poster for his 1885 exhibition of San is even more dramatic (fig. 20). The colored lithograph features a central image in which a group of ostriches dominate the center foreground. The San appear to have been marginalized along with a giraffe in the far background until, looking closer, one notices that the bird in the center right has apparently grown a pair of human legs and is about to use a bow and arrow to ambush the poor creature opposite. The central scene is surrounded by vignettes from the show. Counterclockwise from the top right, they feature a group of men snaking across the ground while stalking a lion, the lion killing a horned antelope, a victory dance by a man parading the slain beast's skin as a trophy of his prowess, Farini (sporting his unmistakable moustache) standing next to a "pigmy" in order to highlight the latter's diminutive stature, and finally a family in the desert, including a woman carrying her baby on an ample pair of buttocks (an allusion to the reputed purpose of San women's steatopygia).[18] Compared with earlier promotional materials, everything about the poster is more visually arresting; it is larger and colored, and its illustrations form a narrative that renders the poster a visualized playbill for the live performance.

Throughout the century and across the full range of promotional materials, the importance of ethnic singularity in triggering and maintaining consumer interest is confirmed by its prominence on posters, playbills, and handbills, and even in the title of the shows' pamphlets. Invariably, it was highlighted in ways that made it one of the most noticeable elements of promotional materials, making it especially so even if a poster was scanned quickly or positioned so that the smaller text was less visible, or was read by someone with limited literacy. The venue might be the only other piece of information that equaled or, more rarely, exceeded the distinction granted to displayed peoples' ethnic origin. For example, in the poster advertising Sara Baartman's display, the venue, "No. 225 Piccadilly," is as eye-catching as the information regarding her ethnic origin, because the latter is distinguished by the use of italics rather than a significant difference in point size, as in the handbill for the Northern Expedition (figs. 13 and 14).

Such distinctions were common where informational fragments were being differentially emphasized. This technique can be seen especially clearly in the playbill for Charles Caldecott's 1853 Zulu exhibition, where a range of typefaces and point sizes distinguish between the performer's ethnic origin, major tableaux performed, and explanatory text for each scene (fig. 16). These typographic conventions make promotional materials especially useful for exploring which elements of a show were considered of interest to consumers. For instance, even if the smaller type is not read, the playbill for the Zulu exhibition announces a show featuring scenes intended to provide a complete and accurate overview of Zulu life in Natal. The use of recently invented moving panoramic scenery is proudly

flaunted, while named locations, such Kraal near D'Urban or Draagenburg Mountains, provide a geographic specificity that might not have been captured with the use of generic topographic terms. Ceremonies with the translated version of their ostensibly indigenous names, such as the Umlongo Wam (meal song and dance) and Ow Tulaswizwa (charm song), feature in carefully chosen subheadings that attempt to substantiate the claims that patrons will experience an authentic and comprehensive overview of Zulu life. Handbills used similar typographic techniques to tailor their descriptive material. Posters, playbills, and handbills, therefore, vied to establish the ethnic singularity of their subjects and used a range of typographic innovations to ensure that the public paid notice.

Displayed peoples might also be promoted as anatomic curiosities. For example, although Maximo and Bartola were always advertised as being of Aztec origin, they were also frequently exhibited as the "Aztec Lilliputians." Promotional material substantiated the claims by routinely depicting the children as especially diminutive. For example, in G. Wilkinson's promotional lithograph of the pair, they are identified as *Wonderful Beings from*

THE AZTEC'S

These Wonderful Beings were brought to North America in 1849, by **Valasquez** *a Spaniard, who States that he carried them off at the hazard of his life from the mysterious and unknown City of Ixamaya, in central South America, where this Lilliputian race has for many centuries been worshipped by the inhabitants as* **Sacred Objects**.

FIGURE 21
Poster of the "Aztec Lilliputians" in the palm of their manager's hand. (By kind permission of the Wellcome Library, London.)

the mysterious and unknown city of Ixamaya ... where this Lilliputian race has for many centuries been worshipped by the inhabitants as SACRED OBJECTS." In the image, the boy and girl are practically indistinguishable on either physiognomic or sartorial grounds. Meanwhile, they are presented as being so diminutive that they are barely the height of a table decoration and easily supported freestanding in their exhibitor's hand (fig. 21). Such images suggest how the marketing of displayed peoples overlapped with that of human curiosities more broadly, whether it was of elegantly dressed midgets, the morbidly obese, or lanky giants.[19] However, it must be borne in mind that the associations between living foreign peoples and other human curiosities, where desired, had to be actively fashioned.

Examining promotional materials closely reveals multiple potential functions. The use of primarily large display type and minimal text on some posters suggests they were intended, and certainly suited, for use purely as proclamations (fig. 13). The possible versatility of use is most clearly seen in handbills. They often employed display type in larger point sizes, effectively forming headlines that announced an exhibit's ethnicity and the show's venue. The remainder of the page was then devoted to explanatory text in a significantly smaller point size (figs. 14 and 15). Handbills vary in size, but could be as large as 7 × 10" (approximately 18 × 25 cm), although they were commonly slightly smaller (A4, approximately equal to 8 × 11" or 21 × 30 cm). Their text usually contained a brief provenance of the performers ("Just Arrived from the Brazils," fig. 15) and some descriptive material. Frequently, claims regarding the wondrous nature of an exhibit or royal patronage proffered further enticement. On occasion, an order of the show's scenes or a list of performers was included: many of the handbills for American painter George Catlin's exhibitions assiduously detailed "THE NAMES OF THE INDIANS," accompanied by English translations (fig. 22) or a list of scenes to be performed. The presence of headlines suggests that the handbills could easily have been used as posters in the streets or outside the venues. Where the explanatory text included the order of play, handbills may possibly have doubled as programs. Similar versatility may have applied to playbills that detailed the contents of advertised shows (fig. 16). Much of this text was in smaller type, which needed to be read carefully. In addition to playbills being pasted inside and outside the venues, visitors may also have been able to procure them as programs. Such versatility is speculative, but it would clearly have aided any show's proprietor in reducing costs by greatly lessening the need for a range of promotional material.

Newspaper advertisements and reviews offered other opportunities for consumption without attendance. For those displayed humans destined to grace the stage, newspaper advertisements often bore the first mention of future performances:

EGYPTIAN HALL, PICCADILLY.–THE O-JIB-WAY INDIANS–A party of these interesting and romantic "Children of the Forest," from the Western Wilds of North America, will make their first appearance at the above Hall, on Monday next, when they will perform their novel Ceremonies, Games, Dances, &c., in full Native Costume. The interpreter will deliver a Lecture descriptive of Indian character each performance. At Two o'clock each Afternoon, and at Eight o'clock in the Evening. Admission, 1s.; Children and Schools half-price.[20]

Typical entries, such as the notice reproduced here, were concise announcements that would draw attention to the ethnic, and perhaps geographic, origin of the exhibits by using capital letters, while headline capitalization pointed out any other features considered worthy of notice. Physical peculiarities or special talents were almost always included, as were claims that the specimens were entirely unique or the most rare, most perfect, or simply the first of their kind to be exhibited. Such strategies intentionally aroused readers' curiosity while differentiating subjects from the exhibits with which they competed on the page and stage. Occasionally, longer

[☞ Will leave London on 20th March.]

Ojibbeway Indians

EGYPTIAN HALL, PICCADILLY.

The Party of NINE OJIBBEWAY INDIANS, Loyal Subjects of *Her Majesty*, from the North-East Shore of *Lake Huron, Upper Canada*, now on a visit to London, will,

UNTIL 20th MARCH, ILLUSTRATE

Catlin's North-American
INDIAN COLLECTION,

With their **War Dances, Songs, Games, War-whoops**, &c.

AS GIVEN IN PRESENCE OF

HER MAJESTY AND PRINCE ALBERT,

AT WINDSOR CASTLE.

The Party consists of two *Chiefs*—four young Men, *Warriors*, two Women, and a Girl ten years old; all dressed in the curious and picturesque Costumes of their Country; well illustrating the extensive and unique Collection, in the centre of which their Dances and other Amusements are performed.

THE NAMES OF THE INDIANS:—

AH-QUE-WE-ZAINTS,	The Boy—Chief. Age 75 Years.
PAT-AU-AH-QUOT-A-WEE-BE,	The Driving Cloud—War-Chief. Age 51 Years.
WE-NISH-KA-WEE-BE,	Flying Gull.
GISH-EE-GOSH-E-GHEE,	The Moonlight Night.
SAH-MA	Tobacco.
NOT-EEN-A-AKM,	The Strong Wind. (The Interpreter.)
WOS-SEE-AB-E-NEUH-QUA,	Woman, (the Squaw of the Moonlight Night.)
NIB-NAB-E-QUAH,	Girl, (the Daughter of the Moonlight Night.)
NE-BET-NEUH-QUA,	Woman, (the Squaw of Tobacco.)

This extraordinary Group of Nine Wild Indians from the Forests of America, and all full Bloods, with the exception of the Interpreter, a half-breed; and acting out, in their own way, so many of their rude and exciting modes in the heart of the civilized world, is an occurrence that has not happened, and probably will not again happen, in the lifetimes of the Readers, and affording them the opportunity of witnessing, in London, the Wild Feats of the Wildernesses of America.

THE EGYPTIAN HALL has been recently improved, and now affords to the Visitors every convenience and attention required in the most fashionable Exhibitions.

THE INDIAN COLLECTION, (for the short time the Indians will remain.)
WILL BE OPEN DAILY,
FROM 1 TO 4 IN THE DAY, AND FROM 7 TO 10 AT NIGHT.

The Indians in the Room,
FROM HALF-PAST 1 TO 3, AND FROM HALF-PAST 7 TO 9,
GIVING THEIR DANCES, &c.

On which occasions Mr. CATLIN will be in the Room, explaining.

After which, they will mingle with the Visitors in the Room, for the purpose of Shaking Hands, etc.

Admittance, in the Day or in the Evening, One Shilling.   Children, One Shilling.

Printed by J. Mitchell and Co. (late Brettell), Rupert Street, Haymarket.

FIGURE 22
A handbill for an exhibition of American painter George Catlin's collection, featuring performers' names. (By kind permission of the Bodleian Library, University of Oxford, JJ, London Play Places 9[20].)

advertisements would appear either at the beginning of a show's run, in which case they included details of the performance itself, or during the exhibition season, in which case quotations from positive reviews or extraordinary attendance figures were deployed to attest to a show's not-to-be-missed nature. The dates, times, and admission prices were always included. Advertisements were taxed at 3 shillings and sixpence per item, regardless of length, until 1833, when the rate was lowered to 1 shilling and sixpence, with the cost varying somewhat according to length.[21] Consequently, exhibitors may have used such short notices in order to reduce costs and only opted for longer adverts when the shows had proved lucrative or in a final attempt to draw crowds before moving on to provincial or continental tours.

Newspaper reviews performed similar functions to street advertisements by providing a set of highlights before potential patrons even entered the exhibition room or postperformance reminders of their experiences. However, unlike playbills, they were not restricted to the chronological order of a show or to giving a comprehensive overview. They are especially valuable for study, since they are frequently the only available discussion of a show's contents. Whereas reviews could have been written by people who did not attend a show, their descriptions of evidently unscripted events, such as the giving of gifts, peoples' refusal to perform, or even sudden violence (see chapters 4 and 5), suggests that most were eyewitness accounts. Although not entirely unproblematic sources, they provide clues that may be used to gauge audience response—for example, the acts that reviewers selected for discussion may be indicative of the show's features that provided the most amusement—and are a source of comparison with the posters, playbills, and handbills.

Reviews commonly appeared once a show had already enjoyed success. They were almost always positive enough to suggest an exhibition was worthwhile attending, even when individual elements were singled out for criticism. This may have been because reviews were only commissioned or used to promote shows considered worthy of notice rather than as critical notices in general; however, it is more likely that this stems from the economic relationship between newspaper editors, individual showmen, and news agencies (see below). Despite the potential difference between playbills and reviews, in terms of the shows' acts that were highlighted or discussed, there is surprisingly little variation. Several plausible possibilities may account for this convergence. One of the most significant is the use of excerpts from promotional materials or press releases. In shorter reviews, for example, the bulk of the text is often directly paraphrased from handbills or pamphlets, suggesting that writers appropriated text regularly, perhaps to meet pressing deadlines or save research time. Alternatively, newspaper reviews may have been using text from press releases that, along with other promotional materials, formed a common framework of claims used to generate paying interest. Reviewers may have tailored their material to match the scenes that promotional materials highlighted. For instance, when advertisements announced that the show would include the performance of marriage rites or a battle scene, reviewers may have been especially careful to discuss these tableaux.

Newspapers, like London, had an internal geography. They tended to follow an established format, with the various sections appearing in set places week after week. Moving through the pages of a newspaper, home and current affairs nested alongside foreign reports. Following on, reviews of the latest entertainments created a market for the advertised goods at the back of the paper. Thus, reviews and advertisements were not isolated mentions of foreign peoples, but were integrated into the context of foreign news and domestic politics. This wider framework presents a source of description that must be considered in any discussion of the shows' representations of displayed peoples and showmen's promotional strategies.

The press often announced the arrival of unusual foreigners visiting or moving to London. We might expect this coverage in the case of ambassadors, diplomats, and other dignitaries; however, leafing through newspapers quickly reveals that alongside such prominent figures, the arrival of humbler individuals was regularly noted. For example, in 1816 the *Times* reported the arrival of a Sámi family, who were making a living by selling game to London's poulterers.[22] Similarly, in 1853, when two Australian Aborigines from Cape York docked in the city, the *Illustrated London News* reported their arrival and provided readers with a picture of their ritually marked bare torsos and a chart to show the "geographical and commercial importance" of their lands to the imperial enterprise.[23] Such arrivals were often marked because the individuals concerned were argued to be the first available representatives of their kind in England, or because of recent political or military activity in their homelands. It is impossible to verify how many of these arrivals were commercially exhibited, but their perceived notability is suggestive of the curiosity that ethnic difference or political relevance could excite.[24]

The juxtaposition of images of the British middle classes to those of visiting foreigners frequently incorporated them into visual narratives on comparative human development. For example, in 1844 the *Pictorial Times* announced the marriage of Alexander Cadotte to Miss Sarah Haynes at St. Martin's Church, London. The wedding was deemed notable because the groom, otherwise known as Notennaakam, or the "Strong Wind," was the interpreter for the ongoing exhibition of Anishinabe. The entire group attended the ceremony and was shown in a picture in which the bride was not even present (fig. 23).[25] On the same page, the British public was shown attending an Easter exhibition at the Polytechnic Institution.

The image of the Anishinabe was a direct copy of a plate that appeared in the travel writings of Catlin, not an actual depiction of the wedding party.[26] It showed the group carrying weapons and wearing skins

THE INDIAN MARRIAGE AT ST. MARTIN'S CHURCH.

This sacred edifice was on Tuesday the scene of one of the strangest events that has probably ever been witnessed within its walls, namely, the marriage of Alexander Cadotte, otherwise Not-eun-a-akru, or "the Strong Wind," interpreter of the Ojibbeway Indians, now in the metropolis, to Miss Sarah Haynes, aged eighteen, daughter of Mr. Haynes, a respectable carver and gilder, residing in Great George Street, Hampstead Road. In order to prevent public curiosity as much as possible from making the sacred ceremony a mere sight, Mr. Rankin, with very good taste, had arranged that the marriage should take place at the early hour of nine o'clock. His precautions, however, were ineffectual; for long before that hour not only were the windows and balconies of every house in George Street (where the Indians reside) filled, but the street itself crowded by hundreds of people anxious to catch a glimpse of this singular bridal party. The Indians themselves occupied a spring carriage drawn by four horses. The remainder of the party, including the bride and bridegroom, Mr. and Mrs. Haynes (the parents), and a sister of the bride, together with Mr. Rankin, occupied four private carriages. On arriving at St. Martin's Church, the whole of the steps and large area under its noble portico was so densely crowded, that it was with the greatest difficulty a strong body of police could obtain an opening for the wedding procession. Indeed, there could not have been fewer than from 2000 to 3000 persons assembled. As early as seven o'clock in the morning, indeed, so great was the anxiety of the public to view this unprecedented union, that a large concourse of persons, the greatest portion of whom seemed to be of a superior

rank in society, had assembled to obtain admission to the church, and long before the hour appointed for the ceremony the sacred building was crowded. The officiating clergyman, the Rev. Septimus Ramsey, took his seat by the altar precisely at nine o'clock, and at half-past nine the tinkling of the Indians' bells and the buzz of the crowd without announced the arrival of the party at the church porch. At this moment curiosity was so intense that the usual decorum observed in a place of worship was simultaneously though unintentionally forgotten, the whole of the spectators rising on the seats. The

first to enter the aisle was "the Boy Chief," aged seventy-five, Ah-que-we-zaints," attired in his full Indian dress, wearing a large wedding favour with streamers from the left side of his head and breast. He was followed by "the Driving Cloud," war chief, aged fifty-one, Pat-au-ah-quot-a-wee-be, accompanied by a youthful associate, the chief attired in his full war costume and wedding favours, "the Flying Gull," We-nish-ka-wee-be, "the Moonlight Night," Gish-wee-gosh-e-ghee, "Tobacco-sah-ma," and, lastly, "the Squaw of the Moonlight Night," Wos-see-ab-e-neuh-qua, accompanied by Mr. Rankin. We append portraits of the Indians. As the Indians walked up the aisle, their dignified demeanour and placid appearance were the theme of general admiration, and though one of the attendants on them assured the reporter that they had never entered a Christian church before, they exhibited throughout the entire ceremony a devotional observance of all that passed around them that spoke much in their favour. The bride presented a most interesting appearance. She is a delicate looking young lady, of pale complexion, with dark hair. She was attired in flowing white, with a veil which reached from a wreath of orange blossoms encircling her hair to the bottom of her dress. The bridegroom was habited in a robe of blue cloth, handsomely trimmed with shells and Indian needlework round the neck, arms, and edges. He also wore a rich head-dress, but somewhat different from those worn by the Indians, and over his surcoat a scarlet shawl of the brightest colour, and his feet were clothed with a pair of mocassins, presented to him by the war chief, adorned with the most curious needlework, made of the skin of the moose deer. On taking his place at the rails of the

THE OJIBBEWAY INDIANS, NOW IN LONDON (from Daguerreotype Portraits, taken by M. Claudet).

THE POLYTECHNIC INSTITUTION, EASTER WEEK.

FIGURE 23

"The Indian Marriage at St. Martin's Church." The image of the wedding party accompanying this newspaper article was taken from Catlin's printed works and did not feature the bride, despite claiming to be of the bridal party. (*Pictorial Times*, April 13, 1844, p. 233. By kind permission of the Guildhall Library, City of London.)

decorated with beads and feathers, and contrasted sharply with the gentility of the Europeans on the same page and the testament to British progress that was provided by the backdrop of technological innovation in the form of the Polytechnic Institution. We can see a similar contrast in the *Illustrated London News* report of the 1845 grand fête Champetre held at Charlton House.[27] The program, "a yard in length," listed a camping group of "North American Indians" among the amusements (fig. 24). While the revelers enjoyed the grounds, the performers and their tents were plunged into the shadowy darkness cast by the disorderly overgrowth of trees. It has been suggested that technological progress, as made manifest in the material culture of a people, was used to classify the level of civilization a people had reached during colonial expansion.[28] Hence, the more advanced technologies a people possessed, the higher they stood in the human hierarchy. Bearing this in mind, we can appreciate the significance of the British being shown exploring an institution dedicated to technological innovation while the Native Americans hover midpage as if they are excised specimens (fig. 23), or are placed in the depths of a picturesque wilderness with only a glimmer of the country house behind them (fig. 24).

Ethnic origin clearly mattered; however, it would be easy to underestimate the importance of topicality. Anyone who has spent time reading nineteenth-century newspapers will be aware of their extensive international coverage long before telegraphy revolutionized the speed of global communication. Showmen undoubtedly capitalized on these discussions to excite interest in their shows; yet this kind of political timeliness can easily be overlooked when too little attention is paid to displayed peoples' specific ethnicities, and they are unhelpfully subsumed into generic categories such as the "other," "savage," or "non-Western." Alternatively, a focus on ethnic origin that is not accompanied by due consideration for the political, economic, military or social circumstances which inform the transcultural encounters of the shows can be equally misleading. Rather, as the case of displayed Zulus makes especially clear, foreign news was a critical resource on which exhibitors capitalized to drum up interest in their shows.

Between 1779 and 1879, the Xhosa (Kaffirs) and Zulus fought a series of wars in the Eastern Cape region of what is now South Africa in an attempt to fend off European incursions and protect their independence. Lasting almost a century, the Xhosa's nine wars of resistance ("Kaffir Wars") marked the longest period of warfare between settlers and indigenous peoples in the region. The eighth war lasted between 1850 and 1853 and proved to be both the longest and the most bitterly fought of all. Meanwhile, under the reign of the legendary King Shaka, who ruled between 1816 and his assassination in 1828, the Zulus were transformed from a relatively small Nguni Kingdom into a new kind of South African polity. They became a centralized and exceptionally well-trained military state that incorporated many

FIGURE 24
(Facing) "Grand Fete Champetre at Charlton House," which featured a group of performers camping in the grounds. *(Illustrated London News,* July 5, 1845, p. 9. Author's collection.)

GRAND FETE CHAMPETRE AT CHARLTON HOUSE.

On Wednesday, this long-announced *fête champêtre*, in aid of the funds of the Royal Kent Dispensary, was given in the park and grounds of Charlton House; the benevolent proprietor, Sir Thomas Maryon Wilson, having generously granted their use for that purpose. The *Fête* was to have taken place on Tuesday; but the unpropitious weather induced the Committee to postpone it until the following day, when, unfortunately, it rained without intermission from half-past one until nearly five o'clock. Nevertheless, there was a great concourse of company from the neighbourhood, and from the metropolis; and, at different periods during the afternoon, there were between 4000 and 5000 persons present.

The Programme of the day included *Promenades Musicales;* Mr. Lumley, of her Majesty's Theatre, had kindly given permission to the *Danseuses Viennoises* to perform their most favourite *pas* at stated hours; Mr. Batty's *artistes* and troop of horses, with their grand auxiliaries, varied the pedal amusements; the nobility and gentry of the County contributed a grand Floricultural Exhibition; there was classic equestrianism from old Rome; an encampment of Canadian Indians, with their feats and dances; and an almost countless variety of other pastimes, the programme of which was a yard in length.

Refreshments were provided in great abundance in tents and in the conservatory; and their enjoyment seemed to make up for the damper thrown upon the al fresco amusements; and, as the sale of tickets last week was very great, and the attendance considerable, we hope the *Fête* may prove profitable to the funds of the excellent Charity on account of which it was produced.

The park and grounds of Charlton House are exquisitely picturesque; and our artist has sketched two of the scenes, *à la Watteau*, during the *Fête;* introducing a portion of the fine old mansion. A Correspondent has obligingly communicated the following interesting details of this noble domain :—

"Charlton (in Domesday Book, *Cerletone*) lies in the manor of Blackheath, about two miles east of Greenwich. Lysons, in his 'Environs of London,' Vol. IV., p. 326, says :—The manor of Charlton, in 1604, was, by King James, granted, in fee, to John, Earl of Mar, who, in 1606, sold it for £2000, to Sir James Erskine. Sir James, the next year, sold it, for £4500, to Sir Adam Newton. His son, Sir Henry (who had taken the name of *Puckering*) aliened it, in

1659, to Sir William Ducie, afterwards K.B., and Lord Viscount Downe, who died at his manor-house here, in 1679. His representatives sold it, in 1680, to Sir William Langhorne, Bart. Sir William Langhorne then entailed it on his nephew, Sir John Conyers, of Horden Hall, County Durham, Bart., who was the son of his sister, Elizabeth, wife of Sir Christopher Conyers, of Horden, Bart. Charlton remained in this branch of the Conyers family until 1731, when, on the death of Sir Baldwyn Conyers, Bart., it reverted, according to entail, to Wm. Langhorne Games, Esq. (another nephew of Sir Wm. Langhorne), and his heirs male, with remainder to his widowed kinswoman, Mrs. Margaret Maryon, and then to her son John, and to his heirs for ever. Mr. Maryon left it, by his will, to his niece, Margaretta Maria; married, firstly, to John Badger Weller, Esq., of Romford, and, secondly, to John Jones, Esq.; with remainder to her daughter, Jane, who married Sir Thomas Spencer Wilson, Bart., of Eastbourne, County Sussex, a Lieutenant-General (who died in 1798); and to her heirs general. It is in right of this lady, his grandmother, that the present Baronet enjoys Charlton House; he is unmarried, and his brother, John Maryon Wilson, of Fitzjohns, Essex, Esq., is his heir presumptive.

"The mansion of Charlton is considered a fine specimen of the style of building in vogue in the reign of James the First. In the room adjoining the Saloon is a chimney-piece, of black marble, so exquisitely polished, that Lord Downes, when possessor of the manor, is said once to have seen, reflected in it, a robbery committed on Blackheath !—and that, having dispatched his servants, they were able to apprehend the thieves."

The mansion is placed upon a hill of gradual ascent, and commands a noble prospect of the Thames: it is of red brick, with stone finishings, and an open balustrade round its summit; above which rise stacks of chimneys, and two small towers that surmount the projecting wings of the principal front and agreeably diversify the general outline. The centre and the entrance porch are elaborately embellished.

SUDDEN TURN OF FORTUNE.—One of those sudden accessions of fortune that occasionally happens has lately occurred to a poor woman, named Caroline Boothby, living in Earl-street, Seven Dials, who has been discovered to be the rightful owner of valuable freehold property near Bethnal-green, which she will shortly be put in possession of, the estimated value being £30,000. She was previously gaining a precarious living by needle-work, and at times was unable to procure the common necessaries of life.

THE FETE CHAMPETRE AT CHARLTON HOUSE.—SKETCHED BY G. HARRISON.

FETE CHAMPETRE AT CHARLTON HOUSE.—THE NORTH AMERICAN INDIANS ENCAMPED IN THE PARK.—SKETCHED BY G. HARRISON.

formerly subdivided and locally ruled groups. Shaka achieved the expansion and social cohesion by developing novel forms of combat, weaponry, and military training and demanding ultimate allegiance as king from freshly incorporated communities, even where local chiefs were left in place or replaced with a new chief of Shaka's choosing. In 1838, under the rule of Dingane (1828–40), Shaka's half-brother, murderer, and successor, the Zulu were defeated at the Battle of Blood River. Heavy losses led to a weakening of their power and civil divisions while colonialists settled in Natal and established Pietermaritzburg as the capital.

Despite its weakened nature, under the rule of Mpande (1840–72) and Cetshwayo (1872–84), the Zulu Kingdom continued to present an obstacle to European expansion into southeast Africa. Hungry for land and labor, settlers in Natal jealously eyed Zulu lands and began encroaching further north. Anxious to protect his sovereignty, avoid war, and protect his own growing body of subjects, Cetshwayo asked the governor of Natal to undertake an inquiry into the disputed territory. Despite the report fully supporting the Zulus' claims, in 1878 the British high commissioner Bartle Frere used it to foment war. He issued Cetshwayo an ultimatum that demanded the payment of a large fine, the surrender of Zulus accused of minor border intrusions, and the dismantling of the Zulu army within thirty days. Given the importance of the army to Zulu political organization, the demands effectively required the king to disassemble his entire kingdom. With Cetshwayo forced to refuse, on January 11, 1879, British troops initiated the Anglo-Zulu War and suffered notoriously at Isandlwana, Eshowe, and Holbane before razing Ulundi (Ondini), the king's capital, to the ground in July and winning in September. While the Zulu Kingdom was still formally an independent nation, Cetshwayo was deposed and forced into exile (during which he visited London). The kingdom was stripped of its monarchy, military system, and political cohesion as it was broken up into thirteen chiefdoms and ultimately annexed by the British in 1887.[29]

Brimming with stories and images from the battlefronts, the press was instrumental in creating and promoting the notions that the Cape was an unsafe region and that the Zulus were a formidable military power that had to be defeated in order to achieve regional stability. For example, in March 1853, shortly before Charles Caldecott's exhibition opened in May, the *Times* reported on a picnic of several dozen adults and children, most likely all Europeans or British, at the Cape in January. All except two were armed. In passing through the vegetation, the officer Mr. Bowker observed fresh human tracks and became suspicious. Sometime later a child from the party disturbed "five huge Caffres," who immediately disappeared with their guns into the bush. In the exchange of gunfire that ensued, Bowker and another officer, Mr. Robert Hart, shot dead one Xhosa and wounded two others. Hart subsequently tracked through the area and "to his surprise found a huge Caffre fast asleep, wrapped up in his Kaross. He at once shot him dead. The fellow never moved."[30]

Just five days later, the *Times* published extracts from the letters of a private soldier. As part of the Rifle Corps, he was stationed in the Amatola Mountains and wrote of his experiences to his sister in England:

I have been through what the devil himself would not go through—sharp fighting, hard marching, bad living, and no bed for months, and for months at a time nothing for a shelter but the canopy of the heaven.... I have seen many soldiers go—in fact I myself have gone into holes and places that have put me in mind of a ferret going into rat's hole after rats. Such are the places the Caffres get to when they are hard pushed by the soldiers, and these are the difficult places we have to root them out of; but, the greater the difficulty the more credit to those that overcome them.... We have chased them about day and night ... to all quarters and hunted them like wild beasts, and taken their cattle, burnt all their huts, and destroyed all their corn, and whenever we have fallen in with them we have always come off victorious, for nothing can stand before British discipline and the Queen's troops.[31]

The soldier's reports present Xhosa military resistance as that of a remarkably dangerous enemy. Although Hart had killed a sleeping man, the tone of the newspaper account suggests that the journalist fully expected readers' sympathies to lie with the officers. The soldier's letters portrayed Africans not as able fighters who were effectively disrupting and challenging Britain's military efforts, but as vermin who had to be hunted like wild beasts. Rather than concede that their grievances arose from legitimate protest at their dispossession, their threats were argued to be borne of irrational stubbornness. The extensive destruction detailed, of human life and a people's subsistence, was presented as a just means of combating the enemy's frenzied lust for violence. Lest anyone sympathized with the Xhosa, the soldier added that the wreckage caused "serves them well right, for they ought to know better than to go to the war with the British nation."

These postings were substantiated by the illustrated press's use of wartime artists.[32] One full-page layout contrasted Xhosa belligerence with British military might (fig. 25). In the first scene, *Kaffirs Bush-Fighting*, a group of Europeans are shown being assailed by a horde of naked men. The killers' pleasure is made evident by their maniacal grins and their degeneracy by their lack of clothing. The sword brandished by the figure in the far right substantiates the perceived inferiority of Xhosa weaponry. The Xhosa who are using guns do so ineffectually—unlike the centrally placed British soldier, who has successfully shot, and presumably killed, a Xhosa man. The second image, *Rescue of the Ammunition Waggons*, is largely occupied with colonists; the Africans are marginalized in number, composition, and military capability in the colonizer/colonized pairing in the foreground.

The scenes are strongly reminiscent of hunting images from the mid-nineteenth century. During this period, hunters' fantasies of the true hunt

THE KAFFIR WAR.

KAFFIRS BUSH-FIGHTING.

and the Burgher force has been summoned from every district. Levies of Hottentots are also being made, who will be organised into provisional companies. In the meantime, large parties of Kaffirs are entering the colony above and below us, murdering stragglers and couriers on the roads, driving off cattle, and burning the detached farmhouses. There are constant skirmishes between them and the Burghers.

"The ammunition is the great attraction fto 'them now. The adroitness with which they carry off cattle is almost miraculous; you never know they are near till they suddenly appear in the midst, and then, with a peculiar whistle, they make the beasts follow them with a run. They lie hid, and creep along, so that our sentries can seldom see them; only the Hottentots' eyes can match the Kaffirs, and detect them."

RESCUE OF THE AMMUNITION WAGGONS.

depended on face-to-face combat with the prey, since such encounters initiated one into manhood.[33] In both these images, an African man directly faces a gun. In the depiction of "bush-fighting," the colonists are hidden far back in the dense vegetation, as if stalking their quarry. Significantly, although the images are of the Xhosa, the term *bush-fighting* denigrates their mode of combat. Europeans commonly differentiated among African peoples; of those resident at the Cape, the Zulus were considered the most superior, while the Khoekhoe and San were commonly discussed as the most degraded of humans.[34] In this vein, the Xhosa are depicted as being incapable of rational war; instead, they appear as chaotic and ineffectual fighters. In the second image, the soldiers are shown in a superior vantage at every level of the picture, and the whole scene is much less frenzied. The Xhosa are barely visible, while those in the foreground are whipped into submission as if they are circus-trained animals. Throughout 1853, the *Illustrated London News* built on this tradition of wartime illustrations by providing readers with a series of "Scenes from the War in Kaffirland." These "vivid and faithful sketches" were claimed to have been drawn with the "aid of a clever and accredited Artist, resident in the colony," and are indicative of the kinds of discussion of which Caldecott took advantage.[35]

Similarly, in 1879, the press closely tracked the fortunes of King Cetshwayo. On February 22, the *Illustrated London News* featured a woodcut of the king splashed across its front page. So large that it only allowed for a caption that informed readers it had been "drawn from life" and the newspaper's iconic header of London's skyline, the image showcased a proud and adorned foe (fig. 26). The same issue offered a supplement in which a full-page layout featured images of "ZULUS AND KAFFIRS OF SOUTH AFRICA." About two-thirds of this visual museum was occupied by studies of "PONDO WARRIORS" and "ZULU WARRIORS," while the remainder housed a "RAIN MAKER" and "ZULU DOCTOR" (fig. 27). The circulation of such images and discussions of the Xhosa, Zulus, and Mpondo not only reflected wider interest in Britain's exploits abroad but proved an irresistible point of association for showmen. Caldecott's 1853 Zulu exhibition deliberately referenced the ongoing conflict with the Xhosa, while Farini's 1879 Zulu exhibition took advantage of British interest in the Anglo-Zulu War. Caldecott's tactics are particularly revealing since, although the Xhosa and the Zulu were known to be distinctive peoples, he blurred the distinction while simultaneously acknowledging his manipulation. He argued that his exhibition of Zulus would be of "intrinsic interest" because the British "have been engaged in a long and disastrous war with people of the same class although not of the same tribe."[36] Such explicit chains of association tied displayed peoples to wider political developments that cannot be ignored in any account of the shows' marketing or reception—especially since they helped establish and facilitate the metonymic interpretation of displayed peoples as exemplars of political activity.

FIGURE 25
(Facing) Contrasting images of the British fighting the Xhosa: *Kaffirs Bush-Fighting* (above) and *Rescue of the Ammunition Waggons*. (Illustrated London News, July 25, 1846, p. 52. Author's collection.)

FIGURE 26
(Following) The Zulu War in South Africa: Cetewayo, the Zulu King. Drawn from the Life in June, 1877, by the Late Mr. Edward Tilt, During His Visit to Zulu-Land. (Illustrated London News, February 22, 1879. Author's collection.)

FIGURE 27
(Page 75) Zulus and Kaffirs of South Africa. (Illustrated London News, February 22, 1879, supplement, 181. Author's collection.)

Artful Promotion

THE ILLUSTRATED LONDON NEWS,

REGISTERED AT THE GENERAL POST-OFFICE FOR TRANSMISSION ABROAD.

No. 2071.—VOL. LXXIV.
SATURDAY, FEBRUARY, 22, 1879.
WITH SUPPLEMENT
SIXPENCE.
By Post, 6½d.

THE ZULU WAR IN SOUTH AFRICA: CETEWAYO, THE ZULU KING.
DRAWN FROM THE LIFE IN JUNE, 1877, BY THE LATE MR. EDWARD TILT, DURING HIS VISIT TO ZULU-LAND.

ZULUS AND KAFFIRS OF SOUTH AFRICA.

Whatever the combination of ethnic difference and political relevance that drew patrons to the shows, their willingness to accept showmen's invitations to attend is indicated by the number of exhibitions that regularly took place throughout the century and followed London seasons with provincial dates. Caldecott's exhibition proved so successful that its initial run in London, from May through June, was extended a number of times until August, when it embarked on a national tour. Scarcely quoted attendance figures bear witness to public appetite. In 1853, one proprietor claimed that "upwards of three thousand persons" had visited the "Aztec Lilliputians" in just two days, while another claimed that "upwards of fifty thousand persons" had visited the 1847 exhibition of the San while they were in Manchester.[37] These figures are unsubstantiated and taken from promotional materials; nonetheless, claims that exhibitions were successfully attracting audiences that numbered in the thousands, not hundreds, are indicative of considerable public exposure. Moreover, some venues boasted seating capacities that could have accommodated such numbers at a single performance and visitors to world fairs are known to have numbered in the millions: Exeter Hall, for example, could seat four thousand. For the wealthy thousands able to spare a shilling or more, the significance of promotional material in providing interpretative frameworks continued inside exhibition venues.

Peopling the Landscape

Posters and playbills outside the venue foreshadowed imminent delights for the queuing patrons. Those who had arranged admission in advance, or reserved seats, were issued entrance tickets that succinctly reiterated promoters' claims and so functioned as more personal mnemonics or even souvenirs (fig. 28a–c). Once inside, patrons frequently heard a lecture in conjunction with the evening's performance (see chapter 3). Delivered either before the performance or during special intermissions, lectures were intended to shape the experience of simply seeing foreign peoples.

Patrons' potential lack of relevant linguistic or ethnological knowledge might render any live performance a bewildering display of indistinguishable ceremonies, songs, and dances; this created specific needs that effectively invested promotional materials with an easily underestimated role in framing consumers' experiences. Some problems arose partly because most consumers were simply unable to speak the performers' language: one reviewer of Knox's 1847 San exhibition observed, "At the conclusion of the lecture the Bosjesmans . . . walked down the hall, and finally entered into an apparently animated conversation on the platform. Of course, what they said was perfectly unintelligible, but they seemed to express themselves with great vivacity and quickness, or, if we may use the expression, natural eloquence." At a similar disadvantage, another attendee concluded that the shouts were "very Arabic or Irish in their explosiveness." The problem was compounded by the lecturer's "want of physical force"

FIGURE 28 A–C
(*Facing*) (a) Entrance ticket for "Aztecs" and the "Earthmen," ca. 1860s. (By kind permission of the Bodleian Library, University of Oxford, JJ, Tickets Show Places 18.) (b) Entrance ticket for "The Bosjesmen or Bushmen," ca. 1850s. (© The British Library Board. Leicester Handbills 1880.b.25 [13].) (c) Entrance ticket for The "Earthmen," ca. mid-1850s. (© The British Library Board. Leicester Handbills 1880.b.25 [13].)

A

FAVOUR TICKET.

LEICESTER ✤ SQUARE.

Admit TWO for SIXPENCE;

or Two to the Reserved Seats, 1s.

TO BEHOLD THE

AZTECS AND THE EARTHMEN,

Patronized by the Queens of England, France,
and Spain.

Two New Races of People, the First of
either Race ever discovered.

The Aztec Lilliputians are about 2½ and the Erdmanniges
3½ feet high. The Aztecs have been worshipped as Gods in
the great and mysterious City of Iximaya in Central America,
and the Earthmen, or Erdmanniges, burrow under the
earth in South Africa, subsisting upon insects and reptiles.
The existence of both Races has always been greatly disputed. Neither the Aztecs nor the Earthmen have any
Language; they are unlike any Human beings ever before seen.

Daily from 3 to 5, and 7 to 9½. Lectures at 4 and 8.

VOCAL AND INSTRUMENTAL MUSIC EVERY EXHIBITION.

MUSIC ON THE CRYSTAL-OPHONIC EVERY EXHIBITION.

Without this Ticket, the Admission is ONE SHILLING; Stalls, 2s., for every Person.
Children, under 10, Half-price.

B

One Penny Admission.

Patronized by his Imperial Majesty, the Emperor of the French, and
the Royal Family of Holland.

The most Extraordinary People known. Daily from 11 a.m. till 11 p.m., at

6, LEICESTER SQUARE.

Mr. MORRIS, the guardian of the AZTECS,

Grateful for the immense patronage bestowed upon these wonderful little creatures, now being
visited by thousands in Paris, has determined on furnishing to the whole of the citizens of London
a sight for which tens of thousands of persons have paid 1s. and 2s. to behold, for

ONLY ONE PENNY ADMISSION.

THE BOSJESMEN or BUSHMEN

(Two Males and One Female) are, beyond doubt, the most extraordinary human beings known to the
world. Remarkable not only on account of their vernacular tongue, but on account of their formation
differing so materially from all other members of the human family yet discovered alive. So remarkable, indeed, as to have bestowed upon them the appellation of the

MEN MONKIES!

And, without exaggeration, their attempt to communicate with one another is more like the gibbering
of monkies than the language of man.

N.B.—Please observe the exhibition of the Bosjesmen will, in order to avoid the crowd, continue from
11 A.M. till 11 P.M., and the admission only One Penny, except on Saturdays from 12 till 3,
when the admission will be One Shilling; after 3 o'Clock One Penny only.

☞ THE EXHIBITION DAILY.

C

6, LEICESTER SQUARE,

SPLENDID ENTERTAINMENT for a LITTLE MONEY,

EVERY DAY AT THREE AND SEVEN.

The Possessor of this Ticket will be admitted for only 3d. to the
Gallery, Reserved Seats, 6d., and Stalls, 1s., to witness

THE EARTHMEN

A race of People three and a half feet high, who burrow under the
Earth, subsisting upon insects and plants, found in South Africa,
the first ever captured; and

Mr. CHARLES SINCLAIR

Whose powers as a Ventriloquist are unequalled, whose skill in the
Magical art is not to be surpassed, and whose execution on the Ærial
Flutina is without parallel.

Without this Ticket the Admission will be just double the above prices; therefore,
by retaining this Ticket, one half the admission money will be saved.

A VOCAL AND INSTRUMENTAL CONCERT

EVERY EXHIBITION. NO EXTRA CHARGE.

Hours of Exhibition from Three to Five, and Seven to Ten.

and the "extreme rapidity of his delivery," which left the audience viewing a "strange people" with little understanding of their manners and customs, because they simply had not heard the explanatory context provided
by his lecture.[38]

The relatively common nature of such incomprehension is reinforced
by reviews of Caldecott's 1853 exhibition. The show consisted of acts in
which

After a supper of meal, of which the Kaffirs partake with large wooden spoons,
an extraordinary song and dance are performed, in which each performer
moves about on his haunches, grunting and snorting the while like a pair of
asthmatic bellows.... No description can give an idea of the cries and shouts—
now comic, now terrible—by which the Kaffirs express emotions. The scene
illustrative of the preliminaries of marriage and the bridal festivities might
leave one in doubt which was the bridegroom, did not that interesting savage
announce his enviable situation by screams of ecstasy which convulse the audience.[39]

The journalist's derision hints at an audience bellowing with laughter; yet
the review's humor depends on the assumed incapability of readers, and
by extension the shows' patrons, of distinguishing between the show's
scenes without some guidance. The plausibility of shared incomprehension speaks volumes.

These intriguing glimpses indicate audiences that can be differentiated on the basis of prior knowledge. Some patrons may have been familiar with the relevant travel and medical literature or traveled abroad and
had firsthand experience of the peoples they chose to see perform. However, between the late eighteenth and mid-nineteenth centuries, the high
cost of travel and the relatively small and falling sales figures of travel accounts suggest that many more are unlikely to have read them and so have
been dependent on showmen for suitable explanatory contexts.[40] For example, if the playbill named a given scene as a marriage ceremony, then
many members of the audience may have been unable to contest such a
claim, based on either personal experience or substantial ethnological
knowledge; witness the frustration of one reviewer of Caldecott's exhibition who grudgingly commented that the "songs and dances are, as may
be expected, monotonous in the extreme, and without the bill it would be
difficult to distinguish the expression of love from the gesture of martial
defiance."[41] Showmen evidently understood the importance of these materials. Caldecott had begun his pamphlet with the claim that "very few
books are extant concerning their [Zulu] manners or their country; while
their early history still awaits the progress of African discovery, and the
results of patient ethnographical research."[42] As late as 1884, Robert A.
Cunningham, who was exhibiting a group of Australian Aborigines, introduced the show's pamphlet as a "little work ... of an uncivilised race of
whom but few travellers have given any accounts," and most of which were

"scattered at random through their books; moreover, these notices are distributed through a vast number of works, many of them very scarce, many very expensive, and most of them ill arranged."[43] Given the likely lack of a mutually intelligible language, falling sales of travel literature, and the relative expense of foreign travel, especially in the early nineteenth century, the use of promotional materials evidently extended beyond attracting paying customers to playing a fundamental role in providing mutually shared frames of reference that many patrons not only used but depended on to make sense of live performances.

Lectures aside, promotional pamphlets were the most substantial and detailed resources available within exhibition venues. Although relatively neglected by historians, an analysis of their material use and content is revealing.[44] Pamphlets appear to have been adapted for publication from lectures and were related to the guidebooks that were available at museums and galleries.[45] One street vendor believed that the "largest buyers of these [guide] publications were country people, sight-seeing in London, for they bought the book not only as an explanatory guide, but to preserve as a memento of their visit."[46] More recently it has been suggested that the opening up of museums to new sections of the public, particularly the working classes, created a new market for teaching resources that was readily filled by enterprising publishers. This role extended the original use of guidebooks in enabling "country-house visitors to identify items in the painting and sculpture collections when the housekeeper was absent or inadequately informed."[47] Guidebooks for both temporary and permanent exhibitions most commonly sold for between sixpence and 1 shilling and could be bought either officially from the host institution or unofficially from street vendors. Catalogs, especially for museums and galleries, tended to provide lists of objects in a collection with little or no accompanying text. In contrast, guidebooks were often illustrated and featured more substantial passages that provided explanatory material or even routes designed to maximize the didactic value of the collections.[48] Their extensive use of explanatory text marks pamphlets as much more akin to guidebooks than standard exhibition catalogs. However, their adaptation from lectures is likely to be unique, as most visitors to a gallery, museum, or theater were unlikely to have been expected to sit through a lecture contextualizing the prospective displays.

Exhibition pamphlets were short essays providing descriptions of the "manners and customs" of displayed peoples. Contents varied, but as a rule they featured biographical and ethnological histories of the peoples being exhibited. Ranging from twenty to thirty pages each, they most commonly cost sixpence and appear to have been sold within showrooms. They rarely appear in catalogs of printed works of the period, and those that do survive are often disintegrating, rarely bound, and often housed in collections of ephemera. Their relatively thin pages and weak bindings suggest that they were intended for use during the performance and little

A

B

else; however, their survival also suggests that they were not always disposed of and may have been kept as souvenirs.[49] The degree of illustration varies, from being entirely absent, limited to a single title page, or running to several plates, as does the subject, ranging from the performers to
scenes from their homelands (fig. 29a–d). The text is usually in relatively
large point size and divided into short sections with individual subheadings to provide structure. Subheadings often referred to the ceremonies
being performed and thus classified the pamphlets' material according to
the shows' contents. For example, the pamphlet accompanying Caldecott's
Zulu exhibition contained major sections detailing the characteristics of
the Zulus' homelands, laws, and government followed by discussions of a
"ZULU MARRIAGE," "WITCHES AND WITCH-FINDING," and "HUNTING
AND GOING TO BATTLE" (fig. 30). All these sections corresponded to the
tableaux detailed on the playbill (fig. 16). The pamphlet accompanying
Catlin's exhibition of the Bakhoje broke up the text in a similar fashion. It
included brief biographies of exhibited individuals that were divided functionally into the chief, "medicine-man," warriors, and women. Different
sections outlined the significance of material culture that was on display,
and each ceremony that was performed. Since their text was not necessar-

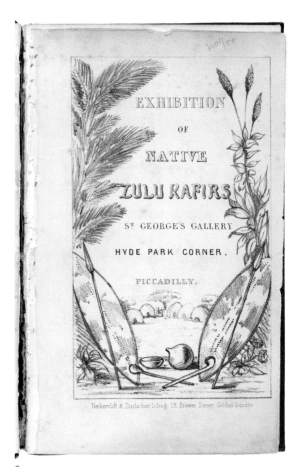

C

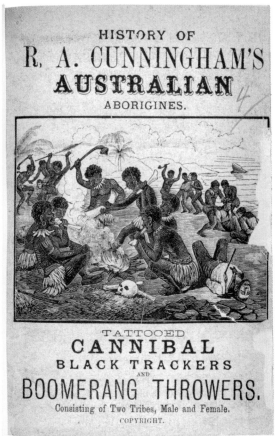

D

ily organized according to staged order, the pamphlets are unlikely to have been used as prolix programs; instead, their format suggests that they offered a reference point for the audience to consult during either the lecture or the performance when a particular scene was being presented.

The pamphlets' descriptive material did not necessarily stem from showmen's personal experience or constitute original pieces of writing; rather, a close reading reveals that they relied heavily on travel literature. Fragments and, more commonly, substantial sections of the text were frequently paraphrased or actively excerpted. For example, as the following two quotations make evident, Caldecott's *Exhibition of Native Zulu Kafirs*, the handbook to his 1853 Zulu exhibition, relied heavily on Nathaniel Isaacs's *Travels and Adventures in Eastern Africa* (1836).[50] An explorer and son of a Jewish merchant based in London, Isaacs visited Natal in 1824. Regarding Zulu government, he writes,

It is monarchical, it is true; but apparently neither hereditary nor elective, the succession depending on the murder of the existing monarch.... In this case, the criminal who performs the bloody deed, or directs its execution, is perhaps a son or some other member of the royal family.... When the monarch of the water first upon the hands of her husband, and then upon those of her friends. She then consigns the calabash to her partner, who in his turn pours some of the water first upon her hands, and then on those of his friends, until it is exhausted, when he returns it to her. The bride then throws the beads at his feet, and any of the party but himself, are at liberty to pick them up and appropriate them. In fact, a general scramble ensues; after which may come another dance, with other manifestations of general felicity, the bride always passing the marriage evening with her own friends, and the bridegroom with his. A representation of a Zulu marriage is given by the Zulus in the course of their performance.

ZULU AMUSEMENTS.

Dancing and singing are pastimes to which the natives are very much attached. Their songs are chiefly of the king's own composition, and in Dingān's reign were varied by him every year. Before opening the concert, they seat themselves in a circle; then, when the song begins, they jerk themselves up and down and to and fro, the movement gradually increasing in quickness. As the song progresses, every singer becomes excited, and jolts his body in the most grotesque manner; puffing all the time with a noise like that of a locomotive coming into a station, and every now and then uttering a shrill whistle, reminding one still more of a steam-engine. There is usually very good rhythm in their music.

During the course of the song, and under the excitement which it occasions, a quarrel frequently occurs. The disputants spring up immediately, settle the dispute with their clubbed sticks, or knob-kerrees, and then rejoin their friends as if nothing had happened.

Their dances are very often got up on a scale of great splendour. Sometimes four or five thousand people assemble, the king on such occasions being always present, and very ambitious to acquit himself well in the national amusement. They dance in a circle, the women being placed in the middle of the ring. In the dance each has his own movement, and the harder he stamps, and the higher he jumps, the cleverer he believes his dancing to be. On festive occasions the king appears in very grand attire, and is accompanied by his *Praiser*, or Poet-laureate; a most uncouth-looking individual, dressed in the skin of a leopard, or a tiger-cat, the head of the animal forming his own head for the nonce, and his occupation being to utter, through the leopard's mouth, and in very deep-toned words, the attributes and excellencies of his super-excellent monarch. The more he disregards the laws of punctuation in performing his duty, the better he acquits himself. We subjoin a portion of his eulogy, printing the epithets as they are spoken, without any intervening pauses—"Thou who art as high as the mountains thou noble elephant thou black one thou who art as high as the heavens thou who art the bird who eats other birds thou who art the great cow and the peace maker! &c. &c. &c."

WITCHES AND WITCH-FINDING.

The Zulus believe illness to be always the result of witchcraft. When any of their tribe are taken ill, the services of the *Inyanger* or witch-finder are called into requisition, to *nooker* or smell out the *Umtugartie* or witch, who has caused the illness of the invalid. They abhor the tiger-cat, or *Imparker*, as they call it, and believe it to be as necessary a companion to the witch of Zulu, as a

FIGURE 30
Two pages from Caldecott's pamphlet accompanying the 1853 exhibition of Zulus. The readable text and use of subheadings that functionally divided the text according to the ceremonies being performed are typical of most promotional pamphlets. (Charles Caldecott, *Exhibition of Native Zulu Kafirs* [1853], 26–27. Reproduced by kind permission of the Syndics of the Cambridge University Library.)

is firmly seated on his throne—which is seldom or never accomplished without, as it were, wading through blood to it—he becomes an absolute king, or "Inquose." His name then becomes sacred and adoration is paid to it.... The power of the monarch is indeed not only despotic, but even atrocious; for he can command indiscriminate massacres by his nod.[51]

In the exhibition pamphlet, this passage became paraphrased as follows:

The king is absolute; there is no liberty of the subject; a nod from the monarch consigns any one to death, no matter guilty or innocent.... It [Zulu rule] is monarchical, but apparently neither hereditary nor elective. The succession depends on the murder of the existing sovereign.... The criminal who performs the deed, or directs it, is usually the son or some other member of the royal family.... When the king becomes firmly seated on his throne, he is called an "Inkosa." His name then becomes sacred and adoration is paid to it.[52]

Caldecott explicitly cited Isaacs as an authority, but frequently the original sources of many passages were silently omitted. For example, the pamphlet accompanying the 1853 exhibition of Flora and Martinus, San children advertised as the "Earthmen," noted,

There is not, perhaps, any class of savages upon the earth that lead lives so near of brutes as the Bosjesmans; none, perhaps, who are sunk so low, who are so unimportant in the scale of existence, whose wants, whose cares, and whose joys, are so low in their nature; and who are consequently so little capable of cultivation. Certainly, no other tribe of savages in whom so high a degree of brutal ferocity is united with so much craft, and so many proofs of real power and mind. To sleep, to eat, and to drink, are the only wants.[53]

Save changes in punctuation and a few words, the same passage originally occurred over forty years earlier in *Travels in South Africa* (1812–15) by Martin Henry Lichtenstein, a German explorer and physician to the Governor of the Cape of Good Hope. Sometimes acknowledged, but frequently not, Lichtenstein, was one of the most cited authorities in the literature on displayed Africans.[54]

Travel literature provided one of the most significant resources used by showmen to frame the visual representations of displayed peoples. In contemporary accounts, the most consistently noted physical features of Maximo and Bartola were the shape of their heads and diminutive stature. Eyewitnesses continually referred to the heads' peculiarity while newspaper articles, medical reports, and pictorial representations reinforced the anatomic focus. The fascination undoubtedly revolved around a debate regarding their intelligence, with many arguing that they suffered from severe mental impairment (see chapter 5). Images of the pair almost always employed a similar and strikingly stylized form of the head. In one image from the *Lady's Newspaper*, the children are shown with their manager and a King Charles Spaniel (fig. 31). Dressed in similar ornately embroidered and lace-trimmed garments, the pair was made to look as alike as possible and was shown in profile to emphasize the shape of their heads. The presence of the dog is intriguing. The breed was becoming more popular in the Victorian period and would have carried some cachet as a toy dog with royal pedigree, since it was named in honor of King Charles II, who particularly favored them. In addition, the breed was so easily identifiable because of its stature and distinctive domed skull. It is no coincidence that the attention paid to the dog's lineage and skull mirrored the interest in the children's being the last of the Aztecs, as well as in their royal heritage and curiously shaped heads.[55] The focus on the children's heads, both in surviving photographs and in the show's pamphlets, drew directly from well-known accounts of Central American art.[56]

FIGURE 31
The "Aztec Lilliputians" with a King Charles spaniel and their manager. (*Lady's Newspaper*, July 9, 1853, p. 2. © The British Library Board. M66099.)

THE AZTECS

The association between the children and Central American travel literature was explicit and encompassed their visual and textual representation. Don Antonio del Rio's *Description of the Ruins of an Ancient City, Discovered near Palenque in the Kingdom of Guatemala, in Spanish America* (1822) and John Stephens's *Incidents of Travel in Central America, Chiapas and Yucatan* (1841) both made well-known claims that an ancient city hitherto lost to European travelers could be found in Central America.[57] Their descriptions of the city's ruins used copious illustrations of altars, wall reliefs, sculptures, and idols to substantiate their claims and were also reproduced in the show's pamphlet. These images from del Rio and Stephens both shared a conventional form of the head remarkably similar to common images of Maximo and Bartola (figs. 32 and 33). The resemblance between circulating images of the children and those of the travel literature indicates that illustrators were using del Rio and Stephens, either directly or indirectly from the show's pamphlet, as a reference work for their own interpretation of Aztec physiognomy (compare figs. 29a, 33, and 54).

The associations between the children and the travel literature extended beyond the promotional literature. One journalist for the *Morning Chronicle* was truly puzzled as to how to describe them, noting a "strongly Jewish" or even "no slight resemblance" to the Assyrian antiquities at Nineveh recently brought to public attention by the explorer Austen Henry Layard.[58] Despite the indecision, the reviewer still felt that "a resemblance more remarkable still is to be traced in the features of the Aztec to the drawings of the *basso-relievos* in Mr. Stephens' volumes."[59] Likewise, when Richard Owen, an anatomist and future curator of London's Natural History Museum, first met Maximo and Bartola he was so "struck with the similarity of the head to those copied from the sculptures in Del Rio's and Stephens valuable works" that he requested Benjamin Brodie, then president of the Ethnological Society, arrange a viewing for "some distinguished men of science." This viewing took place in 1853 at Brodie's home before the children were first exhibited in London. Owen also carried out a separate examination, an account of which he subsequently published in the *Journal of the Ethnological Society of London* (see chapter 6).[60] The accompanying illustration of Maximo's head drawn in comparison to the "skull of an idiot" employed the same stylized head as present in del Rio, Stephens, and the promotional paraphernalia and, with the manipulative use of different scales for the skull and Maximo, alluded to the widespread claim that the children were truly diminutive "Lilliputians" (fig. 34). Such testimony and the images of the children explicitly indicate how showmen, consumers, and ethnologists adapted textual and visual representations of displayed peoples to conform to existing conventions within travel literature.

The use of travel accounts in promotional materials reflects the broader practice of using these and ethnological writings to illustrate foreign news. For instance, not only was Prichard's *Natural History of Man* (1843) among the most respected of nineteenth-century publications on human variety

FIGURE 32

(*Above*) An ancient Aztec altar from a work
by Don Antonio del Rio showing the distinctive shape of their skulls. (Del Rio,
Description of the Ruins of an Ancient City
[1822], plate 9, following p. 128. Reproduced by kind permission of the Syndics
of the Cambridge University Library.)

FIGURE 33

(*Above, right*) An ancient Aztec altar
from a work by John Stephens in which
he claimed to have found the lost city
of Iximaya, where the Aztecs survived.
(Stephens, *Incidents of Travels in Central
America* [1841], 1: facing p. 142. Reproduced
by kind permission of the Syndics of the
Cambridge University Library.)

FIGURE 34

(*Right*) Maximo's head compared with the
skull of an "idiot." Richard Owen used
the illustration to support his claims that
Maximo and Bartola were mentally deficient and akin to the archaeological remains illustrated by del Rio and Stephens.
(Richard Owen and Richard Cull, "A Brief
Notice of the Aztec Race," *Journal of the
Ethnological Society of London* 4 [1856]: facing p. 137. © The British Library Board.
Ac.62334/2.)

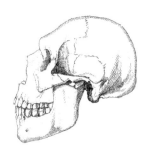

P. 137.

Maximo.
so-called Aztec boy.

Skull of an Idiot.
preserved in St. Bartholomew's Hospital.

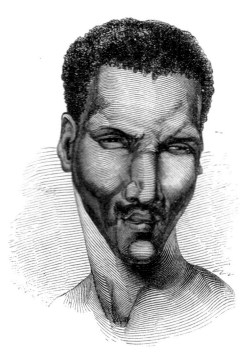

FIGURE 35
John Bull's Last Bargain, an image clearly based on the ethnological writings of James Cowles Prichard. (*Punch* 15 [1848]: 128. By kind permission of Jim Secord.)

FIGURE 36
Kosah Kafir. Prichard's work became an authoritative visual resource for images of human variety. (James Cowles Prichard, *A Natural History of Man*, 2nd ed. enlarged [1845], 315. By kind permission of Jim Secord.)

but it was extensively illustrated with color plates and engravings. Prichard's reputation and his use of images effectively established his work as an authoritative record of foreign peoples' physiognomy and physical nature, making them an ideal basis for creating images of foreign peoples in the press. In 1853, *Punch* featured a piece on the ongoing Xhosa wars accompanied by an image of a man whose head was clearly a reproduction based on Prichard's illustrations (figs. 35 and 36). Even the right-to-left inversion of the image suggests that the artist copied it directly because, like a mirror's reflection, when woodcuts were printed they appeared in reverse on the page. This reproduction and circulation of images is an instructive example of how illustrations were rarely wholly original works but usually an artist's or engraver's reworking of existing images from the dependable resource of travel writings.

Within exhibition venues, live performers peopled travelers' landscapes. Performers were frequently displayed onstage with scenery designed to provide geographic specificity. In the 1847 San exhibition, in "order to show their performances with better effect, especially their manner of fighting," the proprietor erected a small stage "with bushes at intervals," behind which the men "skulk[ed] and dart[ed]" with their "poison arrows."[61] One journalist remarked that it was a "vigorous piece of scenery and greatly relieves the repulsive aspect of the group."[62] The 1853 Zulu exhibition was held against the backdrop of impressive moving panoramic scenery and featured a mock kraal (fig. 37). Significantly, these backgrounds were often based on images within travel literature. A striking example of such imagery being used may be found in William Bullock's

1853

FIGURE 37
A reconstructed
kraal for Caldecott's
exhibition of Zulus.
(Jemima Blackburn
[1823–1909], *Zulus
Dancing in London*,
1853, watercolor on
paper/Private Col-
lection, © Michael
Graham-Stewart/
The Bridgeman Art
Library.)

exhibition of a Sámi family and a herd of reindeer in 1822. The show followed Bullock's fourth attempt to import a herd of live reindeer intended
for use in English husbandry.[63] He also brought along a man named Jens,
a woman named Karina, and an infant. The arrival of the reindeer "excited
so much interest and curiosity, that, in compliance with the wishes of the
public," they were exhibited "by the people themselves."[64] Both the reindeer and people were "decorated in the manner of their country," and an
interpreter was on hand to aid communication with Jens and Karina. The
exhibition took place at the Egyptian Hall in a room large enough to simulate the family's mountainous homelands. Bullock also exhibited numerous items of clothing and material culture. In a well-known print by the
caricaturist Thomas Rowlandson, we can easily see how the exhibition
was set up within the venue. Half the room was hung with the panoramic
painting, creating the snowy and mountainous backdrop against which
the family was exhibited (fig. 38). In the show's pamphlet the family was
also shown against the painting, but the image was composed so that all
references to the technology of display were removed (fig. 39). The scenery
was based on sketches made by the baronet, travel writer, and cofounder
of the Raleigh Club (founded 1827) Arthur de Capell Broke (Brooke). Originally made during a series of Scandinavian tours, they were published in
several works, including *Travels through Sweden, Norway, and Finmark to the*

Artful Promotion

MR. BULLOCK'S EXHIBITION OF LAPLANDERS.

FIGURE 38
Thomas Rowlandson,
Mr Bullock's Exhibi-
tion of Laplanders, 1822.
William Bullock used
panoramic scenery
based on the work of
the traveler Sir Arthur
de Capell Broke. (By
kind permission of
the London Metropoli-
tan Archives, Guild-
hall Library, City of
London.)

FIGURE 39
(Facing, top) The group
of Sámi exhibited
in 1822 at the Egyp-
tian Hall as depicted
by Bullock in the
exhibition pamphlet.
(William Bullock,
An Account of the Fam-
ily of Laplanders [1822],
foldout frontispiece.
Reproduced by kind
permission of the Syn-
dics of the Cambridge
University Library.)

North Cape, in the Summer of 1820 (1823) and *A Winter in Lapland and Sweden* (1827; fig. 40).[65] Bullock explicitly acknowledged his debt to Broke in
an attempt to authenticate the painted backdrop. Meanwhile, Jens, Karina, and their child played out scenes representative of their lifestyle in a
room devoted to simulating their home, while visitors were able to take
reindeer-driven sledge rides through snowy, mountainous peaks. Panoramas were successful forms of entertainment throughout the early and
mid-nineteenth century, but the use of living props was novel.[66]

Undoubtedly, travel literature was of fundamental importance in shaping the conventions of representation shared by showmen, consumers,
and learned men alike. Patrons were clearly encouraged to associate and
interpret their experiences within the ongoing discussions set up by travel
writers, be they explorers, missionaries, colonial officials, naturalists, or
tourists. As mentioned, showmen could rely on a significant portion of the
audience not having read the travel literature to which they referred, and
they capitalized on those willing to pay for the privilege of enlightenment.
The alignment of displayed peoples with contemporary travel literature
was significantly strengthened by promotional pamphlets. Their extensive use of previously published text and images suggests they were either
written relatively quickly or, on occasion, were essentially reprints of substantial sections of other work—perhaps in response to public requests for
more information in the early days of a show's run, or simply as a means of
keeping costs down by not investing time or money into original research.

FIGURE 40
Sir Arthur de Capell Brooke, *Mountain Laplanders Tent*. (Brooke,
A Winter in Lapland and Sweden [1827], 36. Reproduced by kind
permission of the Syndics of the Cambridge University Library.)

Given their space limitations, the information that pamphlets used was highly selective and consequently revealing of the kinds of information that exhibitors believed were important for the audience to have access to (or, perhaps, that consumers demanded). This selective excerpting allows us to observe the means through which exhibitors aligned themselves within specific social and political discussions to legitimate their enterprises as accurate representations of foreign peoples and valuable intercultural encounters. It also allows a partial solution to the problem that eyewitness accounts of the shows are woefully rare. Examining the pamphlets, and other promotional material, in detail indicates how showmen used advertising to invite consumers to associate displayed peoples with specific visual and racialist conventions, political activities, and ethnological research.

While the importance of promotional material may be surmised from this brief examination of the individual uses of posters, playbills, handbills, and pamphlets, understanding their relationship to one another is also necessary if we are to appreciate fully how contemporary methods of production and circulation created a network of closely related artifacts whose public accessibility shaped the shows' receptions.

Promotional Exchanges

Promotional materials were not unrelated scraps of paper but part of a circulating network of claims devoted to successfully creating profitable exhibitions. Textual exchanges and active excerpting between different print forms provides one of the most concrete ways to connect a wide variety of promotional material. Just as showmen relied on travel literature to produce the pamphlets that publicized their exhibitions, journalists regularly used advertising materials as resources from which to write about displayed peoples, often basing the bulk of their articles on promoters' advertising. For example, the descriptions of ceremonies used in reviews were often just paraphrased versions of the text appearing in handbills and playbills. Showmen returned the compliment by frequently employing positive reviews to advertise their wares. Toward the end of an exhibition's run, for instance, showmen might use quotations from particularly approving reviews in their longer advertisements, which attempted to encourage visitors during the final weeks. Exhibitors also often collated and reprinted longer reviews alongside a brief description of a show in very short pamphlets, usually only a few pages in length, which could then be bought by the public.[67] One of the most common reasons for such appropriation was the visit of particularly notable patrons, such as the royal family. In order to attract the crowds, the handbill for Flora and Martinus proudly drew attention to the patronage they had received, noting that "The Natural Grace of the Children, added to the Musical Talent they evince, elicited the Warmest Expressions of Approval" (fig. 41). Reports of auspicious patrons were often reprinted in later editions of the descriptive histories

REGENT GALLERY
71, QUADRANT.

THE

EARTHMEN!

The only Specimens of this Extraordinary Race ever beheld in
Europe, distinguished by the utmost Intelligence and Symmetrical
Beauty, offering a direct Contradiction to the Theory lately set
forth, of the Impossibility of Rendering the Savage a Thinking,
Feeling Being—having been exhibited before

HER MAJESTY
THE QUEEN,
H.R.H. PRINCE ALBERT,
And the Whole of the Royal Family,
Are now being exhibited
From ONE till FIVE o'Clock,
ADMISSION, 2s. 6d. CHILDREN, 1s. 6d.
And from Seven till Ten,
Admission, One Shilling

The Natural Grace of the Children, added to the Musical Talent
they evince, elicited the Warmest Expressions of Approval from
Her Majesty and the other Members of the
Royal Family.

John K. Chapman and Company, 5, Shoe Lane, and Peterborough Court, Fleet Street.

22 Aug 1853

FIGURE 41
A handbill for the ex-
hibition of Flora and
Martinus, the "Earth-
men" children. Pro-
motional materials
proudly capitalized
on the interest of the
royal family, aristoc-
racy, gentry, and the
fashionable to secure
future patrons. (By
kind permission of
the Bodleian Library,
University of Oxford, JJ,
Human Freaks 4[78].)

or in short pamphlets. Textual exchanges demonstrate the movement of
text between materially distinct promotional forms and in the wider press
(such as handbills, pamphlets, and reviews), and so highlight the importance of considering promotional material as an integrated body of material, rather than isolated scraps of showmen's pomp.

The common use of textual exchanges depends largely on the methods
employed to produce newspapers and the nature of journalism as a profession in the nineteenth century.[68] The gap between the production methods
of newspapers with larger circulations and those with smaller print runs
can be striking. The smallest papers, for example, might only be produced

Artful Promotion

[91]

by one editor and one reporter and could not compete with the circulation figures of larger provincial papers or national dailies. Instead, they might offer items of local news, a leading article, and digested forms of the larger papers. The importance of such "scissors-and-paste" journalism is suggested by a letter dated 1855 from a Manchester printer to an associate about a new project: "I shall want the London Times daily, half price will do except Friday. The Field of gardening and agricultural paper, the Manchester Guardian of Wed'y and any other papers we might exchange with. I will undertake the bringing out of the paper, make its selections, see after the local news and editing."[69] Freelance journalists may also be a significant source for textual similarity. These "penny-a-liners" sold written articles to anybody willing to buy them. Frequently impoverished and on the verge of ruin, it is quite likely that they may have sold similar stories, if not exactly the same, to a number of different publications. Although proving how much freelance journalists contributed to a publication is difficult, it is unlikely that they were the sole or even the primary source of textual overlaps; but they remain a possible explanation. In addition, many journalists were routinely employed by a number of periodicals. As such, the production methods involved in the production of news in the nineteenth century may account for the extensive use of textual excerpting.

In conjunction, publications commonly exchanged whole columns of printed material with the advent of stereotyping. Stereotyping involved setting type into columns and using these to cast plates from which prints could be made. Although invented much earlier, it was not in general use until midcentury, but once common, it made textual transfer between publications relatively simple and became especially popular in the 1850s and 1860s as smaller papers attempted to compete with the *Times*. The *Morning Herald* and the *Standard*, for example, cost 4 pence and a penny, respectively, yet most of their printed material was not only shared but identical, "like the Siamese twins."[70] The development of news agencies in the mid- to late nineteenth century is also relevant.[71] They often supplied text as a package that had been written by journalists in their employment, rather than by the newspaper. This ensured that editors could reliably fill their columns without having to undertake the arduous task of finding a dependable writer; instead, they received material that could be inserted, without alteration, directly into their pages. Similarly, advertising agencies were a bridge between clients. They supplied newspapers with press releases and vendors with their required promotional notices. The mutual economic dependence of these parties raises the possibility of arrangements existing between agencies, showmen, and the newspapers to benefit each other and may provide an explanation as to why newspaper reviews of exhibitions appear to have been generally positive.

Informational overlaps were not limited to newspapers and promotional material; pamphlets were equally mined as sources of material for handbills and posters. Advertisements, in the papers and in promotional material, are often worded exactly the same as pamphlets, and the descriptions contained in reviews are frequently dependent on, if not paraphrased versions of, the descriptive histories given in pamphlets. For example, in a *Household Words* review of Caldecott's show, Dickens offered the following account of Zulu government:

The noble savage sets a king to reign over him, to whom he submits his life and limbs without a murmur or question, and whose life is passed chin deep in a lake of blood; but who, after killing incessantly, is in his turn killed by his relations and friends, the moment a gray hair appears on his head.[72]

Dickens was indebted to Caldecott's pamphlet, which, in turn, relied heavily on Isaacs's book, both in this passage and in his descriptions of other ceremonies, such as a Zulu marriage and the instigation of war.[73] Just as showmen actively adapted travel literature to their promotional needs, journalists used the pamphlets as their primary and perhaps only source of descriptive information on displayed peoples when reviewing the shows.

Informational overlaps could also occur across varying stretches of time. For instance, the handbill for Farini's 1879 exhibition of Friendly Zulus featured an approving review (fig. 18):

THE TIMES (speaking of Farini's Zulus) says—"The songs and dances are difficult to distinguish the expression of love from the gesture of martial defiance. Nevertheless as a picture of manners nothing can be more complete; and not the least remarkable part of the exhibition is the perfect training of the wild artists. They seem utterly to lose all sense of their present condition: if English actors could be found so completely to lose themselves in the characters they assumed, histrionic art would be in a state, truly magnificent."[74]

Despite the approbation, the slightly garbled quotation was not a review of Farini's show but of Caldecott's 1853 exhibition of Zulus (see above). Evidently, consumers are exceptionally unlikely to have recalled a newspaper review from twenty-six years ago and therefore discover the misleading claim. Yet the quotation's use raises the question: how did Farini have access to the original review? For instance, did he have copies of some of the original promotional material, or did he have access to a scrapbook, or something similar, in which an interested individual, perhaps Caldecott or himself, had collected materials relevant to human display? Either way, Farini's use of the 1853 review provides a pregnant indication of the varied routes and expanses of time that could be involved in textual exchanges.

The importance of textual exchange and appropriation in providing promotional material across such a diverse range of formats may partly depend on the importance of the anthology as a genre during this period. Writers were often anthologized, with or without their permission, and extracts ranged from whole pages to witty epigrams suited to moral commandment. The widespread use of textual appropriation in the form of anthologizing led to writers, for example George Eliot, adapting their writing styles by including passages especially suited to extraction.[75] It is not surprising that in this culture of exchange so much adaptation took place or that the use of accreditation varied considerably. The appropriation of information in this manner extended to visual material. Pamphlets and the illustrated press both contained images that were directly connected. Caldecott's *Exhibition of the Native Zulu Kafirs*, for example, contained a number of loosely observed lithographs of the colony and Zulu life. One plate differed only in the fine-grained detail from an illustration used by the *Illustrated London News* (figs. 42 and 43). In the pamphlet the image was used as an example of a party going into battle, but in the paper it was used as an example of a wedding party. As the pamphlet does not bear an exact date, it is difficult to know where the original image appeared; however, given the extensive use of pamphlets in reviews, it seems plausible that the image was originally to be found in the promotional literature rather than the newspaper. Either way, it makes clear that images were excerpted and adapted as needed by showmen and journalists.

The dissociation between image and context is also an example of a wider phenomenon in the circulation of images. For example, it has been suggested that contemporary images of Livingstone, once his reputation as an explorer was established, almost always show him wearing the consular cap with which he was peculiarly attached and identified. Images of his famous encounter with an aggressive lion feature the hat as an identifying article, despite the incident having taken place before Livingstone was even appointed to the consulate.[76] These images indicate that pamphlets were used by journalists for their own purposes rather than blindly copied. They also demonstrate that among an illustrator's priorities was

FIGURE 42
This illustration from Caldecott's Zulu exhibition pamphlet claims to show the Zulus preparing for war. (Charles Caldecott, *Exhibition of Native Zulu Kafirs* [1853], facing 28. Reproduced by kind permission of the Syndics of the Cambridge University Library.)

FIGURE 43
*The Zulu Kafirs at
the St. George's Gal-
lery, Knightsbridge.*
The *Illustrated Lon-
don News* used this
image to illustrate a
Zulu wedding party.
Its similarity to the
Caldecott pamphlet's
image shows how
illustrations, as well
as text, were clipped
and reused in a va-
riety of printed ma-
terials. (*Illustrated
London News*, May 28,
1853, p. 409. Author's
collection.)

the creation of a memorable image employing symbols commonly associated with their subject, even if it was at the expense of obvious factual
accuracy.

Textual and visual exchange may be conceptualized as the different
trophic levels of a food chain in which text is continually digested, regurgitated, and consumed. Within this chain, pamphlets provided the crucial
mediating link between travel writing, promotional materials, and jour-
nalistic accounts. They were also the most common starting point for the
circulation of information in London's streets and press, as their contents
were clipped and used across the most diverse range of promotional material with distinctive functions. Thus, although unavailable, the circulation
figures of pamphlets would be unlikely to reflect their importance accurately. Even if they were only available to audience members, or proved too
expensive for those with limited incomes, their use as sources for newspaper articles and promotional materials means the information they contained is likely to have reached a far greater number of people than ever
witnessed a show. Thus, they played a pivotal role in the textual and visual
representation of exhibited peoples, whether directly or through their use
in other print forms.

✳

Promotional material ensured that the shows' impact extended beyond
the boundaries of an exhibition venue's walls into the streets. Many people could not afford the entrance prices exhibitors charged, but any pass-
erby could inspect the posters and playbills that were glued onto available

Artful Promotion

walls. Posters, playbills, handbills, newspaper reviews, and even entrance tickets carried promises of uniqueness, rarity, and ethnic singularity. Using a range of newly emerging techniques, exhibitors ensured that their proclamations were as eye-catching as possible. These encouraged passersby to devote the attention needed to distinguish and read individual posters from the palimpsest that billposting produced.

The primary function of advertising for the shows' proprietors was obviously its role in ensuring commercial success, but how did metropolitan observers willing to take another look use these materials? Advertising in the streets enabled individuals who were unable to afford entrance charges or newspapers a form of consumption as long as they were semiliterate. As illustrated promotional materials became common, even this prerequisite disappeared (although it required new skills associated with visual communication). The geography of promotional materials' use—close to the venue and even on its walls—also allowed passersby to know where a show was taking place. For those able to read, advertising was detailed enough for them to know who was being exhibited, where they came from, and what they would perform. Although limited, this exposure allowed some measure of participation. For those with access to the newspapers, reviews and foreign reports added a significant element to vicarious participation. Reviews detailed the content of lectures, how displayed peoples actually behaved, and how the audience reacted to exhibited individuals. Foreign news added a further contextualizing element and helped make displayed peoples politically relevant.

Patrons wealthy enough to spare a shilling or more on an evening's entertainment would have found that many of the cues showmen used to frame displayed peoples were ultimately rooted in travel literature. It provided background scenery and the descriptive material that was used in lectures and pamphlets. For those unfamiliar with the relevant literature, playbills and pamphlets offered a primer in the manners and customs of the performers. Patrons' lack of prior knowledge may have made them primarily, or even wholly, dependent on promotional material for the information they used to categorize their experiences. Those who were more familiar with the peoples on display, through either reading or personal travel, may not have been dependent on promotional material to make sense of the performances they witnessed, but could still utilize pamphlets as synopses of the relevant literature. Ultimately, such reliance invested showmen with the power to mediate the kinds of knowledge the shows produced and their receptions.

Exhibitors' extensive use of travel literature aligned displayed peoples within the discussions set up by the missionaries, government officials, explorers, and travelers who wrote of their encounters with foreign peoples. Travel literature has long been acknowledged as critical in creating hierarchical views of foreign peoples that might be used to denigrate their humanity and facilitate the justification for imperial expansion.[77] Showmen helped to both create and perpetuate these perceptions by regurgitating whole passages of such accounts in their pamphlets. Travel literature appears to have provided the script for a significant proportion, if not all, of the promotional material used by showmen (such as posters, playbills, and handbills) and provided journalists with a substantial portion of their review material. As such, advertising fashioned a racialist set of expectations that framed the audience's experiences (negative or positive) and thus fundamentally shaped the shows' receptions. Historians have been quick to seize on promotional materials as evidence of the shows' receptions. However, this approach is flawed. As forms of advertising, these materials were wont to emphasize, exaggerate, create, or even fabricate ethnic difference for economic gain. They provide valuable evidence of how showmen marketed displayed peoples (and clearly, ethnic origin mattered here) and how patrons were invited to frame their experiences using racialist stereotypes; however, advertising cannot be taken as evidence for how paying customers actually interpreted the performances they witnessed.

Consumers are highly unlikely to have adopted promotional rhetoric uncritically; however, examining the promotional material closely still provides clues for possible interpretations. The availability of advertising makes it more than likely that the metropolitan population used the racialist stereotypes it employed as a measure against which personal experiences could be judged. Attending a performance might provide a basis for rejecting common stereotypes, but an individual doing so would still be operating from preconceived notions of how a performer might behave, which, ultimately, still depended on advertising. Furthermore, as discussed in chapter 1, since racialist classifications were used to differentiate consumers as much as foreign peoples, patrons were able to use exhibitions to define the habits and customs of foreign peoples and themselves. Showmen capitalized on this by marketing them as unique educational opportunities. Where patrons failed to make such associations, they were made explicit by lecturers, who referred to a backdrop of political activity and foreign affairs. Advertising used posters, bills, and pamphlets, in which showmen attempted to incorporate displayed peoples into the role of the performing "savage." However, exhibition venues were not just sites in which the contact between performers and consumers was polarized in the manner advertising might suggest; rather, exhibitions were significant sites of multiple forms of intercultural encounter.

PART TWO

METROPOLITAN
ENCOUNTERS

FIGURE 44
The frontispiece to George Catlin's *Illustrations of the Manners and Customs of the North American Indians*, vol. 1 (1876). (Reproduced by kind permission of the Syndics of the Cambridge University Library.)

3 Managing Performance

IN THE 1830s, George Catlin, then a young painter from Pennsylvania, spent six years making five journeys across the Great Plains and Rocky Mountains of North America to paint as many indigenous peoples as he could while also amassing an enormous collection of artifacts from the various tribes among whom he found hospitality. Ultimately, Catlin hoped to make his mark and fortune by selling the entire collection to the U.S. government as a comprehensive record of a vanishing people. When this venture failed, he toured the British, European, and American lecture circuits in the 1840s, during which period his collection was accompanied by three groups of Anishinabe and Bakhoje. Catlin's career is indicative of many wider themes in exhibition managers' lives. Driven by his political commitments and financial needs, he used the opportunity to display foreign peoples as a means of making a living after the disappointing turn his speculations had taken. In his writings and tours he traded on personally having trekked the Missouri regions, and recorded for posterity a range of tribes that seemed on the verge of dying out (fig. 44). Yet he also used the shows as a means to promote his cause, consistently seeking to impress on the public the essential humanity of his subjects and the need to protect their traditional ways of life. Although all showmen were concerned with making a profit, many, like Catlin, were also concerned with numerous political, social, and religious causes that informed how they displayed foreign peoples and the lessons they sought to teach the paying public.

In discussions of the shows' receptions, their managers have often been relatively overlooked in favor of the interaction between performers and consumers. The neglect is partly due to a lack of sources from which historians might resurrect their social background, motivations, and success. Aside from a few famous individuals, such as P. T. Barnum or Catlin, most showmen remain anonymous or are known by little more than a name. Yet their marginalization also stems from the way in which their role in shaping the shows' receptions has been conceptualized. Exhibitors are most often credited with producing shows and exploiting any possible opportunities for making a profit, but little else.[1] Early work on human curiosities provides a helpful departure by suggesting that these showmen were instrumental in creating "freaks" and therefore in creating audiences that were willing to pay for the opportunity to see them.[2] Recent research on Barnum also provides a constructive departure.[3] It has been suggested that he pioneered techniques that created and marketed a brand of cheap entertainment in which the public were invited to participate in a never-ending guessing game.[4] Whether he was exhibiting a human curiosity (including anatomic anomalies and foreign peoples) or a curious object (such as a mermaid), Barnum ensured that his promotional claims were couched in carefully crafted equivocation—Is it real or not? Is it man or beast? What is it?—to invite spectators to pay their dime and decide for themselves. When exhibiting anatomic curiosities, such as Tom Thumb, he used specially designed costumes and commissioned furniture to make small people appear diminutive, tall people appear gigantic, and the overweight seem morbidly obese. Barnum has been so closely tied to these emerging techniques of public manipulation that they have come to be defining characteristics of "Barnumism." Such research has been enormously fruitful in understanding how curiosity was both developed and promoted in the nineteenth century, especially as it suggests that Barnum was an active agent in directing the kinds of knowledge show business produced; however, in making Barnum the linchpin of the curiosity business, there is a risk that he will be taken to be more important than both performers and consumers, or that he will be taken to be an exception. Although he was extraordinarily adept at marketing his products, he was, in many senses, by no means unique.

Showmen came from diverse backgrounds and had numerous motivations for displaying foreign peoples; but they all capitalized on their entrepreneurial instincts to bridge the gap between supply and the market demand they created in order to turn a profit. In addition, they invented and shared many techniques to frame human display and which, when fully appreciated, suggest that managers played instrumental roles in shaping the shows' receptions and the knowledge they helped produce.

Entrepreneurial Entertainers

Entrepreneurs who exploited the public's curiosity were critical in producing human displays. Bullock, for instance, trained as a jeweler and goldsmith, but became a traveler and naturalist of repute who was elected to the membership of learned institutions, including the Linnean Society, Edinburgh's Wernerian Society of Natural History, and the Dublin Society. He turned to museum curatorship when, in 1808, he opened the Liverpool Museum.[5] He stocked his museum with objects of armory, natural history specimens, and many curiosities that he had either personally selected or purchased from the sale of other collections (including the closure of the Leverian Museum in 1806). In 1809, following the success of his venture, he moved to London, where he established himself as the proprietor of the Liverpool Museum at no. 22, Piccadilly. The museum quickly proved to be one of the most fashionable places of metropolitan amusement, attracting more than 20,000 visitors in its opening month and 80,000 by June of the same year. Its premises soon proved too small for the growing collection, so in 1811 Bullock moved it to the newly built Egyptian Hall, at nos. 171 and 172, Piccadilly. The museum hosted some of the most famous exhibitions of the nineteenth century, including the Sámi in 1822 and Catlin's shows in the 1840s. As an independent collector living near the trading hustle and bustle of Liverpool's docks, Bullock built up many contacts with traveling salesmen, which demonstrates the importance of the trade and collecting networks to human display (see below). As the Egyptian Hall's owner and manager (until its sale in 1825), he is also an excellent example of an entrepreneur who capitalized on public interest to provide an income sufficient for his financial gain and independence.

Some could only dream of the financial stability Bullock enjoyed and were simply trying to earn a meager living as commercial lecturers. While employed as an anatomy lecturer at a private school in Edinburgh in the 1820s, Robert Knox unwittingly bought corpses from the now infamous murderers William Burke and William Hare. Although later exonerated, by 1842 his involvement with the scandal, radical political commitments, and participation in institutional rivalry between the university and extramural anatomy schools contributed to his ruin. Unable to find professional academic employment, Knox was forced to leave Edinburgh and spent the remainder of his life as a social pariah, earning a hand-to-mouth living as a hack journalist and public lecturer before dying in poverty in 1862.[6] In 1849, however, he gave a series of lectures on the subject of human variety that later formed the basis for his notorious *The Races of Men* (1850), in which Knox argued that race is the most important determinant of human history. Although a somewhat infamous celebrity in his own right, Knox clearly felt he would benefit from the public's added thrill of seeing living curiosities, so he hired a group of San to perform in addition to his regular repertoire of lectures.

Other showmen were driven by political convictions. Catlin publicized the plight of Native Americans, whom he believed were in danger of either being wiped out entirely or losing their cultural identity by becoming assimilated into urban American life. He began his travels just after a significant shift in federal Indian policy. In 1830, under the presidency of Andrew Jackson, the United States passed what came to be known as the Indian Removal Act, which for the first time legalized the forced relocation of tribes from east of the Mississippi to the West. The legislation was publicly rationalized by the claim that if nothing was done, the specter of certain extinction hovered over the tribes of the eastern territories. For instance, in 1829, in his first Annual Message to Congress, Jackson claimed that

Our ancestors found them [Indians] the uncontrolled possessors of these vast regions. By persuasion and force, they have been made to retire from river to river, and from mountain to mountain; until some of the tribes have become extinct, and others have left but remnants, to preserve, for a while, their once terrible names. Surrounded by the whites, with their arts of civilization, which, by destroying the resources of the savage, doom him to weakness and decay; the fate of the Mohegan, the Narragansett, and the Delaware, is fast overtaking the Choctaw, the Cherokee, and the Creek. That this fate surely awaits them, if they remain within the limits of the States, does not admit of a doubt. Humanity and national honor demand that every effort should be made to avert such a great calamity.[7]

These changes in federal Indian policy suggest that the prospects for assimilation, the other available option, were deemed either practically unfeasible or impossible. Instead, since westward expansion could not be halted (or willingly contemplated), Jackson expediently argued, its effects on eastern populations could be alleviated only by creating a designated territory for and enforced relocation of the indigenous peoples.[8] Catlin began his travels up the Missouri River in the wake of these policy shifts, fully convinced of the impending disappearance of his subjects.[9]

Catlin's ramblings led to the accumulation of a vast "Indian collection," with which he toured in America, Britain, and Europe when he turned to public lecturing in the 1840s (fig. 45). In addition, he published accounts of his travels, including *Letters and Notes on the Manners, Customs and Conditions of the North American Indians* (1841). As mentioned, his ultimately frustrated desire was to sell his entire collection to the U.S. government as a monumental record of the pristine American wilderness and its peoples (although much of it found a home in the Smithsonian Institution after his death). Catlin's was not the only voice campaigning on behalf of endangered tribes, but he was unusually willing to publicize their plight. His original exhibition, which made its debut in New York in 1837 and with which he subsequently traveled to London in 1840, involved his acting as a docent for his own collection and lecturing on his travels in the mountains and prairies of North America. Catlin would occasionally dress in tribal clothes and initially hired Cockney performers, in makeup, to perform *tableaux vivants* recreating scenes from his works. By 1844, after a tour of Britain, interest and profits were waning, and Catlin made preparations to leave for America. Just before he left, Arthur Rankin, manager of a group of the Anishinabe, approached him to reach an amicable arrangement for publicly exhibiting the group. Catlin agreed, but after the marriage of Alexander Cadotte, the group's interpreter, Rankin dismissed him from the group and decided to tour the provinces independently (see chapter 4). At this opportune moment, Catlin met the missionary George H. C. Melody, the Bakhoje's manager, with whom he reached a new agreement and reopened his shows with fresh faces. In 1845, he was also approached

by another group of Anishinabe being managed by George Henry (see below). Despite publicizing the damaging effects of westward expansion, it has been suggested that Catlin accepted that the only solution was removal and resettlement of the indigenous peoples. In this light, his exhibitions both promoted the notion of destined extinction and simultaneously validated the interventionist management of imperiled tribes.[10]

Motivated by faith, other managers wanted to save lost souls. Christian philanthropic and missionary projects underpinned the display of many foreign peoples, both publicly and privately. Significantly, converted peoples were often presented to society as evidence of the successful advance of Christianity among the nation's subjects and abroad.[11] Flora and Martinus were entrusted to the care of a man who was believed to be capable of teaching them to be good Christians. The merchant who bought them also intended to return them to Africa as missionaries in order to spread the gospel overseas. In 1844, the Bakhoje were also imported by Melody, whose occupation as a missionary appears to have influenced the U.S. government's decision to grant him permission to travel.[12] Similarly, the promotional material for the Krenak family exhibited in 1822 explicitly indicated missionary involvement: "The object of the Persons who have sent them to Europe being to civilize them, in order to their returning to the Tribe to which they belong, to prepare them to receive the Missionaries, who are at this time so laudably engaged in the good works of Christianity."[13] The show's pamphlet added that the parents, knowing no English, were particularly anxious to return home, where they and their son could be educated in the "principles of the Christian Religion," and to this end they begged public assistance.[14]

The role of missionaries and Christian philanthropy is crucial for understanding displayed peoples' experiences. Missionary intentions were routinely used by showmen to justify both human importation and human display. The possibility of combining conversion with training future Christian ambassadors proved to be a recurrent theme in the early to mid-nineteenth century, but it appears to have become less so by the dawn of the twentieth. Missionaries were also often among the shows' most vocal critics (see chapter 5). In any case, it is clear that just as merchants and military personnel could provide a first point of contact for exhibited peoples with London's show business, so could missionary work.

One of the most interesting examples of a missionary manager is George Henry, better known as Maungwudaus. An Anishinabe who converted to Christianity around 1825, Henry spent much of the 1820s and 1830s attending a Methodist mission school at the recently founded Credit Mission on the banks of the Credit River in Canada, serving at several mission schools, and then moving to Walpole Island in 1837. With his fluent English, he worked as a government interpreter for a local mission before leaving the Methodist Church just three years later. In 1844, in all likelihood inspired by Catlin's entrepreneurialism, he formed a party of local Anishinabe and left for London to exhibit the group. At one performance, Henry noted, "Our war-chief shot a buck in the Park, through the heart, and fell down dead three hundred yards, before four thousand ladies and gentlemen. This was done to amuse them."[15] Unfortunately, three members of the troupe died of smallpox after having refused the vaccination (concerned Quakers had ensured that the rest received treatment), and Henry suffered further loss when his wife and two children also passed away. After the show closed in London, the party left for Paris, where Henry approached and subsequently exhibited with Catlin.

Henry's willingness to act as the agent for an exhibition of his own peoples, his religious development, and his publishing a pamphlet describing his experiences abroad all undermine any attempt to oversimplify the dynamic between mangers and performers into that of Europeans exploiting the colonized solely for their own gain.[16] In contrast, as has been recently observed, "Maungwudaus is a clear example of a First Nations member preferring to act—and being prepared to act—as an impresario for performers who are his own people."[17] This stress on Henry's agency is both valuable and a salutary reminder of the complexity involved in the shows' histories. Meanwhile, Henry's connections to missionary movements provide a suggestive example of how important the infrastructure provided by Christian missionaries proved for the shows.

From the late nineteenth century onward in particular, showmen were often fully fledged professional entertainers. Imre Kiralfy (nee Konigsbaum) was born in Austria into a prosperous Jewish family who were ruined in the 1848 Hungarian Revolution. Along with his brother, Bolossy, he started performing at an early age; by the 1880s, after touring Berlin and Paris, the pair found success producing increasingly extravagant dance spectacles in America. By 1887, Kiralfy and his brother had become estranged, and Imre began producing shows for world's fairs, including the 1893 World's Columbian Exposition in Chicago. Following his success there, Imre moved to London, bought Earl's Court, and rebuilt a small-scale version of Chicago's White City. These experiences made Kiralfy one of the most important exhibition organizers of the late nineteenth century, and his brand of choreographed, showy extravagance not only influenced human displays but significantly changed the nature of world's fairs.

Similarly, William Leonard Hunt, the "Great Farini," was born in Canada and, despite strict parents, appears to have chosen a life in show business after having been captivated by a visit to the circus. He made his name as an acrobat and tightrope walker before showcasing his skills at Niagara Falls in 1850. After touring Europe and the United States and working with Barnum for some time, in 1885 he left for Africa and became famous for becoming the first white man to survive crossing the Kalahari Desert (although a small number of Africans regularly achieved the feat to much less acclaim). During the late 1870s and 1880s, he made his name at the Westminster Aquarium, where his substantial repertoire of acts featured the human cannonball, gymnastics, trained animals, human oddities, and displayed peoples, especially Africans. Farini brought exhibitions of Africans to the fore at a time when the European exploration, colonization, and military control of that continent was gathering momentum, making African exhibitions potentially both politically relevant and commercially lucrative. Exhibiting humans was just one of the many ways in which Farini entertained the public, but the visibility of his shows made them important arenas for encountering performing Africans in the late nineteenth century. Farini is also an excellent example of a flamboyant showman who skillfully took advantage of his own background in performance and the public desire to be entertained, especially by meeting foreign peoples.

Whatever showmen's background or motivations for exhibiting foreign peoples, they shared the desire and the need to make their shows commercially successful. To this end, exhibition proprietors developed a range of techniques to frame live performances as being sufficiently intriguing to be worth paying to see.

Forging Curiosity

Showmen were not just profiteering individuals but critical links in the chain connecting displayed peoples to spectators. They ensured that the nature of live performances complemented the claims of promotional materials in order to satisfy the consumers' curiosity they had helped pique. In doing so, they employed numerous techniques, from lectures to costumes, to invite spectators to be entertained while interpreting displayed peoples within specific political and racialist frameworks. As such, showmen played a significant role in shaping both the shows' receptions and the knowledge they helped produce.

Managers recruiting performers relied on the same international networks of trade and export that governed the circulation of economically important goods such as spices and slaves. Throughout the seventeenth and eighteenth centuries, for example, the Dutch East India Company traded animals as a sideline and became the major supplier of creatures from the Cape of Good Hope. Many animals also arrived in Europe as private entrepreneurial speculations.[18] Throughout the eighteenth and early nineteenth centuries, as economic considerations fueled British imperial expansion, most live animals arrived on these shores as the wards of sailors on trading voyages. The trade flourished as London's menageries and well-heeled aristocratic enthusiasts provided a continual demand for live quadrupeds, often the most popular exhibits in a collection. Menagerie agents frequented the Thames estuary in order to secure the best supplies and dealt directly with the naval men; soon, dealers emerged who specialized in mediating the transactions between supplier and consumer. As territorial acquisition gradually replaced commercial interests as the focus for colonial expansion, new patterns of suppliers reflected the change, with explorers, military men, civil officials, huntsmen, and professional collectors playing an increasingly important role.[19]

Slavery provided a mass market for human commodities that were shipped along the same trade routes as flora and fauna. Although the British slave trade was abolished in 1807, slavery was not outlawed in the British Empire until 1833, with emancipation following in 1838. Until 1807, British merchants dominated the trade, with the greatest number of slaves appearing from Africa's Atlantic coast. Even after abolition, Britons continued to depend on the products of slavery, such as palm oil and sugar, while simultaneously campaigning for it to be ended in America.[20] Meanwhile, the supply of imported goods (American cotton, West Indies sugar, Chinese tea, or North European timber) and exported goods (such as textiles, coal, iron, and steel) depended on viable economic arrangements with foreign countries, while the Stock Exchange and East-End docks ensured that the metropolis functioned as an integral part of both national and global economic activity.[21]

Showmen exploited these existing networks of trade and travel. Many appear to have been overseas agents or individuals who regularly traveled abroad for their profession, such as soldiers, sailors, and merchants, and who commonly acted as agents for metropolitan residents interested in the exotic. Sara Baartman was brought to England by Alexander Dunlop, the surgeon of an African ship and exporter of museum specimens from the Cape of Good Hope. Dunlop had imported Baartman hoping to advantageously dispose of his interest in her to a collector, and made an offer to Bullock before the latter became proprietor of the Egyptian Hall. Although Bullock refused her outright, Dunlop's offer alone reveals the trio's position within the historical network of suppliers, consumers, and consumed. Dunlop's status as a collector with trade contacts and his trade as a naval surgeon meant he could deal in specimens just as other navy employees supplied menagerie proprietors. Crucially, he provided a point of contact for individuals such as Bullock, who relied on exotic specimens for commercial success. Clearly, the access to foreign specimens provided by employment abroad was an advantage, especially for sailors and soldiers, who could speculate on a relatively small scale by importing the odd commodity.

For other showmen, connections to broader networks of trade may also have provided an advantage in that they were known to the colonial authorities, and their mercantile status may have made the difference in securing the permission necessary to export human exhibits. Charles Caldecott's father, A. T. Caldecott, a South African merchant, arranged the travel and accommodations for the thirteen Zulus whom his son exhibited in 1853. Charles noted, "Fortunately, the circumstances of having been known as a merchant of respectability, and a highly honourable man, [had] influenced the government in his favour."[22] Once on Britain's shores, showmen either personally exhibited their human imports or profited by giving up their interests in the enterprise by selling on their purchases or managerial roles. By the late nineteenth century, it became common for humans intended for display to be collected by specialist agents who were commissioned to procure given human types.[23] The most dramatic examples of this kind of importation occurred in the context of world's fairs, where exhibition organizers would essentially import different ethnic groups to order. Their plans read as if they were shopping lists for a global human supermarket, and indicate that by the late nineteenth and early twentieth centuries, importing humans for world's fairs involved complex negotiations between specialized agents, foreign peoples, and government officials rather than acts of trade.[24]

Differentiating displayed peoples from resident ethnic minorities in the metropolis was critical for ensuring paying customers, and so showmen frequently advertised the lengths to which they had gone to import performers. Newspaper reviews and promotional material frequently bore details indicative of how living foreign peoples had been recruited. The extent of the details varied. In all the exhibitions for which pamphlets are available, displayed peoples are, to varying degrees, incorporated into a travel narrative. Handbills advertised the Krenak family exhibited in 1822 as having "Just Arrived from the Brazils, in the Ship Hope, of Liverpool" under the guidance of Captain Stibs (fig. 15). In the exhibition pamphlet, further details emerged regarding their voyage to Europe. They were claimed to have been delivered into the hands of a French adventurer, who brought them over to this country upon speculation, to derive profit from an exhibition of their persons. It is rather to be thought that, in consequence of a bribe to some of the Colonel's domestics [their former owner], the Frenchman obtained possession of these Botocudos, the first of this tribe ever seen in Europe.[25]

However, once on English soil, the "land of liberty" where "the august laws of Great Britain have proscribed slavery," the family was freed from the unscrupulous Frenchman and exhibited under the management of a missionary.[26]

In 1882, Robert A. Cunningham was approached by Barnum's agent while on the lookout for a group of Australian Aborigines to be publicly exhibited in America. Cunningham obliged and also toured Europe with the troupe, bringing them to London in 1884. The show's pamphlet, *History of R. A. Cunningham's Australian Aborigines* (1884), described the performers' "curious habits," followed by reprinted documents from the Australian government and articles from the international press. According to the descriptive material, the performers were the "lowest type of humanity . . . in every particular in which the Negro and Hottentot falls below the white race, the Australian falls still lower than the black African."[27] Before leaving Australia, however, two of the performers had absconded from the steamer bound for San Francisco on which Cunningham had secured their passage. Six days later, they were found wandering in the bush and were approached by a police constable, who offered them food and clothing if they would accompany him. One man fled and, once the constable had caught up with him, produced a knife and stabbed his pursuer. The case was brought to court, and Cunningham was accused of kidnapping, precipitating a flurry of concern (although he was later acquitted and the pair were released into his care).[28]

The final pages of Cunningham's pamphlet featured reprinted articles from the Australian and American papers. The *Sydney Morning Herald* reported that the "poor creatures were evidently in terror and want to run away from their employer," and that the government's representatives were "anxious that these men should not [be] taken away from the Colony" but "sent back from the district from which they were taken." A reprinted letter from W. Camphin ("Inspector of Detectives") claimed, "Two of the males speak English, and say they are willing to go to America. The others do not appear to know where they are going to. . . . [Cunningham] is living at the Hotel, and appears to pay great attention to their wants." The *Sydney Evening News* claimed that the "two found at Manly seem to be utterly wild and on that ground it may be fairly inferred that the case is clearly one of kidnapping. . . . Whatever is to be done, should be done at once. It will never do to have Sydney made the entrepot of a kidnapping trade."[29] The remaining articles from the *Auckland Star*, *Toronto World*, *St. Louis Daily*, and *Pittsburgh Chronicle* were all reprinted reviews praising the show.

Cunningham's presentation was skillful. Details of his troupe's provenance effectively substantiated their authenticity as imported performers. The articles in which Cunningham was accused of kidnapping heightened intrigue, and despite lacking an explicit discussion of how he resolved his difficulties, the sheer existence of the show's reviews strongly implied that he had been absolved of all wrongdoing and allowed to leave the country. In this sense, simply reprinting the documents gave the impression of transparency while, despite lacking the more usual prose narrative describing the recruitment process, the selection of sources effectively created a drama of crime, kidnap, and entertainment.

Maximo and Bartola's exhibitors provided a particularly elaborate history, claiming that the children had been daringly spirited away from the mysterious city of Iximaya in an "eventful expedition."[30] In 1848, Messrs. Huertis of Baltimore and Hammond of Canada were said to have resolved to explore Central America after reading Stephens's *Incidents of Travel*, which made the sensational claims that Iximaya, a secluded, forgotten city in Central America, was still inhabited by the Aztecs who had faithfully preserved the ancient system of political, social, and religious organization from the reign of Emperor Moctezuma (Montezuma). Arriving at Belize in the autumn of 1848, Huertis and Hammond were joined by Pedro Velasquez, a Spaniard from San Salvador, and the party then proceeded in search of Iximaya. In May, the men reached the summit of Mount Sierra, and spying the city's glittering domes and minarets in the distance, said to be of an "Egyptian character," they ventured forth. At length they reached their intended destination and found a city of "vast proportions, with heavy walls and battlements, full of temples, gigantic statues and pagan paraphernalia." The people possessed "Peruvian manners combined with Assyrian magnificence." Bound within the city walls, they sought no "intercourse with the world around." Their custom of killing any travelers who ventured to disturb them meant that "no white man had ever returned." Hammond and Huertis were both slain, while Velasquez, "being more wary, lulled his captors into security, and not only escaped, but brought with him two children."[31] Not only is this travel narrative quite fanciful, but it was consistently challenged as untrue. Moreover, it has been suggested that Hammond and Huertis were based on Stephens and his illustrator Frederick Catherwood. Hammond and Stephens had both traveled in the Near East, while Huertis and Catherwood were both expert surveyors; all four had taken part in a well-funded expedition into the region.[32]

Clearly, performers' biographies were intended to arouse the interest of the paying public; however, the pamphlets' tales were not the only indications of displayed peoples' histories. Showmen frequently reprinted the official correspondence governing human exports, and newspaper reviews often referred to both the adventure stories and legal arrangements behind the exhibitions (see chapter 4). Thus, journalists and showmen ensured that metropolitan residents were made aware of the networks of trade, commerce, and travel in which foreign peoples were procured for exhibition.

Showmen's lectures provided one of the most powerful means of creating, reinforcing, and publicizing the associations between displayed peoples and foreign affairs. Lectures had been an institutionalized form of public address from early on in the nineteenth century, particularly within the community of men of science. It has been argued that between 1800 and 1850, scientific lecturing, medical practice, and technological involvements in trade and industry were especially important for those interested in science but not of gentlemanly standing.[33] Although showmen may not have been directly connected to these communities, gentlemanly or otherwise, the importance of lecturing remains relevant to their enterprise, since it invested the lecturer with credibility and potentially created an audience that was receptive to such forms of public address.

Delivered either before the performance or during special intermissions, lectures were intended to shape the experience of simply seeing foreign peoples. Occasionally an established figure might speak, as with the group of San exhibited in 1847 who were accompanied on their debut by Knox.[34] More often, visitors found that the "various scenes in the entertainment" were "explained by an intelligent young lecturer."[35] These men appear to have been either the shows' proprietors or their close affiliates, such as Charles Caldecott acting as the show's manager on behalf of his father for the 1853 Zulu exhibition. This may have been an attempt to reduce overheads and maximize profits. It may also have allowed members of the audience to put questions directly to the performers' importers and guardians. Proprietors may have been more likely to deliver the lectures personally when they were celebrities in their own right. For example, Catlin, who lectured on "the customs and condition of the North-American Indians, with several figures, in full dress, of different tribes," had written extensively about the many tribes among whom he had traveled.[36] Thus, audience members were not only able to hear about Catlin's personal experiences but, in addition to the smaller pamphlets, purchase his larger works within the showroom.[37]

Since lectures were not routinely reprinted in newspapers or pamphlets, few records survive of their contents; however, some discussion regularly appeared in newspaper reviews. These accounts often explicitly linked displayed peoples and contemporary discussions of human variety, imperialism, and colonial policies. Just as advertising allowed consumption without purchase, the reproduction and circulation of such material allowed lecturers' claims to reach beyond the boundaries of the exhibition venue. Thus, a far larger proportion of the population was encouraged to incorporate exhibitions of living foreign peoples into political discussion than ever attended a show. Although rare, some valuable examples of showmen's lectures survive.[38] The first is the lecture Knox gave regarding the group of San exhibited in 1847.[39] He met them shortly after they arrived from South Africa in Liverpool while he was lecturing at the Manchester Royal Institution. Upon application to the San's guardian, he obtained permission for the group to accompany him on the opening night of his lectures in London which were then held at Exeter Hall. Significantly, in 1850 Knox published the infamous *The Races of Men*, which featured a series of lectures that he had given in Manchester, Birmingham, and London in the preceding years. It is likely that the chapter entitled "Dark Races of Man" was directly adapted for publication from his 1847 lecture on the San, since it bears a striking similarity to press reports and the show's pamphlets.[40] The second surviving lecture is by J. S. Tyler, the guardian of a group of San throughout their stay in England in the late 1840s and early 1850s.[41] This appeared as an eight-page pamphlet and included several anecdotes in addition to the text of the lecture, suggesting that on occasion at least, showmen issued their lectures in published form.

Knox's lecture used the San to discuss his personal theories on human variation and British foreign policy. He began with a brief outline of his belief that hitherto, *race* was a term that had been defined on "artificial distinctions," and called for its reformulation in more scientifically accurate terms. He then briefly outlined his travels as an army surgeon in South Africa to demonstrate the opportunities he had had of observing the San working as servants and living in the wilderness. He introduced the San as belonging to perhaps the most singular of all the races of men, and moved on to a detailed account of their geographic distribution, the derivation of their appellation "Bosjesmans," and a description of how they differed from the Khoekhoe and the Zulus in a brief history of the Cape's occupation since Portuguese explorer Vasco da Gama alighted there at the end of the fifteenth century. This mode of inquiry, he insisted, was proper to any "object of natural history." For the sake of simplicity, Knox argued for the classification of the San and Khoekhoe as the "yellow-skinned" races of Africa following a detailed discussion of the views of other travelers, anatomists, and classical authorities. Significantly, while discussing the form of the skull and the cerebral development of the San, Knox held aloft a cast of the surface of the brain and argued that in Africans the cerebrum was less convoluted, and therefore less developed, than in Europeans; moreover, in the San the two halves of the brain were symmetrical, again a sign of inferior development.[42] He finished with a critical overview of the British government's use of warfare to subdue colonized Africans, and called for the bayonet to be abandoned in favor of economic barter.

Knox's lecture reflected both his racism and his anticolonialism.[43] He believed humans were divided into distinct races that were inherently different on the basis of physical, intellectual, and moral capabilities. Each race was best suited to live in the environment in which it first developed. Humans who attempted to live in habitats falling outside the range of their optimum physiological niche, as in colonialism, were doomed to failure. Thus, Knox believed that the British ought to abandon any attempt to colonize Africa and instead adopt a foreign policy based on trade. Knox's choice of the San as exemplars of his views on human development and classification and their political consequences suggests how living curiosities could be incorporated into discussions germane to human variety and contemporary politics.

Also discussing the San, Tyler's lecture added a religious and moral dimension. He divided his talk into sections on mental, moral, and physical attributes. Within each category he drew mainly from travel literature to illustrate the nature of the San. For example, speaking on their religious practices, he noted, "With the Bushman, however, we have no traces of such [religious] sentiments. All travellers are agreed that they have no perception of a Deity, no knowledge of a futurity, and no religious ceremonies or observances." Of their physical existence he observed, "Few—very few are the instances where man is found without a home or the shelter of a roof—even the wildest savages build their huts. Not so with the Bushman.... He builds himself no dwelling ... [and] is consequently no better than the brutes by which he is surrounded, and like them he springs up before the African traveller when least looked for or expected." Worse still, "they dwindle down into pigmies when compared to most other races of men. In countenance they much resemble the higher tribes of asses; they hardly bear a comparison with even the worst specimens of the human species found elsewhere." Lest these traits encouraged the audience to regard the San as beneath humanity, Tyler ended with a lesson. He asked the audience to recognize the San as deserving the "rank of man" and to "hold out the hand of fellowship, conscious that the same God who invested the Caucasian with the highest attributes, made also the poor benighted Bushman, and gave him claims upon our sympathies, which it were wrong to deny, and impious to abuse."[44]

Like Knox, Tyler used his lecture to direct the audience's attention toward issues for which he felt the San were ideal exemplars. While arguing that they were of comparatively inferior moral or cultural achievement, he emphatically asserted their humanity. His Christian philanthropy impelled him to impress on the audience the importance of both charity and aid to fashion further associations between the San and contemporary debates on human nature, its potential for improvement, and the issue's significance for global missionary action.

Performers were also marketed in visual and material ways. Visual frameworks were most often some form of scenery. The most basic forms often used specimens of flora and fauna native to the performers' homeland. The San children exhibited at the Egyptian Hall in 1845 performed in a room with a "beautiful Collection of DRAWINGS, illustrative of the various KAFIR TRIBES, HOTTENTOTS, &C" and "a fine and curious specimen of the GREAT URSINE BABOON, with some exceedingly rare varieties of the MONKEY TRIBE" (fig. 46). In Cawood's 1850 African exhibition at the Cosmorama, Regent Street, the room was "hung round with

FIGURE 46
(*Facing*) A handbill for the exhibition of the San children in 1845. The children reenacted the process of civilization amid paintings and natural historical specimens. (By kind permission of the Bodleian Library, University of Oxford, JJ, London Play Places 10[47].)

Aug. 45

EGYPTIAN HALL,
PICCADILLY,
Hours of Exhibition, 11 to 1, and 3 to 5.

EXTRAORDINARY
EXHIBITION !

Bushmen Children
OR PIGMY RACE !

Two Bushmen Children from the interior of Africa, a most extraordinary Variety of the Human Race never before Exhibited in Europe.

The Male Specimen only 44 inches high, though nearly full grown, and 16 years of age, presents a perfect Model of a Man in miniature.

The Female but 32 inches high, most elegant and delicate in proportion, 8 years old, and both characterised by remarkable intelligence and gentleness of disposition.

These interesting Children (not related to each other) have no recollection of their parents, who are supposed to have been murdered by the Kafirs, who pursue and exterminate the Bushmen Tribe with the most unrelenting ferocity, and were rescued by a Trader. (Dutch Boer) and brought into the Colony of the Cape of Good Hope, and are now submitted to the Public, having recently arrived in this country.

At the same time will be exhibited, a fine and curious specimen of the GREAT URSINE BABOON, with some exceedingly rare varieties of the MONKEY TRIBE, from Port Natal; also, a beautiful Collection of DRAWINGS, illustrative of the various KAFIR TRIBES, HOTTENTOTS, &c., &c., and curious and beautiful Specimens of RARE BIRDS, from the interior of Africa, and IMPLEMENTS OF WAR of different Tribes.

ORDER OF EXHIBITION;

1st—BUSHMEN CHILDREN in the Dress of their Tribe.
The BUSHMAN will throw his Assigai (or Spear) Dance, &c.

2nd—The BUSHMAN representing a Corporal of the Army, will go through the Manual and Platoon Exercise, with wonderful precision.
The BUSH GIRL appearing as a Soldier's Wife.

3rd—The BUSHMAN as a Gentleman's Servant (Tiger)
The BUSH GIRL as a Lady's Maid.

This will be found to be the most interesting and extraordinary Exhibition ever seen in Europe.

ADMISSION, ONE SHILLING.

G. STUART, Printer, 38, Rupert-street, Haymarket.

skins, and hor[n]s of wild animals of Africa" (fig. 47).[45] Other managers employed oil and canvas to dress their stages. In 1822, for instance, Bullock exhibited the Sámi against a panoramic painting of their homeland (fig. 38). The 1847 exhibition of San sported much sparser scenery in the form of several bushes onstage and a painted backdrop.[46] From the mid-nineteenth century onward in particular, showmen were able to frame displayed peoples using developing techniques in theatrical scenery. In 1853, for instance, Caldecott spared little expense in dramatizing his Zulu exhibition by commissioning moving panoramic scenery based on sketches made in Africa. A relatively recent invention, the scenery was often explicitly complimented in press reviews as a helpful means of illustrating Zulu life. By the later nineteenth century, much more elaborate sets were becoming routine. For instance, in both 1895 and 1899 an entire kraal was reconstructed for an exhibition of Somalis at the Crystal Palace in Sydenham (fig. 48) and the Savage South Africa exhibition at Earl's Court.

Scenery was complemented by material artifacts that were often imported and therefore claimed as authentic. For example, in Isaac Cruikshank's caricature of Bullock's 1822 exhibition, the Sámi family is shown receiving visitors at the Egyptian Hall framed by a border of Sámi clothes, sleighs, weapons, and cooking utensils (fig. 49). These objects were tangible specimens of Sámi life and were used to invite consumers to define their social development using material property. Cruikshank's depiction of artifacts alongside images of sleighing in the snow created a visual narrative of Sámi culture that rationalized their classification within contemporary human taxonomies. In the exhibition pamphlet, it was claimed that Jen and Karina, not Bullock, "exhibited the deer decorated in the manner of their country, and drawing light carriages and sledges."[47] Bullock's self-

SOMALILAND AT THE CRYSTAL PALACE: INSIDE THE SOMALI KRAAL.

excision from the role of manager and organizer was a maneuver aimed at establishing the authenticity of the items consumers relied on to classify the Sámi. Cawood's African exhibition featured various weapons, while the tables in the room were festooned with "some specimens of their domestic implements" (fig. 47).[48] Likewise, Caldecott implied the authenticity of his show by informing patrons that the group wore "the dress of their country" and had "brought with them to England their habiliments and implements of war, their domestic utensils, and everything which, in the course of their representations, may tend to realize to the spectator actual Zulu life."[49] Catlin's exhibitions of the Anishinabe and Bakhoje took place at the Egyptian Hall in the same room as his vast collection. In Farini's 1885 San exhibition, or "Earthmen Pigmies," the group brandished bows and arrows and used them to enact a hunt in which one of the children took on the part of a wild cat (fig. 50). The importance of these props lies in their potential to be used in defining human development. Just as clothing helped to define human variety, material artifacts indicated peoples' technological capabilities and so were used to infer the extent of their human development and intellectual capacity.[50] By exhibiting foreign peoples alongside items of foreign manufacture, often specifically imported alongside performers for the show, managers provided crucial material for consumers to use when reflecting on the nature of displayed peoples.

FIGURE 49
Isaac Cruikshank,
*Laplanders, Rein Deer
&c. as Exhibited at the
Egyptian Hall, Piccadilly,
1822.* The borders of
the illustration show
numerous items of
clothing and instruments that were displayed as representative of Sámi material
culture. (P5395902, by
kind permission of
the London Metropolitan Archives, Guildhall Library, City of
London.)

THE PIGMY EARTHMEN AT THE ROYAL AQUARIUM

HIS WIFE N'arbecy

THE CHIEF N'GO N'QUI

STALKING THE OSTRICH

REJOICING OVER A SLAIN ANIMAL

METHOD OF HUNTING

FIGURE 50
*The Pigmy Earthmen
at the Royal Aquarium.*
The inlaid images
show acts from the
show, including hunt-
ing scenes, that were
intended to drama-
tize the San's every-
day lives. (*Illustrated
Police News*, Septem-
ber 27, 1884. By kind
permission of the
Bodleian Library, Uni-
versity of Oxford, JJ,
Human Freaks 4 [76].)

Throughout the nineteenth century, clothing provided essential markers of ethnic origin and human development; managers capitalized on
this by ensuring that displayed peoples wore suitable costumes. Bullock's Sámi performers were shown in "full Winter Costume of their own
country, with their Summer and Winter residences, and the principal objects of their household furniture."[51] Similarly, in 1850, Cawood shipped
Zulu chief Larcher, his Amapondon wife Homcaumba, and Xhosa soldier
Bourzaquai to England. He had been allowed to recruit them following a
bargain he had made with Sir Harry Smith, "the governor and their chief."
The men were dressed in "cow-skins," but Larcher also wore a "profusion
of animals' tails" and an ostrich-plume headdress. Homcaumba also wore
cow skins, and "her short hair [was shaped] into small tags, kept stiff by
bear's grease."[52] The Zulu women exhibited in 1853 were covered despite
coming from a culture in which showing breasts was both acceptable and
common (compare figs. 37, 66, and 72), while Farini's 1885 exhibition featured performers who wore next to nothing except a few animal-skin capes
and loincloths (fig. 51). Such details were essential, because human variety
was partly defined by clothing in the early to mid-nineteenth century. Of
the performers discussed throughout this work, only Maximo and Bartola
were regularly shown in clothes unadorned by beads, feathers, and animal

Managing Performance

skins (compare figs. 31, 54, and 69).[53] It is telling that every promotional image of performers reproduced here does not depict them in European clothes. The only exception is a portrait of Lobengula accompanying a wedding announcement, which still appears alongside a more conventional image of him in costume (fig. 59).[54]

Costumes played a fundamental role in helping showmen substantiate their promotional claims to be exhibiting authentic performers. For instance, Baartman was advertised as possessing the "kind of shape which is most admired among her countrymen," and when performing she wore a "dress resembling her complexion ... [and] so tight that her shapes above and the enormous size of her posterior parts are as visible as if the said female were naked," with the dress "evidently intended to give the appearance of being undressed."[55] She also wore beads and feathers hung around her waist, the accoutrements associated with her African ancestry, and on occasion would play a small stringed musical instrument (fig. 52). This contemporary testimony unambiguously suggests that the costume had been designed in order to cover Baartman's flesh, and so maintain some semblance of decency, while being as revealing as possible. As such, she wore a garment intentionally fabricated to corroborate her manager's promotional claims and, in doing so, foster interest in her anatomy. It has recently been observed that this image represents an "imagined Hottentot Woman. But for the tortoiseshell necklace and painted face, Sara's costume was more an amalgam than how the Gonaqua dressed before the colonial period." Nonetheless, the depictions were also not "so far off."[56] Her biographers have suggested that the relative accuracy came from Baartman herself, since neither Alexander Dunlop nor Hendrick Cesars would have had the necessary knowledge. The possibility is certainly intriguing. Pertinently it suggests that despite being adapted to substantiate the showmen's claims, the costume was essentially an informed fantasy (possibly created with Baartman's own input). The same could be applied to many of the costumes worn by displayed peoples, as they were often a combination of the performers' personal property and specifically imported items. Meanwhile, patrons' expectations also had to be borne in mind. By the 1890s, and helped substantially by the commercial success of Buffalo Bill's Wild West Show, the horsemanship, feathered headdresses, and ceremonial regalia of Plains groups such as the Lakota (Sioux) became iconographically representative of all American tribes. Shows in which the performers were not dressed as such often came to be rejected as inauthentic because they

FIGURE 52
Sara Baartman in a
costume deliberately
designed to accentu-
ate her figure. (Dan-
iel Lysons, *Collectanea*,
2 vols., unpublished
scrapbook. © The
British Library Board.
C.103.k.11[104].)

did not meet patrons' expectations of how *real* Indians dressed.[57] Thus, costumes were the combined product of managers' needs, the suitability of displayed peoples' own possessions, and patrons' expectations.

Showmen's role in defining the shows' programs provided a significant means of guiding consumers' interpretations. Unlike other living curiosities, foreign peoples performed rites and ceremonies argued to be exemplary of their ethnic heritage. For example, the 1853 exhibition of Zulus consisted of a series of tableaux drawn from Zulu life that were explained by their manager Caldecott.[58] The first scene, in a kraal near Port Natal, featured the Zulus singing and grouping themselves around their huts, displaying game. Next the Zulus would quarrel before sitting down for the "Meal Song" and supper. Afterward they performed the "Charm Song" to ward off evil spirits, and the tableau would close as "night" fell. The second "day" would see the Zulus reassembling and sending for a *sangoma* ("witchdoctor") to heal a member of the party who had fallen ill overnight by foul means. Once the sorcerer's identity had been determined, the accused would be condemned to death. Moving on, there was a Zulu marriage completed with the purchase of a wife for six cows, along with a hunting expedition and the grand finale, in which the warriors attacked Karcloof Fall (fig. 16).[59]

Similarly, when Catlin lectured alongside "a Beautiful Group of Warriors and Braves in full-dress," in this case most likely Catlin's original Cockney stand-ins, they performed several songs and dances (including one with scalps), an enemy attack, the negotiation of a peace treaty, a marriage ceremony, and the rescuing of John Smith by Pocahontas (fig. 53). Later, the Bakhoje also performed ceremonies argued to be representative of their social life and supported by the objects of material culture they had brought with them. They performed tableaux, including the Welcome Dance, the Warrior's Dance, the Scalp Dance, the War Song, and the Wolf Song, each of which illustrated an important event.

The range of ceremonies performed, from meals to acts of warfare, supported showmen's claims to be presenting dramas comprehensively illustrative of displayed peoples' lives. These performances capitalized on showmen's invitations to see metonymy on the stage. Just as displayed peoples were used as exemplars of the differences between human varieties, their performances helped to breathe life into these typologies. Consumers were presented not with static anatomic specimens but with living, breathing people. Crucially, given that these activities were performed regularly and in a set order and included an intentionally broad range of cultural activities, they must have been at least chosen, if not choreographed, by an agent, in all likelihood the proprietor, connected with the exhibition. Furthermore, even if showmen were not directly involved with training displayed peoples to perform on cue, they must have approved of a show's program and so played a pivotal role in defining and policing which performances were considered suitably entertaining, authentic, profitable, and typologically representative.

Exhibitions were commonly marketed as if the performances were unmediated representations of life abroad, yet all were evidently quite carefully choreographed and managed. For instance, the San children's exhibition of 1845 consisted of three acts in which they enacted their progressive civilization onstage, a process in which they developed from belligerent "savages" into useful laborers. In the first act, the pair appeared in "the Dress of their Tribe," and the boy demonstrated the use of the spear. In the second act, the boy appeared in a military uniform and performed a series of platoon exercises while the girl appeared as a soldier's wife. In the final act, the boy performed the role of a gentleman's servant while the girl acted as a lady's maid (fig. 46). In Cawood's 1850 African exhibition, Bourzaquai wielded the "light and sharp assegai [spear], or lance, with great dexterity; and his prowess was often proved against the British rule in the later war." One reviewer remarked that he "hurls the assegai, while

FIGURE 53
(*Facing*) An undated handbill for Catlin's exhibition (ca. 1841) providing details of the shows' tableaux. The range of dances, songs, and rites performed was chosen to substantiate managers' claims to be providing a complete overview of displayed peoples' lives. (By kind permission of the Bodleian Library, University of Oxford, JJ, London Play Places 9[14].)

TABLEAUX VIVANTS OF THE RED INDIANS,

EGYPTIAN HALL, PICCADILLY.

ON TUESDAY, THURSDAY, & SATURDAY;
Afternoons at 3, and Evenings at 8.

Admission in the *Afternoon* or *Evening* One Shilling.

PROGRAMME OF THE FIRST LECTURE.

A brief **Lecture** on the Customs and Condition of the North-American Indians, *with several Figures, in full-dress, of different Tribes.* After which

A Beautiful Group of Warriors and Braves in full-dress, reclining round a fire, regaling themselves with the pipe and a dish of pemican which are passing around. In the midst of their banquet the Chief enters, in full-dress; the pipe is extended to him—he smokes it in sadness, and then breaks up the party by announcing that an enemy is at hand, and they must prepare for war !!

TABLEAUX VIVANTS.

1—Pocahontas rescuing Capt. John Smith, an English Officer, from his Execution, decreed by Pow-ha-tan, the Indian Chief. It had been decreed in council, over which Pow-ha-tan presided, that Captain John Smith should be put to death by having his head placed upon a large stone, and his brains beaten out by two warriors armed with huge painted clubs. His executioners were standing with their clubs raised over him, and in the very instant for giving the fatal blow, Pocahontas, the Chief's favourite daughter, then about 13 years old, threw herself with folded arms around the head of the Captain, who was instantly ordered by the Chief to be released.

2—Warriors Enlisting, by *"smoking through the reddened stem."* The Chief sends *"runners"* or *"criers"* through the tribe with a pipe, the stem of which is painted red; the crier solicits for recruits, and every young man who consents to smoke through *the reddened stem,* when it is extended to him, is considered a volunteer to go to war.

3—Council of War. Chiefs and Doctors deliberating in Council. The Doctors are considered the Oracles of the Nation, and are always consulted by, and seated in council with the Chiefs.

4—War Dance; the ceremony of swearing-in the warriors, who take the most solemn oath, by dancing up to and striking the "reddened post."

5—Foot War-Party on the March. "*Indian File,*" armed with shields, bows, quivers, and lances—the Chief of the party, as is generally the case, going to war in full-dress.

6—War Party Encamped at Night, wrapped in their Robes, with their weapons in their arms; sentinels at their posts.

7—An Alarm in Camp; sentinels rousing the party to arms.

8—War-Party in Council, consulting as to the best mode of attack.

9—Skulking, or advancing cautiously upon the enemy to take them by surprise.

10—Battle and Scalping; the Chief wounded.

11—Scalp Dance, in celebration of a victory; the women in the centre of the group holding up the scalps, and the warriors dancing around them, brandishing their weapons, and yelling in the most frightful manner.

12—Treaty of Peace. The Chiefs and Warriors of the two hostile tribes, in the act of solemnizing the treaty of peace, by smoking mutually through the calumet or pipe of peace, which is ornamented with the Eagle's quills; the calumet resting in front of the group.

13—Pipe of Peace Dance, by the Warriors, with the pipes of peace or calumets in their hands, after the treaty has been concluded. This picturesque scene will be represented with motion, the warriors all joining in the dance, and uniting their voices with the beat of the Indian drum.

the Zoolu uses a short implement, with which he stabs. They go through a sham fight, in which the shaking of shields is very prominent; and howling and stamping to outvie the report of the gunpowder."[60] In the 1899 exhibition Savage South Africa, the Afrikaner and African performers reenacted scenes from the recent Ndebele wars (see chapter 7). In these examples, the performances were deliberately choreographed to retrace the paths of social development for which performers were considered most suited or to make them relevant to specific types of British political activity.

Significantly, performances could be used to place displayed peoples within politicized hierarchical classifications of humanity. In the Zulu or Bakhoje exhibitions, for example, the use of sorcery and ritualistic violence referenced well-known rites.[61] The war dances, folk songs, and other performed ceremonies were all present in the travel literature on which the shows' pamphlets were based. Displayed peoples were always part of broader and ongoing discussions regarding their nature, whether in travel literature or the press. Thus, audience expectations regarding the manners and customs of a particular people were heavily conditioned before they even reached a show's venue (see chapters 2 and 5). Readers of Catlin's published works, for example, are more than likely to have expected that any exhibition of the Anishinabe or Bakhoje would include demonstrations of the various dances and songs discussed in his writings, especially given Catlin's sojourn in the North American wilderness.[62] Similar expectations must have existed for the African performers. For instance, the Zulu were almost always shown in a military context.

These elements suggest how crucial audience expectations were in shaping the contents of a show; we can easily imagine the disappointment that exhibitors risked by failing to include "witch-doctors" or scalpings in their shows, even if it was justified through a commitment to scholarly accuracy. Moreover, the representations of these practices facilitated attempts to define exhibited peoples' position on a developmental human scale. Human varieties were commonly organized into a continuum, with the lowest forms of human social organization capable of being molded into the highest. For example, a hunter-gatherer nomad, if placed within the right environmental conditions, could, through the process of civilization, settle to learn the art of agriculture or commerce and so mature into higher forms of human development. By making displayed peoples perform a range of social customs, showmen established that they had a culture—but one deemed specific to developmental states beneath civilized, commercial, and Christian life.

*

Urban spectatorship made people potentially receptive to opportunities for lingering inspections of human diversity; however, this alone did not ensure a preexisting market for exhibitions of living curiosities. Showmen used promotional material to pique public interest in observing specific kinds of human variation, thereby creating audiences wanting to see living foreign peoples onstage. Ultimately, showmen profited by bridging the gap between the supply of imported peoples and the eagerness to meet and greet "savages" that they had helped to foster. Time and time again, promotional material marketed the shows as opportunities to see performances that were more or less accurate representations of foreign peoples' lives. Reviewers frequently reiterated such claims by encouraging people to pay to see foreign peoples performing in exhibitions of "unusual interest and value."[63] Showmen clearly played an integral role in orchestrating performances. They were potentially able to direct consumers' interpretations of the shows because they exerted considerable control over the kinds of information the patrons were provided with during performances. By choosing, perhaps designing, costumes, props, and background scenery and choreographing performers' routines, showmen invited the viewing public to interpret displayed peoples as authentic ethnic types.

Significantly, showmen may have played an even greater role in shaping the shows' importance by using human display to train viewers to recognize specific human varieties. Discussions of the shows' receptions often assume that spectators knew the defining features of exhibited peoples sufficiently well to both recognize an individual as foreign and distinguish correctly between, say, a Zulu and a San individual.[64] Naturally, spectators could pick up on differences of clothing, complexion, physical stature, and the like; however, observing differences and similarities between humans does not entail the ability to classify humans into specific ethnic types, or the skill required to do so in ways that would have been communally recognized as correct by the lay or learned. Of course, there may have been well-traveled, well-read patrons who were able to perform such tasks easily, but this cannot be assumed for all. At least some, and possibly most, consumers relied on showmen for the necessary cues (see chapters 2 and 5) to categorize exhibited individuals into specific ethnic groupings, because these categories were waiting to be not uncovered but assigned. Consequently, through the consumption of promotional material and repeated visits to the shows, consumers learned what it meant to look or live like a Zulu, Inuit, or Anishinabe and thereby gained the ability to distinguish between them. Cues from showmen did not wholly determine the shows' receptions, since patrons were not passive consumers but active participants who were free to form their own opinions. Nonetheless, it is clear that showmen were significant agents in shaping receptions because they mediated the kinds of knowledge the shows could make available and, in doing so, acted as agents of knowledge production. Yet they were also crucial in more immediate and material senses by recruiting the very people consumers were so eager to meet.

Recruiting
Entertainers

ON THE morning of Wednesday, May 8, 1850, readers of the *Times* were given news of a "most exciting scene" at a recent "Bosjesman Exhibition."[1] The group's manager, Mr. J. S. Tyler, had just completed a lecture on their "habits, &c." when "some person at the further end from the platform caught the eye of one of the male bushmen, and riveted his attention by making grimaces and shaking his face at him in a menacing manner." The performer's "eyes glared" as he stared at the spectator with "rising indignation"; his "nostrils were dilated, and his whole frame became strongly agitated." Many in the audience noticed, and initially mistook the scene for one that had been staged for dramatic effect. The standoff continued until "at last the savage, unable to stand the irritation any longer, suddenly drew an arrow and let fly at the head of his foolish tormentor." Narrowly missing the patron's skull, the weapon became lodged in his hat. Then, "in a frenzy of passion," the performer sprang from the platform "like an ourang-outang," raced toward the offender, and knocked him to the ground. A struggle ensued, with Tyler and some assistants eventually able to stop him from further assaulting the surprised spectator. "Three or four men [had the] little creature (only about four foot high) in their grasp, and it was all they could do to prevent him from getting free." Eventually, Tyler and his assistants were able to subdue the performer and take him away. Meanwhile, the confusion among the audience "baffle[d] all description." Many hurriedly left, women shrieked, and the men also appeared to have been frightened by the sudden turn of the evening's entertainment.

The scene at Tyler's exhibition is extraordinarily suggestive of the kinds of interaction that took place between performers, consumers, and showmen. The sheer extent of the provocation that the audience member felt was acceptable is striking, and one is left thinking it unlikely that he would be so foolish again in a hurry. The San man's evident unwillingness to allow the insult to continue is understandable, and a telling example of the unscripted means performers used to assert themselves by either objecting to how they were being treated or making demands to which they felt entitled or inclined. The dramatic expression of objection also raises the question of how many times he felt similar indignation and was moved to deploy his weapons. Tyler's inability to either prevent the situation from escalating or diffuse it quickly raises questions about how he managed his performers, and whether he had given them any guidance on how he expected them to behave in public. Even if he had provided some rules of conduct, one suspects that they could never have been enough to quell entirely the many grievances which undoubtedly burdened his troupe.

Unfortunately, the evidence required to explore these questions is woefully sparse, especially on the part of the performers. The problem partly lies in the relative lack of interest shown in recording displayed peoples' experiences in the nineteenth century. Even those most concerned with the treatment of performers rarely attempted to collect their testimony either systematically or in quantity.[2] Thus, efforts to reflect on issues of agency, motivation, and consent involved in reconstructing the shows are frequently hampered by the difficulty of finding potentially relevant sources, such as diaries, letters, eyewitness accounts, or interviews.[3] Despite such erasure, nineteenth-century newspapers and periodicals are peppered with rich, albeit frustratingly concise, vignettes that provide foundations from which to begin exploring the complex patterns of formal and informal intercultural contact involved in staging the shows. Building on these glimpses, this chapter explores the ways in which foreign peoples were recruited and transformed into performers while reflecting on why they may have become performers at all and how they experienced life abroad. Such discussion is intended to avoid casting performers as passive victims. Instead, the aim is to trace the many ways in which performers adapted to their new lives, often resisting being confined to the roles expected of them, while also locating these reflections within the broader context of the performers' often heavily circumscribed opportunities for such self-expression.

Making Entertainers

Being exhibited as a curiosity may now seem to be a strange, and even objectionable, profession to many; however, anyone doing so in the nineteenth century would have been following a well-trod and sometimes lucrative path.[4] Although most displayed peoples were adults, many children were exhibited on London's stages. Youngsters were often accompanied by their parents or other family members (on occasion, their lives had begun en route at sea), while others found themselves, parentless, being cared for by their exhibitors.

Flora and Martinus were San children exhibited as the "Earthmen" in 1853. Orphans aged approximately fourteen and sixteen years, respectively, their parents had been killed in ongoing violence in the Cape of Good Hope, South Africa.[5] In 1850 or 1851, a merchant trading in the colony encountered a group of Africans. "Among these he was especially interested with the singular intelligence of the boy and girl," and so "he purchased them, and took them with him to Pietermaritzburg." Traded in Africa, perhaps directly sold as property, it seems virtually certain that the children were not consulted about the possibility of being exhibited. The merchant resolved to educate the pair and arranged for Captain Wetherall, of the brig *Hannah*, to take them safely to England, where they arrived in 1851. They were then entrusted to the care of Mr. George of Croydon, who "determined to educate them, in the hope of that they might become ultimately useful as agents of civilization amongst their benighted countrymen."[6] In later years, they were also exhibited with the most famous foreign children of the nineteenth century, the "Aztecs."

On January 7, 1867, Señor Máximo Váldez Núñez, dressed in evening wear, and Señora Bartola Velásquez, dressed in white satin, were married in London. Afterward, man and wife attended a crowded wedding breakfast in Willis's Rooms (fig. 54).[7] It is almost certain that Maximo and Bartola were the children of Innocente Burgos and Marina Espina, San Salvadorian peasants who were persuaded by Spanish trader Ramón Selva to allow them to travel to the United States to be cured of their learning difficulties. The parents were most probably unable to provide for their children or believed that Selva could help, and so parted with them (whether they benefited financially is unclear). Selva sold Maximo and Bartola to a man named Morris, who acted as their owner and manager. Initially exhibited as Aztec brother and sister in America, in 1853 Morris took them to London, where they were exhibited as the "Aztec Lilliputians" or the last remaining Aztecs. In the late 1850s they were exhibited by P. T. Barnum at his American Museum and toured with the Barnum & Bailey Circus before returning to London in the 1860s. Throughout the 1850s and early 1860s, they attracted considerable crowds and debate regarding their provenance; but with interest waning, the staged marriage attempted to recapture some of their earlier commercial appeal.

Maximo and Bartola were international celebrities. Over the course of their lives, hundreds of thousands of people attended their exhibitions. Charles Eisenmann, a celebrity photographer with a penchant for the curious and a studio conveniently close to Barnum's museum, photographed them several times.[8] Reproduced and used as souvenirs or *carte de visites*, many of these photographs survive, indicating the pair's popularity. Maximo and Bartola provide an excellent example of how individuals in the business of human display could have long careers. It is unknown if they were paid and if so how much, but at the height of their popularity they may have been able to earn a comfortable living, for either themselves or their manager.[9] They toured up until at least 1890, but the details of their later career are sketchy, as are the dates of their deaths. Contemporary accounts suggest that in modern terms, the children suffered permanent and severe learning difficulties caused by a form of microcephaly. As with so many other human curiosities, therefore, entertainment may have

FIGURE 54
(Facing) Promotional poster advertising Maximo and Bartola's wedding breakfast. (By kind permission of the Wellcome Library, London.)

THE AZTECS,
MAXIMO and BARTOLA.

DISCOVERED IN CENTRAL AMERICA 1849

MARRIED, ST GEORGES HANOVER SQUARE, LONDON 7TH JANY 1867

offered them one of the very few, possibly the only, ways in which they were able to support themselves.[10] Although they were generally agreed to be suffering from a lack of mental development rather than lunacy, the institutionalization of "idiots" was becoming more common and remains relevant. In the early nineteenth century, there was a growth in the market for asylums and the number of people committed to institutional care.[11] Thus, the children may have been considered within the domain of the mentally unfit, and given their age and condition, it also seems a virtual certainty that they had little or no understanding of the circumstances in which they were forced to grow up, and were not consulted about the possibility of being exhibited.[12] Other performers were not only capable adults but consenting collaborators.

In 1810, Sara Baartman, the first foreign celebrity exhibit of the century, chose to sail from Cape Town to London.[13] She arrived in England just four years after the British took the Cape of Good Hope from the Dutch, thus ending severe social upheaval. The Dutch East India Company established the Cape as a colony in 1652; it functioned as both a supply port for commercial ships and a vital refreshment and rehabilitation station for scurvy-stricken seamen.[14] Following its colonization, in an effort to minimize costs and inconvenience, the company encouraged agricultural production by European settlers, and by 1700 the colony had grown beyond its capacity to absorb immigrants. Soon after its foundation, some settlers were granted the status of free farmers; quickly growing in numbers, they began intruding further on the land of the nomadic pastoralists, and intense ethnic conflict ensued. The existing settler population rapidly increased, and its dispersion soon followed; by 1778, the settlers had developed a distinctive culture and spoke a local variation of Dutch. In the late eighteenth century, growing dissatisfaction with the rule of the Dutch East India Company led to a period of political and social upheaval as the Khoekhoe, San, and Xhosa continued their opposition to the settlers' encroachment. The British attacked the colony in 1781, later taking it in 1785, and apart from a brief period between 1803 and 1806, confirmed it to be under British rule in 1815. The near endemic conflict over land between colonial settlers and the indigenous populations ensured that the Cape would continue to be a region of considerable turmoil.

Baartman was born in the 1770s fifty miles north of the Gamtoos River Valley, but she grew up in the Camdeboo valley. Here she and her family served on colonists' farms precisely when settlers' encroachment into the traditional Khoekhoe and Gonaqua lands gathered momentum. This colonization contributed to growing tensions, including regular hunts killing local Africans, with survivors increasingly being drawn into the colonial labor force.[15] In the late 1780s, her father passed away and her mother followed shortly afterward in the early 1790s. In 1795 or 1796 she was effectively sold as chattel to Pieter Cesars and soon left for Cape Town.[16] The busy port city created the very demand for female labor that Baartman had been sought to fulfill. Initially she served Cesars's employer, but after his death joined the Cesar household around 1800. In 1803 she moved again, this time to the home of Pieter's brother-in-law, Hendrick Cesars, a free black descended from slaves and the man responsible for her exhibition in London. During her service in the Cesars' households Baartman bore three children, all of whom she lost shortly after birth and barely spoke of in later years.

By 1808, Hendrick had become steeped in debt and, in an effort to stave off his creditor, began to show Baartman to local sailors in the city's military hospital.[17] The following year, Alexander Dunlop, naval surgeon and superintendent of the Slave Lodge in Cape Town, likely witnessed Baartman entertaining the local sailors while attending to his medical duties. To supplement his own meager income, especially in the wake of the closure of the Slave Lodge after the British slave trade was abolished, Dunlop initiated discussions with Cesars regarding the possibility of exhibiting Baartman in London. When finally approached about these plans, Baartman refused to leave unless accompanied by Cesars, who had been intending simply to transfer his rights in her to Dunlop.[18] Baartman's case is particularly interesting because it is possibly the earliest example, certainly from the nineteenth century, of a performer being commercially exhibited at home as part of daily life before traveling abroad.[19] One cannot help wondering how Hendrick had come up with the original arrangement, if this made Baartman more likely to agree to being displayed abroad, and whether Cesars drew on these experiences in staging the London show. Ultimately, Baartman's negotiation worked. Hendrick drew up a contract regarding the terms of Baartman's departure, and she, Dunlop, and Cesars all left Cape Town, hopeful of better fortunes abroad.

Others were also recognized as contracted performers. In 1844 Mewhushekaw (White Cloud), chief of the Bakhoje, entered into an arrangement with the U.S. government and George H. C. Melody, a missionary, to travel with thirteen other Bakhoje to Europe for the purpose of exhibition. It was unusual for the government to grant the necessary permission, because as the secretary of war, J. M. Porter, suggested, "the verbal instructions to the Agents, Superintendents, &c. has been against permitting such tours, for the reason, I presume, that the persons having them in charge are usually men who merely wish to make money out of them by exhibitions, without taking any care of their habits or morals, or inducing them to profit by what they see and hear upon their route."[20] However, in this case it had been decided that Melody's reputable character, in conjunction with the "full assent of the individuals," precluded such evils.[21] Upon the party's arrival in London, Melody quickly called on Catlin, who had been exhibiting his substantial collection at the Egyptian Hall.[22] Catlin agreed, on the condition that the group approved.

Shortly after their arrival in London, the Bakhoje visited Catlin's collection at the Egyptian Hall. Upon entering,

> they all walked silently and slowly to the middle of the room, with their hands over their mouths, denoting surprise and silence.... They had been in a moment transferred into the midst of hundreds of their friends and enemies, who were gazing at them from the walls—amongst wig-wams and thousands of Indian costumes and arms, and views of the prairies they live in—altogether opening to their view, and to be seen at a glance, what it would take them years to see in their own country. They met the portraits of their chiefs and their friends, upon the walls, and extended their hands towards them; and they gathered in groups before their enemies, whom the warriors had met in battle, and now recognized before them. They looked with great pleasure on a picture of their own village, and examined with the closest scrutiny the arms and weapons of their enemies.[23]

The group then sat with Catlin in the middle of the gallery under a Crow tipi, smoking pipes and discussing the proposed exhibition in a Bakhoje council. Catlin was known to the group, as he had lived with Mewhushekaw's family while traveling. During his time in North America, Nuemonya (Walking Rain) and Washkamonya (Fast Dancer) had posed for portraits that to their surprise they found hanging in the gallery. Pleased to meet Chippehola (Catlin) again, the group were well disposed toward him; indeed, Catlin felt he "did not meet them as strangers but as friends."[24]

It is likely that the group appreciated Catlin's knowledge of their culture and language, and, combined with their former acquaintance, this may have encouraged them to enter into an agreement with him. This appreciation is reflected by their recorded reaction upon entering the gallery. It conveys both surprise and recognition of themselves, their homelands, and fellow tribes. In his published account, Catlin presented the encounter as one of transportation to the wilderness. This rhetorical maneuver was clearly aimed at substantiating the authenticity of his collection and the respect he commanded from the Bakhoje. Catlin's choice to employ a council and use an Indian name strongly implies both authoritative knowledge and a privileged means of participation. His description of the group's visit was obviously for the sake of strengthening his own standing; but equally relevant are his remarks regarding the role of the Bakhoje in producing the exhibition. In addition to the explicit documentary evidence, he made the significant claim that the Bakhoje were given an opportunity to question both Catlin and Melody regarding the show's arrangements in a manner that was familiar to them before agreeing to be exhibited.

Similar anxieties regarding recruitment may be seen in A. T. Caldecott's experiences of gathering thirteen Zulus in 1853. It had been his wish for some time, but previous attempts had been thwarted by the locals' "own reluctance, their fear of the voyage," and, significantly, "the difficulties to be overcome before the colonial government would permit them to embark," since it was "necessary that the British Government should sanction their removal. Caldecott memorialized the authorities accordingly." He only secured permission on the condition that he entered into a

recognizance, binding himself in a sum of £500 and two sureties in £250 each, that such natives as he may be able to find willing to accompany him to England shall be well treated on the voyage; and reported, and, if required, produced to the Secretary of State for the Colonies, and finally brought back to, and landed at D'Urban; and further, that before embarking, the said natives be brought before the Diplomatic Agents, to testify their full and voluntary concurrence.[25]

The Zulus were duly taken before the diplomatic agent to give their consent to the endeavor. Caldecott was then issued with a certificate by the authorities that vouched, "Mr. A. T. Caldecott, who is about proceeding to England with some of the natives of this district, is a gentleman of the highest respectability and integrity, and that he has obtained the permission of this Government to take the natives in question, upon condition of his entering into a recognizance" that had been "duly entered into, and now remains filed."[26] The Zulus then traveled to England under the protection of Caldecott's son, who acted as the group's interpreter. As in Catlin's published account, Charles Caldecott's decision to reprint the documentary evidence relating to the importation of Zulu performers attempted to establish the performers' knowing assent and the legality of their embarkation from the Cape of Good Hope. The reassurance that the elder Caldecott had pledged the considerable sum of £1,000 to assure the Zulus' safe return strongly implied that he was willing and able to bear the responsibility of their care and therefore worthy of being granted the necessary permission.

Displayed peoples are also known to have been recruited from colonial prison populations. John Scott was appointed special magistrate on the Northern Border of the Cape Colony, where he served between 1879 and 1887.[27] His task was to address the considerable tension that resulted when the expansion of settlers' farmlands deprived the San of hunting and grazing grounds, often forcing them into stealing livestock for food. It has been argued that by the late nineteenth century there was a significant shift in the relationships between settlers and the San; initially, many local peoples were hunted and killed in a "wholesale system of extermination," but during the 1860s this palpably shifted toward their imprisonment for theft.[28] Meanwhile, it was hoped that the San would be driven into working for farmers. Scott's remit included dealing with the indigenous people's refusal to become part of the colony's cheap labor force. In his position as magistrate, he began selecting child "apprentices" for farmers, specimens for study by the notable German philologist of African languages, Willhelm Bleek, and performers for exhibition abroad.[29]

In 1883 or 1884, on behalf of the Great Farini, W. A. Healey visited the Cape in search of suitable San performers. There, through Scott, he became acquainted with Gert Louw, the "Baster who had captured the Korana leader Klass Lukas at the end of the 1879–80 war."[30] In turn, Louw engaged the services of the six San who were later exhibited by Farini as the "Earthmen Pigmies" at Westminster Aquarium. In 1886, Scott also helped to select artifacts, such as utensils and weapons, and performers for the Colonial and Indian Exhibition held the same year (see chapter 7). Of this group, the San man Klass Tilletjies was described by him as a "stock thief" and "very good specimen indeed." Another woman was "larger but pure bred and possessed of the peculiar female bushman physical characteristics in a well marked degree."[31] In return, the prisoners secured their release and a payment of ten goats (£5) for six months' service at the exhibition.[32] Scott later received gratitude for his services from the Cape Prime Minister, the Royal Astronomer (who was also chairman of the relevant exhibition subcommittee), and a commemorative medal and diploma from the president of the Royal Commission.

Prisoners from India were also recruited to perform at the Colonial and Indian Exhibition of 1886.[33] The Royal Commission responsible for the exhibition hired Messrs. Henry S. King and Company, a private shipping firm, to employ thirty-one skilled craftsmen from the subcontinent. The company was charged with both the costs and the duty of recruitment, transport, and welfare of the performers; in turn, it sought the services of Dr. John William Tyler, the superintendent of the Central Jail in Agra. Tyler selected the men from among his jail's inmates and accompanied them to London, where he received considerable attention as their guardian, including a knighthood in recognition of his administrative achievements. Other than the sheer number of potential recruits, King and Company had good reason for turning to India's jails. In their efforts to rehabilitate criminals, officials in India had begun a program of reform in which convicted individuals were retrained in artisanal skills, such as pottery and weaving, often within the context of factory work. These goods were then sold as exports. Thus, the jail provided both a ready supply of trained individuals and a colonial official to whom the company could essentially subcontract both the role of recruitment and the duty of care. Ultimately, under the aegis of the exhibition, despite being trained "through the industrializing processes of prison reform rather than through the ancient, timeless practices of the village" and being openly acknowledged as inmates in the exhibition literature, the prisoners were transformed into exemplars of traditional Indian artisanship.[34]

By the later nineteenth century, certain individuals made a career as professionals touring internationally and being exhibited at world's fairs. Some of the best examples of such recruitment may be found in Buffalo Bill's Wild West shows of 1883 onward.[35] In the early years of the show, William Cody (Buffalo Bill) visited Pine Ridge Agency (later Pine Ridge

Reservation) each spring to select suitable performers. The process effectively became a ceremony, with hundreds of individuals arriving in their finest tribal attire, but with only a limited number ever chosen. Once selected, bonds had to be posted guaranteeing each performer a new suit of clothes, food, due attention to his health, and safe return.[36] The desire for such employment seems to have been stimulated by the considerably higher wages performers could earn working in the shows. Meanwhile, not only were individuals essentially competing to be in the shows, but from the 1890s onward, exhibitors came to prefer performers that had been previously employed in show business.[37] Such "show Indians" also increasingly came to be recognized as professionals by the U.S. Bureau of Indian Affairs, which began to insist on individual contracts being issued (see below). Of particular relevance here are that some performers chose to be repeatedly employed in the shows; such services became increasingly regulated by the state; and exhibitors came to prefer performers who understood the demands of being displayed over inexperienced individuals. These developments indicate how human displays in the later nineteenth century became an increasingly professionalized business, with dedicated recruitment officers, contractual engagements, and shifting governmental involvement.

Where performers were imported, they frequently required sanction for their travel, which involved complex negotiations between government agencies, performers, and exhibition organizers. From the mid-1800s onward, showmen often included claims regarding the contractual engagements between them and displayed peoples in promotional literature; on occasion, this even extended to reprints of documentary evidence in a show's pamphlet. By the later nineteenth century, contracts had become a standardized element in the process of importing and displaying foreign peoples.[38] A particularly instructive example is provided by the intervention of the Bureau of Indian Affairs in recruitment for the Wild West Shows.

Cody faced considerable opposition on several fronts, especially from policy reformers, who charged that the performers' welfare was being compromised—their untimely deaths often providing ample ammunition for this accusation—and that they were being exposed to morally corruptive influences. He defended himself by arguing that the performers were well paid, they worked voluntarily, and the shows were not conducive to degenerate behavior.[39] Protesters were partly motivated by a shift in federal Indian policy following the Civil War. Before the strife, removal of tribes from the East to dedicated territories in the West had seemed a temporary solution to the desirability of settlement in the East; afterward, as westward expansion and settlement rapidly accelerated, colonizers once again began desiring tribal lands. In view of this, some proposed solutions based on transforming Indian culture into more easily assimilated forms by breaking up tribal affiliations and effectively enforcing agricultural subsistence. Rather irksomely, Cody's shows relied on images of a martial enemy that conflicted with the image of assimilated and "civilized" citizens being promoted by policy reformers. Consequently, reformers began to lobby the Bureau of Indian Affairs to forbid the employment of Indians in the shows.

Complete prohibition would have been illegal, but the bureau did attempt to significantly reduce participation of indigenous peoples in shows by placing restrictions on the terms of employment Cody had to offer and closely monitoring contractual engagements.[40] By 1886, in negotiation with the secretary of the interior, Cody began issuing contracts that stipulated the terms of employment. By 1889 the contracts had also become standardized and issued individually between Cody and performers (rather than just between Cody and the bureau).[41] Such contracts also indicate that exhibited peoples were required to, and did, give their consent in arrangements that were routinely discussed in the wider press. They also demonstrate that in some cases at least, instead of assuming that displayed peoples were exhibited without consent, it might be more appropriate to ask why they gave their consent, if they were able to make a free choice, and what such consent might be worth.

Consent is one of the most problematic issues involved in understanding displayed peoples' histories. Did displayed peoples consent to being exhibited? Were they shown due regard for their personal wishes? If they did permit their display, did they understand what they were doing, and were they coerced in any way? Unfortunately, there is insufficient evidence to conclusively infer the legal status of all performers; however, there is substantial evidence that exhibited peoples were often party to contracts that stated the terms of their employment and the kinds of services they were expected to perform, terms that they actively negotiated.[42] Despite either the broader lack of sources or known contractual engagements, some may argue that displayed peoples cannot have made a free choice. In this vein, the historian David Gerber has drawn heavily on Don Herzog's theoretical work on consent theory to outline a framework for understanding consent in relationship to the display of human curiosities.[43] Both argue that there are certain preconditions which must be in place for an act to count as "effective choice and consent." A person may only be said to have made a free choice when that individual has been able to choose between a "significant range of meaningful choices" and has not been compelled into any one course of action.[44] Here, compulsion is best understood as any form of coercion and circumstance that presses an individual into a particular choice. For instance, if someone lives in a society where social or economic considerations dictate that that a person's options are severely or entirely circumscribed (for example, slavery for black Americans in the nineteenth century), this must be taken into account. Individuals must have sufficient information regarding the different options available and the time and mental capacity necessary to be able to evaluate them. Furthermore, in ascertaining the quality of such consent we cannot assume that giving consent legitimates every consequence of that action. Consent, Herzog argues, is like opening Pandora's box, since it can have many unintended consequences that may mean an individual would have chosen otherwise.[45]

If such criteria are used to evaluate displayed peoples' histories, then it is highly unlikely that they were able to make free choices. In the case of Scott and the African prisoners recruited for the Colonial and Indian Exhibition, correspondence from Mr. Tooke, Private Secretary to the Premier, indicated that "it would not be legal to make his [Tilletjies] release conditional on his going to England but you might privately arrange with him that when he was released he should go to England." Scott brushed aside the objection by claiming that "there is nothing approaching the illegal about the matter."[46] If Scott did make the prisoners' release conditional, which seems entirely plausible and likely, the possibility of free consent being given is absent.[47] In earlier exhibitions, by Charles Caldecott's own admission, the Zulus' cooperation was only secured by "dint of continual perseverance; by telling the poor fellows the grand sights which awaited them; by engaging one this month and another the next; and by promising to each a good and just reward for their services, A. T. Caldecott was at length fortunate enough to secure eleven men, a young woman and a child."[48] Clearly, the Zulus were not especially acquiescent to the elder Caldecott's initial proposals. Perhaps they were simply badgered into giving in or lured on promises of the riches they might be able to acquire without being informed of the long hours and extensive traveling over Europe. Likewise, in the 1880s, Robert A. Cunningham claimed that he had "encountered great danger in going amongst the various tribes [of Australian Aborigines] to offer the creatures on shore all inducements such as tobacco, red handkerchiefs, &c., &c., if they would come with me," but initially at least, it had been "all in vain."[49] Moreover, when members of the Aborigines Protection Society checked the contracts relating to Frank Fillis's show of 1899, they discovered that they were "not with the natives themselves, but with their custodians, who are alone responsible, both to them and to the managers of the 'Savage South Africa' exhibition."[50]

With such testimony available, it may seem unproblematic to conclude that displayed peoples were evidently unable to make free choices; yet this is an issue if one is trying to recover past perspectives. Showmen made frequent and explicit claims that their performers consented to being exhibited, and in nineteenth-century terms, they are likely to have done so to the satisfaction of some authorities (but, critically, not others). If Catlin is to be believed, on occasion it was also done in a manner that his performers would have understood and which drew on their own customs of reaching agreements. Moreover, by the later nineteenth century, performers effectively became professional entertainers and repeatedly chose to be exhibited abroad. Acknowledging showmen's claims does not require their acceptance at face value—though it does help to provide a reminder that consent is culturally and historically specific. Therefore, even if sufficient evidence were available to apply Herzog's and Gerber's criteria, it is not entirely clear how this would help clarify the issue in terms of knowing how those involved conceived of the situation. Moreover, there is the added complication of knowing what might have counted as consent for each cultural group under consideration, since we cannot assume that displayed peoples would all have shared the same notions of, or even means of reaching, consent as either one another or their exhibitors.

It is especially important to remember that many of the exhibitions considered here occurred in a period when the legal status of humans as property and the nature of labor contracts were under considerable debate. For example, Baartman was displayed in London just three years after the abolition of the British slave trade. In a court case brought by prominent abolitionists, including Zachary Macaulay, her exhibitors were accused of enslavement (see chapter 5). The judge ruled in favor of her manager, but following the legal battle, showmen certainly became more cautious in legitimating the presence of foreign human exhibits in the metropolis. There were also cases later in the century aimed at protecting foreign peoples in which Baartman's case was explicitly cited as a precedent for legal intervention.[51] Even after the abolition of the British slave trade in 1807 and slavery in the British Empire in 1833, complete emancipation followed only in 1838, after a period of "apprenticeship." Meanwhile, not only did a highly profitable illegal trade in humans continue regardless, but other suppliers stepped into the breach to take advantage of the continuing demand for slaves in other parts of the world, and new uses were found for slaves who could no longer be exported. Abolition also bought new shortfalls of labor, which came to be filled with fixed-term indentured workers from Asia, Africa, and the Pacific—a practice many feared would simply replace one system of slavery with another and that, in its earlier years at least, often involved kidnapping and coercion as well as voluntary bondage.[52]

Concern regarding the legal arrangements governing the importation of human labor extended to free laborers. For example, in the late eighteenth and early nineteenth centuries, many Asians arriving in Britain were brought over to England as indentured servants or sailors. At the end of their service, some were sent back, but many were cut adrift and left to become vagrants. In 1814, the extent of the problem prompted the British government to pass legislation forcing the East India Company to provide basic provisions for Asian sailors. As a result, anyone wishing to import a foreign servant had to enter into an agreement by which they deposited a sum sufficient to cover the individual's repatriation. These arrangements were legally binding but poorly enforced, and certainly not put into effect for the benefit of imported laborers.[53] Such agreements may not have been put in place for the benefit of performers either, and it is at least as likely that they provided legal protection for both the government and individuals who chose to import foreign peoples.[54] Even when contracts were signed, some contemporary commentators remained unconvinced that the arrangements prevented exploitation. As late as 1899, the Aborigines Protection Society declared, "All exhibitions of so-called 'savages,' brought from their own country in what is really a condition of bondage, even if voluntarily assented to by them, are, in the opinion of your Committee, very objectionable whether or not legal warrant can be found for them."[55] The legal wrangling was complemented by concerned philanthropists and missionaries who frequently condemned the shows' proprietors and patrons as negligent and profiteering with little or no concern for the welfare of "aborigines."[56] Given the broader tensions over slavery, imported laborers, and impressment, it is no surprise that the issue of how displayed peoples had come to grace Britain's shores and exhibition venues was of immense public interest and that whatever arrangements were made, some campaigners remained deeply concerned that performers remained enslaved, "but of a sort that would probably not be recognised in an English court of law."[57]

In response to the public concern over performers' welfare, showmen frequently furnished their critics with what may be best described as narratives of consent. By categorically stating that performers had willingly agreed to be exhibited and providing details such as reprinted travel documents, showmen effectively tried to substantiate two important claims. First, such narratives usually described how performers had been involved in some form of administrative procedure relating to their travel abroad, such as interviews to obtain consent. While relating to performers' welfare, this strategy also implicitly bolstered showmen's claims to be exhibiting authentic foreigners. Second, the strategy preemptively attempted to allay fears that performers were being exhibited against their will. In such cases, the consent given is highly unlikely to measure up to modern standards of what counts as an informed choice, and whether we choose to accept it as such may depend as much as on our political commitments as the ambiguous historical evidence. This is not to claim that narratives of consent are unproblematic, especially as they were clearly attempts to resolve contemporary tensions relating to legitimate human labor and its importation. However, it is to recognize that what counted as consent, the circumstances under which it would have been required, and the procedures considered most suited for obtaining it were under heated and protracted discussion, and that any agreements reached in these circumstances will, in all likelihood, fail to live up to most modern expectations of appropriate human treatment.

Even when agreements were reached, the parties concerned may have had entirely different understandings of what a given contract entailed.[58] For instance, in September 1853, Zulu chief Manyos found himself in court answering to charges of assault.[59] Reports indicate that the previous day, the chief had gone for a walk in Hyde Park with four other members of the troupe. Caldecott, their manager, asked them to return. Nevertheless, the chief refused and had to be escorted back to their residence at St. George's Gallery by a policeman. Here, instead of going straight indoors, the Zulus stood outside the exhibition venue. A crowd gathered around the group and watched as Caldecott attempted to push the chief inside. Manyos responded with a blow and would have hit Caldecott again if others had not stopped him. Fearing they were unsafe, the group went into the gallery and armed themselves with their weapons. Caldecott, alarmed and concerned that physical violence would quickly ensue, asked the police to take the chief into custody.

In court it was clear that Manyos felt he had been pushed simply for going out, and he argued that there was nothing in his contract to prevent it. He also believed that a man of his social standing should not have been treated with such apparent disrespect, and maintained that if someone pushed him he must retaliate. Caldecott responded that he had acted out of concern for the safety of both the public and the Zulus. Furthermore, he argued that he bore the responsibility of protecting his father's investment of £1,000 in ensuring that the Zulus were well treated while they were in Europe and that they were returned to Natal at the close of the exhibition. The judge, William Broderip, a well-known naturalist, ruled that Caldecott had no legal right to prevent Manyos from choosing to go outdoors, even if it was intended for his protection, as the agreement only referred to the performance of "native dances and other customs for exhibition."[60] Manyos was released once he had promised to behave in the future, and to bring any further complaints to the attention of the court without resorting to violence.

The case of Manyos highlights several issues relating to the contracts that governed human importation. Those that set out the terms of travel arrangements, pay, and working conditions still left considerable scope for disputes and conflicting interpretation. The reports of Manyos's defense indicate that he understood he was under a binding agreement which placed certain limitations and expectations of service on him. However, he and Caldecott interpreted the scope of its restrictions differently, based on their respective responsibilities as exhibitor, performer and authority figure for or within the group of Zulus.

It is also unclear that contracts alone would have been enough to settle disputes. For example, in January 1853 another Zulu chief named Larcher, who was being exhibited in London with his wife and child as the result of a mercantile speculation by Mr. Cawood, appeared in court over a pay dispute.[61] Larcher argued that his family was owed the equivalent of one bullock per month, or 35 shillings, but Cawood believed the correct sum was one cow per month, or 10 shillings; reports of the court proceedings do not record the exact sum resolved on but do indicate that an arbitrator was appointed to oversee the distribution of the profits to the satisfaction of both parties.

Although Manyos and Larcher were able to present their grievances in court, it is not likely that all foreign peoples were always given a similar opportunity, or even knew it existed. In Manyos's case it is clear that he appeared in court as a result of having been arrested, not because he voluntarily filed a complaint. In Larcher's case the situation is more ambiguous. However, these two cases suggest that exhibited individuals were occasionally able to call, intentionally or more serendipitously, on the force of the law to support their personal interests. Whether this was always the outcome of their efforts is debatable; however, such cases do suggest that displayed people were not necessarily resigned about their fate. There is a risk when discussing exhibited peoples of assuming that they were either helpless or so obviously in a degraded position that they were merely passive subjects of past forms of exploitation. As the examples of Manyos and Larcher show, some performers actively and repeatedly made demands that helped them (re)negotiate the terms of their employment, whether these related to what they were able to do in their free time or how much they were paid. Court cases are rather dramatic examples of displayed peoples asserting themselves, but they are also probably unrepresentative of the subtler ways in which most performers adapted to their new lives.

At first Mr. George found looking after Flora and Martinus difficult.[62] The children were obviously afraid of their new environment and family in Croydon. "On first arrival they exhibited the utmost fear and timidity," and "if suddenly spoken to, they would crouch down upon the floor like half-tamed animals, who dreaded the keeper's lash." Consequently, they led a "solitary and apparently miserable existence." For months, they associated primarily with each other. Fortunately, Mr. George was a patient man and "did not despair of winning their confidence." He continually tried to speak to them and encourage them to play and interact with his family. Gradually they abandoned their mother tongue, described by contemporaries as "a few guttural and uncouth sounds," and learned to communicate in English. Indeed, once their fear subsided, the residents of Croydon were occasionally "startled by an apparition, grotesquely attired in beads, feathers, and strips of skin, which flashed across the high road, followed by another similar figure in full chase, with not unfrequently a healthy English boy or two bringing up the rear." By the time they were exhibited as the "Earthmen" in private rooms in 1853, Flora and Martinus had learned to play musical instruments, and would dance and sing "Buffalo Girls," "I'm Going to Alabama," and "Britons Never Shall Be Slaves" for consumers as if they were receiving guests at home (figs. 55 and 56). In the mid-1850s, the children were exhibited alongside Maximo and Bartola. Martinus died shortly afterward, and the remaining three were displayed in Barnum's American Museum in the early 1860s before returning once again to London in the mid-1860s, where Flora died in 1864 (fig. 57).[63]

Flora and Martinus almost certainly had no meaningful choice in being exhibited. Their initial experiences of England were clearly upsetting.

FIGURE 55
(*Above, left*) *Flora and Martinus, Children of the Earthmen Tribe.* Although the children were exhibited in a drawing room, the image depicts them among the ostensibly dense vegetation of their homelands. ("The Erdermänne, or Earthmen of South Africa," *Illustrated Magazine of Art*, 1853, p. 445. © The British Library Board. PP.1931.N.)

FIGURE 56
(*Above, right*) *Earthmen Tribe from Port-Natal:* Flora and Martinus depicted in the drawing room in which they received guests and with a chair to emphasize their diminutive stature. (*Illustrated London News*, November 6, 1853, p. 372. Author's collection.)

FIGURE 57
(*Right*) Title page for the pamphlet for the exhibition of Flora, along with Maximo and Bartola. After Martinus died, Flora continued to be exhibited with Maximo and Bartola in P. T. Barnum's American Museum. (By kind permission of the Bodleian Library, University of Oxford, JJ, Human Freaks 4[53].)

Unable to communicate with anyone, they were afraid and are likely to have had little or no understanding of why they had been removed from their home, the people they knew, and the ways of living to which they were accustomed. As the months passed, they learned new skills, which patrons interpreted as evidence of an improved moral and intellectual capacity. The *Morning Chronicle*, for example, reported that their "native germ of intelligence has shown itself capable of not a little cultivation," probably due in a "great degree to the intercourse of the 'Earthmen' with the family of Mr. George." Especially pleasing was that they had been "taught, in some degree, the usages of civilized life, and won to some extent from that absolute ignorance of the very idea of the existence of a Deity or controlling power which they had manifested on their arrival in England."[64] The approval of their religious education bears witness to George's intention to train them as future missionaries who might be returned to Africa. Their newly learned abilities to speak and sing in English and play musical instruments are just some examples of how they adapted to their new environment while being trained to perform for their guests.

Others acculturated themselves in more intimate ways. In April 1844, Sarah Haynes married Alexander Cadotte at St. Martin's Church.[65] Unusually, the couple met at one of Catlin's exhibitions. Sarah, only eighteen years old, appears to have fallen for Alexander instantly, and the couple courted in secret before informing parents of their relationship. Her father objected but relented, and her mother and sisters appear to have encouraged the union. Despite claims that the wedding had been arranged to take place at nine o'clock to avoid public curiosity making the ceremony a "mere sight," upon their arrival, the wedding party nonetheless found the church portico packed "so densely, that it was with the greatest difficulty a strong body of police could obtain an opening for the wedding procession." The wedding proved notable because the groom, otherwise known as Notennaakam (Strong Wind), "a half-caste, [and] a young man of fine personal appearance and address," was interpreter for the group of Anishinabe being exhibited at the time, and who were all in attendance.[66] Haynes was not Cadotte's only admirer. Catlin noted that "there were several fair damsels who nightly paid their shillings, and took their positions near the platform" to admire the young man. One in particular, referred to by Catlin simply as the "jolly fat dame," had also taken a liking to Cadotte (fig. 58). Night after night she attended the exhibition, bestowed gifts on the party, and left letters for Cadotte. He rejected her, reasoning, Catlin claimed, that "she is making too free with me, and all the people see it. She wants a husband too bad, and I hope she will soon get one."[67] Seven months later, the press reported the end of the marriage and Sarah's sheepish retreat to her parents' home.[68] Yet Sarah had actually emigrated to Canada with her husband. After the wedding, the troupe's guardian, Rankin, attempted to exploit the marriage by advertising that the bride would appear in future shows. The couple had not been consulted, and upon learning of

the plans, Cadotte refused to deal with Rankin any longer. The couple then
settled on a reservation on Walpole Island, but here it appears that Cadotte
turned to drink and abused his wife. She later moved to Sault Sainte Marie,
converted to Roman Catholicism, and opened a small Catholic school, but
later died with the marriage never having improved.[69]

Other performers also found spouses abroad. Baartman's exhibition
moved to the provinces after the show closed in London. It was quite common to follow a London season with a provincial tour, but in this case the
tour may have been brought about in response to unfavorable press and
the court case that followed from accusations that she was being forcibly
exhibited. There is evidence that Baartman was exhibited in Manchester,
Bath, and Limerick in Ireland.[70] Manchester parish records indicate that
in December 1811, "Sarah Bartmann a female Hottentot from the Colony of
the Cape of Good Hope, born on the Borders of Caffaria, [was] baptized this
Day by permission of the Lord Bishop of Chester in a letter from his Lord-
ship to Jos. Brookes Chaplain."[71] During this period she also married, but
the identity of her groom remains elusive.[72]

Similarly, at the tail end of the century, in August 1899, Prince Peter
Kushana Lobengula, reputed son of Ndebele king Lobengula Kumalo and
performer in the Savage South Africa exhibition, was set to marry Florence
Kate Jewell, the daughter of a Jewish mining engineer from Cornwall (fig.
59).[73] The impending wedding secured him notoriety, as much of the public expressed its disapproval of the union in the national and local press.[74]
Initially, letters from the groom's solicitors categorically denied that an engagement even existed, and he was reported to be such a "reluctant bridegroom" that it seemed as if "the god Eros" had "blundered sadly over this
affair."[75] Further intrigue brewed after reports that a pastor had refused to
perform the ceremony and that the marriage license had been revoked.[76]
Hearth and Home, a newspaper for "gentlewomen," found the whole affair "nauseating from beginning to end." Miss Jewell, it claimed, "must be

"Place aux Dames"

By LADY VIOLET GREVILLE

COMINGS OF AGE and home-comings are always pleasing ceremonies. Last week saw the coming of age of Lord Graham and Lord Castlereagh, and the home-coming of Lord and Lady Tullibardine. The latter function is of essentially Scotch origin, and is usually the occasion for a loyal expression of feeling. The married couple are well known, and the husband, at least, has probably already given a foretaste of qualities which have endeared him to his tenantry and his dependents. He is not absolutely untried, he has embraced some profession, and distinguished himself therein. He may have gone through an arduous campaign like Lord Tullibardine, and thus the enthusiasm evoked by his happy marriage has a solid basis of fact.

The coming of age festivities, on the contrary, possess a vicarious meaning. Like father like son is an old proverb, and people judge the coming generation by the past. If the father has been a good landlord, a kind master, thoughtful for his dependents, and wise in his ruling, the chances are his son will follow in his footsteps. In both instances last week such was the case, and the popularity of the parents may be gauged by the enthusiasm displayed towards the son. The festivities in Lord Castlereagh's case were sadly marred by his accident, which caused pity to be tenderly mingled with rejoicing; pity for him, his parents and his newly made *fiancée*. It is seldom that a man's engagement takes place simultaneously with his coming of age, and two such great and pleasurable emotions coinciding must almost overpower a young man, and the accident occurring at the same time shed a proportionate gloom.

In Lord Graham's case everything was propitious, the glorious weather left nothing to be desired, everything smiled on him, the sun, the happy faces of his parents and friends, the spontaneous and hearty enthusiasm of his dependents. Those who believe in the strained and unfriendly relations existing between employers and employed, should have seen the magnificent presents given by tenantry, neighbours, employés, and servants, listened to the hearty speeches and loud acclamations, admired the decorations, illuminations and fireworks contributed by the poorest person in the village, and noted the willing way in which everyone put a helping hand to unharness the horses and pull his carriage on a triumphal progress through the village. The young Marquis has received the very best education—that of practical work. He has served as mate in the mercantile service, and, like Lord Charles Beresford, has the true interests of the seaman at heart. When one sees a young man of the aristocracy thus putting his shoulder to the wheel, and giving his sympathy to those below him in position, it is but fair to surmise that the bonds of union between rich and poor, employer and employed have not yet been severed, and that the ties of loyalty and consideration, truth and honour, will be stronger than the blatant shouts of democracy or the unreasoning demands of Socialism. It is the bad landlord that makes the rebellious tenant, and where harmony is preserved by mutual forbearance, the relationship cannot fail to be a pleasant one.

A patient, suffering from a peculiar disease induced by excessive tea-drinking, now lies in one of the hospitals. This particular instance may be exceptionally severe, but many suffer in the same way. Workgirls, servants, and women leading sedentary lives do themselves immense harm by immoderate tea-drinking. The patient in question had drunk five quarts of strong tea daily for thirty years. Few of us, perhaps, reach that maximum, still, tea taken in excess is as injurious as alcohol. The old Chinese teas are going out of fashion, the delicate, sweet-scented Orange Pekoe which delighted our mothers and gave a subtle fragrance to the brew, is now scarcely employed, and the stronger and coarser Indian and Ceylon teas have replaced these rarer blends. It is the method of tea-making that is at fault. Tea, in China and Japan, hurts nobody, for it never stands. A kettle is boiled, and as soon as the simmering is over, some water is poured over a small quantity of green tea placed at the bottom of another kettle. Directly afterwards the water is poured off into a cup, and the tea drunk without milk or sugar. It is never allowed to stand, and for every cup a fresh brew is made, consequently the injurious element, the tannin, is invariably absent. Another mistake we make in England is not only to drink tea often three or four times a day, beginning with the early cup before breakfast, but also to eat meat with it, a meal called high tea, and the sure method of promoting indigestion.

Ladies certainly are uncomplaining martyrs in the matter of dress. All this year they have worn trailing muslins, so long that they gathered up all the dust and dirt of the streets, so narrow that they could not hold them up, and, of course, pocketless. What women have suffered in carrying their handkerchiefs in their hands, their belts, even up their sleeves, like soldiers, their purses hanging from their wrists or their waists, their card-cases in bags or in their fingers, till they were laden like railway porters, cannot be described.

Not content with this, the mere wearing of jewellery is a heavy burden cheerfully borne. The Queen complained much when young of the weight of the crown, but that was only rarely worn at a public function, and, therefore, partook of the nature of a duty; but what shall we say of the present women of fashion? A popular young duchess, for instance, wears at the smartest balls, a large tiara, a heavy diamond belt of hard and unyielding proportions, a high dogcollar of diamonds encompassing her throat and impeding her breathing, and several rows of massive pearls the weight of which causes red marks on her fair skin? Surely torture can go no further, nor even the truth of the axiom "*Il faut souffrir pour être belle*" be better exemplified.

The victory of Private James Doré, of the 2nd Devonshire, in the Rifle Championship was a pleasant surprise. It is seldom that such a competition is won by a private. He scored 140 points, while Sergeant Williamson, 2nd Scottish Rifles, made 138, and Colcur-Sergeant Ashforth, 1st Lancashire Fusiliers, was third with 136. Private James Doré is a native of Torquay, and has fourteen years' service. He has been best shot in Major Davies' company for four years, and last year tied with the battalion shot. Our portrait is by Charles Knight, Aldershot

PRIVATE JAMES DORE, WINNER OF THE RIFLE CHAMPIONSHIP AT ALDERSHOT

Loben's Courtship

THE old adage which says that the course of true love never did run smooth seems to be exemplified in the strange story that has been revealed bit by bit from Earl's Court. Among the natives forming part of the show called "Savage South Africa" at the

MISS FLORENCE K. JEWELL

PRINCE LOBENGULA

Earl's Court Exhibition was the son of Lobengula, known as Peter Kushana Loben. Report said that he had become engaged to an English lady, and that he was shortly to be married. This was subsequently denied, and a letter appeared in *The Daily Graphic* signed by Loben, who, by the way, cannot read, declaring that he had no such intention. The lady to whom he was said to be engaged was Miss Florence Kate Jewell, who is of Jewish extraction und the daughter of a mining engineer of Redruth, Cornwall. Sh first saw Loben in full war paint at Bloemfontein, and, it is said, fell in love with him on the spot. At Bloemfontein Loben has a farm, to which it was said he was anxious to return with his bride. Loben is twenty-four and Miss Jewell twenty-one years of age. Following rapidly after the denial that there was to be any marriage came a report to the effect that the couple were to be married at the church of St. Matthias, Warwick Road, and a little band of spectators gathered at the church on the morning. But there was no wedding. There had been a hitch. No one quite knew what had happened. It was afterwards ascertained that the Rev. F. H. Lane, the curate in charge, had refused to perform the ceremony, and that his refusal had been supported by the Chancellor of the Diocese, who, it was said, had revoked the licence he had previously issued. And there for the present the matter rests for the time, but Miss Jewell confided to a *Daily Graphic* reporter, who had an interview with her, that in the event of another hitch she would not get married in England at all, but would go straight to South Africa and have the ceremony performed there. Our portraits are by Arthur Weston, Newgate Street.

PRINCE LOBENGULA IN HIS NATIVE COSTUME

The Theatres

By W. MOY THOMAS

WHO are the theatrical enthusiasts who go to the play in these sweltering days of mid-August? They are a not inconsiderable number; for though no fewer than eighteen West End houses have now closed doors, there are still about seven that continue the struggle with more or less success. These are the SAVOY, with *H.M.S. Pinafore* and *Trial by Jury*; the GLOBE, with *The Gay Lord Quex*; the COURT, with *Wheels Within Wheels*; the LYRIC, with *El Capitan*; the SHAFTESBURY, with *The Belle of New York*; the PRINCESS'S, with *One of the Best*; and the CRITERION, with *The Wild Rabbit*. With these there is no need to associate the "Variety" theatres—such as the PALACE, the EMPIRE, and the ALHAMBRA—which are rather after-dinner lounges than theatres properly so called. The CRITERION, though included, may also be left out of the account, for this is for the present in the hands of those experimental summer managements which are more or less independent of the law of supply and demand.

Still seven theatres of the higher class constitute a considerable contingent, and the question arises—how are they filled while London is popularly supposed to be at the seaside or gone abroad? Country and foreign visitors, no doubt, count for a good deal, for there is always a large number of such among us, and in or out of season no class are more constant playgoers. When with these we take into account the two or three houses which—like the GLOBE, the COURT, and the SHAFTESBURY—are fortunate enough to have produced pieces that are exceptionally attractive, the solution of the problem certainly becomes less difficult.

An early token of the coming season will be the re-opening of the ADELPHI to-night by the new manager, Mr. Robert Sleath, who will produce the new romantic drama, *With Flying Colours*, by Mr. Seymour Hicks and Mr. F. G. Latham, the scenes of which are laid at Chatham, Southampton, and Dartmoor. There will, however, be no sudden waking up of the theatrical world like that of the sleepers in Lord Tennyson's enchanted palace. For most of the coming novelties—including Messrs. Parker and Wilson Barrett's play at the LYCEUM, the *Trip to Midget-Town*, by the Lilliputian American Company at the NEW OLYMPIC, *The Last Chapter* at the STRAND, *The Ghetto* at the COMEDY, *A Moonlight Blossom* at the PRINCE OF WALES'S, and Mr. E. A. Morton's new musical comedy at DALY'S, *San Joy; or, The, Emperor's Own*, we must wait till next month; while Mr. Hall Caine's drama, based on his novel, *The Christian*, at the DUKE OF YORK'S, which will be new to this country, and Mr. Sydney Grundy's adaptation of *La Tulipe Noire*, at the HAYMARKET, will not be due till the latter days of October. As to the suburban houses, which are tolerably busy even in the dog days, they depend on the patronage of the suburban playgoer, who, as everyone knows, is a far more robust and heat-resisting personage than his brother of the West End.

It is announced that in Mr. Sydney Grundy's new satirical play, entitled *The Degenerate*, with which Mrs. Langtry will commence her season of management at the HAYMARKET on the 31st inst., an important part will be played by the author's daughter, who has not, if we are not mistaken, yet made her appearance on the public stage. Mr. Henry Arthur-Jones, it will be remembered, has two daughters who are acting in their father's comedies as members of important travelling companies. The new fashion will probably spread—at least among dramatists who have clever daughters.

Mr. George Broadhurst, who re-opens the STRAND on Monday, September 4, will still rely on the attractions of American farces. *The Last Chapter*, which will be produced at that date, is a piece of this kind. On the other hand, the company will be found to be largely reinforced by English performers. Mr. Ben Webster, Mr. John Beauchamp, Mr. Philip Cunningham, Miss May Whitty, Miss Jessie Bateman, and several others will appear in the cast.

Mr. Mouflet's new RICHMOND Theatre, which—like its historical predecessor—stands on Richmond Green, will be formally opened next month, when Mr. Ben Greet's company will appear in *As You Like It*. Miss Dorothy Baird—the charming impersonator of Trilby—will be the Rosalind of the cast.

Mr. Charles Morton, of the PALACE Theatre, who has certainly done more to raise the dignity and status of our variety theatres than any other living manager, has attained this week his eightieth birthday—happily, with no diminution of his managerial energy and fertility in ideas. It is proposed to celebrate the event by a special performance at the PALACE Theatre on the 21st of next month.

Shakespeare's *Richard II.*, which there was once a chance of seeing at the LYCEUM, is to be performed by Mr. F. R. Benson's company on the 21st inst. in the grounds of Flint Castle. This *al fresco* representation, however, will not embrace the entire play, but only the more important scenes. The performance is in celebration of the Quincentenary of the surrender of the unfortunate King to "the great Duke Bolingbroke," which event took place on August 21st, 1399.

so obsessed by the desire for notoriety as to be thrown completely off her mental balance."[77] Despite the false starts, the couple lived as man and wife until they were finally wed on February 28, 1900. By then the press had lost interest as its attention turned to the Second Boer War (1899–1902), and the wedding was only briefly mentioned in the official records of Holborn Register Office.[78] The couple suffered a troubled relationship, with Jewell being physically abused by her husband and accusations of adultery on Lobengula's part; ultimately, they sought a divorce in 1902.[79] By 1901 Lobengula had also begun a relationship with Lily Magowan, a Belfast-born redhead. The couple settled in Salford, where Lobengula worked as a miner, and five children followed before he died in 1913.[80]

These relationships and settlements are indicative of the bonds that performers could develop through informal contact. Within live shows there were opportunities for social interaction, but these were relatively limited. However, showmen frequently offered the public the opportunity to book private appointments with displayed peoples. Furthermore, displayed peoples were not always kept under lock and key. Catlin, for example, arranged for a daily carriage ride for the performers in his care, as well as visits to places of interest including the Bank of England, Windsor Castle, and Surrey Zoological Gardens. In a pamphlet describing the experiences of managing a show in Britain and France, Catlin's colleague George Henry noted that his and his performers' company was continually sought: "The nobility and ministers and the Society of Friends [Quakers] invited us almost every day to take tea with them." On one occasion his troupe had been taken to see "three men out of the Zoological Gardens going up to the country of the stars. They had something very large in the shape of a bladder over their heads; they called it a balloon. One man said to us, 'You see now that we Englishmen can go and see the upper world with our bodies.' Lord Bloomfield invited us to see the big guns at Woolwich; three of us got inside of one of them."[81] Such visits created opportunities for unscripted and unregulated contact in which relationships, fleeting or lasting, emerged. Obviously, not all such relationships lasted beyond the shows' run or even the few hours of demonstration, let alone led to marriage; however, they did offer displayed peoples significant opportunities for interacting with metropolitan residents outside the confining role of the performing "savage."

Escaping Expectations

Shortly after Baartman's arrival on British shores, at no. 225 Piccadilly, members of the public were invited to view the "Hottentot Venus" for 2 shillings. She was displayed as a human curiosity because of the perceived enormity of her breasts, buttocks, and hypertrophied labia, traits believed to be characteristic of the Khoekhoe. The show took place on "a stage two feet high, along which she was led by her keeper, and exhibited like a wild beast; being obliged to walk, stand, or sit as he ordered."[82] The stage also had a small recessed area in which she often stood. In this case, the exhibitor would call her to him, "and when she came would desire her to turn round and would invite the spectators to feel her posterior parts and at other times if she was at a distance from him would desire her to turn round in order that everybody might see her extraordinary shape."[83] Eyewitness accounts indicate that she was unhappy and reluctant to perform. Zachary Macaulay, the prominent abolitionist, observed that

from the unhappy and dejected countenance of the same female and from the expressive disapprobation which she gives when ordered to exhibit herself and from her frequent sighs he considers the said female is unhappy and that she is under the restrain and controul [sic] of the exhibitor ... he particularly observed that the said female by her looks gave evident signs of mortification and misery.[84]

Macaulay's account suggests that Baartman clearly disliked the audience's attentiveness, and that she may have been regularly coerced to perform onstage. His antislavery leanings may have predisposed him to see the relationship as one of slavery, but other testimony corroborates Baartman's reticence and suggests she resisted being treated like an animal by striking back when provoked or being passively uncooperative to her exhibitor's demands.[85]

Baartman maintained a level of control over how her body was viewed, despite attempts to make her comply with the wishes of others in other contexts. Having left England to be exhibited in Paris in 1814 by the animal trainer S. Réaux, she quickly attracted the attention of natural historians at the Musée d'histoire naturelle, including the comparative anatomists Georges Cuvier, Etienne Geoffroy St. Hilaire, and Henri de Blainville. In the spring of 1814, she spent three days at the Jardin des plantes, in which the Musée was based, being observed and drawn.[86] Cuvier and de Blainville were particularly keen to view Baartman's labia. Their interest stemmed from travelers' tales that Khoekhoe women had large buttocks and hypertrophied labia, accounts that had circulated since the first European encounters with African peoples of the Cape of Good Hope.[87] Unable to decide whether her anatomy was the result of nature or of artifice, many anatomists had attempted to resolve the mystery, and the men at the Musée were no exception. Despite their pleas and an offer of payment by de Blainville, Baartman refused to allow an intimate examination. At length, the men present were able to persuade her to pose nude, but she tucked her labia away to obscure their visibility. Baartman clearly felt that such contact was totally unacceptable. Her refusal to comply, even in these heavily restricted circumstances, suggests how she found ways to assert herself in order to maintain a sense of her personal dignity.[88]

Controlling how one's body was maintained could provide considerable challenges for performers. In late August 1899, a Swazi performer from Savage South Africa was chatting to a colleague outside one of the entrances to the venue. Abruptly, an omnibus drove past and crushed his foot, causing an agonizing compound fracture of the ankle. Upon examination at the Queen's Jubilee Hospital, the physician ordered an immediate amputation as the only advisable remedy. However, a "peculiar hitch" occurred. The man's interpreter approached the doctor and asked for the operation to be delayed until the man's tribe at the exhibition venue had been consulted, because "amputation of the limbs was contrary to the Swazi custom and religion, and . . . any member of the tribe undergoing it was regarded as bewitched, and either ostracised or killed." The foot was left bandaged and the operation postponed. The next morning, several Swazi performers visited their colleague and also appealed against the amputation; since the foot appeared to be on the mend, it was left to recover. The article in the *Daily News* noted that the penalty was not "as barbarous in Swaziland as amongst some neighbouring tribes. If the injured man returned to his own country alone he would not suffer the extreme penalty of death. Life in his kraal would however be very unpleasant for him."

The story piqued the interest of the newspaper, who relayed it to its readers as nothing more than an example of a "curious tribal custom."[89] Yet the incident provides an arresting example of a performer refusing prescribed medical treatment in order to preserve both his body and his social status among his colleagues in the show and his tribesmen at home. Simultaneously, it highlights the collaborative agency of performers in securing his leg's reprieve. The press coverage also suggests how such assertions of agency could become the subject of wider discussions on the curiousness of performers' cultures, religions, and social organizations.

Similarly, the Bakhoje and Anishinabe found ways to reject advice. Both groups were continually showered with gift copies of the Bible and received requests from missionaries to discuss the question of religion. One morning, the Anishinabe were visited by Rev. S—— and a friend. The reverend, "in a tone and a manner the most winning, and calculated to impress upon them the sincerity of his views" and in the "briefest manner possible, and in the mode the best calculated for their understanding (and which was literally interpreted [for] them), [explained] the system of the Christian religion and the mode of redemption."[90] The visits by clergy reflected broader missionary attempts to promote Christianity among the peoples of the New World.[91]

Missionary efforts began with the Puritans of New England, for whom potential conversion of the indigenous peoples provided a significant rationalization for settlement; however, the early years bore little fruit, with the total number of converts remaining decidedly low. The dawn of the nineteenth century witnessed a renewed energy among missionaries that was most noticeable among Protestants, with Catholics establishing a significant presence in the later nineteenth century. Between 1787 and 1820, eleven bodies, both denominational and interchurch, were established to further the cause of conversion. The most active group was the American

Board of Commissioners for Foreign Missions. Created in 1810, this inter-denominational agency sponsored missions throughout the United States and overseas. Its efforts were tied to attempts to establish mission schools. In effect, conversion, civilization, and education were not only inextricably linked but entailed changing indigenous subsistence from one based on hunting and gathering to agriculture; introducing practical domestic arts such as spinning and weaving; and teaching skills such as reading, writing, and arithmetic while promoting a Christian religious outlook. Significantly, transatlantic missionary traffic also resulted in a number of high-profile missionary converts touring Britain; these included Rev. Peter Jones (who traveled in 1831, 1837–38, and 1844–46), John Sunday (1837), Peter Jacobs (1842), George Copway (1850), and Pahtahquahong Chase (1876, 1881, 1885). A few, such as Jones and Copway, also published accounts of their travels.[92]

Catlin reported that during the speech of Rev. S——, Ahqueewezaints, the boy chief, smoked a pipe and listened intently. After the speech, the chief handed his pipe to Patauaquotaweebe (Driving Cloud), and replied,

We have heard the same words in our own country, where there have been many white people to speak them, and our ears have never been shut against them. We have tried to understand white man's religion, but we cannot—it is medicine to us, and we think we have no need of it. Our religion is simple, and the Great Spirit who gave it to us has taught us all how to understand it. We believe that the Great Spirit made our religion for us, and white man's religion for white men. Their sins we believe are much greater than ours, and perhaps the Great Spirit has thought it best therefore to give them a different religion. Some white men have come to our country, and told us that if we did not take up white man's religion, and give up our own, we should all be lost. Now we don't believe that; and we think those are bad or blind men.

The chief added that when Europeans came to America to make money, the Anishinabe did not require conversion but allowed them to continue their business. "We are here away from our wives and children to try to get some money for them, and there are many things we can take home to them of much more use than white man's religion. Give us guns and ammunition, that we can kill food for them, and protect them from our enemies, and keep whisky and rum sellers out of our country."[93]

The Bakhoje received similar attentions; they too rejected the missionaries' efforts to procure conversions. Catlin reported that they offered similar criticisms of the disparity between the Europeans' professed beliefs and practices.[94] Visited by a Catholic priest and a Methodist preacher, the Bakhoje found it particularly amusing that these were apparently different religions. After questioning Daniel, Catlin's assistant, they concluded that there were in fact six different religions followed by the Europeans, all of which led to a different place in the hereafter (figs. 60 and 61).

While Catlin's reports of these conversations must be partly understood within the conventions of satire, they may also provide glimpses of the performers' actual experiences. His *Adventures of the Ojibbeway and Ioway Indians in England, France, and Belgium*, in which these conversations were recorded, drew on eighteenth-century traditions in which American Indians were essentially uncorrupted, pristine humans who, living by God's natural law, were able to reflect critically on degenerate forms of civilization.[95] In Catlin's work, the Indian visitors were frequently found to be puzzled by the social mores of the British and sought explanations from Catlin or his assistant. The combination of their incomprehension at the treatment of emaciated beggars and street sweepers or at the differences between Catholics and Methodists, and the content of Catlin's answers, provides a social commentary and also frequently shows the performers in a considerably better light than their European brethren.[96] Catlin's self-presentation is that of informed and paternal intermediary, and many are likely to read his descriptions as a means for him to provide a form of social critique. Nonetheless, it has been recently argued that given his knowledge of the performers' language and extended contact with them, both inside and outside exhibition venues, Catlin's work may be read as an account—albeit one that is highly stylized—of the performers' experiences.[97] Taken in this light, these conversations provide glimpses of the performers' refusal to convert or to be confined to the roles that spectators and resident Londoners found acceptable or appropriate to their circumstances.

Other performers simply could not bear the demands placed on them. In 1899, the Savage South Africa extravaganza at Earl's Court featured "a Horde of Savages ... comprising Matabeles, Basutos, Swazies, Hottentots, &c."[98] Over two hundred Africans, twenty-one Afrikaners, and some members of the Cape of Good Hope police lived and performed on-site in a mock kraal at the venue under circumstances that gave rise to much discontent. Unfortunately, the African performers were kept under constant supervision and not allowed to leave the site for fear of their becoming

FIGURE 60
Catlin's drawing based on the thoughts of Sah-mah, an Anishinabe man, on Christianity. Sah-mah argued, "We know that the Great Spirit made the red men to dwell in the forests, and white men to live in green fields and in fine houses; and we believe that we shall live separate in the world to come. The best that we expect or want in a future state is a clear sky and beautiful hunting-grounds, where we expect to meet the friends whom we loved; and we believe that if we speak the truth we shall go there." (George Catlin, *Adventures of the Ojibbeway and Ioway Indians*, 3rd ed. [1852], 1: facing 166. Quotation is from 1:164. Reproduced by kind permission of the Syndics of the Cambridge University Library.)

drunk. The dissatisfaction grew among the "blacks, whose lives [had been] spent in the freedom of the rolling veldt," and who wished to see the sights of London. One day, the performers armed themselves with "long sticks" and produced an "alarming display of temper" while seeking an extension of their "liberty." The superintendent immediately called for an interpreter while barricading himself in his office, reemerging only when the inter-locutor made a "timely appearance" and "quelled what might have devel-oped into open mutiny." The following day, the performers were allowed to roam the grounds of Earl's Court and see the Greater Britain exhibition that was running concurrently with theirs.[99] In press reports, the violence was explained away as if it were the result of a simple misunderstanding; rather than being prisoners, the Africans were simply wards in need of protection from their own predilections for liquor.

Nonetheless, the resentment simmered at Earl's Court and grew throughout the summer. Less than a month after the near "mutiny," a boy had been "boasting [to another] of the progress of his nation, and of his own cleverness at stick play . . . [when they] became angry, and challenged each other to a bout with the sticks." Once begun, the Sotho boy received a rather nasty gash on his upper lip, causing him to bleed and be removed from that evening's performance. After the show, the two renewed their quarrel; one ended up with a "cracked head" and the other a "damaged eye." In order to settle the dust, one of the boys had to be placed in the empty cage of one of the show's animals.[100]

The quarrel was taken up more widely and gave rise to "bitter racial strife."[101] One reporter felt that "the Zulus, the Swazis, and the Matabele" had "increased in the sense of their self-importance" since arriving on Brit-ish soil. Their perceived audacity had grown so much that they felt the Af-rikaners on-site were "not their superiors, if even the equals." Accordingly, one day some Dutchmen visited the kraal and were told by the Africans to

"Umba Kad Sak ('Clear out, or you are a dead man')." The journalist reporting the event claimed that since "African Savages never arbitrate ... [but] fight until their passion exhausts itself," violence ensued; the colonists left after "some blood letting," and the Swazis and Zulus became particularly agitated with each other on behalf of the two boys stick fighting. The imported Cape police managed to gain control, and the "savage chief in charge" was reported as having declared that justice had been served after two Swazis and sixteen Afrikaners were shipped back to their homes.

In some sense, the discontent and violence at Earl's Court is hardly surprising, since the performers were rarely allowed to leave the site. The restrictions placed on them were clearly difficult to bear and seem somewhat heavy-handed, while their protest seems an understandable response to a situation that could easily be construed as a form of captivity. Bringing together so many different groups of people clearly raised conflicts, which presented showmen with the problem of how to maintain order and control and keep their performers content or entertained enough to bear the demands of being itinerant actors. The Africans may not have achieved completely free reign, but the compromise made suggests that sometimes performers could make demands that successfully allowed them to assert themselves and step outside the confining boundaries in which managers or spectators may have wished to place them, whether passively, violently, or collaboratively.

✳

It is highly unlikely that historians will ever be able to establish unambiguously exactly how and why each foreign person came to be a performer onstage in London; however, we can make significant inferences as to why such individuals may have left their homeland and what their experiences abroad may have been. Some may have left their home in order to escape violence and oppression; others may have chosen to leave on the promise of making a living. Others may simply have had no say in the matter by virtue of being too young, mentally incapable, or sold into a life of servitude, or even being a prisoner forced to choose between exhibition and incarceration. While some individuals may have been pressed into becoming performers, others freely chose to enter into contractual arrangements and exhibit themselves. In these cases it is difficult to know what such consent was worth. The individuals here were exhibited in a period during which the legal status of humans as property was under heated debate. It seems likely that such consent may have been obtained primarily for the benefit of managers and government officials. It is certainly unlikely to measure up to modern standards of free choice or informed consent. Yet it does indicate that the shows involved complex interactions between traders, merchants, government agents, and foreign peoples that cannot be reduced to polarized models of control and passivity, victim and aggressor.

Once exhibited, foreign peoples did not confine themselves to the role of the performing "savage." Rather, they could, and did, refuse to perform, strike back when paid unwanted attention, express warmth, and solicit and accept gifts in acts that could both strengthen and undermine racialist prejudice. Displayed peoples were also observers in their own right as they learned to perform the routines expected of them and on occasion learned to speak English or acquired other new skills. In some cases, displayed peoples and consumers were able to build relationships both inside and outside exhibition venues that led to settlement and possibly even acculturation of the performers. Even within the constraints of evidently restrictive situations, displayed peoples created ways to maintain their agency.

Constructive counterparts to such acts of resistance and adaptation may be found in broader contexts. For instance, one study of nineteenth-century North American slavery suggests that quotidian activities such as singing, feigning illness, and telling stories could provide a means for slaves to offer a form of opposition to the extreme inequalities, terror, and injustices slavery engendered.[102] Without arguing that the situation of slaves and displayed peoples is necessarily equivalent, such work is suggestive of how people with severely circumscribed options found ways to assert themselves, often in subtly subversive ways. Yet highlighting acts of cultural integration and resistance, whether learning to speak English, refusing to undress, or refusing accept a sum of money regarded as unfair payment, is not to suggest that displayed peoples were fully empowered to do as they pleased. Doing so would conflate agency and freedom too readily and ignore the usually unequal power relations in operation. Rather, analyzing such acts suggests that histories of the shows' receptions that rely too heavily on oversimplified notions of passivity or agency need to be revised. Paying attention to the varied forms of coercion, resistance, collaboration, and encounter involved in the shows' histories highlights the subtle and often all too limited means displayed peoples could use to negotiate agency in situations that they disliked or found frightening, or in which they may not have had the option of open revolt, in order to maintain a level of personal dignity while encountering arrays of eager patrons, to whom we now turn.

HOMAGE TO BEAUTY.
(At the Friendly Zulu Reception, St. James's Hall.)

Blushing Fair One.—WHAT DOES HE SAY?
Interpreter.—HE IS PAYING YOU THE VERY HIGHEST ZULU COMPLIMENT.
Blushing Fair One (flattered and delighted).—INDEED!
Interpreter.—YES. HE SAYS YOUR BEAUTY IS SUCH THAT, WERE YOU ONLY OF
HIS COLOUR, YOU WOULD BE WORTH *THREE COWS!*
[Blushing Fair One retires, hardly so flattered or delighted.

FIGURE 62

An Homage to Beauty: Farini's Friendly Zulus making a mark in
high society. (*Funny Folks,* August 2, 1879, p. 205. © The British
Library Board. M77812.)

Interpreting Exhibitions

IN AUGUST 1879, the press reported that Farini's Friendly Zulus had been capitalizing on their London sojourn by bartering for British brides. On one occasion, with the aid of an interpreter, a fair lady found she had been paid "the very highest Zulu compliment." Blushing, flattered, and delighted, she inquired further. The obliging interpreter informed her that the Zulu believed her beauty was so great that had she been "only of his colour, you would be worth *three cows*!" (fig. 62). The lady hastily retired.[1] Meanwhile, another paper reported that a Victorian gentleman had intentionally tried to rid himself of his own women. Upon meeting a Zulu man at a fashionable soiree, Blobbs inquired, "What would you give to this lady in your country?" After a hesitant appraisal, the Zulu offered "one cow." Encouraged, Blobbs presented his mother-in-law, a "fat and well-liking" woman, and solicited another valuation. This time an enthusiastic "Ten cows!" was proposed. Unable to believe his luck, the offer was hastily accepted, since, Blobbs informed his friend Gubbins, he would have happily "taken a shin of beef for her!"[2]

Intended to amuse readers of *Funny Folks* and *Sporting Times*, respectively, these anecdotes are suggestive for any discussion of the shows' receptions. Both jokes revolve around the social discomfort or advantage created by the same assumed differences between Victorian and Zulu perceptions of female beauty, the Zulu measurement of wealth in animal property, and use of *lobola* (dowry). Given that such details feature prominently in both promotional literature and live performances, their striking similarities indicate how patrons may have drawn on these shared resources to shape their discussions of the shows' performers. Meanwhile, the appearance of the anecdotes in satirical periodicals highlights how displayed peoples could become the focus of amusement beyond the venues in which they were exhibited, and for people who might never have witnessed a live performance.

The shared resources that were made available for patrons' use in interpreting the shows have been explored by tracing the use of promotional materials and analyzing showmen's management techniques; but how did consumers use such information, and what did they make of their 2 shillings' worth? The overwhelming majority of spectators bequeathed us no records of their experiences, and the few that did often left no more than anonymous and fleeting traces. Even simple questions such as who attended the shows, why did they want to see displayed peoples, and how did they interpret the performances they witnessed are difficult to answer with conclusive certainty. Leafing through the yellowing pages of nineteenth-century newspapers and periodicals often opens up the clearest path toward recovering this hidden terrain. Further glimpses may be gleaned from images, and memoirs of the shows. Using such sources, this chapter maps the diversity of patrons' responses to both performances and performers.[3] This focus is intended to showcase the ways in which the shows were interpreted as relevant for, among other issues, personal predilections for the curious, discussions of human development, foreign policy, military activity, and social satire.

Inquisitive Multitudes

Perhaps the most appropriate place to start is the issue of who attended the shows. Entrance charges provide some clues. In the early to mid-nineteenth century, admission prices were sometimes as low as a shilling for the cheapest unreserved seats. More commonly, adults were charged between 2 and 3 shillings (most often 2 shillings and sixpence), with children half price (most often 1 shilling and sixpence). Where available, the fee for reserved seats was higher, usually starting from at least 2 shillings and rising to as much as 5 shillings.[4] By the later nineteenth century, showmen usually charged a shilling for adults and half price for children, with more expensive options ranging from 2 to 5 shillings still available. A shilling's admission ensured that the shows were far beyond the means of the urban poor.

For those able to spare a shilling or more, the pricing structure of available tickets, from expensive reserved seats to cheaper stalls, suggests differentiated audiences ranging from the aristocratic or nouveau-riche elite to professionals and portions of the middle classes. The shows evidently served as family entertainment, since the range of advertised admission prices and the images of the shows make it clear that men, women, and children all attended (figs. 63–66). Determining the ethnic background of consumers is more difficult. Images of consumers invariably contrast darker-skinned performers with lighter-hued spectators, but given the ethnic diversity of London, there is insufficient evidence from which to assume that spectators were solely white.[5] Moreover, it is worth bearing in mind that international fairs often attracted "imperial pilgrims": globe-trotting tourists from diverse ethnic backgrounds who attended exhibitions, sometimes systematically, and subsequently published accounts of their travels.[6]

In the early nineteenth century at least, human exhibitions offered connoisseurs of the curious significant opportunities for self-fashioning. Charles Mathews, actor, comedian, and "all his life a great sight-seer," frequented the "Exeter 'Change, the Tower, and the fairs in the neighbourhood of London, for the sole purpose of beholding such beings as were not elsewhere to be found."[7] His quest led to his befriending many of the stars of the London shows. For instance, the "Spotted Boy," a young black boy whose skin was mottled with patches of white, "loved him very much" and would play with him for hours; his death greatly saddened Mathews. Daniel Lambert, a man weighing more than 50 stone (700 lbs., 317 kg), and the Polish "dwarf," Count Boruwalski, were also friends, and Mathews and his wife would frequently entertain the count at their home. Mathews also went to see the emaciated "Living Skeleton" and Miss Crackham, a young lady measuring just 22 inches tall (55 cm, 1ft. 10 in.) and whose stage name, the "Sicilian Fairy," encapsulated her size and frailty. In 1810, he visited Sara Baartman and found her

surrounded by many persons, some females! One pinched her; one gentleman poked her with his cane; one lady employed her parasol to ascertain that all was, as she called it, "nattral." This inhuman baiting the poor creature bore with sullen indifference, except upon some provocation, when she seemed inclined to resent brutality, which even a Hottentot can understand. On these occasions it took all the authority of the keeper to subdue her resentment.[8]

By relating this encounter alongside visits to other living curiosities whom Mathews befriended, Baartman is effectively located within the broader context of metropolitan human display. Mathews's association was not a personal peculiarity, since foreign peoples and other human curiosities were often exhibited together. In *Sketches by "Boz"* (1836), Charles Dickens's description of Greenwich Fair illustrated the variety a single show could encompass: "The dwarfs are also objects of great curiosity, and as a dwarf, a giantess, a living skeleton, a wild Indian, and a 'young lady of singular beauty, with perfectly white hair and pink eyes,' and two or three natural curiosities, are usually exhibited together, for the small charge of a penny, they attract very numerous audiences."[9] Mathews's encounter also suggests that displays of foreign peoples complemented displays of anatomic curiosities and thus appealed to spectators who shared his proclivity for beholding the rare, unusual, or different. It has been suggested that by the mid-eighteenth century and through to the early nineteenth century, "the consumption of curiosity through experiences and objects denoted connoisseurship."[10] By the late nineteenth century, curiosity appears to have lost such connotations and become pejoratively associated with the spectacles of the emerging mass-market leisure industry.[11] However, while the

link between curiosity and connoisseurial interest remained, attending an
exhibition of living curiosities may have allowed consumers to express legitimate intellectual interest in the human exhibits while simultaneously
reinforcing their social status as virtuosos.

By the mid-nineteenth century, both press reviews and images suggest that displayed peoples' ethnic origin was consumers' primary attraction to the shows. In 1845, the *Pictorial Times* reported on the exhibition of
San children at the Egyptian Hall, Piccadilly. The boy, a physically mature
sixteen-year-old, was described as being 44 inches tall (1.12 m, 3 ft. 8 in.), and
the eight-year-old girl as being 32 inches tall (81 cm, 2 ft. 8 in.), encouraging their promotion as "perfect Model[s] of Man in miniature."[12] In the article's illustration, the children are depicted on a raised platform that, despite reaching the onlookers' waists, is still not high enough for the pair to
stand taller than the ladies and gentlemen gathered around (fig. 63). The
boy stands in the pose of the classical Apollo Belvedere sculpture, suggesting that he is an artwork to be closely examined and inviting comparisons
with the aesthetic and bodily perfection that Apollo came to represent in
the nineteenth century.[13] His sinewy muscles are sheathed in animal skins,
and the girl is wrapped in a cloak: both are said to wear the "dress of their
tribe (Hottentots)."[14] He holds aloft a spear to suggest he is both a hunter
and a warrior. In contrast, the girl's kneeling posture makes her appear
even more diminutive. She stares out from the center of the image, arresting the viewers' gaze, while her bare, developed breasts suggest premature
sexual maturity. On the left, a couple and a man smile; on the right, a man
and another couple look decidedly less pleased. The children's dark complexion and partial nudity are juxtaposed against the spectators' lighter
hue and covered flesh. The removed stance of the gathered men and

women effects and reinforces the social and cultural separation by marking them as observers rather than participants. Like promotional materials, the image uses stark contrasts (tall/short, clothed/unclothed, white/black, observers/subjects) to suggest that the exhibition is successful primarily because of the observational opportunities it provides.

Interest in displayed foreign peoples may be partly explained by the relative lack of such peoples on the British stage in the early to mid-nineteenth century.[15] Foreign peoples were played with enthusiasm, but "'natives' had to be *depicted*, not seen"; onstage, they were played by imitators, and many of the lead roles were prized.[16] The ethnic variety of the metropolitan population and traveling exhibitions provided ample opportunity to allow foreign peoples to tread the boards, but clearly this was resisted. London's black population is a notable exception, since Londoners' experience of black peoples was inextricably tied up with performance over a broad range of social situations, from buskers in the street to professional entertainers. From the 1820s, the association between black peoples and performance was strengthened by the number of actors painting themselves for theatrical roles, the emergence of Jim Crow theater, and the enormously successful minstrels that became a mainstay of mass entertainment for decades.[17] Yet despite the growing success of blackface entertainment, London's stages did not reflect the ethnic diversity of the streets until the later nineteenth and early twentieth centuries. Thus, commercial exhibitions may simply have been the best means of witnessing foreign peoples perform.

Whereas simply seeing foreigners perform may have been a thrill, other evidence suggests that consumers wanted to do more than merely look. In another image of the 1845 San children's exhibition, they are shown performing for a Victorian couple, but not on a platform or stage (fig. 64). While the lady looks attentively at the boy, her posture is distanced, and she appears decidedly unimpressed by him and his impotent spear. Meanwhile, the girl is holding the hand of the man and appears to be signaling, perhaps even talking, to him. He leans down attentively. In the background, another man examines a collection of prints illustrating African ethnic diversity that, along with numerous stuffed and mounted animals, were exhibited with the children.

Another image of the shows from 1899 presents an intriguing model of reciprocal observation (fig. 65). It depicts what appears to be a Victorian family attending the Savage South Africa exhibition at Earl's Court. The whole family is either bending or kneeling down at the entrance to a "native" hut in the site's mock kraal. As they stare into the hut, their gazes are met and returned by three Africans with heavily stereotyped expressions. In the late nineteenth and early twentieth centuries, representations of Africans employed new and, to modern eyes, increasingly crude caricatures; for example, they were often shown with large open-mouthed smiles and eating slices of watermelon.[18] The image of the "natives" peeping out of

FIGURE 64
*Bushmen Children,
Egyptian Hall, Picca-
dilly. (Illustrated Lon-
don News*, Septem-
ber 6, 1845, p. 160.
Author's collection.)

FIGURE 65
*(Facing) "Savage South
Africa" at Earl's Court:
A Peep at the Natives.
(Graphic*, June 24,
1899, p. 803. Author's
collection.)

the hut reflects these shifts; they almost melt into the black darkness and are only made visible by the whites of their eyes, their teeth (visible in semicircular smiles), and minimal reflections of light on their skin. At the same time, with its title "*Savage South Africa*" *at Earl's Court: A Peep at the Natives*, the image implies that both performers and spectators have been given the opportunity to meet "real natives." It and the *Pictorial Times* illustration (fig. 63) present the shows as encounters between different peoples; yet both also suggest a more complicated model of interaction between performers and patrons. While some consumers may have been content to observe, others clearly wished to converse and physically engage with foreign peoples, as alluded to in the background of *A Peep at the Natives* (fig. 65).

Eyewitness accounts confirm the central importance of interaction between consumers and exhibited peoples. For instance, in reports of the 1847 San exhibition (two men, two women, and a child) comments on these interactions figure prominently. During performances, consumers were able to shake hands with the troupe and often offered them small gifts of beads, cakes, toys, and trinkets.[19] These were received and rewarded with kisses on the hand of the bestower. During one performance, a woman from the audience held and played with the San baby while the women danced onstage. Upon the child's return, the mother kissed the hands of both the baby and the impromptu babysitter. At another performance, a man in possession of a musical snuffbox secretly wound it up and released the mechanism, startling a San man, who then examined it with interest.

"SAVAGE SOUTH AFRICA" AT EARL'S COURT : A PEEP AT THE NATIVES

DRAWN FROM LIFE BY W. T. MAUD

After performances, parties were permitted to apply to the troupe's guardian, Mr. Bishop, to gain admittance to their living quarters, where the San might be seen eating and smoking. Similarly, Scottish artist and popular illustrator Jemima Blackburn visited the Zulu exhibition of 1853 and produced a watercolor of her encounter (fig. 66). It depicts a throng of people surrounding the mother and child. The women appear to be captivated by the baby, with whom they eagerly play, while their own little boy appears ready to reach up and join in the game. The eager women appear to have forced several men, identifiable only by the hovering crowns of numerous tophats, to the back of the crowd. Meanwhile, the *sangoma* (wearing the animal-skin tunic) chats to a Zulu man, while yet another seems to be asleep. The sheer delight the audience found in interacting with the foreign peoples, whether it was surprising them with musical toys or mothering their infants, is the most striking aspect of eyewitness accounts and reviews. That such interaction was encouraged with whatever gifts were to hand, such as beads or food, bears witness to consumers' eagerness. Showmen facilitated such interactions by ensuring the appropriate behavior on the part of exhibit, employing translators to overcome language barriers, and even reprinting vocabularies in printed promotional materials.[20]

In some cases, the social interaction was considered to have overstepped the bounds of propriety. In August 1899, for instance, women were excluded from the Savage South Africa exhibition at Earl's Court. The problem arose when "rumours of discreditable proceedings" surfaced. "There had been cases of dames taking a savage for a drive in Hyde Park; and presents of bracelets and other trinkets were not uncommon." The press had inspired a moral panic, with the *Daily Mail* even launching a campaign to have the kraal closed. The London Exhibition Company, which managed the Earl's Court exhibition, initially introduced new regulations barring physical contact and begging for tips and establishing a new dress code, but these measures still failed to quell public concern; it then excluded women from the kraal altogether. The director of the show had protested, arguing that "after the most stringent enquiries" he had not been able to find anything to substantiate the accusations of indecency, "except the fact that some few women" had "from time to time touched the arms of the natives for the purposes of testing their biceps, which the natives had occasionally displayed" in a manner like the "photographs of [the first celebrity bodybuilder] Sandow," and that the women had "given pennies to and occasionally shaken hands with the natives." Nonetheless, any such "familiarities" had been entirely innocent, and he proposed that "these kindly attentions and sympathetic recognitions of the black man are likely to do good."[21]

Although the show's proprietors attempted to allay fears and the British press marked its disapproval, the ladies' conduct inspired fervent disgust in the Cape Town periodical the *Owl*. Its gossipy feature "It was the Owl that Shrieked" furiously observed,

FIGURE 66
Jemima Blackburn
at Charles Calde-
cott's 1853 exhi-
bition of Zulus.
(Jemima Blackburn
[1823–1909], *Meeting
the Zulus in London*,
1853, watercolor on
paper/Private Col-
lection, © Michael
Graham-Stewart/
The Bridgeman Art
Library.)

For a right down emetic some of the reading contained in the mail papers concerning the amatory adventures of the "ladies" at Earl's Court with the Kaffirs in the Savage South Africa Show about takes the biscuit. Ladies lolling in their victorias down West with a great hulking Kaffir beside them. Faugh, the dirty sluts ought to be whipped at the cart's tail for making such a loathsome exhibition of themselves. So they would be probably in the western States, whilst their paramours would be run up the nearest tree.[22]

The crassly explicit racism of the *Owl* typifies the publication's disapproval of the show; more interestingly, it picked up on the same tensions of what could be deemed acceptable behavior within exhibition venues and how this might, in turn, cause social disruption outside their confines. The article was one in a number that was highly critical of the show and its potential to upset social order, particularly on the part of performers. On one occasion, for instance, the *Owl* reported that the African men involved in the show had formed a habit of stopping and insulting white women passing by Earl's Court. Such behavior implied that the men had forgotten their true social station and instead become dangerously uppity: "It strikes me rather forcibly that, before this thing is done with, it is going to be a perfect curse to the country."[23] The concern prompted both an attempted policing of contact and assurances that all was, and had been, aboveboard. After having failed to convince the owner of the site that all was scrupulous, the show's proprietor, Frank Fillis, moved the exhibition to the Olympia, but by then the Boer War had begun eliciting a new raft of concerns as the British started to lose battle after battle.

By considering the experiences of performers as they took to the stage and acculturated to life abroad, chapter 4 suggested ways in which performers both unsettled and redrew the social distinctions involved in human displays. Yet, as the discussion over ladies' admission to Earl's Court suggests, spectators might also be seen to have failed to observe conventional social norms—or at least created situations in which their motives were questioned, causing raised eyebrows far beyond the shows' venues. As chapter 1 suggested, wandering the streets of London involved distanced and fleeting observational practices in which the histories of passersby were reconstructed solely from glances; but clearly, many urban spectators were left wishing for more. Exhibitors capitalized on the thirst for interaction by charging these spectators for the privilege of being able to stare at, talk to, shake hands with, and bestow gifts on displayed peoples; their willingness to allow and facilitate such interaction suggests its importance for commercial success. Patrons could satisfy their curiosity but also demonstrate humanity by asking questions about a performer's health, eating habits, or emotional well-being. Simultaneously, patrons asserted power, since exhibits were required to answer questions in exchange for being paid or further rewarded with tips. When performers did assert themselves, they were often recorded as being ill tempered or intractable. Paying a shilling or more absolved one of observing many social conventions that governed public politeness. It is safe to assume, for example, that most if not all patrons would never have dreamed of approaching a woman in the street and poking her buttocks to assess their true size (as with Baartman), no matter how curious. Equally, publicly addressing a complete stranger to question him about his dietary requirements and physical exercise—a common question posed to obese curiosities—would have elicited suspicion.[24] Showmen removed such barriers to investigation while legitimating actions that would otherwise have proved improper.

Social interaction extended beyond the boundaries of commercial exhibition venues to more private spaces. George Catlin and the Bakhoje, for example, received numerous invitations to attend dinner parties at the residences of fashionable members of society. Quaker physician Thomas Hodgkin invited them to partake of "an excellent dinner," where they "tried the use of the knife and fork in the English style. Dr. Hodgkin being of the Society of Friends, they received much kind and friendly advice from him, which they never forgot; and from the unusual shape of his dress, they called him afterwards (not being able to recollect his name) Tchonawappa (the straight coat)."[25] Hodgkin had a long-standing passion for reforms in medical education and a keen interest in foreign affairs. A founding member of the Aborigines Protection Society (established 1837) and the Ethno-

BEN SIDONIA SMOKING THE CALUMET WITH THE IOWAYS.

FIGURE 67
*Ben Sidnonia Smoking
the Calumet with
the Ioways. (Punch 7
[1844]: 100. Author's
collection.)*

logical Society of London (established 1843), his dinner invitation suggests that he used the presence of the Bakhoje in London to combine his interest in philanthropy and human variety.[26]

The group was also invited to breakfast at the Park Lane home of Benjamin Disraeli, then a Member of Parliament.[27] After "a little conversation," Disraeli personally gave the group a grand tour of the property. He led them "through the different apartments of his house, where he put in their hands, and explained to them, much to their gratification, many curious daggers, sabres, and other weapons and curiosities of antiquity." A champagne breakfast followed the tour. The party's doctor kept pronouncing that certain items, especially the champagne, were "good." The Disraelis and their friends were clearly delighted with their guests, and for the final dish served a plate of gifts, including jewelry and ornaments. Before leaving, the Bakhoje smoked a pipe while chatting with their hosts, an event that *Punch* deemed worthy of commemoration (fig. 67).

Afterward, Catlin noted that altogether "the pictured buffalo robes—the rouged heads and red feathers—the gaudy silks, and bonnets, and ribbons—glistening lances and tomahawks—and black coats, formed a novel group for the gaze."[28] Although his comment is a conventional and stylized means of drawing social comparisons, it also hints at the possibility that informal contact with exhibited peoples provided patrons with an unusual means of defining their social status. Attending a show or arranging a private viewing may have been as much about participating in the season's latest fashionable amusement, and thus reinforcing one's own standing, as about seeing the living curiosities. Disraeli's invitation certainly confirmed his position as a man whose wealth and connections assured him a private audience with London's latest celebrities, in which case the contrasting dress of his guests demarcated between their distinct ethnicities and roles as fashionable people and fashionable amusements.

Clearly, ethnic differences between displayed peoples and patrons mattered in achieving the shows' commercial success; however, consumers did not simply lump displayed peoples together into uniform categories such as "foreign," "different," or "other." Instead, patrons came to distinguish many fine-grained ethnic differences. In turn, such differences, whether they were viewed as existing between spectators or among the different varieties of performers, gave rise to multiple, and sometimes conflicting, interpretations of the shows' significance.

"Unquestionable natives"

The authenticity of performers appears to have been one of the consumers' most pressing initial concerns. The physician John Conolly, for instance, believed that of the "second group of asserted American aborigines, Ioways and Ogibbeways, the genuineness of a portion appeared doubtful"; despite his misgivings, he conceded that "the greater number were unquestionable natives of a wild land, whose unmitigated shouts and exciting war-dances bore the stamp of fierce reality."[29] The notion that exhibitions could be deemed authentic because they were performed by untrained people found an exponent in a reviewer of the 1853 Zulu exhibition, who argued that the "efforts of these rude actors, ... out of their very lack of training, give a manifestly truthful representation of savage life."[30] Yet these criticisms were relatively minimal when compared with the furor stirred by the claims of Joseph Morris, who exhibited the "Aztec Lilliputians." Maximo and Bartola were displayed as the last surviving representatives of the Aztecs from the forgotten city of Iximaya (see chapters 2 and 3). They were claimed to be of a priestly caste venerated by the city's inhabitants but dwindling in number because they were forbidden from marrying outside their social standing. Thus, the children were not only the last surviving examples of the Aztecs but also objects of religious worship. Exhibitors were quick to capitalize on this distinctive ethnicity and social status, declaring that

They do not appeal to the public as dwarfs, hunchbacks, Tom Thumbs, Siamese Twins or other distorted curiosities: but belong to another category. While to a European public they are sui generis, they are placed before the public as exemplars of a race of people hitherto unknown—a race unlike in form and feature all the modern inhabitants of the earth.[31]

The claims were immediately subject to considerable skepticism and "soon made them objects of interest" with "Anatomists, physiologists, and men of science," who were all duly invited to "see these novelties of nature."[32] However, the critical attention also created a situation in which even lay consumers were expected to assess the exhibitors' sensational claims regarding Maximo and Bartola's provenance and heritage.

For those who were content to accept performers as authentic, the invariable question was, what kind of people were they? In answering, spectators used the shows as opportunities for critical reflection on the nature and significance of human variety. In 1844, one reviewer of the Bakhoje encouraged "lovers of nature in its primitive state" to visit the noble troupe as examples of "rude and half-wild children of the forest," since their "natures exhibit[ed] mingled elements of man's innate worth and vices, independent of civilization," and as such were "subjects of peculiar interest to thinking mind."[33] Just a year later, regarding an exhibition of the San, the editor of the *English Gentleman* informed readers that he had heard "the *humanity* of these pigmies most learnedly disputed" at a recent meeting of the Ethnological Society of London. "It was argued that they could not be other than monkeys, and the language by which they expressed their thoughts, and established their affinity to the great family of man, was treated as the *chattering* of the simian tribe!" Clearly shocked at the bold assertion, the gentleman invited the "curious in these matters" to avail themselves of the "opportunity of determining the knotty point by a close examination of the *physique* of the poor little things."[34] The journalist for the *Times* was far more forthright in expressing a sense of disgust: "[They are a] stunted family of African dwarfs." "In appearance," he remarked, they were "little above the monkey tribe, and scarcely better than the mere brutes of the field. They are continually crouching, warming themselves by the fire, chattering or growling, smoking, &c. They are sullen, silent, and savage—mere animals in propensity, and worse than animals in appearance."[35] The reviewer for the *Athenaeum* shared similarly mixed feelings of repugnance and intellectual fascination:

[They are] the most curious of all the human curiosities that in an age abounding in such importations have solicited the attention of the sight-seers or scientific inquirers of the metropolis. They are of the very lowest type of humanity—little above the monkey-tribe—and with habits and propensities scarcely distinguishing them from the brutes. Here in the midst of an overdone civilisation, is the natural man caught in his very lowest stage of development; and the moral philosopher may speculate usefully on the analogies between the brutes whom civilisation in its excesses *makes* and those who are so for want of it.[36]

Even when consumers shared an evident dislike of performers, as here, they could be expected to be intellectually stimulated, because the shows offered "admirers of 'pure nature'" an opportunity to "confirm their speculations on unsophisticated man, and woman also, or repudiate them, by a visit to these specimens."[37] Indeed, one reviewer believed the San exhibition was so "well calculated to remove prejudices" that it would "make people think aright of the times when 'wild in his woods the noble savage ran.'"[38]

Others deployed a more benevolent tone. One journalist for the *Morning Advertiser* noted that the eldest San woman had a "lovely-looking infant at the breast, to which she seemed greatly attached, and which she fondled with all the care and tenderness of the most affectionate of European mothers." Another reviewer, for *John Bull*, also mentioned the mother's kisses, her suckling of her baby, and the "manner in which each of the four took the hand of any of the company who proffered that token of good will" as evidence of the San's capacity for "kindly and gentle emotions." One reviewer was especially sympathetic, since he believed that

a more painfully striking spectacle can hardly be imagined than was the advance of the four bewildered savages (two men, two women). Their fear was evident from their reluctant and crouching approach, and their stealthy glances, characterised both by ferocity and terror. One of them held his hand horizontally over his eyes, as if he were dazzled by the lights and scared by the company.[39]

An individual with missionary or philanthropic leanings, the reviewer further observed, "We trust that the appearance in this land of these wild and most inferior specimens of mankind, will instruct us in our duty to their nearly helpless and half-famished brethren in South Africa." Suggestively, the comments indicate how disconcerting and distressing the group found the process of being exhibited. They also demonstrate how the same exhibition could give rise to conflicting interpretations of both the displayed individuals and the significance of their actions. Many of the reviewers already cited used the San as exemplars of the kind of physical and social development they thought justified their derogation. Others interpreted the San's behavior, such as the crouching approach or the suckling of the child, more favorably as an indication of innate emotional capacity and the fear bred of being in such an alien environment.

Such reviews suggest that consumers, whether interested in "popular gratification" or "rational curiosity," were often expected to reflect on, and perhaps choose between, two contrasting views of savagery: noble and barbaric.[40] Advocates of the former were most common around the mid-nineteenth century, when the theory of the noble savage gained renewed interest. It had originally achieved prominence in the eighteenth century when many, such as French philosopher Jean-Jacques Rousseau, argued that humans were at their most pure when unencumbered by the trappings of civilization and education.[41] In this sentimentalized view, indigenous peoples were argued to possess many desirable characteristics, including innocence, moral fortitude, innate wisdom, and untutored understanding of the natural world; civilization simply degraded these original virtues. Proponents of the latter, less romantic view were also recurrent commentators on the shows. By the late nineteenth century in particular, distinctly unsentimental images of displayed peoples become more commonly acceptable.[42] Perhaps inevitably, these views have been routinely promoted as conclusively emblematic of the show's receptions. Indeed, their usually deeply racist tone can easily be made to qualify arguments that try to homogenize the show's receptions into unequivocal examples of racist spectatorship relying on voyeuristic gazing to consume its passive victims. Yet, as this discussion suggests, spectators exercised a form of observational judgment when attending the shows and did not simply adopt or regurgitate the claims of either advertising or journalists or moral philosophers wholesale. Rather, these sources were often the starting points from which to reflect critically on human developmental stages, and evidently, many remained unconvinced that displayed peoples were either noble or beyond redemption or inhuman.

For others, the most pressing concern was not the performers' authenticity or capacity to act as exemplars of human development but the moral and religious obligation to safeguard their spirituality and welfare. For instance, in 1899 the Aborigines Protection Society argued that whether for "amusement or alleged instruction," "all such exhibitions" were "on every ground objectionable." The year's most prominent chance to see foreign peoples, Savage South Africa, had been causing so "much anxiety" that the society's members appointed themselves the task of checking the pastoral care provided for the African performers by the show's manager.[43] Responding to the concern, the show's organizers invited the society to personally inspect arrangements, and cited several factors in their favor: the performers had agreed to be exhibited and had not been engaged under "false representations"; they were being taught useful trades so that they could return home with useful new skills; they were also "better fed, clothed, housed, cared for and protected in a moral way" than ever before; they were not allowed to leave the grounds for their own safety; Rev. Charles Johnson, of Rorke's Drift and resident in Africa for over forty years, had been engaged to provide a Sunday service for the performers' "religious welfare"; and the show's proprietor had provided a guarantee to return every one of them to their respective homes at the close of the show. Upon inspection, the society acknowledged that "in the present case exceptional care appears to be taken, in most respects, as regards the health and comfort of the natives"; nonetheless, it remained unconvinced that being cooped up at Earl's Court would not demoralize the performers; that their health would remain unthreatened by any "inclement" weather; that any useful trades were being learned, "unless skill as theatrical performers in begging for money, and in bartering the simple articles which some of them manufacture in their own fashion" could be deemed so; and that such care would be taken once the performer left London to be exhibited abroad.[44] Such anxieties were not uncommon but did find their most vocal expression in the criticisms of missionaries and philanthropists.

The steps taken by the Aborigines Protection Society are highly suggestive of how human displays could both focus and become the subjects of broader debates on the treatment of foreign peoples.[45] For such discussions to make sense, the shows had to be made, and consistently interpreted, as relevant to contemporary political and military activity; such associations were not an inherent feature of the shows but forged by the shows' patrons and critics responding to displayed peoples' presence abroad and onstage. One of the most instructive examples of how such relevance was achieved and maintained may be found in the case of displayed Africans.

Timely Appearances

Of all the displayed peoples discussed in the press, the Zulus are most likely to have been deemed praiseworthy. Many writers argued that they were exceptional warriors that were "superior to both [the Bushman and Hottentot], in personal appearance, bodily strength and martial spirit." Indeed, their "physical characteristics" in both "external form and figure" were often said to be "wholly at variance with those of the other natives of Africa," since they were "neither a Bushman nor a Hottentot.... [The Zulu] has a peculiar countenance:—the elevated forehead and prominent nose of the European, the high cheek-bones of the Hottentot, and the thick lips of the Negro."[46] Paying such close attention to differences in facial structure, bodily form, and complexion in order to draw hierarchical distinctions between African peoples was a common practice in both reviews and travel literature. For example, another journalist remarked that the Zulus were "finely-formed men, lithe and active in their movements, their skin being a dark copper colour."[47] Yet another argued that the group was "for the most part a handsome well-formed race, not deficient of a certain natural grace" which was well complemented by "wearing a picturesque and rather becoming costume."[48] Still another felt that so "much gentleness, such extraordinary skill in the native games, and such noble muscular development tend to make these people peculiarly interesting."[49] Yet despite the Zulus' distinctive physique, the popularity of their exhibitions doubtless stemmed from, and was strengthened by, British activity in the Cape of Good Hope.

Circulated in the show's advertising, the press, and travel literature, tales of violence, border conflict, and British military activity ensured that spectators were attracted by the possibility of witnessing the Zulus' martial capabilities. In both 1853 and 1879, the public was given the chance to meet the mighty Zulus, and the managers of both shows (Caldecott and Farini, respectively) capitalized on both the ethnic novelty and the military connections. The frisson was partly fueled by the relative lack of contact between Europeans and the Zulus until the mid-nineteenth century. Although the San and the Khoekhoe had been known to Europeans since the earliest Portuguese travelers had set foot on the Cape's coast in the sixteenth century, the Zulus lived further inland and were only routinely observed by settlers from the early to mid-nineteenth century onward. Thus, Caldecott claimed his exhibition was of "intrinsic interest," since it brought an "African savage" from "beyond the confines of civilisation" before the public. He carefully informed his audience that the Zulus came from the "very verge of the unexplored deserts of a great continent," and that it was "only within the last thirty years, and since the colonization of Natal, that they have become known to the enterprising traveler from the shores of Europe."[50] Given the novelty of the performers, the audience was encouraged to view their participation as akin to the experiences of an "enterprising traveler." This created a sense of privilege, since members of the audience regardless of their status within Britain were encouraged to feel on a par with an intrepid few in the field. Furthermore, as already noted, Caldecott deliberately conflated the Zulus with the Xhosa to take advantage of contemporary interest in the Xhosa Wars (see chapter 2). His strategy was not missed by the press. Reports often focused on the scenes of battle in the show and the weapons used, such as the war shield and the iconic assegai, which the men dexterously wielded while threatening to thwart British ambitions in the region.[51]

Farini's exhibition was scheduled to open in July 1879 to take advantage of the news of Cetshwayo's removal from the throne; however, the military connection almost forestalled it entirely. Richard Assheton Cross, Home Secretary of Prime Minister Benjamin Disraeli's second Conservative government, objected to the show on the grounds that given the "circumstances" of the ongoing Anglo-Zulu War, the exhibition "would not meet the approval of the country or be in consonance with the general feeling of the community." Parliament's rowdy lower house resounded with cries of "Hear, hear."[52] While fellow Members of Parliament cooed approval, Cross's objections became the focal point of much sarcasm in the press (see below). Eventually, the exhibition continued, but only when there had been a change in venue.

Similarly, the interest in Baartman's exhibition must partly lie in her relevance to discussions of slavery. Indeed, its pertinence was cemented when her exhibition aroused intense public interest after abolitionists objected to her display.[53] On October 12, 1810, the *Morning Chronicle*, a reforming newspaper, published a letter of indictment from "AN ENGLISHMAN," who believed it was "contrary to every principle of morality and good order" to allow Baartman's exhibition, as it connected "offence to public decency, with that most horrid of all situations, Slavery."[54] Hendrick Cesars responded with two letters, one of which forcefully asked, "Has she not as good a right to exhibit herself as an Irish Giant or a Dwarf?"[55] The abolitionist interest prompted a court case. Baartman's self-appointed protectors argued that the exhibit was indecent and, crucially, that she was being held and exhibited against her will. In conjunction with the African Association, the abolitionists arranged for Baartman's repatriation to the Cape. Ultimately, the court ruled in favor of the defendant, Cesars, upon the presentation of a contract between him, Baartman, and Alexander Dunlop—the naval surgeon who had accompanied her to England, the show's manager, and with whom Cesars had set up the London show.[56] With the contract in hand, the judge felt it inappropriate to press charges, and so the show continued.

The court case came at an especially important juncture in the relationship between the Khoekhoe and European settlers in the Cape of Good Hope. Early settlers at the Cape employed a system of indentured servitude to supply labor for their farms. Throughout the eighteenth century, however, it became increasingly difficult to find people willing to enter into such arrangements, since many colonial immigrants aspired to be masters of their own land.[57] Settlers were forced to look to African peoples for labor. Initial attempts at enslavement failed, and alternative sources of labor were imported from West Africa. Over the eighteenth century, chattel slavery became an essential part of the socioeconomic makeup of the Cape region. The Khoekhoe initially survived by exchanging livestock for goods with the Europeans who occupied their grazing lands. However, by the late eighteenth century, African peoples had largely disappeared as autonomous societies through a number of smallpox epidemics and European intervention breaking up local socioeconomic structures. Thus, African peoples became increasingly likely to be tied to settlers' land as chattel slaves. Although the Khoekhoe had not been systematically enslaved since the foundation of the colony, they were continually subjugated. In 1809, the "new rulers enacted the Caledon Code which placed limits on the 'powers colonists had previously had over their laborers' as it reaffirmed in law the servile status of the Khoekhoe and legitimated the use of unfree labor as the basis of the colonial economy."[58] Just two years after the abolition of the British slave trade, three years after the British took over government of the Cape, and one year before Baartman's exhibition, the legislation deliberately attempted to define the status of the Khoekhoe as laborers; consequently, the press coverage of Baartman's court case made her explicitly relevant to contemporary issues, such as labor shortages in the Cape Colony and slavery.

Appreciating the associations between contemporary reportage and the shows is essential to understanding their commercial appeal. Despite the substantial and growing heterogeneity of London's streets discussed in chapter 1, it is important to remember that the world's peoples were not equally represented there. For example, London's black population may have been one of the most visible ethnic minority groups in residence; however, most of these were originally slaves and thus of African American, Caribbean, or West Indian extraction. Able to speak English, dressed in European attire, and often converts to Christianity, they were relatively integrated into urban life, whether as servants or more equally as among the lower classes. Yet when Baartman arrived on these shores, even Londoners with considerable experience of the city's black population would have been extremely unlikely to have had any acquaintance with a resident Khoekhoe woman.[59]

Similarly, when Robert Knox introduced a group of San to the metropolis he carefully established that they were the first of their kind to be brought over for the purpose of exhibition. The San were ethnically distinct, and Londoners knew it; indeed, Knox was able to list every San individual whom the public could have viewed before his show arrived on the scene. Apart from Baartman, who he argued was of a mixed caste, he mentioned just three other individuals, all of whom were brought over by missionaries rather than commercially exhibited.[60] Whatever the exact truth of Knox's claim to novelty, it makes clear that there were still people, such as the San, whose arrival on British shores was exceptional. It is easy to forget that these differences existed, since accounts of displayed peoples often imply that a different color alone is sufficient to relegate exhibits to the status of exotic. This ignores not only the heterogeneity of London but also ethnic differences between peoples of the same color—differences of which the public was aware and showmen capitalized on. It is true that displayed black peoples could be made to correspond with the resident black population, but this was not a given. Thus, patrons were paying to view difference, but not difference resulting from color or even ethnic origin alone; rather, they were often paying to participate in exhibitions with immediate political relevance.

Reportage may have associated displayed peoples with ongoing political, military, and imperial activity, but the shows were made relevant to even broader themes by their appropriation of travel literature.

Travelers' Tales

The public's fascination with travel and exploration, and the print culture it generated, was critical in shaping the shows' receptions. Produced by explorers, missionaries, colonial officials, and tourists, not only was travel literature widely appropriated in exhibition advertising, but it appears to have been the resource consumers used most frequently to interpret human displays. Just as physiognomic manuals helped train urban spectators to decode peoples' histories from brief glances in London's streets, travel literature could be used as an authoritative guide to ostensively train spectators to classify displayed peoples into specific ethnic groups. This use is vital, because being viewed as "foreign," "savage," or "uncivilized" is not the equivalent of being categorized as belonging to a particular ethnic group. It is particularly important for the earlier half of the century, when foreign travel was considerably more expensive and available to far fewer people than became possible in the later nineteenth century.[61] As a result, travelers' observations on peoples' natural habitats, religion, and social organization were routinely compared with the live performances spectators attended. Managers ensured that this material was tailored to meet consumer needs by distilling the passages they believed were most relevant and making them more accessible than the originals in the shows' promotional literature. In addition, they drew direct associations between such literature and topical events, such as the Anglo-Zulu War of 1879. Such associations firmly located displayed peoples within broader social and political discussions in the press while helping consumers to learn about differences between ethnic types.

That displayed peoples were unequivocally interpreted as vivified illustrations of travelers' tales is most evident in press reviews. Witness an 1845 *Morning Herald* reviewer of the San's performance:

The accounts which travelers have given of this nomadic race are justified by the examples which Mr. Bishop shows us. They seem dull and apathetical, but have an expression indicative of latent craftiness and suspicion. The two women are terribly ugly, and will not be likely to challenge the attention of gallants in this country and provoke the jealousy of their flat-nosed partners. They occasionally harangue the audience, and exhibit the "clacking sound of the tongue, and the drawling way of ending their sentences," which historians have described.[62]

Here the San's perceived expressions of cunning, physical ugliness, and speech patterns are interpreted as living embodiments of countless anecdotes. Moreover, by explicitly citing the performers within the framework of travel accounts, the journalist recasts his observations from isolated instances into evidence of broader maxims that, in turn, both reflected and created contemporary racialism.

Likewise, in reviewing the same group of San performers, the *Morning Chronicle* argued that "many of the inferior animals" exhibited

a greater development of the higher faculties than this savage specimen of the human kind. The beaver, for example, possesses the faculty of constructiveness to a very marked extent. The Bosjesman on the contrary, do not appear, as far as we can ascertain, to have any notion of raising huts or cabins, but they wander about in herds or tribes, in search of food and the exigencies of the hour.[63]

The reviewer concluded that the San's lack of personal property and indolence placed them on the very lowest rung of social and moral development.[64] Moreover, the group was unfavorably compared to the industrious beaver, whose natural habit of building log dams was anthropomorphized in order to naturalize the values associated with Christian morality.[65] Taking up a point made in the show's accompanying lecture, the journalist cited the "singular fact" that the San brain had the same convolutions on both sides, "a mark peculiar to the lower animals," as further evidence of their poor development and "marked resemblance to the baboon, ourang-outang, or chimpanzee."[66] By reiterating these common tropes, the reviewer articulated the relevance of the shows in observing human variety. Furthermore, by using the values associated with hard work and personal property as the criteria for judging human social development, he created, shaped, and perpetuated a view of humanity in which the San were considered distinctly lacking in the rudiments of full human development.

The routine derogation of the San relied heavily on the published work of Martin Henry Lichtenstein, a German explorer and physician to the governor of the Cape of Good Hope. His *Travels in South Africa* (1812–15) was often either referred to or partially reprinted, making it possibly the most widely used publication in discussions of exhibited Africans.[67] One passage in particular is worth examining in detail, because it encapsulates some of the most recurrent observations in discussions of the San. After meeting a group of San, Lichtenstein noted,

They were all strikingly low in stature, and seemed as if half famished. One of them, and by no means the least of the party, was measured and found to be only four feet three inches high [51 in., 1.31 m]: he appeared between forty and fifty years of age. The women were still less, and ugly in the extreme.... [In comparison with the Hottentots] their eyes are infinitely more wild and animated, and their whole countenance far more expressive, exhibiting stronger symptoms of suspicion and apprehension; all their actions indicate strong passion much more forcibly.... They have no property to furnish them with food in an easy and convenient manner ..., but are obliged constantly, by means of fraud and artifice, to procure a supply of the most pressing necessaries.... [They have invented] poisoned arrows, with which they can hit to a certainty those wild animals of the field whose strength and swiftness would otherwise be an overmatch for them.... [When the poisoned animal has been tracked] to kill it entirely, to cut out the poisoned part, and to begin devouring the prey, are acts which follow each other with the utmost possible rapidity; nor is the spot quitted till the last bone is entirely cleaned.[68]

Many of these observations, such as the San's diminutiveness, wild eyes, and ugliness, resonate with press reviews.[69] Their physical appearance in particular became such a focal point that years later, Livingstone lamented that "the Bushmen specimens brought to Europe have been selected, like costermongers' dogs, on account of their extreme ugliness; consequently English ideas of the whole tribe are formed in the same way as if the ugliest specimens of the English were exhibited in Africa as characteristic of the entire British nation."[70] Meanwhile, many of Lichtenstein's observations on San social organization became regarded as definitive traits, and contributed to their classification as among the most poorly developed of all humans. Adaptations to the San's nomadic hunter-gatherer lifestyle, such as few material possessions to aid mobility, fueled discussions that presumed the superiority, certainly the preferability, of a sedentary and commercial way of life.[71] The San's cunning as hunters who used poison (rather than the more noble spear or bow), precariousness of their existence (as entailed by their want of future planning and agriculture), and lack of material wealth and personal property were all tropes that became ammunition for those who argued that they were, at best, humans in need of improvement or, at worse, akin to beasts guided only by their passions and at the mercy of the elements.[72]

Managers skillfully tailored the material they used from travel literature in order to make it as relevant as possible to Britain's military operations. For instance, in 1853 the Zulus' manager, Caldecott, provided a brief
lecture on their manners and customs before the performers appeared onstage. One reviewer remarked,

From his [Caldecott's] description of the Zulus, a residence among them must
be anything but agreeable; for though they are hospitable, and much given
to song and dance of the sort, they have an awkward habit of cracking skulls
on the slightest provocation, or, just as often, on no provocation at all, which
would seem to make a native Zulu something like old Lambro, "a good friend,
but bad acquaintance." The thirst of Zulu kings for blood seems almost in-
satiable, it being no uncommon occurrence for a few thousands of his Majesty's subjects to be slaughtered by his warriors in one royal *battue*; and the
wars they carry on against neighbouring tribes are, as far as possible, wars of
extermination, neither age nor sex being spared.[73]

The satirization of Zulu government as simultaneously treacherous and
violent was reinforced by alluding to Lambro, a pirate who captured slaves
and "surprised men with a sword" in Lord Byron's epic poem *Don Juan*.[74]
More important, Caldecott's lecture and the reviewer's account drew directly from Isaacs's *Travels and Adventures in Eastern Africa* (1836).[75]

Isaacs's published observations were mined for information on the Zulus much as Lichtenstein was cited as an authoritative source on the San.
Clearly paraphrasing Isaacs, the show's pamphlet described Zulu government as "perfect despotism."[76] The reports of brutality were substantiated
by Isaacs's account of meeting Shaka. Isaacs noted that when "ordering
any of his subjects to be killed, Chaka [sic] never gave his reason for con-
signing them to death until it was too late to recal [sic] the sentence of execution." He ruled in a climate of such fear that a single "sign, given by
the pointing of his finger, or by the terrible declination of his head, was
promptly obeyed, and as promptly executed, by any one present."[77] It is unclear whether the killings were to slake a limitless bloodlust or a carefully
calculated means of displaying Shaka's control to a man he knew would
be able to regale outsiders and enemies with tales of his power. Either way,
both Caldecott's lecture and the show's pamphlet publicized Shaka as man
whose reign relied on shockingly brutal means of maintaining control. In
turn, this was reiterated and disseminated by the reviewer of the Zulu exhibition as an exemplary case of despotic capriciousness.

Drawing again on Isaacs, the reviewer further substantiated his views
on the perceived irrationality and cruelty of Zulu customs in a discussion
of royal succession. "The King, in his turn, must keep a sharp lookout for
himself after he has passed the half-way house of life, for, according to Zulu
notions of poetic justice, when grey hairs and wrinkles begin to overtake
the royal savage, it is lawful for his nearest relatives to put him to death."[78]
Again, this passage drew on Isaacs and the show's pamphlet, describing the

"barbarous customs" associated with electing a new king. He "must neither have wrinkles nor grey hairs," as they disqualified anyone from "becoming a monarch of a warlike people." Given such limitations, it was "equally indispensable" that the ruling king "never exhibit those proofs of having become unfit and incompetent to reign," and so seek to "conceal these indications" as long as he possibly could.[79] The importance of disguising age was reinforced by Isaacs's anecdotal insistence that Shaka had secretly asked him to procure some hair dye as soon as he had become aware that such a tonic existed.[80] Essentially, Isaacs's travelogue, like so many others, became a multipurpose tool. It could be used to garner relevant information on displayed peoples' cultures, provide an insight into Britain's military opposition, and bolster broader culturally chauvinist attitudes.

Tracing the appropriation of travel literature, as seen here, is critical in understanding how consumers interpreted the shows. Clearly, travelers' writings were one of the most significant resources spectators used to acquire the culturally specific information they needed to understand live performances. Without this descriptive material, even if they were able to identify specific songs or dances as part of a marriage ceremony or preparations for battle or medical treatment (from personal experience or promotional material), they were unlikely to be able to relate their experiences to a broader cultural context, such as the imperative placed on a ruling Zulu monarch's being able to conceal or disguise any signs of aging. Such widespread appropriation of travel literature also suggests that spectators are likely to have been far more informed than we might expect if we were to assume that consumers uncritically accepted and regurgitated the claims of promotional materials.[81] Rather, as even this brief discussion suggests, spectators were often able to draw on quite detailed and specific information regarding displayed peoples' physical attributes, histories, and social organization to critique and contextualize their performances. Whereas some consumers took obvious interest in displayed peoples' lives, others relied on the cultural gulf between spectators and displayed peoples to discuss matters a little closer to home.

Telescopic Philanthropy and Fashionable Amusement

In May 1853, Dickens wrote to his friend and illustrator John Leech, asking him to join him for dinner the coming Thursday, after which he intended to pay a visit to the "savages at Hyde Park Corner."[82] Just over two weeks later, he penned "The Noble Savage" for readers of the weekly periodical he edited, *Household Words*. Ostensibly a review of the Zulu exhibition, it aired his views on missionary philanthropy, imperial expansion, and the impending death of the "noble savage." Other reviewers had been impressed. The journalist for the *Times*, for instance, remarked that "if 11 English actors could be found so completely to lose themselves in the characters they assumed, histrionic art would be in a state truly magnificent."[83] However, Dickens remained decidedly more reticent in his praise:

What a visitor left to his own interpretings and imaginings might suppose these noblemen might be about, when they give vent to that pantomimic expression which is quite settled to be the natural gift of the savage, I cannot possibly conceive; for it is much too luminous for my personal civilisation that it conveys no idea to my mind beyond a general stamping, ramping and raving, remarkable (as everything in savage life is) for its dire uniformity.[84]

The simmering sarcasm was intended to undercut any discussion of the show in the positive terms associated with attributing a natural sense of morality or grace to peoples he considered savage. Using the terminology of pantomime rather than drama, he undermined both the Zulus as performers and attempts to interpret the show as anything other than farcical. The "savage" was not only a "prodigious nuisance" but "something highly desirable to be civilised off the face off the earth."[85] Far from being a call to arms for mass genocide, however, the comment alluded to the possible extinction of "savage" lifestyles by progressively extending Britain's civilizing influence and reforming the cultural practices he found so undesirable.

Dickens's review also addressed his fellow consumers: "It is not the miserable nature of the noble savage that is the new thing; it is the whimpering over him with maudlin admiration, and the affecting to regret him, and the drawing of any comparison of advantage between the blemishes of civilisation and the tenor of his swinish life."[86] By extending his attention to fellow consumers' "maudlin admiration," Dickens painted as uncomplimentary a picture of their behavior as of the Zulus' performance. His antipathy exposed an intense personal dislike of missionary philanthropy. The year before, Dickens had begun publishing *Bleak House* (1852–53) in serial form. In the novel, a character named Mrs. Jellyby ignored the needs of her own family while she fussed and fretted over building a model farm to provide humanitarian aid to the residents of Borrioboola-Gha, a town located on the banks of the Niger.[87] It had been written in the wake of an infamous missionary and commercial trade expedition to the Niger, begun in 1841 and sponsored by the Society for the Extinction of the Slave Trade and for Civilisation of Africa.[88] It proved to be a disaster and, in Dickens's view, wasted considerable material and financial resources on telescopic philanthropy that could have been put to good use at home.

Punch also lampooned the fashionable socialites who fussed over the Zulus:

We see in each movement such truth of expression,
　　Their stampings and kickings are done with such grace,
That ladies of title e'en make the confession
　　That they in the Savage—nobility trace![89]

As the magazine pointed out, London's own savages lived in slums and rookeries only a short distance away from the gallery in which the Zulus attracted so much attention:

It is all very proper to say that a baby
     Might be found nearer to home, if we sought for a pet,
And that in the back courts of St. Giles's, it may be,
     Hordes of young savages there we could get:
But, they've no fancy dresses to set off their figures,
     And nothing is thought of an every-day sight;
And "UNCLE TOM"'s roused such a *penchant* for niggers,
     That dark skins must now take precedence over white.[90]

Both Dickens and *Punch* used the commercial success of the Zulu exhibition to satirize and outright attack long-sighted humanitarianism. By employing the trope of the urban savage, they alienated the urban poor and drew direct comparisons between the Irish living in the rookeries of St. Giles and Africans abroad. Such annoyances were further reinforced by the commercial and political success of Harriet Beecher Stowe's abolitionist novel, *Uncle Tom's Cabin* (1852). By 1853 the book had been widely read and lent impetus to the American abolitionist cause while angering the proslavery camp, which complained that Stowe's portrayal of slavery was inaccurate because of the author's poor acquaintance with working plantations.[91] By weaving associations between displayed peoples, slavery, and the perceived misplacement of Christian sympathy, journalists such as Dickens used the shows to generate debate regarding the prejudices and injustices governing contemporary attitudes toward London's outcasts, and invited consumers to reexamine their own sympathies. Others followed suit.

In the same year, a showman self-styled as Diogenes, an Athenian beggar who made a virtue of being destitute, presented Londoners with a lantern show that depicted the "Earthmen of the London cellars, [and] the Aztecs of the London streets." Its purpose was to draw attention to "the many 'missions,' the ready pity never refused to the little savages abroad," which was "sternly denied to the little savages at home" because "Friends of National Education and Lovers of Ethnological Exhibitions" had become enamored of gazing with the "eye of curious speculation, rather than of Christian interest."[92] Such satire suggests how the shows' receptions were not limited to discussions focused entirely on the nature of displayed peoples or imperial activity. Clearly, the shows could also be used by domestic crusaders to publicize issues closer to home, such as urban poverty and the social ills to which it contributed.

While satire could be directed toward stirring the public's moral conscience, it was also exploited for more frivolous purposes. The case of Baartman is notorious for the many jokes about large buttocks that it inspired.[93] Similarly, whereas the *Household Words* review of the Zulu show may have been politically motivated, it was also written to make readers laugh and belittle the focus of Dickens's sarcasm, be they performers or spectators. In some ways, the shows presented ideal opportunities to poke

OUR SOUTH AFRICAN PETS.

THE HOME SECRETARY HAVING DECLARED EXHIBITIONS BY THE FRIENDLY ZULUS "OUT OF HARMONY WITH THE
GENERAL FEELING OF THE COUNTRY," THEY ARE, OF COURSE, ALL THE RAGE IN SOCIETY. STILL, IT WAS EMBARRASSING
WHEN, AS THEY WERE BEING ENTERTAINED AT THE DUCHESS OF DASH'S THE OTHER NIGHT, THE SERVANT ANNOUNCED
"THE RIGHT HONOURABLE MR. CROSS!'"

fun at fashionable folk, because the wealthier portions of society were the
most active patrons of the shows. For instance, although the Home Secretary had objected to Farini's exhibition of Friendly Zulus, many failed
to share his qualms. According to *Funny Folks,* the objection had even ensured that the Zulus were "all the rage in Society." Moreover, their popularity had caused a somewhat embarrassing stir one night at the home
of the Duchess of Dash. The Zulus were being entertained by the duchess
and her guests when the servant announced the arrival of "the Right Honourable Mr Cross!"[94] *Funny Folks* illustrated the socially awkward moment
with *Our South African Pets* (fig. 68). Although an imaginary scene, the appearance of the article in a satirical periodical and the accompanying illustration suggest that while Cross's objections were impotent as a form
of opposition, they were an effective catalyst for securing the Zulus a place
in society's drawing rooms. In these spaces, the illustration implies, the
mighty Zulus were destined to be fussed and fawned over by ladies as if
they were harmless domesticated pets.

On the same page, another article appeared on the "signs and Tokens
of Zuluism." It described how Mr. Cross had "cast more anti-Zulu glances"
around him since the now well-known parliamentary session, and discovered things "equally obnoxious to the truly patriotic mind" already present
in England. For instance, in a recent walk in London's streets he had come
across a male donkey or, as he named it, an "ass-he-gay," that he "longed
to suppress" accordingly.[95] Alongside *assegai,* words commonly associated with the Zulus, such as *kraal* and *Kaffir,* became the basis for further
laborious puns and so reinforced the magazine's implication that Cross's

patriotic enthusiasm needed tempering before it found another equally ludicrous and misdirected subject. Modern readers are unlikely to bellow in laughter at these jokes, but in all likelihood will interpret them as quaint examples of Victorian self-importance or, less charitably, as indicative of racialized superiority. However, it is important not to lose sight of the role of laughter. Humor played an essential element in the shows' receptions, because displayed peoples could be so easily used as a foil with which to compare the mores of domestic life or high society and to criticize their perceived sentimentality, foolishness, or hypocrisy; and, for some, exhibitions proved to be a rather unflattering looking glass.

✳

Dickens's tirade is perhaps the best-known response evoked by displayed peoples; yet many of his observations were echoed by the eyewitness testimony of other spectators. His unabashed racialism and use of displayed peoples as exemplars of human "savagery," along with the associations he creates between displayed peoples, foreign policy, and domestic troubles, are all recurrent themes in the shows' histories. Yet there are other aspects of his review that are wholly unrepresentative. Most spectators simply did not leave behind such rich testimony, either in published form or in personal memoirs. As such, it is difficult to explore the shows' receptions either in minute detail or in broad scope; what does remain is suggestively littered throughout newspapers, biographies, and periodicals. Surmising the ways in which display invited spectators to create chains of association between themselves, performers, and humans abroad is simpler than understanding how such associations functioned at an individual level. Although eyewitness accounts suggest that showmen were successful in establishing displayed peoples as ethnic types, it is much more difficult to establish what such types may have come to signify. Evidently, patrons delighted in interacting with performers and took advantage of the opportunities for lingering inspection; yet they were not passive consumers but critically engaged participants. Moreover, the shows' receptions were characterized by a diversity that is fundamentally irreducible to either a single or a typical consumer response, and so they present complex interpretative differences that must be accounted for, rather than erased by, the shows' histories.

Rather than believing promotional claims without question, consumers used their experiences to bring their judgment to bear on promotional claims and issues relating to human nature, social customs, and political activity that they felt were raised by the performances they witnessed. Cues such as travel literature or the performers' clothing, material culture, and reenacted ceremonies were used to support consumers' personal and critical reflection with the live performances. Some consumers reacted with empathetic concern for displayed peoples' plights; others were clearly disgusted with individuals they believed to be instances of the lowest form of human development or, more simply, aesthetically displeasing. As this chapter has suggested, one of the most recurrent themes in the shows' receptions was the tendency to interpret displayed peoples as exemplars, whether of political activity, typological human differences, or even the wealthy elite's penchant for novel amusements. Although some were interested in using performers as living case studies from which the truth of the "noble savage" hypothesis could be tested, others were more concerned with trying to decide if the performers were authentic. As the next chapter suggests, the use of displayed peoples as specimens was most important for and prominent among those interested in human natural history.

PART THREE

THE NATURAL HISTORY OF RACE

Transforming "Unfruitful Wonder"

IN 1855, John Conolly, a physician and a superintendent of the insane, observed that "scarcely a year [passed] in which, among the miscellaneous attractions of a London season," one could not find "some exhibition illustrative of the varieties of mankind." Their abundance stemmed from the "commercial relations of England," which allowed duly "extensive opportunities of intercourse with all the races of men." Delivering his presidential address to the Ethnological Society of London, Conolly no doubt echoed the thoughts of his audience when he argued that given such opportunities, "no country should be expected to prosecute the study of Ethnology with more success; and in no metropolis ought we to expect to find, from time to time, such instructive illustrations of all parts of this science as in London." Despite such auspicious prospects, he lamented that until recently, the "observations made on voyages and travels" seemed to have been considered interesting "chiefly in proportion to their marvellous character," and "the natives of such regions when brought to our country, seem to have been merely regarded as objects of curiosity or of unfruitful wonder." Thus, some exhibitions proved unsatisfactory, while others were "deceptive" because they were not publicly instructive. Disgracefully, the possible improvement of displayed peoples had "scarcely occupied" their thoughts; instead, human curiosities were commercially exhibited for a while, or "even invited for inspection in fashionable drawing-rooms among the novelties of the Spring," and then they left, "having gained small notice from the ethnologist, and excited no moral interest even among the most serious or the most philanthropic" individuals. Instead, displayed peoples "arrive[d] in a state of barbarism, and without possessions or knowledge; and they depart[ed] from civilized communities equally ignorant and equally destitute." Disapproving greatly of the squandered opportunities for ethnological research, Conolly called on his fellow colleagues to subject displayed peoples to their own rational, inquiring gazes.[1]

Conolly strikingly affirmed the great importance of human displays for ethnologists, the public, and exhibited peoples. London's exhibitions offered the opportunity for all three groups to gain knowledge, albeit different kinds for each. For displayed peoples, time abroad offered the opportunity to be exposed to the virtues of Christianity and a commercial society so that they too could improve their minds and find salvation. For the public and ethnologists, performers might be used as living specimens from which to learn about typological human variation. For ethnologists in particular, displayed peoples could be observed, classified, and described for the benefit of a broader community bound by shared scholarly interests. Yet the contention that displayed peoples played no significant role in ethnological theorization is worth reexamining in light of the redefinitions that marked British ethnology in the mid-nineteenth century.[2] Between the mid-1840s and early 1870s, the scholarly study of human variety was institutionalized with the emergence of dedicated learned societies. The Ethnological Society of London (founded 1843) and Anthropological Society of London (founded 1863) provided scholars with the possibility of formal affiliation. Meanwhile, the wrangling between them that led to their amalgamation under the auspices of the Anthropological Institute of Great Britain and Ireland (founded 1871) contributed to formative discussions on the discipline's practitioners, methodologies, and theoretical scope.

Given that commercial exhibitions of living curiosities in mid-nineteenth-century London took place within the context of growing intellectual interest and institutional restructuring in the study of human variety, it is curious that they have not been more fully incorporated into histories of the disciplinary development of anthropology. This may be due partly to the polemical self-fashioning of early social anthropologists, who distanced themselves from ethnologists by looking to the eighteenth century for suitable intellectual ancestors.[3]

In more recent scholarship, the shows have been conceptualized as popular spectacles that symbolize the nature and prevalence of racialist theories of human variation without having played a formative role in their scientific development.[4] For example, George W. Stocking's seminal classic *Victorian Anthropology* (1987) contains a chapter on the data anthropologists used but overlooks displayed peoples, despite later observing that one of the "special treats the [Ethnological] Society offered its members—whose ethnographic experience was largely second-hand" was an "evening devoted to the examination of a living aboriginal, usually from the polyglot crew of some sailing vessel then in London."[5] In discussions of late nineteenth-century world's fairs, when anthropologists were often responsible for curating the displays of foreign peoples in sequences representing racialist evolutionary hierarchies, anthropologists are usually argued to have used the fairs merely to display or publicly validate, not make, anthropological knowledge.[6] An exception to this broader trend is the incorporation of the *Völkerschauen* (people shows) into the history of German anthropology, in work that demonstrates how practitioners and institutions, such as Rudolf Virchow and the Berlin Anthropological Society, actively sought to examine exhibited peoples and publish their findings.[7] This enthusiasm was reflected by the significant proportion of German publications that used the *Völkerschauen* as experimental resources. More recently, there has been a systematic examination of the work of William John McGee, first president of the American Anthropological Association (founded 1902), in curating the human displays at the Louisiana Purchase Exposition, the 1904 St. Louis World's Fair.[8] Nonetheless, these studies are all concerned with German and American anthropology in the later nineteenth century. Not only are they unrepresentative of the earlier British context but, as this chapter seeks to show, British debates between the 1830s and 1860s were at a particularly significant crossroads for the remaking of the natural history of "race."

Rather than taking Conolly's claims as an accurate historical record of the relationship between human exhibitions and mid-nineteenth-century ethnological practice, they are recast here as a zealously partisan attempt to redefine that relationship in ways that would have significantly boosted the standing of both his colleagues and the Ethnological Society. After all, he was speaking to a group of people dedicated to establishing, promoting, and strengthening their relatively young discipline. Accordingly, the chapter begins by considering the ways in which the shows were made amenable to being used as opportunities for ethnological research in the early half of the nineteenth century. It then explores how displayed peoples were formally incorporated into ethnological education and practice by Robert Gordon Latham's curatorship of the court of natural history at the Crystal Palace in Sydenham. Exploring these often forgotten relationships between mass culture and ethnological practice suggests that despite Conolly's claims to the contrary, exhibited peoples were made into ethnological specimens that became both the objects and the means of ethnological investigation among the lay public, phrenologists, physicians, anatomists, and ethnologists and in a range of settings, from institutionally backed private examinations to personal connections made at commercial performances.

Making Exhibitions Ethnological

By the early 1840s, commercial exhibitions began to be routinely advertised as educational opportunities for budding ethnologists. By making such claims, journalists were engaging in and contributing to debates on human variety and encouraging consumers to follow suit. For example, a review of the 1847 San exhibition for the *Illustrated London News* betrayed a sense of disgust tempered with intellectual fascination: "The first effect, on entering the room, may be repulsive; but the attentive visitor soon overcomes this feeling, and sees in the benighted beings before him a fine subject for scientific investigation, as well as a scene for popular gratification, and rational curiosity." Regardless of one's moral, aesthetic, or religious inclinations, the reviewer emphasized that those who could overcome their initial shock and disgust would find an abundance of interpretative possibilities that could frame the experience of seeing such distinctive humans. He observed further: "It was strange, too, in looking through one of the windows of the room into the busy street, to reflect that by a single turn of the head might be witnessed the two extremes of humanity—the lowest and highest of the race—the wandering savage, and the silken baron of civilisation."[9] Both savagery and aristocracy were, he deliberated, two points on a developmental spectrum that was potentially universally applicable to human societies; yet they were extremes that, in their own ways, were peculiar forms of human life which in all likelihood were both alien to the shows' patrons and readers of the newspaper. From the mid-nineteenth century onward in particular, reviews of human exhibitions were increasingly likely to draw conclusions regarding human nature and variation in their discussions of exhibited peoples; however, the shows were amenable to being used as opportunities for ethnological musings long before such claims became routine.

In X. Chabert's *A Brief Historical Account of the Life and Adventures of the Botocudo Chieftain*, the pamphlet accompanying the Bond Street exhibition of a Krenak family in 1822, the descriptive material is tellingly focused on their habits, customs, physical form, and biographies. It starts by geographically locating the family "in the forests on the banks of the Rio Doce, as far as the source of that river in the province of Minas Gëraes." In a remark that simultaneously hints at military adeptness and naturalizes it as a typological trait, the pamphlet notes that these "savages are highly renowned for their warlike spirit and their dexterity at shooting the arrow." Shortly afterward, a detailed description of their appearance notes their lack of clothing; copper complexion; jet-black hair that is "straight and stiff, and [worn] cropped close, except a round tuft on the crown of the head"; form of their heads; oblique eyes that are like the Chinese; and finally the "great plugs of wood, in a circular shape, curiously fastened to the lower lip and ears, the tip of which reaches their shoulder." Further on, it is observed that in the "course of their wanderings they destroy game, and gather, wild fruits, which serve to quench their thirst, after they have devoured voraciously the produce of their chace [*sic*]. Such tribes of Botocudos as are more civilized, rear Turkey wheat, beans, and mandiocca."[10] By detailing their geographic distribution, complexion, immodesty, and lowly, albeit slowly improving, stage of social development (as indicated by their hunter-gatherer and partially agricultural subsistence), the pamphlet rationalizes Chabert's decision to classify and advertise the family as a group of South American savages. Meanwhile, the descriptive material also helps substantiate his invitation to patrons to share in the creation, consolidation, and promotion of this taxonomic grouping in both the reading of the pamphlet and the viewing of the performances.

All the printed pamphlets accompanying the shows contained similar information on physical form, geography, means of subsistence, and social customs (such as marriage). The importance of describing peoples' "manners and customs" was greatly indebted to eighteenth-century notions of human variation and shifting patterns of writing history. Throughout the eighteenth century, a wide variety of factors, including complexion, physiognomy, language, religion, physical makeup, clothing, and political, social, and economic organization, provided the necessary information for classifying humans into distinct varieties.[11] By the late eighteenth century, scholars incorporated these factors into a model of social development in which humans naturally passed through four distinctive stages characterized by a nation's modes of subsistence. These four stages were usually defined by hunting, pasturage, agriculture, and, finally, commerce, and were each associated with given practices of social, political, and civil organization as well as manners and morals.[12] In work on eighteenth-century antiquarianism, it has been argued that as these theories were incorporated into historical analysis the nature of explaining the past changed: "The philosophical narratives of the Scottish Enlightenment had elevated the description of manners and customs of a particular age from simply a matter of curiosity—a digression of the main narrative—to an issue of central importance." History withdrew from the "tyranny of facts and dates" to focus on the "opinions, customs and inclinations of a people. Such features were often considered the most salient features when describing a nation because they were representative of the relative civilisation, the social organisation or the state of religious belief."[13] In the nineteenth century, theories of human variation proliferated substantially; however, the often twinned notions of diachronic human variation and developmental civilization (stadial or otherwise) remained both powerful and relevant to discussions of human history and national difference.[14] In this light, pamphlets' discussions of "manners and customs," and frequent use of the phrase in their titles, effectively aligned them with an older generic form of comparative historical writing that was of fundamental relevance for early to mid-nineteenth-century discussions on human variation.

Surviving testimony unambiguously indicates that some paying customers used the shows as opportunities to regard performers as natural historical specimens. Between 1845 and 1855, for example, Conolly saw at least three groups of San (including Flora and Martinus), Maximo and Bartola, and groups of Inuit and Zulus; moreover, he clearly used them as a means to observe "specimens of distinct races of mankind." His personal accounts deserve extended attention, because they provide exceptionally rare eyewitness accounts and demonstrate how he spent years using the shows to collect encounters with foreign peoples and to stimulate his personal and scholarly interest in typological human variation. Upon meeting the Anishinabe women, he was particularly struck by their "unexpected and untaught grace," and their acknowledgments of patrons' greetings that "were made with such a mixed expression of grateful feeling and of dignified politeness" as to suggest "that courtliness of manner was among the natural products of savage life, rather than the artificial result of civilized institutions." Similarly, upon greeting a group of San, including two men, two women, and an infant, he observed their skills of "quick observation," "swift comprehension," and "impressionable character." He made numerous observations regarding their physical development, including musculature, the formation of the head, the arrangement of their tufts of hair, and the coloring of their dark-brown skin. The younger of the men appeared to possess a particular ability to "apprehend all that was said and done, although no pains had been taken to teach him one word of English." Thus, when some visitors were permitted to "tease and perplex him with small conjuring tricks the varied indications in his face and gesture, of surprise, or pleasure, or anger, presented curious illustrations of the natural language of the emotions."[15] Likewise, the "Earthmen" were named for their supposed habit of burrowing holes in the ground to sleep in without the use of any implements. Conolly observed that the delicacy of their hands and feet seemed ill-fitted for the task.

Conolly's commentary demonstrates how he used the shows to assess critically theories of human difference, such as the "noble savage," choose between them, and, significantly, create new ones of his own. His observations regarding the Anishinabe's politeness and the San's facial expressions supported the inference that some social graces and forms of emotional expression are the natural products of human development rather than the fruits of civilization. His remarks on the San's quickness of perception and ability to learn were used to support his sense that they were a people, and by implication all uncivilized peoples, who possessed the capacity for improvement. Finally, his observations regarding the delicacy of Martinus's and Flora's anatomy suggested that "Earthmen" was a potential misnomer that was best abandoned.

Collecting specimens (or in this case encounters with them), designating certain cases as typological exemplars (such as the available performers), carefully comparing them to one another and other specimens, critically evaluating possible explanatory frameworks (such as the "noble savage"), and creating new ways of understanding, categorizing, or defining specimens are all essential components of the taxonomic process. As this testimony confirms, as far as certain classes of human beings were concerned, accomplishing all these crucial tasks was made possible by attending human exhibitions. Conolly is unusual in having left such an explicit and extensive account of his visits to the shows; however, he clearly was not unique, nor is he likely to have been especially unusual, in his use of exhibited peoples as human specimens suitable for ethnological investigation.

The initial appearance of Maximo and Bartola in London is one of the most striking instances of exhibited people being used as ethnological specimens. Before they made any public appearances, the pair visited the families of the colonial administrator Sir James Clarke, the physiologist and surgeon Sir Benjamin Brodie, Latham, and "all the heads of the faculty generally."[16] Brodie, then president of the Ethnological Society, arranged the meeting at his home for "some distinguished men of science" in June 1853. Richard Owen first met Maximo and Bartola here. Interested in making observations that the crowded room could not allow, he arranged to conduct a more detailed examination of the children at the home of Joseph Morris, their exhibitor, on June 30. His report was presented at a special meeting of the Ethnological Society a week later, and published in the society's journal. The report was primarily a technical account of the children's dentition, physiognomy, bodily formation, and cranial development. Owen dismissed the claims that they were Aztecs—his coup de grâce provided by an article that had appeared in the *Philadelphia Bulletin* of July 13 in which Innocent Burgos, a Spaniard living in San Salvador, claimed that he was the father of the children. Owen stressed that the pair were clearly human and not "brutes." That such a claim needed to be explicitly denied gives a pregnant indication not only of its plausibility in some circles but also of how the demarcating line between human and animal had not necessarily been agreed on.[17] He also noted that the "chief and most striking characteristic of both children is due to the abnormal arrest of the brain and brain-case, which gives them the character of hemi-cephalous monsters."[18] Thus, he concluded they were "instances of [an] exceptional arrest of development, not representatives of any peculiar human race."[19]

The children also excited the interest of Robert Knox. He examined them but published a significantly different interpretation of their development. The majority of his essay was devoted to incorporating the children into a general discussion of his own theories on human descent and variety. Knox concurred with Owen that Maximo and Bartola were human and paid little heed to the supposed origins from Iximaya. However, he did associate them with the Aztecs, drawing similarities between their heads and the Central American sculptures, as illustrated by John Stephens's *Incidents of Travel*, and also the physiognomy of the "form of the idiotic head" which occasionally appeared in all the "races of men." Thus, Knox argued that their children were representatives of the Aztec race, who were now "extinct as a race" but had been reproduced in Maximo and Bartola by virtue of the "law of 'interrupted descent.'"[20] According to Knox, this law governed all forms of natural generation and thus the formation of species. Essentially, he argued that the embryos of a natural family were similar and contained within them all the characters required to form any member of a given genus. During development, features were differentially expressed (with some features suppressed), and so deformations of the embryonic form, or monstrosities, were constantly generated. New species arose when, rather than dying, monstrosities flourished within a given environmental or physiological niche and so became viable organisms. Human varieties, which he termed species, were the product of such developmental differentiation.[21] Thus for Knox, Maximo and Bartola were monstrous specimens that demonstrated how human embryos could revert to an archetypical human type rather than just simple arrests of development.[22]

The children's mental capacity stirred wider medical interest. In 1853, the children were examined by the phrenologist Cooter Donovan. He reported that the "extremely defective condition of their mental constitution" rendered them almost entirely without any sign of intelligence. Furthermore, "the organs of the moral and mental faculties are either totally wanting, or in so rudimental a condition as to admit of no effort to manifest any cognizable degree of either moral sentiment or reasoning capacity, beyond what may be allowed to exist in the mind of an infant one month old."[23] In his address to the Ethnological Society, Conolly also presented an extended account of his thoughts on their mental capabilities. He observed that their "first appearance" created a "feeling approaching to awe; and their helplessness, their good-humour, and their vivacity, soon made them objects of interest, and almost of affection." The children's "stooping gait, the unsteady run, the incapacity to walk, and the awkwardness of all the movement were the equally natural accompaniments of imperfect osseous structure and development, and of other imperfections, associated with a nervous system arrested in some stage of embryo life" leading him to conclude that the children were in fact "idiots."[24]

Between 1839 and 1844, Conolly had been in charge of Hanwell Asylum, where he established his medical reputation by ordering that all forms of mechanical restraint, such as chains, manacles, and straitjackets, be destroyed, to be replaced by treatment through discipline and moral persuasion.[25] Having worked with the insane for most of his professional life, he was "at once struck" by the similarities between the mentally ill in his care and Maximo and Bartola, especially between Maximo and a young boy whose "small cranium, peculiar features, manner, vivacity, and mode of walking, were all such, that, if his skin had been blackened, he might have passed for a third example of this new and unknown nation." Conolly collated data regarding cranial circumferences and shape from an examination of a child at Highgate Asylum and Owen's report to conclude that Maximo and Bartola were not Aztecs but "more or less idiotic" children whose histories had been fabricated in order to render them "objects of profitable curiosity."[26]

The controversy regarding Maximo and Bartola's ethnic origin and mental acuity (or lack thereof) is suggestive of how displayed peoples could be used as specimens and where the debates regarding human variety were being generated. It has been argued that the differences of interpretation between Knox and Owen can be analyzed in terms of Owen's social conservatism and Knox's materialistic, radical politics: while insightful, of equal relevance here are the indications they provide of the range of social settings in which the nature of human variety was being reforged.[27]

THE AZTEC CHILDREN.

The circumstances of Owen's and Knox's examinations differed significantly. Owen was an
established anatomist, served on a number of
government committees, and was a member of
the Ethnological Society. In short, he was part
of the elite social network that informally governed London's men of science.[28] His examination of Maximo and Bartola took place with the
institutional backing of the Ethnological Society. At least two such examinations took place at
the house of Brodie, and many more may have
been arranged by budding students who were
prepared to pay for private demonstrations. In
contrast, Knox had been prevented from joining the Ethnological Society in 1855 when the
dominant Quaker element blackballed his application on account of his materialism (he was
later admitted in 1858). Thus, he lacked Owen's
institutional backing and may even have had relatively restricted access
to the children. Possibly, he may not even have examined them himself,
in which case he may have drawn his anatomical discussion from Owen's
published paper or by attending an exhibition.[29] These examinations were
also reported in learned journals such as the *Lancet* and the *Journal of the
Ethnological Society of London*. Such publications made ethnological information available to a wider audience and created a situation in which both
the lay and the learned were expected to assess the conflicting interpretations of the children's anatomy, mental development, and provenance
(fig. 69). Meanwhile, whereas the press had spent years touting the ethnological potential of the shows, in the early 1850s fresh efforts began to incorporate displayed peoples within the domain of institutionalized ethnological practice.

Introducing the Natural History of Nations

In 1854, the Crystal Palace reopened in Sydenham in a building newly designed by Joseph Paxton, twice the size of the original 1851 venue and with
a substantially different catalog of exhibits (fig. 70). Its major displays included courts devoted to the Egyptian, Italian, Greek, Roman, Pompeian,
medieval, Byzantine, and Renaissance periods, with additional courts spe-
cializing in modern sculpture, portraits, and industry.[30] The palace was set
in the midst of vast landscaped gardens adorned with babbling fountains,
and a lake that featured an island inhabited by full-scale models of antediluvian monsters and extinct reptiles uncovered by geologists.[31]

Although a private enterprise, the palace was committed to the ideal of
national education that had underpinned its parent, the Great Exhibition
of 1851.[32] Yet, unlike Paxton's original glass edifice, the one in Sydenham

was a pantheon of national edification and entertainment rather than an international trade fair; it was conceived as "a three-dimensional encyclopaedia of both nature and art, with a much wider syllabus than at Hyde Park, that would help visitors to understand evolution and civilisation in relation to their own times."[33] Significantly, the Crystal Palace's displays were substantially cheaper than most London exhibitions, including human displays, and so here the wealthier elite could be found rubbing shoulders with the working classes, and many more people are likely to have been to Sydenham than could ever hope to see a show. This public accessibility was critical, since from the outset Sydenham was the private enterprise of the Crystal Palace Company. It was intended to "make a profit by reforming the public's habits of observation," and thus encouraged education and moral improvement through visual means while also catering to visitors' less cerebral needs in the courts devoted to eating and drinking.[34] The public quickly took advantage of the opportunities offered, with 1,322,000 visitors in the first year alone, including 71,000 children.[35]

Guidebooks to the palace usually suggested that visitors start their tour from the south wing entrance. Those heeding the advice entered the court of natural history that included tableaux designed to visually catalog the world's flora, fauna, and peoples. Erected under the directorship of Latham and Edward Forbes, professor of botany at King's College, London, the court was a major innovation for the new Crystal Palace. A small-scale museum of man displayed in his natural habitats, it had been designed to offer an ethnological education. Moving through the court of natural history, visitors were greeted with stuffed and mounted animals, growing plants, and models of foreign peoples arranged against a backdrop of painted images. The court's displays were split into the New World on the southwest side and the Old World on the southeast; the geography had been calculated so that a visitor could "place himself in respect to the objects before him in the same relation as he would be to a map of the world" (fig. 71).[36] Starting from the entrance in the south wing, visitors were led into the New World. In the display for Australia they could see a platypus, a Tasmanian wolf, an emu, a cassowary, a group of Papuans, and two Australian men, one of whom was shown on the verge of hurling a stick. The display for the Indian Islands included three Javanese people from the lower classes smoking opium, groups of people from Sumatra and Borneo, and bears and birds. For India, a group of Hindus, birds, a hog, and an elaborate display of a tiger hunt were chosen, while the Chinese display included a yak and some Tibetans. The most extensive tableau was devoted to Africa, with examples of peoples from the eastern coasts, Niger, Sierra Leone, and South Africa, including the San and Zulus. The animals included a hippopotamus, camel, giraffe, hyena, lion, monkeys, antelopes, and gazelles. In the South American corner, a Mexican was shown saving a fellow countryman from danger, with a jaguar killing a deer, an alpaca, ostriches, and a tapir dotted around. In the North American display, Anishinabe were

FIGURE 71
The Natural History Department at the Crystal Palace, Sydenham. (After Samuel Philips, *Guide to the Crystal Palace and its Park* [1854]. By kind permission of Kevin Levell.)

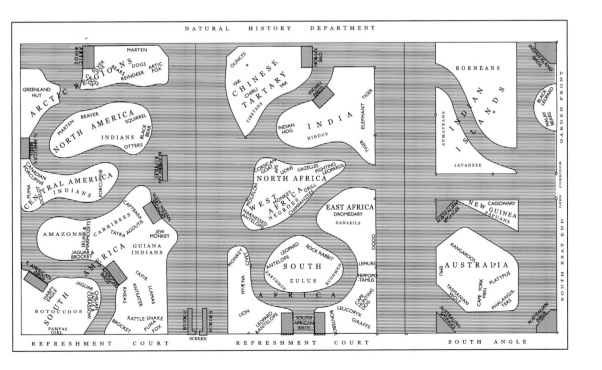

[195]

engaged in a war dance to emphasize their ferocity and were surrounded by a beaver, squirrel, black bear, puma, ocelot, porcupines, and otters. Finally, in the far end of the southwest transept, the visitor could see a display of the Arctic regions populated by reindeer, dogs, an arctic fox, birds, and a Greenland hut.

The human models were extraordinary objects and clearly the primary attraction. The white plaster casts were painted in tones simulating skin, while features such as hair, eyebrows, eyes, fingernails, jewelry, and individualized faces and expressions all contributed to their remarkably "life-like appearance" (figs. 72 and 73).[37] Originally, the models were intended to be nude, but objections from the church prompted the adoption of a more modest approach. Crusaders may have been pleased at the alterations, but others were deeply annoyed at the interference: "It is not, we regret to add, the general opinion that their appearance has been at all improved by the grotesque and incongruous garments in which Dr. Latham has been obliged to swathe them in order to remove the objections of the clergy."[38] Thwarted, Latham arranged the models into visual narratives that he deemed representative of their respective ethnicities. For instance, the Zulus were engaged in the search for a lost article, in which case, he clarified, "a Fetish-man, a medium-man, mystery-man, or conjuror ... is called in, and set upon the suspected parties, who sit around a circle. The conjuror then works himself, like the Pythoness of the old oracles, into a state of rabid excitement, and keeps it until he fixes upon the culprit" (fig. 72).[39] Significantly, Latham may have been borrowing from the highly successful live show of the Zulus by casting into plaster the same story of witchcraft that they performed onstage (see 1853 playbill, fig. 16).

Latham's three-dimensional narratives drew heavily on travel literature. For instance, in the arrangement of the San family, the adult male is shown on high ground and looking into the expansive horizon (fig. 73). The pose is clearly an allusion to the reputed visual acuity of the San, who were frequently described as having astonishing long-range vision that was most apparent and useful when hunting. Lichtenstein's *Travels in South Africa*, for example, recorded that the San's sight was "rendered so acute, by spying continually around them from a great height, after their prey, that they perceive objects clearly at a distance, which no European, even with the best eyes, could see without the assistance of glasses.... Our Bosjesman servants have sometimes discerned flocks of antelopes at the distance of a mile and a half."[40] In the display for the Krenak, a group were shown quarreling, in which case, Latham explained, the wooden plugs adorning their lips and ears were frequently "torn out" and the fleshy shreds "to which they belong[ed] left hanging."[41] Rather than being fictionalized, he chose to reify a disagreement that was originally reported in *Travels in Brazil* by Prince Maximilian of Wied-Neuwid. Latham used the book's original illustration, supplemental drawings from Johann Baptist von Spix and

Carl Friedrich Philipp von Martius's *Travels in Brazil* (1824), and casts from
the anatomy professor Anders Retzius.[42] Just as in the show's promotional
materials, travel literature was critical in providing relevant details about
peoples' manners and customs, painted scenery and even the narratives
into which the models were manipulated and displayed.

A guidebook specifically for the court of natural history helped viewers to interpret the models, stuffed animals, and vegetation.[43] Significantly, its accessibility in terms of both cost and style makes it likely that it was one of the most widely used ethnological works of the 1850s. Written by Latham and Forbes, it cost just sixpence and contained ninety-two pages. Its cover illustration recapitulated the geographic arrangement of the court and located its subjects within the disciplinary domain of natural history (fig. 74). On the left (west) of the picture, a South American stood, with a llama and cactus both framing and obscuring his barely clothed body. In the middle, a seemingly nude Zulu held aloft a tell-tale assegai and shield, albeit bearing the Crystal Palace Company's initials. On the right (east), a turbaned Arab man was shown with a pipe billowing smoke against the backdrop of a camel and date tree. The arrangement of dense exotic vegetation, animals, and humans schematically mapped out the globe's biogeography, while the interweaving of the humans, animals, and plants both reflected and promoted their status and classification as natural historical specimens.

Given the novelty of ethnology, Latham devoted seventy-four pages of the guidebook to explaining his subject. In a move ridiculed by *Punch*, he began by explaining that the term had been derived from two Greek words, *ethnos* and *logos*, and denoted the "science, not exactly of the different nations of the world, but of the different varieties of the human species."[44] Throughout, the guidebook was divided into subsections explaining the habits and customs of each nation of displayed peoples. Each description included details of the people's physiognomy, personality, clothing, geographic range, religion, language, means of subsistence, architecture, social customs, and ceremonies. The group of Tibetans, for example, was classified as representative of the Mongolian human type (in addition to European and Negro) and could be recognized as such because of the breadth of their cheekbones and flattened noses. A pastoral nation, they were "quite peaceable," and as Latham argued, of all the Mongolians, the Chinese were the most civilized, although "after their own peculiar fashion."[45] For the Malaysians, Latham added details of tattooing, dental filing, and distension of the ears.[46] The Papuans were described as a frizzy-haired people, living without woven cloth and possessing "political organisation of the lowest and simplest kind; that of small tribes living in a state of chronic hostility with each other."[47] Latham also reproduced illustrations of Papuan huts and sailing vessels to illustrate their technological capabilities (fig. 75). Like the shows' pamphlets, Latham's guidebook served as an educational manual; crucially, it provided the public with descriptive material that both supported his classification scheme and invited viewers to interpret the models within his favored ethnological framework.

Defining ethnology as the study of human varieties was a barbed indication of Latham's position within contemporary debates regarding the plausibility of dividing humans into more than one species.[48] The belief that all human beings were descended from common ancestors, which

FIGURE 74
(*Facing*) The cover to the guidebook for the courts of natural history at the Crystal Palace, Sydenham. (Robert Gordon Latham and Edward Forbes, *A Hand Book to the Courts of Natural History Described* [1854]. Reproduced by kind permission of the Syndics of the Cambridge University Library.)

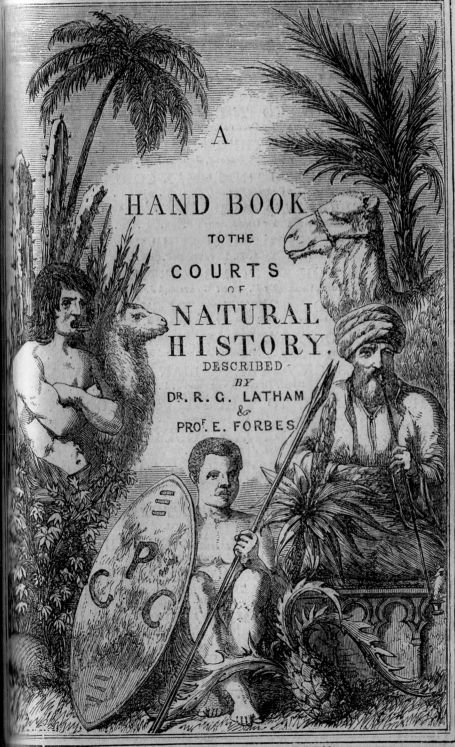

A
HAND BOOK
TO THE
COURTS
OF
NATURAL
HISTORY.
DESCRIBED
BY
DR. R. G. LATHAM
&
PROF. E. FORBES.

CRYSTAL PALACE LIBRARY.

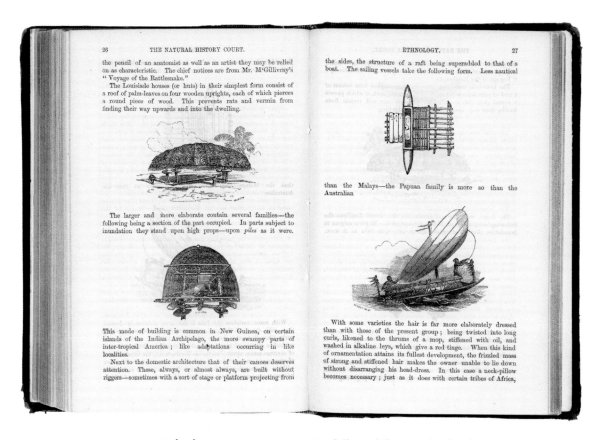

FIGURE 75
The material culture of New Guinea peoples as depicted in Robert Latham's guidebook. (Robert Gordon Latham and Edward Forbes, *A Hand Book to the Courts of Natural History Described* [1854], 26–27. Reproduced by kind permission of the Syndics of the Cambridge University Library.)

came to be known as monogenesis, followed from orthodox interpretations of the book of Genesis, in which Adam and Eve were the ultimate progenitors of humanity.[49] Proponents of human unity did routinely distinguish between different varieties, although the exact number varied: the eighteenth-century comparative anatomist Johann Friedrich Blumenbach favored five (Caucasian, Malayan, Mongolian, American, and Ethiopian), London surgeon John Hunter argued for seven, the philosopher Immanuel Kant defined four separate types, while Latham followed Georges Cuvier in outlining three (Caucasian, Mongolian, and Negro).[50] In Britain, the latter was both the most respectable and the most commonly held position throughout the eighteenth and nineteenth centuries. Nevertheless, a number of scholars proposed multiple acts of creation or centers of survivors of the postdiluvian mooring of Noah's Ark to account for observed variation. As early as 1655, Isaac de la Peyrère's *Prae-Adamitae* proposed that humans had existed before Adam.[51] In the late eighteenth century, Lord Kames (Henry Home) proposed several creative acts to account for the different human nations. For others, now most commonly known as polygenists, even if there had been a single act of creation, the variations between humans constituted sufficient grounds to classify them as separate species. Such works quickly became the focus of refutations intended to maintain religious orthodoxy and remained so for decades.[52] Mobilizing the official guidebook to the court of natural history at the Crystal Palace, Latham contributed to these discussions by consistently stressing human unity while also promoting and reinforcing his use of the taxonomic matrices created by cleaving humanity along the lines of civilized and savage; heathen and Christian; hunting-gathering, agricultural, and commercial; European, Mongolian, and Negro.[53]

Although the study of Britain and Europe formed a significant subdivision of British ethnology, the natural history court only illustrated the peoples of Asia, Africa, and the New World. The omission may have appeared as particularly puzzling, given Latham's own research on the subject, including *Ethnology of the British Colonies and Dependencies* (1851) and *Ethnology of Europe* (1852).[54] Latham excused himself by arguing that visitors would already be sufficiently acquainted with at least a rudimentary knowledge of how British and European peoples were differentiated from one another.[55] In recognition of the lack of European tableaux, *Punch* suggested a suitable display for British natural history that featured a costermonger, donkey, and thistle (fig. 76). Alternatively, the magazine suggested that perhaps it was not necessary after all, since there would "always be found among the visitors themselves a collection of living curiosities of the various populations of Europe" (fig. 77).[56]

The substitution of visitors for specimens of British types neatly encouraged visitors to compare themselves with the peoples on display and note their progress from assumed states of relatively lowly states of social organization and moral purpose. Intriguingly, critics of the working-class visitors acidly compared them to the models and snobbishly proposed that they were more likely to enjoy the natural history court than the Greek sculpture because, since the models were not art, they were more easily appreciated by the plebeian multitudes.[57] Meanwhile, lest visitors were tempted to assume too great a distance between themselves and the exhibited nations, Samuel Philips's official guidebook noted that visitors ought to remember that foreign peoples were also "endowed with immortal souls." Remonstrating further, he added,

It is not yet two thousand years since the forefathers of the present European family tattooed their skins, and lived in so savage a state that late archaeological researches induce us to suspect that they were not wholly free from one of the worst charges that is laid to savage existence; viz. the practice of cannibalism.[58]

This injunction was supported by Latham's guidebook. Although it sometimes accentuated cultural differences by including vivid descriptions of cannibalism, headhunting, decapitations, and worryingly unfettered sexual morality, it also praised the Krenak's ability to improve by embracing missionary activity in South America and some peaceful people in Java.

Transforming "Unfruitful Wonder"

CRYSTAL PALACE—SOME VARIETIES OF THE HUMAN RACE.

Both official and unofficial guidebooks to the Crystal Palace suggested
the potential for improvement believed to be inherent in all humans, while
the overarching theme of progress was reinforced by the overall arrangement of the palace's gardens and courts. For instance, the antediluvian
monsters were arranged in a temporal narrative showing their emergence from the waters onto terra firma. Once visitors had passed through
these scenes from "deep time," they were able to walk uphill to the palace entrance and physically retrace life's development from bygone cata-
clysms.[59] Next they entered the court of natural history before moving on
to the other displays devoted to human civilization in its progressive historical manifestations. The intertwined narratives of temporal and moral
development reflected and consolidated the common attempt to define
human variation as the outcome of processes that operated diachronic-
ally; thus, human exoticism came to be used as a sign of historical lag behind those such as the Victorians, who felt they had successfully achieved
the most developed forms of human civilization, even when such variation was presented in a synchronic space.[60] In this light, the official tableaux presented displays of peoples in need of moral and mental improvement within an intended sequence that reaffirmed the overall theme of

temporal and moral development from a visitor's first steps onto the pal-ace's grounds.[61] Despite the directors' intentions, it would be easy to over-look Sydenham's potential to offer multiple narratives of the past. Visitors did not necessarily follow the advice of guidebooks; instead, they could use one of several entrances and move between and through courts in nu-merous paths. Thus, the peripatetic tracings of history could chart the de-cline and fall of empires, or ahistorical relationships between them, just as easily as performing the linear progression from monsters to Victorians.[62]

Latham did not content himself with simply promoting human unity but drew on contemporary scientific research to substantiate his posi-tion. Doing so ensured that his guidebook encapsulated some of the de-bates that formed the basis of his ethnological project, and presented them in more digestible form to a broader lay audience than many more tradi-tional scholarly works. For instance, in discussions of human variation the cause of skin pigmentation remained an unresolved issue.

In the eighteenth century, complexion had often been explained with reference to physical geography. Common observations, such as humans become darker-skinned as one approaches the equator, and thus hotter climes, helped sustain arguments that skin coloration was a function of exposure to heat rather than an intrinsically different feature of darker complexions. However, by the late eighteenth and early nineteenth cen-turies critics began raising their voices.[63] In 1800, the French anatomist Julien-Joseph Virey published the *Histoire Naturelle du Genre Humain*, in which he argued that in "whatever light we consider Negroes, we cannot deny that they present characteristics of a race distinct from the white."[64] One of his strategies involved disputing the ancient wisdom of climate-related coloration, arguing that however "conclusive this observation may appear, it is certainly not sufficient [to explain variations in pigment], and others contradict it." Moreover,

amidst our own population, and in the same family, we see brown and light colored persons, some with a fair skin, others of a darker color, although liv-ing together in the same manner, and even under the same roof. Negroes born in European and American colonies do not lose their black color. Dutch settlers at the Cape of Good Hope, who live nearly after the Hottentot fashion, but without ever intermarrying with the natives, have retained their original *white* color for two centuries without any alteration.[65]

Thus, for Virey and like-minded individuals, the structure of the human skin, rather than climate or environment, gained ground in the attempt to resolve how coloring developed. Although Virey limited himself to ar-guing that black peoples were different in degree, others were willing to propose a more radical distinction. French physiologist Marie-Jean-Pierre Flourens argued that the skin of "white races" was made of "three distinct laminae or membranes—the derm, and two epiderms," while in the "skin of the black race" there was "an apparatus which is altogether wanting in the man of the white race, an apparatus of two layers, the external of which is the seat of pigmentum or colouring matter of the Negroes." Thus, white and black were "two essentially and specifically distinct races," and as Flourens took pleasure in noting, no one could argue that the effect of climate was sufficient to give or take away tissue.[66]

Latham used his guidebook to present this ongoing debate to the public, using detailed information regarding the skin's structure, including cross-sections of skin taken from a contemporary German histological manual, to dismiss any anatomic distinction between human varieties. He argued, therefore, that Europeans and Negroes differed in "degree only" (fig. 78).[67] Latham's references to contemporary ethnological debates, mobilization of technical literature, and decision to stress human unity unequivocally indicate both the intended educational aspect of the court and the perceived utility of the guidebook in introducing ethnology to the lay public.

Significantly, there are indications that the public did take up these invitations to muse on human variation. One reviewer noted,

The real object of interest presented to the shilling visitor are the eating and drinking courts, where he can be taught to contemplate the requirements of his inner man, after which, by an easy suggestion, you will find him amongst the stuffed animals, intensely taken up with the strange and questionable shapes of his fellow-man; he can do without Blumenbach and Pritchard [sic], or even Latham, their own great progenitor here, because he can make his own comparisons; like the monkey at the looking-glass, he can study his own views of the development theory on the spot; he is touched with a fellow-feeling as he exclaims before the chimpanzee "is he not a man and a brother."[68]

The rhetorical questioning of the chimpanzee's relationship to humanity sarcastically made light of the shilling visitors' eating, drinking, and ostensibly intellectual musings. By denigrating the uses such visitors made of the natural history court, the journalist's comments nevertheless suggest that, despite his disapproval, there were some patrons who felt that the court presented them with sufficient material to stimulate their own thoughts on the natural history of humans without resorting to scholarly tomes, such as those by James Cowles Prichard or Latham, no matter how august, authoritative, or irritating to other observers. The journalist's allusions are indicative of the range of contemporary debates to which the material at Sydenham's Crystal Palace could be made relevant. For instance, development had been made the talk of Victorian society as early as 1844, when the anonymous publication of *Vestiges of the Natural History of Creation* proposed an explanation of the Creation dependent on the natural law of evolution through development.[69] By 1853, the book had been through ten editions and generated considerable discussion regarding the possible identity of the author and the nature of natural development in

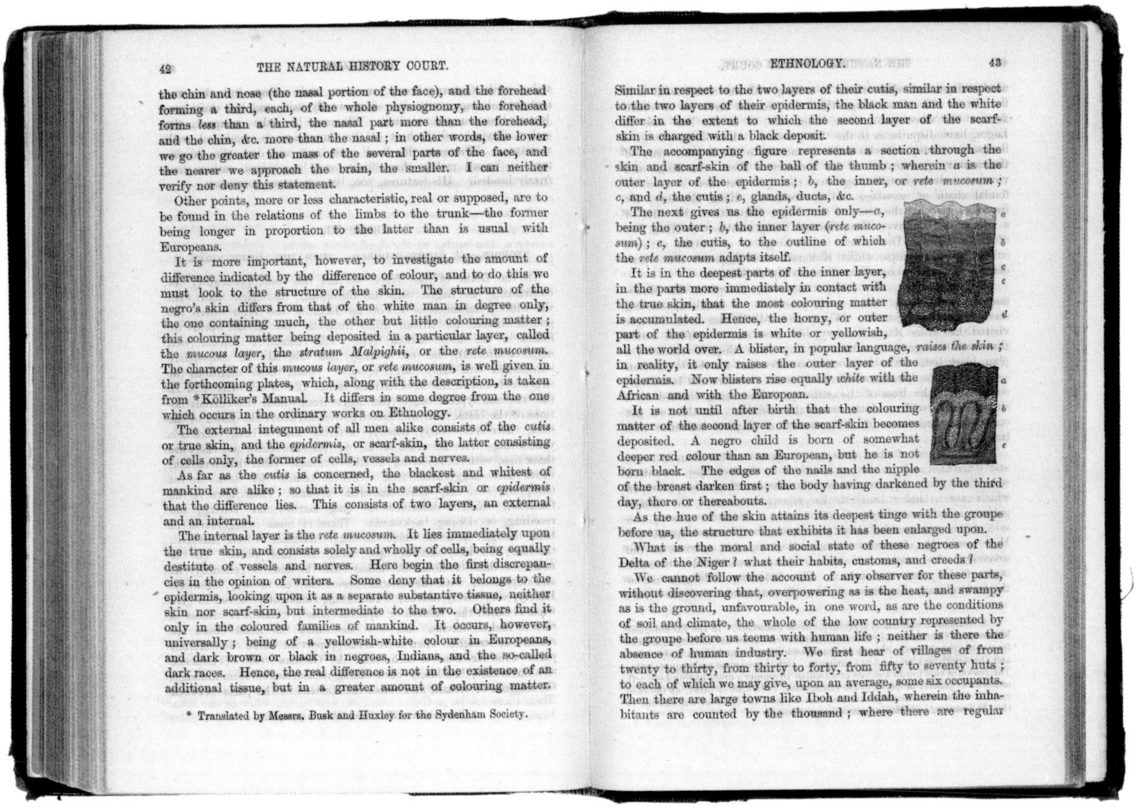

42 THE NATURAL HISTORY COURT.

the chin and nose (the nasal portion of the face), and the forehead forming a third, each, of the whole physiognomy, the forehead forms *less* than a third, the nasal part more than the forehead, and the chin, &c. more than the nasal; in other words, the lower we go the greater the mass of the several parts of the face, and the nearer we approach the brain, the smaller. I can neither verify nor deny this statement.

Other points, more or less characteristic, real or supposed, are to be found in the relations of the limbs to the trunk—the former being longer in proportion to the latter than is usual with Europeans.

It is more important, however, to investigate the amount of difference indicated by the difference of colour, and to do this we must look to the structure of the skin. The structure of the negro's skin differs from that of the white man in degree only, the one containing much, the other but little colouring matter; this colouring matter being deposited in a particular layer, called the *mucous layer*, the *stratum Malpighii*, or the *rete mucosum*. The character of this *mucous layer*, or *rete mucosum*, is well given in the forthcoming plates, which, along with the description, is taken from *Kölliker's Manual. It differs in some degree from the one which occurs in the ordinary works on Ethnology.

The external integument of all men alike consists of the *cutis* or true skin, and the *epidermis*, or scarf-skin, the latter consisting of cells only, the former of cells, vessels and nerves.

As far as the *cutis* is concerned, the blackest and whitest of mankind are alike; so that it is in the scarf-skin or *epidermis* that the difference lies. This consists of two layers, an external and an internal.

The internal layer is the *rete mucosum*. It lies immediately upon the true skin, and consists solely and wholly of cells, being equally destitute of vessels and nerves. Here begin the first discrepancies in the opinion of writers. Some deny that it belongs to the epidermis, looking upon it as a separate substantive tissue, neither skin nor scarf-skin, but intermediate to the two. Others find it only in the coloured families of mankind. It occurs, however, universally; being of a yellowish-white colour in Europeans, and dark brown or black in negroes, Indians, and the so-called dark races. Hence, the real difference is not in the existence of an additional tissue, but in a greater amount of colouring matter.

* Translated by Messrs. Busk and Huxley for the Sydenham Society.

ETHNOLOGY. 43

Similar in respect to the two layers of their cutis, similar in respect to the two layers of their epidermis, the black man and the white differ in the extent to which the second layer of the scarf-skin is charged with a black deposit.

The accompanying figure represents a section through the skin and scarf-skin of the ball of the thumb; wherein *a* is the outer layer of the epidermis; *b*, the inner, or *rete mucosum*; *c*, and *d*, the cutis; *e*, glands, ducts, &c.

The next gives us the epidermis only—*a*, being the outer; *b*, the inner layer (*rete mucosum*); *c*, the cutis, to the outline of which the *rete mucosum* adapts itself.

It is in the deepest parts of the inner layer, in the parts more immediately in contact with the true skin, that the most colouring matter is accumulated. Hence, the horny, or outer part of the epidermis is white or yellowish, all the world over. A blister, in popular language, *raises the skin*; in reality, it only raises the outer layer of the epidermis. Now blisters rise equally *white* with the African and with the European.

It is not until after birth that the colouring matter of the second layer of the scarf-skin becomes deposited. A negro child is born of somewhat deeper red colour than an European, but he is not born black. The edges of the nails and the nipple of the breast darken first; the body having darkened by the third day, there or thereabouts.

As the hue of the skin attains its deepest tinge with the groupe before us, the structure that exhibits it has been enlarged upon.

What is the moral and social state of these negroes of the Delta of the Niger? what their habits, customs, and creeds?

We cannot follow the account of any observer for these parts, without discovering that, overpowering as is the heat, and swampy as is the ground, unfavourable, in one word, as are the conditions of soil and climate, the whole of the low country represented by the groupe before us teems with human life; neither is there the absence of human industry. We first hear of villages of from twenty to thirty, from thirty to forty, from fifty to seventy huts; to each of which we may give, upon an average, some six occupants. Then there are large towns like Iboh and Iddah, wherein the inhabitants are counted by the thousand; where there are regular

FIGURE 78
Two pages from Latham's guidebook describing the structure of human skin and dismissing the notion that human beings might be divided into more than one species. (Robert Gordon Latham and Edward Forbes, *A Hand Book to the Courts of Natural History Described* [1854], 42–43. Reproduced by kind permission of the Syndics of Cambridge University Library.)

"drawing rooms, libraries, churches, pubs, clubs, and railway carriages."[70] Likewise, the writer echoed the slave's cry that had become an iconic rallying cry for abolitionists: "Am I not a man and a brother?" The pointed reference was to the raging debates on slavery in the United States, where the notion of multiple human species found much greater sympathy than in Britain, and which ultimately contributed to the American Civil War between 1861 and 1865.[71] Such broad discussion is just one example of the potential for visitors to wander the court closely examining models of foreign peoples while reflecting on the relationship between development, progress and human variety.

Guidebooks, magazines, and newspapers also provided extensive descriptions of the natural history court. Samuel Philips noted that it was "instructive and amusing," and would provide a "clearer conception" than could be "obtained elsewhere of the manner in which the varieties of man, animals, and plants, are distributed over the globe." Edward McDermott, author of Routledge's guidebook, believed it to be "highly interesting," with numerous "leading diversions."[72] Another journalist likened it to a form of virtual tourism: "the ornamental piece of water at the south end must be supposed to represent the Atlantic Ocean separating the two hemispheres. Sailing down the nave from the Polar regions the old world is upon the left and the New World upon the right." Moving on, one could visit the "vast plains of Chinese Tatary," "burning climes of India," and the "vast arid and unexplored continent of Africa."[73] One of the most popular displays proved to be the tiger hunt, in which

the Tiger, seen extended on his back, has been wounded from the howdah, or car, on the elephant's back, and in his struggle has rolled over into that position. The other tiger seeks to revenge his companion by an attack upon the persons in the howdah, whilst the Elephant is in the act of uttering a roar of fear, and starting off with the speed of terror from the scene of the action. Under such circumstances, the keeper, seated on the neck of the animal, has no control over him, and the riders are in imminent peril of being jolted out of their seats, and of falling into the clutches of the Tiger.[74]

The animals had been procured from the zoological gardens at Regent's Park and were noted for their "life-like appearance." Their apparent authenticity and value were reinforced in magazine and newspaper illustrations in which the animals were represented as if still alive and fighting in the Indian jungle. One journalist believed that a "better subject than this could scarcely be selected for India; for in no other country are elephants so much used, neither is there any country more pestered with tigers, or where they more abundantly thrive than among its interminable jungles."[75] The hunt was specially marked on Philips's guidebook map and also featured on the cover of George Measom's *Crystal Palace Alphabet* (1855), where it entertained and educated "good children" (fig. 79a).[76] Measom's little instruction manual also used images of the court to illustrate Y for Yak and Z for Zoology (fig. 79b–c). The reproduction and circulation of such descriptions not only reflected interest in the court but laid the foundations for widespread public consumption of the ethnological material by ensuring that the court displays a vibrant life beyond the palace's shimmering walls.

The Crystal Palace's human displays were particularly important for those interested in ethnology and who craved formal instruction beyond that provided by showmen. London boasted anatomy museums such as Dr. Kahn's, in which one could peruse wax models of human anatomy (including shockingly explicit examples of afflictions to which only sinful flesh was vulnerable).[77] Occasionally, foreign peoples were featured alongside the more usual fare; for instance, Kahn exhibited Maximo, Bartola, Martinus, Flora, and the "Niam-Niams," a race of men from Abyssinia ostensibly sporting tails.[78] During 1853 at Savile House, Leicester Square, Reimers' Anatomical and Ethnological Museum had exhibited over three hundred wax models, including a "Gallery of Nations," featuring Maximo and Bartola, which claimed to exhibit "at one glance the varied types of the Great Human Family."[79] The review in *Reynolds's Newspaper* was positive, and advised "all to visit it as quickly as possible."[80] Despite such auspicious beginnings and a European tour throughout the 1850s, the museum had passed into Londoners' memory by the time the Crystal Palace in Sydenham flung open its doors.[81] The British Museum made some ethnological and natural

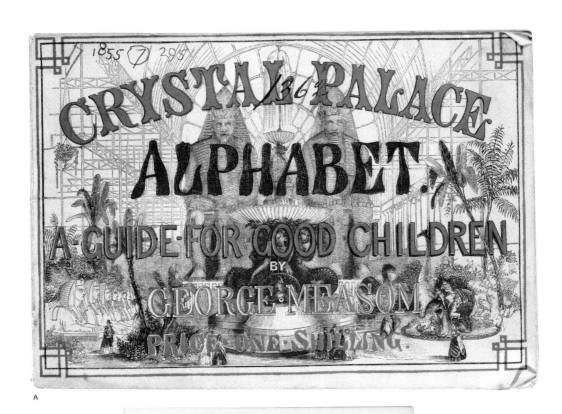

A

Y stands for Yak, whose tails from Thibet
On Turkish high officers' caps are now set.

B

Z for Zoology, study of life,
With which all this beautiful world is so rife.

C

historical material publicly available, but despite having an Ethnographical Room, the relevant artifacts were scattered about the building and not arranged in order to illustrate ethnological theory. Meanwhile, even the most enthusiastic showmen could not match either Latham's expertise in communicating the latest research on human variety or the resources of his museum in displaying such a broad spectrum of ethnic groups. Thus, in the mid-1850s, Sydenham offered an unrivaled object lesson in contemporary ethnology that competed with—and, given its lower entrance fees, likely won—London's shows for custom.[82] With such rivalry in the fray, Latham's possible reliance on the live shows as a source of narrative becomes even more pertinent. Intriguingly, since Zulu performers from Charles Caldecott's 1853 exhibition were used to make the casts, the scene and models may even have been individually recognizable for some visitors. Either way, in the live shows patrons met living peoples who were interactive and potentially challenged their preconceptions (chapters 4 and 5). At the Crystal Palace, the same people were frozen into poses illustrating sometimes sensational, and possibly even the same, stories of foreign peoples' lives, bound together under the banner of contemporary ethnology.

The press regularly suggested that the shows were of special interest for a study of human variety; yet it was Latham who ultimately expended considerable efforts to make such material available to a diverse audience and to incorporate formally displayed peoples into contemporary debates regarding human classification and development. Although clearly successful in attracting the crowds, the Crystal Palace in Sydenham did pose other problems. Latham presented his museum as an uncontentious project; but as his colleagues soon made clear, the public presentation of ethnological theory caused tension, because scholars had yet to agree on the nature of ethnology itself and the best way to present it to both learned and lay audiences.

The Ethnologists' Manifesto

The importance of Latham's directorship is suggested by his alteration of the Crystal Palace Company's original plans. Originally, William Thomson, the curator of the Museums of Natural History and Anatomy at King's College, London, was charged with overseeing the ethnological, zoological, and raw produce collections at Sydenham. Moreover, by 1852 the company had published three short pamphlets in which Thomson outlined plans for the collections. Initially, the company sought donations, and its "list of desiderata" for the ethnological collection included donations of casts of hands and faces, weapons, national costume, drawings, indigenous art, and religious or devotional objects.[83] Yet, once appointed in 1852, Latham adjusted the nature of the enterprise by conceiving of his museum. Meanwhile, 1853 provided a particularly rich selection of exhibited foreign peoples in the metropolis, and Latham quickly took advantage of their presence. Many of the models of people in the palace's natural history court were in fact casts made from individuals either being exhibited or living in London between 1853 and 1854. These included some members of Caldecott's Zulu troupe, Maximo and Bartola, Flora and Martinus, and two Australians, Dick and Tom.[84] Where local examples were less forthcoming, Latham attempted to obtain copies of casts that had been made from life from other ethnological collections, such as those of Anders Retzius, from whom examples of the Krenak and a young Pampa girl were taken. Similarly, he also included indigenous peoples from British Guiana (now Guyana) modeled from life during an expedition by Sir Robert H. Schomburgk, a German naturalist and explorer later knighted by Queen Victoria.[85] The effort to which Latham went to procure casts in preference to awaiting donations or using sculpted models is revealing: not only were displayed peoples considered legitimate ethnological specimens that might be used fruitfully, but the opportunities they provided for research were being actively exploited.

Latham's approach was seen as both admirably innovative and a promising basis for future research. Before the opening ceremony of the Crystal Palace, one journalist was positive about the project but felt that it needed further development, because "Dr. Latham cannot expect to complete his ethnological collection from the types of races brought to the port of London in one year."[86] After having visited the court, another reviewer felt that a portion of "Dr. Latham's ethnological collection is nearly perfect," with the "varied races of mankind, from the most savage and intellectual, to the states verging on civilisation" exhibited in their "appropriate conditions."[87] Conolly argued that although he had lacked "sufficiently numerous opportunities of seeing the various groups of Ethnological models at the Crystal Palace, at Sydenham, to enable me to say more than that they are, artistically, much to be admired," he felt that "the idea of illustrating the Ethnology, Zoology, and Botany of various regions of the earth" was "calculated to be largely instructive." His comment indicates that he felt it was worthwhile to make repeated visits to the court in an effort to take advantage of the models' presence. Significantly, he believed that the court's displays were accurate and relevant enough for a "detailed critical report of the figures, &c.," to be "very interesting" for ethnologists.[88]

Conolly also used the Crystal Palace in Sydenham as an example to bolster his argument that a national collection, possibly housed in the British Museum, and arranged "with a view to the particular illustration of different branches of ethnological inquiry, would greatly facilitate the progress" of ethnology.[89] In making such claims, he highlighted another possible function of such collections: namely, training. Essentially, ethnologists might become figures of authority able to use such collections to ostensibly teach both the lay and the learned how to recognize, and distinguish between, the different human varieties. In this guise, the Crystal Palace, and later fairs such as the Colonial and Indian Exhibition of 1886 (see chapter 7), served multiple, often complementary, functions as ephemeral museums, training grounds, research centers, opportunities to meet colleagues, and educational showcases.[90] Even after the doors shut on the exhibition, the displays continued to prove useful. In later years, Edward Burnett Tylor, the first British anthropologist to obtain a university readership, felt that the models were useful enough to keep photographs of them in his personal collection (figures 72 and 73 are from his private papers). In this context, the models entered and circulated within a new visual economy of photographs and their collectors while helping to create and reinforce their role in the study of human variation. Intriguingly, it also raises the possibility that Tylor may have felt that they were at least as useful as anthropometric photographs which, in the mid-1860s, became the focus of attempts to create new methods of obtaining anthropologically useful information.[91] Meanwhile, Latham's own reputation was significantly enhanced by his curatorship of the museum.

There were detractors. A member of the Ethnological Society, Richard Cull, was irritated that "models of the wretched little idiots exhibited in London last year as Aztecs" had been included, since they were not "types of any race." Similarly, he was concerned that the natural history court was "calculated to mislead," since too much attention had been paid to physical differences and not enough to linguistic or mental attributes: "The exhibition of physical man is merely the natural-history part of man. It is to be hoped that means are adopted to teach the spectators, that however important this may be as a part, it is only a part of the great science of Ethnology." Cull acknowledged that the problem lay partly in the sheer difficulty of addressing his interests, since features "of the mind and its productions, especially that earliest and wonderful production, verbal language, cannot be displayed."[92] The lack of attention to language must have been especially disappointing given Latham's philological talents and experience. After all, between 1839 and 1845, Latham was a professor of English language and literature at University College, London, and well known as the author of the successful textbook *The English Language* (1841).[93] Thus, despite Latham's desires and the guidebook's confident profession on what ethnology *was*, Cull undermined attempts to promote the natural history court as a wholly representative enterprise.[94]

In later years, a conflagration of unknown cause reduced the human models to ashes; the loss was great enough to be mourned by the *Anthropological Review*, which noted, "Amongst the important anthropological events which have taken place during the past year [1866] the destruction by fire of the statues of various savage tribes in the Crystal Palace, deserves to be chronicled. Inaccurate as these representations no doubt were," the educational loss would be immense, the journal stated, since they had been the "only materials generally accessible to the public in London, by which the popular mind could render itself familiar with the aspect of many of the races of man." The *Review* hoped that replacement models would be commissioned, and that they would be in the vein of those forming the

Paris Gallery of Anthropology at the Jardin des Plantes. Just as Latham had done, it called for the casts in all cases to be "coloured with the precise tints of the original skin." Furthermore, the *Review* said it was especially important that "the greatest possible care should be taken, not merely to surround [the models] with all necessary accessories of costume and furniture, but to maintain the expression of the living subject as far as possible," since casts made from dead faces did not always "indicate the true physiognomy of the individual."[95]

Given the objections raised by Cull and the *Anthropological Review*, it is significant that neither party extended them to the decision to create a court of natural history in the first place, or its potential utility for both ongoing and future research. Instead, Cull's frankly expressed qualms were based on the issue of who constituted an ethnic type (certainly not Maximo and Bartola) and his fears that the brand of ethnology presented would simply be too visual to do justice to the theoretical and methodological diversity of contemporary ethnological practice. Meanwhile, anthropologists called for the models to be quickly replaced after their loss. The cross-Channel search for inspiration was not surprising, since James Hunt, the founder of the Anthropological Society, was a devotee of Paul Broca, an influential French anatomist who helped found the institutional framework of mid-century French anthropology; yet the self-conscious alignment with Paris did not stop the *Review* from calling for the emulation of Latham's choice to use live human subjects, realistically painted casts, and naturalistic backgrounds modeled on natural habitats. Meanwhile, writing in 1867, the writer Alphonse Esquiros felt that the "intention was certainly excellent, but the carrying out" left "much to be desired." He acknowledged that exhibits had been "moulded and copied to the very life" and the skins "well prepared"; however, he still felt that the overall effect was "meagre," and that the "details themselves seem sometimes puerile and even ridiculous." Intriguingly, he claimed that a "great English naturalist" had suggested that the museum would have benefited from the introduction of "actual savages of real flesh and blood."[96] Despite the anxiety and disagreement about how best to present the material to the public or ethnologists, Latham's guidebook glossed over the tensions regarding the Crystal Palace's displays and, in turn, the heated negotiations concerning the discipline's future.

Between the 1840s and 1870s, the institutional framework associated with the scholarly study of human variety underwent considerable transformations, helping to redefine the practitioners, intellectual scope, and methodologies of ethnology. In 1837, Thomas Hodgkin helped found the Aborigines' Protection Society.[97] The organization was established in the wake of the 1836 report of the Parliamentary Select Committee on Aborigines, originally set up to conduct an inquiry into the ravages colonial governments had visited on indigenous populations worldwide.[98] Hodgkin was convinced that the moral obligation to protect indigenous peoples would be strengthened and supported by the scientific study of humanity.[99] His interests were complemented by members such as Prichard, and helped draw others to the society who, while sharing the philanthropic commitments, were primarily interested in pursuing their scholarly interests in human difference.

In 1843 a breakaway faction formed the Ethnological Society of London.[100] Moral philanthropy and the scholarly study of human variety were hardly mutually exclusive; nevertheless, those primarily interested in pursuing the sciences of "man" felt the need to generate a distinctive institutional identity. By establishing a forum dedicated to pursuing their interest, members of the new society also helped to bring together previously disparate interests and individuals. Throughout the eighteenth and early nineteenth centuries, scholars interested in biblical hermeneutics, natural history, political economy, philology, liberal politics, theology, abolitionism, and missionary and travel literature all contributed to the study of human variety.[101] Thus, from its inception, ethnology emerged as a synthetic discipline, which is partly reflected by the makeup of the original members of the society, who were primarily military officers, civil servants, clergymen, and physicians. Although the Ethnological Society failed to win recognition by the British Association for the Advancement of Science as a separate subsection in 1844, from 1846 it shared a subsection with zoology and botany. In 1848, it gained further institutional backing when the geologist and scientific bureaucrat extraordinaire Roderick Murchison created a new section for geography and ethnology. The society's publications included the *Journal of the Ethnological Society of London* (1848–56, new series 1869–70), the *Ethnological Journal* (1848–66), and *Transactions of the Ethnological Society of London* (1861–69). The society's periodical literature and meetings helped bring coherence to the emerging discipline and facilitated broader intellectual exchange. However, in the early 1850s the activity and membership of the early years declined, leading to considerable uncertainty as to its future. By the 1860s, a fresh influx of a new and relatively young generation of professionals in their twenties and thirties (total membership rising from 40 1860 to 211 in 1863) overwhelmed the original members of the Ethnological Society and contributed to growing tensions within the group.[102]

In 1863, under the leadership of Hunt, speech therapist and then secretary of the Ethnological Society, another rupture formed the Anthropological Society of London. The final straw appears to have been the illustrations for Robert Clarke's article on Sierra Leone (fig. 80).[103] Hunt was placed in charge of investigating the cost of engravings, and after some discussion the issue was referred to a committee (also featuring Thomas Hodgkin and fellow Quaker philanthropist Henry Christie), where there was disagreement about whether to use the images that eventually appeared. Comparing "the soft and slightly romanticized lines of the engravings eventually published with the harsh and almost bestial representa-

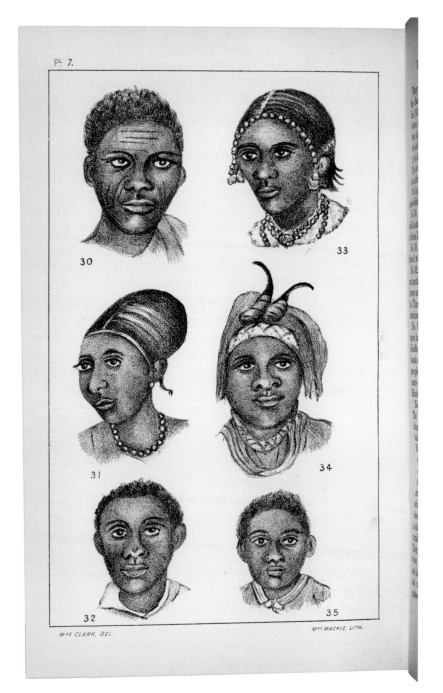

Pt. 7.

30   33

31   34

32   35

M.ᴿˢ CLARK, DEL.   M.ᴿˢ MACKIE, LITH.

FIGURE 80
Robert Clarke's images of the inhabitants of Sierra Leone. (Robert Clarke, "Sketches of the Colony of Sierra Leone and its Inhabitants," *Transactions of the Ethnological Society of London* 2 [1863], plate 7, preceding p. 357. (© The British Library Board. ST 1087.)

tions of blacks in some of the racist works of the period" has given rise to the speculation that Hunt must have felt the selected images were highly unsuitable.[104] Yet we need not look to the more racist or bestial images of the period as the most likely alternatives Hunt wished to use to see why the exaggerated features and naive style of the published engravings may have jarred. The odd proportions undermine any sense of realism which, in Hunt's view, may well have left them wanting as a source either for learning about human variation or for accurate depictions of a particular human type. It has also been suggested that since the article was on Sierra Leone, a free black colony, the images would have been deeply problematic for Hunt, since they depicted Europeanized black peoples who had successfully achieved self-government, a feat of which Hunt believed "Negroes" incapable.[105] In any case, Hunt tendered his resignation from the Ethnological Society at the same meeting and moved on to pastures anew.

Hunt wasted no time in outspokenly promoting his vision of anthropology's future as a scientific discipline. He commissioned translations of foreign works such as Carl Vogt's *Lectures on Man* (1864; Hunt edited and dedicated the work to Broca) and founded (and often secretively edited and financially subsidized) a substantial periodical literature, including the *Transactions of the Anthropological Society of London* (1863), *Anthropological Review* (1863–70), and *Journal of the Anthropological Society of London* (1864–70).[106] Hunt's dissent has often been seen as an attempt to create a home for those opposed to the political, intellectual, and humanitarian commitments of the Ethnological Society.[107] Yet given the dispute over images, it seems likely that the importance of the visual representation, certainly of communication, has been underestimated in the society's fissure. For Hunt, the use of images was a critical consideration in the public presentation of research and, by extension, in establishing the sound foundations of a new discipline. Given his departure over the published images and subsequently his zealous stewardship of such a large and newly established periodical literature, it may also be argued that he left the Ethnological Society in order to create and exert greater editorial control over both images and publications.[108] This seems especially important when the illustrations of Clarke's article are compared with the images that did appear in the periodicals of the Anthropological Society. These were invariably line drawings that look like camera obscura diagrams and stand in stark contrast to the style of the Clarke lithographs. Between 1863 and his premature death in 1869, Hunt provided a figurehead for the new science. Shortly after, despite coexisting uneasily for several years, the Ethnological Society and the Anthropological Society merged in 1871 to form the Anthropological Institute of Great Britain and Ireland, and the diversity of the societies' periodicals was subsumed into the newly founded *Journal of the Anthropological Institute of Great Britain and Ireland* (1872–1906).

These institutional wranglings have traditionally been seen as taking place during, and contributing to, the reconceptualization of "race" from an elastic category based on physical, social, and cultural considerations to an unchangeable, inherited trait based primarily, or even solely, on physiological, anatomic, or biological differences and the emergence of "scientific racism."[109] These shifts are often argued to have been coupled with the ostensible transformation of "armchair" ethnology into modern anthropology; or, in methodological terms, the assumed shift from humanistic textual and philological approaches to scientific investigation rooted in biological science and, ultimately, fieldwork.[110] The anatomist Thomas Henry Huxley's *Man's Place in Nature* (1865) appears to confirm the new disciplinary landscape:

Ethnology is the science which determines the distinctive characters of the persistent modifications of mankind; which ascertains the distribution of those modifications in present and past times, and seeks to discover the causes, or conditions of existence, both of the modifications and of their distribution. . . . Ethnology, as thus defined, is a branch of Anthropology, the great science which unravels the complexities of human structure; traces out the relations of man to other animals; studies all that is especially human in the mode in which man's complex functions are performed; and searches after the conditions which have determined his presence in the world. And anthropology is a section of Zoology, which again is the animal half of Biology—the science of life and living things.[111]

Like Conolly on the shows, we must remember that Huxley was by no means an independent commentator; in contrast, he was instrumental in negotiating the merger between the two societies.[112] His well-known account of the relationship between ethnology and anthropology, and by implication their appropriate institutional alignments, was not simply an outline of the disciplines' future topographies but a partisan appraisal of the polemical refashioning that ultimately contributed to the creation of the Anthropological Institute and late nineteenth-century anthropology.

Between the 1840s and the 1860s, the theorists most emblematically associated, or credited, with the shifting disciplinary landscape of ethnological and anthropological practice are Prichard, Knox, and Hunt. Prichard is an exceptionally important figure. Raised a devout Quaker and subsequently an Anglican convert, over his lifetime he came to be regarded as the "greatest writer" that "treated of the Science of Ethnology, and investigated and classified the nations and kindreds and tongues of voice-varying men."[113] His major works, *Researches into the Physical History of Mankind* (1813; 3rd ed. 1836–47) and the more widely known and digestible *Natural History of Man* (1843), drew on his Edinburgh medical training, voracious reading in multiple languages, and exceptional linguistic skills to fend off the challenge from religious heterodoxy while helping to lay the methodological and intellectual foundations of British ethnology.

Knox's *The Races of Men* (1850) and Hunt's "On the Physical and Mental Characters of the Negro" (1863) are frequently cited as exemplars of a new tide of Victorian racism and aggressive imperialism in the mid-nineteenth century.[114] It is not difficult to see why. Knox is infamous for opening *The Races of Men* with the sensational claim "Race is everything."[115] Meanwhile, Hunt's paper, presented at the annual meeting of the British Association for the Advancement of Science (founded 1831) pronounced, first, that there is as good reason for classifying the negro as a distinct species from the European as there is for making the ass a distinct species from the zebra; secondly, that the negro is inferior intellectually to the European; thirdly, that the analogies are far more numerous between the negro and the ape than between the European and the ape. There was in the negro that assemblage of evidence which would induce an unbiased observer to make the European and negro distinct species.[116]

Yet Knox's and Hunt's views are not only deeply offensive now but were both highly controversial and deemed utterly unacceptable by many of their contemporaries. After all, Hunt's paper was immediately "met by hisses and catcalls for defending the subjection and slavery of African-Americans, and supporting belief in the plurality of human species."[117] Similarly, Knox was widely criticized for his politics and materialism, and despite being exonerated of all charges, remained tainted from guilt by association after being caught buying murdered bodies for his Edinburgh anatomy school. It was precisely this stigmatization that meant he initially failed to be admitted to the Ethnological Society (Hunt later negotiated his acceptance in 1858).[118] Meanwhile, Latham's work has been variously seen as primarily philological, an outmoded form of descriptive natural history heavily indebted to, or even imitative of, Prichard, glossed over in favor of the sensational racism of Knox and Hunt or ignored altogether.[119] However, there are more constructive ways to frame Latham's work.

Latham both retrained as a physician and built his medical career while still a professor of English before pursuing his interests in ethnology. Among men of science, particularly those interested in ethnology, he rose to prominence after the death of Prichard (1848). Elected to the Royal Society in the same year, he quickly published *The Natural History of the Varieties of Man* (1850, the same year as Knox's *Races of Man*); he also served as vice-president of the Ethnological Society and was commissioned to begin work on the Crystal Palace's court of natural history in 1852. Publicly, his profile was enhanced by his curatorship of the palace, writing the court's guidebook with Forbes, and contributing to other works, such as *Orr's Circle of the Sciences* (1854), devoted to explicating science for the broader public.[120]

Latham's assumed public role and personal presentation as heir apparent to Prichard is tellingly suggested by the first illustration of the ethnology section for *Orr's Circle*. In it, Latham is part of a triumvirate of ethnology's luminaries (fig. 81). Even six years after his death, Prichard's prominence is abundantly clear. His centrally located bust is flanked by his intellectual ancestor Blumenbach, gazing into the future on his right. Prichard looks, more indirectly, ahead to his disciple Latham on the left, while Latham simply addresses the reader's gaze in the present. The image both chronologically records ethnology's development from eighteenth-century German comparative anatomy to nineteenth-century

FIGURE 81
Ethnology's past
(Blumenbach), pres-
ent (Prichard), and
future (Latham).
(Robert Gordon
Latham, *The Variet-
ies of Human Species*, 1.
Reproduced by kind
permission of the
Syndics of the Cam-
bridge University
Library.)

British philology and traces a direct intellectual genealogy between the
figures. Meanwhile, Latham's curatorship of the Crystal Palace in Sydenham is indicative of how his work cannot be fully accommodated within
frameworks that propose that the 1850s, and particularly the work of Knox,
ushered in a new era of scientific racism and the successful overthrow of
older approaches in favor of anatomic, physiological, or biological notions
of "race."[121]

Latham bridged the world between the scholarly elite and the lay public with both his writings and his practice. As a trained philologist and a
self-conscious follower in Prichard's footsteps, he did make heavy use of
language and natural history in his ethnological research; however, his
curatorship of the court of natural history demonstrates why he cannot
be accurately characterized as taking a primarily humanistic, text-based
approach (as Prichard ostensibly did) or as having adopted anatomy and
physiology as his primary rationale for defining human variation (as
Knox and Hunt were wont). Rather, it is clear that Latham's research was a
heterogeneous mix of many elements, including natural history, philology,
anatomy, and physiology. Rather than witnessing the emergence or consolidation of a single approach to the study of human variety, his work suggests it would be more accurate to argue that the mid-nineteenth century
saw a substantial *proliferation*, not a homogenization, of intellectual and
methodological approaches accompanying the scholarly study of human
variation. Such diversity is suggested by Latham's own work and affirmed
by the dissent voiced over the displays in the Crystal Palace's court of natural history. Likewise, Latham's connections within the gentlemanly network of scholars interested in ethnology and public presence suggests that
during the 1850s, both ethnologists and polite society looked to Latham,

Transforming "Unfruitful Wonder"

not Knox, for their ethnological educations. It is in this vein, and in Latham's hands in particular, that human displays became resources that were drawn on in the effort to redefine both what "race" actually meant and how it could be productively studied by the lay and the learned.

*

It may be tempting to read John Conolly's address as an accurate description of ethnological practice in the mid-nineteenth century and of the relationship between displayed people, ethnologists, and paying customers; however, in light of the institutional and intellectual redefinitions involved in the study of human variety during this period, it is clear that his argument can be interpreted as a passionate polemic intended to use displayed peoples to bolster the social standing of the Ethnological Society of London. He complained that despite the availability of exhibited peoples in London, they were not habitually examined by ethnologists. Therefore, he argued, the public was left to believe the extraordinary stories used by showmen without exposure to a critical review from those who considered themselves most suited to the task. The lack of systematic study also meant that few accounts of exhibited peoples' anatomy or ethnic provenance appeared in the learned journals, and that ethnologists were left complaining that they had little usable material on which to base their discussions of the shows.

In contrast, Conolly argued for the shows to be subjected to investigations he and his colleagues deemed rational, and opened up two desirable possibilities. First, ethnologists would be able to produce accounts of the full range of exhibited peoples that were specifically designed to address their theoretical and methodological interests. Second, ethnologists might play a role in certifying the authenticity of the showmen's advertised claims. Undoubtedly, achieving such a regulatory function would have allowed the Ethnological Society to exert considerable control over how exhibited peoples were displayed, promoted, and studied. The benefit for paying patrons, Conolly believed, would lie in the educative value of transforming exhibited peoples from "specimens showing the progress made in arts or in science among rude people and in remote regions" into "manifestations of human intellect and modifications of human development in various parts of the same globe, and illustrative of man's unwritten history and progress."[122] Tellingly, his address was subsequently published in pamphlet form as *The Ethnological Exhibitions of London* (1855). In this guise, it became available as a manifesto for ethnology's future, with its very name betraying an anxiety about how the exhibitions ought to be used and by whom. Ultimately, such a highly polemical intervention in the debates over the use of displayed peoples essentially caricatured a highly complex network of critically engaged intellectual interest on the part of the lay public and ethnologists.

Displayed peoples could potentially be used as specimens during any period, but as the language of the new sciences of man emerged in the 1840s, they were quickly appropriated into its discussions by being both routinely and explicitly touted as opportunities to see specimens of typological human variation. The descriptive material included in exhibition pamphlets and promotional material from the early nineteenth century suggests that showmen regularly provided patrons with the kind of information they needed (such as notes on language, clothing, religion, and physiognomy) to think critically about displayed peoples in relationship to human variation. Furthermore, they also offered opportunities to book private appointments where extended examinations could take place. It is highly likely that the shows' attraction lay partly in their ability to provide those interested in ethnology with living examples of peoples to whom they may not otherwise have had personal access, since, despite the heterogeneous population and urban spectators' claims, not all peoples were equally represented in London's resident population.

Conolly's own testimony bears powerful witness to the use of displayed peoples as the basis of personal speculations on human variation. Information regarding exhibits circulated widely, and sometimes made its way into journals and standard texts in discussions of human variety. Upon her death, Sara Baartman was exposed to Georges Cuvier's scalpel, and her autopsy became the subject of a now infamous paper on female Khoekhoe anatomy.[123] Cuvier's triumphant account was well known and became part of a wider currency of ethnological data that was used by ethnologists to inform their theorizing, even when they had not seen Baartman being exhibited. For instance, Prichard's *Natural History of Man* (1843) used examples of displayed peoples, including Baartman and, in later editions, the groups of Bakhoje and Anishinabe exhibited by Catlin, to support his ethnological vision.[124] Similarly, the controversy regarding Maximo and Bartola's ethnic origin and intellectual development indicates how displayed peoples could become the subjects of considerable debate while they were still being exhibited. Thus, displayed peoples came to be used in ethnological theorizing regarding the nature of human variety in a range of social situations and publications.

By the 1850s, Latham's natural history court at Sydenham indicates that exhibited peoples were used within the emerging science of ethnology in institutional settings as well as private rooms. His displays were available until 1866, when a fire badly damaged the majority of the collection and the directors decided not to replace it due to a lack of funds. However, between the palace's opening and the blaze, the natural history court contributed toward promoting an ideal of education by visual means and promoting displayed peoples as legitimate and useful natural historical specimens. The court's importance has been considerably underestimated. Attendance figures alone suggest that a significant proportion of the population walked among the courts, examining the models. Many more are likely to have known about the displays through the press. Coupled with Latham's guidebook, the exhibition endorsed a partisan vision of the subject matter and investigative mode that was most suitable for ethnological research. Simultaneously, it provided Victorians with one of the most accessible and widely consumed nineteenth-century displays of ethnological theory and practice while materially demonstrating how ethnologists felt "rational" investigations of exhibited peoples were to be achieved. In discussing the human models, a modern history of the Crystal Palace proposes that "London had only recently become accustomed in recent years to the sight of living 'savages.'"[125] Unfortunately, this ignores the long-standing tradition of exhibiting foreign peoples.[126] Seeing living foreign peoples on display was not novel; however, it was new to see them as inanimate casts used in a highly accessible, institutionalized setting to illustrate contemporary ethnological debates and so formally incorporate displayed peoples into the study of human variation as both subjects and experimental objects.

Acknowledging displayed peoples' use as scientific resources is especially important, given the considerable activity in the mid-nineteenth century aimed at defining what counted as human difference, the significance of such variation, and how it should be studied. The lasting significance of these debates has been overshadowed by the interest historians have devoted to the legacy of the Anthropological Society and sensational figures such as Knox or Hunt. Although it is fair to regard ethnology as a disciplinary predecessor to anthropology, it is problematic to disregard the late 1850s and figures such as Latham because they appear to have been superseded in the 1860s by a new generation of anthropologists.[127] This is especially so in light of the fact that Latham continued to publish into the late nineteenth century and provided the lay public with the most accessible and widely read introduction to Victorian ethnological theory in the form of his commercially successful guidebook to the natural history court in Sydenham.[128] Similarly, arguing that human differences shifted toward being defined and studied, primarily or solely, in physical terms erases significant diversity between ethnological practitioners in the 1850s. However, it is important to recognize that from the late 1850s onward ethnologists were engaged in a period of disciplinary redefinition which involved fresh demarcations of their subject matter, analytical framework, and methodology.[129] Examining commercial exhibitions of displayed peoples within this climate of dispute highlights how they and the Crystal Palace were both made relevant and contributed to changes in the way that research into human difference was conducted. In the press, displayed peoples were consistently and openly declared to be pertinent to ethnological practice, and the same was said in the notice paid to them by ethnologists in lectures and publications. Such claims were supported by attempts of men such as Owen, Knox, and most particularly Latham to convert the shows into usable observational and experimental material.

Tellingly, once home in Africa, one exhibited Zulu man later recalled that when in England, his group was taken to see the "doctoring houses" where the dead were taken to be "cut up and dried." He remembered that when "we were at the door we saw dead men standing up as if they were alive, so we feared to go in." When asked why the English cut up their dead, he recalled,

I heard that the doctors were the people who liked dead men, and that if the graves were not taken care of their people stole the bodies for them; we were also told that the man of our party who died at Berlin was only buried because we were there, and that he was afterwards taken out and cut up, to see if he was made inside like the white people.[130]

Whether this interview is taken to be the words of the Zulu or the missionary who transcribed his words and subsequently arranged for their publication, the comment suggests a widespread realization that displayed peoples were considered usable experimental material and that, where possible, the opportunities they provided for research were being taken up with enthusiasm. For instance, when Flora died in London in 1864, her body was rushed off for dissection by London's medical men.[131]

Rather than argue that displayed peoples were the crux of ethnological investigation in the nineteenth century, it would be more appropriate to recognize how valuable many clearly felt they were by campaigning for a more comprehensive descriptive project than the piecemeal examinations we know took place. This is especially important for histories of anthropological thought. Ethnologists' hopes may not initially have materialized into systematic examinations of every exhibited individual, but as the final chapter suggests, this began to change in the late nineteenth century as anthropologists played an increasingly important role in exhibiting foreign peoples at international fairs. German anthropology in particular used the *Völkerschauen* as abundant sources of experimental material.[132] However, the shows of London considered here were not only of an earlier period but, more significantly, one that was formative to the very notion of what should constitute suitable material for ethnological, and subsequently anthropological, investigation. Ultimately, by playing a role in redefining human variety and the means used to study it, displayed peoples helped secure the future value of their bodies to anthropological research—dead or alive.

The End of an Affair

IN 1899, a *Pall Mall Gazette* correspondent ventured "into the very heart of South Africa" to meet "subjects of the Cape, Natal, the Orange Free State, and the Transvaal."[1] Once there among the "horde of savages," he encountered "Matabeles, Basutos, Swazies, Hottentots," and "a colossal aggregation of wild fauna of South Africa," including lions, leopards, tigers, bucks, cranes, baboons, and elephants. Fortunately, he was spared the inconvenience of a lengthy sailing trip, having simply taken the Metropolitan Railway to Earl's Court. All this had been made possible due to the "courtesy" of Imre Kiralfy, the owner of Earl's Court, and Frank Fillis, the manager of the Savage South Africa exhibition. Although not an international exhibition in its own right, Fillis's extravaganza was set up as an unofficial accompaniment to the Greater Britain Exhibition at Earl's Court by being held virtually cheek by jowl at the six-thousand-seat Empress Theatre on the same grounds. It also borrowed from conventions relating to displayed peoples that by 1899 had been tried and tested worldwide.

Human displays were immediately incorporated into and ultimately transformed under the aegis of international exhibitions. By the later nineteenth century, organizers began to envisage fairs as encyclopedic educational tools that could help educate the public to become ideal consumers and citizens. As such, they soon became highly successful arenas for public engagement with the political, social, cultural, and commercial agendas of the exhibition organizers and hosts. Among the most commonly cited reasons for hosting such events were promoting peace among nations, aiding mass public education, stimulating trade, and contributing to progress. Yet whatever the professed aims, all exhibition organizers and financiers tried to maximize attendance, publicize the host's social and political agendas, and provide investors with a healthy profit. The funding for these events varied between government support, private sponsorship, public lotteries, and exhibition companies. The sheer scale of the fairs became breathtaking. By the end of the nineteenth century, sites might take up thousands of acres, exhibits numbered in the hundreds of thousands, and attendance figures were regularly reported in tens of millions.[2] By exploring the relationship between Savage South Africa, international fairs, and later nineteenth-century conventions of entertainment and spectacle, this chapter traces how human displays developed in that period. Simultaneously, by exploring their shifting associations with institutionalized anthropology, it suggests how the kinds of knowledge the shows produced were transformed in the final decades of the nineteenth century.

Imperial Metropolis

By the late Victorian period, London had become the biggest city the world had ever seen. It had been a cosmopolitan center throughout its history, but it was in the nineteenth century that it underwent its most substantial transformations, particularly in terms of size and demographic diversity. The first metropolis in history to house a million souls, between 1883 and 1884 its population surpassed 5 million, and far from abating, the growth continued: "There were more Londoners in 1914 than in 2000, living in an area about half the size of modern London, but roughly double the size of London in 1883." By 1881, of a population of approximately 3.8 million, almost 107,000 (2.7%) were classified as foreign, with the largest resident immigrant populations designated as "German (22,000), French (8,250), Polish (6,930), Dutch (4,200), Italian (3,500) and Swiss (2,300)."[3] In addition, smaller but discernible foreign communities were dotted around the city. In Limehouse there was a small Chinese community, Polish and Jewish immigrants found homes in Whitechapel, Italians were resident in Saffron Hill, and a mix of Europeans, mainly Swiss, Italian, and French, lodged in Soho. The growing ethnic heterogeneity and population changes were evocatively captured in 1902 when the journalist George Sims renamed portions of the city as "China Town" and "Little Italy."[4] London's districts were never formally demarcated according to ethnicity, yet Sims's epithets capture the evolving concentrations of ethnic groups in specific metropolitan locales.

Resident immigrants aside, London also played host to a considerable number of foreign visitors and dignitaries. As early as 1710, four "Indian Kings" traveled from their homeland (now eastern New York State) to attempt to forge an alliance with the British and to stave off the encroachment of American settlers on their lands.[5] Between 1882 and 1894, their precedent was followed by envoys from the Zulu, Ndebele, Gaza, and Swazi. With strong ties cemented by a shared heritage, kinship, language, culture, and military organization, these Nguni kingdoms had the common problem of potentially losing their independence in the face of colonial advancement.[6] It has been argued that the "primary mission of all African envoys who came to England in the latter part of Victoria's reign was to mitigate or modify the tide of European imperialism that was engulfing their continent."[7]

After losing the Anglo-Zulu War of 1879, Zulu king Cetshwayo was removed from the throne and faced exile in London. He was both the first and the most high profile of the African envoys. The press brimmed with details of his defeat, commentaries on the most appropriate course of action, and enthusiastic warnings encouraging Cetshwayo and his subjects to accept the loss of their independence and their new status as Britain's subjects. Before his arrival, one letter to the editor of the *Times* asked, "Sir,— Cannot Cetywayo be brought to England, and, as a prisoner on parole, allowed to estimate the resources of the nation by who he has been taken?" A. S. H. further observed that ordinary "Caffre servants" who returned to Natal were always disbelieved, but if the Zulu king, and perhaps some accompanying chiefs, could be impressed on them, their recollections would carry more weight. The suggestion was grounded in the anticipated "effect of a visit to this country on the Caffre mind," an effect that, A. S. H. believed, would "get rid of a troublesome prisoner" and perhaps "make a useful ally."[8] To some extent, the experiences of both Cetshwayo and the other African emissaries reflected the attitude that a display of power might help quell resistance: all of them were shown carefully selected sights, such a Royal Navy ship furnished with guns that could be fired by the press of a single button, army bases where soldiers practiced their maneuvers and fired their weapons, and, naturally, the Great White Queen.[9]

Such high-profile diplomatic visits to London were tied to the late nineteenth-century extension and consolidation of Britain's empire and London's role as an administrative, trading, and financial hub. Known as Britain's "imperial century," the period between 1815 and 1914 witnessed an enormous expansion of British sovereignty borne of an increasingly aggressive and expansionist attitude toward territorial acquisition in the later nineteenth century.[10] Following the violent uprisings of 1857, the British dissolved the East India Company and assumed direct control of India. Between the 1880s and 1914, the "scramble for Africa" resulted in a shoring up of the continent between several European nations; Britain held on to the Cape of Good Hope and extended control into East, West, and Central Africa. These gains saw maps of the period increasingly swathed in pink (fig. 82), the traditional color for representing the British Empire, and ultimately the emergence of a vast realm.

Just as London's connections to colonial territories and peoples were being transformed, so too were the ways in which information about foreign peoples could be obtained. In 1820, for example, it would have taken from five to eight months to sail from London to Calcutta by sailship. By 1825, with the use of steam-assisted ships, the journey had been reduced to just over three months. By 1852, one could go from Southampton to Singapore in forty-five days, to Shanghai in fifty-seven, and Sydney in just seventy-five. Meanwhile, a one-way trip from England to Cape Town, South Africa, was reduced from forty-two days in 1857 to just nineteen days in 1893.[11] In 1869, the opening of the Suez Canal in Egypt considerably reduced journey times, since shipping routes to India and Australia no longer involved circling around the Cape of Good Hope; instead, ships were

FIGURE 82
(Facing) *The British Dominions beyond the Seas at the Date of the Coronation.* Map of the British Empire at the close of the Victorian era, published in honor of King Edward VII. (*Illustrated London News*, June 9, 1902, following 44. Author's collection.)

261

THE BRITISH DOMINIONS BEYOND THE SEAS AT THE DATE OF THE CORONATION.

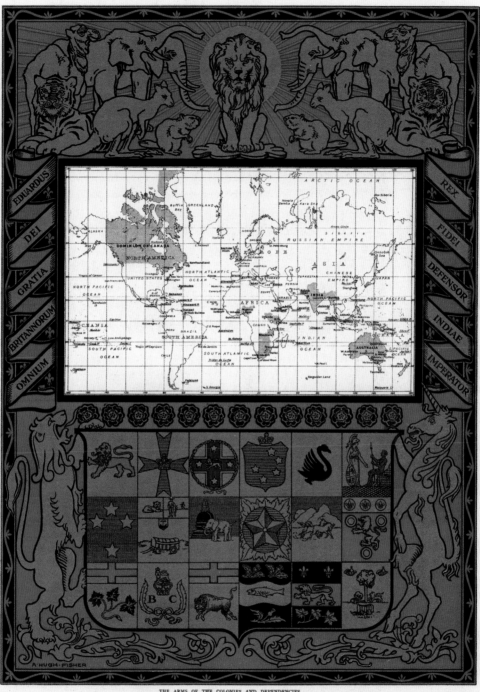

THE ARMS OF THE COLONIES AND DEPENDENCIES.

TASMANIA.	QUEENSLAND.	NEW SOUTH WALES.	VICTORIA.	WESTERN AUSTRALIA.	SOUTH AUSTRALIA.
NEW ZEALAND.	THE TRANSVAAL.	CEYLON.	INDIA.	NATAL.	CAPE COLONY.
ONTARIO.	BRITISH COLUMBIA.	MANITOBA.	NOVA SCOTIA.	QUEBEC.	ORANGE RIVER COLONY.

able to pass through directly between the Mediterranean and Red Seas. A rapidly developing railway network also reduced journey times overland. Between 1850 and the 1870s, for instance, the British laid more than five thousand miles of railway track in India, providing transcontinental links between Bombay and Calcutta. Meanwhile, telegraphy was rolled out overland, particularly in India and Africa, and beneath the sea, notably with the transatlantic connection and direct communications to Cape Town (via Africa's east coast) by 1879. It has been argued that these "technologies, especially when combined, enhanced the state's abilities to expand and dominate."[12] Of particular relevance here is that the advent of the new printing technologies and their tax-free distribution, a global network of telegraphic wires, and cheaper and speedier forms of travel such as steamships all made it quicker, easier, and less expensive to learn about increasingly far-flung places and their inhabitants.

Meanwhile, London's entertainment landscape was considerably reshaped with the emergence of cheap mass-market entertainment that attempted to cater to the growing working and lower middle classes. Music halls, sporting events, and cinema were just some of the new entertainments that became the mainstay of London's show culture in the later nineteenth and early twentieth centuries. The music hall was by far the most accessible of the new entertainment forms: the Alhambra in Leicester Square, one of the earliest and most popular, opened in 1860 with a seating capacity of 3,500.[13] Meanwhile, from the 1860s onward, "sport" shifted from denoting hunting pursuits to signifying recreational, athletic, and competitive activity. By the end of the century, sport had become a commercialized venture, with its own celebrities, large-scale events (such as the Derby horse race and Varsity boat race between the ancient universities of Cambridge and Oxford), and connections to ritualized forms of festivity and human display.[14] Both the motion-picture camera and the projector were available by the late 1880s, and films were commercially exhibited by the mid-1890s. The earliest films were short, unedited records of everyday activities such as walking down streets or the arrival of a train at a rail station. By the 1900s, films were transformed into longer edited recordings with a narrative structure. By 1896, the London papers began to carry advertisements for "Living Pictures" courtesy of the pioneering partnership of the Lumière brothers and their Cinématographe.[15]

The emergence of the mass market fueled reformers' renewed attempts to control and rationalize public entertainments. At the start of the nineteenth century, many of London's accessible diversions could be found either in the street, where itinerant showmen would set up booths on any busy pavement, or at the boisterous and noisy fairs.[16] The fairs were perceived by many to stimulate public disorder and immorality. Consequently, between the seventeenth and mid-nineteenth centuries an extensive program of abolition had been undertaken: Southwark was abolished in 1762, Mayfair in 1764, Peckham in 1827, and Bartholomew's in 1855. The Metropolitan Fairs Act of 1871 declared that fairs "are unnecessary, are the cause of grievous immorality, and very injurious to the inhabitants of the towns where they are held."[17] Meanwhile, as traditional forms of entertainment were reformed, new spaces such as museums, art galleries, and zoological and botanical gardens were all made more publicly accessible. Often the leisure pursuits they offered had only been available to restricted portions of society; however, reformers argued that improved access would provide more rational, hence educative, pursuits than the hurly-burly of fairs and pleasure gardens.[18] The new entertainment forms of the late nineteenth century, such as the music hall and sport, failed to escape the philanthropists' reach and so too became the focus of attempts to rationalize, and thereby ostensibly improve, the amusements of the lower classes.[19]

The changing entertainment landscape shifted the viewing context associated with displayed peoples. For example, in 1868 a group of aboriginal Australian cricketers toured Britain. During matches, play was regularly suspended while the Australians hurled spears, danced, and performed mock fights; to this day, one of the weapons, a leowell, is still displayed at Lord's Cricket Ground.[20] The ostensibly sporting nature of the tour partly reflects the shifting nature of sport and its new role in public entertainment. Similarly, displayed peoples quickly became the focus of the camera's lens with the emergence of film. In 1899, for instance, the Warwick Trading Company produced *Savage South Africa—Savage Attack and Repulse*, depicting the reenactment of a battle between a group of African warriors and the Afrikaner infantry. It features an array of men squatting with their guns at the ready. Within moments, they begin shooting at an off-screen enemy, which is quickly revealed to be a large horde of Africans storming toward them. The Africans are quickly repelled by the firing of guns and the arrival of men on horseback. Finally, the infantry and cavalry reassemble, and the victorious men signal their delight by waving their hats in the air and cheering. Just seventy-five seconds long and silent (sound was introduced in 1927), the film's existence is highly significant. Critically, the performers were drawn from the Savage South Africa exhibition and filmed at the Empress Theatre in Earl's Court; evidently, filming displayed peoples was an attractive enough possibility for them to have been filmed so early on in the development of film.

Just as the viewing context for displayed peoples changed, so did the consumer experience of attending the shows. *Savage South Africa—Savage Attack and Repulse*, for instance, was one of the first on-screen depictions of Africans and has, at times, been mistaken for faked footage of the Boer War. It presented new opportunities for showmen to commodify displayed peoples, yet it also meant that consumers lost the opportunities for unregulated contact that were such a prominent feature of the shows in the early to mid-nineteenth century. The loss of face-to-face contact was obviously inevitable with film, but it also became increasingly difficult with some of the larger venues in which displayed peoples performed (such as

Lord's). In early eyewitness accounts, such contact was evidently one of the main ways in which the stereotyped claims of advertising were called into question or critically reflected on; after all, while promotional material frequently highlighted the "savage" or "barbarous" nature of performers, in-person performers might be described as full of warmth, intelligence, or parental affection. The new dynamic between performers and spectators was reinforced by the lack of invitations to meet performers outside the live performances. Although common earlier in the century, by the later period they began to disappear. They certainly did not feature on promotional materials with any frequency or prominence, and it became increasingly difficult to secure private appointments (see below). Even in international fairs, where spectators could wander through staged villages, exhibitors attempted to control the contact between performers and consumers; sometimes it was curbed altogether by public campaigning or showmen's will, such as the ban placed on female visitors to Savage South Africa after rumored impropriety (see chapter 5).

Moreover, the shifting nature of London's entertainments associated displayed peoples with pastimes that came to be seen as increasingly frivolous. As we have seen, between the 1840s and 1860s exhibitions of foreign peoples began to be explicitly and routinely advertised as ideal opportunities to indulge a scholarly or philosophical interest in human natural history and development. The emergence of large-scale exhibitions and the adoption of display conventions pioneered within the context of international fairs suggest that human displays were becoming primarily associated with entertainment and visual spectacles. It certainly became less common for either the press or managers to rely on claims that their shows were anthropologically relevant to draw the crowds, although they were by no means absent. It was in this distinctively new matrix that the public first encountered Frank Fillis's extravaganza.

London's Kraal

Savage South Africa was an extraordinary affair; set up by a South African circus owner and expert horseman, it was easily the largest African exhibition the metropolis had ever hosted.[21] It had been months in the planning and had required considerable expense and organization to obtain the government permission required to import the necessary personnel.[22] Of these there were many: over two hundred Africans and dozens of Afrikaners had been drafted into service as performers. In addition, Fillis had imported hundreds of animals, including examples of the largest African game. All had to live somewhere, and so, before the cargo ships had docked at Southampton, Fillis arranged for work to begin on a vast mock homestead within the grounds of Earl's Court. In addition, he had expended a great deal of time and money gathering clothes and objects with which to costume and furnish the kraal's inhabitants.

The kraal was a concerted attempt to fabricate an environment that Fillis felt he could promote as authentically African. In addition to setting up a series of huts in the heart of Earl's Court, he surrounded them with painted backdrops of the African veldt. Images of performers on the grounds give some indication of the nature of the enterprise. In the photograph entitled "CHIEF AND GROUP OF SWAZIES" and stamped with "FRANK FILLIS'S SAVAGE SOUTH AFRICA," ten men and a boy are all closely huddled together in full show regalia and adorned with feathers and animal skins (fig. 83). Almost every individual brandishes either an assegai or a knobkierie (club)—the essential weapons of South African, particularly Zulu, warfare and classic reminders of their military prowess. The inclusion of the two huts and the rural plains in the background of the composition implies that the viewer is gazing into the African countryside, yet the bare ground and huts suggest that the photograph was taken at Earl's Court. If one considers that these performers are only eleven of over two hundred people and hundreds of animals in the show, the image provides an arresting glimpse into the nature of consumers' encounters with Savage South Africa.

FIGURE 83
Chief and Group of Swazies, featuring performers from Frank Fillis's Savage South Africa exhibition, 1899. (By kind permission of Michael Stevenson.)

Not content with furnishing Earl's Court with hundreds of performers and animals, Fillis also staged reenactments of the recent Ndebele War (1893) and Ndebele and Shona revolt (1896).[23] Founded as a result of the only major division within the Zulu Kingdom, between the 1820s and mid-1800s the Ndebele established a powerful and expansionist military state along the Zulu model in Matebeleland (now Zimbabwe) that incorporated Nguni speakers, the Sotho-Tswana and Shona. European incursions into the region had long depended on the trade in ivory and slaves, but by the reign of Lobengula (acceded in 1868), the Ndebele king was besieged by Europeans seeking land and mineral rights. In 1888, the staunch colonialist, mineral prospector, and founder of De Beers diamond company, Cecil Rhodes, deceptively claimed to have secured the mineral rights to Lobengula's entire kingdom. In 1889, in the face of bitter opposition from Lobengula, the newly formed British South Africa Company was granted a royal charter to exploit its new concession, effectively extending its administrative control over a substantial portion of the region. In order to maximize profit, the company felt the need to remove Ndebele power altogether and initiated war under the guise of defensive protection. Descendants of the Zulu, the Ndebele were well versed in the military techniques originally developed by Shaka; nevertheless, as the war wore on their forces were devastated by their opponents' newly developed firepower. Following the war and the "deceptively easy" removal of Lobengula from the throne, the British felt the Ndebele were no longer rulers of the region by virtue of concessions granted by a local king but by right of conquest, and so imposed a new political order which they believed the Africans had submissively accepted as superior.[24] The Ndebele may have lost power, but the British had failed to quell, and so profoundly misunderstood, the importance of the Ndebele's self-identification with military supremacy and the Shona's political and religious allegiances to their former rulers. Thus, when the Ndebele and Shona both revolted against the authority of the British South Africa Company in the second conflict, the British were taken aback at the organized and violent expression of the peoples' resentment. Ultimately, despite the angry resistance of both the Shona and the Ndebele, the territories of both Matabeleland and Mashonaland became Rhodesia.

The press kept the public abreast of developments and trumpeted the eventual success of the colonialists in defeating the insurgency. For instance, in October 1893 the *Graphic* published an account of the war by Archibald R. Colquhoun, the administrator of Mashonaland (fig. 84). The page featured a rather resigned-looking Lobengula sitting in his "favourite seat," flanked by two warriors, and floating above an image of a "typical" defensive post (laager) as used by the settlers. The whole article was headed by the image of a South African soldier directly pointing a firearm at close range at an Ndebele warrior defending himself with a shield, knobkierie, and assegai. Images contrasting the traditional weaponry of the Ndebele with the guns and ammunition of the settlers were common,

FIGURE 84
(Facing) *The War in Matabele-Land.* (*Graphic*, October 28, 1893, supplement. Author's collection.)

THE WAR IN MATABELE-LAND.

WRITTEN BY

ARCHIBALD R. COLQUHOUN,

F.R.S., M.R.A.S., A.M.I.C.E., GOLD MEDALIST, R.G.S.,

FIRST ADMINISTRATOR OF MASHONALAND,

Author of "Across Chryse," "Among the Shans," etc., etc.

LO BENGULA, KING OF THE MATABELE, IN HIS FAVOURITE SEAT

THE responsibility for the war rests neither with the British South Africa Company nor with Lo Bengula. The blame lies with the "war-party" in Matabeleland—in other words, the "matjaka," the young unmarried soldiery who have been at all times impatient of control by their indunas, or chiefs, and even by the King himself. There has been from the first on the part of the High Commissioner (Sir Henry Loch), Mr. Rhodes, and Dr. Jameson, prudence, patience, and skill in the conduct of our relations with the Matabele, with the view of averting collision so long as it could be avoided or even postponed. Lo Bengula has throughout been subject to circumstances which occasionally overmaster the very ablest and most powerful of rulers—the will of the people; or, as in Matabeleland, that of the native hierarchy, of which the most dangerous section, again, is the "matjaka." I well recollect when the Pioneer Expedition started on its journey to effect the occupation of Mashonaland, it was a matter of grave doubt whether Lo Bengula would be able to control the "war-party," and the situation at various times during the progress of the Expedition was undoubtedly critical. He had no desire to fight; not that he was particularly friendly to the Expedition, but he under stood the strength of the white man and the inevitable result of collision. He had a most difficult part to play; to retain his seat on his throne, and to keep upon his shoulders; and, in order to accomplish this, he was obliged to manage the "matjaka" with great tact and adroitness. Any symptom of either yielding or wavering might at any second have cost him his life. At last, three years after the occupation of Mashonaland, the "matjaka" got the upper hand, and forced what was practically a declaration of war. That my view is well founded is borne out by what Sir Sidney Shippard, the Administrator of Bechuanaland, wrote in 1888 on the condition of Matabeleland when on a mission to Buluwayo:—

Lo Bengula's power of restraining the matjaka is said by those best acquainted with the country to be greatly diminished within the last few years. The older indunas, the companions of his boyhood, are said to be still devoted to their chief, but the younger regiments, many of which can boast of no Zulu blood, and consist entirely of maghole, *i.e.*, slave boys or captives taken in war, and trained up to become matjaka, are said to be anything but loyal to Lo Bengula. It is impossible to forecast the future in such a country as this. A matjaka rebellion, attempted revolution, and civil war appear to me to be not unlikely. . . . Some of the older Matabele indunas and indodas are confessedly sick of carnage, and desire nothing so much as a peaceful government with security for life and property, not to be obtained under the present *régime*; but the restless and bloodthirsty matjaka are perpetually craving for the fresh slaughter of helpless victims, who attempt no resistance, and make but feeble efforts to escape by flight or by betaking themselves to hiding-places, and Lo Bengula dare not withstand the impetuosity of his troops, even if he would.

A DECISIVE BLOW AND ITS EFFECTS

It is now a life and death struggle between the pioneers and their neighbours, and a decisive blow must be struck at the Matabele power which will shatter the military prestige and power of that nation. This accomplished, the greater portion of the people would, I believe, remain in Matabeleland, and settling down to peaceful pursuits—of which mining would be an important one—become incorporated in Zambesia, while probably some of the irreconcilable indunas and their warrior-followers would move northwards and establish themselves in some district north of the Zambesi. I certainly do not think the whole Matabele nation will trek bodily

northwards. The Matabele are not all warriors. They possess much of the raw material of a tolerably peaceful and hardworking people, and of this a certain proportion has already tasted the sweets of justice and regular payment of wages in the Transvaal and Mashonaland; but the greater part is locked up in the military system prevailing in the country. Once the military system is broken up the more peaceful and industrious elements will detach themselves and settle down. I am sure it will be the policy of Mr. Rhodes to prevent anything like this much-talked-of trek, for two very good reasons: firstly, to prevent the establishment of another standing menace north of the Zambesi, which would prove most disadvantageous to the territory south of that river and to that controlled by Mr. H. H. Johnston at Nyassa; secondly, to retain an adequate native population for the development of Mashonaland, so absolutely necessary a desideratum. The future prosperity of the country depends largely upon a sufficient supply of native labour; and once the Company's forces have broken the military caste the rest of the people will not delay, in my opinion, to come to terms with Mr. Rhodes, who has always shown a strong disposition towards compromise when compromise is the wise course. White labour, it must be remembered, is out of the question in these distant regions. Even at Johannesburg and Kimberley the mines would have to close to-morrow if native labour were not available.

CHARACTER OF THE COUNTRY

The public is sufficiently acquainted with the general geography of Matabeleland and Mashonaland, by means of the maps which are almost daily appearing in the Press, to render any lengthy description of these countries superfluous within the brief limits of this Supplement. A few words on the subject, however, are necessary. The country both south and east of Buluwayo presents considerable difficulties, the main approach from the south being through a pass which it would be, I have always understood, highly dangerous to traverse, while the region between Forts Victoria and Charter and the rivers and streams, and, therefore, not well suited for the operations of mounted troops. It is to be hoped that the opportunity will present itself to the Company's forces to engage the Matabele troops in the open high veldt in the neighbourhood of Buluwayo, or at the capital itself. The two columns from

THE TYPICAL "LAAGER" (DEFENSIVE POST), AS USED BY THE FORCES MOVING ON BULUWAYO

especially in promoting the use of new military technology. An automated killing machine, the Maxim gun was essentially a second-generation machine gun whose wartime use was inaugurated during the conflict. Needing less manpower and more efficient than its predecessors, the Gatling and Gardner, it could be operated by one person and automatically loaded a new cartridge every time one was spent.[25] Furthermore, over long ranges it proved more effective than the Ndebele's weapons, since they were designed to be used primarily for hand-to-hand or short-range combat. The circulation of such images attempted to substantiate the assumption that the Ndebele and Shona must heel or else find themselves in the sight of a rifle or, worse still, a Maxim gun (fig. 85).

While the conflict with the Ndebele provided a critical sense of historical relevance for the show, Fillis's choice of material also reflects the role of entertainment in creating and consolidating the perceived historical value of events. The importance of timeliness and immediate political relevance for ensuring the commercial appeal of human displays has already been noted (chapters 2 and 5). Shows such as Charles Henry Caldecott's Zulu exhibition or Farini's Friendly Zulus both capitalized on contemporary military activity at the Cape of Good Hope. Likewise, Fillis's show took advantage of British interest in the Ndebele and was calculated to create a stir. At times, literally dozens of Afrikaners on horseback were chased by even more numerous and flamboyantly costumed Africans. However, although recent events, the wars were hardly news in the same sense as the Anglo-Zulu conflict had been for Farini, and so it would be more accurate to think of Savage South Africa as a form of theatrically tempered historical reconstruction.

The show's sense of occasion was reinforced by the presence of Peter Lobengula, the reputed son of the former king, and the Gwelo coach that "was attacked by the Matabele in the war of 1896 and almost hacked to pieces by battle axes." Now repaired after "considerable trouble," the coach was assailed twice daily by the Ndebele *impis* (fig. 86).[26] From the outset, Peter attracted interest and suspicion. Although he claimed to be the son of King Lobengula, it is more likely that he was an African man who was able to take advantage of Fillis's venture.[27] By January 1900, the show closed in the wake of negative press regarding Peter's marriage and the banning of ladies from the kraal; despite embarking on a national tour, takings suffered as the Boer War transfixed the nation's attention. Clearly, in both scale and scope, Savage South Africa was unlike anything Londoners had seen earlier in the century. In order to understand how and why such shifts occurred, it is essential to understand how the conventions governing human display shifted in the context of the British, French, and U.S. international fairs that emerged after 1851.

FIGURE 85
(Facing) The Campaign against the Matabele: A horse and cart drag along a Maxim gun, ready to wreak devastation on the unsuspecting Ndebele hidden in the mountains. (*Graphic*, October 21, 1893, p. 300. Author's collection.)

" The Company's troops, composed of police and a large body of volunteers, are equipped not as regular soldiers, but in everyday working-dress, forming in every respect a thoroughly
effective, mobile body of 'irregular horse,' well-fitted for South African border warfare ; while the Maxim-gun artillery will prove a most deadly weapon for dealing with the close column
attack formation hitherto employed by Lobengula's warriors, or for destroying his kraals "

THE BRITISH SOUTH AFRICA COMPANY'S FORCES MOVING INTO THE INTERIOR.   DRAWN BY FRANK DADD, R.I., FROM SKETCHES BY ARCHIBALD COLQUHOUN

THE CAMPAIGN AGAINST THE MATABELE

A CORNER IN "EGYPT"

SAVAGE SOUTH AFRICA. STUDY OF A "BOER"

SKETCH IN THE AFRICAN VILLAGE

SAVAGE SOUTH AFRICA. ATTACK ON THE GWELO COACH

SKETCHES AT THE GREATER BRITAIN EXHIBITION AT EARL'S COURT.

The Citizens of the World

The notion that trade exhibitions were opportunities to see unusual or foreign peoples was prevalent at the Great Exhibition. Henry Mayhew's *1851; or, The Adventures of Mr and Mrs Sandboys* (1851) poked fun at contemporary enthusiasm for the wonders of Hyde Park. Meanwhile, the London they encountered had become a "curious sight even to Londoners":

In almost every omnibus, some two or three foreigners were seen among the passengers—either some light-haired Germans, or high-cheeked Americans, or sallow Turks, with their "fez-caps" of scarlet cloth. In the pit of the theatres, Chinamen, with their peculiar slanting eyes, and old-woman-like look and dress, might occasionally be perceived gaping with wonder at the scene; while from the number of gentlemen in beards, felt hats, and full pantaloons, visible at the West-end, Regent-street had much of the Anglo-Frenchified character of the Boulogne-sur-Mer.[28]

Illustrated by George Cruikshank, the book's frontispiece depicted the earth from the perspective of outer space and made light of the sense that, from the furthest reaches of the globe, peoples of all nations were swarming toward the Palace whether on foot from their mud huts, on beasts of burden (including horses, camels, and elephants), or aboard ships across stormy seas. Mayhew was not alone, and in the press, Londoners were quickly portrayed as being as interested in seeing the foreign visitors as they were the official exhibits.

Originally published in *Punch* in 1851, John Tenniel's *The Happy Family in Hyde Park* is an example of the ways in which the heterogeneity of visitors became essential to the exhibition's consumption (fig. 87). At first glance the image appears to confirm that the Crystal Palace houses Tenniel's eponymous international happy family. Alongside the European visitors, many foreign people are easily distinguishable, including a Chinese man, a Native American, a turbaned Turk, and a rather hairy Cossack. Yet if we look closer, an ethnic divide is clearly visible.[29] Alongside Mr. Punch, the Europeans are all outside the palace, looking in on the foreigners as if they were exotic botanical specimens in a colossal greenhouse. Moreover, on the center right, a smartly dressed young gentleman appears to be offering the others some form of educational instruction by using his cane to pick out an especially interesting specimen. Inside the palace, the foreigners are not examining the exhibited goods, as one would expect of paying visitors, but performing national dances as if they were displayed wares in their own right. These elements undermine the image of Tenniel's happy family by highlighting a sense of separation between European visitors as observers and foreign visitors as public spectacles. In addition, Mr. Punch stares directly at the viewer and offers an invitation to share in the voyeuristic consumption of foreign tourists.

For patrons intent on taking up Mr. Punch's invitation, foreign tourists were complemented by foreign attendants. Alongside the better-known

FIGURE 86
(Facing) Sketches at the Greater Britain Exhibition at Earl's Court. (*Illustrated London News*, May 20, 1899, p. 724. Author's collection.)

THE HAPPY FAMILY IN HYDE PARK.

FIGURE 87
John Tenniel, *The Happy Family in Hyde Park*. (*Punch*, July 19, 1851, p. 38. By kind permission of Jim Secord.)

FIGURE 88
(*Facing*) *The Tunis Court*, featuring an attendant. The court marked the first use of living foreign peoples within the context of international fairs. (*Illustrated London News*, May 31, 1851, p. 294. Author's collection.)

Indian displays, the Crystal Palace also featured smaller courts devoted to the Ottoman Empire, most notably its Egyptian, Turkish, and Tunisian territories.[30] The Ottoman artifacts included silk textiles, jewelry, woodwork, leather, books, woven carpets, guns, swords, feathers, and garments "as one might expect to see in a native old clothes' shop at Algiers or at Cairo." Within these displays, the Tunisian court featured an "extremely picturesque and obliging native *custodien*" who, being a "good-natured Turk," freely dispensed sweetmeats and guided visitors around articles of "rudest description," but which were "admirably calculated to afford illustration of the *ménage* and *convenances* of the North African tribes." In the *Illustrated London News*, the attendant was shown surrounded by the articles as if he were manning a small-scale bazaar (fig. 88).[31] His living presence was in addition to the models of foreign peoples that were displayed within the Crystal Palace's walls. For instance, the Indian court featured a collection of more than sixty groups of models designed to showcase the various Hindu castes, and the fine art court featured wax models of North and South American peasants clothed in their national costumes and cast into tableaus of their respective customs.[32] These displays were augmented by the numerous foreign peoples featured in London's entertainments as showmen attempted to compete with attraction of Hyde Park. For instance, Vauxhall Gardens hosted an Algerian family in Arab and adapted for prompt removal, are scattered about in admired disorder. In strange contrast to this tatterdemalion lot stand two glass cases, which contain some very splendid specimens of gold embroidered dresses and horse caparisons, and other articles of *vertu* selected, probably, from the Bey's private collection. Nor must we omit to address attention to some very curious models of arabesque carvings in gypsum, intended for the decoration of the interior of Moorish rooms. The workmanship is of a bold character, the devices elaborate and pleasing, and the material being pierced through, must have a very light and graceful effect when applied to the purposes intended. Preparatory to the process of carving, the gypsum is enclosed in a wooden frame, with a back to it, which supports and protects it till the design is completed.

We must now quit the Tunis bay and its extremely picturesque and obliging native *custodes*, hoping we have said enough to induce many of our readers to spend an hour in exploring its diversified and truly novel contents, as we have done.

THE CANADA COURT.

A HUNDRED years ago, supposing a great international and industrial exhibition to have been possible at that time, Canada would have furnished a very different assortment from that with which she now presents us. Then we should have had a rude and miscellaneous lot of native manufactures and native finery, something after the fashion of that now collected in the Tunis bay—a wigwam, some wooden or horn spoons, rough earthen pots, a few embroidered mocassins, a few tomahawks, and a dozen or so of scalps and other military trophies; but nothing indicative of the natural resources of this vast and almost virgin tract of territory; nothing that spoke of the honest industry or intelligent enterprise of its inhabitants. Very different from this, however, is now the case. Civilisation has begun its useful work in the far west; European industry has planted the spade there, and some of the fruits are now before us—speaking much and creditably for the past, but speaking still more cheeringly of what is yet to come.

The Canada division is situated to the south side of the Western Nave, next beyond the East Indian division. Its products are not so showy, but are yet more valuable as evidences of social wealth and social advancement. They are the spoils of peace, not of war, the industrial beginnings of a junior branch of the great civilising family of the universe, not the gaudy remains of an effete barbarism, which has been demolished, but not yet replaced by anything better. The Canadians send us abundant samples of natural wealth drawn from the bowels of the earth—specimens of iron, copper, and silver ore, besides a case of native gold obtained from the gravel on the south-east side of the pro-

longation of the Green Mountains specimens of magnesite rock, of stones of fine quality for the purpose of lithography, of agates, soapstones, gypsum, slates, and serpentines. Of timber there is a large assortment (the major part forming a large pile in the midst of the main avenue)—oak, curled ash, bass-wood black walnut, pine, curled maple bird's-eye maple, hemlock, elm, spruce, &c., all fine specimens, and of which the black walnut struck us as especially beautiful, both for its colour, its rich and varied grain, and the high degree of polish of which it is susceptible. The maples also are extremely rich, and, as well as the black walnut, are well adapted for furniture and other decorative works. Of agricultural products we have numerous samples, the Canadian exhibitors evidently attaching a due importance to this branch of their national wealth: barrels filled with corn, Indian meal, barley, oats, peas, beans, flax, potatoes preserved for sea voyage; with Siberian oil-seed, hemp, hops, and sugar from the maple tree, all show the varied richness of a land which, put to good account, might effectually relieve the distress of the older communities of the world.

Lastly, in unmanufactured, or but partially manufactured, products, there are specimens of moose hide and leather, moose deer's head and horns, calf-skin, porpoise-skin, &c.

In addition to these resources of natural wealth, the Canadian colonists are favourably represented as regards their skill of handicraft—particularly as relates to furniture and articles of domestic and general use. Of furniture there are several most creditable specimens—substantial in make, whilst aiming at some trick of style in decoration, which, although of course not claiming to compete with the more finished and artistic articles of *luxe* produced in London, Vienna, and Paris, show an aptness of handling, which a little study of improved models, abundant opportunities for which the present Exhibition affords, will doubtless, in future, direct more happily. Amongst the articles of furniture deserving of special mention, from the loyal associations connected with them, are half-a-dozen chairs, the seats and back worked in worsted and silk by the ladies of Montreal, "for England's Queen." There are also a handsome pianoforte and some other musical intruments, showing that Saxon industry in Canada does not intend to restrict itself for the future to mere articles of utility.

In the midst of the room are some very stylish sleighs, with harness and sleigh-robes complete; and a fire-engine of unusually large proportions, and remarkably elegant design and workmanship, capable of throwing two streams of water 156 feet high, or a single stream 210 feet high. There is attached to it a hose containing necessary tools, and with a seat for the accommodation of the firemen; but this adds greatly to the length, and,

THE TUNIS COURT

THE TUNIS COURT.—GENERAL VIEW.

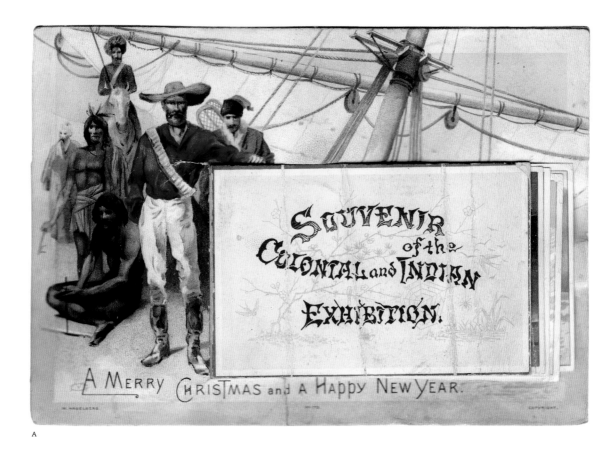

A

costume, and the Egyptian Hall hosted a Syrian troupe who performed in the Holy Land panorama.[33]

Although immediately incorporated into international exhibitions, the diverse ways in which displayed peoples were featured in British events is best illustrated by the Colonial and Indian Exhibition of 1886.[34] Running for six months in South Kensington, it provided the most extensive use of displayed foreign peoples within the context of a nineteenth-century British fair. A total of 89 living "natives" were featured in the program, in-cluding 46 Indians, 10 "Ceylonese," 10 "Red Indians" from British Guiana, 5 Cypriots, 5 "Malays," 9 Africans from the Cape of Good Hope, and 4 individuals from the "Straits Settlements."[35] The living performers were complemented by human models that were scattered around the site and arranged in "native groups" that bear significant similarities to Latham's models at the Crystal Palace in Sydenham (see chapter 6). For example, the Australian displays featured an encampment from the "olden time," com-plete with models of Australian Aborigines in the midst of native flora and fauna.[36] Other models included a "short statured Andamanese woman, bedecked with shells and leaves, the white skull of a near relation dangling on her jet black breast," close to her husband with spear in hand; a "Bhud-distic mendicant priest, clad in a torn yellow rope and holding his begging bowl"; "portrait-models of representative soldiers and native officers of the

B

C

D

E

F

G

H

I

Indian Army," and an Australian Aborigine spearing fish.[37] These models were to be found in the "Ethnology Sub-Courts" of the exhibition. The importance of the models and performers is suggested by a Christmas-season souvenir from the exhibition in which images of living performers, models, and natural history displays were grouped together and, on this occasion, sent with "Jamie's love to Lady" (fig. 89a–i). Several themes in the exhibition's displays of foreign peoples are worth dwelling on.

As a celebration of Britain's overseas possessions, the Colonial and Indian Exhibition focused on performers' status as British subjects. Most of the living individuals performed as laborers, servants, or artisanal craftsmen producing marketable commodities. The Indians were almost all shown as weavers, printers, stonemasons, carpenters, painters, and metalworkers (fig. 90). Three Cypriots were shown weaving silk on a loom (fig. 91). The Africans, along with many of the other displayed peoples onsite, worked daily in a diamond mine (fig. 92). Discovered at the Cape in 1867, diamonds transformed the economy and labor patterns of the region and, by the early 1870s, had established Kimberley as the second-largest city in South Africa. Unsurprisingly, in the "middle of the Cape Court," the "washing for diamonds, the diamonds in the rough, and the polishing of the diamonds" attracted the "greatest attention."[38] The interest in mineral resources extended to other sections, most noticeably in the Australian courts, which featured a "Queensland gold-digger" washing alluvium in the search for the metal's yellow glimmer.[39] The fruits of his labors were displayed in a large glass cabinet and augmented with a "large and varied collection" of precious stone and minerals. 1886 also proved to be the year in which gold was discovered in the Witwatersrand—a discovery that led to the foundation of Johannesburg.[40] Other foreign peoples worked as attendants: for example, a few of the Sinhalese men worked in a teahouse

FIGURE 90
Carpet-Weaving.
(*Courtyard of Indian Palace*). Indian prisoners performing as artisans at the Colonial and Indian Exhibition. (*Illustrated London News*, July 17, 1886, p. 88. Author's collection.)

adjacent to the Ceylon court, while a group of seven "Bombay servants" provided the same service in the Indian courts. The Indian subcourts also featured four "native shops," manned by Indians and "similar to those found in the average Indian village."[41]

Crucially, displayed peoples at the Colonial and Indian Exhibition were portrayed in both their ostensibly natural and their built environments. For example, visitors to the "Native Department" of the Cape of Good Hope were presented with a "Kafir Kraal and Bushman Hut" that were "occupied by four Kafirs, and by a bushman and his wife," who provided daily perfor-mances of their "respective native industries, including the manufacture of weapons, sticks, baskets, wickerwork mats, sieves, beadwork, and wire ornaments." Moreover, an additional performer was expected to join this "interesting community" during the exhibition's run.[42] Likewise, the ethnology subcourts featured a "native hut" from Cyprus, an "Indian lodge made from buffalo hide" in the Canadian court, and houses fashioned from bamboo, as were to be found in "Eastern India and the Malay peninsula," and that had been erected from imported material by Malaysian carpenters who had left before the exhibition opened.[43] These models were complemented by substantial natural history collections featured in the ethnology subcourts, with some of the largest displays of flora and fauna coming from the Seychelles, Queensland, New Guinea, and British Guiana (fig. 93). Across the range of nations displayed, the ethnology subcourts also featured a vast array of material artifacts such as weapons, manufactured objects, clothing, domestic utensils, and photographs of the colonies. The diversity of exhibited objects suggests the range of context in which displayed peoples could be encountered within the ethnology subcourts, from a mock kraal to a miniature marketplace and tableaux of natural history collections. Moreover, as the case of the kraal indicates, displayed peoples might perform a variety of activities designed to showcase their lifestyle in ways that made them ethnologically representative of their origins.

In other displays, and with the ethnological subcourts in particular, displayed peoples were presented as historical artifacts. In some cases, such as the Indian artisans, they were ostensibly timeless, and therefore authentic,

FIGURE 93
Roland Ward's natural history displays for the Colonial and Indian Exhibition. (John Dinsdale, *Sketches at the Colonial and Indian Exhibition* [1886], 1: plate 2. Author's collection.)

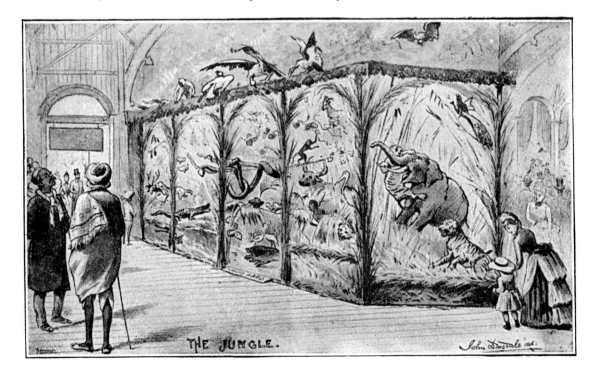

THE JUNGLE.

examples of "native" craftsmanship.[44] In other displays, more disturbing chronologies reduced the exhibited humans to being exemplars of the human past. For instance, as the exhibition literature explained, the models of Australian Aborigines represented a scene from Australia's uncivilized "olden time"—just four decades ago: "To Englishmen who reckon by centuries the title 'Encampment of the olden time—forty years ago,' seems strangely quaint.... The encampment is an exact representation of those made by the natives when the white men first arrived in Victoria" (fig. 94).[45] For the *Illustrated London News*, the scenes "forcibly" demonstrated the "wondrous civilisation of Victoria" and were made especially instructive by "contrasting the native groups delineated with the cultivated beauty of the Melbourne Botanic Gardens, picturesquely reflected" in a series of "excellent photographs" featured at South Kensington.[46] Celebrating the rapid colonization of Victoria depended on contrasting Aborigines, as relics of the past, with the settlers of the future. In turn, it promoted as desirable the rapid territorial dispossession faced by Australian Aborigines in the 1840s.[47]

Foreign peoples were incorporated into the Colonial and Indian Exhibition in a variety of ways. Crucially, they were integrated into the wider context of the exhibition rather than being segregated into a dedicated subcourt. Many were living performers, but their numbers were augmented by the substantial use that was made of human models. In the ethnology subcourts, indigenous populations were shown as forms of past human development and even relics of recent territorial expansion. Yet displayed peoples at South Kensington were shown primarily not as natural historical specimens of specific human types (as Latham had done at Sydenham) but as representatives of a range of political and natural historical relationships, most obviously as subjects of the British Crown. Within this larger context, one of the most important themes was the economic importance of foreign peoples, which, in turn, reflected the broader interest in cataloging and displaying Britain's overseas possessions.[48] As noted previously, some of the African and Indian performers were prisoners recruited from jails in the Cape and Agra (see chapter 4). In the roles assumed for the exhibition, they were transformed from being problematic individuals into economically useful workers. In the case of the San, they had been imprisoned for theft when they stole food to survive after refusing to work as laborers on settlers' farms.[49] Their status as prisoners confirmed their resistance to settlers' attempts to reform their means of subsistence from nomadic hunting to paid agricultural hands; yet at the exhibition they performed new public roles as "Cape Kafirs at work."[50] Likewise, the recruitment of Indian prisoners was partly the product of larger reforms of Indian prisons in which inmates were retrained as craftsmen to help transform them into economically productive individuals.[51] Despite these attempts, as the official catalog noted, expert "lovers of Oriental art" found

COLONIAL AND INDIAN EXHIBITION: VICTORIA.

CASE OF GOLD NUGGETS.

may be derived from a glance at the two adjoining wall-pictures in the principal entrance-hall of the Exhibition — the paintings which mirror the pastoral condition of the site of Melbourne in 1839, and the city of bricks and mortar, embellished with fine Government offices, churches, chapels, and noble public buildings, existing in 1886. But still more forcibly is the wondrous growth of civilisation in Victoria brought home by contrasting the native groups delineated with the cultivated beauty of the Melbourne Botanic Gardens, picturesquely reflected in the excellent photographs of Mr. J. W. Lindt. Mr. James Thomson avers that in no other large town in the world has a working man so many enjoyments or so many privileges as in Melbourne. He says, and produces a map smothered with red dots in support of his assertion, the whole country, as well as the me-

tropolis, is dotted with State schools. The Free Library, Museum, and Picture Galleries, and the Botanic and Zoological Gardens afford gratuitous recreation and instruction to the labourer and mechanic, as well as to the clerk or shopman. In the matter of indoor amusement, the inhabitants are furnished with four theatres and several music-halls; and grand concerts are given weekly in the Townhall and Exhibition Building. Maintaining that, proud as Victorians are of their colony, "they are also proud of being Australians of British blood," Mr. Thomson seasonably adds, "that the British race in Victoria does not suffer deterioration is amply proved by the fact that in each of the University boats in the memorable race of the Third of April last was a Victorian born oarsman—Mr. S. Fairbairn, who rowed No. 5 for Cambridge; and Mr. Robertson, who pulled No. 3

NATIVE ENCAMPMENT.

"grave deterioration in the productions of the present day, both in design, texture, and clothing," which they directly attributed to the use of prison labor.[52] Nonetheless, most of the carpets at the exhibition had been produced by inmates. Thus, whether as laborers, craftsmen, or servants, displayed peoples were being incorporated into the wider imperial economy of trade and labor, even where they had specifically rejected such an economy in their homelands.

One of the most interesting examples of how recruitment transformed problematic individuals into economically useful workers is provided by Tulsi Ram; he performed as a "sweetmeat maker" from Agra but was a Punjabi peasant who had traveled to London in 1885 in the hope of securing an audience with Queen Victoria in order to settle a local land dispute.[53] Destitute and vagrant, in the months leading up to the exhibition he was arrested over a dozen times and frustrated officials with his incessant demands to meet the queen. His transformation from a vexingly vocal immigrant into an exemplar of Indian artisanal skill is a pregnant indication of the role exhibition organizers played in the recruitment, training, and management of performers' stage identities. Ram was carefully selected to perform as a means of stifling his demands. Meanwhile, his identification as a sweetmeat maker signaled how his personal history had been intentionally fabricated, both to corroborate the histories ascribed to the other Indian performers and to support the broader aims of the exhibition in displaying Britain's overseas possessions and subjects. By training Ram in the skills deemed appropriate for his professed trade and then requiring him to perform them, the exhibitors made further attempts to substantiate his newly invented employment history. Similar processes of invention and improvisation were involved in transforming the other African and Indian performers from prisoners into their newly designated roles as potters, weavers, diamond washers, carpet makers, or, in other terms, suitably productive colonial labor.

Visitors' interest in the foreign performers and the ethnological material at the Colonial and Indian Exhibition is evocatively captured by Trilokya Nath Mukharji.[54] Whereas the majority of exhibition commissioners were Anglo-Indians or government officials, a number of princes and South Asians were also involved in curating the Indian material at international exhibitions. A Bengali from the upper castes, Mukharji proved to be one of the most important figures drawn from the Raj's subjects. He lectured as an exhibition assistant and helped write various official publications for the Indian displays at a number of European events, including the Colonial and Indian Exhibition. Upon his return to India, he also wrote a fascinating account of his visit to Europe.

Of the displays of foreign peoples at South Kensington, Mukharji noted that the "Indian Bazaar" was always attended by a "dense crowd" that was "as much astonished to see the Indians produce works of art with the aid of rude apparatus they themselves had discarded long ago as a Hindu would

FIGURE 94
(Facing) Case of Gold Nuggets and Native Encampment from "olden time." (Illustrated London News, August 7, 1886, p. 157. Author's collection.)

be to see a chimpanzee officiating as a priest in a funeral ceremony and reading out Sanskrit texts from a palm leaf book spread before him." Moreover, it was from the ladies that Mukharji and the foreign peoples received most attention: "We were pierced through and through by stares from eyes of all colours—green, gray, blue and black—and every movement and act of ours, walking, sitting, eating, reading, received its full share of 'O, I, Never!'"[55] Mukharji's account is riven with details on the complexity and reciprocal acts of looking evoked by the human displays. He watches the English watching the foreigners. In turn, the foreigners watch the English and, all the while, the English return the inquisitive glances of the performers and Mukharji. Meanwhile, Mukharji's account reveals a deeply seated sense of discomfort borne of visitors' eagerness to meet foreign peoples.

As an official delegate from India, Mukharji was not one of the performers but was frequently mistaken as one by visitors. For example, on one occasion while reading a newspaper, he became aware of being watched by a group at a nearby table that included a girl of seventeen, whom he overheard saying, "Oh, how I wish I could speak to him?" After approaching her and once she had overcome her "bashfulness," she spoke with unexpected "vivacity" and, Mukharji noted, "was delighted with everything I said, expressed her astonishment at my knowledge of English, and complimented me for the performance of the band from *my country*, *viz.*; the West Indian band composed of Negroes and Mulattoes." The lady's ignorance of the difference between Mukharji, the official performers, and the West Indian band made him "wince a little," but nonetheless, he furnished her with enough anecdotes to "brag among her less fortunate relations for six months to come of her having actually seen and talked to a genuine 'Blackie.'" On another occasion, Mukharji was harassed by a sailor who begged him to speak to his wife and badgered him into compliance after Mukharji initially refused. Significantly, he added that outside the confines of the exhibition "we never experienced one act of kindness."[56]

Mukharji found the ease with which visitors assumed he was a performer profoundly uncomfortable. In response, he transformed his own role within the exhibition from a government official into an observer of the English.[57] His account of the attendees' interest in foreign peoples both confirms their appeal and, pertinently, provides a salutary lesson for those keen on discussing the reception of the shows in terms of white patrons observing colored subjects. Not only did the shows involve reciprocal observation but, within the context of international exhibitions at the very least, displayed peoples were sometimes Europeans and not necessarily imported foreigners, while viewers were of varied ethnicities.[58] Moreover, in souvenir publications, visitors and exhibited peoples alike were promoted as available for "refreshing recollections" (fig. 95).

The use of displayed peoples at the Great Exhibition and the Colonial and Indian Exhibition raises problems for existing accounts of how

A

B

FIGURE 95A–B
(a) *Odds and Ends* and (b) *Refreshing Recollections* from the Colonial
and Indian Exhibition, in which displayed peoples were featured
alongside the "Beauty & the Beast" and "Interesting if not interested visitors." (John Dinsdale, *Sketches at the Colonial and Indian
Exhibition* [1886], 2: plates 4 and 6. Author's collection.)

human displays evolved under the aegis of world's fairs. Traditionally, the Parisian Exposition Universelle of 1867 has been identified as the first time foreign peoples were formally integrated into international fairs (as either shopkeepers or servants), and the Exposition Universelle of 1889 as the inauguration of the practice of importing foreign peoples specifically and solely for the purpose of displaying human variety in indigenous villages on their fairgrounds; yet the importance of the earlier British exhibitions of both 1851 and 1886 needs to be reevaluated.[59] In order to understand why, it is worth briefly revisiting French and U.S. innovations in the 1880s.

In attempts to emulate the commercial success of human displays in the wider Parisian community, most obviously at the Jardin d'Acclimatation, the organizers of the 1889 exposition set up camps of foreign peoples at the foot of the Eiffel Tower.[60] Here, groups of Congolese, New Caledonians, Dahomeyans, Gaboonese, Senegalese, and a settlement of Cochin-China and a Kampong-Javanese were overshadowed by the towering iron testament to French material and technological progress. At the Parisian fair, two Egyptian tourists found a street ostensibly in medieval Cairo through which imported Egyptian herdsmen hurried dozens of donkeys. It also included houses, a masjid (mosque), shops, and an imitation bazaar where "Egyptians" (Frenchmen dressed in "native" garb) sold trinkets to tourists. Manifestly disgusted, the Egyptian tourists stayed away. They were particularly offended by the masjid's facade being used for a coffeehouse filled with whirling dervishes and belly dancers.[61] Yet as the exhibition organizers soon realized, for most patrons the foreign peoples were the most memorable and successful element of the entire exposition.

After witnessing the commercial potential of displayed peoples in France, U.S. fair organizers quickly followed suit, but introduced innovations that materially associated such displays with mass spectacle and evolutionary notions of progress. Americans were introduced to displayed peoples within the context of the World's Columbian Exposition held in Chicago in 1893 to commemorate the four-hundredth anniversary of Columbus's founding voyage. Effectively divided into two sections, the White City and the Midway Plaisance, the dual personality of the fair significantly changed the viewing context for human displays. The White City contained fourteen showcase buildings designed in the Beaux-Arts style that contributed to a unified architectural aesthetic. The whole city was adjoined by the mile-long Midway, which acted as a conduit to the peripatetic traffic. It harbored displayed peoples, belly dancers, the Ferris wheel and other fairground rides, caged animals, jugglers, and traveling performers.

Significantly, the Midway was arranged to provide a visual synopsis of human evolution, from savagery through barbarism to civilization, in an attempt to contribute to the fair's overarching theme of progressive human civilization.[62] At the far end, furthest from the White City, Africans and Native Americans provided twinned examples of savagery. The Dahomeyan Village nestled among Tatanka Iyotanka's (Sitting Bull's) cabin (he had been killed just three years earlier by state reservation police), a Sámi village, Chinese village, Brazilian concert hall, and Wild West show. The Islamic and Asian world occupied the central midway. A display for Algeria and Tunisia was adjacent to a Cairo street scene and was located opposite a Moorish palace and Turkish village. Further on and closest to the main fairground was a Javanese village, Japanese bazaar, German village, Irish village, and Dutch settlement. Meanwhile, in between the model Eiffel Tower and Aztec village, a zoo with performing animals had been set up by the Hagenbeck-Wallace Circus.

Rather than providing a perfect gradation from black to white, the Midway's arrangement reflected, broadly speaking, contemporary evolutionary schemes in which humans were hierarchically graded from the lowest forms of human development toward the zenith of civilized whiteness, as materially manifested in the White City. The division between the White City and the Midway enabled the inclusion of many popular and financially lucrative elements without detracting from the visual coherence of the main fair; yet ultimately, this effectively demarcated between an official educative space and an unofficial amusement zone replete with mass entertainments. In particular, since the Midway was imitated by later organizers, the Columbian fair created a convention that, by the early twentieth century and despite the involvement of anthropologists (see below), helped disassociate displayed peoples from contemporary scientific practice and, in so doing, altered the interpretative context in which fairgoers viewed them.

As the examples of the Crystal Palace and the Colonial and Indian Exhibition make clear, there were several notable differences in the way foreign peoples were displayed at these British fairs and those that adopted the Parisian and U.S. models after 1889–93. Critically, given the presence of foreign attendants (and models) at the Crystal Palace, displayed peoples were evidently incorporated into international exhibitions from their outset, not after the Parisian exposition of 1867.[63] Within nineteenth-century British exhibitions, displayed peoples were not necessarily used solely, or even primarily, as ethnic types but were also commonly used as attendants, laborers, and guides. Moreover, by not being segregated into a separate subsection devoted solely to displayed peoples or "amusements," performers were tightly integrated into the display environment of an exhibition venue rather than appearing as almost unofficial adjuncts. Finally, although British anthropologists were involved in curating the Colonial and Indian Exhibition, the performers were not necessarily displayed according to anthropological or evolutionary criteria (as at Chicago or St. Louis; see below). Instead, the exhibition catalog and press reports paid much less attention to the displayed peoples' utility as ethnological specimens, and far more to the kinds of political or economic relationships that they were used to represent; this seems to be the case even though some performers were displayed within subcourts devoted to ethnology.

The End of an Affair

[249]

U.S. and Parisian conventions were largely imported by Imre Kiralfy, Britain's most prominent exhibition organizer from the end of the nineteenth century until his death in 1919. Kiralfy explicitly modeled Earl's Court on the World's Columbian Exposition of 1893, and between 1908 and the start of World War I he also presided over London's very own White City.[64] Kiralfy developed a brand of visual entertainment that relied on special effects and substantial cohorts of onstage dancers. This approach was exemplified by shows such as Venice, which opened at London's Olympia in 1891. Advertised as featuring over fourteen hundred performers, it also boasted reconstructions of the Venetian canals and a hundred gondolas to transport those willing to spend anything between 1 shilling and 3 pounds, 3 shillings through the reproduced glories of Italy.[65] In 1894, Kiralfy's Orient show at the Olympia featured a parade of ambassadors from the East since Henry V had held court. The grand spectacle reproduced the "Eastern magnificence and splendour of bygone days" in the "'grandest show on earth'" (fig. 96).[66]

One of Kiralfy's most pertinent shows was the 1895 Empire of India Exhibition (held again in 1896 as the Empire of India and Ceylon Exhibition), the first devoted solely to India and set up by a showman (albeit in collaboration with the government). As part of the exhibition, Kiralfy custom built an entire site and imported South Asians to work as performers and craftsmen (fig. 97). He also recreated a Bombay street scene, storefronts from Lahore, and a Hindu temple from Benares. The exhibition program also contained *India*, an imperial melodrama written and produced by Kiralfy that showcased a thousand years of Indian history in an effort to promote the British Raj. Although India was hardly a novel theme for the theater of exhibitions, Kiralfy's production has been seen as significant because it differed in "scale—it had a cast of a thousand professional performers; authenticity—it was part of an exhibition presided over by many Indian princes and British government officials; and intention— it aspired to historical verisimilitude in an unprecedented way."[67] Under Kiralfy's guidance, exhibitions at international fairs became increasingly lavish and elaborate in terms of both scale and expense. Their primary goal was to ensure commercial success through visual impact. It is this shifting context of human display to which Frank Fillis's exhibition must be related and in which his patrons encountered Savage South Africa.

Fillis's choice to advertise the exhibition as an opportunity to see "Africa" is an indication of the shift in the scale and nature of human displays. As became increasingly typical of shows in the later nineteenth century, Savage South Africa was conceived as an entertaining visual extravaganza. To this end, consumers were indebted to Fillis's considerable experience in the circus. The dramatizations of the Ndebele conflicts were framed by circus acts, including tightrope walkers, people playing polo on bicycles, and equestrian feats made possible by Fillis's expert horsemanship. Meanwhile, the vast scale of the enterprise also reflected shifting

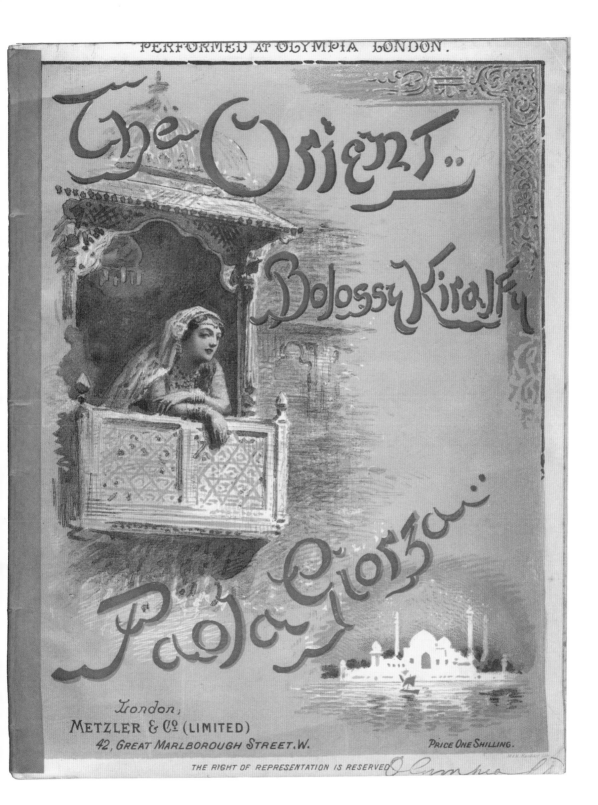

FIGURE 96
A musical score for Imre Kiralfy's exhibition The Orient, 1895. (Author's collection.)

THE EMPIRE OF INDIA EXHIBITION AT EARL'S COURT.

patterns of display. Earlier in the nineteenth century, exhibitions were routinely advertised using specific appellations such as "Zulu" or "Bosjesman." This was partly because the use of the umbrella term *African* became more common only in the later period; even so, showmen often exhibited individuals from only one ethnic group. Even when individuals of more than one ethnicity were exhibited together, such as in Cawood's African exhibition of 1850, which featured just three individuals, consumers would have been hard pressed to find more than one or two from each group. In contrast, Fillis had imported dozens of each ethnicity he exhibited, including the Zulu, Ndebele, Sotho, and Swazi. The grand scale and diversity of the show were typical of human displays in later international fairs.

The changes in magnitude and variety altered the interpretative possibilities associated with human displays. For consumers it became feasible to view several, and possibly many dozens, of human varieties in the space of a short walk. Earlier in the century, unless one dedicated years to the task, it would have been difficult for even the most ardent consumer to witness such diversity solely by attending shows. Not dependent on extensive travel or collected memories, the miscellaneous nature of human displays at international fairs made them ideal for those interested in making comparative assessments between peoples and added convenience by allowing such comparisons to be made on the spot. After all, where else might have one have gone to see such contextualized diversity in such a brief period of time or in such a confined locality? Even in the most ethnically diverse cities it would have been a challenge to see so many people wearing "native" dress, living in "native" buildings, and conducting "native" ceremonies, let alone view them in a manner conducive to comparative assessment. Instead, one might easily have seen some of these elements, such as dress—but it would have been far more difficult, if not impossible, to have been exposed to the ceremonial and architectural range on offer, even in the most cosmopolitan urban centers.

The decision to build a "kraal" in the heart of Earl's Court also signaled the shift toward displaying foreign peoples within the context of ostensibly authentic indigenous villages. Rarely allowed to leave for fear of subsequent misbehavior, licentiousness, or inebriation, over two hundred Africans were housed within the confines of Kiralfy's pleasure dome. The exhibition of foreign peoples living on-site and performing mundane acts echoes the use of "native" villages to frame displayed peoples. In 1885, the department store Liberty's had seen fit to promote its latest Eastern-inspired offerings by setting up an Indian village in Battersea Park (fig. 98). The exhibition proved commercially disastrous, and the performers, suffering from a bitter winter and harassment from patrons, attracted considerable attention in both the London and Bombay papers.[68] Later on, the displays of the Colonial and Indian Exhibition of 1886, Parisian exposition of 1889, and Chicago World's Fair of 1893 all helped make the convention of the "native village" so successful that it continued to be followed

FIGURE 97
(Facing) The Empire
of India Exhibition at
Earl's Court. (Illus-
trated London News,
July 27, 1895, p. 109.
Author's collection.)

1. Snake-charmer.   3. Silk-embroiderers.   5. A run through the village.   7. Musical instrument maker.   9. Potter.
2. Nautch-dancing.   4. Brass-ware moulder.   6. Knife-tosser.   8. Juggler.   10. Elementary boy.

SKETCHES AT THE INDIAN VILLAGE, ALBERT PALACE, BATTERSEA PARK.

until the demise of the fairs following World War I (although later fairs never reached the grandeur of the St. Louis World's Fair of 1904, the Louisiana Purchase Exposition).

Indigenous villages enabled the reinvention of human displays in order to take full advantage of the fairs' larger size and better funding while providing vast open-air theaters that attempted to simulate foreign cultures. The immediate results of more money and larger spaces were a much greater investment in the theatrical environment of human displays (namely the reproduction architecture of the village itself) and many more ethnicities and individuals on display. Yet despite their obvious interventions, exhibition organizers, including Fillis, consistently maintained that indigenous villages were authentic and unmediated representations of how foreign peoples lived. These claims were designed to erase systematically their extensive involvement in setting up the displays; for instance, fair organizers would often design the villages, sometimes with the input of the represented nations, and then require performers to build them during the lengthy months of an international fair.[69] In addition, organizers frequently designed the costumes displayed peoples wore, and managed the food they ate and the ceremonies they performed.[70]

Showcasing performers within mock villages transformed the dynamics of intercultural contact for both consumers and performers. While the official dramatizations of Savage South Africa took place twice daily at the Empress Theatre, visitors regularly walked through the grounds and watched the Africans engaged in quotidian activities such as cooking, playing, and smoking. Here too, the African exhibition was typical of the late nineteenth century. Although audience participation had almost always been possible, and was usually encouraged in smaller-scale shows, the nature of such interactions changed within the context of later fairs. For consumers, indigenous villages and their inhabitants were able to function as three-dimensional object lessons that could be touched, looked at, talked to, and, critically, walked around and through. Initially, this allowed organizers to remove some of the spatial separation that inevitably came into play when displayed peoples performed onstage while seated audiences watched. However, by the end of the nineteenth century, physical barriers such as fences began to regulate the kinds of contact made possible at the shows by formally demarcating between patrons and performers.[71] Meanwhile, the London kraal also reflected the broader development of exhibition spaces that relied on "immersive" environments to display and entertain.[72] For performers, indigenous villages demanded that they live and work on the same site for considerable periods. Here the boundary between living and working was deeply ambiguous (one might say close to absent), and performers found themselves in a liminal space continually negotiating between their daily needs, consumers' wants, and managers' requirements.

FIGURE 98
(Facing) Sketches at the Indian Village, Albert Palace, Battersea Park. (Illustrated London News, November 21, 1885, p. 527. Author's collection.)

Despite the similarities, there were significant differences between Savage South Africa and the human displays of international fairs. The most obvious and important contrast is that Fillis exhibited only Africans and Afrikaners. Although his exhibition provided consumers with significant diversity, it still could not compare with the sheer range seen at the Colonial and Indian Exhibition and other world's fairs of the later nineteenth century. Savage South Africa was funded by neither government coffers nor a group of investors. Instead, as an entrepreneur Fillis bore the considerable costs and reaped what few rewards there were.[73] In addition, the show was held as an unofficial adjunct to, not a component of, the Greater Britain Exhibition of 1899. The separation was intentionally effected by the organizers of the international fair in order to distance themselves from Fillis's venture.[74] Despite these efforts, the two exhibitions were frequently conflated, both in advertising and in the press. For instance, when the *Graphic* reported on the show it provided readers with sketches of both exhibitions at Earl's Court.[75] In its visual synopsis of the event, it placed scenes from the opening of the Greater Britain Exhibition, at which the Duke of Cambridge was present, alongside several vignettes from Fillis's show, including two Africans washing, an "African chieftain" parading himself on the grounds, and a group of Xhosa smoking. Likewise, the *Illustrated London News* produced a full-page spread featuring a "corner in Egypt," complete with Arabs and Victorian visitors at the Greater Britain Exhibition sandwiched between Fillis's African village and the show's reenactment of the attack of the Gwelo coach (fig. 86).

Although the public enthusiastically patronized Fillis's show, at least one group appears to have stayed away. Savage South Africa seems to have attracted little anthropological interest; this might seem rather curious, since anthropologists either personally curated or were closely associated with the international exhibitions held in London (1886, see below), Paris (1889), Chicago (1893), and St. Louis (1904).[76] We might expect that Britain's anthropologists would have been keen to take advantage of the presence of over two hundred Africans in London. Yet just as the nature of human displays were changing, so too was their relationship to institutionalized anthropology.

Crossroads

The greatest organized anthropological interest in displayed peoples within the context of a nineteenth-century international exhibition in Britain occurred at the Colonial and Indian Exhibition, due in large part to the "wishes of the authorities" that the Anthropological Institute "hold a series of conferences" in South Kensington. Addressing the institute, its president, the eugenicist and statistician Francis Galton (a cousin of Charles Darwin's), no doubt echoed the thoughts of many of his colleagues when he spoke of the invitation having evinced "much pleasure." Moreover, the opportunity of "meeting men from all parts of the Empire who are familiarly acquainted with its native races, and of inspecting collections of high ethnological interest that have been arranged with cost and pains in the various courts," was, he insisted, "unprecedented."[77] Hopes for the fruitful use of the exhibitions' resources led to several meetings of the institute being held throughout June and July at South Kensington. Initially, members met at the venue and heard "from gentlemen connected with the ethnological exhibits a brief account of the most typical specimens, together with any other ethnological remarks they may wish to make."[78] At each conference many of the "textile fabrics, weapons, and other objects illustrating the customs of the peoples was removed from its place in the exhibition to the conference room for inspection"; members later dispersed to examine the courts for the remainder of the day and hear "further explanations."[79] These talks included several discussions of the African collections from both the Cape of Good Hope and West Africa, the collection from Cyprus, and exhibits from the West Indies and the Caribbean. Some of the courts were personally curated by members of the Anthropological Institute; for instance, Robert James Mann, an expert on South African ethnology, superintended the display of the ethnological collection from Natal.[80] Once the exhibition had closed its doors, its resources continued to prove useful, since the lion's share of the 1887 volume of *Journal of the Anthropological Institute of Great Britain and Ireland* featured papers either presented at the exhibition or based on its official exhibits, ranging from foreign performers to material artifacts.[81]

Most pertinently, foreign performers at the Colonial and Indian Exhibition provided experimental subjects and complemented the research potential of the displayed artifacts. For example, when hearing about the Cape Colony, the anthropologists were given a talk illustrated by "some characteristic specimens of Bantu workmanship", including pottery, "old-fashioned fetisch objects" [*sic*], musical instruments, and three performers.[82] During the talk, one of the performers had his strength tested using the same instrument Galton had used to measure the strength of "nearly 10,000 persons" in the anthropometric laboratory he had set up at South Kensington's International Health Exhibition in 1884.[83] The man, identified only as a "Bushman," had already been weighed and his height determined. He then squeezed and pulled on the apparatus, adapted from fairground machines designed to test muscle strength. Galton concluded that he was "barely of the average strength of an Englishman, even when allowance is made for his small weight."[84]

As well as making use of the foreign performers' presence, many of the anthropologists in attendance based their papers on the material artifacts from the exhibition and used them as evidence for their broader generalizations. Miss A. W. Buckland, for example, presented a paper on tattooing in which she argued for the importance of studying the bodily adornments as a means of tracing human history.[85] When explaining that there were two types of tattooing (cicatrized marks and the drawing of a pattern that was then pricked with colored matter), she referred her colleagues to Australia, "where some of the natives are scarred in a remarkable manner, [and like] some of those exhibited in England last year having the shoulder cut and scarred." Moreover, when referring to the practice of tattooing among west coast Africans, Buckland referred her colleagues to the "masks and other representations brought over for the Colonial and Indian Exhibition."[86]

The diversity of anthropological activity at the Colonial and Indian Exhibition is both striking and instructive. The exhibition provided opportunities for anthropologists to act as curators, while the displays could be used to both conduct research and provide the basis for future publications. Yet for the majority of the Anthropological Institute's members, the displays did not result in either a publication or curatorial responsibility; if we were to argue that this rendered the exhibition of limited relevance for the nation's anthropologists, we would be overlooking other potentially significant uses of the official exhibits, most importantly in training and building an anthropological research community. Leafing through the 1887 and 1888 volumes of the *Journal of the Anthropological Institute of Great Britain and Ireland* leaves little doubt that the exhibits were just as likely to be used as resources from which anthropologists could acquire new skills of observation as they were to conduct research.[87] For example, after the lectures, members of the institute would be guided around the exhibition grounds by the expert speakers and invited to interpret the displays as both illustrative of the theoretical claims under discussion and relevant to ongoing research within anthropological circles. A useful way of understanding the importance of such training is to think of it as a means of "learning to *attend* to the world" in ways that were communally recognized as being anthropologically relevant and skilled.[88] Just as with Latham's displays at the Crystal Palace in Sydenham, the foreign peoples, artifacts, and natural history collections at the exhibition were made into both experimental objects and object lessons. Meanwhile, the displays also became the focus of discussions on how to improve the discipline's future prospects.

Despite being a "great event of anthropological interest," the anthropologists were disgruntled nonetheless; their disquiet was related directly to contemporary concerns with establishing and training both contemporary and future generations of practitioners. The "chief difficulty" with conducting research at the exhibition lay in the "narrowly limited time" at their disposal.[89] Yet even with unlimited access, significant problems would have remained. Galton opined that "few sections of the Exhibition would have been more attractive, not only to the anthropologist, but also to the general public," than one that "effectually represented the domestic life, the arts and the usages of the Red Indian." Even so, rather irritatingly, the Canadian authorities had focused almost entirely on the "white man," and the material devoted to the "whole of the Red Indian" occupied "no more horizontal space than would be afforded by a moderately-sized dinner table."[90] The exhibition had also led to discussions for the foundation of an Imperial Institute, plans in which Galton felt his colleagues ought to express the greatest interest. Speaking just before the public opening of Oxford's Pitt Rivers Museum and in the wake of the recent reorganization of the Ethnographical Gallery at the British Museum necessitated by the establishment of the Natural History Museum (1881), he urged that a "prominent feature of the Imperial Institute should be an Ethnological Museum of the races in the British Dominions."[91]

Galton had no reason to suspect that the planned Imperial Institute might feature such a collection; nonetheless, his calling for a permanent anthropological collection to complement the material at both the Pitt Rivers and the British Museum is significant because it grew, at least partly, out of the frustrations caused by conducting research at the Colonial and Indian Exhibition. Not only had there not been enough time, but the displayed material was deemed insufficient to be considered properly representative of the variety of peoples on display. Moreover, if successful, the anthropologists would have managed to secure one of the earliest permanent collections displayed according to anthropological criteria. Significantly, Galton's comments followed the by-then-successful campaigning of the archaeologist and prolific collector Augustus Henry Lane Fox to establish an anthropological museum. Having changed his name to the more familiar Pitt-Rivers after inheriting his cousin's fortune, he spent much of his later years arguing, to an initially rather unenthusiastic range of colleagues, for the importance of museums to the discipline, in terms of providing training and research objects.[92] That such discussions were taking place gives some indication of just why the exhibition had been greeted with such enthusiasm, and why anthropologists eagerly made as much use as possible of the available artifacts and performers.

Despite the recognized importance of international exhibitions for anthropological research by contemporary practitioners, British anthropologists' use of their resources appears to have remained far more haphazard than the systematic investigations attempted and hoped for at the Colonial and Indian Exhibition. For example, in the mid-1880s while in London, three performers named Billy, Jenny, and "Little Toby" from Robert A. Cunningham's troupe of Australian Aborigines appeared before the Anthropological Institute. Cunningham provided a lecture for the anthropologists, while the performers showcased their skills with weapons, sang "native" songs, were asked to count objects presented to them, and had their photographs taken. In 1883, a group of Krenak was both explicitly advertised as an anthropological exhibition and examined by A. H. Keane (fig. 99). When a group of Sioux performed in London in the 1890s, the physician Wilberforce Smith examined their teeth and used his findings to provide fodder for his broader conclusions on human dentition. Likewise, between 1899 and 1900, a group of Inuit were being exhibited at London's Olympia. The Cambridge-based W. L. H. Duckworth took advantage

of their stay to procure detailed measurements of their skulls. His findings were later presented at the Cambridge Philosophical Society. Cunningham, Keane, Smith, and Duckworth all published reports in the *Journal of the Anthropological Institute of Great Britain and Ireland*.[93] These individual researchers' activities suggest that where possible, anthropologists enthusiastically continued in their efforts to take advantage of displayed peoples for anthropological research into the later nineteenth century. Nonetheless, others felt such efforts were woefully insufficient.

In 1900, Cambridge psychiatrist, anthropologist, and future physician to the shell-shocked soldiers of World War I, William H. R. Rivers, wrote a rather frustrated letter to the Anthropological Institute in which he complained,

Nearly every year members of savage or barbarous races are exhibited in London in large numbers. At present, little or nothing is done to utilise the anthropological material which is thus brought to our doors, although in other countries, and especially in Germany, much useful work has been done.[94]

Rivers was clearly envious of the dividends that studies of displayed peoples had paid elsewhere; although anthropologists were involved in displaying foreign peoples in both France and the United States, by far the most sustained use of performers was to be found in Germany. The doctor, politician, and anthropologist Rudolf Virchow took great care to attend exhibitions, examine displayed peoples, and present his findings publicly. As head of the Berlin Anthropological Society, Virchow was able to utilize the society's journal to publicize his approach widely and champion the value of performers as living anthropological specimens. His labors were the most methodical and sustained efforts in Europe and the United States to take advantage of the opportunities provided by public interest in the *Völkerschauen*.[95] Clearly, Rivers, and in all likelihood many others like him, respected Virchow's research as an exemplary case of what might be achieved, and desired opportunities to follow suit.

The problem with British anthropology, Rivers argued, was not necessarily a lack of interest but a lack of organization on the part of the anthropologists, and exhibitors' reticence to grant private individuals the freedom to conduct their investigations. It is tempting and easy to view Rivers's epistolary lament as simply a restatement of Conolly's earlier research manifesto, *The Ethnological Exhibitions of London* (1855; see chapter 6); however, this would fail to acknowledge that Rivers was writing in a new era of institutionalized anthropology, of which he sought to take advantage. For instance, he suggested that exhibition proprietors would be more likely to allow "accredited representatives of the Institute facilities for investigation." That such accreditation could be appealed to indicates a significant alteration in anthropologists' fortunes. After the amalgamation of the Ethnological Society of London and the Anthropological Society of London to form the Anthropological Institute of Great Britain and Ireland

The End of an Affair

(1871), anthropologists were united under the umbrella of a single learned society. Similarly, the founding of the *Journal of the Anthropological Institute of Great Britain and Ireland* (1872–1906) created a common publication that superseded older periodicals. This did not erase intellectual or methodological differences, though it did provide a common institutional framework for a new generation. Meanwhile, the cultural evolutionist Edward Burnett Tylor took up the first British readership in anthropology at the University of Oxford in 1884.[96] In 1900, the young zoologist and ethnologist Alfred Cort Haddon was appointed to a lectureship in ethnology at Cambridge, and in 1909 he was promoted to a readership. As such, the later nineteenth century witnessed the consolidation of efforts, begun between the 1840s and the 1860s, to promote and institutionalize the scholarly study of human variation and which foreran anthropology's institutional eminence in 1930s London.[97]

Intriguingly, Rivers was especially concerned that such research should take place "soon after the arrival of the natives in England before they have been ruined for purposes of scientific study by the British Public."[98] Although not explicit about either the causes or the effects of the ruination, the warning is suggestive. Rivers is unlikely to have been referring to displayed peoples' physical features. Unlike the late eighteenth and early nineteenth centuries, by the time Rivers put pen to paper the physical expression of ethnic difference was considered stable or even immutable rather than subject to changes in climate, subsistence, or lifestyle.[99] Therefore, displayed peoples remained useful to anthropologists interested in physical difference, because their physical makeup was unaltered by being imported or displayed or through the intercultural contact of the shows.

Rivers may have been referring to how displayed peoples' adaptations to life abroad hampered research efforts by making them unwilling subjects. Spectators often gave gifts, money, or trinkets to performers in order to encourage them to engage with their eager benefactors. Over time, many performers, rather than simply accepting what was given, began to negotiate for tips and other benefits.[100] Similarly, when anthropologists were able to examine displayed peoples firsthand, they did not necessarily find compliant collaborators. Newspapers and eyewitness accounts often note that displayed peoples were difficult to control; perhaps they refused to perform, were unwilling to tolerate the restrictions of being confined to given living quarters, or questioned the pay they were being given. Such acts of resistance highlight the possibility that Rivers may have been referring to the difficulty of getting performers to do what anthropologists would have liked.[101] After all, common practices such as taking photographs (particularly nude studies), making physical measurements, producing plaster casts of body parts, and interviewing were all time-consuming and required a degree of (coerced or willing) collaboration between performers and anthropologists, without which a performer could not be transformed into a useful specimen.

Authenticity also provides a possible source for Rivers's concern. He may have felt that the processes of being imported and displayed would inevitably reduce the value of displayed peoples as anthropological specimens because of the cultural and social adaptations they often made while abroad. This seems especially likely, given that just over ten years later, Rivers proposed that reliable ethnography depended on a specific and small window of opportunity:

Probably the most favorable moment for ethnographical work is from ten to thirty years after a people has been brought under the influence of official and missionary [agents]. Such a time is sufficient to make intensive work possible, but not long enough to have allowed any serious impairment of the native culture and, even if it has been changed, full and trustworthy information about the past can still be obtained from those who have participated in the rites and practices which have disappeared or suffered change.[102]

Rivers's methodological advice is revealing. The preexisting infrastructure provided by earlier colonial contact or missionaries is evidently essential for facilitating the kind of intensive activity Rivers believed was most suited to ethnographic study. He also explicitly voiced concerns regarding the effect of extended intercultural contact.

Problematically, the "rapid spread of Western culture" and its associated "destructive change" was causing the disappearance of "native culture" and so extinguishing the very objects of his study.[103] Once performers became accommodated to alien cultures, anthropologists may no longer have found them useful for garnering observations on those peoples who had managed to preserve older customs, religions, and arts irrespective of transcultural contact. By the early to mid-twentieth century, the view that anthropological studies were best conducted *in situ* and with pristine subjects had become firmly entrenched and significantly bolstered by the appearance of Polish émigré Bronislaw Malinowski's research on the Trobriand Islands (1916–29) and the extensive graduate training he oversaw as a lecturer at the London School of Economics.[104] Yet Rivers's colleague Haddon was the first to define "intensive work," to use Rivers's own phrase, in anthropological terms and argue for its importance in new anthropological research. Critically, this is not to argue that earlier generations were somehow unaware or unconcerned with obtaining information from *in situ* or participant observation and the methodological issues raised by ensuring such information was reliable. Alternatively, it is not to privilege fieldwork either as a more scientific methodology than its predecessors or as a way of demarcating between sound anthropological work and otherwise in the late nineteenth century (this only occurred in the twentieth century). However, it is to recognize that around the turn of the century, anthropologists such as Rivers and Haddon began to argue that intensive ethnographic work done *in situ* was the best, and in some cases only, way to resolve many of the disciplines' problems and the perceived shortcomings of earlier generations.[105] As such, it is likely that Rivers's concern stemmed from conducting intensive work with subjects whose memories extended to precolonial or early missionary contact.

The exhortation fell on sympathetic ears. The Anthropological Institute resolved to "make representations to the proprietors of such exhibitions, and to issue letters of introduction to qualified observers who wish for special facilities." Moreover, if anybody wished to communicate information "as to the arrival of natives for exhibition," they were asked to write directly to the institute's offices.[106] Clearly, the fellows found themselves in sufficient agreement with Rivers to announce that they would provide "qualified" individuals with a form of accreditation and sponsorship when approaching exhibition organizers. They were also willing to collect information on the arrival of suitable "natives." That such arrangements should be made at all bears witness to the perceived value of displayed peoples for ongoing anthropological research. Yet, as with earlier attempts and unlike the work of Virchow, these institutionally sanctioned efforts still did not translate into the systematic utilization of displayed peoples as experimental resources. Given the proclivities of Rivers and his colleagues, why was this the case? There are many possibilities, with at least some linked to the changing nature of London and the British Empire in the late nineteenth century, as already discussed; but there are also significant reasons that relate to the changing nature of British anthropology.

By the end of the nineteenth century, British anthropological interest became heavily focused on notions of culture, social organization, religion, myth, ritual, and kinship. Tylor's *Primitive Culture* (1871) became an early example of this approach and was later complemented by the appearance of James George Frazer's great tome *The Golden Bough* (1890).[107] Tylor's work was important for his notion of "survivals" and also his ideas about culture. *Primitive Culture* opened with the assertion: "Culture or Civilization, taken in its wide ethnographic sense, is that complex whole which includes knowledge, belief, art, morals, law, custom and any other capabilities and habits acquired by man as a member of society."[108] Based on this, Tylor developed an evolutionary perspective in which culture was theorized as a continuum; in turn, this led to the search for the origins of culture and the laws of cultural progress. "Survivals" were habits, metaphors, and customs that had been retained from earlier stages of human development. Essentially, Tylor argued that the identification of survivals provided clues for the reconstruction of past states of mind and the explanation of seemingly inexplicable practices in European civilization. Survivals became Tylor's primary tool for tracing the progress of one stage of human thought to the next. Frazer's project aimed to provide a comparative account of the development of mythology, magic, and religion in order to trace the shared, and therefore fundamental, tropes of religious belief from ancient to modern peoples. These theoretical interests became linked to the emergence of new methodologies.

Within histories of anthropology at least, Rivers is best known as a member of the Cambridge Anthropological Expedition to the Torres Straits in 1898. Led by Haddon, the expedition has come to be seen as one of the first anthropological studies that was largely empirical in nature. It is noted also for its methodological innovations, particularly the intensive ethnographic research conducted *in situ*, the development of the "genealogical method," and the innovative use of film and photography.[109] The venture was Haddon's brainchild and was conceived after he had been on a seven-month zoological expedition to the same area of the Pacific in 1888. The goal of that expedition was to conduct a comprehensive anthropological study that embraced ethnology, physical anthropology, psychology, linguistics, sociology, and musicology. For the Cambridge venture, Haddon assembled a team of accompanying professionals, including Sidney Ray, an authority on the languages of Oceania; the musicologist Charles Samuel Myers; the naturalist Charles Gabriel Seligman; the medical expert William McDougall; and Rivers. They were also equipped with the latest scientific instruments for recording images and sound: wax-cylinder phonographs through which they were able to make almost one hundred recordings of islanders' speech and song; photographic kits that included equipment for taking both stills and movies; and an experimental kit for color photography.

Rivers's research in the Torres Straits provides examples of two distinctive anthropological preoccupations of the period: physical anthropology and the study of genealogical relationships. He began by testing islanders' visual acuity through experiments comparing their ability to identify different colors to that of Europeans. These investigations were designed to test the hypothesis that the indigenous islanders would be able to perform such tasks better than Europeans because of their more acute senses. The notion that sensory skills and human development were inversely related grew out of mid-nineteenth-century writings such as those of Herbert Spencer, who argued, "Testimonies to the acute senses and quick perceptions of the uncivilized, are given by nearly everyone who describes them."[110] Meanwhile, in reconstructing the islanders' familial connections, Rivers developed a technique that became known as the genealogical method.[111] On this research he reported,

In Torres Straits, as in so many other parts of the world, the system of kinship is so wholly different from that of ourselves that many of our simplest terms of relationship cannot be used without the danger of great confusion and error. In collecting the genealogies I therefore limited myself to as few terms as possible, and found that I could do all that was necessary with the five terms, father, mother, child, husband, and wife. Care had of course to be taken to limit these terms to their English sense. The term which was open to the most serious liability to error was that of father, but I was able to make the natives understand very thoroughly that I wanted the "proper father." ... I took one individual as the starting-point of a genealogy, found the name of his real father and mother, then if either had been married more than once; then the names of their children in proper order and ascertained the marriages and families of each child.[112]

One such data was obtained, Rivers cross-checked it with at least two other individuals. With the use of this systematic interviewing, he gradually built up "a complete collection of the genealogies as far back as they could be traced," in order to "study many sociological problems more exactly than would be otherwise possible."[113]

Upon returning to Britain, Haddon began arguing that anthropologists must undertake extended *in situ* research as a matter of some urgency. In 1903, for example, he used his Presidential Address to the Anthropological Institute to discuss "Anthropology, its Position and Needs."[114] He was particularly concerned that students spent "laborious hours in reading, transcribing, and collating the records of travellers and in endeavouring to make them yield their secrets." Yet he argued that such sources were of questionable reliability because of the scattered and incomplete descriptions they provided of relevant ceremonies, rituals, and material artifacts. There were, Haddon claimed, "but two remedies for this state of affairs—trained observers and fresh investigations in the field." Clearly, he was attempting to bolster his argument that a new generation of specially trained, accredited, and professional anthropologists was needed to energize the institutional standing of his discipline; however, it is significant that investigations in the field were seen to be a critical ingredient in formulating the corrective tonic.

Haddon also argued that it was imperative that such investigations be conducted with haste, since a great deal of anthropological knowledge was on the verge of being permanently lost. He had observed the problem while in the Torres Straits:

Very soon after my arrival I found … [the natives] had of late years been greatly reduced in number, and that, with the exception of one or two individuals, none of the white residents knew anything about the customs of the natives, and not a single person cared about them personally. When I began to question the natives I discovered that the young men had a very imperfect acquaintance with the old habits and beliefs, and that only from the older men was reliable information to be obtained. So it was made clear to me that if I neglected to avail myself of the present opportunity … it was extremely probable that the knowledge would never be gleaned.[115]

Haddon set about salvaging as much information as possible.[116] In many senses, the fear of imminent loss was well founded, as numerous human societies found themselves ravaged by the new diseases, territorial dispossession, warfare, and genocide they suffered due to imperial expansion. Most famously, in 1869 William Lanney, widely perceived at the time as the last Tasmanian man, and in 1876, Truganini, described as the last Tasmanian woman, passed away.[117] Haddon's Presidential Address alluded to these broader currents when he lamented that each year witnessed "a decrease in the lore we might have garnered, and this diminution of opportunity is taking place with accelerating speed."[118] Just over ten years later, Rivers was repeating the same mournful elegy when he argued that knowledge of older languages, religious ceremonies, and arts was increasingly becoming the province of old men whose aging created a ticking time bomb: "In many parts of the world the death of every old man brings with it the loss of knowledge never to be replaced."[119] Following the work of Tylor in particular, evolutionary views of culture helped to establish some living societies as living exemplars of earliest stages of human development. Although much more evident in the early twentieth century, anthropologists also began seeking peoples and societies that were unaffected by colonial contact or the modern world. By the early twentieth century, this search helped fuel a change in anthropologists' focus and research interests.

When considering how shifting conventions of anthropological research altered the experimental and research potential of displayed peoples, it is useful to bear in mind the emergent national differences and disciplinary subdivisions within anthropology. Regardless of where displayed peoples performed, be they exhibition venues, fairs, or smaller shows, once performers' ethnic provenance could be confirmed, they could be used to provide the raw measurements that were so crucial to physical anthropology. As such, displayed peoples were potentially most useful as specimens for physical anthropologists. This utility is reflected by the predominance of physical anthropology within the published research that did employ displayed peoples as a resource.[120] Although physical anthropology was by no means absent from British research, by the later nineteenth century such inquiry maintained a stronger foothold in the United States, France, and Germany.[121] Meanwhile in Britain, some anthropologists became increasingly interested in information that was much more difficult to obtain from displayed peoples or existing texts written by authors with significantly different research interests. After all, using displayed peoples to employ the genealogical method would have presented enormous difficulties, because performers were not necessarily imported in family groups. Even where familial relationships had been respected and preserved, the number of related individuals needed to cross-check a single genealogical tree would rarely, if ever, have been present at a single show. Not all ethnographic data would have been as difficult to collect, but such problems are relevant. Meanwhile, the growing interest in conducting intensive research *in situ* further fueled the desire to look beyond the shows for anthropological information.[122] When combined with the lack of sufficient access to performers and their resistance to being made the subject of experimental investigations, such difficulties provide some indication of why, in late nineteenth-century Britain, displayed peoples were not wholly abandoned as useful resources but were used *relatively* haphazardly in comparison with institutionalized anthropology in United States, France, and Germany in the same period.[123]

✳

Savage South Africa exemplified the format of many human exhibitions in the later nineteenth century. Foreign peoples were shown on a much larger scale and often kept on-site in mock indigenous villages. These emerging conventions provided spectators with new opportunities to view displayed peoples within ostensibly authentic environments, make comparative assessments of ethnic difference, and see increasingly extravagant visual displays. Yet at the same time, displayed peoples were becoming increasingly dissociated from intellectual interest in human natural history. Although performers' ethnic origin maintained a critical role in ensuring commercial interest, the shows were no longer routinely promoted as opportunities to test theories of human development. Moreover, as the nature of London's entertainment landscape changed and became associated with visual extravagance, displayed peoples were increasingly likely to be coupled with this qualitative shift. The tendency toward viewing human display either primarily or solely in terms of entertainment or spectacular performance is partly suggested by the apparent lack of interest shown by anthropologists in Fillis's performers at Earl's Court. Nonetheless, the shows were not abandoned wholesale by scholars interested in human variation.

The use of displayed peoples as anthropological specimens in the later nineteenth century is best illustrated by the example of the Colonial and Indian Exhibition. Most obviously, it provided a cornucopia brimming, for the lay and the learned, with human models, artifacts, natural history collections, and performers that could be made relevant to anthropologists' concerns. As curators or consultants, they were able to help steer the displays in ways that would prove helpful for their interests. Even without such direct input, the exhibits provided object lessons during their conference lectures and evidence for broader anthropological theorizing and training. The resources of the exhibition also became the basis for a substantial number of papers in the *Journal of the Anthropological Institute of Great Britain and Ireland* and, in doing so, became part of the currency of anthropological data in the late 1880s. Meanwhile, dissatisfaction with the exhibition and the conducting of research using its resources underpinned calls for the establishment of a new permanent anthropological collection. Even after the exhibition had closed its doors, numerous research publications demonstrate that anthropologists continued to make use of displayed peoples where possible throughout the 1880s and 1890s.

As the rallying cry of Rivers suggests, despite the anthropological interest in performers, British attempts to take advantage of displayed peoples for their own research appear to have been relatively haphazard when compared with their international colleagues. Considering the efforts of earlier generations and the connections made between displayed peoples and human natural history, this seems rather curious. However, we must bear in mind that displayed peoples were not self-evident specimens. Rather, they could be made relevant to scholarly research; but whether this was even attempted or achieved depended on the methods and intellectual preoccupations of the discipline's practitioners. Published research based on performers falls within the domain of physical anthropology, while linguistic, genealogical, or similar research appears to have been conducted on a smaller scale, not attempted, abandoned, or simply not published.

Suggestively, by the late nineteenth century British anthropologists had become more interested in social and cultural development and were beginning to look to *in situ* research as the best means of conducting their research. This significantly changed the potential utility of displayed peoples for anthropological research. Displayed peoples could, and evidently were, used as physical specimens and object lessons to train anthropologists to observe in disciplinarily productive ways; nonetheless, performers were less useful for those interested in studying certain cultural and social dimensions of indigenous peoples' lives, such as religion or kinship, or employing new techniques, such as the genealogical method. Bearing this in mind, it would be misleading to argue that displayed peoples were abandoned wholesale by anthropologists; however, *relative* to their European, transatlantic, and ancestral colleagues, late nineteenth-century British anthropologists were increasingly likely to find displayed peoples less useful for their new research agendas.

Meanwhile, London's changing demography, show culture, and high-profile diplomats, along with changing technologies of travel and communication, all transformed the potential market associated with human displays. In the early to mid-nineteenth century, viewing ethnic diversity, especially in urban spaces and port cities, was not difficult; yet by the late nineteenth century the telegraph and the steamship ensured unprecedentedly fast access to information about foreign peoples and the chance to meet them. Meanwhile, by taking advantage of the telegraphic network and daily publication schedules, the press had carved out a new role as the dominant, if not sole, source of the most up-to-date information possible. The shows retained a sense of contemporary relevance, but unlike earlier in the century, they no longer competed for timely significance as the press took over as the source of the news. This access to timely information became especially evident during times of political rupture, such as the Anglo-Zulu War (1879) and Boer Wars (1880–81 and 1899–1902), when papers kept the public abreast of daily developments and trains hurtling across the countryside quickened and cheapened their distribution.

All this was a far cry from the 1830s, when Prichard was unable to accept a rare opportunity (and possibly the only one he might ever be given) to finally meet a Mandinka (Mandingo) performer; or 1853, when Charles Caldecott claimed that his Zulu exhibition was of a people virtually unknown to most Europeans (even those resident at the Cape of Good Hope); or the early nineteenth century, when scholars often looked to missionary literature as the most reliable discussions of foreign peoples' "manners and customs."[124] In addition, by the late nineteenth century the shows had become increasingly dissociated from stimulating interest in human development and increasingly associated with spectacle, visual extravagance, and public frivolity. Promoters no longer relied so heavily on claims that their shows were suitable for widespread public engagement with contemporary theories of ethnic difference; in contrast, displayed peoples appear to have been made increasingly and primarily relevant to displaying the unequal relationships between Britain and its colonized subjects. Yet rather than indicating that such shows were no longer closely tied to knowledge production, especially of an anthropological nature, as the dawn of the twentieth century beckoned, it would be more accurate to argue that the kind of knowledge that was being produced had itself metamorphosed.

Afterlives

AS I WAS writing this book, I came across promotional material for "Africa! Africa!" an "evening of traditional Zulu music and dance" that captured the "essence of the mighty Zulu nation." The show's poster featured a man dressed in various animal skins posing with an assegai and shield in hand. In another leaflet, potential customers were promised that the exhibition would take them through the "fascinating proposal customs" and on to the "engagement and wedding ceremonies" in a "glimpse of Zulu culture, as seen through the eyes of the traditional Witch Doctor." The claims were accompanied by an image of the Zulus gathered in a semicircle with the "Witch Doctor" in the center. He looked up at the sky, his face obscured by an elaborate headdress and contorted as if in the throes of shamanic communion. The arresting images, allusion to ritual magic, use of ornate costumes, and invitation to view the exhibition as an authentic glimpse into Zulu life were uncannily familiar, and as on so many other occasions, my pleasure at having found new material was accompanied by a concern about the role of such shows in the public realm. However, the show was not a Victorian sensation but a theatrical production staged by the Mighty Zulu Nation, and was being promoted as a celebration of Zulu culture as part of the 2002 spring program at the Cambridge Corn Exchange (fig. 100).[1] It is tempting to read the similarities between "Africa Africa!" and nineteenth-century shows as indicative of an underlying historical equivalence or a direct genealogical relationship. Yet this would fail to fully acknowledge that the production was being staged as an educational outreach program run by an African theater company. It would also overlook the distinctive ways in which the commercial exhibition of foreign peoples developed over the course of the 1800s.

The nineteenth century witnessed numerous and significant transformations in these shows. The most obvious is the move from small-scale entrepreneurial ventures to vast undertakings, usually within the context of international fairs. In their own lifetimes, many patrons were likely to have noticed the differing opportunities provided by showmen for meeting a single performer or small group versus those provided by the largest

AFRICA AFRICA!

'...the Zulu experience was absolutely fantastic'
THE EXPRESS

'An utterly brilliant evening.'
THE TIMES

AN EVENING OF TRADITIONAL ZULU MUSIC AND DANCE

Enjoy the vibrant sights and sounds of **The Mighty Zulu Nation** with this evening of traditional music and dance. Taking us from the fascinating proposal customs through to engagement and wedding ceremonies, the show offers a glimpse of Zulu culture, as seen through the eyes of the traditional Witch Doctor.

Blending drama, song and dance, **Africa Africa!** is a musical extravaganza that echoes wonderfully the heartbeat and essence of the mighty Zulu nation.

7.30PM TICKETS £15.00 LCA LCB

ANY NEW SHOWS WILL BE LISTED ON · www.cornex.co.uk

FIGURE 100
Spring Program, Cambridge Corn Exchange, 2002. (By kind permission of the Mighty Zulu Nation and the Cambridge Corn Exchange.)

fairs, where hundreds of performers lived and worked on-site. Likewise, patrons would have seen the shift of venue—from the adaptation of a local lecture theater or museum hall with minimal scenery, such as a few carefully chosen objects or painted panoramic backdrop, to the construction of purpose-built villages on sites in which foreign peoples appeared to have been "immersed" in the grassy plains, parched savannahs, or rocky slopes

[272]

of their homelands' natural environment.[2] Rising levels of literacy and the availability of cheaper printing technologies changed how the shows could be promoted and consumed. By the 1830s, advertising swathed London's streets in letterpress announcing the arrival of the latest novelty. By the 1880s, large color posters began contributing to the palimpsests created by eager flyposters. While advertising allowed consumption without purchase, the shows also became more accessible, as the most common entrance fees changed from 2 shillings and sixpence midcentury to 1 shilling in the later decades. Meanwhile, whereas earlier ventures were usually privately financed, international fairs drew on a greater range of financing streams, including private investments, commercial sponsorship, public subscriptions, and state funding. Individual entrepreneurs remained significant, as the careers of William Cody (Buffalo Bill), Frank Fillis, and Imre Kiralfy attest; but they faced stiffer forms of competition from the expansion of cheap mass-market entertainment, such as the music hall and early films, as well as novel opportunities to take advantage of emerging markets and the new consumers they created. Thus, over the course of the century, the shows maintained their commercial appeal, became increasingly accessible, and presented a growing range of peoples onstage.

The shifting ways in which displayed peoples were recruited and marketed both reflected and contributed to an expanding imperial presence. In the most material sense, the British Empire provided an increasingly developed infrastructure that proved crucial for both recruiting entertainers and choosing which ethnicities to exhibit. Similarly, over the course of the century, the permission required from the government to allow performers to travel and be employed in Britain became increasingly regulated and standardized. The labor contracts that set out the terms and conditions of employment also became not only more common but necessary and regulated elements of the recruitment process. Meanwhile, the showmen's increasing reliance on professionalized suppliers traipsing the globe in search of exhibitors' desiderata reflected the developing networks provided by the wider context of an expanding formal empire. Displayed peoples often hailed from regions in which Britain either had or was broadening its interests. Tellingly, of all the Africans who might have been chosen to perform on London's stages, the peoples of the Cape of Good Hope were the most frequently featured. This directly reflected Britain's expanding political and territorial presence in South Africa.[3] In turn, the timing of such exhibitions regularly reflected ongoing, particularly military, activity in the region, such as the Anglo-Zulu War. Showmen worked hard to make patrons aware of such connections and so capitalize on them for commercial success. Their promotional materials frequently featured details regarding the lengths to which they had gone to secure the governmental permission required to recruit performers, including narratives of consent that attempted to establish the recruited peoples' willingness to become traveling performers and descriptions of Britain's political, military, or trade interests in the performers' homelands. Such strategies were essential in both creating and maintaining the shows as politically relevant.

Understanding the shows' development over the nineteenth century has often been made difficult by the attention focused on either individual case studies or the later international exhibitions; the imbalance has created both chronological and analytical problems. Traditionally, histories of human display have looked to the examples of Paris (Exposition Universelle, 1867 and 1889), Chicago (World's Columbian Exposition, 1893), and St. Louis (Louisiana Purchase Exposition, 1904) as the best means of discussing the use of displayed peoples within the context of international fairs, particularly when discussing their connections to anthropological study.[4] However, the Great Exhibition of 1851 inaugurated the practice of displaying living foreign peoples within international fairs, 1854 witnessed one of the earliest and most significant attempts to incorporate displayed peoples into ethnological practice for both the lay and learned at the Crystal Palace in Sydenham, while the 1886 Colonial and Indian Exhibition provides an exemplary case of the diverse ways in which displayed peoples were presented in international fairs and used by anthropologists within late nineteenth-century Britain. The formative role of the British story within the larger context of both the history of anthropology and that of world's fairs needs to be revisited.

Meanwhile, many features of the later period have been taken as representative of the earlier historical context. For instance, discussions of the shows' receptions often rely on color-based or biological definitions of "race"; however, these are simply too narrow to accurately reflect the broader definitions of both the eighteenth and early to mid-nineteenth centuries, and fail to account for the persistence of older ways of framing human variety. Likewise, the association with spectacle has been strengthened by analyzing the shows in relation to the visual techniques of spectacular theater and immersive displays, which became the preferred way to frame displayed peoples by the end of the century. Tracing the development of the shows over the course of the nineteenth century suggests that this focus on spectacle can be misleading. For instance, the notion of spectacle often implies a distanced, and possibly passive, consumption of visual experience. Distance is helpful for understanding urban spectatorship, since the continual movement of crowds and the constraints of etiquette thoroughly discouraged interaction. In contrast, patrons attending live shows were presented with performers who, however limited their means, were interactive. As discussed below, being aware of the historical specificity and shifting perceptions of "spectacle," "science," and "race" allows the shows' histories to be reconstructed in terms that foreground the perspectives of historical actors and account for the shows' changing significance for intercultural encounter and knowledge production.

In terms of the shows' receptions, the most significant point of consensus to have emerged is that exhibitions of living foreign peoples helped

CONCLUSION

to perpetuate Western, usually imperial, notions of superiority through shaping, reinforcing, and popularizing hierarchical arrangements of the world's peoples that were fundamentally racialist. Displayed peoples are argued to have been "pressed into the service of imperialism through the medium of the savage freak show."[5] Similarly, it has been contended that "in the course of their travels," the Australian Aborigines Robert A. Cunningham displayed in the late 1880s "were regarded as objects of curiosity, which by the late-nineteenth century was a curiosity blinkered by the preconceptions of an age that saw them as representatives of type— a 'savage' type—rather than as individuals."[6] The association with past racism and typological alterity has been reinforced by schematizing the shows as examples of a "self" observing the "other," and mapping this dichotomy onto a divide between white and black.[7] For instance, it has been suggested that the world's fairs "told the story of mankind, the very same narratives that accompanied and legitimated colonial expansion. In this epic, staged by themselves, white, rational, civilized European citizens cast themselves in the role of hero."[8] Similarly, in discussing the fairs' living anthropological displays it has been argued that "science represented 'native' peoples as non-interiorized 'others' who existed outside the common bonds of humanity and the flow of history."[9]

By modeling the shows on the dynamics of white selves observing black others, historians have consistently categorized consumers and performers into ethnic groupings based on complexion; in doing so, they have often unhelpfully employed biologically based definitions of human variety and stable notions of "white" and "black" as a historical standard.[10] In the eighteenth and the early nineteenth centuries, human variety was defined by a wide set of criteria, including nonphysical characteristics such as clothing, religion, and language.[11] Moreover, mid- to late-nineteenth-century debates of how best to define *race* substantially proliferated the ways in which it was conceived; thus, even when chromatic or biological definitions were proposed they did not wholly supplant older traditions but often competed with them. Meanwhile, the ethnic diversity of London's population undermines attempts to argue that consumers' interest was generated by differences of ethnic origin as signaled by color. After all, contemporary writers routinely described London as a cosmopolitan city, so many patrons would have been accustomed to seeing a range of foreign peoples on the streets, and some may even have employed foreign labor in their townhouses or country retreats. Similarly, as the writings of many "imperial pilgrims" confirm, foreign peoples were also consumers of such displays, particularly within the context of international fairs, where they may even have been involved in their management.

It is worth being especially wary of employing color-based dichotomies. *Whiteness* and *blackness* are problematic terms of unification, because they can erase significant differences between the peoples of the same color, and they are historically contingent and contested categories. For example, most of the African peoples discussed were usually referred to as ethnically distinct peoples, such as the San, Zulu, or Ndebele, rather than black or African.[12] Similarly, Britons were subdivided into many groups, including the Irish, Anglo-Saxon, and Caledonian.[13] These differences are historically significant, because they were often considered sufficient to create human hierarchies between peoples now regarded as of the same or similar color (such as the base San and mighty Zulu or the Negroid Irish and superior Anglo-Saxon). Recapturing these fine-grained distinctions is essential for analyzing the shows' receptions, since not only were patrons aware of them but showmen routinely capitalized on them by promoting their performers as peoples whose presence in Britain was still exceptional.

While acknowledging that ethnic difference clearly played a critical role in the shows' promotion and receptions, this work has suggested that such associations were not inherent, self-evident, or uniformly adopted. Instead, the focus has been on the work that showmen, journalists, and patrons invested into constructing and interpreting the shows and the intellectual effort that had to be mobilized for displayed peoples to suggest anything of political, cultural, or scientific significance. Posters, playbills, handbills, and entrance tickets were often emblazoned with claims of uniqueness, rarity, ethnic singularity, and political relevance. Their slogans and claims attempted to persuade consumers to part with their money by offering rare opportunities to see peoples hitherto unknown to the European world, Britain's latest military enemies, or exemplars of specific states of human development. Many have been quick to seize on such claims as evidence of the shows' receptions. However, as forms of advertising, these materials were wont to emphasize, exaggerate, create, or even fabricate difference for economic gain. They provide valuable evidence regarding showmen's marketing techniques and the frameworks within which patrons were expected to consume, but they cannot be taken as evidence for how patrons interpreted the performances they witnessed.

Managers used many cues, such as printed promotional material, lectures, highly stylized images, costumes, and background scenery, to frame displayed peoples; thus, they ensured that the shows functioned as a context that helped attribute meaning to the performers. If and when displayed peoples were introduced into this matrix, they were made into exemplars that, through repeated acts of "showing and telling," might be used as object lessons to ostensibly train consumers about a given issue. Critically, this context encompassed enormous diversity; thus, displayed peoples served as, among other options, objects of commercial exchange, skilled performers, natural historical specimens, political subjects, military foes, benighted and irreligious victims awaiting philanthropic and missionary intervention, and evidence in the debates over human origins. Eyewitness testimony suggests that showmen's invitations to use displayed peoples as ethnic exemplars were successful, sometimes long after they exhibited. For instance, in 1888 Auguste Racinet produced an authoritative guide on

FIGURE 101
(Facing) Sara Baartman's show costume as used to illustrate African national costumes. (Adolf Rosenberg, *Geschichte des Kostüms*, after Auguste Racinet, 1888, plate 128. Author's collection.)

[276]

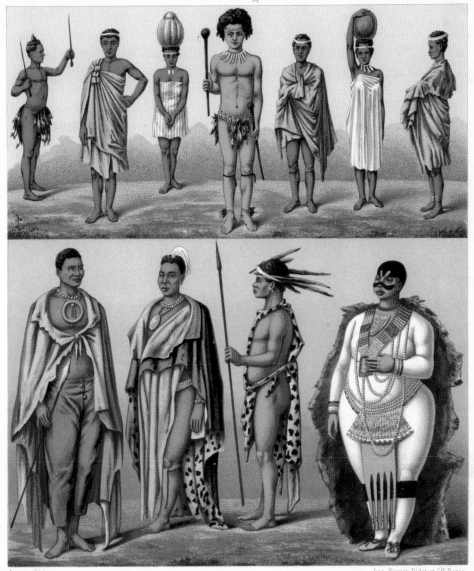

Jauvin lith   Imp. Firmin Didot et Cie Paris.

the history of clothing in which various individuals were shown in representative national costumes. In one of the many plates devoted to African clothing, Sara Baartman is featured sporting her show costume when exhibited in Piccadilly (fig. 101).

While acknowledging such uses of displayed peoples, it is of fundamental importance to remember that they were simultaneously and inextricably linked to patrons interpreting the shows as evidence for multiple and often competing theories of the nature of humanity or appropriate foreign policies. Some consumers were disgusted with the performers; others were touched by their humanity and good nature. Even when displayed peoples were discussed in terms of civilized and savage, it is worth bearing in mind that these states were not discrete, binary opposites but part of a developmental spectrum used to taxonomize human social and cultural organization. Likewise, missionaries and philanthropists clearly contributed to, and relied on, the political relevance of displayed peoples, though they were often deeply critical of such shows as a form of entertainment. Instead, they rallied together to call on managers and patrons to be more mindful of their moral and religious obligations. This complexity is glossed over too hastily in searches for a unified or typical voice. It is more productive to acknowledge that the shows' receptions were contingent on the specific circumstances of each show, manager, patron, and performer. Woefully, such details are all too often irrecoverable, but enough evidence exists to piece together a history of human display that takes into account not just the possibility but also the reality of the multiple interpretations any given show generated.

Interpretative diversity was underpinned by the opportunities the shows provided for dynamic intercultural encounters. Urban spectatorship produced a potential clientele that was both attentive to human variation and accustomed to using people as objects of visual inspection and consumption. Showmen profited from this by offering the opportunity for lingering inspection. By charging a shilling, or more, they absolved spectators from abiding by the boundaries of common propriety and allowed patrons to talk to, bestow gifts on, dance with, shake hands with, and even play tricks on entertainers. Performers could—and did—refuse to perform, strike back, show warmth, and solicit and accept gifts in acts that both strengthened and undermined promotional claims and patrons' expectations. Significantly, such contact frequently formed the basis of both fleeting and lasting relationships. Performers were frequently taken for day trips about town and treated as tourists. In conjunction, they were entertained at the homes of distinguished guests, fashionable folk, and even the royal family. Some built relationships that lasted far beyond the polite, conversational dinner party: performers are known to have married, settled and started families with spouses they met while earning a living abroad. Dispensing with the notion that displayed peoples' histories are best understood as spectacles helps highlight the fundamental importance of these diverse and dynamic relationships.[14] It also helps reframe the shows as significant arenas for the production of scientific knowledge.

Throughout the eighteenth and nineteenth centuries, scholars were engaged in protracted and vigorous debates that attempted to define the category of human. In the mid-nineteenth century, these debates were reformulated into the central theoretical conundrum of a new discipline, ethnology (and later anthropology). Displayed peoples were amenable to being used as opportunities for viewing human difference throughout the century, but at midcentury their potential utility as specimens began to be tied to new debates as ethnologists attempted to promote the disciplinary and institutional status of their subject by establishing shared forums for intellectual exchange, defining the remit of their theoretical concerns in human variety, and determining a suitable methodology. As part of these shifts, ethnologists called increasingly loudly for displayed peoples to be subjected to their probing gazes, and so competed for intellectual prestige by attempting to become the arbiters of ethnic authenticity. Within this climate of methodological debate, individuals from a broad spectrum of expertise, from established ethnologists to members of the lay public, used displayed peoples as living natural historical specimens to "speculate usefully" on human variety and thereby generate ethnological knowledge.[15] In the later nineteenth century, many anthropologists either personally curated or were closely associated with international exhibitions. As the presence of the Anthropological Institute at the Colonial and Indian Exhibition suggests, displayed peoples continued to provide experimental subjects, object lessons to train new practitioners, the basis for publications, and a rallying point for consolidating and promoting disciplinary status. Significantly, the available eyewitness accounts and scientific reports suggest that this is how the shows were often used. In this sense, the peoples on display became observational, experimental, and teaching resources that could be used by the lay and the learned. Of course, not all patrons may have viewed displayed peoples as specimens, but they were certainly encouraged to, and a significant number appear to have done so enthusiastically.

By recognizing the importance of the shows for the production of natural knowledge, this work both draws on and contributes to a growing literature that examines how scientific knowledge was made in multiple sites, or a "marketplace," described as "popular" by both historians and historical actors, including periodicals, museums, and exhibitions.[16] Building on this work, human displays may be seen as both formative for anthropological knowledge production as well as one of the most significant arenas in which the lay public engaged with nineteenth-century anthropological debates. Although there has been substantial interest in the links between the world's fairs and anthropology, anthropologists' involvement was conceptually limited to one of public communication—or, more simplistically, the diffusion or misinterpretation of expert knowledge within the popular realm. One recent collection of essays has argued, "In fact, anthropologists did not 'orchestrate' such exhibitions, they validated them, initially in a spirit of opportunism, chiefly out of interest in the 'specimens' displayed, and in the anticipation that such shows would make the general public, as political decision-makers, more aware of scientific research."[17] Such claims dismiss the use of the shows to conduct research while simultaneously assuming that anthropology was institutionally well enough established and secure to be in a position to validate the shows. Moreover, they fail to account for the ways in which early anthropological practitioners and institutions consistently attempted, with varied success, to promote and consolidate their own status as a result of their involvement with the fairs.[18]

Accordingly, investigations of displayed peoples are often dismissed as pseudoscientific, predominantly because of the modern dismissal of race as a scientifically meaningful category and proposed objective nature of scientific investigation.[19] Characterizing past scientific theories as pseudoscientific because they have been superseded or because they are no longer considered politically acceptable implies that "real" science is, and can be, immune to the political and social climates in which it is conducted; however, this has been consistently shown to be a fundamentally problematic position, since scientific practices are inextricably bound to wider political and social concerns across an array of historical and geographic contexts.[20] Moreover, the nineteenth-century exhibitions considered here occurred in a period when who could be a legitimate contributor to the making of natural knowledge and what counted as science were being reforged. Recognizing the pliable disciplinary landscape of the mid-nineteenth century allows a better understanding of the relationship between the shows and debates regarding ethnological and anthropological practice, because they were embedded within these wider upheavals.

Many elements of displayed peoples' histories often seem strangely familiar, since the fascination, pleasure, and curiosity excited by human difference continues to ensure a living for many worldwide. Both "Africa Africa!" and nineteenth-century exhibitions of displayed peoples advertised performers as representatives of specific ethnic groups and capitalized on assumed and created cultural differences between consumers and performers for a range of commercial and educational purposes. Modern folk festivals, tourist package holidays visiting the reservations of indigenous peoples, and the National Geographic television channel and magazine are just some examples of contexts in which humans continue to be marketed, and consumed, using ethnic typologies. The "native" village continues to be deployed in worrying and even violent contexts. In June 2005, the Augsburg Zoo hosted a four-day festival that featured a mock African village in the heart of the zoo. Manned by various performers, it was marketed as a taste of African life and caused a scandal, with detractors accusing the authorities of racist exploitation.[21] More recently, the War on Terror rages in Afghanistan and Iraq at the time of writing; having conspicuously failed to root out the ostensible threats to security and ensure the postinvasion stability of these regions with appalling consequences, politicians threaten the escalation of the conflict and expansion into further reaches of world. As part of its strategy for training troops, the British Ministry of Defense has established a mock Afghan village in the heart of Thetford Forest in Norfolk, East Anglia. Fourteen million pounds have been spent in recreating dusty streets that are pumped full of suitable aromas and which ring with the *adhan* (Muslim call to prayer) while robed "Taliban insurgents" roam around, colluding in Farsi. The site has enjoyed a history of replica environments, having initially served as a Nazi village and then taking on Northern Irish and Bosnian guises before being revamped for its current role.[22] Such uses of living foreign peoples may mean that some feel little has changed.

Alternatively, it is tempting to imagine that as citizens of modern multicultural societies we are free from, certainly less tainted by, the prejudice and voyeurism that fed the commercial success of displayed peoples in the nineteenth century; but assuming too much distance can be just as problematic as assuming none at all. For example, in 1992 the exhibit Two Undiscovered Amerindians Visit toured the United States, Australia, and London. A male and a female Amerindian lived inside a golden cage and were claimed to originate from an island that had been overlooked by explorers and travelers for over five centuries.[23] A fake *Encyclopaedia Britannica* entry, map of the island, and chronology of human display contextualized the exhibit. The only means of obtaining further information was from the protective guards. The pair performed "traditional" tasks ranging from making voodoo dolls, exercising with weights, watching television, and working at a laptop computer. For a small fee, the woman performed a "traditional" dance to rap music and the man momentarily revealed his "primitive" genitalia. The installation was previously unadvertised and, crucially, presented as a museum exhibit rather than performance art, thus forcing visitors to reflect on their relationship with the caged people, aided only by didactic information given. Coco Fusco, who performed as the "Amerindian" woman, writes, "As we assumed the stereotypical role of the domesticated savage, many audience members felt *entitled* to assume the role of the colonizer."[24] Many paid the requisite fee to view the genitalia or watch the ritual dance, some walking away when their expectations of "authenticity" were disappointed. Others questioned the guards in an attempt to verify the exhibits' provenance. Once convinced, these viewers easily assumed positions of control and superiority, some even hurling abuse or sexually harassing the pair. After realizing that the performance was an installation, many participants became angry and upset. Unable to cope with the implications of their behavior, visitors castigated the exhibitors for their "immoral" deception of the public.[25] The performance raises many interesting issues, but particularly intriguing is the ease with which consumers were able to behave in ways that they later acknowledged to be unacceptable and that undermined their self-perception as free from certain kinds of prejudice. When reading of displayed peoples' histories, it is easy to assume that we would never have patronized such shows or treated displayed peoples with anything other than appropriate humanity, dignity, and respect; yet without the benefit of hindsight to justify ourselves, the situation clearly becomes more complicated.

Issues relating to moral responsibility and cultural sensitivity tie in to the considerable political significance of displayed peoples' histories. This has been partly created by analyzing these issues within the context of developing ideas of race, nation, and empire. Baartman has become an icon for oppressed Africans. Her tale has been consistently taken to be emblematic of the Western denigration and exploitation of colonized black, particularly African, peoples and the construction of black female sexuality as deviant by historians, modern artists, and political groups.[26] After Georges Cuvier's triumphant autopsy, Baartman's skeleton and a painted plaster cast made from her cadaver were displayed at the Museé de l'Homme. These were removed in the 1970s when there were feminist objections to her display. In 1995, a campaign to repatriate her remains began. The ensuing political row took eight years to be resolved. In 2002, she was finally returned to Africa and laid to rest. At her funeral, chosen to coincide with International Day of the World's Indigenous People and South Africa's National Women's Day (August 9), President Thabo Mbeki maintained that the "story of Sarah Baartman is the story of the African people." It was, he declared, "the story of the loss of our ancient freedom" and of "our reduction to the state of objects who could be owned, used and discarded by others."[27] The (problematic) implication is that not only was there one (negative) image of blackness in the early nineteenth century, but Baartman was representative of this image.[28] Yet even now there is no consensus on exactly who Baartman was, let alone whose history she might best exemplify. Once the French government agreed to her repatriation, many competing claims emerged from communities as to whom she belonged to, most obviously from groups claiming Khoekhoe descent, such as the Griqua. The fraught negotiations over how she should be buried and by whom provide a fascinating and a potent reminder of the differences that are all too often erased when Baartman is discussed as simply "black" or "African."[29]

The recent return and burial of the Queensland, Australia, man now known as Tambo sparked similar debates. Exhibited in Europe and America in the 1880s by Robert Cunningham, he died in the United States, where his body was embalmed and subsequently displayed at dime museums and exhibition halls into the twentieth century. Rediscovered in the basement of a funeral home in Cleveland, Ohio, in 1993, he was buried shortly after on Palm Island in 1994. Regarding the burial's significance for the local community, it has been suggested that "within the family and community it activated processes of cultural renewal," since it signaled the "symbolic return of other 'lost ones' who had been removed during the period when Aboriginal lives were controlled under the Protection Act introduced in Queensland in 1897." Furthermore, "the present economic and social injustices endured by Aborigines that have their roots in that past must be addressed. Only then will the symbolically charged event of Tambo's return stand confidently as a redemptive moment in Indigenous and non-Indigenous relations."[30] These particular histories reflect wider developments relating to the emergence of postcolonial nationalism and the issues of exploitation, identity, and agency that are being addressed worldwide as historically marginalized communities force museums to reassess the ethics of displaying or storing their communities and handling human remains.[31]

The broad consensus that exhibitions of living foreign peoples reinforced racist attitudes coupled with political investment has created histories that are both emotionally and politically potent. Anxieties that one might become complicit in displayed peoples' derogation or reenact and thereby contribute to the dissemination of racialist and voyeuristic views are both well founded and, one suspects, common. As such, it is likely, perhaps inevitable, that historians discussing the subject feel under pressure to distance themselves from the attitudes under investigation, so as not to appear to be resurrecting the shows as opportunities for further voyeuristic consumption or in order to denounce the shows as pseudoscientific entertainment.[32] With such powerful responses in the fray, it is not difficult to see why many have taken the shows to be unproblematic icons of Western racist exploitation of foreign, often colonized, peoples. Prima facie, characterizing the practice of exhibiting foreign peoples as scientifically insignificant, racist spectacles may seem accurate and desirable. It certainly supports many contemporary notions of what constitutes acceptable entertainment and human treatment, consolidates the ostensible objectivity of scientific investigation, and is also amenable for certain political ends. It is not difficult to empathize with this use or the political commitments of those who, quite rightly, support campaigns against continuing racist oppression and modern forms of cultural imperialism, and seek recompense for past wrongs. Nonetheless, it is worth being more critical of the criteria currently used to establish displayed peoples' status within these projects; otherwise, these people risk being reestablished as freaks renamed as cultural icons. All too often, the arguments that individuals such as Baartman or Tambo are iconic of historically marginalized communities have been premised on problematic arguments, such as color was central to the ascription of ethnic difference; historically there was a single image of the "black," "savage," or "other" operating; and displayed peoples were interpreted as typologically representative of this image. However, as discussed, suggestions that living foreign peoples were uniformly interpreted as "freaks" or "others" or within the context of imperialist nationalism are worth revising.

Peoples on Parade has attempted to offer a history of displayed peoples that accounts for why they proved so commercially successful, how they were transformed from small entrepreneurial speculations into government-sponsored initiatives, and what their lasting significance has been to scientific debates on the nature of human variation in the nineteenth century. Consequently, it has sought to avoid simply adding the shows to an already long list of examples of endemic nineteenth-century racism; rather, it has suggested that more compelling accounts are needed of how the association between displayed peoples and human variety was created and maintained. Highlighting limitations in some of the criteria currently used to conceptualize displayed peoples' histories is not intended to imply that they cannot or should not be politicized. Rather, it is to suggest that being more critically reflective about the contingency of common analytical terms, such as *race*, *science*, *entertainment*, or even *human*, offers the option of a far more powerful and contextually sensitive basis for the ascription of modern political significance. In doing so, it has explored how displayed peoples' lives were representative of historical patterns of knowledge production, exploitation, oppression, and dispossession while remaining alert to the diverse ways in which the shows were experienced and interpreted by performers and patrons alike. Thus, extended attention has been paid to suggesting how processes such as recruitment, trade, performance, and promotion all helped to tie the shows to broader political and social debates. In turn, this fueled the interpretation of the shows as relevant to a diverse range of discussions, including, but not limited to, British presence abroad, be it military, imperial, or missionary; slavery and philanthropic obligation; entertainment, whether perceived as rational or spectacular; and human development within the framework of natural history or, as the century wore on, anthropology. By recasting the shows as significant sites for the production of natural and intercultural knowledge, the suggestion is that they created a lasting legacy by shaping early anthropological inquiry, encounters between peoples, and broader public attitudes toward ethnic difference, and in so doing, helped define what it means to be human.

ACKNOWLEDGMENTS

ANYONE WRITING a work of this nature will understand that it is, in many senses, a collaborative venture aided in innumerable ways by family, friends, and colleagues. During this project's long gestation, I have accrued many debts, which it is my pleasure to acknowledge.

Being a member of the Department of History and Philosophy of Science at the University of Cambridge has been my good fortune. Under the charismatic and much-missed leadership of the late Peter Lipton, the department quickly became my intellectual home, shaped my historical interests, and provided opportunities to meet and share with many colleagues and friends.

I am profoundly indebted to Jim Secord. Working with an eminent scholar is always an honor, but working with Jim has also been an enormous pleasure. A teacher of unrivaled brilliance and a simply wonderful colleague, he has been unfailingly generous in more ways than words can possibly express. Without him this book would never have been completed, and I am eternally grateful for all that he has helped me achieve.

Many readers have kindly shared their expertise while reading my work. Their burdens have varied from reviewing the earliest incarnations of this work to commenting on numerous chapters from the final manuscript; all have been enormously helpful. Simon Schaffer has always been an inspiration. Anyone who has worked with him will be familiar with his extraordinary historical and philosophical learning, knowledge that he has always shared with enthusiasm. Sam Alberti, Christopher Bayly, Susan Bayly, Richard Drayton, Jim Endersby, Mike Esbester, Patricia Fara, Nick Hopwood, Nick Jardine, Ludmilla Jordanova, Bernth Lindfors, Billie Melman, Kate Nichols, Sharrona Pearl, Anne Secord, and Efram Sera-Shriar all made beneficial suggestions. Michael Bravo, Michael Bresalier, Victoria Carroll, Elizabeth Edwards, Cathy Gere, and Rob Ralley all read earlier work on Sara Baartman that has been incorporated here. Sujit Sivasundaram and two anonymous referees valiantly read the entire manuscript and provided many invaluable comments. As a research fellow with the Cambridge Victorian Studies Group, I have also profited immensely from the combined wisdom of Peter Mandler, Mary Beard, Jocelyn Betts, Helen Brookman, Rachel Bryant Davies, Adelene Buckland, David Gange, Simon Goldhill, Michael Ledger-Lomas, Clare Pettitt, Astrid Swenson, and Anna Vaninskaya. Kevin Levell shared his enormous talent and kindly helped prepare many of the images.

For financial assistance, I am obliged to the Arts and Humanities Research Board, Christ's College, the Isaac Newton Trust, the Raymond and Edith Williamson Fund, and the University of Cambridge, who all supported the earliest stages of this work. The book was completed during a Leverhulme Trust fellowship, an opportunity for which I am deeply grateful. The Getty Foundation has also charitably supported the reproduction of so many images.

Many archivists and librarians have patiently borne my requests for information and archival material. The staff of the superb John Johnson Collection of Printed Ephemera, Oxford, were particularly helpful in making my research trip there fruitful. I also benefited from the assistance of staff at the Whipple Library, University Library, and Haddon Library in Cambridge and the British Library in London. I am especially pleased to acknowledge the support of the Wellcome Library, London; Guildhall Library, London; and Michael Stevenson in allowing the reproduction of their images gratis.

The University of Chicago Press has been magnificent. Karen Merikangas Darling has been a consistently supportive and understanding editor, and I am deeply grateful to her for taking this project on board. I am also appreciative of the work of Christie Henry, Abby Collier, Sandy Hazel, Matt Avery, the editorial board, and the production staff. I could not be more thrilled with their work, and the final outcome.

Finally, although they may not have directly contributed as readers, I am sincerely thankful for the support of many others, of whom only a few many be mentioned here. Douglas Barker, Kelvin Bowkett, Gareth Rees and Nicholas Gay all helped give me the opportunity to come up to Cambridge and pursue a long-held dream. Tim Brighouse and Rosslyn Nelson continue to provide inspiration. Salina Begum, Noreen Jahangir, Uzma Mukhtar, and Ayesha Maclean have all offered friendship and understanding along the way. Vicky Levell has been a truly magnanimous Princess. Rob Humphreys has shown both inordinate patience and untold kindness.

I owe a great deal to my family, especially Sumayyah, Umar, Khalid, Sumera, and Sidrah. My final and greatest debt is to my beloved *ammi* and *abbu ji*.

APPENDIX: TERMINOLOGY

Listed below are modern ethnological terms alongside their nineteenth-century variants, including various spellings as used in the text, press material, and periodicals. Yet modern terms are also problematic, since there is not necessarily any consensus on which is the most appropriate or accurate. For instance, in Britain *Native American* is usually considered the least offensive term possible, while *Indian* is almost never used; however, in the United States the term *Indian* has been reappropriated in some contexts, as in the name of the recently established National Museum of the American Indian (and so is used in the text). Likewise, although modern terms are often drawn from indigenous languages, they might bear pejorative connotations or still erase considerable differences between peoples, such as with the use of *San* or *Sioux*. While acknowledging these problems, this book has used modern terms and, where possible, attempted to make use of names drawn from indigenous languages throughout.

Anishinabe	Ojibbeway, Ojibwe, Ojibway
Asian	Asiatic
Bakhoje	Ioway
Krenak	Botocudos
Khoekhoe	Hottentot
Ndebele	Matabele
Mandinka	Mandingo
Mfengu	Fingo
Mpondo	Pondo
Sámi	Laplanders
San	Bushmen, Bosjesmans, "Earthmen"
Shona	Mashona
Sotho	Basuto
Tswana	Bechuana
Xhosa	Caffres, Kafirs, Kaffirs
Zulu	Zoolu

ABBREVIATIONS

BAAS, British Association for the Advancement of Science
ESL, Ethnological Society of London
ILN, Illustrated London News
JJ, John Johnson Collection of Printed Ephemera, Bodleian Library, Oxford
ODNB, Oxford Dictionary of National Biography
OED, Oxford English Dictionary
OHBE, The Oxford History of the British Empire
LLLP, London Labour and the London Poor

NOTES

Introduction

1. Advertisement, *Times*, May 13, 1847, 1. Exeter Hall had a seating capacity of four thousand and so, if full, the audience would have been quite considerable. For a contemporary description see Charles Knight, *London Pictorially Illustrated*, 6 vols. (London: Charles Knight, 1841–44), 6:241–56.

2. For this account of the shows, including all quotations, see the fullest contemporary account in Anon., *Now Exhibiting at the Egyptian Hall, Piccadilly …* (London: Chapman, Elcoate, 1847), 1–2.

3. For an indication of the range of ethnic groups displayed in London during the nineteenth century, see the JJ, Human Freaks, 1–5; Daniel Lysons, "Collectanea; or, A Collection of Advertisements and Paragraphs from the Newspapers Relating to Various Subjects," 2 vols., and "Collectanea: Or a Collection of Advertisements and Paragraphs from the Newspapers Relating to Various Subjects," 5 vols., unpublished scrapbooks, British Library, London.

4. In addition to Richard D. Altick, *The Shows of London: A Panoramic History of Exhibitions,* 1600–1862 (Cambridge, MA: Harvard University Press, Belknap Press, 1978), see Ben Weinreb and Christopher Hibbert, *The London Encyclopedia*, rev. ed. (London: Macmillan, 1993), for information on the addresses, opening hours, and admission prices for these institutions. Although not formally defined, the season ran, roughly speaking, from the end of March (the end of the fox-hunting season) or April to July (the start of parliamentary sessions). See Stephen Inwood, *A History of London* (London: Macmillan, 1998), 640–41.

5. Ian Ousby, *The Englishman's England: Taste, Travel and the Rise of Tourism* (Cambridge: Cambridge University Press, 1990). For an example of internal tourism see Victoria Carroll, "The Natural History of Visiting: Responses to Charles Waterton and Walton Hall," *Studies in History and Philosophy of Biological and Biomedical Sciences* 35 (2004): 31–64.

6. For a chronological list of exhibitions between 1493 and 1992, see Coco Fusco, "The Other History of Intercultural Performance," in *English is Broken Here* (New York: New Press, 1995), 37–63 (especially 41–43).

7. Presently, there are no published monographs devoted to commercial exhibitions of foreign peoples during the early nineteenth century. Some of the most useful material may be found in Thomas Frost, *The Old Showmen and the Old London Fairs* (London: Tinsley Brothers, 1874), and Altick, *The Shows of London*. For an excellent collection of ephemeral material see the JJ, especially Human Freaks 1–5. Helpful

contextual material on London's entertainments and the old fairs may be found in Thomas Frost, *Circus Life and Circus Celebrities* (London: Tinsley Brothers, 1875); William Biggs Boulton, *The Amusements of Old London* ... (London: Nimmo, 1901), and Robert W. Malcolmson, *Popular Recreations in English Society, 1700–1850* (Cambridge: Cambridge University Press, 1973).

8. For the most comprehensive available biography of Baartman, see Clifton Crais and Pamela Scully, *Sara Baartman and the Hottentot Venus: A Biography and a Ghost Story* (Princeton, NJ: Princeton University Press, 2008).

9. X. Chabert, *A Brief Historical Account of the Life and Adventures of the Botocudo Chieftain, and Family, Now Exhibiting at No. 23, New Bond Street* (London: C. Baynes, 1822).

10. For introductory overviews of the use of humans in international fairs, see Paul Greenhalgh, *Ephemeral Vistas: The Expositions Universelles, Great Exhibitions and World's Fairs, 1851–1939* (Manchester: Manchester University Press, 1988), 82–111, and Raymond Corbey, "Ethnographic Showcases 1870–1930," *Cultural Anthropology* 8 (1993): 338–69. See also Peter H. Hoffenberg, *An Empire on Display: English, Indian, and Australian Exhibitions from the Crystal Palace to the Great War* (Berkeley and Los Angeles: University of California Press, 2001).

11. Although there were some precedents in the local and national trade fairs of the eighteenth and early nineteenth centuries, the emergence of international trade fairs is usually attributed to the 1851 opening of the Great Exhibition.

12. For the observation of foreign visitors to world's fairs, see Jeffrey A. Auerbach, *The Great Exhibition of 1851: A Nation on Display* (New Haven, CT: Yale University Press, 1999), and Hoffenberg, *An Empire on Display*.

13. Nigel Rothfels, *Savages and Beasts: The Birth of the Modern Zoo* (Baltimore: Johns Hopkins University Press, 2002), and Eric Ames, *Carl Hagenbeck's Empire of Entertainments* (Seattle: University of Washington Press, 2009).

14. For accounts of nineteenth-century racialism, see Christine Bolt, *Victorian Attitudes to Race* (London: Routledge and Kegan Paul, 1971); Douglas A. Lorimer, *Colour, Class, and the Victorians: English Attitudes to the Negro in the Mid-Nineteenth Century* (Leicester: Leicester University Press, 1978); and Nancy Leys Stepan, *The Idea of Race in Science: Great Britain, 1800–1960* (London: Macmillan, 1982). For a selection of primary sources, see Hannah F. Augstein, ed., *Race: The Origins of an Idea, 1760–1850*, Key Issues, no. 14 (Bristol: Thoemmes, 1996). For a helpful article regarding the use of race see Nancy Leys Stepan, "Race and Gender: The Role of Analogy in Science," *Isis* 77 (1986): 261–77.

15. On human displays in international fairs, see Burton Benedict, *The Anthropology of World's Fairs: San Francisco's Panama Pacific International Exposition of 1915* (Berkeley, CA: Scolar, 1983); Greenhalgh, *Ephemeral Vistas*; Robert W. Rydell, *All the World's a Fair: Visions of Empire at American International Expositions, 1876–1916* (Chicago: University of Chicago Press, 1984); Robert W. Rydell, *World of Fairs: The Century-of-Progress Expositions* (Chicago: University of Chicago Press, 1993); Nancy J. Parezo and Don D. Fowler, *Anthropology Goes to the Fair: The 1904 Louisiana Purchase Exposition* (Lincoln: University of Nebraska Press, 2008); Roslyn Poignant, *Professional Savages: Captive Lives and Western Spectacle* (New Haven, CT: Yale University Press, 2004); Rothfels, *Savages and Beasts*; Bernth Lindfors, ed., *Africans on Stage: Studies in Ethnological Show Business* (Bloomington: Indiana University Press, 1999); Annie Coombes, *Reinventing Africa: Museums, Material Culture and Popular Imagination in Late Victo-*

rian and Edwardian England (New Haven, CT: Yale University Press, 1994); Anne Maxwell, Colonial Photography and Exhibitions: Representations of the "Native" People and
the Making of European Identities (London: Leicester University Press, 1999); and Andrew Zimmerman, Anthropology and Antihumanism in Imperial Germany (Chicago:
University of Chicago Press, 2001). Zimmerman, Rydell, Rothfels, and Parezo and
Fowler provide among the most extended discussions of the connections between
the sciences and displayed peoples. Despite this attention, many historians of the
shows are dismissive of the possibilities for scientific research, often arguing that
such research is insignificant because it is pseudoscientific; alternatively, the shows
are argued to be sites for publicly communicating (as opposed to making) anthropological knowledge. See chapters 6 and 7 and the conclusion for further discussion.

16. Robert Knox, The Races of Men: A Fragment (London: Henry Renshaw, 1850), preface;
and Robert Knox, The Races of Men: A Philosophical Inquiry into the Influence of Race
over the Destinies of Nations, 2nd ed. (London: Henry Renshaw, 1862). For more on
Knox's politics and the making of his reputation, see Evelleen Richards, "The 'Moral
Anatomy' of Robert Knox: The Interplay between Biological and Social Thought in
Victorian Scientific Naturalism," Journal of the History of Biology 22 (1989): 373–436;
Cora Kaplan, "White, Black, and Green: Racialising Irishness in Victorian England,"
in Victoria's Ireland?: Irishness and Britishness, 1837–1901, ed. Peter Gray (Dublin: Four
Courts, 2004), 51–68; and Cora Kaplan, "'A Heterogeneous Thing': Female Childhood
and the Rise of Racial Thinking in Victorian Britain," in Human, All Too Human, ed.
Diana Fuss (London: Routledge, 1996), 169–202. For the fullest outline of the lecture
see chapter 4 of the present text and Anon., Now Exhibiting at the Egyptian Hall.

17. In Britain, the laboratory had been in use since the seventeenth century, but it only
gained dominance as an experimental arena and training ground in the late nineteenth century. For more on how it was established as a legitimate and suitable place
for the production of reliable natural knowledge and then transformed in a space
used to demarcate scientific practice, see Steven Shapin and Simon Schaffer, Leviathan and the Air-Pump: Hobbes, Boyle and the Experimental Life (Princeton, NJ: Princeton University Press, 1985); Graeme Gooday, "Nature in the Laboratory: Domestication and Discipline with the Microscope in Victorian Life Science," British Journal
of the History of Science 24 (1991): 304–41; and Soraya de Chadaverian, "Laboratory
Science versus Country-House Experiments: The Controversy between Julian Sachs
and Charles Darwin," British Journal of the History of Science 29 (1996): 17–41.

18. Roger Cooter, The Cultural Meaning of Popular Science: Phrenology and the Organization of Consent in Nineteenth-Century Britain (Cambridge: Cambridge University Press,
1984), and Alison Winter, Mesmerized: Powers of Mind in Victorian Britain (Chicago:
University of Chicago Press, 1998).

19. For more on women in the sciences, see Sally Gregory Kohlstedt and Helen Longino,
eds., "Women, Gender, and Science: New Directions," special issue, Osiris 12 (1997),
and Sally Gregory Kohlstedt, "Women in the History of Science: An Ambiguous
Place," Osiris 10 (1995): 39–60. For more on the historical participation of ethnic minorities in science, see Darlene Clark Hine, "Co-Labourers in the Work of the Lord:
Nineteenth-Century Black Women Physicians," in The "Racial" Economy of Science:
Towards a Democratic Future, ed. Sandra Harding (Bloomington: Indiana University
Press, 1993), 210–27; Joan Mark, "Francis La Flesche: The American Indian as An-
thropologist," Isis 73 (1982): 495–510; and Stuart McCook, "It May Be Truth, but It

Is Not Evidence: Paul du Chaillu and the Legitimation of Evidence in the Field Sciences," *Osiris* 11 (1996): 177–97. For technicians see also N. C. Russell, E. M. Tansey, and V. Lear, "Missing Links in the History and Practice of Science: Teams, Technicians and Technical Work," *History of Science* 38 (2000): 237–41; and Richard Sorrenson, "George Graham, Visible Technician," *British Journal for the History of Science* 32 (1999): 203–21.

20. For an overview of these developments, see Jan Golinski, *Making Natural Knowledge: Constructivism and the History of Science* (Cambridge: Cambridge University Press, 1998). For more specific examples relating to space, see the following. For natural history see Nicholas Jardine, James A. Secord, and E. C. Spary, eds., *The Cultures of Natural History* (Cambridge: Cambridge University Press, 1996). For royal courts see Mario Biagioli, *Galileo Courtier: The Practice of Science in the Culture of Absolutism* (Chicago: University of Chicago Press, 1993). For botanical gardens see Richard Drayton, *Nature's Government: Science, Imperial Britain and the "Improvement" of the World* (New Haven, CT: Yale University Press, 2000), and Jim Endersby, *Imperial Nature: Joseph Hooker and the Practices of Victorian Natural History* (Chicago: University of Chicago Press, 2008). For public lectures see Simon Schaffer, "Natural Philosophy and Public Spectacle in the Eighteenth Century," *History of Science* 21 (1983): 1–35. For the coffeehouse see Jeffrey R. Wigelsworth, "Competing to Popularize Newtonian Philosophy: John Theophilus Desaguliers and the Preservation of Reputation," *Isis* 94 (2003): 435–55. For the pub see Anne Secord, "Science in the Pub: Artisan Botanists in Early-Nineteenth-Century Lancashire," *History of Science* 32 (1994): 269–315. For fieldwork see George W. Stocking, ed., *Observers Observed: Essays on Ethnographic Fieldwork* (Madison: University of Wisconsin Press, 1983). For the museum see Peter Vergo, ed., *The New Museology* (London: Reaktion, 1989); Susan Pearce, ed., *Interpreting Objects and Collections* (London: Routledge, 1994); Tony Bennett, *The Birth of the Museum: History, Theory, Politics* (London: Routledge, 1995); George W. Stocking, ed., *Objects and Others: Essays on Museums and Material Culture* (Madison: University of Wisconsin Press, 1985); and John V. Pickstone, "Museological Science? The Place of the Analytical/Comparative in Nineteenth-Century Science, Technology and Medicine," *History of Science* 32 (1994): 111–38.

21. For the conceptualization of human variety before the nineteenth century, see Roxann Wheeler, *The Complexion of Race: Categories of Difference in Eighteenth-Century Culture* (Philadelphia: University of Pennsylvania Press, 2000); David Bindman, *From Ape to Apollo: Aesthetics and the Idea of Race in the 18th Century* (London: Reaktion, 2002); Colin Kidd, *British Identities before Nationalism: Ethnicity and Nationhood in the Atlantic World, 1600–1800* (Cambridge: Cambridge University Press, 1999); Mark Harrison, *Climates and Constitutions: Health, Race, Environment and British Imperialism in India, 1600–1850* (Oxford: Oxford University Press, 1999); and Dror Wahrman, "Climate, Civilization and Complexion: Varieties of Race," in *The Making of the Modern Self: Identity and Culture in Eighteenth-Century England* (New Haven, CT: Yale University Press, 2006), 83–126. For more on the nineteenth century, see Seymour Drescher, "The Ending of the Slave Trade and the Evolution of European Racism," *Social Science History* 14 (1990): 415–450; George W. Stocking, *Victorian Anthropology* (London: Free Press, 1987); George W. Stocking, "What's in a Name? The Origins of the Royal Anthropological Institute, 1837–71," *Man* 6 (1971): 369–90; George W. Stocking, "From Chronology to Ethnology: James Cowles Prichard and British Anthropology, 1800–1850," in James C. Prichard, *Researches into the Physical*

History of Man, ed. George Stocking (Orig. pub. 1813; Stocking edition, Chicago: University of Chicago Press, 1973), ix–cx; Hannah F. Augstein, *James Cowles Prichard's Anthropology: Remaking the Science of Man in Early-Nineteenth-Century Britain* (Amsterdam: Rodopi, 1999); Bolt, *Victorian Attitudes to Race*; Lorimer, *Colour, Class, and the Victorians*; Stepan, *The Idea of Race in Science*; and Augstein, ed., *Race*. For a helpful discussion of the shifting fortunes of environmentalism, see Warwick Anderson, *The Cultivation of Whiteness: Science, Health and Racial Destiny in Australia* (New York: Basic Books, 2003).

22. See Corbey, "Ethnographic Showcases." Likewise, Lindfors, ed., *Africans on Stage*, glosses such shows as "ethnological showbusiness." I also used the term in earlier work. See Sadiah Qureshi, "Displaying Sarah Baartman, the 'Hottentot Venus,'" *History of Science* 42 (2004): 233–57.

23. Robert Knox, quoted in Anon., *Now Exhibiting at the Egyptian Hall*, 1.

24. The British and Foreign Anti-Slavery Society (1839) continued the work of William Wilberforce's Society for the Mitigation and Gradual Abolition of Slavery throughout the British Dominions (1823), while the Aborigines' Protection Society (1837) was set up in the wake of the 1836 Parliamentary Select Committee on Aborigines. For more on the 1836 committee, see Zoë Laidlaw, "Aunt Anna's Report: The Buxton Women and the Aborigines Select Committee 1835–37," *Journal of Imperial and Commonwealth History* 32 (2004): 1–28.

25. Charles Dickens, "Review: 'Narrative of the Expedition Sent by her Majesty's Government to the River Niger in 1841, under the Command of the Captain H.D. Trotter, RN,'" *Examiner*, August 19, 1848, pp. 531–35; quotation is from p. 532.

26. [Thomas Carlyle], "Occasional Discourse on the Negro Question," *Fraser's Magazine for Town and Country* 40 (1849): 670–79; quotations are from pp. 671–72.

27. For seminal studies on popular culture, see John M. Mackenzie, *Propaganda and Empire: The Manipulation of British Public Opinion, 1880–1960* (Manchester: Manchester University Press, 1984), and John M. Mackenzie, ed., *Imperialism and Popular Culture* (Manchester: Manchester University Press, 1986). For the museum see Ivan Karp and Steven D. Lavine, eds., *Exhibiting Cultures: The Poetics and the Politics of Museum Display* (Washington, DC: Smithsonian Institution Press, 1991); Tim Barringer and Tom Flynn, eds., *Colonialism and the Object: Empire, Material Culture and the Museum* (London: Routledge, 1998); James Clifford, *The Predicament of Culture: Twentieth-Century Ethnography, Literature and Art* (Cambridge, MA: Harvard University Press, 1988); Vergo, *The New Museology*; Bennett, *The Birth of the Museum*; and Carol Duncan, *Civilising Rituals: Inside Public Art Museums* (London: Routledge, 1995). For zoological gardens see Harriet Ritvo, *The Animal Estate: The English and Other Creatures in the Victorian Age* (Cambridge, MA: Harvard University Press, 1987); Robert J. Hoage and William A. Deiss, eds., *New Worlds, New Animals: From Menagerie to Zoological Park in the Nineteenth Century* (Baltimore, MD; London: Johns Hopkins University Press, 1996); Eric Baratay and Elisabeth Hardouin-Fugier, *Zoo: A History of Zoological Gardens in the West* (London: Reaktion, 2002); and Ames, *Carl Hagenbeck's Empire of Entertainments*. For more on natural history in general, see Jardine, Secord, and Spary, eds., *The Cultures of Natural History*. For the department store see Geoffrey Crossick and Serge Jaumain, eds, *Cathedrals of Consumption: The European Department Store, 1850–1939* (Aldershot, UK: Ashgate, 1999). For the theater and music hall see J. S. Bratton et al. eds., *Acts of Supremacy: The British Empire and the Stage, 1790–1930* (Manchester: Manchester University Press, 1991); David Mayer, *Harlequin*

in *His Element: The English Pantomime, 1806–1836* (Cambridge, MA: Harvard University Press, 1969); and Gillian Russell, *The Theatres of War: Performance Politics and Society,* 1793–1915 (Oxford: Oxford University Press, 1995).

28. For an indication of the range of living curiosities the public was able to see on London's stages, see Frost, *The Old Showmen and the Old London Fairs*; Altick, *The Shows of London*; and Ricky Jay, *Learned Pigs and Fireproof Women* (London: Hale, 1986).

29. This association is common (and often assumed) in discussions of the commercial exhibitions of foreign peoples. See Lindfors, ed., *Africans on Stage*; Robert Bogdan, *Freak Show: Presenting Human Oddities for Amusement and Profit* (Chicago: University of Chicago Press, 1988); Rosemarie Garland Thomson, ed., *Freakery: Cultural Spectacles of the Extraordinary Body*. New York: New York University Press, 1996; Alice D. Dreger, *One of Us: Conjoined Twins and the Future of Normal* (Cambridge, MA: Harvard University Press, 2004); Michael Mitchell, *Monsters: Human Freaks in America's Gilded Age; The Photographs of Chas. Eisenmann*, 2nd ed. (Toronto: ECW, 2002); Gahan Wilson, *The Big Book of Freaks: 50 Amazing True Tales of Human Oddities* (New York: Paradox, 1996); and Martin Howard, *Victorian Grotesque: An Illustrated Excursion into Medical Curiosities, Freaks and Abnormalities—Principally of the Victorian Age* (London: Jupiter, 1977). Nadja Durbach, *The Spectacle of Deformity: Freak Shows and Modern British Culture* (Berkeley and Los Angeles: University of California Press, 2009), provides a recent and helpful discussion of the ways in which exhibitions of foreign peoples overlapped with those of other human curiosities, laying the groundwork for further work in the area.

30. Durbach, *The Spectacle of Deformity*, 8.

31. Yvette Abrahams, "Images of Sara Bartman: Sexuality, Race and Gender in Early-Nineteenth-Century Britain," in *Nation, Empire, Colony: Historicizing Gender and Race*, ed. Ruth R. Pierson and Nupur Chaudry (Bloomington: Indiana University Press, 1998); 220–36 quotation is from p. 225. See also Rosemarie Garland Thompson, "From Wonder to Error: Monsters from Antiquity to Modernity," in *Human Zoos: Science and Spectacle in the Age of Colonial Empires*, ed. Pascal Blanchard et al., trans. Teresa Bridgeman (Liverpool: Liverpool University Press, 2008), 52–61.

32. For instance see Philips Verner Bradford and Harvey Blume, *Ota Benga: The Pygmy in the Zoo* (New York: St. Martin's Press, 1992); Harvey Blume, "Ota Benga and the Barnum Complex," in Lindfors, ed., *Africans on Stage*, 188–202; Crais and Scully, *Sara Baartman and the Hottentot Venus*; and Ben Shephard, *Kitty and the Prince* (London: Profile Books, 2003). Aided by an extensive family archive, Bradford and Blume, for example, present one of the most extended discussions of the dynamic relationship between Ota Benga, an African man exhibited at New York's zoological gardens and the Lousiana Purchase Exposition (the 1904 St. Louis World's Fair), and Samuel Philips Verner, his manager. Likewise, based on the first systematic scouring of the African archives, Crais and Scully provide the most comprehensive account of Baartman's life both before and after leaving Cape Town.

33. See Dhurba Ghosh, "Decoding the Nameless: Gender, Subjectivity, and Historical Methodologies in Reading the Archives of Colonial India," in *A New Imperial History: Culture, Identity and Modernity in Britain and the Empire, 1660–1840*, ed. Kathleen Wilson (Cambridge: Cambridge University Press, 2004), 297–316. Ghosh's article is particularly helpful in demonstrating how patterns of erasure can be used constructively to map out past social topographies and so demonstrate both agency and subjugation.

34. For a superb example of just how subtly political and racialist messages can be encoded, see Simon Schaffer, "On Astronomical Drawing," in *Picturing Science, Producing Art*, ed. Peter Galison and Caroline A. Jones (New York: Routledge, 1998), 441–74.

35. The only cases in which I have intentionally refrained from reproducing the relevant images are when I know they have been produced using coercion and unwilling subjects. Pertinent examples include the nude images of Baartman produced when she was at the Jardin des Plantes in 1814. The professors present at the examination pleaded with her for to remove her clothing, and she only did so reluctantly and after considerable pressure. For an account of her visit to the gardens see Georges Cuvier, "Extrait d'Observations Faites sur le Cadavre d'une Femme Connue á Paris et á Londres Sous le Nom de Vénus Hottentotte," *Mémoires des Muséum d'Histoire Naturelle*, 3 (1817): 259–74. The original images appeared in Georges Cuvier, "Une Femme de Race Boschismanne," in *Histoire Naturelle des Mammifères*, by Etienne Geoffroy St. Hilaire and Frédérick Cuvier (Paris: A. Belin, 1824), 1:1–4.

36. The concern with language has long informed studies of imperialism, with much being written regarding the use of linguistic appropriation and abrogation as a means of maintaining agency and offering resistance. For a discussion of such literary strategies, see Bill Ashcroft, Gareth Griffiths, and Helen Tiffin, *The Empire Writes Back: Theory and Practice in Post-Colonial Literatures*, 2nd ed. (London; New York: Routledge, 2002).

37. For one of the most helpful discussions of this issue, see Barbara J. Fields, "Ideology and Race in American History," in *Region, Race and Reconstruction: Essays in Honour of C. Vann Woodward*, ed. J. Morgan Kousser and James M. McPherson (Oxford: Oxford University Press, 1982), 143–77.

38. For a succinct analysis of these terms, see Colin Kidd, "Ethnicity in the British Atlantic World, 1688–1830," in Wilson, ed., *A New Imperial History*, 260–77. Fuller accounts may be found in Wheeler, *The Complexion of Race*; Bindman, *From Ape to Apollo*; and Kidd, *British Identities before Nationalism*. For a helpful account of why "races" are no longer seen as discrete natural entities among scientists, see Colin Kidd, *The Forging of Races: Race and Scripture in the Protestant Atlantic World, 1600–2000* (Cambridge: Cambridge University Press, 2006), 1–18.

39. This terminology follows on from the work of Graham Richards, *"Race," Racism and Psychology: Towards a Reflexive History* (London: Routledge, 1997).

Chapter One

1. "Mr Pips's Diary," *Punch* 17 (1849): 82. The diary satirized Samuel Pepys and provided a series of sketches of English life, each accompanied by a humorous picture.

2. Walter Benjamin, *Charles Baudelaire: A Lyric Poet in the Era of High Capitalism*, trans. Harry Zohn (London: New Left Books, 1973).

3. For an account of *flânerie* that is much more broadly contextualized than that of Benjamin, see Dana Brand, *The Spectator and the City in Nineteenth-Century American Literature* (Cambridge: Cambridge University Press, 1991). She argues that the conditions necessary for *flânerie* existed in England as early as the seventeenth century and that elements of the activity can be found in England, and subsequently America, in addition to the traditional French context. For other accounts of the *flâneur* see Susanna Barrows, *Distorting Mirrors: Visions of the Crowd in Late Nineteenth-Century France* (London: Yale University Press, 1981); Richard D. E. Burton, *The Flaneur and his City: Patterns of Daily Life in Paris, 1815–1851*, Durham Modern Languages Series

(Durham, UK: University of Durham Press, 1994); and Keith Tester, ed., *The Flâneur* (London: Routledge, 1994). More recently, Chris Otter, *The Victorian Eye: A Political History of Light and Vision in Britain*, 1800–1910 (Chicago: University of Chicago Press, 2008), argues that by focusing on the *flâneur* and the panopticon, histories of modern vision have often overemphasized the notions of spectacle and surveillance.

4. It is beyond the scope of this work to explore fully why the category of the urban spectator is a profitable extension of Benjamin's project. For more see Brand, *The Spectator and the City*.

5. [Eliza Lynn], "Passing Faces," April 14, 1855; *Household Words* 11 (1855): 261–64; quotation is from p. 261. Lynn is more commonly known as Lynn Linton, but did not adopt that name until she married William James Linton in 1858.

6. "'City Arabs' and 'Home Heathens,'" *ILN*, January 8, 1853, pp. 17–18. It is possible that this article was written by Henry Mayhew or his brother, as both occasionally contributed to the *ILN* in the early 1850s. For a discussion of their involvement with the paper, see Ann Hofstra Grogg, "The 'Illustrated London News,' 1842–1852" (Ph.D. diss., Indiana University, 1977), 94–95. The appearance of the phrase "City Arab" appears to be among its earliest usages and parallels the use of "Street Arab," which the *OED* notes was coined in 1848 and popularized in the early 1850s, particularly by Dickens.

7. Henry Mayhew, *London Labour and the London Poor; A Cyclopædia of the Condition and Earning of those that Will Work, those that Cannot Work, and those that Will Not Work*, 2 vols. (London: Woodfall, 1851–52). See also Henry Mayhew, *London Labour and the London Poor ...*, 4 vols. (London: London: Griffin, Bohn, 1861–62). The first two volumes of the 1861–62 edition were the same as the 1850s work. Volume 3 was begun but not published in 1856. Mayhew only wrote the introductory thirty-seven pages to the fourth volume, the rest being the work of various collaborators. Unless otherwise indicated, all further page references are to the 1861–62 edition, abbreviated hereafter as *LLLP*. For quotations see Mayhew, *LLLP*, preface. This note on the various editions of the work follows on from Anne Humpherys in Henry Mayhew, *Voices of the Poor: Selections from the* Morning Chronicle *"Labour and the Poor,"* 1849–1850, ed. Anne Humpherys (London: Cass, 1971), xvii.

8. Mayhew, *Voices of the Poor*, ix–x.

9. This account of London's geography is based on Andrew Saint, "The Building Art of the First Industrial Metropolis," in *London: World City*, 1800–1840, ed. Celina Fox (New Haven, C: Yale University Press, 1992), 51–76; J. Mordaunt Cook, "Metropolitan Improvements: John Nash and the Picturesque," in ibid., 77–96; and Inwood, *A History of London*.

10. See Anne Humpherys, *Travels into the Poor Man's Country: The Work of Henry Mayhew* (Athens, GA: University of Georgia Press, 1977); Anne Humphreys, *Henry Mayhew* (Boston, MA: Twayne, 1984); and Henry Mayhew, *The Unknown Mayhew: Selections from the* Morning Chronicle, 1849–50, ed. E. P. Thompson and Eileen Yeo (London: Merlin, 1971).

11. Mayhew, *LLLP*, 1:2.

12. See Andrew Smith, *Report of the Expedition for Exploring Central Africa from the Cape of Good Hope* (Cape Town: [Government Gazette Office], 1836), and *ODNB*.

13. For Prichard's reputation at the time of his death, see Anon., "Obituary of Dr. Prichard," *Journal of the Ethnological Society of London* 2 (1850): 182–207, quotation from

182; and Thomas Hodgkin, "Obituary: Dr. Prichard," *Lancet* 1 (1849): 18–19. For the changing fortunes of Prichard's reputation, see Stocking, "From Chronology to Ethnology," and Augstein, *James Cowles Prichard's Anthropology*. See also James C. Prichard, *The Natural History of Man: Comprising Inquiries into the Modifying Influence of Physical and Moral Agencies on the Different Tribes of the Human Family* (London: Hippolyte Bailliere, 1843).

14. James C. Prichard, *The Natural History of Man: Comprising Inquiries into the Modifying Influence of Physical and Moral Agencies on the Different Tribes of the Human Family*, 4th ed., ed. and enlarged by Edwin Norris (London: Hippolyte Bailliere, 1855), 1:101–14. Prichard's three divisions mapped onto three basic varieties of humans: the Negro, the Mongolian, and the European, respectively.

15. Mayhew, *LLLP*, 1:2.

16. See Charles Herbert, "Mayhew's Cockney Polynesia," in *Culture and Anomie: The Ethnographic Imagination in the Nineteenth Century* (Chicago: University of Chicago Press, 1991), 204–52. Herbert's research is valuable in unraveling the use of travel literature to demonstrate Mayhew's ethnological leanings and in providing a literary analysis of Mayhew's work. This chapter builds on Herbert's insights by situating Mayhew within the broader framework of nineteenth-century social observation. For further references to Mayhew as a social investigator, see Thompson and Yeo, *The Unknown Mayhew*.

17. Mayhew, *LLLP*, 1:2. Mayhew defined *Sonqua* as a pauper in the language of the San and Khoekhoe and *Fingoes* as wanderers, beggars, or outcasts in the language of the Zulu.

18. Mayhew, *LLLP*, 1:2.

19. Richard Phillips, cited in Roy Porter, *London: A Social History* (London: Penguin, 2000), 197.

20. Gustave Doré and Jerrold Blanchard, *London: A Pilgrimage* (London: Grant, 1872; reprint, New York: Dover, 1970), 187.

21. Thomas Babington Macaulay, review of [*Die römische Papste*], trans. S. Austin (London, 1840); *Edinburgh Review* 72 (1840): 227–58.

22. This discussion of costers and rovers is heavily indebted to Herbert, "Mayhew's Cockney Polynesia."

23. All quotations from Mayhew, *LLLP*, 1:20–21, 43.

24. Ibid., 1:21.

25. For more on how culture was defined and used to assess civilizational states in the nineteenth century, see Herbert, *Culture and Anomie*.

26. The saying reflects the adoption of this principle in English common law and was established in the sixteenth century.

27. Catherine Hall, *Civilising Subjects: Metropole and Colony in the English Imagination, 1830–1867* (Cambridge: Polity, 2002), 120–39.

28. Thomas Guthrie, *A Plea for Ragged Schools: Prevention Better than Cure* (Edinburgh: John Elder, William Collins, and James Nisbet, 1847), 19.

29. All quotations from Mayhew, *LLLP*, 1:213–14, 320–21. See also 1:2.

30. For a summary of some of these tropes, see Ter Ellingson, *The Myth of the Noble Savage* (Berkeley and Los Angeles: University of California Press, 2001), and Stocking, *Victorian Anthropology*.

31. For a helpful account of the changing iconography of the Khoekhoe, see Zöe S.

Strother, "Display of the Body Hottentott," in *Africans on Stage: Studies in Ethnological Show Business*, ed. Bernth Lindfors (Bloomington: Indiana University Press, 1998), 1–61.

32. Peter Kolben, *The Present State of the Cape of Good-Hope; or, a Particular Account of the Several Nations of the Hottentots* ... translated by Mr. Medley, 2 vols. (London: W. Innys, 1731), 1:46.

33. Mayhew, *LLLP*, 1:111.

34. Ibid.

35. Herbert, "Mayhew's Cockney Polynesia", especially 209–22.

36. Mayhew, *LLLP*, 4:35–210, 210–69.

37. Ibid., 4:56.

38. Edward Napier, *Excursions in Southern Africa* ... (London: W. Shober1,1849); Harriet Ward, *Five Years in Kaffirland* ... (London: H. Colburn, 1848); Charles Sturt, *Narrative of an Expedition into Central Australia* ... (London: T. and W. Boone, 1849); and M. Lucett, *Rovings in the Pacific from 1837 to 1849* ... (London: Longman, 1851).

39. For a helpful set of articles that help situate Mayhew in wider discussions of Victorian ethnography, see James Buzard and Joseph Childers, eds., "Victorian Ethnographies," special issue, *Victorian Studies* 41 (1998).

40. This account of Mayhew's research practices is based on Thompson and Yeo, *The Unknown Mayhew*.

41. William Booth, *In Darkest England and the Way Out* (London: Salvation Army, 1890).

42. Ibid., 13–15.

43. Clare Pettitt, *Dr Livingstone, I Presume? Missionaries, Journalists, Explorers and Empire* (Cambridge, MA: Harvard University Press, 2007).

44. Tim Jeal, *Stanley: The Impossible Life of Africa's Greatest Explorer* (London: Faber and Faber, 2007), especially 337–415.

45. Henry Morton Stanley, *In Darkest Africa; or, The Quest, Rescue, and Retreat of Emin, Governor of Equatoria* (London: Sampson Low, Marston, Searle and Rivington, 1890).

46. Brian Murray, "Savages and Street Arabs: Henry Morton Stanley in Darkest England," unpublished paper, 2008; private correspondence. I am thankful to Mr. Murray for allowing me access to his work.

47. Ibid.

48. Mrs H. M. Stanley [Dorothy Tennant], *London Street Arabs* (London: Cassell and Company, 1890), 5–7.

49. Oliver Goldsmith, *The Citizen of the World; or, Letters From a Chinese Philosopher, Residing in London, to his Friends in the Country* (London: C. Cooke, 1799); Charles de Secondat Montesquieu, *Persian Letters*, trans. Mr. Ozell (London: [J. Tonson], 1722); and Robert Southey [Don Manuel Alvarez Espriella, pseud.], *Letters from England* (London: Longman, 1807).

50. Saloni Mathur, *India by Design: Colonial History and Cultural Display* (Berkeley and Los Angeles: University of California Press, 2007), 62. See for instance Zine Magubane's *Bringing the Empire Home: Race, Class and Gender in Britain and Colonial South Africa* (Chicago: University of Chicago Press, 2003).

51. Quotation is from Doré and Blanchard, *London*, 2.

52. Llewellyn Woodward, *The Age of Reform, 1815–1870*, The Oxford History of England, 2nd ed. (Oxford: Oxford University Press, 1962), 1.

53. Robert Mudie, *Babylon the Great: A Dissection and Demonstration of Men and Things in the British Capital*, 2 vols. (London: Charles Knight, 1825), 1:2.

54. For more on urban spectatorship during the nineteenth century, see Lynda Nead, *Victorian Babylon: People, Streets and Images in Nineteenth-Century London* (New Haven, CT: Yale University Press, 2000), and Brand, *The Spectator and the City*.

55. John Bee [John Badock], *A Living Picture of London for 1828, and Stranger's Guide through the Streets of the Metropolis . . .* (London: W. Clarke, 1828), 11.

56. William Wordsworth, *The Prelude*, bk. 7, lines 594–99. First published between 1799 and 1805, a revised version of the poem was published after Wordsworth's death in 1850. Given that the discussion here is concerned with the first half of the nineteenth century, the original version has been used throughout. Both versions may be found in William Wordsworth, *The Prelude: A Parallel Text*, ed. J. C. Maxwell (London: Penguin, 1971).

57. William Thesing, *The London Muse: Victorian Poetic Responses to the City* (Athens, GA: Georgia University Press, 1982).

58. Charles Lamb, "The Londoner," essay to the editor of the *Reflector* [1801]; reprinted in *The Collected Essays of Charles Lamb* with an introduction by Robert Lynd and notes by William Macdonald (London: Dent, 1929), 2:6–8; quotation is from p. 7.

59. Bee, *A Living Picture of London.*

60. Mudie, *Babylon the Great*, 1:2.

61. Charles Lamb, letter to William Wordsworth, [January 30,1801], in *Selected Letters of Charles Lamb*, ed. G. T. Clapton (London: Methuen, 1925), 75–79; quotation is from p. 78.

62. "Life in London," *Mirror of Literature, Amusement and Instruction* 3 (1824): 173.

63. Mudie, *Babylon the Great*, 1:4.

64. Brand, *The Spectator and the City*, 41; and Jon P. Klancher, *The Making of English Reading Audiences, 1790–1832* (Madison: University of Wisconsin Press, 1987), 83.

65. John Fisher Murray, *The World of London* (London: William Blackwood and Sons, 1843), 1:25. Murray's quotation is from William Shakespeare, *Macbeth*, 4.1.111.

66. Murray, *The World of London*, 1:4.

67. Ibid.

68. Bee, *A Living Picture of London*, 56.

69. Louis Simond, *Journal of a Tour and Residence in Great Britain, During the Years 1810 and 1811*, 2nd ed. (Edinburgh: Archibald Constable, 1817), 2:32.

70. [Hermann] Pückler-Muskau, *A Regency Visitor: The English Tour of Prince Pückler-Muskau Described in his Letters, 1826–1828*, ed. E. M. Butler, trans. Sarah Austin (London: Collins, 1957), 48.

71. Heinrich Heine, "London," in *English Fragments from the German of Heinrich Heine*, trans. Sarah Norris (Edinburgh: R. Grant & Son, 1880); reprinted in *London, 1066–1914*, ed. Xavier Baron (The Banks, East Sussex: Helm Information, 1997), 2:230–34; quotation is from p. 231.

72. Bee, *A Living Picture of London*, 73.

73. Bee, *A Living Picture of London*, is just one example. See also Frank Wadleigh Chandler, *The Literature of Roguery* (London: B. Franklin, 1958), and John Marriott, ed., *Unknown London: Early Modernist Visions of the Metropolis, 1815–1845*, 6 vols. (London: Pickering & Chatto, 2000).

74. Bee, *A Living Picture of London*, 56.

75. Simond, *Journal of a Tour and Residence in Great Britain*, 1:22.

76. Ibid., 1:36.

77. Inwood, *A History of London*, 542–46.

78. Pückler-Muskau, *Regency Visitor*, 37–38.

79. Flora Tristan, *Flora Tristan's London Journal: A Survey of London Life in the* 1830s, trans. Dennis Palmer and Giselle Pinceti (London, 1840; reprint, London: Prior, 1980), 4.

80. George Henry [Maungwudaus], *Remarks Concerning Ojibway Indians, by One of Themselves Called Maungwudaus* ... (Leeds: C. A. Wilson, 1847), 1. Later reprinted as *An Account of the Chippewa Indians, who have been Travelling Among the Whites, in the United States, England, Ireland, Scotland and Belgium* ... (Boston: published by the Author, 1848). The American edition is reprinted in Bernd C. Pyer, ed., *American Indian Nonfiction: An Anthology of Writings,* 1760s-1930s (Norman: University of Oklahoma Press, 2007), 197–204; quotation is from p. 197. All subsequent page references are to the 1847 British edition.

81. Najaf Koolee Meerza, *Journal of a Residence in England, and of a Journey from and to Syria* (London: privately printed, [1839]), 280.

82. This account of foreign visitors is based on Simond, *Journal of a Tour and Residence in Great Britain*; Tristan, *Flora Tristan's London Journal*; James Baillie Fraser, *Narrative of the Residence of the Persian Princes in London, in* 1835 *and* 1836 (London: Richard Bentley, 1838); Meerza, *Journal of a Residence in England*; Pückler-Muskau, *A Regency Visitor*; Henry, *An Account of the Chippewa Indians*; Theodore Fontane, *Journeys to England in Victoria's Early Days*, trans. Dorothy Harrison (London: Massie Publishing, 1939; ed. E. M. Butler, London: Collins, 1957); Baron, *London*; and Marriott, *Unknown London*.

83. Fontane, *Journeys to England*, 19.

84. "Life in London," *Mirror of Literature, Amusement and Instruction* 3 (1824): 173.

85. For more on the ethnic diversity of sailors, see Peter Linebaugh and Marcus Rediker, *The Many Headed Hydra: Sailors, Slaves, Commoners, and the Hidden History of the Revolutionary Atlantic* (London: Verso, 2000).

86. For the best introductory account of the cosmopolitan population, see Nick Merriman, ed., *The Peopling of London: Fifteen Thousand Years of Settlement from Overseas* (London: Museum of London, 1993). Porter, *London*, and Inwood, *A History of London*, also provide useful material. More specific accounts may be found as follows. For black peoples see Peter Fryer, *Staying Power: The History of Black People in Britain* (London: Pluto, 1984); Gretchen Gerzina, *Black England: Life before Emancipation* (London: John Murray, 1995); Gretchen Gerzina, ed., *Black Victorians/Black Victoriana* (New Brunswick, NJ: Rutgers University Press, 2003); James Walvin, *The Black Presence: A Documentary History of the Negro in England,* 1555–1860 (London: Orbach and Chambers, 1971); Paul Edwards and James Walvin, *Black Personalities in the Era of the Slave Trade* (Baton Rouge: Louisiana State University Press, 1983); and Philip D. Morgan and Sean Hawkins, eds., *Black Experience and the Empire*, Oxford History of the British Empire Companion Series (Oxford: Oxford University Press, 2004). For Asians see Rozina Visram, *Ayahs, Lascars and Princes: Indians in Britain,* 1700–1947 (London: Pluto, 1986) and *Asians in Britain:* 400 *Years of History* (London: Pluto, 2001), and A. Martin Wainwright, *"The Better Class" of Indians: Social Rank, Imperial Identity and South Asians in Britain,* 1858–1914 (Manchester: Manchester University Press, 2008). For Jews see Pamela Fletcher Jones, *The Jews of Britain: A Thousand Years of History* (Gloucestershire: Windrush Press, 1990). For more on the Irish see Roger Swift and Sheridan Gilley, eds., *The Irish in Britain,* 1815–1939 (London: Pinter Publishers, 1989), and Graham Davis, *The Irish in Britain,* 1815–1914 (Dublin: Gill and Macmillan, 1991). This account of historical immigration is indebted to Nick Merri-

man and Rozina Visram, "The World in a City," in Merriman, *The Peopling of London*, 3–27; and Inwood, *A History of London*.

87. However, there were some restrictions. For example, individuals born abroad could not own land. For Jews this was not changed until 1825. Other restrictions were lifted gradually until none remained in the late nineteenth century. For a brief history of the Jewish presence in London, see Anne Kershen, "The Jewish Community in London," in Merriman, ed., *The Peopling of London*, 138–48.

88. See Visram, *Ayahs, Lascars and Princes* and *Asians in Britain*. See also Elizabeth M. Collingham, *Imperial Bodies* (Cambridge: Polity, 2001).

89. "Strangers' Home," *Lady's Newspaper*, June 7, 1856, p. 364.

90. Joseph Salter, *The Asiatic in England; Sketches of Sixteen Years' Work Among Orientals* (London: Seeley, Jackson and Halliday, 1873), 83.

91. For more on Anglo-Indian relationships, see Durba Ghosh, *Sex and the Family in Colonial India: The Making of Empire* (Cambridge: Cambridge University Press, 2006).

92. For a now classic account of the slave trade, see Philip D. Curtin, *The Atlantic Slave Trade: A Census* (Madison: University of Wisconsin Press, 1969). For more recent perspectives on both slavery and abolition, see David Eltis and James Walvin, eds., *The Abolition of the Atlantic Slave Trade: Origins and Effects in Europe, Africa, and the Americas* (Madison: University of Wisconsin Press, 1981); David Eltis, *The Rise of African Slavery in the Americas* (Cambridge: Cambridge University Press, 2000); Seymour Drescher, *The Mighty Experiment: Free Labour versus Slavery in British Emancipation* (Oxford: Oxford University Press, 2002); and David Brion Davis, *Inhuman Bondage: The Rise and Fall of Slavery in the New World* (Oxford: Oxford University Press, 2006).

93. [Edward Long], *Candid Reflections upon the Judgement Lately Awarded by the Court of King's Bench in Westminster-Hall on What is Commonly Called the Negro-Cause, by a Planter* (London: T. Lowndes, 1772), 47–49. Long's attitudes are not necessarily broadly representative but are sensational and well-known examples of some of the most vehement racism of the period.

94. Fryer, *Staying Power*, 120–26.

95. Benjamin Silliman, *A Journal of Travels in England, Holland and Scotland and of Two Passages Over the Atlantic, in the Years of 1805 and 1806 …*, 3rd ed. (New Haven, CT: S. Converse, 1820), 1:272.

96. David Dabydeen, *Hogarth's Blacks: Images of Blacks in Eighteenth Century English Art* (Manchester: Manchester University Press, 1987).

97. For Wedderburn see Robert Wedderburn, *The Horrors of Slavery, and Other Writings*, ed. Iain McCalman (Edinburgh: Edinburgh University Press, 1991), and Iain McCalman, *Radical Underworld: Prophets, Revolutionaries, and Pornographers in London, 1795–1840* (Cambridge: Cambridge University Press, 1988), 50–72. For Equiano see James Walvin, *An African's Life : The Life and Times of Olaudah Equiano, 1745–1797* (London: Cassell, 1998), and Edwards, *Black Personalities in the Era of the Slave Trade*, 119–41.

98. Kidd, *British Identities before Nationalism*.

99. For more on how the Irish were visually distinguished in print, see L. Perry Curtis Jr., *Apes and Angels: The Irishman in Victorian Caricature*, rev. ed. (Washington, DC: Smithsonian Institution Press, 1997), and Robert F. Foster, *Paddy and Mr Punch: Connections in Irish and English History* (London: Penguin, 1993).

100. The first British king was formerly appointed the Lord of Ireland in 1171. Between 1541 and 1800, Ireland was ruled as a subordinate kingdom. In 1800, Ireland and

Great Britain were united into a single kingdom, and this situation continued until 1922. See Seán Hutton, "The Irish in London," in Merriman, *The Peopling of London*, 118–28.

101. Michael Ball and David Sutherland, *An Economic History of London* (London: Routledge, 2001), especially 41–85.

102. For more on phrenology see Roger Cooter, *The Cultural Meaning of Popular Science*, and John van Whye, *Phrenology and the Origins of Victorian Scientific Naturalism* (Aldershot, UK: Ashgate, 2004). For Camper see Bindman, *From Ape to Apollo*. For more on nineteenth-century physiognomy, see Mary Cowling, *The Artist as Anthropologist: The Representation of Type and Character in Victorian Art* (Cambridge: Cambridge University Press, 1989); Lucy Hartley, *Physiognomy and the Meaning of Expression in Nineteenth-Century Culture* (Cambridge: Cambridge University Press, 2001); Anthea Callen, *The Spectacular Body: Science, Method and Meaning in the Work of Degas* (New Haven, CT: Yale University Press, 1995); Graeme Tytler, *Physiognomy in the European Novel: Faces and Fortunes* (Princeton, NJ: Princeton University Press, 1982); Bindman, *From Ape to Apollo*; and Sharrona Pearl, *About Faces: Physiognomy in Nineteenth-Century Britain* (Cambridge, MA: Harvard University Press, 2009).

103. These were the standard stereotyped features of Jewish peoples. For more on Haydon and his use of racialist stereotypes, see David Higgins, "Art, Genius and Racial Theory in the Early-Nineteenth Century," *History Workshop Journal* 58 (2004): 17–40.

104. Mayhew, *LLLP*, 6:35–210.

105. For more on Hogarth and social satire, see Mark Hallett, *The Spectacle of Difference: Graphic Satire in the Age of Hogarth* (New Haven, CT: Yale University Press, 1999).

106. This discussion of the Cries is drawn from Sean Shesgreen, *Images of the Outcast: The Urban Poor in the Cries of London* (Manchester: Manchester University Press, 2002).

107. Ibid., 90–117 for Hogarth and 149–73 for Beard.

108. Wordsworth, *The Prelude*, bk. 7, lines 228–43. Interestingly, in the 1850 version of the poem Wordsworth added "The begging scavenger, with hat in hand" to this section in a move that equated the urban poor with other foreign peoples. See Wordsworth, *The Prelude* (1850), bk. 7, line 313.

109. Merriman, *The Peopling of London*, 130 and 139–40.

110. Mudie, *Babylon the Great*, 1:64–65.

111. Thomas Woolnoth, *Facts and Faces: Being an Enquiry into the Connection between Linear and Mental Portraiture, with a Dissertation on Personal and Relative Beauty*, 2nd ed. (London: published by the author, 1854), 40.

112. Ibid., 130.

113. Cowling, *The Artist as Anthropologist*, and Pearl, *About Faces*, 26–56.

114. For more on ostension as a basis for learning, see Barry Barnes, "On the Conventional Character of Knowledge and Cognition," *Philosophy of the Social Sciences* 11 (1981): 303–33; "Social Life as Bootstrapped Induction," *Sociology* 17 (1983): 524–45; and "Ostensive Learning and Self-Referring Knowledge," in *Cognition and Social Worlds*, ed. Angus Gellatly, Don Rogers, and John A. Sloboda (Oxford: Clarendon Press, 1989), 190–204.

115. Pearl, *About Faces*, 4 and 42–43.

116. For a selection of contemporary writings illustrating these attitudes, see Baron, *London*, and Marriott, *Unknown London*.

117. Gerzina, *Black England*, 3.

118. This is not to deny that considerable work has been done on immigrant populations. Merriman, *The Peopling of London*; Fryer, *Staying Power*; Gerzina, *Black England*; Gerzina, *Black Victorians/Black Victoriana*; Walvin, *The Black Presence*; Visram, *Ayahs, Lascars and Princes*; and Wainwright, *"The Better Class" of Indians*, as used in this book, are just some examples. However, these studies are often limited to a single ethnic group, and historians have been slower to integrate discussions of an ethnically heterogeneous population into accounts of British society, especially in relationship to the shows' receptions. Linda Colley, *Britons: Forging the Nation, 1707–1837* (New Haven, CT: Yale University Press, 1992), for example, does not address the ethnic heterogeneity of Britain with regard to international migrating populations. The exception here is the history of Irish migration and settlement in Britain. See Swift and Gilley, *The Irish in Britain*, and Davis, *The Irish in Britain, 1815–1914*.

119. In her analyses of travel literature, Mary Louise Pratt has defined a "contact zone" as "the space of colonial encounters." It is "an attempt to invoke the spatial and temporal copresence of subjects previously separated by geographic and historical disjunctures, whose trajectories now intersect." Mary Louise Pratt, *Imperial Eyes: Travel Writing and Transculturation* (London: Routledge, 1992), 7.

120. For more on intercultural contact see Linda Colley, *Captives: Britain, Empire and the World, 1600–1850* (London: Jonathan Cape, 2002), and Jas Elsner and Joan Pau-Rubies, eds., *Voyages and Visions: Towards a Cultural History of Travel* (London: Reaktion, 1988); Martin J. Daunton and Rick Alpern, eds., *Empire and Others: British Encounters with Indigenous Peoples, 1600–1850* (London: UCL, 1999); and Catherine Hall, *The Cultures of Empire, A Reader: Colonizers in Britain and the Empire in the Nineteenth and Twentieth Centuries* (Manchester: Manchester University Press, 2000).

121. Catherine Hall's *Civilising Subjects* and Magubane's *Bringing the Empire Home* provide helpful examples of how such histories may be written symmetrically.

122. Even though Abrahams, "Images of Sara Baartman," acknowledges that black peoples lived in Britain, she still argues that their color marked them as exotic or alien and, in doing so, conflates them into a single ethnic group. In turn, the neglect of resident ethnic diversity in discussions of the shows' receptions has facilitated the oversimplification and homogenization of diverse consumer responses into the framework of a white self observing the black other (see conclusion). This model is becoming far less common but remains dominant. For instance, see its use across an enormous range of contexts in Pascal Blanchard et al., eds., *Human Zoos: Science and Spectacle in the Age of Colonial Empires*, trans. Teresa Bridgeman (Liverpool: Liverpool University Press, 2008).

Chapter Two

1. "The Billstickers" Exhibition," *Punch* 12 (1847): 226.

2. Anon., *The Language of the Walls: And a Voice from the Shop Windows; Or, The Mirror of Commercial Roguery, By One who Thinks Aloud* (Manchester: Abel Haywood, 1855).

3. For more on early means of advertising, see the launch issue of the *Illustrated London News*, May 14, 1842. See also Diana Hindley and Geoff Hindley, *Advertising in Victorian England, 1837–1901* (London: Wayland, 1972); Thomas Richards, *The Commodity Culture of Victorian England: Advertising and Spectacle, 1851–1914* (Stanford, CA: Stanford University Press, 1990); and Michael Twyman, *Printing 1770–1970: An Illustrated History of Its Development and Uses in England*, 2nd ed. (London: British Library, 1998).

For more on racialist advertising, see Jan Piertese, *White on Black: Images of Africa and Blacks in Western Popular Culture* (New Haven, CT: Yale University Press, 1992), and Anandi Ramamurthy, *Imperial Persuaders: Images of Africa and Asia in British Advertising* (Manchester: Manchester University Press, 2003).

4. "Advertising," *Athenaeum*, July 13, 1833, 459–60. T. Richards, *The Commodity Culture of Victorian England*, 6, has argued that the Great Exhibition "found advertising in a primitive state.... The trade had a few old tricks, a fixed repertoire a few hundred years old, and nothing more." While recognizing the role of the theater, arguing that "most advertising was an off-shoot of theatre advertising," his interest in the rise of the commodity means that he sidelines the use of this promotional material and so underestimates its importance, for both exhibition proprietors and potential patrons.

5. None of the histories of human exhibitions cited in this book provides a substantial critical analysis of the entire cycle of production, circulation, and use of promotional material (although some touch on these phases to varying degrees). Many do not even distinguish between the wide variety of promotional materials they have used or the sources that were available to them. An exception is the analysis of the Zulu pamphlet in relationship to travel literature and Dickens's journalism in Bernth Lindfors, "Charles Dickens and the Zulus," in Lindfors, *Africans on Stage*, 62–80. On a broader note, see Sara Thornton, *Advertising, Subjectivity and the Nineteenth-Century Novel: Dickens, Balzac and the Language of the Walls* (Basingstoke, UK: Palgrave Macmillan, 2009).

6. See Elizabeth Edwards, ed., *Anthropology and Photography, 1860–1920* (New Haven, CT: Yale University Press, 1994), and Elizabeth Edwards, *Raw Histories: Photographs, Anthropology and Museums* (Oxford: Berg, 2001).

7. The majority of the promotional materials used in this book are from the John Johnson Collection of Printed Ephemera, held at the Bodleian Library, Oxford, and the Evanion Collection at the British Library, London. Readers wishing to consult printed collections of primary materials are directed toward Leonard de Vries, *Victorian Advertisements* (London: John Murray, 1968), and Catherine Haill, *Fun without Vulgarity: Victorian and Edwardian Popular Entertainment Posters* (London: HMSO, 1996).

8. For examples see Karp and Lavine, *Exhibiting Cultures*; Barringer and Flynn, *Colonialism and the Object*; Clifford, *The Predicament of Culture*; Vergo, *The New Museology*; and Bennett, *The Birth of the Museum*.

9. Aileen Fyfe, for example, has attempted to recover how guidebooks for the British Museum shaped working-class visitors' experiences. Ralph O'Connor and Robert Aguirre have examined how guidebooks were used in the interpretation of panoramas. These discussions are helpful, particularly in providing a comparative perspective on the use of promotional materials in London's shows. In building on this work, this chapter hopes to lay the groundwork for further considerations of the production, circulation, and intertextuality of such promotional materials across the full range of pamphlets, guidebooks, handbills, playbills, and newspaper reviews available. See Aileen Fyfe, "Reading Natural History at the British Museum and the *Pictorial Museum*, in *Science in the Marketplace: Nineteenth-Century Sites and Experiences*, ed. Aileen Fyfe and Bernard Lightman (Chicago: University of Chicago Press, 2007), 196–230; Ralph O'Connor, *The Earth on Show: Fossils and the Poetics of Popular Science, 1802–1856* (Chicago: University of Chicago Press, 2008), 263–324;

and Robert D. Aguirre, *Informal Empire: Mexico and Central America in the Victorian Culture* (Minneapolis: University of Minnesota Press, 2005), especially 35–60.

10. Posters were commonly the largest printed formats and usually contained the least information. Handbills were commonly smaller and included more detailed text outlining the nature of the show. Playbills (later, theater bills) varied in length but commonly contained the most text and provided a detailed outline of the show's contents. All three could be pasted up either in the street or outside an exhibition venue, while handbills and playbills were usually handed out to passersby. For more on the definitions of these forms, see Maurice Rickards, *Encyclopaedia of Ephemera: A Guide to the Fragmentary Documents of Everyday Life for the Collector, Curator and Historian*, ed. Michael Twyman (London: British Library, 2000).

11. Hindley and Hindley, *Advertising in Victorian England*, 90.

12. The lack of posters promoting exhibitions of foreign peoples may be because the painting was executed in the mid-1830s when, to my knowledge, there were no major exhibitions of this kind (although smaller shows may still have taken place).

13. Twyman, *Printing 1770–1970*.

14. For more on the history of typography, see David C. Greetham, *Textual Scholarship: An Introduction* (London: Garland, 1994), 225–70; and Philip Gaskell, *A New Introduction to Bibliography*, 2nd en. (Winchester: St Paul's Bibliographies, 1995), 207–14.

15. Twyman, *Printing 1770–1970*, 10–14.

16. For the standard account of the history of photography, see Beaumont Newhall, *A History of Photography from 1839 to the Present*, 5th ed. (New York: Museum of Modern Art, 1984).

17. E. Edwards, *Raw Histories*.

18. Baartman, one of the most famous exhibits of the nineteenth century, was advertised as an example of female steatopygia. For more on both her display and the development of this visual stereotype, see Strother, "Display of the Body Hottentot," and John R. Baker, *Race* (Oxford: Oxford University Press, 1974), 313–19.

19. Durbach, *The Spectacle of Deformity*.

20. Advertisement, *ILN*, May 10, 1845, p. 302.

21. Hindley and Hindley, *Advertising in Victorian England*, 10.

22. "The Laplanders . . . ," *Times*, February 8, 1816, p. 3.

23. "Cape York Aborigines," *ILN*, October 8, 1853. I have found no record of these two men being exhibited at a later date, although models were made of them for displays at the Crystal Palace in Sydenham. For more on the importance of these models, see chapter 6.

24. Even where no evidence can be found of such individuals being publicly exhibited, it is tempting to argue that they were likely to have been displayed in some context, for example in the domestic sphere or even in the streets of London themselves.

25. "The Indian Marriage at St. Martin's Church," *Pictorial Times*, April 13, 1844, p. 233.

26. See George Catlin, *Adventures of the Ojibbeway and Ioway Indians in England, France and Belgium . . .*, 3rd ed., 2 vols. (London: published by the author, 1852), and George Catlin, *Unparalleled Exhibition: The Fourteen Ioway Indians and their Interpreter . . .* (London: W. S. Johnson, 1844), vol. 1, facing p. 136.

27. "Grand Fete Champetre at Charlton House," *ILN*, July 5, 1845, p. 9.

28. Michael Adas, *Machines as the Measure of Men: Science, Technology, and Ideologies of Western Dominance* (Ithaca, NY: Cornell University Press, 1989).

29. Donald R. Morris, *The Washing of the Spears: The Rise and Fall of the Mighty Zulu Nation*

(London: Jonathan Cape, 1965; reprint, London: Pimlico, 1994; Noel Mostert, *Frontiers: The Epic of South Africa's Creation and the Tragedy of the Xhosa People* (London: Jonathan Cape, 1992); J. D. Omer-Cooper, "The Nguni Outburst," in *The Cambridge History of Africa: Volume 5, c.1790–c.1870*, ed. John E. Flint (Cambridge: Cambridge University Press, 1985), 359–421; and Shula Marks, "Southern Africa, 1867–1886," in *The Cambridge History of Africa: Volume 6, c.1870–c.1905*, ed. Roland Oliver and G. N. Sanderson (Cambridge: Cambridge University Press, 1985), 359–421. These developments were also tied to large-scale internal migration, known as the *mfecane*, the exact causes of which are highly controversial. Compare Julian Cobbing, "The Mfecane as Alibi: Thoughts on Dithakong and Mbolompo," *Journal of African History* 29 (1988): 487–519; and Elizabeth Eldregde, "Sources of Conflict in Southern Africa, c. 1800–30: The 'Mfecane' Reconsidered," *Journal of African History* 33 (1992): 1–35.

30. "A Picnic at the Cape," *Times*, March 2, 1853, p. 6.

31. "A Soldier's view of the Caffre War," *Times*, March 7, 1853. This passage is taken from the first letter. The second provides a more differentiated account of African peoples, including the San, the Khoekhoe, and the Zulus, and the military strategies they used.

32. For more on the use of images in the *ILN*, see Peter W. Sinnema, *Dynamics of the Pictured Page: Representing the Nation in the* Illustrated London News (Aldershot, UK: Ashgate, 1998).

33. For more on nineteenth-century hunting, see Ritvo, *The Animal Estate*; John M. Mackenzie, *The Empire of Nature: Hunting, Conservation and British Imperialism* (Manchester: Manchester University Press, 1998); Joseph Sramek, "'Face Him Like a Briton': Tiger Hunting, Imperialism, and British Masculinity in Colonial India, 1800–1875," *Victorian Studies* 48 (2006): 659–80; and Jamie Lorimer and Sarah Whatmore, "After the 'King of Beasts': Samuel Baker and the Embodied Historical Geographies of Elephant Hunting in Mid-Nineteenth-Century Ceylon," *Journal of Historical Geography* 35 (2009): 668–89.

34. One account of Dutch settlers on a hunting excursion related how they shot dead and ate a San man, believing they were eating large game rather than a human. Mathias Georg Guenther, "From 'Brutal Savages' to 'Harmless People': Notes on the Changing Western Image of the Bushmen," *Paideuma* 26 (1980): 123–40. For more on European representations of the San, see Pippa Skotnes, ed., *Miscast: Negotiating the Presence of the Bushmen* (Cape Town, South Africa: University of Cape Town, 1996). In a lecture on Africans, Knox argued that "no two races differ as much as do the Hottentot and Bushman race and the Kaffir; the latter, tall stout, robust of a deep bronze colour, enterprising, chivalrous and bold; freemen, in fact, who have more than once driven in British troops, and with whom we wage a war of extermination—for, be assured of this: the Kaffir, will never become the slave of the white man; he will never with his life yield his lands to the British and Dutch now gaping for them." From Anon., *Now Exhibiting at the Egyptian Hall*, 2.

35. "Scenes from the War in Kaffirland," *ILN*, July 18, 1853, p. 39. Initially, the *ILN* did not have its own foreign correspondents, and most of its foreign news reports were contributions sent in from around the world by freelance writers. For more see Grogg, "The 'Illustrated London News.'"

36. Charles Henry Caldecott, *Exhibition of Native Zulu Kafirs: St Georges Gallery, Hyde Park Corner, Piccadilly* (London: John Mitchell, 1853), 3. The press used similar tactics by describing the exhibited troupe as Zulu Kaffirs or just Kaffirs.

37. "Aztec Lilliputians," advertisement, *ILN*, July 16, 1853, p. 22; and Anon., *Now Exhibiting at the Egyptian Hall*, 1.

38. Anon., *Now Exhibiting at the Egyptian Hall*, 1.

39. "The Zulu Kaffirs, at the St. George's Gallery, Knightsbridge," *ILN*, May 28, 1853.

40. For a discussion of the falling sales figures of travel literature, see Nigel Leask, *Curiosity and the Aesthetics of Travel Writing, 1770–1840: "From an Antique Land"* (Oxford: Oxford University Press, 2002). Such dependence may have been particularly acute for exhibitions of foreign peoples because of the unfamiliar material they relied on. However, the need for or use of explanatory context was hardly absent for other exhibitions or forms of display. See Fyfe, "Reading Natural History at the British Museum and the *Pictorial Museum*"; O'Connor, *The Earth on Show*; and Carroll, "The Natural History of Visiting."

41. "The Caffres at Hyde-Park-Corner," newspaper clipping dated May 18, 1853, JJ, Human Freaks 4 (83d).

42. Caldecott, *Exhibition of Native Zulu Kafirs*, 4.

43. R. A. Cunningham, *History of R. A. Cunningham's Australian Aborigines, Tattooed Cannibal Black Trackers and Boomerang Throwers, Consisting of Two Tribes, Male and Female* (London, J. Elliot, 1884), 2.

44. Helpful exceptions may be found in Aguirre, *Informal Empire*, particularly 109–11, where he discusses the pamphlet for Maximo and Bartola; and Lindfors, "Charles Dickens and the Zulus."

45. Lindfors, "Charles Dickens and the Zulus." In the pamphlet accompanying the exhibition of Flora and Martinus, the text appears to contain stage directions: "The map to which I point will explain this to you," suggesting the pamphlet was adapted from a lecture or even referred to as the lecture was given. See Anon., *The Erdermänner; or, Earthmen from the Orange River in Southern Africa* (London: John K. Chapman, 1853), 6.

46. Mayhew, *LLLP*, 1:299–300.

47. Fyfe, "Reading Natural History at the British Museum and the *Pictorial Museum*," 214.

48. Ibid., 214–17.

49. Of the pamphlets cited in this book, only two were in bound format. However, these were at the British Library and at Cambridge University Library and were clearly bound not by the original owners but in order to preserve them for library users.

50. This discussion draws on Lindfors, "Charles Dickens and the Zulus." Lindfors also provides a more detailed analysis of the similarities between Caldecott, Isaacs, and Dickens and also discusses these quotations.

51. Nathaniel Isaacs, *Travels and Adventures in Eastern Africa, Descriptive of the Zoolus, their Manners, Customs, with a Sketch of Natal* (London: E. Churton, 1836), 2:295–97.

52. Caldecott, *Exhibition of Native Zulu Kafirs*, 19.

53. Anon., *The Erdermänner*, 9–10.

54. For the English translation see [Martin] Henry Lichtenstein, *Travels in South Africa, in the Years* 1803, 1804, 1805, 1806, trans. Anne Plumtre (London: [Henry Colburn], 1812–15), 2:194–95. To see examples of its textual appropriation, see Anon., *Now Exhibiting in the Egyptian Hall*; J. S. Tyler, *The Bosjesmans: A Lecture, on the Mental, Moral, and Physical Attributes of the Bush Men* (Leeds: C. A. Wilson, [1847]); Anon., *The Erdermänner*; and Anon., "The Erdmannings; or, Earthmen of Africa; Their Country and History," in *Life of the Living Aztec Children, Now Exhibiting at Barnum's American Museum, New York* (New York: Wynkoop, Hallenbeck and Thomas, 1860), 41–48.

Other examples of travel literature cited in the pamphlets discussed here include James Backhouse, *Observations Submitted in Brotherly Love to the Missionaries and other Gospel Labourers in South Africa*, 1840 (Cape Town: Saul Solomon, 1840); Robert Moffat, *Missionary Labours and Scenes on Southern Africa* (London: John Snow, 1842); T. Arbousset and F. Daumas, *Narrative of an Explanatory Tour to the North East of the Colony of the Cape of Good Hope ...*, trans. John Corumbie (Cape Town: A. S. Robertson and S. Solomon, 1846).

55. Aguirre, *Informal Empire*, 123–31, also suggests that interest in the children's lineage reflected wider concerns with interracial mixing during the period, particularly in the context of South America. For more on the King Charles Spaniel, see David Allan Feller, "Gentlemen Comforters," *America Kennel Club Gazette*, December 2007, 30–35.

56. For photographs of the pair, see M. Mitchell, *Monsters*, 71.

57. Don Antonio del Rio, *Description of the Ruins of an Ancient City ...* (London: Henry Berthoud, 1822), and John L. Stephens, *Incidents of Travel in Central America, Chiapas and Yucatan*, 2 vols. (London: John Murray, 1841). Stephens knew of the del Rio publication and drew on it in his own work, although subsequent writers have tended to overlook the earlier text. See Aguirre, *Informal Empire*, 74.

58. Layard shipped back many antiquities that are now housed in the British Museum. His findings were well known from their public display and his extensive illustrated publications for the mass market. See the following by Austen Henry Layard: *Nineveh and its Remains* (London: John Murray: 1849); *The Monuments of Nineveh* (London: John Murray, 1849–53); and *A Popular Account of Discoveries at Nineveh* (London: John Murray, 1852).

59. "The Aztecs," *Morning Chronicle*, July 12, 1853, p. 5.

60. Richard Owen and Richard Cull, "A Brief Notice of the Aztec Race, and a Description of the So-Called Aztec Children," *Journal of the Ethnological Society of London* 4 (1856): 120–37.

61. Anon., *Now Exhibiting at the Egyptian Hall*, 2.

62. "The Bosjesmans, at the Egyptian Hall, Piccadilly," *ILN*, June 12, 1847, p. 381.

63. William Bullock, *An Account of the Family of Laplanders ...* (London: James Bullock, 1822).

64. Ibid., 5.

65. Sir Arthur de Capell Brooke, *Travels through Sweden, Norway, and Finmark to the North Cape, in the Summer of* 1820 (London: Rodwell and Martin, 1823), and Sir Arthur de Capell Brooke, *A Winter in Lapland and Sweden ...* (London: John Murray, 1827). The *ODNB* notes that Broke preferred the older spelling of his name to the more commonly used Brooke (which was used in his publications).

66. See Stephen Oetterman, *The Panorama: History of a Mass Medium*, trans. Deborah Lucas Schneider (New York: Zone Books, 1997); Ralph Hyde, *Panoramania: The Art and Entertainment of the "All-Embracing" View* (London: Trefoil Publications, 1988); and Altick, *The Shows of London*. For some beautiful reproductions, including foldout plates, see Bernard Comment, *The Panorama* (London: Reaktion, 1999).

67. See for example Anon., *Final Close of the St. George's Gallery, Hyde Park Corner, Piccadilly. Zulu Kafirs. Last Few Days in London* (London: W. J. Goulbourn, 1853). This short pamphlet is almost entirely a compilation of reviews.

68. See Lucy Brown, *Victorian News and Newspapers* (Oxford: Clarendon Press, 1985), and

Jeremy Black, *The English Press, 1621–1861* (Gloucestershire: Sutton, 2001). See also Hindley and Hindley, *Advertising in Victorian England*.

69. Cited in Brown, *Victorian News and Newspapers*, 83–84.
70. Cited in ibid., 116.
71. See Brown, *Victorian News and Newspapers*, and Hindley and Hindley, *Advertising in Victorian England*.
72. Charles Dickens, "The Noble Savage," *Household Words* 7 (1853): 337–39; quotation is from p. 338.
73. An extensive discussion of the similarities is beyond the scope of this chapter. For a more detailed analysis see Lindfors, "Charles Dickens and the Zulus."
74. "Farini's Friendly Zulus," handbill, Evan. 876, Evanion Collection, British Library.
75. For the importance of anthology as a means of disseminating a writer's work, see Leah Price, *The Anthology and the Rise of the Novel: From Richardson to George Eliot* (Cambridge: Cambridge University Press, 2000).
76. Felix Driver, *Geography Militant: Cultures of Exploration and Empire* (Oxford: Blackwell, 2001), 70–71.
77. M. Pratt, *Imperial Eyes*.

Chapter Three

1. Considerable work has been done on the importance of exhibition organizers in the context of international fairs, as in Hoffenberg's *An Empire on Display*. Likewise, managers' roles in producing the shows are well documented, as Crais and Scully's *Sara Baartman and the Hottentot Venus*, Poignant's *Professional Savages*, and Bradford and Blume's *Ota Benga* all indicate. However, Barnum aside, far less attention has been paid to how managers played a role in knowledge production and in shaping the shows' receptions by choosing scenery, costumes, props, and scenes, as discussed here.
2. Bogdan, *Freak Show*.
3. James W. Cook, *The Arts of Deception: Playing with Fraud in the Age of Barnum* (Cambridge, MA: Harvard University Press, 2001), and Benjamin Reiss, *The Showman and the Slave: Race, Death and Memory in Barnum's America* (Cambridge, MA: Harvard University Press, 2001).
4. There are historical precedents that Cook explicitly acknowledges. One example is the automaton of a Turkish chess player that toured Britain and the United States in the late eighteenth century. For more on the chess exhibition and the intriguing puzzle it presented to consumers, see J. Cook, *The Arts of Deception*, and Simon Schaffer, "Enlightened Automata," in *The Sciences in Enlightened Europe*, ed. William Clark, Jan Golinski and Simon Schaffer (Chicago: University of Chicago Press, 1999), 126–65.
5. For more on Bullock see Altick, *The Shows of London*, 235–52; Susan Pearce, "William Bullock: Collections and Exhibitions at the Egyptian Hall, 1816–25," *Journal of the History of Collections* 20 (2007): 1–19; and Susan Pearce, "William Bullock: Inventing a Visual Language of Objects," in *Museum Revolutions: How Museums Change and are Changed*, ed. J. Knell, Suzanne Macleod, and Sheila E. R. Watson (London: Routledge, 2007), 15–27.
6. See E. Richards, "The 'Moral Anatomy' of Robert Knox."
7. Andrew Jackson, "First Annual Message, Dec. 8 1829," in *Messages of Gen. Andrew*

Jackson with a Short Sketch of his Life, ed. N. H. Concord (Boston [MA?]: John F. Brown and William White, 1837) 39–68; quotation is from p. 61. Also see Ronald N. Satz, *American Indian Policy in the Jacksonian Era* (Lincoln: University of Nebraska Press, 1974).

8. For an excellent discussion of how the trope of endangerment was used to rationalize indigenous removal, see Mark David Spence, *Dispossessing the Wilderness: Indian Removal and the Making of the National Parks* (Oxford: Oxford University Press, 1999). and Philip Burnham, *Indian Country, God's Country: Native Americans and the National Parks* (Washington, DC: Island Press, 2000).

9. Spence, *Dispossessing the Wilderness*; John Hausdoerfer, *Catlin's Lament: Indians, Manifest Destiny and the Ethics of Nature* (Lawrence: University of Kansas Press, 2009); and Kathryn S. Hight, "'Doomed to Perish': George Catlin's Depictions of the Mandan," *Art Journal* 49 (1990): 119–24.

10. Hight, "'Doomed to Perish.'"

11. See for example Sujit Sivasundaram, "Natural History Spiritualised: Civilising Islanders, Cultivating Breadfruit and Collecting Souls," *History of Science* 39 (2001): 417–43. He discusses the display of three converted Khoekhoe, two women and a man, who were bought to London by missionaries.

12. See Catlin, *Unparalleled Exhibition.*

13. Poster, JJ, Human Freaks 4 (59), reproduced in fig. 15.

14. Chabert, *A Brief Historical Account of the Life and Adventures of the Botocudo Chieftain*, 20.

15. Henry, *Remarks Concerning Ojibway Indians*, 4–5.

16. Ames, *Carl Hagenbeck's Empire of Entertainments*, 47–49, presents a similar case of Somali performer Hersi Egeh Gorseh. Gorseh originally worked for Hagenbeck as a performer but later went on to manage his own troupes.

17. Kate Flint, *The Transatlantic Indian*, 1776–1930 (Princeton, NJ: Princeton University Press, 2009), 82; see also 82–85.

18. Hoage and Deiss, *New Worlds, New Animals*, 98.

19. Ritvo, *The Animal Estate*, 241–47.

20. David Richardson, "The British Empire and the Atlantic Slave Trade, 1660–1807," in *The Eighteenth Century*, ed. Peter J. Marshall, vol. 2 of *OHBE* (Oxford: Oxford University Press, 1998), 440–64.

21. See J. Cain, "Economics and Empire: The Metropolitan Context," in *The Nineteenth Century*, ed. Andrew Porter, vol. 3 of *OHBE* (Oxford: Oxford University Press, 1998), 31–52; B. R. Tomlinson, "Economics and Empire: The Periphery and the Imperial Economy," in Porter, *The Nineteenth Century*, 3:53–74; K. T. Hoppen, "A Maturing Economy," in *The Mid-Victorian Generation, 1846–1886*, The New Oxford History of England (Oxford: Oxford University Press, 1998), 275–315; and Martin Daunton, "London and the World," in Fox, *London*, 21–38.

22. Caldecott, *Exhibition of Native Zulu Kafirs*, 4.

23. The first exhibitor to employ this strategy was the German entrepreneur and menagerie manager Carl Hagenbeck. See Rothfels, *Savages and Beasts*, and Ames, *Carl Hagenbeck's Empire of Entertainments*. Other examples, including Barnum, can be found in Lindfors, *Africans on Stage*; Bradford and Blume, *Ota Benga*; and Parezo and Fowler, *Anthropology Goes to the Fair*.

24. Parezo and Fowler, *Anthropology Goes to the Fair*, 52–57.

25. Chabert, *A Brief Historical Account of the Life and Adventures of the Botocudo Chieftain*, 19.
26. Ibid, 20.
27. Cunningham, *History of R. A. Cunningham's Australian Aborigines*, 4.
28. For a discussion of how Cunningham may have assembled the troupe, see Poignant, *Professional Savages*, 66–76.
29. Cunningham, *History of R. A. Cunningham's Australian Aborigines*, 10–13.
30. Pedro Velasquez, *Memoir of an Eventful Expedition into Central America, Resulting in the Discovery of the Idolatrous City of Iximaya, in an Unexplored Region* ... (London, 1853). For a briefer statement see "The Aztec Lilliputians," *Times*, July 7, 1853, p. 8; and "Discovery of Ruined Cities," *Times*, November 22, 1853, p. 8. See also "Aztec Lilliputians," advertisement, *Times*, July 19, 1853, p. 8. The advert was a response to criticism from the exhibitors, Joseph Morris and John Henry Anderson. It used various letters and newspaper articles to defend the exhibition. At almost one and a half columns long, it must have been expensive and bears witness to the importance the men attached to refuting their critics.
31. All quotations are from "The Aztec Lilliputians," *Times*, July 7, 1853. See also Velasquez, *Illustrated Memoir of an Eventful Expedition into Central America*, and Stephens, *Incidents of Travel*.
32. Aguirre, *Informal Empire*, 110.
33. J. N. Hays, "The London Lecturing Empire, 1800–50," in *Metropolis and Province: Science in British Culture, 1780–1850*, ed. Ian Inkster and Jack Morrell (London: Hutchinson, 1983), 91–119. For a recent discussion of the importance of scientific lecturing in London's show culture, see Bernard Lightman, "Lecturing in the Spatial Economy of Science," in Fyfe and Lightman, *Science in the Marketplace*, 97–132.
34. Anon., *Now Exhibiting at the Egyptian Hall*.
35. "The Zulu Kaffirs," *ILN*, May 28, 1853.
36. Handbill, JJ, London Play Places 9 (20). George Catlin, *Catlin's North American Indian Portfolio: Hunting Scenes and Amusements of the Rocky Mountains and Prairies of America* ... (London: [published by the author], 1844), and George Catlin, *Notes of Eight Years' Travel and Residence in Europe, with his North American Indian Collection*, 2 vols. (London: published by the author, 1848).
37. Some of Catlin's writings were privately printed, and promotional materials for his shows frequently indicate that patrons will be given the opportunity to buy several of his published works at the show.
38. It is highly likely that pamphlets were adapted from lectures and so might be used to judge their contents; however, this discussion has been restricted to material that has been explicitly identified as being from lectures. Reprinting lectures considered worthy of special interest in newspapers or as small pamphlets was a common practice. These would have been either prepared from manuscripts in the lecturers' possession, often with modifications or corrections, or based on notes taken by a journalist during the performance. As such, they cannot be used as exact replicas of the lecture. One of the best-known cases of this is John Tyndall's infamous Belfast Address, his presidential speech to the BAAS in 1874. It inspired considerable contemporary criticism due to its discussion of materialism, but the definitive text of the lecture, as read by Tyndall, remains elusive. See Ruth Barton, "John Tyndall, Pantheist: A Rereading of the Belfast Address" *Osiris* 3 (1987): 111–34.

39. Reprinted in Anon., *Now Exhibiting at the Egyptian Hall*, 2. Compare with Knox, *The Races of Men*.

40. Knox, *The Races of Men*, 145–241. Compare with Anon, *Now Exhibiting at the Egyptian Hall*, and Anon., *History of the Bosjesmans, or Bush people: The Aborigines of Southern Africa* ... ([London]: Chapman, Elcoate, 1847).

41. Tyler, *The Bosjesmans*.

42. The text is unclear regarding whose brain was being used, but from Knox's discussion, it was probably of an African and intended to show "poor" development of the convolutions of the cerebrum. See Anon., *Now Exhibiting at the Egyptian Hall*.

43. For more on Knox and anticolonialism, see E. Richards, "The 'Moral Anatomy' of Robert Knox," and Evelleen Richards, "A Political Anatomy of Monsters, Hopeful and Otherwise: Teratogeny, Transcendentalism, and Evolutionary Theorizing," *Isis* 85 (1994): 377–411.

44. Tyler, *The Bosjesmans*, 2–7.

45. "African Exhibition," newspaper clipping, JJ, Human Freaks 4 (82).

46. Anon., *Now Exhibiting at the Egyptian Hall*, 2.

47. Bullock, *An Account of the Family of Laplanders*, 6.

48. "African Exhibition," newspaper clipping, JJ, Human Freaks 4 (82).

49. Caldecott, *Exhibition of Native Zulu Kafirs*, 7.

50. Adas, *Machines as the Measure of Men*.

51. Bullock, *An Account of the Family of Laplanders*, 33.

52. "African Exhibition," newspaper clipping, JJ, Human Freaks 4 (82).

53. For the importance of clothing as a means of defining human variety, see Wheeler, *The Complexion of Race*. For more on the replacement of indigenous garments with European clothing as a symbol of conversion, see Sujit Sivasundaram, *Nature and the Godly Empire: Science and Evangelical Mission in the Pacific, 1795–1850* (Cambridge: Cambridge University Press, 2005), 192–96; and C. Hall, *Civilising Subjects*. In some cases, converted peoples willingly appropriated European clothes as a symbol of conversion, even when missionaries did not encourage them to do so. See Nicholas Thomas, *Colonialism's Culture Anthropology, Travel and Government* (Cambridge: Polity Press, 1994).

54. I have found almost no images of the displayed peoples I discuss being depicted in European clothes, and certainly not when shown onstage.

55. See the Baartman court records as reprinted in Strother, "Display of the Body Hottentot", 41–48.

56. Crais and Scully, *Sara Baartman and the Hottentot Venus*, 75.

57. For an excellent discussion of the role of consumer expectation see Ames, *Carl Hagenbeck's Empire of Entertainments*, 105–15.

58. "The Zulu Kafirs at the St. George's Gallery, Knightsbridge," *ILN*, May 28, 1853.

59. Playbill, JJ, Human Freaks 4 (84).

60. "African Exhibition," newspaper clipping, JJ, Human Freaks 4 (82).

61. For examples of the relevant travel literature for these two exhibitions, see Isaacs, *Travels and Adventures in Eastern Africa*, and Catlin, *Notes of Eight Years' Travel*.

62. See Catlin, *Catlin's North American Indian Portfolio* and *Notes of Eight Years' Travel*.

63. "The Bosjesman, at the Egyptian Hall, Piccadilly," *ILN*, June 12, 1847, p. 381.

64. I have yet to find an extended discussion of how spectators learned to create and apply specific ethnic classifications and consequently use them as a means of

personally interpreting the shows. For this account of ostensive learning, see the following by Barnes: "On the Conventional Character of Knowledge and Cognition"; "Social Life as Bootstrapped Induction" and "Ostensive Learning and Self-Referring Knowledge."

Chapter Four

1. "Scene at a Bosjesman Exhibition," *Times*, May 8, 1850, p. 7. The article was reprinted from the *Cheltenham Journal*, suggesting that the exhibition was held in the town hall. However, it notes that Mr. Tyler had witnessed a similar scene while exhibiting the group in London.

2. There are rare and valuable exceptions, such as the several court cases discussed in this chapter—namely those of Baartman, Manyos, and Larcher. However, these accounts were only gathered once the performers had become involved in a court case. Testimony gathered for the sake of recording displayed peoples' experiences is much rarer and difficult to locate (although more exists for the later nineteenth century onward). Most relevant to the displayed peoples discussed here are Lindfors, "A Zulu View of Victorian London," *Munger Africana Library Notes* 9 (1979): 1–8; and Shephard, *Kitty and the Prince*, for his use of personal letters between Lobengula and Jewell. Also see Hilke Thode-Arora, "Abraham's Diary—a European Ethnic Show from an Inuk Participant's Viewpoint," *Journal of the Society for the Anthropology of Europe*, 2 (2008): 2–17.

3. For accounts that attempt to reconstruct performers' experiences, see Crais and Scully, *Sara Baartman and the Hottentot Venus*; Abrahams, "Images of Sara Bartman"; Yvette Abrahams, "Disempowered to Consent: Sara Bartman and Khoisan Slavery in the Nineteenth-Century Cape Colony and Britain," *South African Historical Journal* 35 (1996): 89–114; Ames, *Carl Hagenbeck's Empire of Entertainnments*; Rothfels, *Savages and Beasts*; Zimmerman, *Anthropology and Antihumanism*; Poignant, *Professional Savages*; Blume and Bradford, *Ota Benga*; Parezo and Fowler, *Anthropology Goes to the Fair*; and Thode-Arora, "Abraham's Diary."

4. Altick, *The Shows of London*; Bogdan, *Freak Show*; Thomson, *Freakery*; M. Mitchell, *Monsters*; and Michael Howell and Peter Ford, *The Illustrated True History of the Elephant Man*, 2nd ed. (London: Butler and Tanner, 1983).

5. This biography is based on "The Erdermänne, or Earthmen of South Africa," *Illustrated Magazine of Art*; JJ, Human Freaks 4 (79). For more on the children, see "Earthmen from Port Natal," *ILN*, November 6, 1853, pp. 371–72 and the exhibition pamphlets; Anon., *The Erdermänner*; and Anon., "The Erdmanninges."

6. "The Erdermänne, or Earthmen of South Africa," *Illustrated Magazine of Art*; JJ, Human Freaks 4 (79).

7. Bogdan, *Freak Show*, 127–35. Unless otherwise indicated, this biography is based primarily on Bogdan and the primary sources, cited as relevant.

8. For more on Eisenmann and his portraits, see Mitchell, *Monsters*.

9. For more on Barnum see Neil Harris, *Humbug: The Art of Barnum* (Boston: Brown, 1973); James Cook, *The Arts of Deception*; and Reiss, *The Showman and the Slave*.

10. Bogdan, *Freak Show*, and Dreger, *One of Us*, both suggest that the shows offered a means of professional employment for individuals who would otherwise not have been likely to find such work. They also suggest that the shows allowed human curiosities to cast off the stigma of shame and find value in their anatomy. While

certainly possible for many human curiosities, it seems highly unlikely that any form of intentional desire to perform played a role in Maximo and Bartola's exhibition, due to the severity of their developmental problems. For a discussion of why such exhibition of human curiosities must be considered in terms of circumstantial coercion, see David A. Gerber, "The 'Careers' of People Exhibited in Freak Shows: The Problem of Volition and Valorization," in Garland, *Freakery*, 38–54.

11. For a useful account of the changes in the market for the institutionalized treatment of mental illness, see Roy Porter, *Mind Forg'd Manacles: A History of Madness from the Restoration to the Regency* (London: Athlone, 1987), 110–68.

12. The anatomist Richard Owen, physician John Conolly, and anthropologist Rudolf Virchow all examined the children at various stages in their lives and concluded that they suffered severe learning difficulties. See Owen and Cull, "A Brief Notice of the Aztec Race"; John Conolly, *The Ethnological Exhibitions of London* (London: John Churchill, 1855); and Nigel Rothfels, "Aztecs, Aborigines and Ape-People: Science and Freaks in Germany, 1850–1900," in Garland, *Freakery*, 158–72.

13. Abrahams, "Disempowered to Consent," suggests that Baartman was a slave. Yet the most exhaustive and recent biography of her suggests that she actually had negotiated the terms on which she left Cape Town. See Crais and Scully, *Sara Baartman and the Hottentot Venus*, 55–57. The following account of Baartman's life in Africa is indebted to Crais and Scully's impressively researched biography.

14. For more on the history of colonial occupation at the Cape, see Leonard Thompson and Monica Wilson, eds., *A History of South Africa to 1870*, vol. 1 of *The Oxford History of South Africa* (Oxford: Clarendon Press, 1969), especially 183–232; and Clifton Crais, *White Supremacy and Black Resistance in Pre-Industrial South Africa: The Making of the Colonial Order, 1770–1865* (Cambridge: Cambridge University Press, 1992). Although not specifically about the Khoekhoe, a helpful discussion of the period and the role of intercultural contact in shaping African politics during a similar period may be found in Jean and John Cormaroff, *Of Revelation and Revolution: Christianity, Colonialism and Consciousness in South Africa* (Chicago: University of Chicago Press, 1991).

15. On the hunting of Africans in this region, see Crais and Scully, *Sara Baartman and the Hottentot Venus*, 19–21; and Martin Legassick, "From Prisoners to Exhibits: Representations of Bushmen of the Northern Cape, 1880–1900" in *Rethinking Settler Colonialism: History and Memory in Australia, Canada, Aotearoa New Zealand and South Africa*, ed. Annie Coombes (Manchester: Manchester University Press, 2006), 63–84.

16. Although sold, she was not legally recognized as a slave, since the Khoekhoe were nominally free laborers.

17. Crais and Scully, *Sara Baartman and the Hottentot Venus*, 50.

18. Ibid., 55.

19. This was known in the case of Native Americans, although they may not always have been exhibited in their home states. For example, when Glacier National Park was set up in Montana, the Blackfeet were employed to perform for visiting tourists. In some cases, the performers lived on-site in designated areas, but in others they were not allowed to reside within the park itself. The performances supported the fiction that these national parks were wildernesses to be preserved free of human use, which in turn helped dispossess so many indigenous populations of their ancestral and traditional homelands. See Spence, *Dispossessing the Wilderness*.

20. J. M. Porter, letter, September 14, 1843; reprinted in Catlin, *Adventures of the Ojibbeway and Ioway Indians*, 4.

21. Catlin, *Adventures of the Ojibbeway and Ioway Indians in England, France, and Belgium*, 2:2.

22. For a descriptive catalog of the collection, see ibid., 1:248–93. For reproductions of Catlin's paintings, including portraits of some of the individuals exhibited in London, see Robert J. Moore Jr., *Native Americans, A Portrait: The Art and Travels of Charles Bird King, George Catlin, and Karl Bodmer* (New York: Stewart, Tabori and Chang, 1997).

23. Catlin, *Adventures of the Ojibbeway and Ioway Indians in England, France, and Belgium*, 2:4–5.

24. Ibid., 2:5.

25. Caldecott, *Exhibition of Native Zulu Kafirs*, 4–5.

26. Ibid., 6.

27. For this discussion of African prisoners, see Legassick, "From Prisoners to Exhibits."

28. Louis Anthing, magistrate in Namaqualand, April 21, 1863, Cape Archives Repository, Cape Town, A39–1863, 3; cited in ibid., 66.

29. For more on Bleek see Skotnes, *Miscast*, and Pippa Skotnes, ed., *Claim to the Country: The Archive of Wilhelm Bleek and Lucy Lloyd* (Athens, OH: Ohio University Press, 2007).

30. On W. A. Healey see Peacock, *The Great Farini*, 305–8. On Louw see Legassick, "From Prisoners to Exhibits," 75.

31. Letter from John Scott to Mr. Tooke, January 29, 1886, Cape Archives Repository NBC17; cited in ibid., 76.

32. Ibid., 83n57.

33. Mathur, *India by Design*, and Saloni Mathur, "Living Ethnological Exhibits: The Case of 1886," *Cultural Anthropology* 15 (2001): 492–524.

34. Mathur, *India by Design*, 66.

35. Between 1872 and 1876, William Cody began his stage career, acting in a series of melodramas. His first show featuring Indians began its run in 1883, and the first London appearance was held in 1887. For the most detailed discussion of these issues in relationship to Cody, see L. G. Moses, *Wild West Shows and the Images of American Indians, 1883–1933* (Albuquerque: University of New Mexico Press, 1996), especially 60–79.

36. Ibid., 23–25.

37. Ibid., 137–39.

38. For Cody see ibid., 60–79; for Hagenbeck see Ames, *Carl Hagenbeck's Empire of Entertainments*, 47–52.

39. Moses, *Wild West Shows*, 38–39.

40. In 1879, the Standing Bear decision allowed peaceable Indians freedom of movement from their reservations. This was ignored in 1887, when Cody's agents were told that Indians could not leave the reservations without formal approval. Moses, *Wild West Shows*, 64–66.

41. Ibid., 32 and 138.

42. See Ames, *Carl Hagenbeck's Empire of Entertainments*, 47–52, for an excellent discussion of these issues in the context of late nineteenth-century Germany; one of Hagenbeck's original contracts is reprinted on p. 48.

43. Gerber, "The 'Careers' of People Exhibited in Freak Shows," and Don Herzog, *Happy Slaves: A Critique of Consent Theory* (Chicago: University of Chicago Press, 1989).

44. Gerber, "The 'Careers' of People Exhibited in Freak Shows," 42.

45. Herzog, *Happy Slaves*, 231.

46. John Scott to Mr. Tooke, January 29, 1886, Cape Archives Repository NBC17; and Private Secretary to the Premier to John Scott, January 29, 1886, Cape Archives Repository NBC9; cited in Legassick, "From Prisoners to Exhibits," 83n56.

47. It should be noted that when Scott began sending prisoners to Bleek, J. Rose Innes of the Department of Native Affairs in Cape Town "had no objection, provided the 'Bushmen' were 'willing to enter into the engagement proposed.'" Cited in Legassick, "From Prisoners to Exhibits," 74. Given this, it is likely that Scott would have had to obtain some form of consent, but it may easily have been coercively secured by making it conditional on the prisoners' co-operation with Scott's plans.

48. Caldecott, *Exhibition of Native Zulu Kafirs*, 4.

49. Cunningham, *History of R. A. Cunningham's Australian Aborigines*, 3.

50. "Savage South Africa," *Transactions of the Aborigines Protection Society*, June 1, 1899, p. 438.

51. For example, "Court Of Exchequer, Thursday, Jan. 24 Motions.—In Re The Canadian Prisoners," *Times*, January 25, 1839; "In Re Jean Besset—Habeas Corpus," *Times*, November 4, 1844; and Driver, *Geography Militant*, 150–63. Crais and Scully have recently shown that her court case is still cited in modern legal actions such as *Handman vs. Rumsfeld* (2006). See Crais and Scully, *Sara Baartman and the Hottentot Venus*, 142–44.

52. For contemporary perspectives on the issue of abolition, see C. P. Ripley, ed., *The Black Abolitionist Papers*, 5 vols. (Chapel Hill: University of North Carolina Press, 1985), especially vol. 1, *The British Isles, 1830–1865*. Indentured labor was not an innovation, since many British colonies in the Americas had used European indentured labor in the seventeenth and eighteenth centuries. However, after 1838 the nature of indentured labor changed, with different ethnicities being shipped to more-distant destinations and given additional benefits, such as wages and medical care. Moreover, there was no direct historical continuity, as the introduction of African slavery had largely replaced European indenture. For a comparative perspective on indentured labor, see David Northrup, *Indentured Labour in the Age of Imperialism, 1834–1922* (Cambridge: Cambridge University Press, 1995). For an example of the transition from slave to free labor in the colonies, see Richard B. Allen, "Capital, Illegal Slaves, Indentured Labourers and the Creation of a Sugar Plantation Economy in Mauritius, 1810–60," *Journal of Imperial and Commonwealth History* 36 (2008): 151–70.

53. See Visram, *Ayahs, Lascars and Princes*, and Visram, *Asians in Britain*. See also Collingham, *Imperial Bodies*.

54. One is reminded of the genesis of informed consent, which is often argued to have originated as a form of legal protection to prevent health care officials from being sued and not for the patients' benefit. For more on the history of informed consent, see Ruth R. Faden and Tom L. Beauchamp, *A History and Theory of Informed Consent* (New York: Oxford University Press, 1986).

55. "The Aborigines Protection Society," *Transactions of the Aborigines Protection Society*, November 1, 1899, p. 450.

56. See "Zoolus, Earthmen, and the Aztec Imposition," *Colonial Intelligencer; or, Aborigines' Friend* (London), June 1, 1853, pp. 262–65; and Conolly, *The Ethnological Exhibitions of London*.

57. "Savage South Africa," *Transactions of the Aborigines Protection Society*, June 1, 1899, p. 438.

58. Any difference of understanding may easily be the result of cultural rather than in-dividual differences. One of the most pertinent cases here is the Treaty of Waitangi between the British and the Maori that was signed in 1840. Although the treaty's existence has not been disputed, there is considerable conflict over how the terms should be interpreted and put into action in modern New Zealand, with the Maori claiming that their participation in the treaty was not intended to, and should not be used to, deny them land and cultural property rights. For a recent account see Paul Moon, *Te Ara Ki Te Tiri: The Path to the Treaty of Waitangi* (Auckland: Ling, 2002).

59. For a report of the court proceedings, see "Police," *Times*, September 29, 1853, p. 10.

60. Ibid.

61. For a report of the court proceedings, see "Police," *Times*, January 25, 1853, p. 7.

62. All quotations from "The Earthmen," *ILN*, November 6, 1852, pp. 371–72; and "The Erdermänne, or Earthmen of South Africa," *Illustrated Magazine of Art*; JJ, Human Freaks 4 (79).

63. W. H. Flower and J. Murie, "Account of the Dissection of a Bushwoman," *Journal of Anatomy and Physiology* (1867): 189–208. C. W. D., "Flower and Murie on the Dissec-tion of a Bushwoman," *Anthropological Review* 5 (1867): 319–24.

64. "The Earthmen of the Orange River," *Morning Chronicle*, May 10, 1853, p. 6.

65. For this account of the wedding and courtship, see "Marriage Extraordinary," *Times*, April 2, 1844; "The Indian Marriage at St. Martin's Church," *Pictorial Times*, April 12, 1844; "The Indian Marriage at St. Martin's Church," *Times*, April 15, 1844, p. 5; "Im-portant. To the Ladies," *Punch* 6 (1844): 179; and "The 'Strong Wind,' in St. Martin's Church," *Punch* 6 (1844): 173. See also Catlin, *Adventures of the Ojibbeway and Ioway Indians in England, France, and Belgium*, vol. 2.

66. Catlin, *Adventures of the Ojibbeway and Ioway Indians in England, France, and Belgium*, 1:110. In the press, there was confusion over Cadotte's ethnic origin. Most of the pa-pers implied he was partly Anishinabe; however, a letter to the editor of the *Times* stressed he was French Canadian. See Septimus F. Ramsey, letter to the editor, "The Indian Marriage at St. Martin's Church," *Times*, April 13, 1844.

67. Cadotte, quoted in Catlin, *Adventures of the Ojibbeway and Ioway Indians in England, France, and Belgium*, 1:180. For a helpful discussion of sexual attraction and Catlin's show, see Flint, *The Transatlantic Indian*, 63–73.

68. "What Might Have Been Expected," *Times*, October 5, 1844, p. 5.

69. Two contemporary writers met Haynes in the 1850s and noted the disintegrating nature of their marriage. See Flint, *The Transatlantic Indian*, 69–70.

70. Baartman's exhibition is lampooned in "The Ballad of John Higginbottom of Bath," which is frequently cited in the literature. See Percival Kirby, "The Hottentot Venus," *Africana Notes and News* 6 (1949): 57; and Abrahams, "Images of Sara Bartman," 232–33. Lysons, "Collectanea," records references in the Manchester papers. Baart-man's appearance in Ireland is recorded in Maurice Lenihan, *Limerick, its Histories and Antiquities, Ecclesiastical, Civil and Military* (Dublin: Hodges, Smith, 1866), 416.

71. This quotation is from the original certificate of baptism as reproduced in Kirby, "The Hottentot Venus," and Crais and Scully, *Sara Baartman and the Hottentot Venus*, 109. The original is held at the Musée del'Homme.

72. Cuvier, "Extrait d'Observations," 262. See also Crais and Scully, *Sara Baartman and the Hottentot Venus*, 106–9.

73. Shephard, *Kitty and the Prince*; "Loben's Courtship," *Graphic*, August 19, 1899, p. 262. Shephard presents the most extensive discussion of Lobengula's identity, but has

been unable to resolve whether he was related to Ndebele royalty or whether his lineage was fabricated for promotional purposes; the latter seems to be the most probable.

74. Shephard, *Kitty and the Prince*.

75. "An Earl's Court Romance," *Western Mail* (Cardiff), August 11, 1899, p. 7.

76. "Loben's Courtship," *Graphic*, August 19, 1899, p. 262.

77. "At Earl's Court," *Hearth and Home*, August 24, 1899, p. 603.

78. Shephard, *Kitty and the Prince*, 149.

79. Ibid., 159–77. According to Shephard, the divorce may never have been finalized.

80. Ibid., 196–204. Shephard found no record of the couple being married, possibly because the divorce from Jewell may never have taken place.

81. Henry, *Remarks Concerning Ojibway Indians*, 4–5.

82. [Robert Chambers], *The Book of Days: A Miscellany of Popular Antiquities in Connection with the Calendar*, 2 vols. (London: W. & R. Chambers, 1863), 2:621.

83. Zachary Macaulay, Thos. Gisborne Babington, and P. van Wageninge, PFF 747 (KB1/36), National Archives (London), as reprinted in Strother, "Display of the Body Hottentot," 43–46; quotation is from p. 44.

84. Ibid, 44.

85. Mrs. [Anne] Mathews, *Memoirs of Charles Mathews, Comedian*, 4 vols. (London: Richard Bentley, 1839), 4:133–40.

86. The images, along with a shortened version of Cuvier's autopsy report, appeared as Cuvier, "Une Femme de Race Boschismanne."

87. For more on interest in Khoekhoe genitalia in travel literature, see J. Baker, *Race*, 313–19.

88. Cuvier only succeeded after her death. See Cuvier, "Extrait d'Observations."

89. "Remarkable Story from Earl's Court," *Daily News*, August 28, 1899, p. 6.

90. For the full account of this meeting, see Catlin, *Adventures of the Ojibbeway and Ioway Indians in England, France, and Belgium*, 1:163–65; quotation is from 1:163–64. Catlin often noted that a reverend gentleman wanted to visit the performers and discuss Christianity, but often did not specify the denomination. On two occasions he noted that a Catholic priest and two Methodists visit, but this specificity is unusual. It has been suggested that these reported discussions are in fact stylized conversational set pieces rather than genuine transcripts of the discussion. Given that the account was written some years after the exhibitions and that the conversations are, in part, rhetorically similar, this seems the most likely possibility. For a discussion of these set pieces and why they are still useful for documenting performers' experiences, see Christopher Mulvey, "Among the Sag-anoshes: Ojibwa and Iowa Indians with George Catlin in Europe, 1843–1848," in *Indians and Europe: An Interdisciplinary Collection of Essays*, ed. Christian F. Feest (Aachen, Germany: Edition Herodot, 1987), 253–75.

91. Francis Paul Prucha, *The Great Father: The United States Government and the American Indians*, 2 vols. combined (Lincoln: University of Nebraska Press, 1995), 9–11 and 135–58; Henry Warner Bowden, *American Indians and Christian Missions: Studies in Cultural Conflict* (Chicago: University of Chicago Press, 1981), 164–99.

92. Flint, *The Transatlantic Indian*, 192–225.

93. Chief Ahqueewezaints, quoted in Catlin, *Adventures of the Ojibbeway and Ioway Indians in England, France, and Belgium*, 1:163–65; quotation is from 1:165.

94. For the visit of a missionary to the Bakhoje, see ibid., 2:54–56.

95. Mulvey, "Among the Sag-anoshes," 256.

96. For an extended discussion of how Catlin's work can be read as an example of this form of satire, see ibid. Mulvey also discusses how the different reports are uncannily similar, suggesting that the conversations are highly stylized set pieces. See also Anthony Pagden, "The Savage Critic: Some European Images of the Primitive," *Yearbook of English Studies* 13 (1983): 32–45.

97. Flint, *The Transatlantic Indian*, 78–85.

98. "Greater Britain Exhibition," *Horse and Hound*, May 6, 1899, p. 278.

99. "Mutiny at Earl's Court," *Lloyd's Weekly Newspaper*, May 14, 1899, p. 13.

100. "Disturbance at 'Savage South Africa,'" *Daily News*, June 26, 1899, p. 3.

101. "Trouble at Earl's Court," *Belfast News-Letter*, June 26, 1899, p. 6.

102. Saidiya Hartman, *Scenes of Subjection: Terror, Slavery and Self-Making in Nineteenth-Century America* (Oxford: Oxford University Press, 1997). See also James C. Scott, *Weapons of the Weak: Everyday Forms of Peasant Resistance* (London: Yale University Press, 1985).

Chapter Five

1. "Homage to beauty," *Funny Folks*, August 2, 1879, p. 245.

2. "Multiple News Items," *Sporting Times*, August 2, 1879, p, 2.

3. This approach is intended to avoid pressing the shows' receptions into a single mold. The most obvious and widely used form of homogenization is the use of the self/other divide to characterize the receptions. For instance, see its use across multiple national, ethnic, geographic, and chronological contexts in Blanchard et al., *Human Zoos*.

4. For a selection of advertisements confirming these costs, see "Egyptian Hall, Piccadilly …," *ILN*, May 10, 1845, p. 302; "The Wild Man of the Prairies …," *ILN*, August 29, 1846, p. 143; "Zulu Kaffirs … " and "The Earthmen ….," *ILN*, May 14, 1853, p. 375; and "Aztec Lilliputians …," *ILN*, July 16, 1853, p. 22.

5. I have not come across any images of the shows in which patrons and performers share skin tone or ethnic origin. However, Hoffenberg's *An Empire on Display*, especially pp. 242–71, confirms that at the very least, within the context of international exhibitions patrons were not necessarily white. Rydell's *All the World's a Fair*, 53–55, also documents how some world's fairs set aside special days for "colored" peoples to attend.

6. Most relevant here is T[rilokya] N[ath] Mukharji, *Visit to Europe* (Calcutta: W. Newman, 1889).

7. Mathews, *Memoirs of Charles Mathews*, 4:133–40. For more on Miss Crackham see Gaby Wood, *The Smallest of All Persons Mentioned in the Records of Littleness* (London, Profile Books, 1998).

8. Mathews, *Memoirs of Charles Mathews*, 4:137.

9. Charles Dickens, *Sketches by "Boz," Illustrative of Every-day Life and Every-day People* (London: John Macrone, 1836; reprint, London: Penguin, 1995), 143.

10. Barbara Benedict, *Curiosity: A Cultural History of Modern Enquiry* (Chicago: University of Chicago Press, 2001), 158.

11. Peter Bailey, *Leisure and Class in Victorian England: Rational Recreation and the Contest for Control, 1830–1885* (London: Routledge, 1987).

12. Handbill, JJ, London Play Places 10 (47), reproduced in fig. 46; measurements are from "Bushmen Children," *ILN*, September 6, 1845, p. 160.

13. For the use of classical poses in images that otherwise aspired to be wholly accurate representations of foreign peoples. see Hugh Honour, *The Image of the Black in Western Art*, 4 vols. (Houston: Menil Foundation, 1989).

14. "Bushmen Children," *ILN*, September 6, 1845, p. 160.

15. John Brewer, *The Pleasures of the Imagination* (London: HarperCollins, 1997), 330 and 384–423.

16. Bratton, *Acts of Supremacy*, 136.

17. Michael Pickering, "Mock Blacks and Racial Mockery: The 'Nigger' Minstrel and British Imperialism," in ibid.,179–236.

18. Piertese, *White on Black*, 199–200.

19. See Anon., *Now Exhibiting at the Egyptian Hall*.

20. In both ibid. and Anon., *An Interesting Account of Those Extraordinary People the Esquimaux Indians …* (Sheffield: George Ridge, n.d. [ca. 1820s]), vocabularies are reprinted, suggesting that there was a demand for such information and that some consumers may have used it to interact with displayed peoples. Newspaper reviews and promotional literature indicate that almost all the showmen discussed in this book used translators to aid conversation between consumers and performers.

21. "Savage South Africa," *Western Mail* (Cardiff), August 30, 1899, p. 7; "Savage South Africa," *Daily News*, August 29, 1899, p. 4; and "'Savage South Africa': The Kaffir Kraal Scandal," *Aberdeen Weekly Journal*, August 23, 1899, p. 10. See also Shephard, *Kitty and the Prince*, 130–45. Part of the problem may have lain in changing notions of what was deemed acceptable physical contact. Americans in the nineteenth century (see Silliman in chapter 1) often noted that the British were far more permissive regarding interracial coupling; however, it has been argued that over the course of the 1800s, changing perceptions of miscegenation helped foster a greater disapproval for such unions. See Ronald Hyam, *Empire and Sexuality: The British Experience* (Manchester: Manchester University Press, 1990). and Ghosh, *Sex and the Family in Colonial India*, especially 69–108.

22. "It was the Owl that Shrieked," *The Owl* (Cape Town), August 25, 1899, p. 558.

23. "It was the Owl that Shrieked," *The Owl* (Cape Town), September 29, 1899, p. 640.

24. For an account of both these forms of behavior, see Mathews, *Memoirs of Charles Mathews*, 4:133–40.

25. Catlin, *Adventures of the Ojibbeway and Ioway Indians in England, France, and Belgium*, 2:29.

26. Amalie M. Kass and Edward H. Kass, *Perfecting the World: The Life and Times of Dr Thomas Hodgkin, 1798–1866* (New York: Harcourt Brace Jovanovich, 1988).

27. For more on this visit, see Catlin, *Adventures of the Ojibbeway and Ioway Indians in England, France, and Belgium*, 2:42–52; "The Ioway Indians," *Times*, August 17, 1844, p. 5; "The Ioways—'The Lost Tribe'—And Young England," *Punch* 7 (1844): 95; and "Ben Sidonia Smoking the Calumet with the Ioways," *Punch* 7 (1844): 100.

28. Catlin, *Adventures of the Ojibbeway and Ioway Indians in England, France, and Belgium*, 2:48.

29. Conolly, *The Ethnological Exhibitions of London*, 7.

30. "The Zulu Kaffirs," *John Bull*, May 21, 1853, p. 332.

31. "Aztec Lilliputians," advertisement, *Times*, July 19, 1853, p. 8.

32. Conolly, *The Ethnological Exhibitions of London*, 12. This account of the debate is based on: "The Aztec Children," *ILN*, July 9, 1853, p. 11–12; "The Aztec People," *Athenaeum*,

July 9, 1853, pp. 824–25, which includes a letter from Latham discussing their ethnic origin; "The Aztecs," *Lancet*, July 9, 1853, p. 44; "The Aztec Lilliputians," *Athenaeum*, July 16, 1853, pp. 860–61; "The Aztec Children," *ILN*, July 23, 1853, pp. 43–44; "Can the Aztecs speak," *ILN*, July 30, 1853, p. 66; "The Aztec Children," *Athenaeum*, October 1, 1853, p. 1170; "The Aztec Children," *Illustrated Magazine of Art* (1853): 77–78; "Dentition of the Aztecs," *Lancet*, May 20, 1854, p. 548; Owen and Cull, "A Brief Notice of the Aztec Race," originally read by Owen at a special meeting of the ESL, July 6, 1853; and Robert Knox, "Some Remarks on the Aztecque and Bosjieman Children, Now Being Exhibited in London, and on the Races to Which They Are Presumed to Belong," *Lancet*, April 7, 1855, pp. 357–60.

33. "The Ioway Indians," *Age and Argus*, August 24, 1844, p. 12.

34. "The Bushmen Children, or Pigmy Race," *English Gentleman*, August 16, 1845, p. 263.

35. "The 'Bosjesmans,' or Bush People," *Times*, May 19, 1847, p. 7.

36. "Our Weekly Gossip," *Athenaeum*, May 29, 1847, pp. 573–74.

37. "The 'Bosjesmans,' or Bush People," *The Times*, May 19, 1847, p. 7.

38. Ibid.

39. Reprinted in Anon., *Now Exhibiting at the Egyptian Hall*, 1.

40. "The Bosjesman, at the Egyptian Hall, Piccadilly," *ILN*, June 12, 1847, p. 381.

41. Ellingson, *The Myth of the Noble Savage*.

42. Piertese, *White on Black*, especially 152–65 and 212–23.

43. Aborigines Protection Society, *Annual Report of the Aborigines Protection Society*, 1899, p. 7.

44. "Savage South Africa," *Transactions of the Aborigines Protection Society*, June 1, 1899, pp. 436–39.

45. For example, the Sunday service for the Savage South Africa performers was reported on in "Notes of the Month," *Mission Field*, August 1, 1899, pp. 309–10. See also the follow-up article "Notes and Comments," *Transactions of the Aborigines Protection Society*, April 1, 1900, p. 526.

46. "St. George's Gallery, Hyde Park—Zulu Kaffirs," *Lady's Newspaper*, July 23, 1853, p. 39.

47. "The Zulu Kaffirs," *Lady's Newspaper*, May 21, 1853, p. 327.

48. "The Zulu Kaffirs," *Bell's Life in London and Sporting Chronicle*, May 22, 1853, p. 8.

49. "St. George's Gallery, Hyde Park—Zulu Kaffirs," *Lady's Newspaper*, July 23, 1853, p. 39.

50. Caldecott, *Exhibition of Native Zulu Kafirs*, 4.

51. See "The Zulu Kaffirs at the St. George's Gallery, Knightsbridge," *ILN*, May 28, 1853. The illustration in particular (reproduced in the present text as figure 42) reinforces the warrior image by showing the men all bearing shields and assegais.

52. "House of Commons—Tuesday," *Reynolds's Newspaper*, July 13, 1879, p. 3.

53. See the court records as reprinted in Strother, "Display of the Body Hottentot," 41–48; and the following newspaper articles: "An Englishman," letter to the editor, *Morning Chronicle*, October 12, 1810, p. 3; Hendrick Cesars, "The Hottentot Venus," letter to the editor, *Morning Chronicle*, October 13, 1810, p. 3; Humanitas, "Female Hottentot," letter to the editor, *Morning Chronicle*, October 17, 1810, p. 3; A Man and a Christian, letter, *Morning Post*, October 18, 1810, p. 3; Hendrick Cesars, letter to the editor, *Morning Chronicle*, October 23, 1810, p. 4; Humanitas, "Female Hottentot," *Morning Chronicle*, October 24, 1810, p. 3; White Man, letter, *Morning Post*, October 29, 1810, p. 3; "Law report; Court of King's Bench," *Times*, November 26, 1810, p. 3; "Law intelligence; Court of King's Bench, Sat., Nov. 24; the Hottentot Venus," *Morning Chronicle*,

November 26, 1810, p. 3; "Law intelligence; Court of King's Bench, Nov. 28; the Hottentot Venus," *Morning Chronicle*, November 29, 1810, p. 3; "Law report; Court of King's Bench," *Times*, November 29, 1810, p. 3.

54. *Morning Chronicle*, October 12, 1810.

55. *Morning Chronicle*, October 23, 1810.

56. For more detail on the arrangements see Crais and Scully, *Sara Baartman and the Hottentot Venus*, 55–78.

57. On labor shortages and British emigration see Crais, *White Supremacy and Black Resistance*, 87–96.

58. Ibid., 59.

59. See Fryer, *Staying Power*, and Walvin, *The Black Presence*.

60. Anon., *Now Exhibiting at the Egyptian Hall*.

61. On the development of cheaper forms of travel and the emergence of more accessible tourism, see Paul Smith, *The History of Tourism: Thomas Cook and the Origins of Leisure Travel*, 4 vols. (London: Routledge, 1998).

62. Reprinted in Anon., *Now Exhibiting at the Egyptian Hall*, 1.

63. Reprinted in ibid.

64. For an account of the cross-cultural conflict engendered by differences between the hunter-gatherer and pastoral lifestyles in the Cape, see Crais, *White Supremacy and Black Resistance*.

65. For more on the image of the industrious beaver and lazy sloth in reference to missionary work, see Sujit Sivasundaram, "The Periodical as Barometer: Spiritual Measurement and the Evangelical Magazine," in *Science and Culture in the Nineteenth-Century Media*, ed. Geoffrey Cantor et al. (Aldershot, UK: Ashgate, 2003), 43–56.

66. Reprinted in Anon., *Now Exhibiting at the Egyptian Hall*, 1.

67. Lichtenstein, *Travels in South Africa*. To see examples of its textual appropriation, see Anon., *Now Exhibiting at the Egyptian Hall*; Tyler, *The Bosjesmans*; Anon., *The Erdermänner*; and Anon, "The Erdmanninges."

68. Lichtenstein, *Travels in South Africa*, 2:42–43.

69. The review from the *Morning Post* was reprinted in the promotional paper Anon., *Now Exhibiting at the Egyptian Hall*.

70. David Livingstone, *Missionary Travels and Researches in South Africa …* (New York: Harper and Brothers, 1858), 55.

71. Wheeler, *The Complexion of Race*; Ronald Meek, *Social Science and the Ignoble Savage* (Cambridge: Cambridge University Press, 1976).

72. Skotnes, *Miscast*.

73. "The Zulu Kaffirs," *Lady's Newspaper*, May 21, 1853, p. 327.

74. Lord Byron, *Don Juan*, canto 3, stanza 37, line 3. See especially cantos 3–4.

75. Caldecott, *Exhibition of Native Zulu Kafirs*, and Isaacs, *Travels and Adventures in Eastern Africa*.

76. Caldecott, *Exhibition of Native Zulu Kafirs*, 19.

77. Isaacs, *Travels and Adventures in Eastern Africa*, 1:331.

78. "The Zulu Kaffirs," *Lady's Newspaper*, May 21, 1853, p. 327.

79. Isaacs, *Travels and Adventures in Eastern Africa*, 1:295–96.

80. Ibid., 1:232–33, 289–90.

81. This is not to claim that the information they were provided with would necessarily live up to modern understandings of reliable ethnographic descriptions of indig-

enous societies; but it is to avoid retrospectively expecting consumers to have had such knowledge, and to avoid discussions of whether the shows were or were not authentic. Rather, the focus here is on what kinds of resources patrons had available, what use they made of them, and how this can help us reevaluate the historiography of the shows' receptions.

82. Charles Dickens, letter to John Leech [May 23, 1853]; reprinted in *The Letters of Charles Dickens*, ed. Madeline House and others (Oxford: Clarendon Press, 1993), 7:91.

83. "The Caffres at Hyde-Park Corner," *Times*, May 18, 1853, p. 8.

84. Charles Dickens, "The Noble Savage," *Household Words* (June 11, 1853): 338.

85. Ibid., 337.

86. Ibid., 338.

87. For more on Mrs. Jellyby, see Rodney-Stenning Edgecombe, "Dickens and Addison: A Possible Source for Mrs. Jellyby," *Dickensian* 98 (2002): 153–55; and Joel Gold, "Mrs. Jellyby: Dickens's Inside Joke," *Dickensian* 79 (1983): 35–38.

88. For Dickens's views on the expedition, see Charles Dickens, "Review: 'Narrative of the Expedition Sent by her Majesty's Government to the River Niger in 1841,'" and Malvern van Wyk Smith, "'What the Waves Were Saying': 'Dombey and Son' and Textual Ripples on African Shore," in *Dickens and the Children of Empire*, ed. Wendy S. Jacobson (New York: Palgrave Macmillan, 2000), 128–52.

89. A Friend and a Brother, "Thoughts on the Savage Lions of London," *Punch* 25 (1853): 38.

90. Ibid.

91. Stowe, a Northerner, never visited a plantation but based her novel on interviews with runaway slaves and published works on the practice, including a former slave's autobiography. On the writing of the novel and the development of her abolitionism, see Joan D. Hedrick, *Harriet Beecher Stowe: A Life* (Oxford: Oxford University Press, 1994), 218–52.

92. "Diogenes," *Lady's Newspaper*, September 10, 1853, p. 150.

93. For examples of the visual material, see Altick, *The Shows of London*, 271–72.

94. "Our South African Pets", *Funny Folks*, July 26, 1879, p. 236.

95. "Signs and Tokens of Zuluism", *Funny Folks*, July 26, 1879, p. 236.

Chapter Six

1. Conolly, *The Ethnological Exhibitions of London*, 5–7.

2. Conolly was not the only one. In 1844, for example, Richard King used his presidential address to the ESL to argue that commercial exhibitions were rich resources that could be drawn on. He estimated that three hundred foreign people of ethnological interest had been in London in the previous year alone. While it is not clear if they were all commercially exhibited, and one suspects not, his claim suggests that arguments similar to Conolly's were being explicitly made in the early 1840s. Furthermore, like Conolly, King was particularly concerned that such shows often occurred without leaving a trace in the records of scientific men; thus, his estimate is suspiciously large. This interest in the involvement of science must be seen as partly due to his position as president of the ESL and the society's attempts to establish itself and ethnology as an academic discipline. See Richard King, *Address to the Ethnological Society of London, Delivered at the Anniversary Meeting, 1844* (London: W. Watts, 1844).

3. George W. Stocking, for example, argues that from the mid-nineteenth century onward, anthropologists tended to ignore their intellectual debts to ethnologists in favor of eighteenth-century luminaries such as Johann Friedrich Blumenbach. In this historiographical tradition, the early 1800s were frequently characterized as a "dark age" for anthropology. See Stocking, *Victorian Anthropology*, 9–10.

4. As Ames, *Carl Hagenbeck's Empire on Entertainments*, points out, there is a substantial interest in science in histories of human displays—often, he argues, to the detriment of discussions of leisure and entertainment. Despite this focus, much of the discussion remains poorly informed by histories of science and thus is predicated on the assumption that the shows were arenas in which science was not made but displayed or applied. See the conclusion of the present text.

5. Stocking, *Victorian Anthropology*, 246. The comment on second-hand ethnography belies Stocking's interest in the emergence of fieldwork as the emblematic methodology of anthropological research.

6. Rydell, *All the World's a Fair*, and Parezo and Fowler, *Anthropology Goes to the Fair*, provide excellent examples in which the involvement of anthropologists in curating the displays is abundantly clear, most obviously in the 1893 Chicago and 1904 St. Louis exhibitions. See also Greenhalgh, *Ephemeral Vistas*, and Lee D. Baker, *From Savage to Negro: Anthropology and the Construction of Race, 1896–1954* (Berkeley and Los Angeles: University of California Press, 1988), 79–80.

7. Rothfels, *Savages and Beasts*, and Zimmerman, *Anthropology and Antihumanism*.

8. Parezo and Fowler, *Anthropology Goes to the Fair*.

9. "The Bosjesman, at the Egyptian Hall, Piccadilly," *ILN*, June 12, 1847, p. 381.

10. Chabert, *A Brief Historical Account of the Life and Adventures of the Botocudo Chieftain*, 3–5.

11. Wheeler, *The Complexion of Race*; Bindman, *From Ape to Apollo*; Kidd, *British Identities before Nationalism*. For more on the challenges to environmentalism, see Harrison, *Climates and Constitutions*, and W. Anderson, *The Cultivation of Whiteness*.

12. Meek, *Social Science and the Ignoble Savage*. Crucially, changing the material circumstances of a people, by introducing commerce for example, would change their moral and social makeup and, crucially, could be used to change how humans were classified. For instance, of the factors used to designate human difference, only one's place of birth was fixed. Consequently, an African who learned to speak English, converted to Christianity, and dressed in European clothes could be classified as European. As Wheeler's *The Complexion of Race* argues, this broad basis for defining human variation and its potential elasticity is often overlooked when biological or color-based notions of ethnic difference are anachronistically adopted for earlier periods, as is the case in much writing on the eighteenth century.

13. Rosemary Sweet, *Antiquaries: The Discovery of the Past in Eighteenth-Century Britain* (London; New York: Hambledon and London, 2004), 27.

14. This is especially true for some ethnologists, such as James Cowles Prichard and Conolly, who studied at Edinburgh in the early nineteenth century when the moral philosopher Dugald Stewart (1753–1828) was promoting stadial theories of human development. Also see Peter Mandler, "'Race' and 'Nation' in Mid-Victorian Thought," in *History, Religion and Culture: British Intellectual History 1750–1950*, ed. Stefan Collini, Richard Whatmore and Brian Young (Cambridge: Cambridge University Press, 2000), 224–44.

15. Conolly, *The Ethnological Exhibitions of London*, 7–10. The address mentions all these

exhibitions and gives anecdotal accounts that make clear that he must have seen them, either in public venues or in private demonstrations.

16. "Aztec Lilliputians," *Times*, July 19, 1853.

17. For an excellent and extended discussion of what it might mean to compare humans to animals during this period in the Australian context, see Kay Anderson, *Race and the Crisis of Humanism* (London: Routledge, 2007).

18. Owen and Cull, "A Brief Notice of the Aztec Race," 134.

19. Ibid., 36.

20. Knox, "Some Remarks on the Aztecque and Bosjieman Children," 359.

21. Despite Knox's use of the term *species* to distinguish between different human varieties, Caplan has argued that since he believed all human embryos could potentially become any of the different human races, Knox is more appropriately seen as a monogenist than polygenist. For an elaboration of her argument, see Kaplan, "White, Black, and Green" and "'A Heterogeneous Thing.'"

22. For more on Knox's theories of anatomy, see E. Richards, "The 'Moral Anatomy' of Robert Knox." For the sake of explanatory clarity, modern terms have been used to explain Knox's theory of embryonic development.

23. "The Aztec Children," *ILN*, July 23, 1853.

24. Conolly, *The Ethnological Exhibitions of London*, 12–13.

25. As early as 1830, Conolly had argued that many of the treatments meted out to the mad were highly detrimental. Although he gained fame for removing mechanical restraints, it was not his invention but a system he adopted after seeing its use in 1838 by Robert Gardiner Hill in a provincial asylum in Lincoln. See *ODNB*.

26. Conolly, *The Ethnological Exhibitions of London*, 14–17.

27. For more on how Knox's and Owen's interpretation of the children's development correlated with their social standing and political affiliation, see E. Richards, "A Political Anatomy of Monsters."

28. For a useful discussion of the role of elite clubs in governing London's gentlemen of science, see Ruth Barton, "'Huxley, Lubbock, and Half a Dozen Others': Professionals and Gentlemen in the Formation of the X-Club, 1851–1864," *Isis* 89 (1998): 410–44, and "'An Influential Set of Chaps': The X-Club and Royal Society Politics, 1864–85," *British Journal for the History of Science* 23 (1990): 53–81.

29. Given the lack of anatomic detail in Knox's paper, E. Richards, "A Political Anatomy of Monsters," suggests he drew directly from Owen's paper. While this is entirely plausible, he may have also had the opportunity to make limited observations at a show and used these to underpin his arguments.

30. Unless otherwise stated, this discussion is based on Jan R. Piggott, *Palace of the People: The Crystal Palace at Sydenham, 1854–1936* (London: Hurst, 2004); Robert G. Latham and Edward Forbes, *A Hand Book to the Courts of Natural History Described* (London: Bradbury and Evans, 1854); Philip H. Delamotte, *Photographic Views of the Crystal Palace Sydenham, Taken during the Progress of the Works*, 2 vols. (London: Photographic Institution, 1854); Samuel Philips, *Guide to the Crystal Palace and its Park, Sydenham*, 2nd ed. (London: Bradbury and Evans, [1854]); and [Edward McDermott], *Routledge's Guide to the Crystal Palace and Park at Sydenham ...* (London: George Routledge, 1854).

31. James A. Secord, "Monsters at the Crystal Palace," in *Models: The Third Dimension of Space*, ed. Soraya de Chadarevian and Nick Hopwood (Stanford, CA: Stanford University Press, 2004), 138–69; and O'Connor, *The Earth on Show*.

32. The literature on the 1851 exhibition is vast. For examples see Auerbach, *The Great Exhibition of 1851*; Greenhalgh, *Ephemeral Vistas*; and Hoffenberg, *An Empire on Display*. For a contemporary guide see John Tallis, *Tallis's History and Description of the Crystal Palace and the Exhibition of the World's Industry in 1851*, 3 vols. (London: Tallis, 1852).

33. Piggott, *The Palace of the People*, v.

34. Secord, "Monsters at the Crystal Palace," 139.

35. Piggott, *The Palace of the People*, 61. Piggott notes that between 1854 and 1886, 60 million visitors passed through the Crystal Palace in Sydenham.

36. Latham and Forbes, *A Hand Book to the Courts of Natural History*, 6.

37. "A Visit to the Crystal Palace," *Lady's Newspaper*, June 10, 1854, p. 364.

38. "The Crystal Palace at Sydenham," *Daily News*, June 9, 1854, p. 5.

39. Latham and Forbes, *A Hand Book to the Courts of Natural History*, 54.

40. Lichtenstein, *Travels in Southern Africa*, 196. See chapter 7 and note 110 of chapter 7 of the present work.

41. Latham and Forbes, *A Hand Book to the Courts of Natural History*, 60.

42. Prince Alexander Philip Maximilian (zu Wied), *Travels in Brazil in the Years 1815, 1816 and 1817*, trans. H. E. Lloyd (London: Henry Colburn, 1820); Joh[ann] Bapt[ist] von Spix and C[arl] F[riedrich] Phil[ip] von Martius, *Travels in Brazil in the Years 1817–1820*, trans. H. E. Lloyd (London: Longman, Rees, Hurst, Orme, Brown and Greene, 1824).

43. Latham and Forbes, *A Hand Book to the Courts of Natural History*. Many of the courts had a specific guidebook issued for visitors' benefit. The geological guidebook, intended to explain the models of extinct reptiles, was written by the anatomist Richard Owen, another notable man of science and first curator of the British Museum of Natural History.

44. Ibid., 6. *Punch* argued that Latham was expanding on a word "which every schoolboy knows." See "Punch's handbooks to the Crystal Palace," *Punch* 27 (1854): 8–9; quotation is from p. 8.

45. Latham and Forbes, *A Hand Book to the Courts of Natural History*, 7–8.

46. Ibid., 10.

47. Ibid., 25–30; quotation is on p. 28.

48. David N. Livingstone, *Adam's Ancestors: Race, Religion and the Politics of Human Origins* (Baltimore: Johns Hopkins University Press, 2008), and Augstein, *Race*.

49. See Kidd, *The Forging of Races*, for an illuminating discussion of the importance of biblical hermeneutics for understandings of human variety in this period.

50. Augstein, *Race*, ix–xxxiii.

51. Stephen D. Snobelen, "Of Stones, Men and Angels: The Competing Myth of Isabelle Duncan's Pre-Adamite Man," *Studies in the History and Philosophy of the Biomedical Sciences* 32 (2001): 59–104; and Livingstone, *Adam's Ancestors*.

52. Throughout his career, Prichard explicitly tried to fend off such heterodoxy. See Augstein, *James Cowles Prichard's Anthropology*, and Prichard, *The Natural History of Man*.

53. In Robert G. Latham, *The Natural History of the Varieties of Man* (London: John van Voorst, 1850), humans were divided into three basic types: the European, Mongolian, and Negro.

54. Robert. G. Latham, *Ethnology of the British Colonies and Dependencies* (London: John van Voorst, 1851) and *The Ethnology of Europe* (London: John van Voorst, 1852). See also James C. Prichard, *The Eastern Origin of the Celtic Nations* ...(Oxford: S. Collingwood, 1831).

55. Latham and Forbes, *A Hand Book to the Courts of Natural History*, 5.

56. "Punch's handbooks to the Crystal Palace," 8.

57. Kate Nichols, *Greece and Rome at the Crystal Palace: Classical Sculpture and Modern Britain, 1854–1936* (Oxford: Oxford University Press, forthcoming). I am grateful to her for sharing her work.

58. Philips, *Guide to the Crystal Palace and its Park*, 188.

59. Martin Rudwick, *Scenes from Deep Time: Early Pictorial Representations of the Prehistoric World* (Chicago: University of Chicago Press, 1992); J. Secord, "Monsters at the Crystal Palace"; and O'Connor, *The Earth on Show*.

60. The importance of diachronic human variation is particularly evident in the work of Prichard, for whom ethnology was, "in fact, more neatly allied to history than to natural science," because it was concerned with "describing and classifying past modifications of humanity through a comparative approach." In addition, "Ethnology professes to give an account, not of what nature produces in the present day, but of what she has produced in times long past. It is an attempt to trace the history of tribes and races of men from the most remote periods which are within the reach of investigation, to discover their mutual relations, and to arrive at conclusions, either certain or probable, as to their affinity or diversity of origin." See James C. Prichard, "On the Various Methods of Research Which Contribute to the Advancement of Ethnology, and of the Relations of that Science to Other Branches of Knowledge," in *BAAS Official Report* (London: John Murray, 1847), 230–53; quotation is from p. 231. The paper was based on one read at the anniversary address of the ESL, June 22, 1847 (the BAAS meeting took place three days later), and which was later published in the society's journal. See "On the Relations of Ethnology to Other Branches of Knowledge," *Journal of the Ethnological Society of London* 1 (1848): 301–29. The BAAS meeting took place just three days after the initial reading; see "British Association For The Advancement Of Science," *Times*, June 28, 1847. See also James C. Prichard, "Abstract of a Comparative Review of Philological and Physiological Researches as Applied to the History of the Human Species," in *BAAS Official Report* (London: John Murray, 1831–32), 529–44. For an indication of how typical this view was of other ethnologists during the 1840s, see Thomas Hodgkin, "The Progress of Ethnology," *Journal of the Ethnological Society of London* 1 (1848): 27–45; and Ernest Dieffenbach, "The Study of Ethnology," *Journal of the Ethnological Society of London* 1 (1848): 15–26.

61. Piggott, *The Palace of the People*, 126.

62. Nichols, *Greece and Rome at the Crystal Palace*.

63. For broader accounts of the challenges to environmental determinism, see Harrison, *Climates and Constitutions*; Wahrman, "Climate, Civilization and Complexion"; and W. Anderson, *The Cultivation of Whiteness*.

64. Julien-Joseph Virey, *Natural History of the Negro Race*, trans. J. H. Geunebault (Charleston, SC: D. J. Dowling, 1837), 19.

65. Ibid., 21–22.

66. Marie-Jean-Pierre Flourens, "On the Natural History of Man," *Edinburgh New Philosophical Journal* 27 (1839): 351–58; quotation is from p. 353.

67. Latham and Forbes, *A Hand Book to the Courts of Natural History*, 42. The images of skin tissue originally appeared in A. Kolliker, *Manual of Human Histology*, trans. and ed. George Busk and Thomas H. Huxley (London: Sydenham Society, 1853), 106.

68. "Leader," *Crystal Palace Herald*, new series, August 1854, p. 33.

69. [Robert Chambers], *Vestiges of the Natural History of Creation* (London: John Churchill, 1844).

70. James A. Secord, *Victorian Sensation: The Extraordinary Publication, Reception and Secret Authorship of "Vestiges of the Natural History of Creation"* (Chicago: University of Chicago Press, 2000), 522. Secord's magisterial work presents the most thorough and sophisticated overview of the book's reception and its role in making development theories the focus of extensive and fierce debate in the mid-nineteenth century.

71. See, for instance, J[osiah] C[lark]. Nott and Geo[rge]. R. Gliddon, *Types of Mankind; or, Ethnological Researchers based upon the Ancient Monuments, Paintings, Sculptures, and Crania of Races …* (Philadelphia: Lippincott, Grambo, 1854). For a discussion of these debates in a transatlantic context and an indication of how American theorizers were much more prone to split humans into multiple species, partly because of the continuing support for slavery in the antebellum period, see Adrian Desmond and James Moore, *Darwin's Sacred Cause: How a Hatred of Slavery Shaped Darwin Shaped Darwin's Views on Human Evolution* (Boston: Houghton Mifflin Harcourt, 2009).

72. For a range of unofficial descriptions, see Delamotte, *Photographic Views of the Crystal Palace*, which includes some photographs of the courts' displays, including Africa, the yak, and the snow leopard; Philips, *Guide to the Crystal Palace and its Park*, 117; and [McDermott], *Routledge's Guide to the Crystal Palace and Park at Sydenham*, 170.

73. "The Crystal Palace, Sydenham," *Morning Chronicle*, April 24, 1854, p. 3.

74. Philips, *Guide to the Crystal Palace and its Park*, 127.

75. "Tiger Hunt," *Illustrated Crystal Palace Gazette*, July 1, 1854, pp. 168–69.

76. George Measom, *Crystal Palace Alphabet: A Guide for Good Children* (London: [n.p.], 1855).

77. Altick, *The Shows of London*, 341–42.

78. Bernth Lindfors, "Dr Kahn and the Niam-Niams," in Blanchard et al., *Human Zoos*, 229–28.

79. Handbill 1853, JJ, Waxworks, 3 (41).

80. "Anatomical Museum," *Reynolds's Newspaper*, June 5, 1853, p. 16.

81. Handbill 1853, JJ, Waxworks, 3 (41).

82. Of course, London boasted other displays of natural history, most obviously at the Egyptian Hall and the Zoological Gardens. Models of human races also appeared in other contexts, for example at the original Crystal Palace (see chapter 7); however, the palace in Sydenham was unique in providing a museum of human types, shown in their ostensibly natural environments and curated by an ethnologist with a view to educating patrons about contemporary ethnological theory. Once the models were destroyed in a fire in 1866, it could be said that the public was not given a similar opportunity to visit a permanent anthropological exhibition until the foundation of the Pitt Rivers Museum in Oxford in 1884.

83. William Thomson, *Crystal Palace, Sydenham: Natural History Department; Ethnological Collection (A list of desiderata.)* (London: [Crystal Palace Company], 1852); *Crystal Palace, Sydenham: Natural History Department; Raw Produce Collection (A list of desiderata.)* (London: [Crystal Palace Company], 1852); and *Crystal Palace, Sydenham: Natural History Department; Zoological Collection. (A list of desiderata.)* (London: [Crystal Palace Company], 1852). See also Piggott, *The Palace of the People*, 127.

84. Latham and Forbes, *A Hand Book to the Courts of Natural History*; Robert G. Latham, "Ethnological Remarks upon Some of the More Remarkable Varieties of Human Species, Represented by Individuals Now in London," in *BAAS Official Report* (London: John Murray, 1853), 88. The paper was later reprinted as "Ethnological Remarks upon

Some of the More Remarkable Varieties of Human Species, Represented by Individuals Now in London," *Journal of the Ethnological Society of London* 4 (1856): 148–50.

85. D. Graham Burnett, "Exploration, Performance, Alliance: Robert Schomburgk in British Guiana," *Journal of Caribbean Studies* 15 (2000): 11–37.

86. "The Crystal Palace," *Reynolds's Newspaper*, April 23, 1854, p. 7.

87. "A Visit to the Crystal Palace," *Lady's Newspaper*, June 10, 1854, p. 364.

88. Conolly, *The Ethnological Exhibitions of London*, 38–39.

89. Ibid., 41–42.

90. For a similar argument in relationship to French fairs of the 1930s, see Benoît de l'Estoile, "From the Colonial Exhibition to the Museum of Man: An Alternative Genealogy of French Anthropology," *Social Anthropology* 11 (2003): 341–61. The role of the Crystal Palace in Sydenham in training ethnologists is developed in Efram Sera-Shriar, "Beyond the Armchair: Early Observational Practices and the Sciences of Man in Britain, 1813–1871" (Ph.D. diss., University of Leeds, 2011).

91. E. Edwards, *Raw Histories* and "Evolving Images: Photography, Race and Popular Darwinism," in *Endless Forms: Darwin, Natural Sciences and the Visual Arts*, ed. Diana Donald and Jane Munro (New Haven, CT: Yale University Press, 2009), 166–93.

92. Richard Cull, "On the Recent Progress of Ethnology: Being the Annual Discource for 1852," *Journal of the Ethnological Society of London* 3 (1854): 297–316, especially 297.

93. ODNB.

94. It is worth remembering that Cull aired his views before having seen the finished court and based them on reports, not personal experience, since the article mentioned that Latham was in the business of preparing the handbook (which was complete for the opening ceremony, as it had to be presented to Queen Victoria). However, one suspects he held to his views: the article was published in 1856, two years after the Crystal Palace opened.

95. "Disastrous Fire at the Crystal Palace," *Daily News*, December 31, 1866, p. 5; and "Anthropological News," *Anthropological Review* 5 (1867): 240–56 (especially 241–42). Given that Hunt edited the *Anthropological Review*, it is almost certain that he wrote the article and that it represented his personal view of Latham's models. For a contemporary account of the Parisian gallery, see Karl Baedeker, *Paris and its Environs: With Routes from London to Paris, and from Paris to the Rhine and Switzerland*, 6th ed. (Leipsic: Karl Baedeker, 1878), 246–47.

96. Alphonse Esquiros, *Religious Life in England* (London: Chapman and Hall, 1867), 213.

97. For more on Hodgkin's philanthropic project, see Zoë Laidlaw, "Heathens, Slaves and Aborigines: Thomas Hodgkin's Critique of Missions and Anti-slavery," *History Workshop Journal* 2007 (64): 133–61; and Kass and Kass, *Perfecting the World*.

98. Laidlaw, "Aunt Anna's Report," and Select Committee on Aborigines (British Settlements), *Report from the Select Committee on Aborigines (British Settlements)* ... (London: House of Commons, 1837).

99. Laidlaw, "Heathens, Slaves and Aborigines," 136–37.

100. For this history of the ESL, see Stocking, *Victorian Anthropology*, especially 239–73; and "What's in a Name?"

101. Wheeler, *The Complexion of Race*, and Kidd, *The Forging of Races*.

102. For more on the early origins of the ESL, see Stocking, "What's in a Name?" and William F. Bynum, "Time's Noblest Offspring: The Problem of Man in the British Natural Historical Sciences, 1800–1863" (Ph.D. diss., University of Cambridge, 1974).

103. Robert Clarke, "Sketches of the Colony of Sierra Leone and its Inhabitants," *Transactions of the Ethnological Society of London* 2 (1863): 320–363.

104. Stocking, *Victorian Anthropology*, 247. Even if one does not join Stocking in looking to the more racist images of the period as the obvious comparison, the images are distinctive when compared with standard ethnological texts of the period, such as Prichard, *The Natural History of Man*.

105. Sera-Shriar, "Beyond the Armchair," argues that the images would have been severely at odds with Hunt's political views. I am grateful to him for sharing his work and views.

106. Carl Vogt, *Lectures on Man: His Place in Creation and in the History of the Earth* (London: Longman, Green, Longman and Roberts, 1864).

107. Stocking's *Victorian Anthropology* has proved to be seminal in this respect.

108. For more on Hunt and periodical literature, see Sera-Shriar, "Beyond the Armchair."

109. Stepan, *The Idea of Race in Science*.

110. Henrika Kuklick, *The Savage Within: The Social History of British Anthropology, 1885–1945* (Cambridge: Cambridge University Press, 1991), and Fredrik Barth et al, *One Discipline, Four Ways: British, German, French and American Anthropology* (Chicago: University of Chicago Press, 2005). In these publications, institutionalized anthropology is essentially seen as a fieldwork-based practice, and so earlier approaches are frequently characterized as "armchair anthropology." It is beyond the scope of this work to offer a substantial revision of this historiography; however, see Sera-Shriar, "Beyond the Armchair."

111. Thomas H. Huxley, "On the Methods and Results of Ethnology," in *Man's Place in Nature: And Other Anthropological Essays* (London: Macmillan, [1865] 1900), 209–52; quotation is from pp. 209–10.

112. Stocking, *Victorian Anthropology*.

113. For Prichard's reputation, including quotation, see Hodgkin, "Obituary: Dr. Prichard," and Thomas Hodgkin, "Obituary of Dr. Prichard," *Journal of the Ethnological Society of London* 2 (1850): 182–207; quotation is from p. 182.

114. For more on the development of imperialism in the mid- to late nineteenth century, see A. Porter, *The Nineteenth Century*.

115. Knox, *The Races of Men*, preface.

116. James Hunt, "On the Physical and Mental Characteristics of the Negro," in *BAAS Official Report* (London: John Murray, 1863), 140.

117. Cited in *ODNB*. For a contemporary account of the debate following Hunt's paper, see Anon., "Exchange by William Craft and Dr. James Hunt at the Annual Meeting of the British Association for the Advancement of Science, Newcastle-upon-Tyne, England, August 27, 1863," in *The Black Abolitionist Papers*, ed. C. P. Ripley. 1:537–43 (Chapel Hill: University of North Carolina Press, 1985).

118. E. Richards, "The 'Moral Anatomy' of Robert Knox."

119. For the classic account of the role of Prichard, Latham, Knox, and Hunt, see Stocking, *Victorian Anthropology*, especially 239–73. For instance, "Latham still hoped to cope with this data within the ethnological paradigm: classification, in terms of connection by descent and affiliation [a classic Prichardian strategy], was his 'chief end.' But as the decade wore on, Latham's data seemed to overwhelm him.... With Latham ethnology had thus virtually retreated into a purely descriptive 'natural history' of the sort pursued by early-eighteenth-century botanists." Stocking argues

that the resolution to this "crisis" in Prichardian ethnology came with the "transformation of 'ethnology' and the emergence of synthetic disciplinary rubric that in the
Anglo-American tradition has been called 'anthropology.'" See Stocking, *Victorian
Anthropology*, 103 and 74–77, respectively. Since *Victorian Anthropology* is both a seminal and a standard text, Stocking's argument has been enormously influential and
consistently reproduced since its publication.

120. *Orr's Circle of the Sciences: A Series of Treatises on the Principles of Sciences with their
Application to Practical Pursuits* (London: Wm. S. Orr, 1854). Later reprinted as Robert
G. Latham, *The Varieties of Human Species: Being A Manual of Ethnography: Introduc-
tory to the Study of History* (London: Charles Griffin and Company, [ca. 1860].

121. For some influential examples of this historiography, see the following: Robert C.
Young, *Colonial Desire: Hybridity in Theory, Culture and Race* (London: Routledge, 1995),
makes substantial use of Knox to discuss nineteenth-century theories of race; Philip
D. Curtin, *The Image of Africa: British Ideas and Action, 1780–1850*, 2 vols. (Madison:
University of Wisconsin Press, 1964), "The first great proponent [of racial history] in
Great Britain was Dr. Robert Knox, the real founder of British racism and one of the
key figures in the general Western movement toward a dogmatic pseudo-scientific
racism," 2:377; Catherine Hall, *Defining the Victorian Nation: Class, Race, Gender and
the Reform Act of 1867* (Cambridge: Cambridge University Press, 2000), notes that
"by the 1840s . . . the emphasis moved to the fundamental heterogeneity of mankind,
the natural differences between men, fixed by immutable biological laws. . . . Symp-
tomatic of this new approach to 'race' and the ways in which it was popularised was
the work of Robert Knox," 191–92. Significantly, Hall's later work, especially *Civilising Subjects*, 48–49 and 275–76, shifts focus away from this view of Knox. For further
discussion of the historiography of Knox, see Peter Mandler, "The Problem with Cultural History," *Cultural and Social History* 1 (2004): 94–117.

122. Conolly, *The Ethnological Exhibitions of London*, 5–6.

123. Georges Cuvier, "Extrait d'Observations."

124. Prichard, *Natural History of Man*, 2nd ed., 123–28 for Baartman and 584–85 for the
Anishinabe. Compare with the use of Baartman in John Marshall, "On the Brain of
a Bushwoman: And on the Brains of Two Idiots of European Descent," *Philosophi-
cal Transactions of the Royal Society of London* 154 (1864): 501–58; Flower and Murie,
"Account of the Dissection of a Bushwoman"; and C. W. D., "Flower and Murie on the
Dissection of a Bushwoman."

125. Piggott, *The Palace of the People*, 126.

126. For example Altick, *The Shows of London*; Lindfors, *Africans on Stage*; and the contemporary writings of Frost, *The Old Showmen and the Old London Fairs*.

127. Stocking, *After Tylor*; Kuklick, *The Savage Within*.

128. Latham and Forbes, *A Hand Book to the Courts of Natural History*.

129. For more on this self-fashioning in the ESL's publications, see Brent R. Henze,
"Scientific Rhetorics in the Emergence of British Ethnology, 1808–1848: Discourses,
Disciplines and Institutions" (Ph.D. diss., Pennsylvania State University, 2001).

130. Quoted in Anon., "A South African Native's Picture of England," *Munger Africana
Library Notes* 9 (1979): 17; originally published in *Natal Journal* 2 (1858): 126–38.

131. Flora died in 1864 and was dissected at the Royal College of Surgeons. The account
of her dissection explicitly compared her to Baartman, as detailed in Cuvier's paper
"Extrait d'Oservations." It was also taken up as a valuable source of information for

writers interested in San anatomy. See Flower and Murie, "Account of the Dissection of a Bushwoman"; C. W. D., "Flower and Murie on the Dissection of a Bushwoman"; and Joseph Barnard Davis, "Contributions towards Determining the Weight of the Brain in Different Races of Man," *Philosophical Transactions of the Royal Society of London* 158 (1868): 505–27.

132. Rothfels, *Savages and Beasts*, and Zimmerman, *Anthropology and Antihumanism*.

Chapter Seven

1. "Savage South Africa," *Pall Mall Gazette*, May 4, 1899, p. 4; "Greater Britain Exhibition," *Horse and Hound*, May 6, 1899, p. 278.

2. Greenhalgh, *Ephemeral Vistas*, and Hoffenberg, *An Empire on Display*.

3. Stephen Inwood, *City of Cities: The Birth of Modern London* (London: Macmillan, 2005), 9. The following discussion of London's demography is heavily indebted to Inwood's account.

4. Merriman and Visram, "The World in a City."

5. Stephanie Pratt, "The Four 'Indian Kings,'" in *Between Worlds: Voyagers to Britain, 1700–1850*, by Jocelyn Hackforth-Jones et al. (London: National Portrait Gallery, 2007), 22–35.

6. Neil Parsons, "No Longer 'Rare Birds' in London: Zulu, Ndebele, Gaza and Swazi Envoys to England, 1882–1894," in *Black Victorians/Black Victoriana*, ed. Gerzina Gretchen (New Brunswick, NJ: Rutgers University Press, 2003), 110–44. See also Neil Parsons, *King Khama, Emperor Joe and the Great White Queen* (Chicago: University of Chicago Press, 1998).

7. Neil Parsons, "No Longer 'Rare Birds' in London," 112.

8. A. S. H., "The Zulu King," *Times*, October 13, 1879, p. 8.

9. Parsons, "No Longer 'Rare Birds' in London," 112.

10. A. Porter, *The Nineteenth Century*.

11. Robert Kubicek, "British Expansion, Empire and Technological Change," in A. Porter, *The Nineteenth Century*, 247–69, especially 254–55.

12. Ibid., 248.

13. Bailey, *Leisure and Class in Victorian England*, 154–74.

14. Mike Huggins, *The Victorians and Sport* (London: Hambledon and London, 2004).

15. "Continuous Photography," *Daily News*, February 21, 1896, p. 8.

16. Frost, *The Old Showmen and the Old London Fairs*, provides a useful contemporary account of the origin and nature of London's fairs.

17. Cited in R. Porter, *London*, 351.

18. For more on the campaign for rational entertainment in the mid-nineteenth century, see Altick, *The Shows of London*.

19. Bailey, *Leisure and Class in Victorian England*.

20. David Sampson, "Strangers in a Strange Land: The 1868 Aborigines and Other Indigenous Performers in Mid-Victorian Britain" (Ph.D. diss., University of Technology, Sydney, 2000).

21. For this account of the Savage South Africa exhibition, see Shephard, *Kitty and the Prince*; Ben Shephard, "Showbiz Imperialism: The Case of Peter Lobengula," in *Imperialism and Popular Culture*, ed. John M. Mackenzie (Manchester: Manchester University Press, 1986) 94–112; and newspaper articles as cited.

22. Shephard, *Kitty and the Prince*.

23. This account draws on Terence O. Ranger, *Revolt in Southern Rhodesia, 1896–7* (London: Heinemann, 1967); Marks, "Southern Africa, 1867–1886"; and Shula Marks, "Southern and Central Africa, 1886–1910," in Oliver and Sanderson, *The Cambridge History of Africa: Volume 6*, 422–92.

24. Ranger, *Revolt in Southern Rhodesia*, 97.

25. Iain McCallum, *Blood Brothers: Hiram and Hudson Maxim; Pioneers of Modern Warfare* (London: Chatham, 1999).

26. "Greater Britain Exhibition," *Horse and Hound*, May 6, 1899, p. 278.

27. Shephard, *Kitty and the Prince*.

28. Henry Mayhew, *1851; or, The Adventures of Mr and Mrs Sandboys and Family, who Came up to London to Enjoy themselves and See the Great Exhibition* (London: David Bogue, 1851), 132.

29. Hoffenberg, *An Empire on Display*, 203, also notes this racial divide.

30. Francesca Vanke, "Degrees of Otherness: The Ottoman Empire and China at the Great Exhibition of 1851," in *Britain, the Empire, and the World at the Great Exhibition of 1851*, ed. Jeffrey A. Auerbach and Peter H. Hoffenberg (Aldershot, UK: Ashgate Publishing, 2008), 191–206.

31. "The Tunis Court," *ILN*, May 31, 1850, pp. 493–94.

32. Edward Ziter, *The Orient on the Victorian Stage* (Cambridge: Cambridge University Press, 2003), 110.

33. Ibid., 94–131, also notes the presence of foreign attendants at the Great Exhibition and discusses displays of the Orient within the context of international fairs.

34. Unless otherwise stated, this account of the Colonial and Indian Exhibition is based on newspaper references as cited and Frank Cundall, *Reminiscences of the Colonial and Indian Exhibition* (London: William Clowes and Sons, 1886); John Dinsdale, *Sketches of the Colonial and Indian Exhibition*, 2 vols. (London: Jordison, 1886); Mathur, *India by Design*; Legassick, "From Prisoners to Exhibits"; Mukharji, *Visit to Europe*; and Hoffenberg, *An Empire on Display*.

35. For the complete list of "Natives," see Cundall, *Reminiscences of the Colonial and Indian Exhibition*, 114–15.

36. Compared with the image from the *ILN* (fig. 94), Cundall, *Reminiscences of the Colonial and Indian Exhibition*, 54, has an image with only one Aborigine lying down, a large bird (in all likelihood a rhea) in the background, and many more smaller birds, and the dog appears to be two puppies. It is likely that the newspaper's illustration features some embellishments (including the dog), since Cundall claimed that all his illustrations were made "on the spot" and "reproduced mechanically without the intervention of any hand but the artist's" (vii). The additional figures in the *ILN* image may have been drawn from another display featuring Aborigines and a kangaroo (49).

37. For more on the Andamanese models, see Claire Wintle, "Model Subjects: Representations of the Andaman Islands at the Colonial and Indian Exhibition, 1886," *History Workshop Journal* 67 (2009): 194–207; and Mukharji, *Visit to Europe*, 71. For all other descriptions and quotations, see Cundall, *Reminiscences of the Colonial and Indian Exhibition*, 36 (monk), 24 (soldiers), 62 (fishing), and 25 (subcourts), respectively.

38. "A Ramble through the Cape of Good Hope Court," *ILN*, October 16, 1886, pp. 412–13; quotation is from p. 412.

39. Cundall, *Reminiscences of the Colonial and Indian Exhibition*, 57.

40. Ibid., 56.

41. Ibid., 114, 26.

42. [Colonial and Indian Exhibition], *Catalogue of the Exhibits of the Colony of the Cape of Good Hope* (London: Richards, Glanville, 1886), 7. For a more extensive account of the exhibits for the Cape of Good Hope, see John Noble, ed., *Official Handbook: History, Productions and Resources of the Cape of Good Hope* (Cape Town: Solomon and Company, 1886). The handbook features essays on the history, production, and resources (see preface) of the Cape, with particular reference to aspects, such as diamond mining and ostrich farming, that featured among the official exhibits.

43. Cundall, *Reminiscences of the Colonial and Indian Exhibition*, 17, 75, and 25.

44. Mathur, *India by Design*, 59.

45. Cundall, *Reminiscences of the Colonial and Indian Exhibition*, 55.

46. "Colonial and Indian Exhibition: Victoria," *ILN*, August 7, 1886, p. 157.

47. For more on the encounters between aboriginal Australians and colonizers in the Melbourne region, see Richard Broome, *Aboriginal Victorians: A History since 1800* (Crows Nest, New South Wales: Allen and Unwin, 2005), 1–94.

48. A considerable portion of the exhibition literature discussed trade and natural resources in reference to each colony. See [Colonial and Indian Exhibition], *Colonial and Indian Exhibition: Official Catalogue* (London, William Clowes and Sons, 1886).

49. Legassick, "From Prisoners to Exhibits."

50. Cundall, *Reminiscences of the Colonial and Indian Exhibition*, 88.

51. Mathur, *India by Design*, 66.

52. [Colonial and Indian Exhibition], *Colonial and Indian Exhibition*, 17–18.

53. For the quotations see Cundall, *Reminiscences of the Colonial and Indian Exhibition*, 114. For the most detailed discussion of Tulsi Ram, see Mathur, *India by Design* and "Living Ethnological Exhibits."

54. A full account of Mukharji's activities is beyond the scope of this work. For the most extended discussion, see Hoffenberg, *An Empire on Display*; and Mathur, *India by Design* and "Living Ethnological Exhibits."

55. Mukharji, *Visit to Europe*, 99–100.

56. Ibid., 105–7.

57. These responses are discussed more fully in Mathur, "Living Ethnological Exhibits," 507–9.

58. On the display of Indians in India, see Crispin Bates, "Race, Caste and Tribe in Central Asia: The Early Origins of Indian Anthropometry," in *The Concept of Race in South Asia*, ed. Peter Robb (New Delhi: Oxford University Press, 1995), 219–59 (see especially 238–40). On the display of Europeans within international fairs, see Rydell, *All the World's a Fair*, 65 and 179.

59. The Parisian Exposition of 1878 also featured the "Rue de Caire": a street lined with shops and a bazaar manned by many North Africans. Greenhalgh, *Ephemeral Vistas*, 102.

60. William H. Schneider, *An Empire for the Masses: The French Popular Image of Africa, 1870–1900* (Westport, CT: Greenwood, 1982), especially 125–51.

61. Timothy Mitchell, *Colonising Egypt* (Cambridge: Cambridge University Press, 1988), 1–33.

62. These three stages (savagery, barbarism, and civilization) were often used to describe human development by American anthropologists. See Lewis Henry Morgan, *Ancient Society; or, Researches in the Lines of Human Progress From Savagery, Through*

Barbarism To Civilization (New York: Henry Holt, 1877): "It can now be asserted on convincing evidence that savagery preceded barbarism in all the tribes of mankind, as barbarism is known to have preceded civilization. The history of the human race is one in source, one in experience, and one in progress," v–vi; and L. Baker, *From Savage to Negro*. For more on American anthropology, see Curtis M. Hinsley Jr., *Savages and Scientists: The Smithsonian Institution and the Development of American Anthropology, 1846–1910* (Washington, DC: Smithsonian Institution Press, 1981).

63. Ziter, *The Orient on the Victorian Stage*, 108, also notes the same chronology for the use of foreign peoples as official exhibits within the context of international exhibitions.

64. Bolossy Kiralfy, *Creator of Great Musical Spectacles: An Autobiography*, ed. Barbara M. Barker (Ann Arbor: UMI Research Press, 1988).

65. "Venice at Olympia," *Sporting Times*, December 12, 1891, p. 4.

66. "Olympia, London: The Orient," *Dart: The Birmingham Pictorial*, January 18, 1894, p. 13.

67. Breandon Gregory, "Staging British India," in Brattons and others, *Acts of Supremacy*, 150–78, quotation is from p. 152. Gregory also provides a detailed discussion of the play and its relationship to spectacular theater. See also Hoffenberg, *An Empire on Display*, 151–65, for comparative material on India at international fairs.

68. Mathur, *India by Design*, 27–51.

69. For the involvement of represented nations, see Hoffenberg, *An Empire on Display*, especially 50–62; and Rydell, *All the World's a Fair*, especially 48–52.

70. One of the most spectacular examples of this is at the 1904 world's fair held in St. Louis, at which the government mounted a forty-seven-acre exhibit to show the peoples from the Philippines alone. They erected six villages and imported eleven hundred people from the Philippines to live on the site for the duration of the exhibition and to provide living illustrations of typical Philippine life. See Parezo and Fowler, *Anthropology Goes to the Fair*.

71. Ames, *Carl Hagenbeck's Empire of Entertainments*, 88–94.

72. Ibid., especially 141–97, provides a helpful discussion of this dynamic in terms of the development of "immersive" spaces of entertainment in the context of the Hagenbeck's *Tierparks* (zoos).

73. Shephard, *Kitty and the Prince*.

74. Ibid., 73–76.

75. "Greater Britain," *Graphic*, May 13, 1899, p. 590.

76. Rydell, *World of Fairs* and *All the World's a Fair*; Parezo and Fowler, *Anthropology Goes to the Fair*.

77. Francis Galton, "Opening Remarks by the President," *Journal of the Anthropological Institute of Great Britain and Ireland* 16 (1887): 175–77; quotation is from p. 175.

78. Ibid., 176.

79. "Anthropological Notes," *Athenaeum*, July 24, 1886, p. 120.

80. Francis Galton, "Address Delivered of the Anniversary Meeting of the Anthropological Institute of Great Britain and Ireland, January 25th, 1887," *Journal of the Anthropological Institute of Great Britain and Ireland* 16 (1887): 386–402; Robert James Mann, "The Kaffir Race of Natal," *Transactions of the Ethnological Society of London* 5 (1867): 277–97; and Robert James Mann, "Remarks on Some of the Races of South Africa Represented at the Exhibition," *Journal of the Anthropological Institute of Great Britain and Ireland* 16 (1887): 177–78.

81. Almost all the articles in the sixteenth volume (1887) and some in the seventeenth

volume (1888) of the *Journal of the Anthropological Institute of Great Britain and Ireland* were based on papers originally presented within the context of the Colonial and Indian Exhibition. Citing all the relevant articles here would be unnecessarily unwieldy, and so only those from which quotations have been used are individually cited.

82. Galton, "Opening Remarks by the President," 176.

83. Jim Endersby, *"Homo Sapiens*: Francis Galton's Fairgound Attraction," in *A Guinea Pig's History of Biology* (London: William Heinemann, 2007), 61–94.

84. Galton, "Opening Remarks by the President," 177.

85. A. W. Buckland, "On Tattooing," *Journal of the Anthropological Institute of Great Britain and Ireland* 17 (1888): 318–328.

86. Ibid., 319–20. Buckland repeatedly referred to the exhibition's displays as a means of providing comparative evidence for her paper.

87. This is directly analogous to the didactic uses made of the 1893 Chicago fair for training students. Rydell, *All the World's a Fair*, 166. On observational practices in nineteenth-century anthropology, see Sera-Shriar, "Beyond the Armchair".

88. To use Tim Ingold's phrase, we might think of this kind of training as a form of "enskilment." See Tim Ingold, "The Art of Translation in a Continuous World," in *Beyond Boundaries: Understanding, Translation and Anthropological Discourse*, ed. Gísli Pálsson (Berg: Oxford, 1993); 210–30; quotation is from 222. The literature on learning to see in the laboratory also provides a useful counterpoint. For the importance of mutual agreement on what is recognized as relevant or of significance within science, see Shapin and Schaffer, *Leviathan and the Air-Pump*.

89. Galton, "Opening Remarks by the President," 175.

90. Francis Galton, "Opening Remarks by the President," *Journal of the Anthropological Institute of Great Britain and Ireland* 16 (1887): 189–90; quotation is from 189.

91. Galton, "Address Delivered of the Anniversary Meeting," 391.

92. For more on Pitt-Rivers, his collections, and the founding of the Pitt Rivers Museum, see William Ryan Chapman, "Arranging Ethnology: A. H. L. F. Pitt Rivers and the Typological Tradition," in *Objects and Others: Essays on Museums and Material Culture*, ed. George W. Stocking (Madison: University of Wisconsin Press, 1985), 15–48; and Alison Petch, "'Man as He Was and as He Is': Pitt Rivers's Collections," *Journal of the History of Collections* 1 (1998):75–85 and "Chance and Certitude: Pitt Rivers and His First Collection," *Journal of the History of Collections* 18 (2006): 257–66.

93. R. A. Cunningham, "Exhibition of Natives of Queensland," *Journal of the Anthropological Institute of Great Britain and Ireland* 17 (1888): 83–84; A. H. Keane, "On the Botocudos," *Journal of the Anthropological Institute of Great Britain and Ireland* 13 (1884): 199–213; Wilberforce Smith, "Teeth of Ten Sioux Indians," *Journal of the Anthropological Institute of Great Britain and Ireland* 24 (1895): 109–16; and W. L. H. Duckworth, "A Contribution to Eskimo Craniology," *Journal of the Anthropological Institute of Great Britain and Ireland* 30 (1900): 125–40.

94. W. H. R. Rivers, "[Communication from Dr. W. H. R. Rivers Regarding Exhibition of Human Specimens]," *Journal of the Anthropological Institute of Great Britain and Ireland* 30 (1900): 6–7.

95. Zimmerman, *Anthropology and Antihumanism*, especially 15–37.

96. In France, the Société Ethnologique de Paris was founded in 1839 and was followed by the Société d'Anthropologie de Paris in 1859. In the United States, although not a

primarily scholarly organization, the Bureau of Indian Affairs (founded 1824) contributed to the foundation of scholarly studies by supporting research into human variety. Later, the Smithsonian Institution's Bureau of American Ethnology was founded by an act of Congress in 1879. Meanwhile, the *Transactions of the Anthropological Society of Washington* (1879–83), *American Anthropologist* (founded 1888), and *Journal of the American Folklore* (founded 1888) all gave disciplinary voices to American anthropology.

97. Adam Kuper, *Anthropology and Anthropologist: The Modern British School* (London: Allen Lane, 1973); George W. Stocking, *After Tylor: British Social Anthropology, 1888–1951* (London: Athlone, 1995); and Kuklick, *The Savage Within*. Many histories of anthropology propose the late nineteenth century as the most appropriate period in which one can see the emergence of institutionalized anthropology, particularly due to the emergence of paid posts and the entrenchment of the discipline within political circles and higher education. The chronology given here differs in that it includes the establishment of the earliest learned societies, such as the ESL and ASL, within the discussion of institutionalization.

98. Rivers, "[Communication from Dr. W. H. R. Rivers Regarding Exhibition of Human Specimens]."

99. Wheeler, *The Complexion of Race*.

100. This has been noted in many histories of the shows. See Ames, *Carl Hagenbeck's Empire of Entertainments*; Zimmerman, *Anthropology and Antihumanism*; Rothfels, *Savages and Beasts*; and Parezo and Fowler, *Anthropology Goes to the Fair*.

101. German anthropologist Felix von Luschan found the same problem. Bismark Bell (Kwelle Ndumbe), a Duala dignitary, refused to be photographed in "native" garb, preferring a European dinner jacket as a sign of his social status. Luschan frequently vented against this resistance with the pejorative "trouser nigger." See Zimmerman, *Anthropology and Antihumanism*, 30–33.

102. William Rivers, "Report on Anthropological Research Outside America," in *Reports on the Present Condition and Future Needs of the Science of Anthropology*, ed. W. H. R. Rivers, A. E. Jenks, and S. G. Morley, Carnegie Publication 200 (Washington, DC: Carnegie Institution, 1913) 5–28; quotation is from p. 7.

103. Ibid., 6. For a classic discussion of this aspect of anthropological collecting, see Jacob W. Gruber, "Ethnographic Salvage and the Shaping of Anthropology," *American Anthropologist*, n.s., 72 (1970): 1289–99.

104. Bronislaw Malinowski, *Argonauts of the Western Pacific: An Account of Native Enterprise and Adventure in the Archipelagoes of Melanesian New Guinea* (London: Routledge, 1922); George W. Stocking, ed., *Rivers, Benedict, and Others: Essays on Culture and Personality* (Madison: University of Wisconsin Press, 1986); Michael W. Young, *Malinowski: Odyssey of an Anthropologist, 1884–1920* (New Haven, CT: Yale University Press, 2004); and Kuper, *Anthropology and Anthropologist*.

105. Compare Stocking, *Victorian Anthropology*; Stocking, *After Tylor*; and Kuklick's *The Savage Within* with Sera-Shriar, "Beyond the Armchair." In many histories of anthropology, fieldwork defines anthropological practice and is usually argued to have been transformed by, and after, the Torres Strait expedition of 1898 or the work of Malinowski. However, this overlooks the considerable effort earlier investigators expended to obtain information from reliable and direct observers, especially when they were unable to procure it personally. Prichard, for example, consistently

preferred the work of missionaries, because he felt their extended contact with indigenous peoples made them more reliable sources than other travelers. In some senses the discussion of in-situ observation presented here is analogous to how historians of science have characterized the rise of the laboratory in the natural sciences in the nineteenth century. Despite having been in existence from the early modern period, laboratories did not become the defining feature of work deemed scientific until the late 1800s. See Shapin and Schaffer, *Leviathan and the Air-Pump*; Gooday, "Nature in the Laboratory"; and de Chadaverian, "Laboratory Science versus Country-House Experiments."

106. Rivers, "[Communication from Dr. W. H. R. Rivers Regarding Exhibition of Human Specimens]," 7.

107. Edward B. Tylor, *Primitive Culture: Researches into the Development of Mythology, Philosophy, Religion, Art and Custom*, 2 vols. (London: John Murray, 1871); Sir James Frazer, *The Golden Bough: A Study in Comparative Religion* (London: Macmillan, 1890).

108. Tylor, *Primitive Culture*, 1:1.

109. Anita Herle and Sandra Rouse, eds., *Cambridge and the Torres Strait: Centenary Essays on the 1898 Anthropological Expedition* (Cambridge: Cambridge University Press, 1998).

110. Herbert Spencer, *The Principles of Sociology*, 2 vols. (New York: D. Appleton, 1882), 1:87; and W. H. R. Rivers, "Primitive Color Vision," *Popular Science Monthly* 59 (1901): 44–58.

111. W. H. R. Rivers, "A Genealogical Method of Collecting Social and Vital Statistics," *Journal of the Anthropological Institute of Great Britain and Ireland* 30 (1900): 74–82.

112. Ibid., 75.

113. Ibid., 74.

114. A. C. Haddon, "President's Address: Anthropology, its Position and Needs," *Journal of the Anthropological Institute of Great Britain and Ireland* 33 (1903): 11–23; quotation is from pp. 22–23.

115. A. C. Haddon, "The Ethnography of the Western Tribe of Torres Straits," *Journal of the Anthropological Institute of Great Britain and Ireland* 19 (1890): 297–440; quotation is from pp. 297–298.

116. Gruber, "Ethnographic Salvage and the Shaping of Anthropology."

117. Patrick Bratlinger, *Dark Vanishings: Discourse on the Extinction of Primitive Races, 1800–1930* (Ithaca, NY: Cornell University Press, 2003), and Lyndall Ryan, *The Aboriginal Tasmanians* (St. Lucia, Queensland, Australia: University of Queensland Press, 1981).

118. A. C. Haddon, "President's Address," 23.

119. Rivers, "Report on Anthropological Research Outside America," 6. For Rivers, these old men were the only hope for a generation of anthropologists. "The brightest side of the matter is the extent and fidelity of the memories of ancient times. Nearly everywhere, among rude peoples whose culture is vanishing, there are to be found old men, often more alert and mentally vigorous than their juniors, who seem to be inspired by a fervor fit to be called religious, as it is found how closely and exactly they have preserved in their memories the minute details of rites and customs which they have had no opportunity of practising for years. Such old men have only to meet one in whom they recognize an interest akin to their own to become fountains of knowledge which seem almost inexhaustible, and yet each case of

this kind only brings more forcibly to the mind how great would be the loss when these fountains have been dried by the inevitable consequences of a few years' delay" (ibid.). Moreover, these laments were not new. See, for example, James Cowles Prichard, "On the Extinction of Human Races," *Edinburgh New Philosophical Journal* 28 (1839): 166–70.

120. Duckworth, "A Contribution to Eskimo Craniology," and W. Smith, "Teeth of Ten Sioux Indians."

121. For U.S. anthropology see L. Baker, *From Savage to Negro*, and Rydell, *All the World's a Fair*; for French anthropology see Elizabeth Williams, *The Physical and the Moral: Anthropology, Physiology and Philosophical Medicine in France, 1750–1850* (Cambridge: Cambridge University Press, 1994); for German anthropology see Zimmerman, *Anthropology and Antihumanism*.

122. "A typical piece of intensive work is one in which the worker lives for a year or more among a community of perhaps four or five hundred people and studies every detail of their life and culture; in which he comes to know every member of the community personally; in which he is not content with generalized information, but studies every feature of life and custom in concrete detail and by means of the vernacular language. . . . It is only by such work that it is possible to discover the incomplete and even misleading character of much of the vast mass of survey work which forms the existing material of anthropology." Rivers, "Report on Anthropological Research Outside America," 7.

123. See Rydell, *All the World's a Fair*; Rydell, *World of Fairs*; Greenhalgh, *Ephemeral Vistas*; and Zimmerman, *Anthropology and Antihumanism*.

124. On Prichard and the Mandinka, see Augstein, *James Cowles Prichard's Anthropology*, 10.

Conclusion

1. Poster and leaflet for the Cambridge Corn Exchange, spring 2002; author's collection.

2. Ames, *Carl Hagenbeck's Empire of Entertainments*.

3. By contrast, French exhibitions were far more likely to feature performers drawn from West Africa, especially the Dahomey. See Schneider, *An Empire for the Masses*, 125–51; and Dana S. Hale, *Races on Display: French Representations of Colonized Peoples, 1886–1940* (Bloomington: Indiana University Press, 2008).

4. Rydell, *World of Fairs* and *All the World's a Fair*; Parezo and Fowler, *Anthropology Goes to the Fair*.

5. Abrahams, "Images of Sara Bartman," 225.

6. Poignant, *Professional Savages*, 4.

7. These histories are, of course, drawing on the widespread use of binary oppositions as a means of historical analysis. For a particularly pertinent, and now classic, example of such a model, see the use of *Orient* and *Occident* in Edward Said, *Orientalism: Western Conceptions of the Orient* (London: Routledge and Kegan Paul, 1978). See also the characterization of imperialism as masculine and white in Anne McClintock, *Imperial Leather: Race, Gender and Sexuality in the Colonial Context* (London: Routledge, 1995). Although, as suggested here, these models are still widely used, the polarization they engender has been subject to considerable and longstanding criticism. For a discussion of how the use of *Orient* and *Occident* shapes

an essentialist view of European peoples, see James Clifford, "On Orientalism," in *The Predicament of Culture*, 255–76. For an overview of recent critical approaches, see D. A. Washbrook, "Orients and Occidents: Colonial Discourse Theory and the Historiography of the British Empire," in *Historiography*, ed. Robin W. Winks, vol. 5 of *OHBE* (Oxford: Oxford University Press, 1999), 597–611; and Patrick Wolfe, "History and Imperialism: A Century of Theory, from Marx to Postcolonialism," *American Historical Review* 102 (1997): 388–420. See also Homi K. Bhabha, *The Location of Culture* (London: Routledge, 1994). Following the lead of Bhabha, there has also been a considerable literature devoted to detailing the phenomenon of hybridity that helps to break down polarized models of intercultural contact.

8. Corbey, "Ethnographic Showcases," 341.

9. Maxwell, *Colonial Photography*, 2–3.

10. Examples of historians using color as a means of defining human variety before the late nineteenth century include Sander Gilman, *Difference and Pathology: Stereotypes of Sexuality, Race and Madness* (Ithaca, NY: Cornell University Press, 1985); Anne Fausto-Sterling, "Gender, Race and Nation: The Comparative Anatomy of "Hottentot" Women in Europe, 1815–1817," in *Deviant Bodies: Critical Perspectives on Difference in Science and Popular Culture*, ed. Jennifer Terry and Jacqueline Urla (Bloomington: Indiana University Press, 1995), 19–48; and Abrahams, "Disempowered to Consent" and "Images of Sara Baartman." For just some examples of literature dealing with the contingency of "whiteness" and "blackness," see Stuart Hall, "New Ethnicities," in *Black Film, British Cinema*, Institute of Contemporary Arts Documents 7 (London: Institute of Contemporary Arts, 1989), 27–31; David R. Roediger, *Working toward Whiteness: How America's Immigrants Became White; The Strage Journey from Ellis Island to theSuburbs* (New York: Basic Books, 2005); Algernon Austin, *Achieving Blackness: Race, Black Nationalism and Afrocentrism in the Twentieth Century* (New York: New York University Press, 2006); and Ruth Frankenberg, ed., *Displacing Whiteness: Essays in Social and Cultural Criticism* (Durham, NC: Duke University Press, 1997).

11. For a recent discussion of the problems associated with such anachronistic chromatism, with specific reference to literary and historical studies of the eighteenth century, see Wheeler, *The Complexion of Race*.

12. For examples see accounts of Robert Knox's lecture in chapter 4 of the present text; Anon., *Now Exhibiting at the Egyptian Hall*; Lichtenstein, *Travels in South Africa*; and Prichard, *The Natural History of Man*. For a more extended account of how the notion of blackness has been developed as an ahistorical category that erases differences between people of the same color in relationship to human display, see Magubane, "Which Bodies Matter?"

13. For an account of differences in British populations, see Kidd, *British Identities before Nationalism*.

14. Otter's *The Victorian Eye* provides a recent and helpful critique of the notion of spectacle.

15. "Our Weekly Gossip," *Athenaeum*, May 29, 1847, pp. 573–74.

16. Fyfe and Lightman, *Science in the Marketplace*. For an overview of these debates, see Jonathan Topham, ed., "Focus: Historicizing 'Popular Science,'" *Isi* 100 (2009): 310–68.

17. Blanchard et al., *Human Zoos*, 1–49; for quotation see 44n48.

18. In addition to the British efforts documented in chapters 6 and 7, it is worth noting that Harvard professor F. W. Putnam wanted to use his involvement in 1893 Chicago World's Fair to campaign for a permanent ethnological museum. Moreover, anthropologists' efforts were not limited to educating the public but extended to training a new generation of students. For example, at the University of Chicago anthropology students could receive credit for completing "The Louisiana Purchase Exposition Class in Ethnology," for which "the living exhibits along the Pike, in the Philippines exhibit, and in the Anthropology Department proper formed the nucleus of the course." Rydell, *All the World's A Fair*, 166.

19. For a helpful summary of the reasons scientists no longer routinely use the term *race*, see Kidd, *The Forging of Races*, 1–18.

20. Regrettably, despite its otherwise impressive documentation of anthropological involvement in the 1904 St. Louis World's Fair, Parezo and Fowler's *Anthropology Goes to the Fair* (307, 321, and 348) still employs the notion of pseudoscience to characterize such interest. For a discussion of the developments with respect to the history of science, see Golinski, *Making Natural Knowledge*. Among the earliest and most seminal works in this respect remains Shapin and Schaffer, *Leviathan and the Air-Pump*, and Steven Shapin, *A Social History of Truth: Civility and Science in Seventeenth-Century England* (Chicago: University of Chicago Press, 1994). For an introductory overview of some of the philosophical perspectives on this issue, see A. F. Chalmers, *What Is this Thing Called Science?*, 2nd ed. (Mliton Keynes, UK: Open University Press, 1982).

21. Nina Glick Schiller, Data Dea, and Markus Höhne, *African Culture and the Zoo in the 21st Century: The "African Village" in the Augsburg Zoo and Its Wider Implications* (Halle: Max Planck Institute for Social Anthropology, 2005).

22. "MoD builds Afghan Village in Norfolk," *Telegraph*, May 1, 2009; online at http://www .telegraph.co.uk/news/newstopics/onthefrontline/5256219/MoD-builds-Afghan-village-in-Norfolk.html; "Soldiers on Excercise at Mock Afghan Village," online at http://www.army.mod.uk/news/15236.aspx; and Deborah Haynes, "Afghan War Games Shatter Peace in Deepest Norfolk Countryside," *Times*, June 11, 2009; online at http://www.timesonline.co.uk/tol/news/uk/article6474648.ece. All articles accessed November 9, 2009.

23. Coco Fusco, "The Other History of Intercultural Performance," in *English is Broken Here* (New York: New Press, 1995), 37–63; quotation is from p. 39.

24. Ibid., 47; added emphasis. For more on Fusco's work, see Ruth Behar and Bruce Mannheim, "In Dialogue: The Couple in the Cage; A Guatinaui Odyssey," *Visual Anthropology Review* 11 (1995): 118–27; and Barbara Kirshenblatt-Gimblett, "The Ethnographic Burlesque," *Drama Review* 42 (1998): 175–80.

25. Fusco's analysis of visitor responses is most interesting when she begins to differentiate them on the basis of gender, social background, and ethnic origin. Despite the sometimes significant differences, the concern with authenticity and literalism emerges as an almost universal response.

26. Gilman, *Difference and Pathology*, has been the root of much of this research. For an overview of these developments, see Magubane, "Which Bodies Matter?" and Qureshi, "Displaying Sara Baartman."

27. Obed Zilwa, "Sold as a Slave, Exhibited as a Freak, Sarah Finds Dignity After 200 Years," *Independent*, August 10, 2002, p. 12.

28. Magubane, "Which Bodies Matter?"
29. Crais and Scully, *Sara Baartman and the Hottentot Venus*, 149–69, is a fascinating account of the many interest groups involved in Baartman's return.
30. Poignant, *Professional Savages*, 241 and 254, respectively.
31. For the most recent government report on the issue of human remains in British collections, see Great Britain, Working Group on Human Remains in Museum Collections, *The Working Group on Human Remains Report* (London: Department for Culture, Media and Sport, 2003).
32. Abrahams, for instance, argues that the "fairly typical ... approach of white male academics to the study of Sara Bartman" is best described as "analysis [replaced] with name calling." Abrahams, "Images of Sarah Bartman," 222.

BIBLIOGRAPHY

Collections of Ephemera and Advertising

Evanion Collection, British Library, London
John Johnson Collection of Printed Ephemera, Bodleian Library, Oxford
Print Collections, Guildhall Library, London
Prints Collections, London Metropolitan Archives

Periodicals

Unless otherwise indicated, all periodicals were published in London.

Aberdeen Weekly Journal
Age and Argus
Athenaeum
Belfast News-Letter
Bell's Life in London and Sporting Chronicle
Crystal Palace Herald
Daily News
Dart: The Birmingham Pictorial
Eclectic Review
Edinburgh Review
English Gentleman
Funny Folks
Graphic
Guardian
Hearth and Home
Horse and Hound
Household Words
Illustrated Crystal Palace Gazette
Illustrated London News
Illustrated Magazine of Art
Illustrated Police News
Independent
John Bull
Judy
Lady's Newspaper
Lloyd's Weekly Newspaper
Lancet
Mirror of Literature, Amusement and
    Instruction
Morning Advertiser
Morning Chronicle
Morning Herald
Morning Post
Owl (Cape Town)
Pall Mall Gazette
Pictorial Times
Punch, or the London Charivari
Quarterly Review
Reynolds's Newspaper
Sporting Times
Telegraph
Times
Western Mail (Cardiff)

Primary Sources

Sources that were reprinted after 1914 but originally published before 1914 are included here.

Anonymous. "Anthropological News." *Anthropological Review* 5 (1867): 240–56.

———. *The Erdermänner; or, Earthmen from the Orange River in Southern Africa*. London: John K. Chapman, 1853.

———. "The Erdmannings; or, Earthmen of Africa; Their Country and History." In *Illustrated Memoir of an Eventful Expedition into Central America Resulting in the Discovery of the Idolatrous City on Iximaya, in an Unexplored Region; and the Possession of Two Remarkable Aztec Children, Maximo (the Boy) and Bartola (the Girl) Descendants and Specimens of the Sacerdotal Caste (Now Nearly Extinct) of the Ancient Aztec Founders of the Ruined Temples of that Country, Described by John L. Stephens; Esq. and Other Travellers*, by Pedro Velasquez, 41–48. New York: Wynkoop, Hallenbeck and Thomas, 1860.

———. "Exchange by William Craft and Dr. James Hunt at the Annual Meeting of the British Association for the Advancement of Science, Newcastle-upon-Tyne, England, 27 August, 1863." In *The Black Abolitionist Papers*, edited by C. P. Ripley, 1:537–43. Chapel Hill: University of North Carolina Press, 1985.

———. *Final Close of the St. George's Gallery, Hyde Park Corner, Piccadilly. Zulu Kafirs. Last Few Days in London*. London: W. J. Goulbourn, 1853.

———. *History of the Bosjesmans, or Bush people: The Aborigines of Southern Africa; With Copious Extracts from the Best Authors, Showing the Habits and Disposition of the Above-Named Extraordinary Race of Human Being*. [London]: Chapman, Elcoate, 1847.

———. *An Interesting Account of Those Extraordinary People the Esquimaux Indians, from Baffin's Bay, North Pole: To Which is Affixed, a Vocabulary of Esquimaux Words, Translated into English by George Niagungitok; And a Catalogue of the Museum of Natural and Artificial Curiosities, Which Accompany the Exhibition of the Esquimaux Indians*. Sheffield: George Ridge, n.d. [circa early 1820s].

———. *The Language of the Walls: And a Voice from the Shop Windows; Or, The Mirror of Commercial Roguery, By One who Thinks Aloud*. Manchester: Abel Haywood, 1855.

———. *Now Exhibiting at the Egyptian Hall, Piccadilly: The Bosjesmans, or Bush People, from the Interior of South Africa, Who First Appeared at the Exeter Hall, on Monday, 17th May; The only Real Specimens of This Extraordinary and Rapidly Decreasing Race of Human Beings Who Have Ever Visited Europe*. London: Chapman, Elcoate, 1847.

———. "Queries Respecting the Human Race, to be Addressed to Travellers and Others: Drawn up by a Committee of the British Association for the Advancement of Science, appointed in 1839." In *BAAS Official Report*, 332–39. London: John Murray, 1841.

———. "A South African Native's Picture of England." *Munger Africana Library Notes* 9 (1979): 8–19. Originally published in *Natal Journal* 2 (1858): 126–38.

Arbousset, T., and F. Daumas. *Narrative of an Explanatory Tour to the North East of the Colony of the Cape of Good Hope by the Revs T. Arbousset and F. Daumas, of the Paris Missionary Society*. Translated by John Corumbie. Cape Town: A. S. Robertson and S. Solomon, 1846.

Backhouse, James. *Observations Submitted in Brotherly Love to the Missionaries and other Gospel Labourers in South Africa, 1840*. Cape Town: Saul Solomon, 1840.

Baedeker, Karl. *Paris and its Environs: With Routes from London to Paris, and from Paris to the Rhine and Switzerland*. 6th ed. Leipsic: Karl Baedeker, 1878.

Bee, John [John Badock]. *A Living Picture of London for 1828, and Stranger's Guide through the Streets of the Metropolis: Shewing the Frauds, the Arts, the Snares and Wiles of All Descriptions of Rogues, that Every Where Abound; with Suitable Admonitions, Precautions and Advice How to Avoid or Defeat their Attempts; Interspersed with Sketches of Cockney Manners, Life, Society, and Customs; And Supported Throughout by Numerous Cases, Anecdotes, and Personal Adventures.* London: W. Clarke, 1828.

Booth, William. *In Darkest England and the Way Out.* London: Salvation Army, 1890.

Boulton, William Biggs. *The Amusements of Old London: Being a Survey of the Sports and Pastimes, Tea Gardens and Parks, Playhouses and Other Diversions of the People of London from the 17th to the Beginning of the 19th Century.* London: Nimmo, 1901.

Brodie, Benjamin C. "Address to the Ethnological Society of London, Delivered at the Anniversary Meeting on the 27th May 1853, by Sir B. C. Brodie, Bart. D.C.L. F.R.S. President." *Journal of the Ethnological Society of London* 4 (1856): 98–103.

Brooke, Sir Arthur de Capell. *Travels through Sweden, Norway, and Finmark to the North Cape, in the Summer of 1820.* London: Rockwell and Martin, 1823.

———. *A Winter in Lapland and Sweden, with Various Observations Relating to Finmark and its Inhabitants; Made during a Residence at Hammerfest, near the North Cape.* London: John Murray, 1827.

Buckland, A. W. "On Tattooing." *Journal of the Anthropological Institute of Great Britain and Ireland* 17 (1888): 318–28.

Bullock, William. *An Account of the Family of Laplanders: Which with their Summer and Winter Residences, Domestic Implements, Sledges, Herd of Living Reindeer; and Panoramic View of the North Cape (from a Drawing Lately Made on the Spot by Capt. Brooke, to Whom the Proprietor is Indebted for Permission to Exhibit it) are Now Exhibiting at the Egyptian Hall, Piccadilly.* London: James Bullock, 1822.

———. *A Companion to the London Museum and Pantherion Containing a Brief Description of Upwards of Fifteen Thousand Natural and Foreign Curiosities, Antiquities and Productions of Fine Arts.* London, 1813.

Caldecott, C[harles] H[enry]. *Descriptive History of the Zulu Kafirs, their Customs and their Country, with Illustrations.* London: John Mitchell, 1853.

———. *Exhibition of Native Zulu Kafirs: St Georges Gallery, Hyde Park Corner, Piccadilly.* London: John Mitchell, 1853.

Catlin, George. *Adventures of the Ojibbeway and Ioway Indians in England, France, and Belgium: Being Notes of Eight Years' Travels and Residence in Europe with his North American Indian Collection.* 3rd ed. 2 vols. London: published by the author, 1852.

———. *Catlin's North American Indian Portfolio: Hunting Scenes and Amusements of the Rocky Mountains and Prairies of America, From Drawings and Notes of the Author, Made during Eight Years' Travel amongst Forty-Eight of the Wildest and Most Remote Tribes of Savages in North America.* London: [published by the author], 1844.

———. *Illustrations of the Manners, Customs & Condition of the North American Indians. With Letters and Notes, Written During Eight Years of Travel and Adventure Among the Wildest and Most Remarkable Tribes Now Existing.* 2 vols. London: Chatto and Windus, Piccadilly, 1876.

———. *Notes of Eight Years' Travel and Residence in Europe, with his North American Indian Collection.* 2 vols. London: [published by the author], 1848.

———. *Unparalleled Exhibition: The Fourteen Ioway Indians and their Interpreter, Just Arrived from the Upper Missouri, near the Rocky Mountains, North America.* London: W. S. Johnson, 1844.

Chabert, X. *A Brief Historical Account of the Life and Adventures of the Botocudo Chieftain, and Family, Now Exhibiting at No. 23, New Bond Street: Together with a Faithful Description of the Manners and Customs of the Savage Inhabitants of the Country They Come From*. London: C. Baynes, 1822.

[Chambers, Robert]. *The Book of Days: A Miscellany of Popular Antiquities in Connection with the Calendar*. 2 vols. London: W. & R. Chambers, 1863.

———. *Vestiges of the Natural History of Creation*. London: John Churchill, 1844.

Clarke, Robert. "Sketches of the Colony of Sierra Leone and its Inhabitants." *Transactions of the Ethnological Society of London* 2 (1863): 320–63.

[Colonial and Indian Exhibition]. *Catalogue of the Exhibits of the Colony of the Cape of Good Hope*. London: Richards, Glanville, 1886.

———. *Colonial and Indian Exhibition: Official Catalogue*. London: William Clowes and Sons, 1886.

Conolly, John. *The Ethnological Exhibitions of London*. London: John Churchill, 1855.

Cull, Richard. "A Description of Three Esquimaux." *Journal of the Ethnological Society of London* 4 (1854): 215–25.

———. "On the Recent Progress of Ethnology: Being the Annual Discource for 1852." *Journal of the Ethnological Society of London* 3 (1854): 165–77.

Cundall, Frank. *Reminiscences of the Colonial and Indian Exhibition*. London: William Clowes and Sons, 1886.

Cunningham, R[obert] A. "Exhibition of Natives of Queensland." *Journal of the Anthropological Institute of Great Britain and Ireland* 17 (1888): 83–84.

———. *History of R. A. Cunningham's Australian Aborigines, Tattooed Cannibal Black Trackers and Boomerang Throwers, Consisting of Two Tribes, Male and Female*. London: J. Elliot, 1884.

Cuvier, Georges. "Extrait d'Observations faites sur le Cadavre d'une Femme Connue á Paris et á Londres sous le Nom de Vénus Hottentotte." *Mémoires des Muséum d'Histoire Naturelle* 3 (1817): 259–74.

———. "Une Femme de Race Boschismanne." In *Histoire Naturelle Des Mammifères*, by Etienne Geoffroy Saint-Hilaire and Frédérick Cuvier, 1:1–4. Paris: A. Belin, 1824.

C. W. D. "Flower and Murie on the Dissection of a Bushwoman." *Anthropological Review* 5 (1867): 319–24.

Davis, Joseph Barnard. "Contributions towards Determining the Weight of the Brain in Different Races of Man." *Philosophical Transactions of the Royal Society of London* 158 (1868): 505–27.

Delamotte, Philip H. *Photographic Views of the Crystal Palace Sydenham, Taken during the Progress of the Works*. 2 vols. London: Photographic Institution, 1854.

Dickens, Charles. Letter to John Leech [23 May 1853]. In *The Letters of Charles Dickens*, edited by Madeline House and others, 7:91. Oxford: Clarendon Press, 1993.

———. *Sketches by "Boz," Illustrative of Every-day Life and Every-day People*. London: John Macrone, 1836. Reprint, London: Penguin, 1995.

Dieffenbach, Ernest. "The Study of Ethnology." *Journal of the Ethnological Society of London* 1 (1848): 15–26.

Dinsdale, John. *Sketches of the Colonial and Indian Exhibition*. 2 vols. London: Jordison, 1886.

Doré, Gustave, and Jerrold Blanchard. *London: A Pilgrimage*. London: Grant and Co., 1872. Reprint, New York: Dover, 1970.

Duckworth, W. L. H. "A Contribution to Eskimo Craniology." *Journal of the Anthropological Institute of Great Britain and Ireland* 30 (1900): 125–40.

Equiano, Olaudah. *The Interesting Narrative of the Life of Olaudiah Equiano; or, Gustav Vassa, the African: An Authoritative Text Written by Himself.* London: printed for and sold by the author, 1789.

Esquiros, Alphonse. *Religious Life in England.* London: Chapman and Hall, 1867.

Flourens, Marie-Jean-Pierre. "On the Natural History of Man." *Edinburgh New Philosophical Journal* 27 (1839): 351–58.

Flower, W[illiam] H[enry], and J[ames] Murie. "Account of the Dissection of a Bushwoman." *Journal of Anatomy and Physiology* (1867): 189–208.

Fontane, Theodore. *Journeys to England in Victoria's Early Days.* Translated by Dorothy Harrison. London: Massie Publishing, 1939. Edited by E. M. Butler, London: Collins, 1957.

Fraser, James Baillie. *Narrative of the Residence of the Persian Princes in London, in 1835 and 1836.* London: Richard Bentley, 1838.

Frazer, Sir James. *The Golden Bough: A Study in Comparative Religion.* London: Macmillan, 1890.

Frost, Thomas. *Circus Life and Circus Celebrities.* London: Tinsley Brothers, 1875.

———. *The Old Showmen and the Old London Fairs.* London: Tinsley Brothers, 1874.

Galton, Francis. "Address Delivered of the Anniversary Meeting of the Anthropological Institute of Great Britain and Ireland, January 25th, 1887." *Journal of the Anthropological Institute of Great Britain and Ireland* 16 (1887): 386–402.

———. "Opening Remarks by the President." *Journal of the Anthropological Institute of Great Britain and Ireland* 16 (1887): 175–77.

———. "Opening Remarks by the President." *Journal of the Anthropological Institute of Great Britain and Ireland* 16 (1887): 189–90.

Goldsmith, Oliver. *The Citizen of the World; or, Letters from a Chinese Philosopher, Residing in London, to his Friends in the Country.* London: C. Cooke, 1799.

Guthrie, Thomas. *A Plea for Ragged Schools: Prevention Better than Cure.* Edinburgh: John Elder, William Collins, and James Nisbet, 1847.

Haddon, A. C. "The Ethnography of the Western Tribe of Torres Straits." *Journal of the Anthropological Institute of Great Britain and Ireland* 19 (1890): 297–440.

———. "President's Address: Anthropology, its Position and Needs." *Journal of the Anthropological Institute of Great Britain and Ireland* 33 (1903): 11–23.

Hausdoerfer, John. *Catlin's Lament: Indians, Manifest Destiny and the Ethics of Nature.* Lawrence: University of Kansas Press, 2009.

Heine, Heinrich. "London." In *London, 1066–1914,* edited by Xavier Baron, 2:230–34. The Banks, East Sussex: Helm Information, 1997. Originally published in *English Fragments from the German of Heinrich Heine,* translated by Sarah Norris (Edinburgh: R. Grant and Son, 1880).

Henry, George, [Maungwudaus]. *An Account of the Chippewa Indians, who have been Travelling Among the Whites, in the United States, England, Ireland, Scotland and Belgium: With Very Interesting Incidents in Relation to the General Characteristics of the English, Irish, Scotch, French and Americans, with Regard to Their Hospitality, Peculiarities, etc.* Boston: published by the author, 1848.

———. *Remarks Concerning Ojibway Indians, by One of Themselves Called Maungwudaus, Who Has Been Travelling in England, France, Belgium, Ireland, and Scotland.* Leeds: C. A. Wilson, 1847.

Hodgkin, Thomas. "The Progress of Ethnology." *Journal of the Ethnological Society of London* 1 (1848): 27–45.

———. "Obituary: Dr. Prichard." *Lancet* 1 (1849): 18–19.

———. "Obituary: Dr. Prichard." *Journal of the Ethnological Society of London* 2 (1850): 182–207.

Hodgkin, Thomas, and Richard Cull. "A Manual of Ethnological Inquiry: Being a Series of Questions concerning the Human Race, Prepared by a Sub-Committee of the British Association for the Advancement of Science, Appointed in 1851 (Consisting of Dr. Hodgkin and Richard Cull, Esq.) and Adapted for the Use of Travellers and Others in Studying the Varieties of Man." In *BAAS Official Report*, 243–52. London: John Murray, 1852.

[Hodgkin, Thomas, Richard Cull, and James C. Prichard]. *A Manual of Ethnological Inquiry: Being a Series of Questions concerning the Human Race, Prepared by a Sub-Committee of the British Association for the Advancement of Science, Appointed in 1851, and Adapted for the Use of Travellers and Others, in Studying the Varieties of Man.* London: Taylor and Francis, 1852.

Hunt, James. *Introductory Address on the Study of Anthropology, Delivered before the Anthropological Society of London, February 24th, 1863.* [London], 1863.

———. "On Anthropological Classification." In *BAAS Official Report*, 139–40. London: John Murray, 1863.

———. "On the Physical and Mental Characteristics of the Negro." In *BAAS Official Report*, 140. London: John Murray, 1863.

Huxley, Thomas H. "On the Methods and Results of Ethnology." In *Man's Place in Nature: And Other Anthropological Essays*, 209–52. London: Macmillan, [1865] 1900.

Isaacs, Nathaniel. *Travels and Adventures in Eastern Africa, Descriptive of the Zoolus, their Manners, and Customs, with a Sketch of Natal.* 2 vols. London: E. Churton, 1836.

Jackson, Andrew. "First Annual Message, Dec. 8 1829." In *Messages of Gen. Andrew Jackson with a Short Sketch of his Life*, edited by N. H. Concord, 39–68. Boston [MA?]: John F. Brown and William White, 1837.

Keane, A. H. "On the Botocudos." *Journal of the Anthropological Institute of Great Britain and Ireland* 13 (1884): 199–213.

King, Richard. *Address to the Ethnological Society of London, Delivered at the Anniversary Meeting, 1844.* London: W. Watts, 1844.

Kiralfy, Bolossy. *Creator of Great Musical Spectacles: An Autobiography.* Edited by Barbara M. Barker. Ann Arbor: UMI Research Press, 1988.

Knight, Charles. *London Pictorially Illustrated.* 6 vols. London: Charles Knight, 1841–44.

Knox, Robert. *The Races of Men: A Fragment.* London: Henry Renshaw, 1850.

———. *The Races of Men: A Philosophical Inquiry into the Influence of Race over the Destinies of Nations.* 2nd ed. London: Henry Renshaw, 1862.

———. "Some Remarks on the Aztecque and Bosjieman Children, Now Being Exhibited in London, and on the Races to Which They Are Presumed to Belong." *Lancet*, April 7, 1855, pp. 357–60.

Kolben, Peter. *The Present State of the Cape of Good-Hope: or, a Particular Account of the Several Nations of the Hottentots: Their Religion, Government, Laws, Customs,*

Ceremonies, and Opinions; Their Art of War, Possessions, Language, Genius, &c., translated by Mr. Medley, 2 vols. London: W. Innys, 1731.

Kolliker, A. *Manual of Human Histology*. Translated and edited by George Busk and Thomas H. Huxley. London: Sydenham Society, 1853.

Lamb, Charles. Letter to William Wordsworth [30 January 1801]. In *Selected Letters of Charles Lamb*, edited by G. T. Clapton, 75–79. London: Methuen, 1925.

———. "The Londoner." In *The Collected Essays of Charles Lamb*, with an introduction by Robert Lynd and notes by William Macdonald, 2:6–8. London: Dent, 1929.

Lamprey, John. "On a Method of Measuring the Human Form for Students of Ethnology." *Journal of the Ethnological Society*, n.s., 1 (1869): 84–85.

Latham, Robert Gordon. *Descriptive Ethnology*. 2 vols. London: John van Voorst, 1859.

———. *The English Language*. London: [Taylor and Walton], 1841.

———. *The Ethnology of the British Colonies and Dependencies*. London: John van Voorst, 1851.

———. *The Ethnology of the British Islands*. London: John van Voorst, 1852.

———. *The Ethnology of Europe*. London: John van Voorst, 1852.

———. "Ethnological Remarks upon Some of the More Remarkable Varieties of Human Species, Represented by Individuals Now in London." In *BAAS Official Report*, 88. London: John Murray, 1853.

———. "Ethnological Remarks upon Some of the More Remarkable Varieties of Human Species, Represented by Individuals Now in London." *Journal of the Ethnological Society of London* 4 (1856): 148–50.

———. *History and Ethnology of the English Language*. London, 1849.

———. "On the Present State and Recent Progress of Ethnographical Philology." In *BAAS Official Report*, 154–29. London: John Murray, 1847.

Latham, Robert Gordon, and Edward Forbes. *A Hand Book to the Courts of Natural History Described*. London: Bradbury and Evans, 1854.

———. *The Natural History of the Varieties of Man*. London: John van Voorst, 1850.

Layard, Austen Henry. *The Monuments of Nineveh*. London: John Murray, 1849–53.

———. *Nineveh and its Remains*. London: John Murray, 1849.

———. *A Popular Account of Discoveries at Nineveh*. London: John Murray, 1852.

Lenihan, Maurice. *Limerick, its Histories and Antiquities, Ecclesiastical, Civil and Military*. Dublin: Hodges, Smith, 1866.

Lichtenstein, [Martin] Henry. *Travels in South Africa, in the Years 1803, 1804, 1805, 1806*. Translated by Anne Plumtre. 2 vols. London: [Henry Colburn], 1812–15.

Livingstone, David. *Missionary Travels and Researches in South Africa: Including a Sketch of Sixteen Years' Residence in the Interior of Africa, and a Journey from the Cape Of Good Hope to Loanda on the West Coast; Thence Across the Continent, Down the River Zambezi, to the Eastern Ocean*. New York: Harper and Brothers, 1858.

[Long, Edward]. *Candid Reflections upon the Judgement Lately Awarded by the Court of King's Bench in Westminster-Hall on What is Commonly Called the Negro-Cause, by a Planter*. London: T. Lowndes, 1772.

Lucett, M. *Rovings in the Pacific from 1837 to 1849, with a Glance at California, by a Merchant, Long Resident at Tahiti*. London: Longman, 1851.

Lysons, Daniel. "Collectanea; or, A Collection of Advertisements and Paragraphs from the Newspapers Relating to Various Subjects." 2 vols. Unpublished scrapbook, British Library, London.

———. "Collectanea; or, A Collection of Advertisements and Paragraphs from the Newspapers Relating to Various Subjects." 5 vols. Unpublished scrapbook, British Library, London.

Mann, Robert James. "The Kaffir Race of Natal." *Transactions of the Ethnological Society of London* 5 (1867): 277–97.

———. "Remarks on Some of the Races of South Africa Represented at the Exhibition." *Journal of the Anthropological Institute of Great Britain and Ireland* 16 (1887): 177–78.

Marshall, John. "On the Brain of a Bushwoman: And on the Brains of Two Idiots of European Descent." *Philosophical Transactions of the Royal Society of London* 154 (1864): 501–58.

Mathews, Mrs. [Anne]. *Memoirs of Charles Mathews, Comedian*. 4 vols. London: Richard Bentley, 1839.

Mayhew, Henry. *1851; or, The Adventures of Mr and Mrs Sandboys and Family, who Came up to London to Enjoy themselves and See the Great Exhibition*. London: David Bogue, 1851.

———. *London Labour and the London Poor: A Cyclopædia of the Condition and Earning of those that Will Work, those that Cannot Work, and those that Will Not Work*. 2 vols. London: Woodfall, 1851–52.

———. *London Labour and the London Poor*. 4 vols. London: Griffin, Bohn, 1861–62.

———. *The Unknown Mayhew: Selections from the* Morning Chronicle, *1849–50*. Edited by E. Thompson and Eileen Yeo. London: Merlin, 1971.

———. *Voices of the Poor: Selections from the* Morning Chronicle *"Labour and the Poor," 1849–1850*. Edited by Anne Humpherys. London: Cass, 1971.

[McDermott, Edward]. *Routledge's Guide to the Crystal Palace and Park at Sydenham: With Descriptions of the Principal Works of Science and Art, and of the Geological Formations, and Restoration of Extinct Animals, Therein Exhibited*. London: George Routledge, 1854.

Measom, George. *Crystal Palace Alphabet: A Guide for Good Children*. London, 1855.

Meerza, Najaf Koolee. *Journal of a Residence in England, and of a Journey from and to Syria*. London: privately printed, [1839].

Moffat, Robert. *Missionary Labours and Scenes on Southern Africa*. London: John Snow, 1842.

Montesquieu, Charles de Secondat. *Persian Letters*. Translated by Mr. Ozell. London: [J. Tonson], 1722.

Morgan, Lewis Henry. *Ancient Society; or, Researches in the Lines of Human Progress From Savagery, Through Barbarism To Civilization*. New York: Henry Holt, 1877.

Mudie, Robert. *Babylon the Great: A Dissection and Demonstration of Men and Things in the British Capital*. 2 vols. London: Charles Knight, 1828.

Mukharji, T[rilokya] N[ath]. *Visit to Europe*. Calcutta: W. Newman, 1889.

Murray, John Fisher. *The World of London*. 2 vols. London: William Blackwood and Sons, 1843.

Napier, Edward. *Excursions in Southern Africa: Including a History of the Cape Colony, an Account of the Native tribes*. London: W. Shoberl, 1849.

Noble, John, ed. *Official Handbook: History, Productions and Resources of the Cape of Good Hope*. Cape Town: Solomon, 1886.

Nott, J[osiah] C[lark] and Geo[rge]. R. Gliddon. *Types of Mankind: Or Ethnological*

Researchers based upon the Ancient Monuments, Paintings, Sculptures, and Crania of Races, and upon their Natural Geographical, Philological, and Biblical History; Illustrated by Selections from the Edited Papers of Samuel George Morton, MD (Late President of the Academy of Natural Sciences at Philadelphia) and by Additional Contributions from Prof. L. Aggassiz, LLD; W. Usher, MD; and Prof. H. S. Patterson, MD. Philadelphia: Lippincott, Grambo, & Co., 1854.

Owen, Richard, and Richard Cull. "A Brief Notice of the Aztec Race, and a Description of the So-Called Aztec Children." *Journal of the Ethnological Society of London* 4 (1856): 120–37.

Philips, Samuel. *Guide to the Crystal Palace and its Park, Sydenham.* 2nd ed. London: Bradbury and Evans, [1854].

Prichard, James Cowles. "Abstract of a Comparative Review of Philological and Physiological Researches as Applied to the History of the Human Species." In *BAAS Official Report*, 529–44. London: John Murray, 1831–32.

———. *The Eastern Origin of the Celtic Nations Proved by a Comparison of their Dialects with the Sanskrit, Greek, Latin, and Teutonic Languages, Forming a Supplement to Researches into the Physical History of Mankind.* Oxford: S. Collingwood, 1831.

———. *The Natural History of Man: Comprising Inquiries into the Modifying Influence of Physical and Moral Agencies on the Different Tribes of the Human Family.* London: Hippolyte Bailliere, 1843.

———. *The Natural History of Man: Comprising Inquiries into the Modifying Influence of Physical and Moral Agencies on the Different Tribes of the Human Family.* 2nd ed. enlarged. 2 vols. London: Hippolyte Bailliere, 1845.

———. *The Natural History of Man: Comprising Inquiries into the Modifying Influence of Physical and Moral Agencies on the Different Tribes of the Human Family.* 4th ed. Edited and enlarged by Edwin Norris. 2 vols. London: H. Bailliere, 1855.

———. "On the Extinction of Human Races." *Edinburgh New Philosophical Journal* 28 (1839): 166–70.

———. "On the Relations of Ethnology to Other Branches of Knowledge." *Journal of the Ethnological Society of London* 1 (1848): 301–29.

———. "On the Various Methods of Research Which Contribute to the Advancement of Ethnology, and of the Relations of that Science to Other Branches of Knowledge." In *BAAS Official Report*, 230–53. London: John Murray, 1847.

———. *Researches into the Physical History of Man.* London: J. and A. Arch, 1813.

———. *Researches into the Physical History of Mankind.* 2nd ed. 2 vols. London: J. and A. Arch, 1826.

———. *Researches into the Physical History of Mankind.* 3rd ed. London: Sherwood, Gilbert and Piper Arch 1836.

Pückler-Muskau, [Hermann]. *A Regency Visitor: The English Tour of Prince Pückler-Muskau Described in his Letters, 1826–1828.* Edited by E. M. Butler. Translated by Sarah Austin. London: Collins, 1957.

Rio, Don Antonio del. *Description of the Ruins of an Ancient City, Discovered near Palenque in the Kingdom of Guatemala, in Spanish America: Translated from the Original Manuscript Report by Captain Don Antonio Del Rio; Followed by Teatro Critico Americano; or, A Critical Investigation and Research into the History of the Americans, by Doctor Paul Felix Cabrera, of the City of New Guatemala.* London: Henry Berthoud, 1822.

Rivers, W. H. R. "[Communication from Dr. W. H. R. Rivers Regarding Exhibition of Human Specimens]." *Journal of the Anthropological Institute of Great Britain and Ireland* 30 (1900): 6–7.

———. "A Genealogical Method of Collecting Social and Vital Statistics." *Journal of the Anthropological Institute of Great Britain and Ireland* 30 (1900): 74–82.

———. "Primitive Color Vision." *Popular Science Monthly* 59 (1901): 44–58.

———. "Report on Anthropological Research Outside America." In *Reports on the Present Condition and Future Needs of the Science of Anthropology*, edited by W. H. R. Rivers, A. E. Jenks, and S. G. Morley, 5–28. Carnegie Publication 200. Washington, DC: Carnegie Institution, 1913.

Rosenberg. Adolf. *Geschichte des Kostüms in Chronologischer Entwicklung von A. Racinet*. Berlin: Verlag von Ernst Wasmuth, 1888.

Salter, Joseph. *The Asiatic in England: Sketches of Sixteen Years' Work Among Orientals*. London: Seeley, Jackson and Halliday, 1873.

Select Committee on Aborigines (British Settlements). *Report from the Select Committee on Aborigines (British Settlements): With the Minutes of Evidence, Appendix and Index*. London: House of Commons, 1837.

Simond, Louis. *Journal of a Tour and Residence in Great Britain, During the Years 1810 and 1811*. 2nd ed. Edinburgh: Archibald Constable, 1817.

Silliman, Benjamin. *A Journal of Travels in England, Holland and Scotland and of Two Passages Over the Atlantic, in the Years of 1805 and 1806: With Considerable Additions, Principally From the Original Manuscripts of the Author*. 3rd ed. 3 vols. New Haven, CT: S. Converse, 1820.

Smith, Andrew. *Report of the Expedition for Exploring Central Africa from the Cape of Good Hope*. Cape Town: [Government Gazette Office], 1836.

Smith, Wilberforce. "Teeth of Ten Sioux Indians." *Journal of the Anthropological Institute of Great Britain and Ireland* 24 (1895): 109–16.

Southey, Robert [Don Manuel Alvarez Espriella, pseud.]. *Letters from England*. London: Longman, 1807.

Spencer, Herbert. *The Principles of Sociology*. 2 vols. New York: D. Appleton, 1882.

Spix, Joh[ann] Bapt[ist] von, and C[arl] F[riedrich] Phil[ip] von Martius. *Travels in Brazil in the Years 1817–1820*. Trans. H. E. Lloyd. London: Longman, Rees, Hurst, Orme, Brown and Greene, 1824.

Stanley, Henry Morton. *In Darkest Africa; or, The Quest, Rescue, and Retreat of Emin, Governor of Equatoria*. London: Sampson Low, Marston, Searle and Rivington, 1890.

Stanley, Mrs H. M. [Dorothy Tennant]. *London Street Arabs*. London: Cassell, 1890.

Stephens, John L. *Incidents of Travel in Central America, Chiapas and Yucatan*. 2 vols. London: John Murray, 1841.

Sturt, Charles. *Narrative of an Expedition into Central Australia: During the Years 1844, 5 and 6, Together with a Notice of the Province of South Australia in 1847*. London: T. and W. Boone, 1849.

Tallis, John. *Tallis's History and Description of the Crystal Palace and the Exhibition of the World's Industry in 1851*. 3 vols. London: Tallis, 1852.

Thomson, William. *Crystal Palace, Sydenham: Natural History Department; Ethnological Collection*. (*A list of desiderata*.) London: [Crystal Palace Company], 1852.

———. *Crystal Palace, Sydenham. Natural History Department; Raw Produce Collection*. (*A list of desiderata*.) London: [Crystal Palace Company], 1852.

———. *Crystal Palace, Sydenham: Natural History Department; Zoological Collection.* (*A list of desiderata.*) London: [Crystal Palace Company], 1852.

Tiedemann, Frederick. "On the Brain of a Negro Compared with that of the European and the Ourang-Outang." *Philosophical Transactions of the Royal Society of London* 126 (1836): 497–558.

Tristan, Flora. *Flora Tristan's London Journal: A Survey of London Life in the 1830s.* Translated by Dennis Palmer and Giselle Pinceti. London, 1840. Reprint, London: Prior, 1980.

Tyler, J. S. *The Bosjesmans: A Lecture, on the Mental, Moral and Physical Attributes of the Bush Men.* Leeds: C. A. Wilson, [1847].

Tylor, Edward B. *Primitive Culture: Researches into the Development of Mythology, Philosophy, Religion, Art and Custom.* 2 vols. London: John Murray, 1871.

Velasquez, Pedro. *Life of the Living Aztec Children, Now Exhibiting at Barnum's American Museum, New York.* New York: Wynkoop, Hallenbeck and Thomas, 1860.

———. *Memoir of an Eventful Expedition into Central America, Resulting in the Discovery of the Idolatrous City of Iximaya, in an Unexplored Region: and the Possession of Two Remarkable Aztec Children, Maximo (the Man) and Bartola (the Woman) Descendents and Specimens of the Sacerdotal Cast (Now Nearly Extinct) of the Ancient Aztec Founders of the Ruined Temples of that Country Described by John L. Stephens, Esq. and Other Travellers.* London, 1853.

———. *Pagan Rites and Ceremonies of the Mayaboon Indians in the City of Iximaya in Central America.* London, 1853.

Virey, Julien-Joseph. *Natural History of The Negro Race.* Translated by J. H. Guenebault. Charleston, SC: D. J. Dowling, 1837.

Vogt, Carl. *Lectures on Man: His Place in Creation and in the History of the Earth.* London: Longman, Green, Longman and Roberts, 1864.

Ward, Harriet. *Five Years in Kaffirland: With Sketches of the Late War in that Country, to the Conclusion of Peace.* London: H. Colburn, 1848.

Wedderburn, Robert. *The Horrors of Slavery, and Other Writings.* Edited by Iain McCalman. Edinburgh: Edinburgh University Press, 1991.

(zu Wied), Prince Alexander Philip Maximilian. *Travels in Brazil in the Years 1815, 1816 and 1817.* Translated by H. E. Lloyd. London: Henry Colburn, 1820.

Woolnoth, Thomas. *Facts and Faces: Being an Enquiry into the Connection between Linear and Mental Portraiture, with a Dissertation on Personal and Relative Beauty.* 2nd ed. London: published by the author, 1854.

Wordsworth, William. *The Prelude: A Parallel Text.* Edited by J. C. Maxwell. London: Penguin, 1971.

Secondary Sources

Abrahams, Yvette. "Disempowered to Consent: Sara Bartman and Khoisan Slavery in the Nineteenth-Century Cape Colony and Britain." *South African Historical Journal* 35 (1996): 89–114.

———. "Images of Sara Bartman: Sexuality, Race and Gender in Early-Nineteenth-Century Britain." In *Nation, Empire, Colony: Historicizing Gender and Race*, edited by Ruth R. Pierson and Nupur Chaudry, 220–36. Bloomington: Indiana University Press, 1998.

Adas, Michael. *Machines as the Measure of Men: Science, Technology and Ideologies of Western Dominance*. Ithaca, NY: Cornell University Press, 1989.

Aguirre, Robert D. *Informal Empire: Mexico and Central America in the Victorian Culture*. Minneapolis: University of Minnesota Press, 2005.

Alexander, Michael. *Omai: Noble Savage*. London: Collins and Harvill Press, 1977.

Allen, Richard B. "Capital, Illegal Slaves, Indentured Labourers and the Creation of a Sugar Plantation Economy in Mauritius, 1810–60." *Journal of Imperial and Commonwealth History* 36 (2008): 151–70.

Altick, Richard D. *The Shows of London: A Panoramic History of Exhibitions, 1600–1862*. Cambridge, MA: Harvard University Press, Belknap Press, 1978.

Ames, Eric. *Carl Hagenbeck's Empire of Entertainments*. Seattle: University of Washington Press, 2009.

Anderson, Benedict. *Imagined Communities: Reflections on the Origins and Spread of Nationalism*. Rev. ed. London: Verso, 1991.

Anderson, Kay. *Race and the Crisis of Humanism*. London: Routledge, 2007.

Anderson, Patricia. *The Printed Image and the Transformation of Popular Culture, 1790–1860*. Oxford: Clarendon Press, 1991.

Anderson, Warwick. *The Cultivation of Whiteness: Science, Health and Racial Destiny in Australia*. New York: Basic Books, 2003.

Arberry, Arthur J. *The Library of the Indian Office: A Historical Sketch*. London: Secretary of State for India at the India Office, 1938.

Ashcroft, Bill, Gareth Griffiths, and Helen Tiffin. *The Empire Writes Back: Theory and Practice in Post-Colonial Literatures*. 2nd ed. London: Routledge, 2002.

Auerbach, Jeffrey A. *The Great Exhibition of 1851: A Nation on Display*. New Haven, CT: Yale University Press, 1999.

Augstein, Hannah F., ed. "From the Land of the Bible to the Caucasus and Beyond: The Shifting Ideas of the Geographical Origin of Humankind." In *Race, Science and Medicine, 1700–1960*, edited by Waltraud Ernst and Bernard Harris, 58–79. London: Routledge, 1999.

———. *James Cowles Prichard's Anthropology: Remaking the Science of Man in Early Nineteenth-Century Britain*. Amsterdam: Rodopi, 1999.

———, ed. *Race: The Origins of an Idea, 1760–1850*. Key Issues, no. 14. Bristol: Thoemmes, 1996.

Austin, Algernon. *Achieving Blackness: Race, Black Nationalism and Afrocentrism in the Twentieth Century*. New York: New York University Press, 2006.

Badou, Gérard. *L'Enigme de la Vénus Hottentote*. [Paris]: Lattès, 2000.

Bailey, Peter. *Leisure and Class in Victorian England: Rational Recreation and the Contest for Control, 1830–1885*. London: Routledge, 1987.

Baker, John R. *Race*. Oxford: Oxford University Press, 1974.

Baker, Lee D. *From Savage to Negro: Anthropology and the Construction of Race, 1896–1954*. Berkeley and Los Angeles: University of California Press, 1988.

Ball, Michael, and David Sutherland. *An Economic History of London*. London: Routledge, 2001.

Baratay, Eric, and Elisabeth Hardouin-Fugier. *Zoo: A History of Zoological Gardens in the West*. London: Reaktion, 2002.

Barnes, Barry. "On the Conventional Character of Knowledge and Cognition." *Philosophy of the Social Sciences* 11 (1981): 303–33.

———. "Ostensive Learning and Self-Referring Knowledge." In *Cognition and Social Worlds*, edited by Angus Gellatly, Don Rogers, and John A. Sloboda, 190–204. Oxford: Clarendon Press, 1989.

———. "Social Life as Bootstrapped Induction." *Sociology* 17 (1983): 524–45.

Baron, Sabrina Alcorn, ed. *The Reader Revealed*. Washington, DC: Folger Shakespeare Library, 2001.

Baron, Xavier, ed. *London, 1066–1914*. 3 vols. The Banks, East Sussex: Helm Information, 1997.

Barringer, Tim, and Tom Flynn, eds. *Colonialism and the Object: Empire, Material Culture and the Museum*. London: Routledge, 1998.

Barrows, Susanna. *Distorting Mirrors: Visions of the Crowd in Late Nineteenth-Century France*. London: Yale University Press, 1981.

Barth, Fredrik, et al. *One Discipline, Four Ways: British, German, French and American Anthropology*. Chicago: University of Chicago Press, 2005.

Barton, Ruth. "'Huxley, Lubbock, and Half a Dozen Others': Professionals and Gentlemen in the Formation of the X-Club, 1851–1864." *Isis* 89 (1998): 410–44.

———. "'An Influential Set of Chaps': The X-Club and Royal Society Politics, 1864–85." *British Journal for the History of Science* 23 (1990): 53–81.

———. "John Tyndall, Pantheist: A Rereading of the Belfast Address." *Osiris* 3 (1987): 111–34.

Bates, Crispin. "Race, Caste and Tribe in Central Asia: The Early Origins of Indian Anthropometry." In *The Concept of Race in South Asia*, edited by Peter Robb, 219–59. New Delhi: Oxford University Press, 1995.

Baxandall, Michael. *Painting and Experience in Fifteenth-Century Italy: A Primer in the Social History of Pictorial Style*. Oxford: Oxford University Press, 1988.

Bayly, Christopher A. *The Birth of the Modern World, 1780–1914: Global Connections and Comparisons*. Malden, MA: Blackwell, 2004.

———. "The First Age of Global Imperialism, 1760–1830." *Journal of Imperial and Commonwealth History* 26 (1998): 28–48.

———. *Imperial Meridian: The British Empire and the World, 1780–1830*. London: Longman, 1989.

Behar, Ruth, and Bruce Mannheim. "In Dialogue: The Couple in the Cage; A Guatinaui Odyssey." *Visual Anthropology Review* 11 (1995): 118–27.

Benedict, Barbara. *Curiosity: A Cultural History of Modern Enquiry*. Chicago: University of Chicago Press, 2001.

Benedict, Burton. *The Anthropology of World's Fairs: San Francisco's Panama Pacific International Exposition of 1915*. Berkeley, CA: Scolar Press, 1983.

———. "International Exhibitions and National Identity." *Anthropology Today* 7 (1991): 5–9.

Benjamin, Walter. *Charles Baudelaire: A Lyric Poet in the Era of High Capitalism*. Translated by Harry Zohn. London: New Left Books, 1973.

Bennett, Tony. *The Birth of the Museum: History, Theory, Politics*. London: Routledge, 1995.

———. "The Exhibitionary Complex." *New Formations* 4 (1988): 74–102.

Bhabha, Homi K. *The Location of Culture*. London: Routledge, 1994.

Biagioli, Mario. *Galileo, Courtier: The Practice of Science in the Culture of Absolutism*. Chicago: University of Chicago Press, 1993.

Bindman, David. *From Ape to Apollo: Aesthetics and the Idea of Race in the 18th Century*. London: Reaktion, 2002.

Black, Jeremy. *The English Press, 1621–1861*. Gloucestershire: Sutton, 2001.

Blanchard, Pascal, et al., eds. *Human Zoos: Science and Spectacle in the Age of Colonial Empires*. Translated by Teresa Bridgeman. Liverpool: Liverpool University Press, 2008.

Blondheim, Menahem. *News over the Wires: Telegraph and the Flow of Public Information in America, 1844–1897*. Cambridge, MA: Harvard University Press, 1994.

Blume, Harvey. "Ota Benga and the Barnum Complex." In Lindfors, ed., *Africans on Stage*, 188–202.

Blunt, Wilfred. *The Ark in the Park: The Zoo in the Nineteenth Century*. London: Hamilton, 1976.

Bogdan, Robert. *Freak Show: Presenting Human Oddities for Amusement and Profit*. Chicago: University of Chicago Press, 1988.

Bolt, Christine. *Victorian Attitudes to Race*. London: Routledge and Kegan Paul, 1971.

Bowden, Henry Warner. *American Indians and Christian Missions: Studies in Cultural Conflict*. Chicago: University of Chicago Press, 1981.

Bradford, Philips Verner, and Harvey Blume. *Ota Benga: The Pygmy in the Zoo*. New York: St. Martin's Press, 1992.

Brand, Dana. *The Spectator and the City in Nineteenth-Century American Literature*. Cambridge: Cambridge University Press, 1991.

Bratlinger, Patrick. *Dark Vanishings: Discourse on the Extinction of Primitive Races, 1800–1930*. Ithaca, NY: Cornell University Press, 2003.

———. "Victorians and Africans: The Genealogy of the Myth of the Dark Continent." In Gates Jr., ed., *"Race," Writing and Difference*, 185–222.

Bratton, J. S., and others, eds. *Acts of Supremacy: The British Empire and the Stage, 1790–1930*. Manchester: Manchester University Press, 1991.

Breckenridge, Carol. A. "The Aesthetics and Politics of Colonial Collecting: India at World Fairs." *Comparative Studies in Society and History* 31 (1989): 195–216.

Brewer, John. *The Pleasures of the Imagination*. London: HarperCollins, 1997.

Broome, Richard. *Aboriginal Victorians: A History since 1800*. Crows Nest, New South Wales: Allen and Unwin, 2005.

Brown, Lucy. *Victorian News and Newspapers*. Oxford: Clarendon Press, 1985.

Burke, Peter. *Eyewitnessing: The Use of Images as Historical Evidence*. London: Reaktion, 2001.

Burnett, D. Graham. "Exploration, Performance, Alliance: Robert Schomburgk in British Guiana." *Journal of Caribbean Studies* 15 (2000): 11–37.

Burnham, Philip. *Indian Country, God's Country: Native Americans and the National Parks*. Washington, DC: Island Press, 2000.

Burton, Richard D. E. *The Flaneur and His City: Patterns of Daily Life in Paris, 1815–1851*. Durham Modern Languages Series. Durham, UK: University of Durham, 1994.

Buzard, James, and Joseph Childers, eds. "Victorian Ethnographies." Special issue, *Victorian Studies* 41 (1998).

Bynum, William F. "Time's Noblest Offspring: The Problem of Man in the British Natural Historical Sciences, 1800–1863." Ph.D. diss., University of Cambridge, 1974.

Cain, P. J. "Economics and Empire: The Metropolitan Context." In A. Porter, ed., *The Nineteenth Century*, 31–52.

Callen, Anthea. *The Spectacular Body: Science, Method and Meaning in the Work of Degas*. New Haven, CT: Yale University Press, 1995.

Cameron, David Kerr. *London's Pleasures: From Restoration to Regency*. Gloucestershire: Sutton, 2001.

Carlson, Marvin. "Theatre Audiences and the Reading of Performance." In *Interpreting the Theatrical Past: Essays in the Historiography of Performance*, edited by Thomas Postlewait and Bruce A. McConachie, 82–98. Iowa City: University of Iowa Press, 1989.

Carroll, Victoria. "The Natural History of Visiting: Responses to Charles Waterton and Walton Hall." *Studies in History and Philosophy of Biological and Biomedical Sciences* 35 (2004): 31–64.

Chadaverian, Soraya de. "Laboratory Science versus Country-House Experiments: The Controversy between Julian Sachs and Charles Darwin." *British Journal of the History of Science* 29 (1996): 17–41.

Chakrabarty, Dipesh. "Postcoloniality and the Artifice of History: Who Speaks for 'Indian' Pasts?" *Representations* 32 (1992): 1–26.

Chalmers, A. F. *What Is This Thing Called Science?* 2nd ed. Milton Keynes, UK: Open University Press, 1982.

Chandler, Frank Wadleigh. *The Literature of Roguery*. London: B. Franklin, 1958.

Chapman, William Ryan. "Arranging Ethnology: A. H. L. F. Pitt Rivers and the Typological Tradition." In *Objects and Others: Essays on Museums and Material Culture*, ed. George W. Stocking, 15–48. Madison: University of Wisconsin Press, 1985.

———. "Ethnology in the Museum: A.H.L.F. Pitt Rivers (1827–1900) and the Institutional Foundations of British Anthropology." Ph.D. diss., University of Oxford, 1982.

Clark, William, Jan Golinski, and Simon Schaffer, eds., *The Sciences in Enlightened Europe*. Chicago: University of Chicago Press, 1999.

Clifford, James. "On Orientalism." In *The Predicament of Culture*, 255–76.

———. *The Predicament of Culture: Twentieth-Century Ethnography, Literature and Art*. Cambridge, MA: Harvard University Press, 1988.

Cobbing, Julian. "The Mfecane as Alibi: Thoughts on Dithakong and Mbolompo." *Journal of African History* 29 (1988): 487–519.

Colley, Linda. *Britons: Forging the Nation, 1707–1837*. New Haven, CT: Yale University Press, 1992.

———. *Captives: Britain, Empire and the World, 1600–1850*. London: Jonathan Cape, 2002.

Collingham, Elizabeth M. *Imperial Bodies*. Cambridge: Polity, 2001.

Comment, Bernard. *The Panorama*. London: Reaktion, 1999.

Cook, J. Mordaunt. "Metropolitan Improvements: John Nash and the Picturesque." In Fox, ed., *London*, 77–96.

Cook, James W. *The Arts of Deception: Playing with Fraud in the Age of P. T. Barnum*. Cambridge, MA: Harvard University Press, 2001.

Coombes, Annie. *Reinventing Africa: Museums, Material Culture and Popular Imagination in Late-Victorian and Edwardian England*. New Haven, CT: Yale University Press, 1994.

Cooter, Roger. *The Cultural Meaning of Popular Science: Phrenology and the Organization of Consent in Nineteenth-Century Britain*. Cambridge: Cambridge University Press, 1984.

Cooter, Roger, and Stephen Pumfrey. "Separate Spheres and Public Places: Reflections on the History of Science Popularization and Science in Popular Culture." *History of Science* 32 (1994): 237–67.

Corbey, Raymond. "Ethnographic Showcases 1870–1930." *Cultural Anthropology* 8 (1993): 338–69.

Cormaroff, Jean, and John Cormaroff. *Of Revelation and Revolution: Christianity, Colonialism and Consciousness in South Africa*. Chicago: University of Chicago Press, 1991.

Cowling, Mary. *The Artist as Anthropologist: The Representation of Type and Character in Victorian Art*. Cambridge: Cambridge University Press, 1989.

Crais, Clifton. *White Supremacy and Black Resistance in Pre-Industrial South Africa: The Making of the Colonial Order, 1770–1865*. Cambridge: Cambridge University Press, 1992.

Crais, Clifton, and Pamela Scully. *Sara Baartman and the Hottentot Venus: A Biography and a Ghost Story*. Princeton, NJ: Princeton University Press, 2008.

Crossick, Geoffrey, and Serge Jaumain, eds. *Cathedrals of Consumption: The European Department Store, 1850–1939*. Aldershot, UK: Ashgate, 1999.

Curtin, Philip D. *The Atlantic Slave Trade: A Census*. Madison: University of Wisconsin Press, 1969.

———. *The Image of Africa: British Ideas and Action, 1780–1850*. 2 vols. Madison: University of Wisconsin Press, 1964.

Curtis, L. Perry, Jr. *Apes and Angels: The Irishman in Victorian Caricature*. Rev. ed. Washington, DC: Smithsonian Institution Press, 1997.

Dabydeen, David. *Hogarth's Blacks: Images of Blacks in Eighteenth Century English Art*. Manchester: Manchester University Press, 1987.

Darnton, Robert. *The Business of Enlightenment: A Publishing History of the "Encyclopédie," 1775–1800*. Cambridge, MA: Harvard University Press, 1979.

Daunton, Martin. "London and the World." In Fox, ed., *London*, 21–38.

Daunton, Martin J., and Rick Alpern, eds. *Empire and Others: British Encounters with Indigenous Peoples, 1600–1850*. London: UCL, 1999.

Davis, David Brion. *Inhuman Bondage: The Rise and Fall of Slavery in the New World*. Oxford: Oxford University Press, 2006.

Davis, Graham. *The Irish in Britain, 1815–1914*. Dublin: Gill and Macmillan, 1991.

Davison, Patricia. "Human Subjects as Museum Objects: A Project to Make Life-Casts of 'Bushmen' and 'Hottentots,' 1907–1924." *Annals of the South African Museum* 102 (1993): 165–83.

Desmond, Adrian, and James Moore. *Darwin's Sacred Cause: How a Hatred of Slavery Shaped Darwin's Views on Human Evolution*. Boston: Houghton Mifflin Harcourt, 2009.

Desmond, Ray. *The India Museum, 1801–1879*. London: Her Majesty's Stationery Office, 1982.

Drayton, Richard. *Nature's Government: Science, Imperial Britain and the "Improvement" of the World*. New Haven, CT: Yale University Press, 2000.

Dreger, Alice D. *One of Us: Conjoined Twins and the Future of Normal*. Cambridge, MA: Harvard University Press, 2004.

Drescher, Seymour. "The Ending of the Slave Trade and the Evolution of European Racism." *Social Science History* 14 (1990): 415–50.

———. *The Mighty Experiment: Free Labour versus Slavery in British Emancipation*. Oxford: Oxford University Press, 2002.

Driver, Felix. *Geography Militant: Cultures of Exploration and Empire*. Oxford: Blackwell, 2001.

Duffin, Jacalyn, and Alison Li. "Great Moments: Parke, Davis and Company and the Creation of Medical Art." *Isis* 86 (1995): 1–29.

Duncan, Carol. *Civilising Rituals: Inside Public Art Museums*. London: Routledge, 1995.

Durbach, Nadja. *The Spectacle of Deformity: Freak Shows and Modern British Culture*. Berkeley and Los Angeles: University of California Press, 2009.

Edgecombe, Rodney-Stenning. "Dickens and Addison: A Possible Source for Mrs Jellyby." *Dickensian* 98 (2002): 153–55.

Edwards, Elizabeth, ed. *Anthropology and Photography, 1860–1920*. New Haven, CT: Yale University Press, 1994.

———. "Evolving Images: Photography, Race and Popular Darwinism." In *Endless Forms, Darwin, Natural Sciences and the Visual Arts*, edited by DianaDonald and Jane Munro, 166–93. New Haven, CT: Yale University Press, 2009.

———. *Raw Histories: Photographs, Anthropology and Museums*. Oxford: Berg, 2001.

Edwards, Paul, and James Walvin. *Black Personalities in the Era of the Slave Trade*. Baton Rouge: Louisiana State University Press, 1983.

Eldredge, Elizabeth. "Sources of Conflict in Southern Africa, c. 1800–30: The 'Mfecane' Reconsidered." *Journal of African History* 33 (1992): 1–35.

Ellingson, Ter. *The Myth of the Noble Savage*. Berkeley and Los Angeles: University of California Press, 2001.

Elsner, Jas, and Joan Pau-Rubies, eds. *Voyages and Visions: Towards a Cultural History of Travel*. London: Reaktion, 1988.

Eltis, David. *The Rise of African Slavery in the Americas*. Cambridge: Cambridge University Press, 2000.

Eltis, David, and James Walvin, eds. *The Abolition of the Atlantic Slave Trade: Origins and Effects in Europe, Africa and the Americas*. Madison: University of Wisconsin Press, 1981.

Endersby, Jim. "*Homo Sapiens*: Francis Galton's Fairgound Attraction." In *A Guinea Pig's History of Biology*, 61–94. London: William Heinemann, 2007.

———. *Imperial Nature: Joseph Hooker and the Practices of Victorian Natural History*. Chicago: University of Chicago Press, 2008.

l'Estoile, Benoît de. "From the Colonial Exhibition to the Museum of Man: An Alternative Genealogy of French Anthropology." *Social Anthropology* 11 (2003): 341–61.

Ettema, Michael J. "History Museums and the Culture of Materialism." In *Past Meets Present: Essays about Historic Interpretation and Public Audiences*, edited by Jo Blatti, 62–93. London: Smithsonian Institution Press, 1987.

Fabian, Johannes. *Time and the Other: How Anthropology Makes Its Object*. New York: Columbia University Press, 1983.

Faden, Ruth R., and Tom L. Beauchamp. *A History and Theory of Informed Consent*. New York: Oxford University Press, 1986.

Fausto-Sterling, Anne. "Gender, Race and Nation: The Comparative Anatomy of 'Hottentot' Women in Europe, 1815–1817." In *Deviant Bodies: Critical Perspectives*

on *Difference in Science and Popular Culture*, edited by Jennifer Terry and
Jacqueline Urla, 19–48. Bloomington: Indiana University Press, 1995.

Feest, Christian F., ed. *Indians and Europe: An Interdisciplinary Collection of Essays*.
Aachen, Germany: Edition Herodot, 1987.

Feller, David Allan. "Gentlemen Comforters." *America Kennel Club Gazette*, December 2007, 30–35.

Fields, Barbara J. "Ideology and Race in American History." In *Region, Race and Reconstruction: Essays in Honour of C. Vann Woodward*, edited by J. Morgan Kousser and James M. McPherson, 143–77. Oxford: Oxford University Press, 1982.

Fish, Stanley. *Self-Consuming Artifacts: The Experience of Seventeenth-Century Literature*. Berkeley and Los Angeles: University of California Press, 1972.

Flint, Kate. *The Transatlantic Indian, 1776–1930*. Princeton, NJ: Princeton University Press, 2009.

Forgan, Sophie. "The Architecture of Display: Museums, Universities and Objects in Nineteenth-Century Britain." *History of Science* 32 (1994): 139–62.

Foster, Robert F. *Paddy and Mr Punch: Connections in Irish and English History*.
London: Penguin, 1993.

Fox, Celina, ed. *London: World City, 1800–1840*. New Haven, CT: Yale University Press, 1992.

Frankenberg, Ruth, ed. *Displacing Whiteness: Essays in Social and Cultural Criticism*.
Durham, NC: Duke University Press, 1997.

Fryer, Peter. *Staying Power: The History of Black People in Britain*. London: Pluto, 1984.

Fusco, Coco. "The Other History of Intercultural Performance." In *English Is Broken Here*, 37–63. New York: New Press, 1995.

Fyfe, Aileen. "Reading Natural History at the British Museum and the *Pictorial Museum*." In Fyfe and Lightman, eds., *Science in the Marketplace*, 196–230.

Fyfe, Aileen, and Bernard Lightman, eds. *Science in the Marketplace: Nineteenth-Century Sites and Experiences*. Chicago: University of Chicago Press, 2007.

Galison, Peter, and Caroline A. Jones. *Picturing Science, Producing Art*. New York: Routledge, 1998.

Gaskell, Ivan. *Vermeer's Wager: Speculations on Art History, Theory and Art Museums*.
London: Reaktion, 2004.

Gaskell, Philip. *A New Introduction to Bibliography*, 2nd ed. Winchester: St Paul's Bibliographies, 1995.

Gates, Henry Louis, Jr., ed. *"Race," Writing and Difference*. Chicago: University of Chicago Press, 1985.

Gerber, David A. "The 'Careers' of People Exhibited in Freak Shows: The Problem of Volition and Valorization." In Thomson, ed., *Freakery*, 38–54.

Gerzina, Gretchen. *Black England: Life before Emancipation*. London: John Murray, 1995.

———, ed. *Black Victorians/Black Victoriana*. New Brunswick, NJ: Rutgers University Press, 2003.

Ghosh, Dhurba. "Decoding the Nameless: Gender, Subjectivity and Historical Methodologies in Reading the Archives of Colonial India." In K. Wilson, ed., *A New Imperial History*, 297–316.

———. *Sex and the Family in Colonial India: The Making of Empire*. Cambridge: Cambridge University Press, 2006.

Gilman, Sander. "Black Bodies, White Bodies: Toward an Iconography of Female

Sexuality in Late Nineteenth-Century Art, Medicine and Literature." In Gates Jr., ed., *"Race," Writing and Difference*, 223–61.

———. *Difference and Pathology: Stereotypes of Sexuality, Race and Madness*. Ithaca, NY: Cornell University Press, 1985.

Gold, Joel. "Mrs. Jellyby: Dickens's Inside Joke." *Dickensian* 79 (1983): 35–38.

Golinski, Jan. *Making Natural Knowledge: Constructivism and the History of Science*. Cambridge: Cambridge University Press, 1998.

Gooday, Graeme. "Nature in the Laboratory: Domestication and Discipline with the Microscope in Victorian Life Science." *British Journal of the History of Science* 24 (1991): 304–41.

Gould, Stephen J. "The Hottentot Venus." In *The Flamingo's Smile*, 291–305. New York: Norton, 1985.

Great Britain: Working Group on Human Remains in Museum Collections. *The Working Group on Human Remains Report*. London: Department for Culture, Media and Sport, 2003.

Greenhalgh, Paul. *Ephemeral Vistas: The Expositions Universelles, Great Exhibitions and World's Fairs, 1851–1939*. Manchester: Manchester University Press, 1988.

Greetham, David C. *Textual Scholarship: An Introduction*. London: Garland, 1994.

Gregory, Breandon. "Staging British India." In Bratton and others, eds., *Acts of Supremacy*, 150–78.

Grogg, Ann Hofstra. "The 'Illustrated London News,' 1842–1852." Ph.D. diss., Indiana University, 1977.

Grove, Richard H. *Green Imperialism: Colonial Expansion, Tropical Edens and the Origins of Environmentalism, 1600–1860*. Cambridge: Cambridge University Press, 1995.

Gruber, Jacob. "Ethnographic Salvage and the Shaping of Anthropology." *American Anthropologist*, n.s., 72 (1970): 1289–99.

Guenther, Mathias Georg. "From 'Brutal Savages' to 'Harmless People': Notes on the Changing Western Image of the Bushmen." *Paideuma* 26 (1980): 123–40.

Guest, Harriet. "Ornament and Use: Mai and Cook in London." In K. Wilson, ed., *A New Imperial History*, 317–44.

Hackforth-Jones, Jocelyn, et al. *Between Worlds: Voyagers to Britain, 1700–1850*. London: National Portrait Gallery, 2007.

Hadley, Elaine. *Melodramatic Tactics: Theatricalized Dissent in the English Marketplace, 1800–1885*. Stanford, CA: Stanford University Press, 1995.

Haill, Catherine. *Fun without Vulgarity: Victorian and Edwardian Popular Entertainment Posters*. London: The Stationery Office, 1996.

Hale, Dana S. *Races on Display: French Representations of Colonized Peoples, 1886–1940*. Bloomington: Indiana University Press, 2008.

Hall, Catherine, ed. *Civilising Subjects: Metropole and Colony in the English Imagination, 1830–1867*. Cambridge: Polity, 2002.

———. *The Cultures of Empire, A Reader: Colonizers in Britain and the Empire in the Nineteenth and Twentieth Centuries*. Manchester: Manchester University Press, 2000.

———. *Defining the Victorian Nation: Class, Race, Gender and the Reform Act of 1867*. Cambridge: Cambridge University Press, 2000.

Hall, Stuart. "New Ethnicities." In *Black Film, British Cinema*, 27–31. Institute of Contemporary Arts Documents 7. London: Institute of Contemporary Arts, 1989.

———, ed. *Representation: Cultural Representations and Signifying Practices*. London: Sage Publications, 1997.

Hallam, Elizabeth, and Brian Street, eds. *Cultural Encounters: Representing "Otherness."* London: Routledge, 2000.

Hallett, Mark. *The Spectacle of Difference: Graphic Satire in the Age of Hogarth*. New Haven, CT: Yale University Press, 1999.

Haraway, Donna. "Teddy Bear Patriarchy: Taxidermy in the Garden of Eden, New York City, 1908–36." In *Primate Visions: Gender, Race and Nature in the World of Modern Science*, 26–58. London: Routledge, 1989.

Harris, Neil. *Humbug: The Art of Barnum*. Boston: Brown, 1973.

Harrison, Mark. *Climates and Constitutions: Health, Race, Environment and British Imperialism in India, 1600–1850*. Oxford: Oxford University Press, 1999.

Hartley, Lucy. *Physiognomy and the Meaning of Expression in Nineteenth-Century Culture*. Cambridge: Cambridge University Press, 2001.

Hartman, Saidiya. *Scenes of Subjection: Terror, Slavery and Self-Making in Nineteenth-Century America*. Oxford: Oxford University Press, 1997.

Hausdoerfer, John. *Catlin's Lament: Indians, Manifest Destiny and the Ethics of Nature*. Lawrence: University of Kansas Press, 2009.

Hays, J. N. "The London Lecturing Empire, 1800–50." In *Metropolis and Province: Science in British Culture, 1780–1850*, edited by Ian Inkster and Jack Morrell, 91–119. London: Hutchinson, 1983.

Hayward, Arthur L. *The Days of Dickens: A Glance at Some Aspects of Early Victorian London*. London: Routledge, 1926.

Hazlewood, Nick. *Savage: The Life and Times of Jemmy Button*. London: Hodder and Stoughton, 2000.

Hedrick, Joan D. *Harriet Beecher Stowe: A Life*. Oxford: Oxford University Press, 1994.

Henze, Brent R. "Scientific Rhetorics in the Emergence of British Ethnology, 1808–1848: Discourses, Disciplines and Institutions." Ph.D. diss., Pennsylvania State University, 2001.

Herbert, Christopher. *Culture and Anomie: The Ethnographic Imagination in the Nineteenth Century*. Chicago: University of Chicago Press, 1991.

———. "Mayhew's Cockney Polynesia." In *Culture and Anomie*, 204–52.

———. "Rat Worship and Taboo in Mayhew's London." *Representations* 23 (1988): 1–24.

Herle, Anita, and Sandra Rouse, eds. *Cambridge and the Torres Strait: Centenary Essays on the 1898 Anthropological Expedition*. Cambridge: Cambridge University Press, 1998.

Herzog, Don. *Happy Slaves: A Critique of Consent Theory*. Chicago: University of Chicago Press, 1989.

Hetherington, Michelle. *Cook and Omai: The Cult of the South Seas*. Canberra: National Library of Australia, 2001.

Higgins, David. "Art, Genius and Racial Theory in the Early-Nineteenth Century." *History Workshop Journal* 58 (2004): 17–40.

Hight, Kathryn S. "'Doomed to Perish': George Catlin's Depictions of the Mandan." *Art Journal* 49 (1990): 119–24.

Hindley, Diana, and Geoff Hindley. *Advertising in Victorian England, 1837–1901*. London: Wayland, 1972.

Hine, Darlene Clark. "Co-Labourers in the Work of the Lord: Nineteenth-Century Black Women Physicians." In *The "Racial" Economy of Science: Towards a Democratic Future*, edited by Sandra Harding, 210–27. Bloomington: Indiana University Press, 1993.

Hinsley, Curtis M., Jr. *Savages and Scientists: The Smithsonian Institution and the Development of American Anthropology, 1846–1910*. Washington, DC: Smithsonian Institution Press, 1981.

Hoage, Robert J., and William A. Deiss, eds. *New Worlds, New Animals: From Menagerie to Zoological Park in the Nineteenth Century*. Baltimore: Johns Hopkins University Press, 1996.

Hoffenberg, Peter H. *An Empire on Display: English, Indian and Australian Exhibitions from the Crystal Palace to the Great War*. Berkeley and Los Angeles: University of California Press, 2001.

Holder, Heidi J. "Melodrama, Realism and Empire on the British Stage." In Bratton and others, eds., *Acts of Supremacy*, 129–49.

Honour, Hugh. *The Image of the Black in Western Art*. 4 vols. Houston: Menil Foundation, 1989.

hooks, bell. "Selling Hot Pussy: Representations of Black Female Sexuality in the Cultural Marketplace." In *Writing on the Body: Female Embodiment and Feminist Theory*, edited by Nadia Medina, Katie Conboy, and Sarah Stanbury, 113–28. New York: Columbia University Press, 1997.

Hoppen, K. T. "A Maturing Economy." In *The Mid-Victorian Generation, 1846–1886*, 275–315. The New Oxford History of England. Oxford: Oxford University Press, 1998.

Howard, Martin. *Victorian Grotesque: An Illustrated Excursion into Medical Curiosities, Freaks and Abnormalities—Principally of the Victorian Age*. London: Jupiter, 1977.

Howell, Michael, and Peter Ford. *The Illustrated True History of the Elephant Man*. 2nd ed. London: Butler and Tanner, 1983.

Huggins, Mike. *The Victorians and Sport*. London: Hambledon and London, 2004.

Humpherys, Anne. *Henry Mayhew*. Boston: Twayne, 1984.

———. *Travels into the Poor Man's Country: The Work of Henry Mayhew*. Athens, GA: University of Georgia Press, 1977.

Hunt, Bruce J. "Doing Science in a Global Empire: Cable Telegraphy and Electrical Physics in Victorian Britain." In *Victorian Science in Context*, edited by Bernard Lightman, 312–33. Chicago: University of Chicago Press, 1997.

Hutton, Seán. "The Irish in London." In Merriman, ed., *The Peopling of London*, 118–28.

Hyam, Ronald. *Empire and Sexuality: The British Experience*. Manchester: Manchester University Press, 1990.

Hyde, Ralph. *Panoramania: The Art and Entertainment of the "All-Embracing" View*. London: Trefoil Publications, 1988.

Ingold, Tim. "The Art of Translation in a Continuous World." In *Beyond Boundaries: Understanding, Translation and Anthropological Discourse*, edited by Gísli Pálsson, 210–30. Oxford: Berg, 1993.

Inwood, Stephen. *City of Cities: The Birth of Modern London*. London: Macmillan, 2005.

———. *A History of London*. London: Macmillan, 1998.

Jacobson, Wendy, ed. *Dickens and the Children of Empire*. New York: Palgrave Macmillan, 2000.

Jacobus, Mary, Evelyn Fox Keller, and Sally Shuttleworth, eds. *Body Politics: Women, Literature and the Discourse of Science*. New York: Routledge, 1989.

Jardine, Nicholas, James A. Secord, and E. C. Spary, eds. *The Cultures of Natural History*. Cambridge: Cambridge University Press, 1996.

Jay, Ricky. *Learned Pigs and Fireproof Women*. London: Hale, 1986.

Jeal, Tim. *Stanley: The Impossible Life of Africa's Greatest Explorer*. London: Faber and Faber, 2007.

Johns, Adrian. *The Nature of the Book: Print and Knowledge in the Making*. Chicago: University of Chicago Press, 1998.

Jones, Pamela Fletcher. *The Jews of Britain: A Thousand Years of History*. Gloucestershire: Windrush Press, 1990.

Jordanova, Ludmilla. *Defining Features: Scientific and Medical Portraits, 1660–2000*. London: National Portrait Gallery, 2000.

Kaplan, Cora. "'A Heterogeneous Thing': Female Childhood and the Rise of Racial Thinking in Victorian Britain." In *Human, All Too Human*, edited by Diana Fuss, 169–202. London: Routledge, 1996.

———. "White, Black, and Green: Racialising Irishness in Victorian England." In *Victoria's Ireland? Irishness and Britishness, 1837–1901*, edited by Peter Gray, 51–68. Dublin: Four Courts Press, 2004.

Karp, Ivan, and Steven D. Lavine, eds. *Exhibiting Cultures: The Poetics and the Politics of Museum Display*. Washington, DC: Smithsonian Institution Press, 1991.

Kass, Amalie M., and Edward H. Kass. *Perfecting the World: The Life and Times of Dr. Thomas Hodgkin, 1798–1866*. New York: Harcourt Brace Jovanovich, 1988.

Keller, Evelyn Fox. *Reflections on Gender and Science*. New Haven, CT: Yale University Press, 1985.

Kenny, Robert. "From the Curse of Ham to the Curse of Nature." *British Journal for the History of Science* 40 (2007): 367–88.

Kershen, Anne. "The Jewish Community in London." In Merriman, ed., *The Peopling of London*, 138–48.

Kidd, Colin. *British Identities before Nationalism: Ethnicity and Nationhood in the Atlantic World, 1600–1800*. Cambridge: Cambridge University Press, 1999.

———. "Ethnicity in the British Atlantic World, 1688–1830." In K. Wilson, ed., *A New Imperial History*, 260–77.

———. *The Forging of Races: Race and Scripture in the Protestant Atlantic World, 1600–2000*. Cambridge: Cambridge University Press, 2006.

Kiralfy, Bolossy. *Creator of Great Musical Spectacles: An Autobiography*. Edited by Barbara M. Barker. Ann Arbor: UMI Research Press, 1988.

Kirby, Percival. "A Further Note on the 'Hottentott Venus.'" *Africana Notes and News* 11 (1954): 165–66.

———. "The Hottentot Venus." *Africana Notes and News* 6 (1949): 55–62.

———. "The 'Hottentott Venus' of the Musée de l'Homme, Paris." *South African Journal of Science* 10 (1954): 319–22.

———. "More about the Hottentot Venus." *Africana Notes and News* 10 (1953): 124–34.

Kirshenblatt-Gimblett, Barbara. "The Ethnographic Burlesque." *Drama Review* 42 (1998): 175–80.

———. "Objects of Ethnography." In Karp and Lavine, eds., *Exhibiting Cultures*, 386–443.

Klancher, Jon P. *The Making of English Reading Audiences, 1790–1832*. Madison: University of Wisconsin Press, 1987.

Koerner, Lisbet. *Linnaeus: Nature and Nation*. Cambridge, MA: Harvard University Press, 1999.

Kohlstedt, Sally Gregory. "Women in the History of Science: An Ambiguous Place." *Osiris* 10 (1995): 39–60.

Kohlstedt, Sally Gregory, and Helen Longino, eds. "Women, Gender and Science: New Directions." Special issue, *Osiris* 12 (1997).

Kubicek, Robert. "British Expansion, Empire and Technological Change." In A. Porter, ed., *The Nineteenth Century*, 247–69.

Kuklick, Henrika. *The Savage Within: The Social History of British Anthropology, 1885–1945*. Cambridge: Cambridge University Press, 1991.

Kuper, Adam. *Anthropology and Anthropologist: The Modern British School*. London: Allen Lane, 1973.

Kurin, Richard. "Cultural Conservation through Representation: Festival of India Folk-life Exhibitions at the Smithsonian Institution." In Karp and Lavine, eds., *Exhibiting Cultures*, 315–43.

Laidlaw, Zoë. "Aunt Anna's Report: The Buxton Women and the Aborigines Select Committee 1835-37." *Journal of Imperial and Commonwealth History* 32 (2004): 1–28.

———. "Heathens, Slaves and Aborigines: Thomas Hodgkin's Critique of Missions and Anti-Slavery." *History Workshop Journal* 64 (2007): 133–61.

Latour, Bruno. *The Pasteurization of France*. Translated by Alan Sheridan and John Law. Cambridge, MA: Harvard University Press, 1988.

Leask, Nigel. *Curiosity and the Aesthetics of Travel Writing, 1770–1840: "From an Antique Land."* Oxford: Oxford University Press, 2002.

Legassick, Martin. "From Prisoners to Exhibits: Representations of Bushmen of the Northern Cape, 1880 1900." In *Rethinking Settler Colonialism: History and Memory in Australia, Canada, Aotearoa New Zealand and South Africa*, edited by Annie Coombes, 63–84. Manchester: Manchester University Press, 2006.

Lightman, Bernard. "Lecturing in the Spatial Economy of Science." In Fyfe and Lightman, eds., *Science in the Marketplace*, 97–132.

———. *Victorian Popularizers of Science: Designing Nature for New Audiences*. Chicago: University of Chicago Press, 2007.

———. "The Visual Theology of Victorian Popularizers of Science: From Reverent Eye to Chemical Retina." *Isis* 91 (2000): 650–80.

Linbaugh, Peter, and Marcus Rediker. *The Many Headed Hydra: Sailors, Slaves, Commoners and the Hidden History of the Revolutionary Atlantic*. London: Verso, 2000.

Lindfors, Bernth, ed. *Africans on Stage: Studies in Ethnological Show Business*. Bloomington: Indiana University Press, 1999.

———. "The Afterlife of the Hottentot-Venus." *Neohelicon* 16 (1989): 293–301.

———. "The Bottom Line: African Caricature in Georgian England." *World Literature Written in English* 24 (1984): 43–51.

———. "Charles Dickens and the Zulus." in Lindfors, ed., *Africans on Stage*, 62–80.

———. "Dr Kahn and the Niam-Niams." In Blanchard et al., *Human Zoos*, 229–38.

———. "Ethnological Show Business: Footlighting the Dark Continent." In Thomson, ed., *Freakery*, 207–18.

———. "The Hottentot Venus and Other African Attractions in Nineteenth-Century England." *Australasian Drama Studies* 1 (1983): 83–104.

———. "A Zulu View of Victorian London," *Munger Africana Library Notes* 9 (1979): 1–8.

Livingstone, David N. *Adam's Ancestors: Race, Religion and the Politics of Human Origins*. Baltimore: Johns Hopkins University Press, 2008.

Lorimer, Douglas A. *Colour, Class and the Victorians: English Attitudes to the Negro in the Mid-Nineteenth Century*. Leicester: Leicester University Press, 1978.

Lorimer, Jamie, and Sarah Whatmore. "After the 'King of Beasts': Samuel Baker and the Embodied Historical Geographies of Elephant Hunting in Mid-Nineteenth-Century Ceylon." *Journal of Historical Geography* 35 (2009): 668–89.

Luckhurst, Kenneth W. *The Story of Exhibitions*. London: Studio Publications, 1951.

Lynn, Martin. "British Policy, Trade, and Informal Empire in the Mid-Nineteenth Century." In A. Porter, ed., *The Nineteenth Century*, 101–21.

Macdonald, Sharon, and Gordon Fyfe, eds. *Theorizing Museums*. Oxford: Blackwell, 1996.

Mackenzie, John M. *The Empire of Nature: Hunting, Conservation and British Imperialism*. Manchester: Manchester University Press, 1998.

———, ed. *Imperialism and Popular Culture*. Manchester: Manchester University Press, 1986.

———. *Propaganda and Empire: The Manipulation of British Public Opinion, 1880–1960*. Manchester: Manchester University Press, 1984.

Magubane, Zine. *Bringing the Empire Home: Race, Class and Gender in Britain and Colonial South Africa*. Chicago: University of Chicago Press, 2003.

———. "Which Bodies Matter? Feminism, Poststructuralism, Race and the Curious Theoretical Odyssey of the 'Hottentot Venus.'" *Gender & Society* 15 (2001): 816–34.

Malcolmson, Robert W. *Popular Recreations in English Society, 1700–1850*. Cambridge: Cambridge University Press, 1973.

Malinowski, Bronislaw. *Argonauts of the Western Pacific: An Account of Native Enterprise and Adventure in the Archipelagoes of Melanesian New Guinea*. London: Routledge, 1922.

Mandler, Peter. "The Problem with Cultural History." *Cultural and Social History* 1 (2004): 94–117.

———. "'Race' and 'Nation' in Mid-Victorian Thought." In *History, Religion and Culture: British Intellectual History 1750–1950*, edited by Stefan Collini, Richard Whatmore, and Brian Young, 224–44. Cambridge: Cambridge University Press, 2000.

Mark, Joan. "Francis La Flesche: The American Indian as Anthropologist." *Isis* 73 (1982): 495–510.

Marks, Shula. "Southern Africa, 1867–1886." In *The Cambridge History of Africa: Volume 6, c.1870–c.1905*, edited by Roland Oliver and G. N. Sanderson, 359–421. Cambridge: Cambridge University Press, 1985.

———. "Southern and Central Africa, 1886–1910." In Oliver and Sanderson, eds., *The Cambridge History of Africa: Volume 6*, 422–492.

Marriott, John, ed. *Unknown London: Early Modernist Visions of the Metropolis, 1815–1845*. 6 vols. London: Pickering and Chatto, 2000.

Mathur, Saloni. "Living Ethnological Exhibits: The Case of 1886." *Cultural Anthropology* 15 (2001): 492–524.

————. *India by Design: Colonial History and Cultural Display.* Berkeley and Los Angeles: University of California Press, 2007.

Maxwell, Anne. *Colonial Photography and Exhibitions: Representations of the "Native" People and the Making of European Identities.* London: Leicester University Press, 1999.

Mayer, David. *Harlequin in His Element: The English Pantomime, 1806–1836.* Cambridge, MA: Harvard University Press, 1969.

McCallum, Iain. *Blood Brothers: Hiram and Hudson Maxim; Pioneers of Modern Warfare.* London: Chatham, 1999.

McCalman, Iain. *Radical Underworld: Prophets, Revolutionaries and Pornographers in London, 1795–1840.* Cambridge: Cambridge University Press, 1988.

McClintock, Anne. *Imperial Leather: Race, Gender and Sexuality in the Colonial Context.* London: Routledge, 1995.

McCook, Stuart. "It May Be Truth, but It Is Not Evidence: Paul du Chaillu and the Legitimation of Evidence in the Field Sciences." *Osiris* 11 (1996): 177–97.

Meek, Ronald. *Social Science and the Ignoble Savage.* Cambridge: Cambridge University Press, 1976.

Merriman, Nick, ed. *The Peopling of London: Fifteen Thousand Years of Settlement from Overseas.* London: Museum of London, 1993.

Merriman, Nick, and Rozina Visram. "The World in a City." In Merriman, ed., *The Peopling of London,* 3–27.

Miller, David P., and Peter H. Reill, eds. *Visions of Empire: Voyages, Botany and Representations of Nature.* Cambridge: Cambridge University Press, 1996.

Mitchell, Michael. *Monsters: Human Freaks in America's Gilded Age; The Photographs of Charles Eisenmann.* 2nd ed. Toronto: ECW Press, 2002.

Mitchell, Timothy. *Colonising Egypt.* Cambridge: Cambridge University Press, 1988.

————. "The World as Exhibitions." *Comparative Studies in Society and History* 31 (1989): 217–36.

Moienuddin, Mohammad. *Sunset at Srirangapatam: After the Death of Tipu Sultan.* London: Sangam, 2000.

Moon, Paul. *Te Ara Ki Te Tiri: The Path to the Treaty of Waitangi.* Auckland, NZ: David Ling, 2002.

Moore, Grace. "Reappraising Dickens's 'Noble Savage.'" *Dickensian* 98 (2002): 236–243.

Moore, Robert J., Jr. *Native Americans, a Portrait: The Art and Travels of Charles Bird King, George Catlin and Karl Bodmer.* New York: Stewart, Tabori and Chang, 1997.

Morgan, Philip D., and Sean Hawkins, eds. *Black Experience and the Empire.* Oxford History of the British Empire Companion Series. Oxford: Oxford University Press, 2004.

Morris, Donald R. *The Washing of the Spears: The Rise and Fall of the Mighty Zulu Nation.* London: Jonathan Cape, 1965. Reprint, London: Pimlico, 1994.

Moses, L. G. *Wild West Shows and the Images of American Indians, 1883–1933.* Albuquerque: University of New Mexico Press, 1996.

Mostert, Noel. *Frontiers: The Epic of South Africa's Creation and the Tragedy of the Xhosa People.* London: Jonathan Cape, 1992.

Mulvey, Christopher. "Among the Sag-anoshes: Ojibwa and Iowa Indians with George Catlin in Europe, 1843–1848." In *Indians and Europe: An Interdisciplinary*

Collection of Essays, edited by Christian F. Feest, 253–75. Aachen, Germany: Edition Herodot, 1987.

Murray, Brian. "Savages and Street Arabs: Henry Morton Stanley in Darkest England." Unpublished paper, 2008.

Nead, Lynda. *Victorian Babylon: People, Streets and Images in Nineteenth-Century London*. New Haven, CT: Yale University Press, 2000.

Newhall, Beaumont. *A History of Photography from 1839 to the Present*. 5th ed. New York: Museum of Modern Art, 1984.

Nichols, Kate. *Greece and Rome at the Crystal Palace: Classical Sculpture and Modern Britain, 1854–1936."* Oxford: Oxford University Press, forthcoming.

Northrup, David. *Indentured Labour in the Age of Imperialism, 1834–1922*. Cambridge: Cambridge University Press, 1995.

O'Connor, Ralph. *The Earth on Show: Fossils and the Poetics of Popular Science, 1802–1856*. Chicago: University of Chicago Press, 2008.

Oetterman, Stephen. *The Panorama: History of a Mass Medium*. Translated by Deborah Lucas Schneider. New York: Zone Books, 1997.

Oldroyd, David R. *The Highlands Controversy: Constructing Geological Knowledge through Fieldwork in 19th-Century Britain*. Chicago: University of Chicago Press, 1990.

Omer-Cooper, J. D. "The Nguni Outburst." In *The Cambridge History of Africa: Volume 5, c. 1790–c.1870*, edited by John E. Fint, 359–421. Cambridge: Cambridge University Press, 1985.

Otter, Chris. *The Victorian Eye: A Political History of Light and Vision in Britain, 1800–1910*. Chicago: University of Chicago Press, 2008.

Ousby, Ian. *The Englishman's England: Taste, Travel and the Rise of Tourism*. Cambridge: Cambridge University Press, 1990.

Outram, Darinda. *Georges Cuvier: Vocation, Science and Authority in Post-Revolutionary France*. Manchester: Manchester University Press, 1984.

Pagden, Anthony. "The Savage Critic: Some European Images of the Primitive." *Yearbook of English Studies* 13 (1983): 32–45.

Pang, Alex Soojung-Kim. "Visual Representation and the Post-Constructivist History of Science." *Historical Studies in the Physical and Biological Sciences* 28 (1997): 139–71.

Parezo, Nancy J., and Don D. Fowler. *Anthropology Goes to the Fair: The 1904 Louisiana Purchase Exposition*. Lincoln: University of Nebraska Press, 2008.

Parsons, Neil. *King Khama, Emperor Joe and the Great White Queen*. Chicago: University of Chicago Press, 1998.

———. "No Longer 'Rare Birds' in London: Zulu, Ndebele, Gaza and Swazi Envoys to England, 1882–1894." In *Black Victorians/Black Victoriana*, edited by Gerzina Gretchen, 110–44. New Brunswick, NJ: Rutgers University Press, 2003.

Pearce, Susan, ed. *Interpreting Objects and Collections*. London: Routledge, 1994.

———. "William Bullock: Collections and Exhibitions at the Egyptian Hall, 1816–25." *Journal of the History of Collections* 20 (2007): 1–19.

———. "William Bullock: Inventing a Visual Language of Objects." In *Museum Revolutions: How Museums Change and are Changed*, edited by J. Knell, Suzanne Macleod, and Sheila E. R. Watson, 15–27. London: Routledge, 2007.

Pearl, Sharrona. *About Faces: Physiognomy in Nineteenth-Century Britain*. Cambridge, MA: Harvard University Press, 2009.

Penny, H. Glenn. *Objects of Culture: Ethnology and Ethnographic Museums in Imperial Germany*. Chapel Hill: University of North Carolina Press, 2002.

Petch, Alison. "Chance and Certitude: Pitt Rivers and His First Collection." *Journal of the History of Collections* 18 (2006): 257–66.

———. "'Man as He Was and as He Is': Pitt Rivers's Collections." *Journal of the History of Collections* 1 (1998): 75–85.

Pettitt, Clare. *Dr Livingstone, I Presume? Missionaries, Journalists, Explorers and Empire*. Cambridge, MA: Harvard University Press, 2007.

Pickering, Michael. "Mock Blacks and Racial Mockery: The 'Nigger' Minstrel and British Imperialism." In Bratton and others, eds., *Acts of Supremacy*, 179–236.

Pickstone, John V. "Museological Science? The Place of the Analytical/Comparative in Nineteenth-Century Science, Technology and Medicine." *History of Science* 32 (1994): 111–38.

Piertese, Jan. *White on Black: Images of Africa and Blacks in Western Popular Culture*. New Haven, CT: Yale University Press, 1992.

Piggott, Jan R. *The Palace of the People: The Crystal Palace at Sydenham, 1854–1936*. London: Hurst, 2004.

Pilbeam, Pamela M. *Madame Tussaud and the History of Waxworks*. London: Hambledon, 2002.

Poignant, Roslyn. *Professional Savages: Captive Lives and Western Spectacle*. New Haven, CT: Yale University Press, 2004.

Porter, Andrew, ed. *The Nineteenth Century*. Vol. 3 of *The Oxford History of the British Empire*. Oxford: Oxford University Press, 1998.

Porter, Roy. *London: A Social History*. London: Penguin, 2000.

———. *Mind Forg'd Manacles: A History of Madness from the Restoration to the Regency*. London: Athlone, 1987.

Postlewait, Thomas, and Bruce A. McConachie. *Interpreting the Theatrical Past: Essays in the Historiography of Performance*. Iowa City: University of Iowa Press, 1989.

Prakash, Gyan. "Subaltern Studies as Postcolonial Criticism." *American Historical Review* 99 (1994): 1475–90.

Pratt, Mary Louise. *Imperial Eyes: Travel Writing and Transculturation*. London: Routledge, 1992.

Pratt, Stephanie. "The Four 'Indian Kings.'" In *Between Worlds: Voyagers to Britain, 1700–1850*, by Jocelyn Hackforth-Jones et al., 22–35. London: National Portrait Gallery, 2007.

Price, Leah. *The Anthology and the Rise of the Novel: From Richardson to George Eliot*. Cambridge: Cambridge University Press, 2000.

Prucha, Francis Paul. *The Great Father: The United States Government and the American Indians*. 2 vols. combined. Lincoln: University of Nebraska Press, 1995.

Qureshi, Sadiah. "Displaying Sara Baartman, the 'Hottentot Venus.'" *History of Science* 42 (2004): 233–57.

Ramamurthy, Anandi. *Imperial Persuaders: Images of Africa and Asia in British Advertising*. Manchester: Manchester University Press, 2003.

Ranger, Terence O. *Revolt in Southern Rhodesia, 1896–7*. London: Heinemann, 1967.

Reiss, Benjamin. *The Showman and the Slave: Race, Death and Memory in Barnum's America*. Cambridge, MA: Harvard University Press, 2001.

Rhodes, Richard. *The Making of the Atomic Bomb: The Discovery of Nuclear Energy*. New York: Simon and Schuster, 1987.

Richards, Evelleen. "The 'Moral Anatomy' of Robert Knox: The Interplay between Biological and Social Thought in Victorian Scientific Naturalism." *Journal of the History of Biology* 22 (1989): 373–436.

———. "A Political Anatomy of Monsters, Hopeful and Otherwise: Teratogeny, Transcendentalism, and Evolutionary Theorizing." *Isis* 85 (1994): 377–411.

Richards, Graham. *"Race," Racism and Psychology: Towards a Reflexive History*. London: Routledge, 1997.

Richards, Thomas. *The Commodity Culture of Victorian England: Advertising and Spectacle, 1851–1914*. Stanford, CA: Stanford University Press, 1990.

Richardson, David. "The British Empire and the Atlantic Slave Trade, 1660–1807." In *The Eighteenth Century*, edited by Peter J. Marshall, 440–64; vol. 2 of *The Oxford History of the British Empire*. Oxford: Oxford University Press, 1998.

Richardson, John. *The Annals of London: A Year-by-Year Record of a Thousand Years of History*. London: Cassell, 2000.

Rickards, Maurice. *Encyclopaedia of Ephemera: A Guide to the Fragmentary Documents of Everyday Life for the Collector, Curator and Historian*. Edited by Michael Twyman. London: British Library, 2000.

Ripley, C. P., ed. *The Black Abolitionist Papers*. 5 vols. Chapel Hill: University of North Carolina Press, 1985.

Ritvo, Harriet. *The Animal Estate: The English and Other Creatures in the Victorian Age*. Cambridge, MA: Harvard University Press, 1987.

———. *The Platypus and the Mermaid and Other Figments of the Classifying Imagination*. Cambridge, MA: Harvard University Press, 1997.

Robbins, Louise E. *Elephant Slaves and Pampered Parrots: Exotic Animals in Eighteenth-Century Paris*. Baltimore: Johns Hopkins University Press, 2002.

Roediger, David R. *Working toward Whiteness: How America's Immigrants Became White; The Strange Journey from Ellis Island to the Suburbs*. New York: Basic Books, 2005.

Rossiter, Margaret W. *Women Scientists in America: Before Affirmative Action, 1940–1972*. Baltimore: Johns Hopkins University Press, 1995.

———. *Women Scientists in America: Struggles and Strategies to 1940*. Baltimore: Johns Hopkins University Press, 1982.

Rothfels, Nigel. "Aztecs, Aborigines and Ape-People: Science and Freaks in Germany, 1850–1900." In Thomson, ed., *Freakery*, 158–72.

———. *Savages and Beasts: The Birth of the Modern Zoo*. Baltimore: Johns Hopkins University Press, 2002.

Rudwick, Martin J. S. "The Emergence of a Visual Language for Geological Science, 1760–1840." *History of Science* 14 (1976): 149–95.

———. *Scenes from Deep Time: Early Pictorial Representations of the Prehistoric World*. Chicago: University of Chicago Press, 1992.

Russell, Gillian. "An 'Entertainment of Oddities': Fashionable Sociability and the Pacific in the 1770s." In K. Wilson, ed., *A New Imperial History*, 48–70.

———. *The Theatres of War: Performance Politics and Society, 1793–1915*. Oxford: Oxford University Press, 1995.

Russell, N. C., E. M. Tansey, and P. V. Lear. "Missing Links in the History and Practice of Science: Teams, Technicians and Technical Work." *History of Science* 38 (2000): 237–41.

Ryan, Lyndall. *The Aboriginal Tasmanians*. St. Lucia, Queensland, Australia: University of Queensland Press, 1981.

Rydell, Robert W. *All the World's a Fair: Visions of Empire at American International Expositions, 1876–1916*. Chicago: University of Chicago Press, 1984.

———. *World of Fairs: The Century-of-Progress Expositions*. Chicago: University of Chicago Press, 1993.

Said, Edward. *Orientalism: Western Conceptions of the Orient*. London: Routledge and Kegan Paul, 1978.

Saint, Andrew. "The Building Art of the First Industrial Metropolis." In Fox, ed., *London*, 51–76.

Sampson, David. "Strangers in a Strange Land: The 1868 Aborigines and Other Indigenous Performers in Mid-Victorian Britain." Ph.D. diss., University of Technology, Sydney, 2000.

Satz, Ronald N. *American Indian Policy in the Jacksonian Era*. Lincoln: University of Nebraska Press, 1974.

Schaffer, Simon. "Enlightened Automata." In *The Sciences in Enlightened Europe*, edited by William Clark, Jan Golinski, and Simon Schaffer, 126–65. Chicago: University of Chicago Press, 1999.

———. "Machine Philosophy: Demonstration Devices in Georgian Mechanics." *Osiris* 9 (1994): 157–82.

———. "Natural Philosophy and Public Spectacle in the Eighteenth Century." *History of Science* 21 (1983): 1–35.

———. "On Astronomical Drawing." In *Picturing Science, Producing Art*, edited by Peter Galison and Caroline A. Jones, 441–74. New York: Routledge, 1998.

———. "The Show That Never Ends: Perpetual Motion in the Early Eighteenth Century." *British Journal for the History of Science* 28 (1995): 157–89.

Schiebinger, Londa. *Nature's Body: Gender in the Making of Modern Science*. Boston: Beacon Press, 1993.

Schiller, Nina Glick, Data Dea, and Markus Höhne. *African Culture and the Zoo in the 21st Century: The "African Village" in the Augsburg Zoo and Its Wider Implications*. Halle: Max Planck Institute for Social Anthropology, 2005.

Schneider, William H. *An Empire for the Masses: The French Popular Image of Africa, 1870–1900*. Westport, CT: Greenwood, 1982.

Schudson, Michael. *The Power of News*. Cambridge, MA: Harvard University Press, 1996.

Scott, James C. *Weapons of the Weak: Everyday Forms of Peasant Resistance*. London: Yale University Press, 1985.

Secord, Anne. "Botany on a Plate: Pleasure and the Power of Pictures in Promoting Early Nineteenth–Century Scientific Knowledge." *Isis* 93 (2002): 28–57.

———. "Corresponding Interests: Artisans and Gentlemen in 19th-Century Natural-History." *British Journal for the History of Science* 27 (1994): 383–408.

———. "Science in the Pub: Artisan Botanists in Early-19th-Century Lancashire." *History of Science* 32 (1994): 269–315.

Secord, James A. "Monsters at the Crystal Palace." In *Models: The Third Dimension of Space*, edited by Soraya de Chadarevian and Nick Hopwood, 138–69. Stanford, CA: Stanford University Press, 2004.

———. *Victorian Sensation: The Extraordinary Publication, Reception and Secret Authorship of "Vestiges of the Natural History of Creation."* Chicago: University of Chicago Press, 2000.

Sera-Shriar, Efram. "Beyond the Armchair: Early Observational Practices and the Sciences of Man in Britain, 1813–1871." Ph.D. diss., University of Leeds, 2011.

Shapin, Steven. *A Social History of Truth: Civility and Science in Seventeenth-Century England*. Chicago: University of Chicago Press, 1994.

Shapin, Steven, and Simon Schaffer. *Leviathan and the Air-Pump: Hobbes, Boyle and the Experimental Life*. Princeton, NJ: Princeton University Press, 1985.

Shesgreen, Sean. *Images of the Outcast: The Urban Poor in the Cries of London*. Manchester: Manchester University Press, 2002.

Shephard, Ben. *Kitty and the Prince*. London: Profile Books, 2003.

———. "Showbiz Imperialism: The Case of Peter Lobengula." In *Imperialism and Popular Culture*, edited by John M. Mackenzie, 94–112. Manchester: Manchester University Press, 1986.

Sinnema, Peter W. *Dynamics of the Pictured Page: Representing the Nation in the* Illustrated London News. Aldershot, UK: Ashgate, 1998.

Sivasundaram, Sujit. "Natural History Spiritualised: Civilising Islanders, Cultivating Breadfruit and Collecting Souls." *History of Science* 39 (2001): 417–43.

———. *Nature and the Godly Empire: Science and Evangelical Mission in the Pacific, 1795–1850*. Cambridge: Cambridge University Press, 2005.

———. "The Periodical as Barometer: Spiritual Measurement and the Evangelical Magazine." In *Science and Culture in the Nineteenth-Century Media*, edited by Geoffrey Cantor et al., 43–56. Aldershot, UK: Ashgate, 2003.

Skotnes, Pippa, ed. *Claim to the Country: The Archive of Wilhelm Bleek and Lucy Lloyd*. Athens, OH: Ohio University Press, 2007.

———. *Miscast: Negotiating the Presence of the Bushmen*. Cape Town: University of Cape Town, 1996.

Smith, Bernard. *European Vision and the South Pacific, 1768–1860: A Study in the History of Art and Ideas*. Oxford: Clarendon Press, 1960.

Smith, Malvern van Wyk. "'What the Waves Were Saying': 'Dombey and Son' and Textual Ripples on African Shore." In *Dickens and the Children of Empire*, edited by Wendy S. Jacobson, 128–52. New York: Palgrave Macmillan, 2000.

Smith, Paul. *The History of Tourism: Thomas Cook and the Origins of Leisure Travel*. 4 vols. London: Routledge, 1998.

Snobelen, Stephen D. "Of Stones, Men and Angels: The Competing Myth of Isabelle Duncan's Pre-Adamite Man." *Studies in the History and Philosophy of the Biomedical Sciences* 31 (2001): 59–104.

Sorrenson, Richard. "George Graham, Visible Technician." *British Journal for the History of Science* 32 (1999): 203–21.

Spary, E. C. *Utopia's Garden: French Natural History from Old Regime to Revolution*. Chicago: University of Chicago Press, 2000.

Spence, Mark David. *Dispossessing the Wilderness: Indian Removal and the Making of the National Parks*. Oxford: Oxford University Press, 1999.

Spivak, Gayatri Chakravorty. "Can the Subaltern Speak?" In *Marxism and the Interpretation of Culture*, 271–313. Urbana: University of Illinois Press, 1988.

Sramek, Joseph. "'Face Him Like a Briton': Tiger Hunting, Imperialism, and British Masculinity in Colonial India, 1800–1875." *Victorian Studies* 48 (2006): 659–80.

Stafford, Robert A. *Scientist of Empire: Sir Roderick Murchison, Scientific Exploration and Victorian Imperialism*. Cambridge: Cambridge University Press, 1989.

Stepan, Nancy Leys. *The Idea of Race in Science: Great Britain, 1800–1960*. London: Macmillan, 1982.

———. "Race and Gender: The Role of Analogy in Science." *Isis* 77 (1986): 261–77.

Stocking, George W. *After Tylor: British Social Anthropology, 1888–1951*. London: Athlone, 1995.

———. "From Chronology to Ethnology: James Cowles Prichard and British Anthropology, 1800–1850." In James Cowles Prichard, *Researches into the Physical History of Man*, edited by George W. Stocking, ix–cx. Orig. pub. London: Arch, 1813. Stocking ed., Chicago: University of Chicago Press, 1973.

———, ed. *Objects and Others: Essays on Museums and Material Culture*. Madison: University of Wisconsin Press, 1985.

———, ed. *Observers Observed: Essays on Ethnographic Fieldwork*. Madison: University of Wisconsin Press, 1983.

———. *Rivers, Benedict, and Others: Essays on Culture and Personality*. Madison: University of Wisconsin Press, 1986.

———. *Victorian Anthropology*. London: Free Press, 1987.

———. "What's in a Name? The Origins of the Royal Anthropological Institute, 1837–71." *Man* 6 (1971): 369–90.

Strother, Zöe S. "Display of the Body Hottentott." In Lindfors, ed., *Africans on Stage*, 1–61.

Suleiman, Susan R., and Inge Crosman, eds. *The Reader in the Text: Essays on Audience and Interpretation*. Princeton, NJ: Princeton University Press, 1980.

Sweet, Rosemary. *Antiquaries: The Discovery of the Past in Eighteenth-Century Britain*. London: Hambledon and London, 2004.

Swift, Roger, and Sheridan Gilley, eds. *The Irish in Britain, 1815–1939*. London: Pinter, 1989.

Tester, Keith, ed. *The Flâneur*. London: Routledge, 1994.

Thesing, William. *The London Muse: Victorian Poetic Responses to the City*. Athens, GA: University of Georgia Press, 1982.

Thode-Arora, Hilke. "Abraham's Diary—a European Ethnic Show from an Inuk Participant's Viewpoint." *Journal of the Society for the Anthropology of Europe* 2 (2008): 2–17.

Thomas, Nicholas. *Colonialism's Culture: Anthropology, Travel and Government*. Cambridge: Polity Press, 1994.

———. *Entangled Objects: Exchange, Material Culture and Colonialism in the Pacific*. Cambridge, MA: Harvard University Press, 1991.

Thompson, E. P., and Eileen Yeo. *The Unknown Mayhew: Selections from the* Morning Chronicle, *1849–50*. London: Merlin, 1971. Reprint, Harmondsworth: Penguin, 1984.

Thompson, Leonard, and Monica Wilson, eds. *A History of South Africa to 1870*; vol. 1 of *The Oxford History of South Africa*. Oxford: Clarendon Press, 1969.

Thomson, Rosemarie Garland. "From Wonder to Error: Monsters from Antiquity to Modernity." In Blanchard et al., *Human Zoos*, 52–61.

———. ed. *Freakery: Cultural Spectacles of the Extraordinary Body*. New York: New York University Press, 1996.

Thornton, Sara. *Advertising, Subjectivity and the Nineteenth-Century Novel: Dickens, Balzac and the Language of the Walls*. Basingstoke, UK: Palgrave Macmillan, 2009.

Tomlinson, B. R. "Economics and Empire: The Periphery and the Imperial Economy." In A. Porter, ed., *The Nineteenth Century*, 53–74.

Topham, Jonathan R. "Beyond the 'Common Context': The Production and Reading of the 'Bridgewater Treatises.'" *Isis* 89 (1998): 233–62.

———, ed. "Focus: Historicizing 'Popular Science.'" *Isis* 100 (2009): 310–68.

———. "Scientific Publishing and the Reading of Science in the Nineteenth Century: A Historiographical Survey and Guide to Sources." *Studies in the History and Philosophy of Science* 31 (2000): 559–612.

Twyman, Michael. *Printing 1770–1970: An Illustrated History of Its Development and Uses in England*. 2nd ed. London: British Library, 1998.

Tytler, Graeme. *Physiognomy in the European Novel: Faces and Fortunes*. Princeton, NJ: Princeton University Press, 1982.

Urry, James. *Before Social Anthropology: Essays on the History of British Anthropology*. Philadelphia: Harwood Academic Publishers, 1993.

Vanke, Francesca. "Degrees of Otherness: The Ottoman Empire and China at the Great Exhibition of 1851." In *Britain, the Empire, and the World at the Great Exhibition of 1851*, edited by Jeffrey A. Auerbach and Peter H. Hoffenberg, 191–206. Aldershot, UK: Ashgate, 2008.

Vergo, Peter. *The New Museology*. London: Reaktion, 1989.

Vevers, Gwynne. *London's Zoo: An Anthology to Celebrate 150 Years of the Zoological Society of London, with Its Zoos at Regent's Park in London and Whipsnade in Bedfordshire*. London: Bodley Head, 1976.

Visram, Rozina. *Asians in Britain: 400 Years of History*. London: Pluto, 2001.

———. *Ayahs, Lascars and Princes: Indians in Britain, 1700–1947*. London: Pluto, 1986.

Vries, Leonard de. *Victorian Advertisements*. London: John Murray, 1968.

Wahrman, Dror. "Climate, Civilization and Complexion: Varieties of Race." In *The Making of the Modern Self: Identity and Culture in Eighteenth-Century England*, 83–126. New Haven, CT: Yale University Press, 2006.

Wainwright, A. Martin. *"The Better Class" of Indians: Social Rank, Imperial Identity and South Asians in Britain, 1858–1914*. Manchester: Manchester University Press, 2008.

Walvin, James. *An African's Life: The Life and Times of Olaudah Equiano, 1745–1797*. London: Cassell, 1998.

———. *The Black Presence: A Documentary History of the Negro in England, 1555–1860*. London: Orbach and Chambers, 1971.

———. *Fruits of Empire: Exotic Produce and British Taste, 1600–1800*. New York: New York University Press, 1997.

Washbrook, D. A. "Orients and Occidents: Colonial Discourse Theory and the Historiography of the British Empire." In *Historiography*, edited by Robin W. Winks, 597–611; vol. 5 of *The Oxford History of the British Empire*. Oxford: Oxford University Press, 1999.

Weinreb, Ben, and Christopher Hibbert, eds. *The London Encyclopaedia*. Rev. ed. London: Macmillan, 1993.

Wheeler, Roxann. *The Complexion of Race: Categories of Difference in Eighteenth-Century Culture*. Philadelphia: University of Pennsylvania Press, 2000.

Whye, John van. *Phrenology and the Origins of Victorian Scientific Naturalism*. Aldershot, UK: Ashgate, 2004.

Wigelsworth, Jeffrey R. "Competing to Popularize Newtonian Philosophy: John Theophilus Desaguliers and the Preservation of Reputation." *Isis* 94 (2003): 435–55.

Williams, Elizabeth. *The Physical and the Moral: Anthropology, Physiology and Philosophical Medicine in France, 1750–1850*. Cambridge: Cambridge University Press, 1994.

Wilson, Gahan. *The Big Book of Freaks: 50 Amazing True Tales of Human Oddities*. New York: Paradox Press, 1996.

Wilson, Kathleen. "Introduction: Histories, Empires, Modernities." In K. Wilson, ed., *A New Imperial History*, 1–26.

———. *The Island Race: Englishness, Empire and Gender in the Eighteenth Century*. London: Routledge, 2002.

———. ed. *A New Imperial History: Culture, Identity and Modernity in Britain and the Empire, 1660–1840*. Cambridge: Cambridge University Press, 2004.

Winter, Alison. *Mesmerized: Powers of Mind in Victorian Britain*. Chicago: University of Chicago Press, 1998.

Wintle, Claire. "Model Subjects: Representations of the Andaman Islands at the Colonial and Indian Exhibition, 1886." *History Workshop Journal* 67 (2009): 194–207.

Wolfe, Patrick. "History and Imperialism: A Century of Theory, from Marx to Postcolonialism." *American Historical Review* 102 (1997): 388–420.

Wood, Gaby. *The Smallest of All Persons Mentioned in the Records of Littleness*. London: Profile Books, 1998.

Woodward, Llewellyn. *The Age of Reform, 1815–1870*. The Oxford History of England, 2nd ed. Oxford: Oxford University Press, 1962.

Young, Michael W. *Malinowski: Odyssey of an Anthropologist, 1884–1920*. New Haven, CT: Yale University Press, 2004.

Young, Robert C. *Colonial Desire: Hybridity in Theory, Culture and Race*. London: Routledge, 1995.

Zimmerman, Andrew. *Anthropology and Antihumanism in Imperial Germany*. Chicago: University of Chicago Press, 2001.

Ziter, Edward. *The Orient on the Victorian Stage*. Cambridge: Cambridge University Press, 2003.

INDEX

Page numbers in italics refer to figures.

100, 123, 144, 150–51. *See also* Anishinabe; Bakhoje; Catlin, George
"native" village, 4, 253–55, 280; illustrations of, *117, 161, 229, 234, 252, 254*
Ndebele: foundation of Matabeleland,
230; illustrations of, *231, 233*; Ndebele
Wars, 230–32
newspapers, 188; exhibition reviews in,
65–66, 78, 90, 92–93, 109–12 passim;
eyewitness accounts in, 127, 156, 162,
167–68, 174, 262; geography of, 66;
international coverage, 68–75; production of, 91–92

ostension: 42, 43, 173, 209–10, 276–77,
302n114

pamphlets, 79–83, 92, 94–95, 109, 111,
188–89; illustrated frontispieces, *80–81*;
patrons' use of, 96, 219; travel literature
appropriated by, 81–82, 88–90, 93
patrons: critical engagement with performances and advertising, 97, 125,
143, 165–69, 181–82 passim, 189–90,
204, 218, 276–78 passim; dependence
on advertising, 76, 78–79, 88, 96, 219,
322n81; expectations of, 120–21; identity of, 156, 246, 319n5; observational
training of, 125, 173 (*see also* ostension); relationships with performers,
144–46; reports of notable visits in
advertising, 90–91; social interaction
with performers, 159–65, 253, 278. *See
also* audiences
performers: aesthetic responses to, 170,
174–75; agency and consent of 9, 131–
33, 136–41, 146–53; autopsies of, 219,
221, 331; child, 141–43; as exemplars of
travel literature, 86–88, 96, 174–77;
legal cases involving, 139–41, 171; as
managers, 106, 310n16; marriages of,
143–46; as mothers, 3, 160, 162–63, 167–
68; provenance of, 109–12; recruitment
of, 127–36; social interaction with patrons, 159–65, 253, 278; wage disputes,
140–41. *See also* managers; patrons
philanthropy, 105, 212, 227, 278; Exeter
Hall, 7; telescopic, 177–79. *See also*
Aborigines' Protection Society; missionaries
phrenology, 5, 38; Cooter Donavan and, 192

physiognomy, 38, 41–44, 86, 191, 211
Prichard, James Cowles, 18–19, 23, 212–19
passim, 324n14, 327n60; as ethnological authority, 84, *86*, 204; Mandinka
and, 269; reputation of, 18, 216–17
pseudoscience, 5, 279–80, 283, 290n15,
341n20
Punch, 86, 165, 202, 236

race: Apollo Belvedere in images of, *158*;
climate in defining, 203–4; debates on
skin color and structure, 203–5; diachronic variations in, 189, 202, 327;
early notions of, 6, 188–89; in historiography of exhibitions, 274–76, 283;
mid-nineteenth-century debates on,
211–21; monogenism and polygenism,
198–201, 203–4, 215–16; pre-adamite,
200; stadial theories of, 189, 324n12;
technology in defining, 68; terminology of, 10–11; typology of savagery,
barbarism, and civilization, 248, 334n62
Ram, Tulsi, 245
Rio, Antonio del, 84–85
Rivers, William H. R.: on fieldwork, 263,
338n119; genealogical method, 265–66;
on performers as specimens, 261–64

Sámi, 56, 66, 87–89, 116, *118, 119*, 249
San, 5–7 passim, *39–40*, 189–90; children
at the Egyptian Hall (1845), 114–15, 122,
158–60, 172–74, 189; derogatory views
of, 73, 83, 175, 306n34; exhibition in
1847 (debuted with Knox), 1–2, 76, *80*,
86, 112–14, 116, 160, 162, 187–88; eye-
sight of, 196; Farini's 1885 exhibition of
"Earthmen Pigmies," 60–61, 118–19,
120, 134; Flora and Martinus (the
"Earthmen" in 1853), 77, 82–83, 90–91,
105, 127–28, 141–43, 189–90, 197, 206,
209, 221, 307n45, 331n131; hunting of,
133; rarity of, 40, 172–73. *See also* Lichtenstein, Martin Henry
Savage South Africa, 116, 124, 159–61, 222,
228–34, 250, 253, 256, 268; Aborigines'
Protection Society and, 137, 169; film of
(*Savage South Africa—Savage Attack
and Repulse*), 227; performers' discontent, 150–52; reports in the *Owl* (Cape
Town), 162–64; women banned, 162,
228. *See also* Lobengula, Peter